Tips for Studying with This Book

This textbook has been designed to help you succeed in your U.S. ...
steps to get the most out of reading and studying from *The American Promise: A Compact History*, Third Edition.

- **PREVIEW: Before You Read**

  a. *Orient Yourself:* Look at the chapter title and study the chapter outline to preview the topics in the chapter and the order in which they will be covered.

  b. *Skim "Reviewing the Chapter":* Look at the Reviewing the Chapter section at the end of the chapter. The Who and What lists contain key terms to look for while you read. The Review Questions and Making Connections alert you to topics you should pay close attention to as you read.

- **FOCUS: While You Read**

  a. *Follow the Story:* Read the opening story carefully. It previews topics that will be important in the chapter. Pay attention to section headings as you continue to read; they alert you to what is to come and help you keep track of where the chapter is heading.

  b. *Pay Attention to the Context:* Look at the maps, tables, and figures in the chapter, which can help you understand the national and regional contexts of the story.

  c. *Check Your Reading:* After you read each major section, try to answer the review question at the end. If you have trouble, skim the section again for the answer.

- **REVIEW: After You Read**

  a. *Test Your Knowledge:* Turn to the Reviewing the Chapter section at the end of the chapter and review the list of Key Terms. Can you identify them and explain why they are important to the chapter? If not, flip back to the page number indicated and skim to refresh your memory.

  b. *Review the Timeline:* Review the order of events in the Timeline to make sure you understand the relationships between events in the chapter and their sequence.

  c. *Place the Specifics in the Big Picture:* Answer the Review Questions and Making Connections questions, citing evidence from the text to make sure you understand the important developments in the chapter.

- **TAKE PRACTICE QUIZZES: Online Study Guide**
  bedfordstmartins.com/roarkcompact

  a. *See What You've Learned:* To determine what you know and what you need to review, visit the Online Study Guide, which provides self-assessment quizzes for each chapter with instantly graded results.

  b. *Deepen Your Knowledge:* Develop a rich understanding of the period covered in the chapter and hone your interpretive skills by exploring other online features such as Reading Historical Documents and Visual Activity.

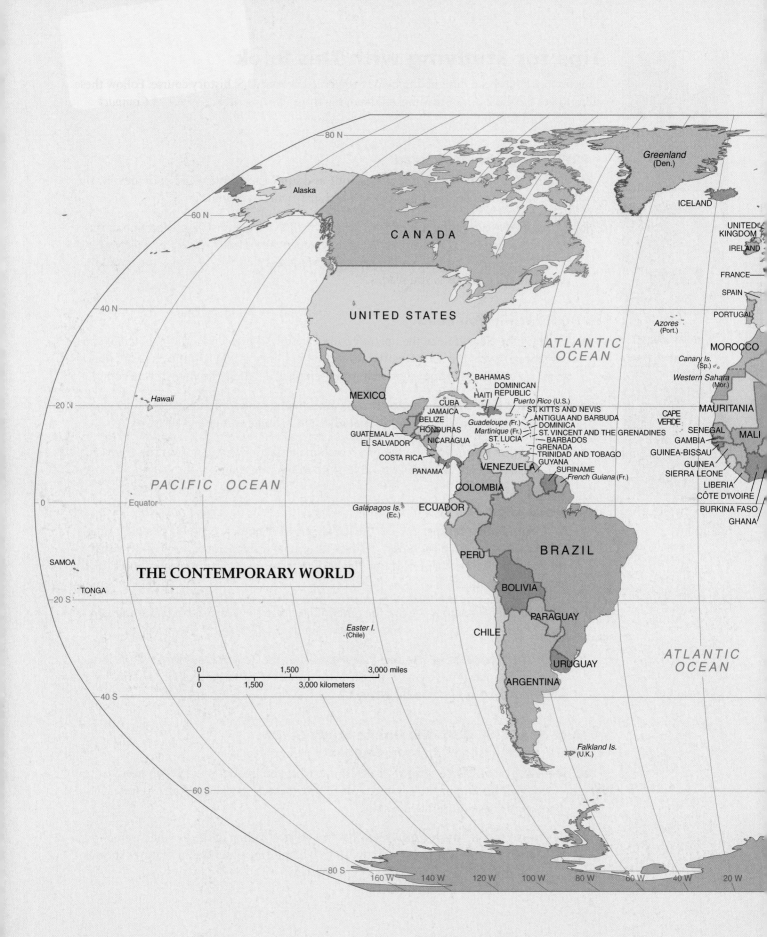

THE CONTEMPORARY WORLD

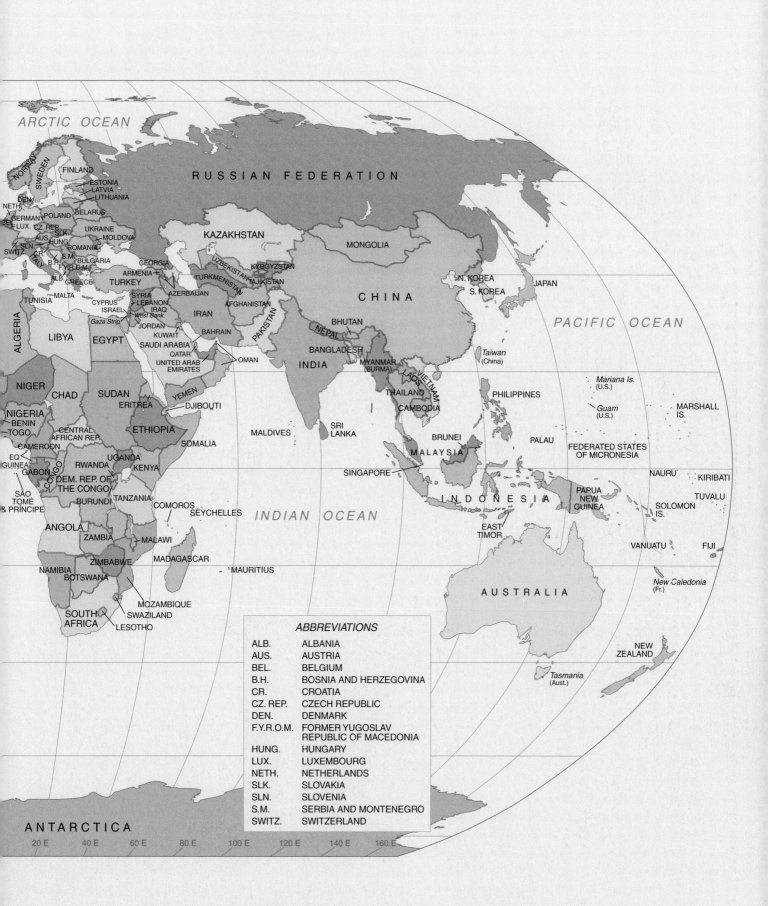

ARCTIC OCEAN

NORWAY
SWEDEN
FINLAND

RUSSIAN FEDERATION

ESTONIA
LATVIA
LITHUANIA
DEN.
NETH.
GERMANY POLAND
BEL. LUX. CZ. REP. BELARUS
AUS. SLK. UKRAINE
HUNG. MOLDOVA
SWITZ. CR. ROMANIA
SLN. B.H. S.M. BULGARIA
ITALY ALB. F.Y.R.O.M. GEORGIA
GREECE TURKEY ARMENIA
TUNISIA MALTA AZERBAIJAN
CYPRUS SYRIA
ISRAEL LEBANON
West Bank IRAQ
Gaza Strip JORDAN
KUWAIT
QATAR
SAUDI ARABIA
UNITED ARAB
EMIRATES
OMAN

KAZAKHSTAN

MONGOLIA

UZBEKISTAN KYRGYZSTAN
TURKMENISTAN TAJIKISTAN
AFGHANISTAN
IRAN PAKISTAN
BHUTAN
NEPAL

N. KOREA
S. KOREA
JAPAN

PACIFIC OCEAN

CHINA

ALGERIA
LIBYA
EGYPT

NIGER
CHAD
SUDAN
ERITREA
NIGERIA
BENIN
TOGO
CENTRAL
AFRICAN REP.
CAMEROON
EQ.
GUINEA
GABON CONGO RWANDA
DEM. REP. OF UGANDA
THE CONGO KENYA
SÃO
TOMÉ
& PRÍNCIPE BURUNDI
TANZANIA

YEMEN
DJIBOUTI
ETHIOPIA
SOMALIA

BAHRAIN

INDIA

BANGLADESH
MYANMAR
(BURMA)
LAOS
THAILAND
CAMBODIA
VIETNAM

MALDIVES

SRI
LANKA

PHILIPPINES

Taiwan
(China)

Mariana Is.
(U.S.)
Guam
(U.S.)

MARSHALL
IS.

BRUNEI
MALAYSIA

PALAU

FEDERATED STATES
OF MICRONESIA

SINGAPORE

NAURU

KIRIBATI
TUVALU

COMOROS
SEYCHELLES

INDIAN OCEAN

INDONESIA

PAPUA
NEW
GUINEA

SOLOMON
IS.

ANGOLA
ZAMBIA
MALAWI
ZIMBABWE
MADAGASCAR
MAURITIUS

EAST
TIMOR

VANUATU

FIJI

NAMIBIA
BOTSWANA
MOZAMBIQUE
SWAZILAND
SOUTH
AFRICA LESOTHO

New Caledonia
(Fr.)

AUSTRALIA

NEW
ZEALAND

Tasmania
(Aust.)

ABBREVIATIONS	
ALB.	ALBANIA
AUS.	AUSTRIA
BEL.	BELGIUM
B.H.	BOSNIA AND HERZEGOVINA
CR.	CROATIA
CZ. REP.	CZECH REPUBLIC
DEN.	DENMARK
F.Y.R.O.M.	FORMER YUGOSLAV REPUBLIC OF MACEDONIA
HUNG.	HUNGARY
LUX.	LUXEMBOURG
NETH.	NETHERLANDS
SLK.	SLOVAKIA
SLN.	SLOVENIA
S.M.	SERBIA AND MONTENEGRO
SWITZ.	SWITZERLAND

ANTARCTICA

20 E   40 E   60 E   80 E   100 E   120 E   140 E   160 E

The American Promise

A COMPACT HISTORY

Third Edition

HAND-COLORED STEREOGRAPH OF SOLDIERS AND AN AFRICAN AMERICAN MAN SITTING AT A CAMP DINNER, c. 1861–65

Camp Dinner (detail), *1861–65* by Thomas C. Roche, negative number 37700, Collection of the New-York Historical Society.

The
American
Promise

A COMPACT HISTORY

Third Edition

Volume I: To 1877

James L. Roark
Emory University

Michael P. Johnson
Johns Hopkins University

Patricia Cline Cohen
University of California, Santa Barbara

Sarah Stage
Arizona State University

Alan Lawson
Boston College

Susan M. Hartmann
The Ohio State University

BEDFORD/ST. MARTIN'S
Boston ◆ New York

FOR BEDFORD/ST. MARTIN'S

Executive Editor for History: Mary Dougherty
Director of Development for History: Jane Knetzger
Senior Developmental Editor: Heidi L. Hood
Senior Production Editor: Karen S. Baart
Production Supervisor: Jennifer Wetzel
Executive Marketing Manager: Jenna Bookin Barry
Associate Editor: Shannon Hunt
Editorial Assistant: Daniel Cole
Production Assistants: Katherine Caruana and Lindsay DiGianvittorio
Copyeditor: Patricia Herbst
Text Design: Wanda Kossak
Photo Research: Pembroke Herbert/Sandi Rygiel, Picture Research Consultants & Archives, Inc.
Indexer: Anne Harbour
Cover Design: Billy Boardman
Cartography: Mapping Specialists Ltd.
Composition: Techbooks
Printing and Binding: R.R. Donnelley & Sons Company

President: Joan E. Feinberg
Editorial Director: Denise B. Wydra
Director of Marketing: Karen Melton Soeltz
Director of Editing, Design, and Production: Marcia Cohen
Managing Editor: Elizabeth M. Schaaf

Library of Congress Control Number: 2005938010

Manufactured in the United States of America.

1 0 9 8 7 6
f e d c b a

For information, write: Bedford/St. Martin's, 75 Arlington Street, Boston, MA 02116 (617-399-4000)

ISBN-10: 0–312–44165–7   ISBN-13: 978–0–312–44165–4 (combined edition)
ISBN-10: 0–312–44841–4   ISBN-13: 978–0–312–44841–7 (Vol. I)
ISBN-10: 0–312–44842–2   ISBN-13: 978–0–312–44842–4 (Vol. II)
ISBN-10: 0–312–45643–3   ISBN-13: 978–0–312–45643–6 (high school edition)

Cover Art: Hand-colored stereograph of soldiers and an African American man sitting at a camp dinner, c. 1861–65. *Camp Dinner* (detail), *1861–65* by Thomas C. Roche, negative number 37700, Collection of the New-York Historical Society.

BRIEF CONTENTS

CONTENTS

CHAPTER 1

Ancient America: Before 1492   3

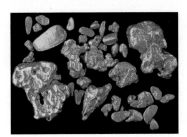

MAPS, FIGURES, AND TABLES

MAPS, FIGURES, AND TABLES

CHAPTER 16

THE THIRD EDITION of *The American Promise: A Compact History* is an occasion for celebration. As authors, we are deeply gratified that our book has become one of the best selling and most popular texts for the U.S. history survey, and we continue to take pride in the book's distinctly useful format, one which combines a brief narrative with all of the art, maps, features, and pedagogical tools of a full-length text. With this particular revision, we feel we have reached a new milestone in our ongoing efforts to present the most teachable and readable book available on the market.

In this edition we not only did our own abridgement to make the book 30 percent shorter, as we have done in the past, but we also created a new in-text study guide. At the end of each major section of a chapter, students will find review questions that also form part of the comprehensive chapter review appearing at each chapter's end. These new Reviewing the Chapter sections offer step-by-step guidance that leads students from basic comprehension to questions for analysis. These elements of the revision derive from our commitment to making this book accessible to students, and they were strengthened by the insights of our adopters and reviewers. We are grateful for their suggestions and confident the resulting text will be even more useful to students and instructors.

From the beginning, *The American Promise* has been shaped by our firsthand knowledge that the survey course is the most difficult to teach and the most difficult to take. Collectively, we have logged more than a century in introductory American history classrooms in institutions that range from small community colleges to large research universities. Drawing on our practical experience, we set an ambitious goal, one that we continue to focus on in the third compact edition: to produce the most teachable and readable introductory American history textbook available. Our experience as teachers informs every aspect of our text, beginning with its framework. Many survey texts emphasize either a social or a political approach to history, and by focusing on one, they inevitably slight the other. In our classrooms, we have found that students need **both** the structure a political narrative provides and the insights gained from examining social and cultural experience. To write a comprehensive, balanced account of American history we have focused on the public arena — the place where politics intersects social and cultural developments — to show how Americans confronted the major issues of their day and created far-reaching historical change.

We also thought hard about the concerns most frequently voiced by instructors: that students often find history boring, unfocused, and difficult and their textbooks lifeless and overwhelming. Getting students to open the book is one of the biggest hurdles instructors face. We asked ourselves how our text could address these concerns and engage students in ways that would help them understand and remember the main developments in American history. To make the political, social, economic, and cultural changes vivid and memorable and to portray fully the diversity of the American experience, we stitch into our narrative the voices of hundreds of contemporaries—from presidents to pipefitters, sharecroppers to suffragists—whose ideas and actions shaped their times and whose efforts still affect our lives. By incorporating a rich selection of authentic American voices, we seek to capture history as it happened and to create a narrative that compels students' interest and sparks their historical imagination.

Our title, *The American Promise*, reflects our emphasis on human agency and our conviction that American history is an unfinished story. For millions, the nation held out the promise of a better life, unfettered worship, representative government, democratic politics, and other freedoms seldom found elsewhere around the world. But none of these promises has come with guarantees. And promises fulfilled for some have meant promises denied to others. As we see it, much of American history is a continuing struggle over the definition and realization of the nation's promise. Abraham Lincoln, in the midst of what he termed the "fiery trial" of the Civil War, pronounced the nation "the last best hope of Earth." Kept alive by countless sacrifices, that hope has been marred by compromises, disappointments, and denials, but it still lives. We believe that *The American Promise: A Compact History,* Third Edition, with its attention to making history come alive, will help students become aware of the legacy of hope bequeathed to them by previous generations of Americans stretching back nearly four centuries, a legacy that is theirs to preserve and build on.

Features

From the beginning, readers have proclaimed this textbook a visual feast, richly illustrated in ways that extend and reinforce the narrative. The third compact edition offers more than 460 contemporaneous **illustrations**, a visual program usually found only in a full-sized text, and many are in full color and large enough to study in detail. Over 250 **artifacts** make the past tangible. Full-page **chapter-opening artifacts** and other captioned artifacts throughout the text emphasize the importance of material culture in the study of the past and enrich the historical account. **New embedded artifacts** (small images of material culture)—from boots and political buttons to guns and sewing machines—are folded into the narrative. Similarly, **new illustrated chapter timelines** provide thumbnail-size images from the chapter to reinforce the narrative and stimulate students' power of recall. A striking **new design** highlights the illustration program and makes the most of our **comprehensive captions** while enticing students to delve deeper into the text itself.

We have expanded our highly regarded **map program** to offer the most effective set of maps available in a compact survey text. More than 160 **full-color maps**—far more than in most full-length books—help students learn geography and its role in history. Each chapter offers, on average, three to four **full-sized maps** showing major developments in a wide range of areas, from environmental and technological issues to political, social, cultural, and diplomatic matters. New maps reflect our increased attention to Native American peoples and to the West in particular. In addition, each chapter includes two or three **spot maps**, small,

single-concept maps embedded in the narrative to strengthen students' grasp of crucial issues. Unique to *The American Promise*, new spot maps highlight such topics as Spanish missions in California, frontier land opened by Indian removal in the 1830s, the Mexican cession, selected Indian relocations from 1950 to 1970, contemporary Israel, and the recent conflict in Afghanistan. Finally, each chapter includes a **critical-thinking map exercise**, almost all of which are new.

As part of our ongoing efforts to make this the most teachable and readable survey text available, we paid renewed attention to imaginative and effective pedagogy. Thus, this third compact edition has increased its reach, lending greater in-text help to all levels of students. All chapters are constructed to preview, reinforce, and review the narrative in the most memorable and engaging way possible. To prepare students for the reading to come, each chapter begins with a **new chapter outline** to accompany the vivid **opening vignette** that invites students into the narrative with lively accounts of individuals or groups who embody the central themes of the chapter. New vignettes in this edition include, among others, Roger Williams being banished from Puritan Massachusetts, runaway slave William Gould enlisting in the Union navy, Native American boarding school students celebrating Indian Citizenship Day, Henry Ford putting America on wheels, Colonel Paul Tibbets dropping the bomb on Hiroshima, Phyllis Schlafly promoting conservatism, and Colin Powell adjusting to the post–cold war world. Each vignette ends with a **narrative overview** of the chapter's main topics. To further prepare students as they read, major sections within each chapter begin with **introductory paragraphs** that preview the subsections that follow and conclude with **new review questions** to help students absorb main points and build confidence in their mastery as they read. Throughout each chapter, **two-tiered running heads** with dates and topical headings remind students where the sections they are reading fall chronologically. In addition, **new thematic chronologies** reinforce and extend points in the narrative, and a **new Glossary of Historical Vocabulary** aids students' comprehension by defining terms that some may find hard to grasp, such as *covenant, laissez-faire,* and *progressivism.* At the end of each chapter, a **conclusion** critically re-examines central ideas and provides a bridge to the next chapter.

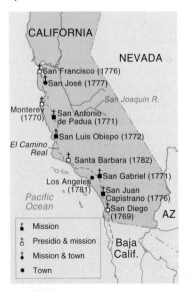

Spanish Missions in California

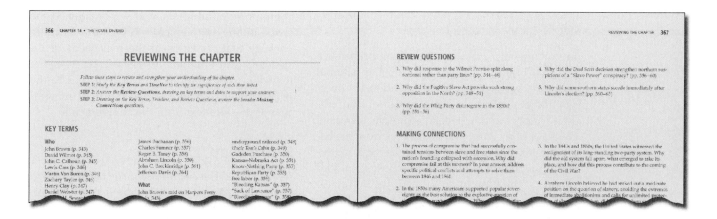

Perhaps the most notable new way this edition reaches out to students is through a substantial **new Reviewing the Chapter** section at the end of each chapter that provides step-by-step study plans to ensure student success. These two-page chapter review guides start with clear **study instructions** that lead students through an incremental approach to reviewing the chapter. Lists of **Key Terms** with page numbers highlight important people, events, and concepts, while illustrated chapter **Timelines** give clear chronological overviews of key events. Two sets of questions prompt students to think critically and make use of the facts they have mastered. The focused **Review Questions** are repeated from within the chapter for reinforcement, while **Making Connections** questions ask students about broad developments in preparation for essay examinations. Finally, the chapter review ends with an **Online Study Guide cross-reference** pointing students to free self-assessment quizzes and other study aids for further help.

Special features reinforce the narrative and offer teachers more points of departure for assignments and discussion. Because students live in an increasingly global world and need help making connections with the world outside the United States, we added ten essays in our **new Beyond America's Borders** feature. These essays seek to widen students' perspectives, to help them see that this country did not develop in isolation. Essays as varied as "American Tobacco and European Consumers," "Filibusters: The Underside of Manifest Destiny," "Transnational Feminisms," and "Jobs in a Globalizing Era" consider the reciprocal connections between the United States and the wider world and challenge students to think about the effects of transnational connec-

tions over time. A broader notion of American history will help students understand more fully the complex development of their nation's history and help prepare them to live in the twenty-first century.

Fresh topics in our three enduring special features further enrich this compact edition. Each **Documenting the American Promise** feature juxtaposes three or four primary documents to dramatize the human dimension of major events and show varying perspectives on a topic or issue. Feature introductions and document headnotes contextualize the sources, while Questions for Analysis and Debate promote critical thinking about primary sources. New topics include "Missionaries Report on California Missions" and "Voices of Protest." **Historical Question** essays pose and interpret historical questions of continuing interest to demonstrate the depth and variety of possible answers, thereby countering the belief of many beginning students that historians simply gather facts and string them together in a chronological narrative. New questions in this edition include "How Long Did the Seven Years' War Last in Indian Country?" and "Why Did the ERA Fail?" **The Promise of Technology** essays examine the social, economic, and cultural ramifications —positive and negative— of technological innovations. New topics in this edition include "Stoves Transform Cooking" and "Better Living through Electricity."

Textual Changes

In our ongoing effort to offer a comprehensive text that braids all Americans into the national narrative, we give particular attention to diversity and the influence of class, religion, race, ethnicity, gender, and region. For example, increased coverage of the West and its peoples from the beginning of American history means fresh material throughout the text and a new post–Civil War chapter, "The West in the Gilded Age." We also give more coverage to the environment, Native Americans, Mexicans, Latinos, and other topics closely related to the history of the West. To strengthen coverage and increase clarity and accessibility, we have reorganized certain chapters. In particular, organizational changes in the chapters on antebellum America and the Gilded Age provide clearer themes with smoother transitions and place the West firmly in the national narrative. We also provide stronger post-1945 chapters, reorganized to make themes more compelling and chronology clearer. These post-1945 chapters also include a fresh array of voices, pay greater attention to the West and related topics, and, of course, present up-to-date coverage of the George W. Bush administration, the Middle East, and the war on terrorism.

Staying abreast of current scholarship is important to us, and this edition reflects that keen interest. We incorporated a wealth of new scholarship to benefit students. Readers will note that we made good use of the latest works on the Spanish borderlands, Native Americans in the Seven Years' War, the role of political wives in the early Republic, the social history of the Gold Rush, the active participation of blacks in their own liberation during the Civil War, mining and commercial farming in the Gilded Age West, race and Americanization, Mexican migration into the American Southwest and how it compares to black migration into the North, the story of the atomic bomb, and the rise of contemporary conservatism.

Supplements

Developed with our guidance and thoroughly revised to reflect the changes in the third edition, the comprehensive collection of print and electronic resources accompanying the textbook represents a host of practical learning and teaching aids. Again, we learned much from the book's community of adopters, and we broadened the scope of the supplements to create a learning package that responds to the real needs of instructors and students. Cross-references in the textbook to the Online Study Guide and to the primary source reader signal the tight integration of the core text with the supplements.

For Students

***Reading the American Past: Selected Historical Documents*, Third Edition.** Edited by Michael P. Johnson (Johns Hopkins University), one of the authors of *The American Promise*, and designed to complement the textbook, *Reading the American Past* provides a broad selection of over 150 primary source documents as well as editorial apparatus to help students understand the sources. Emphasizing the important social, political, and economic themes of U.S. history courses, 31 new documents (one per chapter) were added to provide a multiplicity of perspectives on environmental, western, ethnic, and gender history and to bring a global dimension to the anthology. Available free when packaged with the text.

Online Study Guide at bedfordstmartins.com/ roarkcompact. The popular Online Study Guide for *The American Promise* is a free and uniquely personalized learning tool to help students mas-

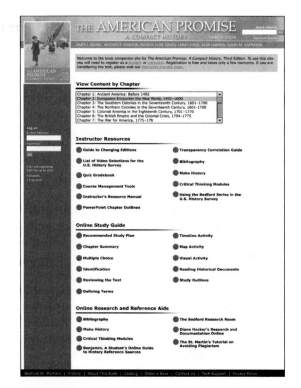

ter themes and information presented in the text-book and improve their historical skills. Assessment quizzes let students evaluate their comprehension and provide them with customized plans for further study through a variety of activities. Instructors can monitor students' progress through the online Quiz Gradebook or receive e-mail updates.

The Bedford Glossary for U.S. History. This handy supplement for the survey course gives students clear, concise definitions of the political, economic, social, and cultural terms used by historians and contemporary media alike. The terms are historically contextualized to aid comprehension. Available free when packaged with the text.

History Matters: A Student Guide to U.S. History Online. This new resource, written by Alan Gevinson, Kelly Schrum, and Roy Rosenzweig (all of George Mason University), provides an illustrated and annotated guide to 250 of the most useful Web sites for student research in U.S. history as well as advice on evaluating and using Internet sources. This essential guide is based on the acclaimed "History Matters" Web site developed by the American History Social Project and the Center for History and New Media. Available free when packaged with the text.

NEW *Maps in Context: A Workbook for American History.* Written by historical cartography expert Gerald A. Danzer (University of Illinois, Chicago), this skill-building workbook helps students comprehend essential connections between geographic literacy and historical understanding. Organized to correspond to the typical U.S. history survey course, *Maps in Context* presents a wealth of map-centered projects and convenient pop quizzes that give students hands-on experience working with maps. Available free when packaged with the text.

Bedford Series in History and Culture. Over 100 titles in this highly praised series combine first-rate scholarship, historical narrative, and important primary documents for undergraduate courses. Each book is brief, inexpensive, and focused on a specific topic or period. Package discounts are available.

Historians at Work Series. Brief enough for a single assignment yet meaty enough to provoke thoughtful discussion, each volume in this series examines a single historical question by combining unabridged selections by distinguished historians, each with a different perspective on the issue, with helpful learning aids. Package discounts are available.

NEW Trade Books. Titles published by sister companies Farrar, Straus and Giroux; Henry Holt and Company; Hill and Wang; Picador; and St. Martin's Press are available at deep discounts when packaged with the text.

Online Bibliography at bedfordstmartins.com/roarkcompact. Organized by book chapter and topic, the online bibliography provides an authoritative and comprehensive list of references to jump-start student research.

Critical Thinking Modules at bedfordstmartins.com/historymodules. This Web site offers over two dozen online modules for interpreting maps, audio, visual, and textual sources, centered on events covered in the U.S. history survey. An online guide correlates modules to textbook chapters.

A Student's Online Guide to History Reference Sources at bedfordstmartins.com/benjamin. This Web site provides links to history-related databases, indexes, and journals, plus contact information for state, provincial, local, and professional history organizations.

Research and Documentation Online at bedfordstmartins.com/resdoc. This Web site provides clear advice on how to integrate primary and secondary sources into research papers, how to cite sources correctly, and how to format in MLA, APA, *Chicago*, or CBE style.

The St. Martin's Tutorial on Avoiding Plagiarism at bedfordstmartins.com/plagiarismtutorial. This online tutorial reviews the consequences of plagiarism and explains what sources to acknowledge, how to keep good notes, how to organize research, and how to integrate sources appropriately. The tutorial includes exercises to help students practice integrating sources and recognize acceptable summaries.

Bedford Research Room at bedfordstmartins.com/researchroom. The Research Room, drawn from Mike Palmquist's *The Bedford Researcher,* offers a wealth of resources—including interactive tutorials, research activities, student writing samples, and links to hundreds of other places online—to support students in courses across the disciplines. The site also offers instructors a library of helpful instructional tools.

Telecourse Guides for *Shaping America: U.S. History to 1877* **and** *Transforming America: U.S. History since 1877.* These guides by Kenneth G. Alfers (Dallas County Community College District) are designed for students using *The American Promise* in conjunction with the Dallas Tele-Learning telecourses *Shaping America* and *Transforming America.* Lesson overviews, assignments, objectives, and focus points provide structure for distance learners, while enrichment ideas, suggested readings, and brief primary sources extend the unit lessons. Practice tests help students evaluate their mastery of the material.

For Instructors

Instructor's Resource Manual. This popular manual by Sarah E. Gardner (Mercer University) and Catherine A. Jones (Johns Hopkins University) offers both experienced and first-time instructors tools for presenting textbook material in exciting and engaging ways—learning objectives, annotated chapter outlines, model answers to review questions, lecture strategies, tips for helping students with common misconceptions and difficult topics, and suggestions for in-class activities, including using film and video, ways to start discussions, topics for debate, and analyzing primary sources. The new edition also features a chapter-by-chapter guide to all of the supplements available with *The American Promise: A Compact History,* an extensive guide for first-time teaching assistants, sample syllabi, and a brief guide for using the book companion site.

Transparencies. This set of over 160 full-color acetate transparencies of full-size maps and many other images from both the full and compact editions of *The American Promise* helps instructors present lectures and teach students important map-reading skills.

Book Companion Site at bedfordstmartins.com/ roarkcompact. The companion Web site gathers all the electronic resources for *The American Promise: A Compact History,* including the Online Study Guide and related Quiz Gradebook, at a single Web address, providing convenient links to lecture, assignment, and research materials such as PowerPoint chapter outlines and the digital libraries at Make History.

Computerized Test Bank. This test bank by Bradford Wood (Eastern Kentucky University), Peter Lau (University of Rhode Island), and Sondra Cosgrove (Community College of Southern Nevada) contains easy-to-use software to create tests. Over 80 exercises are provided per chapter, including multiple-choice, fill-in-the-blank, map analysis, short essay, and full-length essay questions. Instructors can customize quizzes, add or edit both questions and answers, and export questions and answers to a variety of formats, including WebCT and Blackboard. The disc includes correct answers and essay outlines as well as separate test banks for the associated telecourses *Shaping America* and *Transforming America.*

Instructor's Resource CD-ROM. This disc provides instructors with ready-made and customizable PowerPoint multimedia presentations built around chapter outlines, maps, figures, and selected images from the textbook. The disc also includes selected images from the textbook in jpeg format, the *Instructor's Resource Manual,* outline maps in pdf format for quizzing or handouts, and a quick-start guide to the Online Study Guide.

NEW Make History at bedfordstmartins.com/ makehistory. Comprising the content of our five acclaimed online libraries—Map Central, the U.S. History Image Library, DocLinks, HistoryLinks, and PlaceLinks, Make History provides one-stop access to relevant digital content including maps, images, documents, and Web links. Students and instructors alike can search this free, easy-to-use database by keyword, topic, date, or specific chapter of *The American Promise* and can download any content they find. Instructors using *The American Promise* can also create entire collections of content and store them online for later use or post their collections to the Web to share with students.

Using the Bedford Series in History and Culture in the U.S. History Survey at bedfordstmartins .com/usingseries. This online guide helps instructors integrate volumes from the highly regarded Bedford Series in History and Culture into their U.S. history survey course. The guide not only correlates themes from each series book with the survey course but also provides ideas for classroom discussions.

Course Management Content. E-content is available for this book in Blackboard, WebCT, Angel, and Desire2Learn course management systems. This e-content includes nearly all of the offerings from the book's Online Study Guide as well as the book's test bank and the test banks from the associated telecourses *Shaping America* and *Transforming America*.

Videos and Multimedia. A wide assortment of videos and multimedia CD-ROMs on various topics in American history is available to qualified adopters. Also available are 59 short clips from the telecourses *Shaping America* and *Transforming America* in DVD and VHS formats for presentation during lectures.

The American Promise **for Distance Learning via Telecourse.** We are pleased to announce that *The American Promise* has been selected as the textbook for the award-winning U.S. history telecourses *Shaping America: U.S. History to 1877* and *Transforming America: U.S. History since 1877* by Dallas TeleLearning at the LeCroy Center for Educational Telecommunications, Dallas County Community College District. Guides for students and instructors fully integrate the narrative of *The American Promise* into each telecourse. For more information on these distance-learning opportunities, visit the Dallas TeleLearning Web site at http://telelearning.dcccd.edu, e-mail tlearn@dcccd.edu, or call 972-669-6650.

Acknowledgments

We gratefully acknowledge all of the helpful suggestions from those who have read and taught from the previous editions of *The American Promise*, and we hope that our many classroom collaborators will be pleased to see their influence in the third compact edition. In particular, we wish to thank the talented scholars and teachers who gave generously of their time and knowledge to review this book; their critiques and suggestions contributed greatly to the published work: Troy Bickham, *Texas A&M University*; Vincent Clark, *Johnson County Community College*; James Denton, *University of Colorado at Boulder*; Andy DeRoche, *Front Range Community College*; Mark Ellis, *University of Nebraska*; James Good, *North Harris College*; Larry Hartzell, *Brookdale Community College*; Donald Heidenreich, *Lindenwood University*; Adam Howard, *George Mason University*; Jerome Rodnitzky, *University of Texas at Arlington*; Jeffrey Smith, *Lindenwood University*; Richard Sorrell, *Brookdale Community*

College; Richard Ulibarri, *Weber State University*; and Keith Zahniser, *Ohio State University*.

In addition, we wish to thank the reviewers of the full-length third edition of this textbook, whose comments about organization and content informed the compact edition as well: Eric Arnesen, *University of Illinois, Chicago*; Carl H. Boening, *Shelton State Community College*; Tommy L. Bynum, *Georgia Perimeter College*; Lawrence Cebula, *Missouri Southern State College*; Michael Connolly, *Tidewater Community College*; Gary Darden, *Rutgers University*; David Engerman, *Brandeis University*; Maurine W. Greenwald, *University of Pittsburgh*; David Igler, *University of Utah*; Peter F. Lau, *University of Rhode Island*; Charles H. Martin, *University of Texas, El Paso*; April Masten, *State University of New York, Stony Brook*; Jim R. McClellan, *Northern Virginia Community College*; Constance McGovern, *Frostburg State University*; Karen Merrill, *Williams College*; Peggy Renner, *Glendale Community College*; Steven Reschly, *Truman State University*; Leo Ribuffo, *The George Washington University*; Christine Sears, *University of Delaware*; Michael Sherry, *Northwestern University*; Steven Stoll, *Yale University*; Diana Turk, *New York University*; Elliott West, *University of Arkansas*; Jon A. Whitfield, *Central Texas College, Fort Knox*; Thomas Winn, *Austin Peay State University*; and Thomas Zeiler, *University of Colorado at Boulder*.

A project as complex as this requires the talents of many individuals. First, we would like to acknowledge our families for their support, forbearance, and toleration of our textbook responsibilities. Pembroke Herbert and Sandi Rygiel of Picture Research Consultants, Inc., contributed their unparalleled knowledge and diligent research to make possible the extraordinary illustration program.

We would also like to thank the many people at Bedford/St. Martin's who have been crucial to this project. No one contributed more than senior editor Heidi L. Hood, who managed the entire revision and oversaw the development of each chapter. We thank as well associate editor Shannon Hunt for her help with portions of the manuscript. Thanks also go to editorial assistant Daniel Cole, who provided invaluable editorial support and who coordinated the supplements. We are also grateful to Jane Knetzger, director of development for history, and Mary Dougherty, executive editor, for their support and guidance. For their imaginative and tireless efforts to promote the book, we want to thank Jenna Bookin Barry, marketing manager, and Amanda Byrnes, marketing associate. With great skill and professionalism, senior production editor Karen Baart juggled and monitored the many pieces related to copyediting, design, and typesetting. Karen was ably assisted by production intern Lindsay DiGianvittorio and by Katherine Caruana, production assistant; Katherine also saw to the production of the *Instructor's Resource Manual.* Managing editor Elizabeth Schaaf and assistant managing editor John Amburg offered their customary expert guidance. Production supervisor Jennifer Wetzel oversaw the manufacturing of the book. Page makeup artist DeNee Skipper, copyeditor Patricia Herbst, and proofreaders Janet Cocker and Barbara Price attended to the myriad details that help make the book shine. Anne Harbour provided an especially useful index. Associate new media editor Danielle Slevens and new media production coordinator Coleen O'Hanley made sure that *The American Promise* remains at the forefront of technological support for students and instructors. Editorial director Denise Wydra provided helpful advice throughout the course of the project. Finally, president Joan E. Feinberg and former president Charles H. Christensen took a personal interest in *The American Promise* from the start, for which we are grateful.

JAMES L. ROARK

Born in Eunice, Louisiana, and raised in the West, James L. Roark received his B.A. from the University of California, Davis, in 1963 and his Ph.D. from Stanford University in 1973. His dissertation won the Allan Nevins Prize. He has taught at the University of Nigeria, Nsukka; the University of Nairobi, Kenya; the University of Missouri, St. Louis; and, since 1983, Emory University, where he is Samuel Candler Dobbs Professor of American History. In 1993, he received the Emory Williams Distinguished Teaching Award, and in 2001–2002 he was Pitt Professor of American Institutions at Cambridge University. He has written *Masters without Slaves: Southern Planters in the Civil War and Reconstruction* (1977). With Michael P. Johnson, he is author of *Black Masters: A Free Family of Color in the Old South* (1984) and editor of *No Chariot Let Down: Charleston's Free People of Color on the Eve of the Civil War* (1984). He has received research assistance from the American Philosophical Society, the National Endowment for the Humanities, and the Gilder Lehrman Institute of American History. Active in the Organization of American Historians and the Southern Historical Association, he is also a fellow of the Society of American Historians.

MICHAEL P. JOHNSON

Born and raised in Ponca City, Oklahoma, Michael P. Johnson studied at Knox College in Galesburg, Illinois, where he received a B.A. in 1963, and at Stanford University in Palo Alto, California, earning a Ph.D. in 1973. He is currently professor of history at Johns Hopkins University in Baltimore, having previously taught at the University of California, Irvine, San Jose State University, and LeMoyne (now LeMoyne-Owen) College in Memphis. His publications include *Toward a Patriarchal Republic: The Secession of Georgia* (1977); with James L. Roark, *Black Masters: A Free*

Family of Color in the Old South (1984) and *No Chariot Let Down: Charleston's Free People of Color on the Eve of the Civil War* (1984); *Abraham Lincoln, Slavery, and the Civil War: Selected Speeches and Writings* (2001); *Reading the American Past: Selected Historical Documents*, the documents reader for *The American Promise*; and articles that have appeared in the *William and Mary Quarterly,* the *Journal of Southern History, Labor History,* the *New York Review of Books,* the *New Republic,* the *Nation,* and other journals. Johnson has been awarded research fellowships by the American Council of Learned Societies, the National Endowment for the Humanities, and the Center for Advanced Study in the Behavioral Sciences and Stanford University, and the Times Mirror Foundation Distinguished Research Fellowship at the Huntington Library. He has directed a National Endowment for the Humanities Summer Seminar for College Teachers and has been honored with the University of California, Irvine, Academic Senate Distinguished Teaching Award and the University of California, Irvine, Alumni Association Outstanding Teaching Award. He won the *William and Mary Quarterly* award for best article in 2002 and the Organization of American Historians ABC-CLIO *America: History and Life* Award for best American history article in 2002. He is an active member of the American Historical Association, the Organization of American Historians, and the Southern Historical Association.

PATRICIA CLINE COHEN

Born in Ann Arbor, Michigan, and raised in Palo Alto, California, Patricia Cline Cohen earned a B.A. at the University of Chicago in 1968 and a Ph.D. at the University of California, Berkeley in 1977. In 1976, she joined the history faculty at the University of California, Santa Barbara. In 2005–2006 she received the university's Distinguished Teaching Award. Cohen has written *A Calculating People: The Spread of Numeracy in Early America* (1982; reissued

1999) and *The Murder of Helen Jewett: The Life and Death of a Prostitute in Nineteenth-Century New York* (1998). She has also published articles on quantitative literacy, mathematics education, prostitution, and murder in journals including the *Journal of Women's History, Radical History Review,* the *William and Mary Quarterly,* and the *NWSA Journal.* Her scholarly work has received support from the National Endowment for the Humanities, the National Humanities Center, the University of California President's Fellowship in the Humanities, the Mellon Foundation, the American Antiquarian Society, the Schlesinger Library, and the Newberry Library. She is an active associate of the Omohundro Institute of Early American History and Culture, sits on the advisory council of the Society for the History of the Early American Republic, and is past president of the Western Association of Women Historians. She has served as chair of the history department, as chair of the Women's Studies Program, and as acting dean of the humanities and fine arts at the University of California at Santa Barbara. In 2001–2002 she was the Distinguished Senior Mellon Fellow at the American Antiquarian Society. Currently she is working on a book about women's health advocate Mary Gove Nichols.

Sarah Stage

Sarah Stage was born in Davenport, Iowa, and received a B.A. from the University of Iowa in 1966 and a Ph.D. in American studies from Yale University in 1975. She has taught U.S. history for more than twenty-five years at Williams College and the University of California, Riverside. Currently she is professor of Women's Studies at Arizona State University at the West campus in Phoenix. Her books include *Female Complaints: Lydia Pinkham and the Business of Women's Medicine* (1979) and *Rethinking Home Economics: Women and the History of a Profession* (1997), which has been translated for a Japanese edition. Among the fellowships she has received are the Rockefeller Foundation Humanities Fellowship, the American Association of University Women dissertation fellowship, a fellowship from the Charles Warren Center for the Study of History at Harvard University, and the University of California President's Fellowship in the Humanities. She is at work on a book entitled *Women and the Progressive Impulse in American Politics, 1890–1914.*

Alan Lawson

Born in Providence, Rhode Island, Alan Lawson received his B.A. from Brown University in 1955 and his M.A. from the University of Wisconsin in 1956. After Army service and experience as a high school teacher, he earned his Ph.D. from the University of Michigan in 1967. Since winning the Allan Nevins Prize for his dissertation, Lawson has served on the faculties of the University of California, Irvine, Smith College, and, currently, Boston College. He has written *The Failure of Independent Liberalism* (1971) and coedited *From Revolution to Republic* (1976). While completing the forthcoming *Ideas in Crisis: The New Deal and the Mobilization of Progressive Experience,* he has published book chapters and essays on political economy, the cultural legacy of the New Deal, multiculturalism, and the arts in public life. He has served as editor of the *Review of Education* and the *Intellectual History Newsletter* and contributed articles to those journals as well as to the *History of Education Quarterly.* He has been active in the field of American studies as director of the Boston College American studies program and as a contributor to the *American Quarterly.* Under the auspices of the United States Information Agency, Lawson has been coordinator and lecturer for programs to instruct faculty from foreign nations in the state of American historical scholarship and teaching.

Susan M. Hartmann

Professor of history at Ohio State University, Susan M. Hartmann received her B.A. from Washington University and her Ph.D. from the University of Missouri. After specializing in the political economy of the post–World War II period and publishing *Truman and the 80th Congress* (1971), she expanded her interests to the field of women's history, publishing many articles and three books: *The Home Front and Beyond: American Women in the 1940s* (1982); *From Margin to Mainstream: American Women and Politics since 1960* (1989); and *The Other Feminists: Activists in the Liberal Establishment* (1998). Her work has been supported by the Truman Library Institute, the Rockefeller Foundation, the National Endowment for the Humanities, and the American Council of Learned Societies. At Ohio State she has served as director of women's studies, and in 1995 she won the Exemplary Faculty Award in the College of Humanities. Hartmann has taught at the University of Missouri, St. Louis, and Boston University, and she has lectured on American history in Australia, Austria, France, Germany, Greece, Japan, Nepal, and New Zealand. She is a fellow of the Society of American Historians, has served on award committees of the American Historical Association, the Organization of American Historians, the American Studies Association, and the National Women's Studies Association, and currently is on the Board of Directors at the Truman Library Institute. Her current research is on gender and the transformation of politics since 1945.

The American Promise

A COMPACT HISTORY

Third Edition

ANASAZI EFFIGY

Ancient North Americans crafted human likenesses in stone, clay, and wood, as well as depicting human forms on canyon walls, pottery, and elsewhere. An Anasazi Indian in the Southwest carved this artifact from stone sometime around AD 1200. The unmistakably human features of the object tempt us to believe that it might be an ancient American self-portrait. Certainly the carver took care to give the object a recognizably human face, neck, arms, hands, legs, and feet. The brightly colored pigments suggest clothing or body decorations. The Anasazi who painted the object had a clear idea of what should be painted orange, turquoise, and red. Red belonged on wrists, not on lips. This color code that made perfect sense to the Anasazi remains obscure to us, a hint that the carver may have intended to depict a deity or supernatural being who had some human features. For example, the artifact lacks ears and sexual organs. The polished tip of the nose contrasts with the rough surface of the torso and legs, suggesting that Anasazi often rubbed the nose. Experts refer to this artifact and others like it as effigies, that is, objects that presumably had ritualistic or spiritual significance. Instead of showing us what the Anasazi considered a self-portrait, this effigy probably depicts one of their many gods. Yet, since the Anasazi—like other human beings—probably created gods in their own image, the effigy may somewhat resemble Anasazi people.

Ancient America

Before 1492

GEORGE MCJUNKIN, the manager of the Crowfoot Ranch near Folsom, New Mexico, rode out to mend fences and to look for missing cattle after a violent rainstorm in August 1908. An American of African descent, McJunkin had been born a slave in Texas and had been riding horses since he was a boy. After he became free at the end of the Civil War in 1865, McJunkin worked as a cowboy in Colorado and New Mexico before becoming the Crowfoot manager in 1891. Now, as he rode across the ranch land he knew so well to survey damage caused by the recent storm, McJunkin noticed that floodwater had washed away the bank of a gulch called Wild Horse Arroyo and exposed a deposit of stark white bones. Curious, he dismounted and chipped away at the deposit until he uncovered an entire fossilized bone. The bone was much larger than the parched skeletons of range cattle and buffalo that McJunkin often saw, so he saved it, hoping someday to identify it.

Four years later, in 1912, McJunkin met Carl Schwachheim, a white man in Raton, New Mexico. Schwachheim, a blacksmith, shared McJunkin's curiosity about fossils, and the two men became friends. McJunkin told Schwachheim about the fossil deposit he had discovered. Ten years later, a few months after McJunkin's death, Schwachheim finally drove out to Wild Horse Arroyo and dug out several bones. But, like McJunkin, he could not identify any animal that had such big bones.

In 1926, Schwachheim delivered cattle to the stockyards in Denver, and he took some of the fossilized bones to the Denver Museum of Natural History and showed them to J. D. Figgins, a paleontologist who was an expert on fossils of ancient animals. Figgins immediately recognized the significance of the bones and a few months later began an excavation of the Folsom site that revolutionized knowledge about the first Americans.

When Figgins began his dig at Folsom, archaeologists (individuals who examine **artifacts** left by long-vanished peoples as part of the study of **archaeology**) believed that Native Americans had arrived relatively recently in the Western Hemisphere, probably no more than three or four thousand years earlier when, experts assumed, they had paddled small boats across the icy waters of the Bering Strait from what is now Siberia. At Folsom, Figgins learned that the bones McJunkin had first spotted belonged to twenty-three giant bison, a species known to have been extinct for at least 10,000 years. Far more startling, Figgins found among the bones nineteen flint spear points (Folsom points, they have since been called), proof that human beings had been alive at the same time as the giant bison. One spear point remained stuck

George McJunkin

This photo shows McJunkin a few years after he discovered the Folsom site but about fifteen years before anyone understood the significance of his find. He appears here in his work clothes on horseback, as he probably was when he made the discovery. The fossilized bones he discovered belonged to an extinct bison species that was much larger than modern bison; the horns of the ancient animal often spanned six feet, wide enough for McJunkin's horse to have stood sideways between the horns.

Eastern New Mexico University, Blackwater Draw Site, Portales, New Mexico 88130.

Archaeology and History

Archaeologists and historians share the desire to learn about people who lived in the past, but they usually employ different methods to obtain information. Both archaeologists and historians study artifacts as clues to the activities and ideas of the humans who created them. They concentrate, however, on different kinds of artifacts. Archaeologists tend to focus on physical objects such as bones, stones, pots, baskets, jewelry, textiles, clothing, graves, and buildings. Historians direct their attention mostly to writings, which encompass personal and private jottings such as diary entries and love letters, official and public pronouncements such as laws and speeches, as well as an enormous variety of other documents. Although historians are interested in other artifacts and archaeologists do not neglect written sources if they exist, the characteristic concentration of historians on writings and archaeologists on other physical objects denotes a rough cultural and chronological boundary between the human beings studied by the two groups of scholars, a boundary marked by the use of writing.

Writing is defined as a system of symbols that record spoken language. Writing originated among ancient peoples in China, Egypt, and Central America about 8,000 years ago, within the most recent 2 percent of the 400 millennia that modern human beings (*Homo sapiens*) have existed. Writing came into use even later in most other places in the world. The ancient Americans who inhabited North America in 1492, for example, possessed many forms of symbolic representation, but not writing.

The people who lived during the millennia before writing were biologically nearly identical to us. Their DNA was the template for ours. But unlike us, they did not use writing to communicate across space and time. They invented hundreds of spoken languages; they learned to survive and even to thrive in almost every natural environment; they chose and honored leaders; they traded, warred, and worshipped; and, above all, they learned from and taught each other. Much of what we would like to know about their experiences remains unknown because it took place before writing existed. The absence of writing forever muffles their words and thus their history.

Archaeologists specialize in learning about people who did not document their history in writing. They study the millions of artifacts created by these people. They also scrutinize soil,

between two ribs of a giant bison, where a Stone Age hunter had plunged it more than 10,000 years earlier. No longer could anyone doubt that human beings had inhabited North America for at least ten millennia.

The Folsom discovery sparked other major finds of ancient artifacts that continue to this day. Since the 1930s, archaeologists have tried to reconstruct the history of ancient Americans, to understand the hunters who killed giant bison with flint-tipped spears as well as their ancestors who first arrived in North America and their descendants who built southwestern pueblos and eastern burial mounds, and *their* descendants who encountered Europeans in 1492. Although the long history of ancient Americans is incomplete and controversial, scholars have learned the identity of ancient Americans, where they came from, and some basic features of the complex cultures they created and passed along to their descendants who eventually came face-to-face with Europeans.

Anasazi Pictograph
This unusual pictograph was painted about AD 1300 on the wall of an Anasazi dwelling in what is now Canyonlands National Park in Utah. The colorful design presumably had a specific meaning for the Anasazi who created it, but that meaning remains indecipherable to experts today.
J. Q. Jacobs.

geological strata, pollen, climate, and other environmental features to reconstruct the history of ancient peoples. Although no documents chronicle ancient Americans' lives, archaeologists have learned to make artifacts tell a great deal about the people who made them.

Since ancient America was the long first phase of the history of the United States, this chapter relies on the work of archaeologists to sketch a brief overview of this important era. Ancient Americans and their descendants resided in North America for thousands of years before Europeans arrived. They created societies and cultures of remarkable diversity and complexity. Because they did not use written records, their history cannot be reconstructed with the detail and certainty made possible by writing. But it is better to abbreviate and oversimplify their history than to ignore it.

REVIEW   Why do historians rely on the work of archaeologists to write the history of ancient America?

The First Americans

The first human beings to arrive in the Western Hemisphere emigrated from Asia. They brought with them hunting skills, weapon- and tool-making techniques, and a full range of other forms of human knowledge developed millennia earlier in Africa, Europe, and Asia. These first Americans specialized in hunting mammoths, giant elephant-like creatures they had learned in Europe and Asia to kill, butcher, and process for food, clothing, building materials, and many other purposes. Most likely, these first Americans wandered into the Western Hemisphere more or less accidentally, hungry and in pursuit of their prey.

African and Asian Origins

Human beings lived elsewhere in the world for hundreds of thousands of years before they reached the Western Hemisphere. Millions of years before humans evolved anywhere on the globe, North and South America became detached from the gigantic common landmass scientists now call Pangaea. About 240 million years ago, powerful forces deep within the earth fractured Pangaea and slowly pushed the continents apart to approximately their present positions (Map 1.1). This process of continental drift encircled the land of the Western Hemisphere with large oceans that isolated it from the other continents, long before early human beings (*Homo erectus*) first appeared in Africa about 2 million years ago. (Hereafter in this chapter, the abbreviation *BP*—archaeologists' notation for "years before the present"—is used to indicate dates earlier than 2,000 years ago. Dates more recent than 2,000 years ago are indicated with the common and familiar notation *AD*—for example, AD 1492.)

More than a million and a half years after *Homo erectus* appeared, or about 400,000 BP, modern humans (*Homo sapiens*) evolved in Africa. All human beings throughout the world today are descendants of these ancient Africans. Slowly, over many millennia, *Homo sapiens* migrated out of Africa and into Europe and Asia. Unlike North and South America, Europe and Asia retained land connections to Africa, making migration possible for *Homo sapiens*. The vast oceans encircling North and South America kept human beings away for roughly 97 percent of the time *Homo sapiens* have been on earth.

Two major developments made it possible for human beings to migrate to the Western

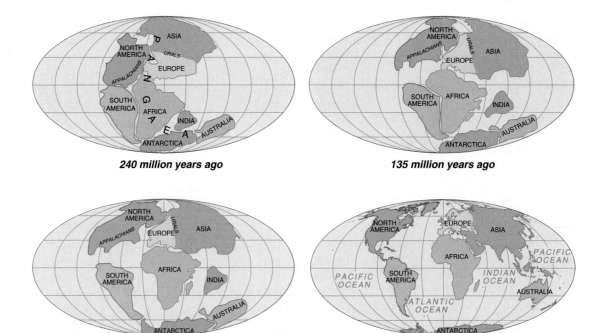

240 million years ago

135 million years ago

65 million years ago

Present-day

MAP 1.1 Continental Drift
Massive geological forces separated North and South America from other continents eons before human beings evolved in Africa in the last 1.5 million years.

Hemisphere. First, humans successfully adapted to the frigid environment near the Arctic Circle. Second, changes in the earth's climate reconnected North America to Asia.

By about 25,000 BP, *Homo sapiens* had spread from Africa throughout Europe and Asia. People, presumably women, had learned to use bone needles to sew animal skins into warm clothing that permitted them to become permanent residents of extremely cold regions like northeastern Siberia. Ancient Siberians walked to North America on land that now lies submerged beneath sixty miles of water that separates easternmost Siberia from westernmost Alaska. During the last global cold spell—the Wisconsin glaciation, which endured from about 80,000 BP to about 10,000 BP—the sea level dropped as much as 350 feet below its current level, exposing what experts refer to as a land bridge between Asian Siberia and American Alaska. This land bridge, which scientists call Beringia, opened a pathway about a thousand miles wide between the Eastern and Western Hemispheres.

Beringia

SIBERIA

Bering Strait land bridge

Bering Sea

NORTH AMERICA

0   300   600 miles
0   300   600 kilometers

Siberian hunters presumably roamed into Beringia for centuries in search of game animals. (See "Beyond America's Borders," page 8.) Grasses and small shrubs that covered Beringia supported herds of mammoth, bison, and numerous smaller animals. As the hunters ventured farther and farther east, they became pioneers of human life in the Western Hemisphere. Unbeknownst to them, their migrations revolutionized the history of the world.

Archaeologists speculate that these Siberian hunters traveled in small bands of no more than 25 people. How many such bands arrived in North America before Beringia once again disappeared beneath the sea will never be known. When they came is hotly debated by experts. The first migrants probably arrived sometime after 15,000 BP. Scattered and inconclusive evidence suggests that they may have arrived several thousand years earlier. Certainly humans inhabited the Western Hemisphere by 13,000 BP.

Archaeologists refer to these first migrants and their

descendants for the next few millennia as Paleo-Indians. While the date of their arrival is somewhat uncertain, they certainly originated in Asia. Some archaeologists have speculated that the Paleo-Indians may have sailed across the South Pacific from Polynesia or across the North Atlantic from Europe, but no evidence conclusively supports such views. Instead, detailed analyses of Native American languages, blood proteins, and DNA patterns, along with extensive archaeological discoveries, provide conclusive evidence of ancient Americans' Asian origins.

Paleo-Indian Hunters

When humans first arrived in the Western Hemisphere, massive glaciers covered most of present-day Canada. A narrow corridor not entirely obstructed by ice ran along the eastern side of Canada's Rocky Mountains, and most archaeologists believe that Paleo-Indians migrated through the ice-free passageway in pursuit of game. They may also have traveled along the coast in small boats, hopscotching from one desirable landing spot to another. At the southern edge of the glaciers, Paleo-Indians entered a hunters' paradise.

North, Central, and South America teemed with wildlife that had never before confronted wily two-legged predators armed with razor-sharp spears. The abundance of game presumably made hunting relatively easy. Ample food permitted the Paleo-Indian population to grow. Within a thousand years or so, Paleo-Indians lived throughout the Western Hemisphere.

Paleo-Indians used a distinctively shaped spearhead known now as a Clovis point, named for the place in New Mexico where it was first excavated. Archaeologists' discovery of Clovis points throughout North and Central America in sites occupied between 11,500 BP and 11,000 BP provides evidence that these nomadic hunters shared a common ancestry and way of life. Paleo-Indians probably hunted smaller animals, but most of the artifacts that have survived from this era indicate that they specialized in hunting mammoths. One mammoth kill supplied meat for weeks or, if dried, for months. Mammoth hide and bones provided clothing, shelter, tools, and much more.

About 11,000 BP, Paleo-Indians confronted a major crisis. The mammoths and other big-game animals they hunted became extinct.

FIGURE 1.1 Human Habitation of the World and the Western Hemisphere
These clock faces illustrate the long global history of modern humans (left) and of human history in the Western Hemisphere since the arrival of the first ancient Americans (right). If the total period of human life on earth is considered, American history since the arrival of Columbus in 1492 comprises less than one minute (or one-tenth of 1 percent) of modern human existence. And if the total period of human life in the New World is converted from millennia to a 12-hour clock, then ancient American history makes up the first 11½ hours, and all history since the arrival of the Europeans in 1492 occupies only the last half hour.

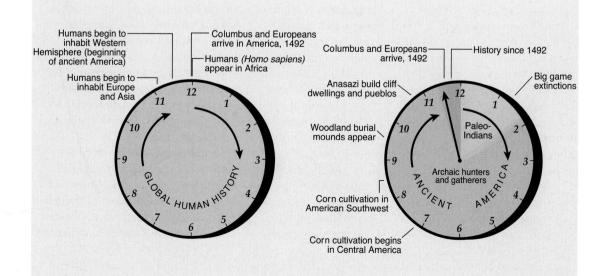

Nature's Immigrants

Like the first human beings who came to the New World, most of the large animals in ancient America were descendants of migrants from elsewhere on the globe. Mammoths, the signature prey of the Clovis hunters of ancient America, illustrate the persistent immigration of animals from Asia to North America. The ancestors of the mammoths that Clovis hunters stalked about 12,000 years ago had emigrated from Asia about 1.7 million years earlier. The first mammoth migrants from Asia followed in the tracks of hundreds of other animal species that had made their way across Beringia to North America for more than 60 million years. These immigrants and their descendants populated the natural environment of America that ancient Americans first encountered. Clearly, America was a land of immigrants long before the first humans arrived.

An extraterrestrial event created the basic precondition for these animal migrations. Scientists have discovered convincing evidence that about 65 million years ago a meteorite about six miles in diameter slammed into the Yucatán peninsula in

Meteor Impact in North America, 65 Million Years Ago

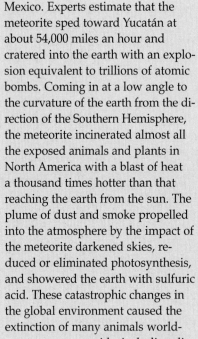

Mexico. Experts estimate that the meteorite sped toward Yucatán at about 54,000 miles an hour and cratered into the earth with an explosion equivalent to trillions of atomic bombs. Coming in at a low angle to the curvature of the earth from the direction of the Southern Hemisphere, the meteorite incinerated almost all the exposed animals and plants in North America with a blast of heat a thousand times hotter than that reaching the earth from the sun. The plume of dust and smoke propelled into the atmosphere by the impact of the meteorite darkened skies, reduced or eliminated photosynthesis, and showered the earth with sulfuric acid. These catastrophic changes in the global environment caused the extinction of many animals worldwide, including dinosaurs who had ruled the earth for more than 100 million years. But outside the fiery blast zone that extended thousands of miles north from ground zero in Yucatán, many animals survived the mass extinction and became the ancestors of animals that eventually migrated to North America.

Among the animals that survived the great extinction were small ratlike creatures, the ances-

tors of mammals that began to multiply and remultiply, ultimately filling many of the environmental niches previously occupied by dinosaurs and other extinct species. For example, a tiny hoofed mammal now called Procerberus made the trek across Beringia from Asia to North America and within about 4 million years spawned dozens of new species of hoofed mammals in the New World, the largest the size of a small pony. Procerberus became the ancient ancestor of both horses and camels, species that evolved first in North America.

In the millions of years that followed ancestor species' initial migration from Asia, distinctive North American descendants evolved, just as horses and camels did. The ancestor of North American cats migrated from Asia about 17 million years ago, but within a few million years, North America had evolved distinctive cat species, including lions roughly twice as large as the largest male African lions today. Similarly, nature's migrants from Asia developed into distinctive North American elephants (including mammoths), rhinoceroses, and pigs, as well as many smaller creatures such as beavers, skunks, and weasels. Although the migration of ancient birds is less well known because of the scarcity of fossil remains, the ancestor of today's common raven made the colossal journey to North America over millions of years by flying through Asia from its starting point in Australia.

Some animals that evolved in North America eventually migrated back to Asia and beyond. Horses and camels illustrate this two-way traffic on the Beringian land bridge. Horses evolved in North America for about

Saber-Toothed Cat Skeleton

Saber-toothed cats ranged throughout North America when the first Americans arrived. This fossilized skeleton came from the La Brea tar pits in present-day Los Angeles, California. For millennia before the arrival of human beings in the New World, these cats and 660 other animal species became bogged down in the tar pits, which ultimately served to preserve their remains. Hundreds of thousands of saber-toothed cat bones have been recovered from the tar pit deposits. The cats probably used their huge incisors to tear open the throats or abdomens of their prey. Unlike the swift-footed big cats of today, saber-toothed cats did not chase down their prey. Since they weighed about twice as much as modern lions, they crouched in ambush and leaped on unsuspecting victims. This mode of attack probably accounts for the many fossils in the tar pits. Cats who attacked prey mired in the sticky tar probably became trapped themselves sometimes. Like many other big mammals that inhabited North America during the Paleo-Indian era, the saber-toothed cat became extinct about 11,000 BP.

George C. Page Museum.

---

migrants was in the other direction, from Asia to North America. The greater variety of well-established species in the larger Asian landmass made it difficult for many North American species to get a foothold there. Conversely, migrants from Asia more readily carved out an environmental niche for themselves in the New World.

On the eve of the arrival of ancient Americans in the New World, the large mammals they would prey upon—and in some cases compete with for prey—were the descendants of migrants who had preceded the first Americans millions of years earlier. The giant bison who roamed the plains—and whose fossilized remains George McJunkin excavated early in the twentieth century—descended from Asian migrants. So did the giant sloths that measured eighteen feet from nose to tail and weighed three tons. So did the massive short-faced bear that ran down its prey despite weighing the better part of a ton. So did the saber-toothed cat that, fossil deposits prove, feasted on young mammoths. And so did the mammoths themselves. The human beings who first set foot in the New World were pioneers of human migration to North America, but they were only the latest of latecomers among the thousands of nature's migrants from Asia that had been pioneering in North America for more than 60 million years.

20 million years before they first wandered across the land bridge to Asia. They didn't stop there. Modern-day zebras on the plains of Africa are the descendants of those ancient American migrant horses. Camels were much more recent out-migrants, wending their way from North America to Asia only about 4 million years ago. Dogs, evidently one of the few native North American mammals, also migrated to Asia, along with other distinctive species. But the dominant stream of nature's

Scientists are not completely certain why the extinction occurred, although the changing environment probably contributed to it. About this time the Wisconsin glacial period came to an end, glaciers melted, and sea levels rose. Some large mammals probably had difficulty adapting to the warmer climate. Many archaeologists also believe, however, that Paleo-Indians contributed to the extinctions in the Western Hemisphere by killing these animals more rapidly than they could reproduce. Within just a few thousand years of their arrival in the New World (the term that Europeans eventually coined for the Western Hemisphere), Paleo-Indian hunters helped bring about a radical change in the natural environment—namely the extinction of large mammals that had existed for millions of years and whose presence had initially drawn hunters west across Beringia.

Paleo-Indians adapted to the drastic environmental change of the big-game extinctions by making at least two important changes in their way of life. First, hunters began to prey more intensively on smaller animals. Second, Paleo-Indians devoted more energy to foraging, that is, to collecting wild plant foods such as roots, seeds, nuts, berries, and fruits. When Paleo-Indians made these changes, they replaced the apparent uniformity of the big-game-oriented Clovis culture* with great cultural diversity. This diversity arose because ancient Americans adapted to the many natural environments throughout the hemisphere, ranging from icy tundra to steamy jungles.

Post-Clovis adaptations to local environments resulted in the astounding variety of Native American cultures that existed when Europeans arrived in AD 1492. By then, more than three hundred major tribes and hundreds of lesser groups inhabited North America alone. Hundreds more lived in Central and South America. These peoples spoke different languages, practiced different religions, lived in different dwellings, followed different subsistence strategies, and observed different rules of kinship and inheritance. Hundreds of other ancient American cultures had disappeared or transformed themselves as their people constantly adapted to environmental and other changes.

> **REVIEW**   Why were humans able to migrate into North America after 15,000 BP?

Archaic Hunters and Gatherers

Archaeologists use the term **Archaic** to describe both the many different hunting and gathering cultures that descended from Paleo-Indians and the long period of time when those cultures dominated the history of ancient America, roughly from 10,000 BP to somewhere between 4000 BP and 3000 BP. The term usefully describes the era in the history of ancient America that followed the Paleo-Indian big-game hunters and preceded the development of agriculture. It denotes a hunter-gatherer way of life that persisted in North America long after European colonization.

Archaic Indians hunted with spears; but they also took smaller game with traps, nets, and hooks. Unlike their Paleo-Indian predecessors, most Archaic peoples used a variety of stone tools to prepare food from wild plants. A characteristic Archaic artifact is a grinding stone used to pulverize seeds into edible form. Most Archaic Indians migrated from place to place to harvest plants and hunt animals. They usually did not establish permanent villages, although they

---

* The word *culture* is used here to connote what is commonly called "way of life." It refers not only to how a group of people supplied themselves with food and shelter but also to their family relationships, social groupings, religious ideas, and other features of their lives. For most prehistoric cultures—as for the Clovis people—more is known about food and shelter because of the artifacts that have survived. Ancient Americans' ideas, assumptions, hopes, dreams, and fantasies were undoubtedly important, but we know very little about them.

Clovis Spear Straightener
Clovis hunters used this bone spear straightener about 11,000 BP at a campsite in Arizona where archaeologists discovered it lying among the butchered remains of two mammoth carcasses and thirteen ancient bison. Similar objects often appear in ancient sites in Eurasia, but this is the only bone artifact yet discovered in a Clovis-era site in North America. Presumably Clovis hunters stuck their spear shafts through the opening and then grasped the handle of the straightener and moved it back and forth along the length of the shaft to remove imperfections and make the spear a more effective weapon.
Arizona State Museum, University of Arizona.

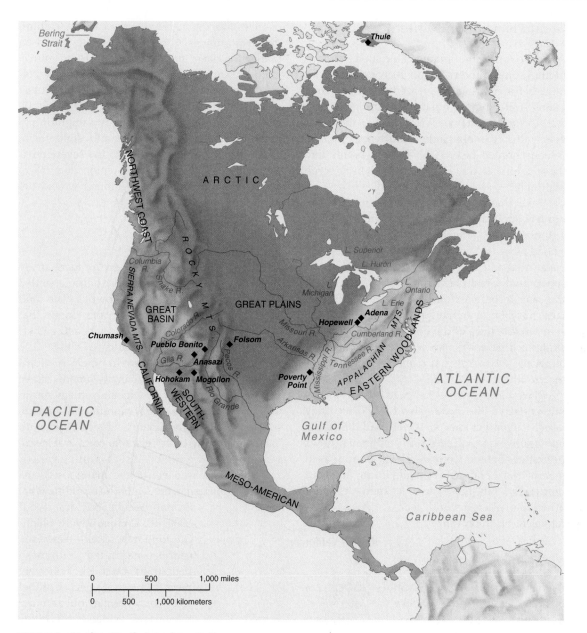

MAP 1.2 Native North American Cultures

Environmental conditions defined the boundaries of the broad zones of cultural similarity among ancient North Americans.

READING THE MAP: What crucial environmental features set the boundaries of each cultural region? (The topography indicated on Map 1.3, "Native North Americans about 1500," may be helpful.)

CONNECTIONS: How did environmental factors and variations affect the development of different groups of Native American cultures? Why do you think historians and archaeologists group cultures together by their regional positions?

FOR MORE HELP ANALYZING THIS MAP, see the map activity for this chapter in the Online Study Guide at bedfordstmartins.com/roarkcompact.

often returned to the same river valley or fertile meadow from year to year. In certain regions with especially rich resources—such as present-day California and the Pacific Northwest—they developed permanent settlements. Many groups became highly proficient basket makers in order to collect and store plant food. Instead of depending on agriculture, they gathered wild plants and hunted wild animals. Archaic peoples followed these practices in distinctive ways in the different environmental regions of North America (Map 1.2).

Great Plains Bison Hunters

After the extinction of large game such as mammoths, some hunters began to concentrate on huge herds of bison that grazed the grassy, arid plains stretching for hundreds of miles east of the Rocky Mountains. For almost a thousand years after the big-game extinctions, Archaic Indians hunted bison with Folsom points like those found at the site discovered by George McJunkin.

Like their nomadic predecessors, Folsom hunters moved constantly to maintain contact with their prey. Often two or three hunters from a band of several families would single out a few bison from a herd and creep up close enough to spear them. Great Plains hunters also developed trapping techniques that made it easier to kill large numbers of animals. At the original Folsom site, careful study of the bones McJunkin found suggests that early one winter hunters drove bison into the narrow gulch and speared twenty-three of them.

Bows and arrows reached Great Plains hunters from the north about AD 500. They largely replaced spears, which had been the hunters' weapon of choice for millennia. Bows permitted hunters to wound an animal from farther away, and arrows made it easy to shoot repeatedly. But these new weapons did not otherwise alter age-old techniques of bison hunting.

Great Basin Cultures

Archaic peoples in the Great Basin between the Rocky Mountains and the Sierra Nevada inhabited a region of great environmental diversity. Some Great Basin Indians lived along the shores of large marshes and lakes that formed during rainy periods. They ate fish of every available size and type, catching them with bone hooks and nets. Other cultures survived in the foothills of mountains between the blistering heat on the desert floor and the cold, treeless mountain heights. Hunters killed deer, antelope, and sometimes bison, as well as smaller game like rabbits, rodents, and snakes.

Despite the variety and occasional abundance of animals, Great Basin peoples relied on plants for their most important food source. Unlike meat and fish, plant food could be collected and stored for long periods to protect against shortages caused by the fickle rainfall. By diversifying their food sources and migrating to favorable locations to collect and store them, Great Basin peoples adapted to the severe environmental challenges of the region and maintained their Archaic hunter-gatherer way of life for centuries after AD 1492.

Pacific Coast Cultures

The richness of the natural environment made present-day California the most densely settled area in all of ancient North America. The land and ocean offered such ample food that California peoples remained hunters and gatherers for hundreds of years after AD 1492. The diversity of California's environment also encouraged corresponding diversity among native peoples. The mosaic of Archaic settlements in California included about five hundred separate tribes speaking some ninety languages, each with local dialects. No other region of comparable size in North America exhibited such cultural variety.

The Chumash, one of the many California cultures, emerged in the region surrounding what is now Santa Barbara about 5000 BP. Comparatively plentiful food resources—especially acorns—permitted Chumash people to establish relatively permanent villages. Conflict frequently broke out among the villages, evidently caused by competition for valuable acorn-gathering territory. Although few other California cultures achieved the population density and village settlements of the Chumash, all shared the hunter-gatherer way of life and reliance on acorns as a major food source.

Another rich natural environment lay along the Pacific Northwest coast. Like the Chumash, Northwest peoples built more or less permanent villages. After about 5500 BP, they concentrated on catching large quantities of salmon, halibut, and other fish, which they dried

Ancient California

Tolowa
Karok
Yurok
Shasta
Wiyot
Achomawi
Hupa
Atsugewi
Wintun
Chimariko
Yana
Nomlaki
Yahi
Yuki
Maidu
Pomo
Konkow
Wappo
Patwin
Miwok
Costano
Esselen
Mono
Salina
Yokut
Tubatulabal
Chumash
Kitanemuk
Serrano
Fernandeno
Gabrielino
Juaneno
Cahuilla
Luiseno
Cupeno
Diegueno
Kamia
Akwa'ala
Nakipa
Kiliwa

NORTH AMERICA

PACIFIC OCEAN

Cochimi
Ignacieno
Waicura
Pericu

0   125   250 miles
0   125 250 kilometers

Chumash Necklace

Long before the arrival of Europeans, ancient Chumash people in southern California made this elegant necklace of abalone shell. The carefully formed, polished, and assembled pieces of shell illustrate the artistry of the Chumash and their access to the rich and diverse marine life of the Pacific coast. Since living abalone cling stubbornly to submerged rocks along the coast, Chumash divers presumably pried abalone from their rocky perches to obtain their delicious flesh; then one or more Chumash artisans recycled the inedible shell to make this necklace. Its iridescent splendor demonstrates that Chumash people wore beautiful as well as useful adornments.

Natural History Museum of Los Angeles County.

to last throughout the year and to trade with people who lived hundreds of miles from the coast. Fishing also freed Northwest peoples to develop sophisticated woodworking skills. They fashioned elaborate wood carvings that denoted wealth and status as well as huge canoes for fishing, hunting, and conducting warfare against neighboring tribes. Much of the warfare among Archaic northwesterners grew out of attempts to defend or gain access to prime fishing sites.

Eastern Woodland Cultures

East of the Mississippi River, Archaic peoples adapted to a forest environment that included many local variants, such as the major river valleys of the Mississippi, Ohio, Tennessee, and Cumberland; the Great Lakes region; and the Atlantic coast (see Map 1.2). Throughout these diverse locales, Archaic peoples followed similar survival strategies.

Woodland hunters stalked deer as their most important prey. Deer supplied Woodland peoples with food as well as hides and bones that they crafted into clothing, weapons, needles, and many other tools. Like Archaic peoples elsewhere, Woodland Indians gathered edible plants, seeds, and nuts. About 6000 BP, some Woodland groups established more or less permanent settlements of 25 to 150 people, usually near a river or lake that offered a wide variety of plant and animal resources. The existence of such settlements has permitted archaeologists to locate numerous Archaic burial sites that suggest Woodland people had a life expectancy of about eighteen years.

Around 4000 BP, Woodland cultures added two important features to their basic hunter-gatherer lifestyles: agriculture and pottery. Gourds and pumpkins that were first cultivated thousands of years earlier in Mexico spread to Woodland peoples through trade and migration. Woodland peoples also began to cultivate local species such as sunflowers, as well as small quantities of tobacco, another import from South America. Corn, the most important plant food in Mexico, became a significant Woodland food crop around 2500 BP. These cultivated crops added to the quantity, variety, and predictability of Woodland food sources, but they did not alter Woodland peoples' dependence on gathering wild plants, seeds, and nuts.

Like agriculture, pottery also probably originated in Mexico. Traders and migrants probably brought pots into North America along with Central and South American seeds. Pots were more durable than baskets for cooking and storage of food and water, but they were also much heavier. The permanent settlements of Woodland peoples made the heavy weight of pots much less important than their advantages compared to leaky and fragile baskets. While pottery and agriculture introduced changes in Woodland cultures, ancient Woodland Americans retained the other basic features of their Archaic hunter-gatherer lifestyle, which persisted in most areas to 1492 and beyond.

REVIEW   Why did post-Clovis Native Americans shift from big-game hunting to foraging and smaller-game hunting?

Agricultural Settlements and Chiefdoms

Among Eastern Woodland peoples and most other Archaic cultures, agriculture supplemented hunter-gatherer subsistence strategies. Reliance on wild animals and plants required most Archaic groups to remain small and mobile. But beginning about 4000 BP, distinctive southwestern cultures slowly began to depend on agriculture and to build permanent settlements. Later, around 2500 BP, Woodland peoples in the vast Mississippi valley began to construct burial mounds and other earthworks that suggest the existence of social and political hierarchies that archaeologists term chiefdoms. Although the hunter-gatherer lifestyle never entirely disap-

peared, the development of agricultural settlements and chiefdoms represented important innovations to the Archaic way of life.

Southwestern Cultures

Ancient Americans in present-day Arizona, New Mexico, and southern portions of Utah and Colorado developed cultures characterized by agriculture and multiunit dwellings called pueblos. All southwestern peoples confronted the challenge of a dry climate and unpredictable fluctuations in rainfall that made the supply of wild plant food very unreliable. These ancient Americans probably adopted agriculture in response to this basic environmental condition.

About 3500 BP southwestern hunters and gatherers began to cultivate their signature

Ancient Agriculture
Dropping seeds into holes punched in cleared ground by a pointed stick, known as a "dibble," this ancient American farmer sows a new crop while previously planted seeds—including the corn and beans immediately opposite him—bear fruit for harvest. Created by a sixteenth-century European artist, the drawing misrepresents who did the agricultural work in many ancient American cultures—namely women rather than men. However, the three-foot dibble would have been used as shown here.

The Pierpont Morgan Library/Art Resource, NY; Jerry Jacka Photography.

food crop, corn, which had been grown in Central and South America since about 7000 BP. During the next 3,000 years, corn became the most important cultivated crop for ancient Americans throughout North America. In the Southwest, the demands of corn cultivation encouraged hunter-gatherers to restrict their migratory habits in order to tend the crop. A vital consideration was access to water. Southwestern Indians became irrigation experts, conserving water and distributing it to thirsty crops.

About AD 200, small farming settlements began to appear throughout southern New Mexico, marking the emergence of the Mogollon culture. Typically, a Mogollon settlement included a dozen pit houses, made by digging out a rounded pit about fifteen feet in diameter and a foot or two deep and then erecting poles to support a roof of branches or dirt. Larger villages usually had one or two bigger pit houses that may have been the predecessors of the circular kivas, the ceremonial rooms that became a characteristic of nearly all southwestern settlements. About AD 1000, Mogollon culture began to decline, for reasons that remain obscure.

Around AD 500, while the Mogollon culture prevailed in New Mexico, other ancient people migrated from Mexico to southern Arizona and established the distinctive Hohokam culture. Hohokam settlements used sophisticated grids of irrigation canals to plant and harvest crops twice a year. Hohokam culture reflected the continuing influence of its origins in Mexico. The people built sizable platform mounds and ball courts characteristic of many Mexican cultures to the south. Hohokam culture declined about AD 1400, for reasons that remain a mystery.

North of the Hohokam and Mogollon cultures, in a region that encompassed southern Utah and Colorado and northern Arizona and New Mexico, the Anasazi culture began to flourish about AD 100. The early Anasazi built pit houses on mesa tops and used irrigation

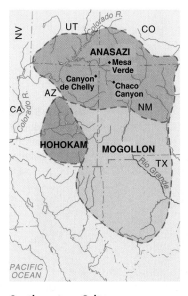

Southwestern Cultures

much like their neighbors to the south. Beginning around AD 1000 (again, it is not known why), Anasazi began to move to large, multistory cliff dwellings whose spectacular ruins still exist at Mesa Verde, Colorado, and elsewhere. Other Anasazi communities—like the one whose impressive ruins can be visited at Chaco Canyon, New Mexico—erected huge, stone-walled pueblos with enough rooms to house everyone in the settlement. Anasazi pueblos and cliff dwellings typically contained one or more kivas used for secret ceremonies, restricted to men, that sought to communicate with the supernatural world.

Drought began to plague the region about AD 1130, and it lasted for more than half a century,

Hohokam "Cigarettes"
Ancient Hohokam smokers in present-day Arizona stuffed these reeds (which probably grew near their irrigation canals) with shredded tobacco. They wrapped cotton thread around each reed to protect their fingers from heat while they inhaled the smoke of the burning tobacco. When hunting or tending their crops, Hohokam smokers probably found these "cigarettes" more convenient than their heavier and more cumbersome stone or ceramic pipes, which were better suited for sedentary occasions.
Jerry Jacka Photography.

Mexican Ball Court Model

The Mexica and other ancient Central American peoples commonly built special courts (or playing fields) for their intensely competitive ball games. This rare model of a ball court, made in Mexico sometime between 2200 BP and AD 250, shows a game in progress, complete with players and spectators. Players wore padded belts and used their hips to hit the hard rubber ball through the goal. Spectators watched intently, not only to admire the skills of the players but also because a lot was at stake. Spectators bet on the game, and losing players were often killed. A few ball courts have been excavated in North America, providing compelling evidence of one of the many connections between ancient Mexicans and North Americans.

Yale University Art Gallery. Stephen Carlton Clark, B.A. 1903, Fund.

Pueblo Bonito, Chaco Canyon, New Mexico

About AD 1000, Pueblo Bonito stood at the center of Chacoan culture that extended over more than 20,000 square miles in the region at the intersection of present-day Utah, Colorado, Arizona, and New Mexico. The numerous circular kivas show the significance of ceremonies and rituals to the people of Chaco Canyon. Major buildings appear to have been aligned to mark the spring and winter solstices and the phases of the lunar cycle, suggesting that the ceremonies at Chaco Canyon may have symbolized the potent connections between earth and sky, between humans and the omnipotent celestial ruler.

Richard Alexander Cooke III.

triggering the disappearance of Anasazi culture. By AD 1200, the large Anasazi pueblos had been abandoned. The prolonged drought probably intensified conflict among pueblos and made it impossible to depend on the techniques of irrigated agriculture that had worked for centuries. Some Anasazi migrated toward regions with more reliable rainfall and settled in Hopi, Zuñi, and Acoma pueblos that their descendants in Arizona and New Mexico have occupied ever since.

Woodland Burial Mounds and Chiefdoms

No other ancient Americans created dwellings similar to pueblos, but around 2500 BP, Woodland cultures throughout the vast area drained by the Mississippi River began to build burial mounds. The size of the mounds, the labor and organization required to erect them, and differences in the artifacts buried with certain individuals suggest the existence of a social and political hierarchy that archaeologists term a chiefdom. Experts do not know the name of a single chief, nor do they know the organizational structure a chief headed. But the only way archaeologists can account for the complex and labor-intensive burial mounds and artifacts found in them is to assume that one person—whom scholars term a chief— had the ability to command the labor and obedience of very large numbers of other people, who comprised the chief's chiefdom.

Between 2500 BP and 2100 BP, Adena people built hundreds of burial mounds radiating from central Ohio. In the mounds, the Adena usually accompanied burials with grave goods that included spear points and stone pipes as well as thin sheets of mica (a glasslike mineral) crafted into shapes of birds, beasts, and human hands. Over the body and grave goods Adena people piled dirt into a mound. Sometimes burial mounds were constructed all at once, but often they were built up slowly over many years.

About 2100 BP, Adena culture evolved into the more elaborate Hopewell culture, which lasted about 500 years. While centered in Ohio, Hopewell culture extended throughout the drainage of the Ohio and Mississippi rivers. Hopewell people built larger mounds and filled them with more

Ashley Creek Petroglyph
Ancient Americans incised this large petroglyph on a rock wall in present-day Utah. The elaborate shield and regalia (the headdress, breastplate, belt, and skirt) suggest that the larger figure depicts a chief or a warrior (who may also have been a chief). Experts do not know the meaning of these and other petroglyphs, although the care with which they were rendered proves that they were significant to the ancient Southwestern artists who made them.
J. Q. Jacobs.

For more help analyzing this image, see the visual activity for this chapter in the Online Study Guide at bedfordstmartins.com/roarkcompact.

magnificent grave goods than had their Adena predecessors.

Burial was probably reserved for the most important members of Hopewell groups. Most people were cremated. Burial rituals appear to have brought many people together to honor the dead person and to help build the mound. Hopewell mounds were often 100 feet in diameter and 30 feet high. Grave goods at Hopewell sites testify to the high quality of Hopewell crafts and to the existence of a thriving trade network that ranged from Wyoming to Florida. Archaeologists believe that Hopewell chiefs probably played an important role in this sprawling interregional trade.

Hopewell culture declined about AD 400 for reasons that are obscure. Archaeologists speculate that bows and arrows, along with increasing reliance on agriculture, made small settlements more self-sufficient and, therefore, less dependent on the central authority of the Hopewell chiefs who were responsible for the burial mounds.

Four hundred years later, another mound-building culture flourished. The Mississippian culture emerged in the floodplains of the major southeastern river systems about AD 800 and lasted until about AD 1500. Major Mississippian sites included huge mounds with platforms on top for ceremonies and for the residences of great chiefs. The largest Mississippian site was Cahokia, whose remnants can be seen in Illinois near the confluence of the Mississippi and Missouri rivers.

At Cahokia, more than one hundred mounds were grouped around large open plazas. Monk's Mound, the largest, covered sixteen acres at its base and was one hundred feet tall. Dwellings may have housed as many as thirty thousand inhabitants, easily qualifying Cahokia as the largest settlement in ancient North America. One Cahokia burial mound suggests the authority a great chief exercised. One man—presumably the chief—was buried with the bodies of more than sixty people who had been killed at the time of burial, including fifty young women who had been strangled. Such a mass sacrifice illustrates the coercive power of a Cahokia chief.

Cahokia and other Mississippian cultures had dwindled by AD 1500. When Europeans arrived, most of the descendants of Mississippian cultures, like those of the Hopewell culture, lived in small dispersed villages supported by hunting and gathering supplemented by agriculture.

REVIEW   How did the availability of food influence the distribution of Native American population across the continent?

Major Mississippian Mounds, AD 800–1500

Native Americans in the 1490s

About thirteen millennia after Paleo-Indians first migrated to the Western Hemisphere, a new migration—this time from Europe—began in 1492 with the journey of Christopher Columbus. In the decades before the arrival of Columbus, Native Americans continued to employ their ancestors' time-tested survival strategies of hunting, gathering, and agriculture. Those strategies succeeded in both populating and shaping the new world Europeans encountered.

By the 1490s, Native Americans lived throughout North America, but their total population is a subject of heated debate among scholars. Some experts claim Native Americans numbered 18 million to 20 million, while others place the population at no more than a million. A prudent estimate is about 4 million. On the eve of European colonization, the small island nation of England had about the same number of people as all of North America. Compared to England and elsewhere in Europe, Native Americans were spread thin across the land, an outgrowth of their survival strategies of hunting, gathering, and agriculture.

Regions in North America with abundant resources had relatively high population. About one-fifth of Native Americans lived along the West Coast in food-rich California and the Pacific Northwest, where the population density was, respectively, six times greater and four times greater than the average for the whole continent. The food-scarce vastness of the Great Plains, Great Basin, and Arctic regions held about one-quarter of Native Americans, but the population density was extremely low, roughly one-tenth the continental average. About a quarter of Native Americans resided in the arid Southwest, where irrigation and intensive agriculture permitted a population density about twice the continental average. But even in California, the most densely inhabited region of North America, population density was just one-twentieth of England's.

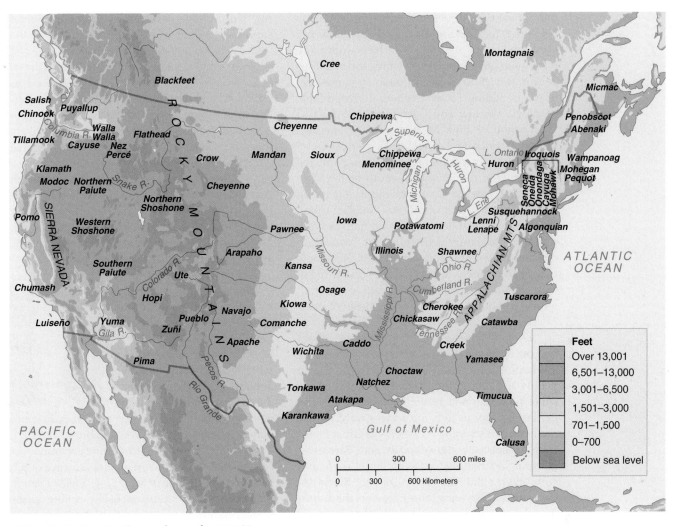

MAP 1.3   Native North Americans about 1500
Distinctive Native American peoples resided throughout the area that, centuries later, would become the United States. This map indicates the approximate location of some of the larger tribes about 1500. In the interest of legibility, many other peoples who inhabited North America at the time are omitted from the map.

The enormous Woodland region east of the Mississippi River was home to about one-third of Native Americans, whose population density approximated the continental average of one person per square mile. Eastern Woodland peoples clustered into three broad linguistic and cultural groups: Algonquian, Iroquoian, and Muskogean.

Algonquian tribes inhabited the Atlantic seaboard, the Great Lakes region, and much of the upper Midwest (Map 1.3). The relatively mild climate along the Atlantic permitted the coastal Algonquians to grow corn and other crops as well as to hunt and fish. Around the Great Lakes and in northern New England, however, cool summers and severe winters made agriculture impractical. Instead, the Abenaki, Penobscot, Chippewa, and other tribes concentrated on hunting and fishing, using canoes both for transportation and for gathering wild rice.

Inland from the Algonquian region, Iroquoian tribes occupied territories centered in Pennsylvania and upstate New York, as well as the hilly upland regions of the Carolinas and Georgia. Three features distinguished Iroquoian tribes from their neighbors. First, their success in cultivating corn and other crops allowed them to build permanent settlements, usually consisting of several bark-covered longhouses up to one hundred feet long and housing five to ten families. Second, Iroquoian societies adhered to matrilineal rules of descent. Property of all sorts belonged to women. Women headed family clans and even selected the chiefs (normally men) who governed tribes. Third, for purposes of war and diplomacy, an Iroquoian confederation—including the Seneca, Onondaga, Mohawk, Oneida, and Cayuga tribes—formed the League of Five Nations, which remained powerful well into the eighteenth century.

Muskogean peoples spread throughout the woodlands of the Southeast, south of the Ohio River and east of the Mississippi. Including Creek, Choctaw, Chickasaw, and Natchez tribes, Muskogeans inhabited a bountiful natural environment that provided abundant food from hunting, gathering, and agriculture. Remnants of the earlier Mississippian culture still existed in Muskogean religion. The Natchez even built temple mounds modeled after those of their Mississippian ancestors.

Great Plains peoples accounted for about one out of seven Native Americans. Inhabiting the huge region west of the Eastern Woodland people and east of the Rocky Mountains, many tribes had migrated to the Great Plains within the last century or two, forced westward by Iroquoian and Algonquian tribes. Some Great Plains tribes—especially the Mandan and Pawnee—farmed successfully, growing both corn and sunflowers. But the Teton Sioux, Blackfeet, Comanche, Cheyenne, and Crow on the northern plains and the Apache and other nomadic tribes on the southern plains depended on buffalo (American bison) for subsistence.

Southwestern cultures included about a quarter of all native North Americans. These descendants of the Mogollon, Hohokam, and Anasazi cultures lived in settled agricultural communities, many of them pueblos. They continued to grow corn, beans, and squash with methods they had refined for centuries. However, their communities came under attack by a large number of warlike Athapascan tribes who invaded the Southwest beginning around AD 1300. The Athapascans—principally Apache and Navajo—were skillful warriors who preyed on the sedentary pueblo Indians, reaping the fruits of agriculture without the work of farming.

About a fifth of all native North Americans resided along the Pacific coast. In California, abundant acorns and nutritious marine life supported high population densities but retarded the development of agriculture. Similar dependence on hunting and gathering persisted along the Northwest coast, where fishing reigned supreme. Salmon was so abundant that at the Dalles site on the Columbia River, Northwest peoples caught millions of pounds of salmon every summer and traded it as far away as California and the Great Plains. Although important trading centers existed throughout North America, particularly in the Southwest, it is likely that the Dalles site was the largest Native American trading center in North America.

While trading was common, all native North Americans in the 1490s still depended on hunting and gathering for a major portion of their food. Most of them also practiced agriculture. People throughout North America used bows, arrows, and other weapons for hunting and warfare. None of them employed writing, expressing themselves instead in many other ways: drawings sketched on stones, wood, and animal skins; patterns woven in baskets and textiles; designs painted on pottery, crafted into bead-work, or carved into effigies; as well as in song, dance, religious ceremonies, and burial rites.

These rich and varied cultural resources of Native Americans did not include features of life common in Europe during the 1490s. Native Americans did not use wheels; sailing ships were unknown to them; they had no large domesticated animals such as horses, cows, or oxen; their use of metals was restricted to copper. However, the absence of these European conveniences mattered less to native North Americans than their own cultural adaptations to the natural environment local to each tribe and to the social environment among neighboring peoples. That great similarity—adaptation to natural and social environments—underlay all the cultural diversity among native North Americans.

It would be a mistake, however, to conclude that native North Americans lived in blissful harmony with nature and each other. Archaeological sites provide ample evidence of violent conflict among Native Americans. Skeletons bear the marks of wounds as well as of ritualistic human sacrifice and even cannibalism. In general, fear and anxiety must have been at least as common among Native Americans as feelings of peace and security.

Native Americans not only adapted to the natural environment; they also changed it in many ways. They built thousands of structures, from small dwellings to massive pueblos and enormous mounds, permanently altering the landscape. Their gathering techniques selected productive and nutritious varieties of plants, thereby shifting the balance of local plants toward useful varieties. The first stages of North American agriculture, for example, probably resulted from Native Americans gathering wild seeds and then sowing them in a meadow for later harvest. It is almost certain that fertile and hardy varieties of corn were developed in this way, first in Mexico and later in North America.

Native Americans also altered the natural environment by setting fires. Great Plains hunters often used fires to force buffalo together and make them easy to slaughter. Eastern Woodland, Southwest, and Pacific coast Indians also set fires to hunt deer and other valuable prey. Over thousands of square miles throughout North America, Indians started fires along the edges of woods to burn off shrubby undergrowth and encroaching tree seedlings. These burns encouraged the growth of tender young plants that attracted deer and other game animals, bringing them within convenient range of hunters' weapons.

Because fires usually burned until they ran out of fuel or were extinguished by rain or wind, enormous regions of North America were burned over. In the long run, fires created and maintained light-dappled meadows for hunting and agriculture, cleared entangling underbrush from forests, and promoted a diverse and productive natural environment. Fires, like other activities of Native Americans, shaped the landscape of North America long before Europeans arrived in 1492.

REVIEW   Why did some Native Americans set fire to the land?

The Mexica: A Meso-American Culture

The indigenous population of the New World (the Western Hemisphere) numbered roughly 80 million in the 1490s, about the same as the population of Europe. Almost all these people lived in Mexico and Central and South America.

Like their much less numerous North American counterparts, they too lived in a natural environment of tremendous diversity. They too developed hundreds of cultures, far too numerous to catalog here. But among all these cultures, the Mexica stood out. (Europeans often called these people Aztecs, a name the Mexica did not use.) Their empire stretched from coast to coast across central Mexico, encompassing as many as 25 million people. We know more about the Mexica than about any other Native American society of the time, principally because of their massive monuments and their Spanish conquerors' well-documented interest in subduing them. Their significance in the history of the New World after 1492 dictates a brief discussion of their culture and society.

The Mexica began their rise to prominence about 1325 when small bands settled on a marshy island in Lake Texcoco, the site of the future city of Tenochtitlán, the capital of the Mexican empire. Resourceful, courageous, and cold-blooded warriors, the Mexica often hired out as mercenaries for richer, more settled tribes. By 1430, the Mexica succeeded in asserting their dominance over their former allies and leading their own military campaigns in an ever-widening arc of empire building. Despite pockets of resistance, by the 1490s the Mexica ruled an empire that covered more land than Spain and Portugal combined and contained almost three times as many people.

The empire exemplified the central values of Mexican society. The Mexica worshipped the war god Huitzilopochtli. Warriors held the most exalted positions in the Mexican social hierarchy, even above the priests who performed the sacred ceremonies that won Huitzilopochtli's favor. In the almost constant battles necessary to defend and extend the empire, young Mexican men exhibited the courage and daring that would allow them to rise in the carefully graduated ranks of warriors. The Mexica considered capturing prisoners the ultimate act of bravery. Warriors usually turned over the captives to Mexican priests, who sacrificed them to Huitzilopochtli by cutting out their hearts.

The empire contributed far more to Mexican society than victims for sacrifice. At the most basic level, the empire functioned as a military and political system that collected tribute from subject peoples. The Mexica forced conquered tribes to pay tribute in goods, not money. Tribute redistributed to the Mexica as much as one-third of the goods produced by conquered tribes. It included everything from candidates for human sacrifice to textiles and basic food products such as corn and beans as well as exotic luxury items such as gold, turquoise, and rare bird feathers.

Tribute reflected the fundamental relations of power and wealth that pervaded the Mexican empire. The relatively small nobility of Mexican warriors, supported by a still smaller priesthood, possessed the military and religious power to command the obedience of thousands of non-noble Mexicans and of millions of other non-Mexicans in subjugated provinces. The Mexican elite exercised their power to obtain tribute and thereby to redistribute wealth from the conquered to the conquerors, from the commoners to the nobility, from the poor to the rich. This redistribution of wealth made possible the achieve-

Salado Ritual Figure
About AD 1350—more than a century before Columbus arrived in the Western Hemisphere—this figure was carefully wrapped in a reed mat with other items and stored in a cave in a mountainous region of New Mexico by people of the Salado culture, descendants of the Mimbres, who had flourished three centuries earlier. The face of this figure is as close to a self-portrait of ancient Americans on the eve of their encounter with Europeans as we are ever likely to have. Adorned with vivid pigments, cotton string, bright feathers, and stones, the effigy testifies to the human complexity of all ancient Americans, a complexity visible in artifacts that have survived the millennia before the arrival of Europeans.
© 2000 The Art Institute of Chicago.

ments of Mexican society that eventually amazed Spaniards: the huge cities, fabulous temples, teeming markets, and luxuriant gardens, not to mention the storehouses stuffed with gold and other treasures.

On the whole, the Mexica did not interfere much with the internal government of conquered regions. Instead, they usually permitted the traditional ruling elite to stay in power—so long as they paid tribute. The conquered provinces received very little in return from the Mexica, except immunity from punitive raids. Subjugated communities felt exploited by the constant payment of tribute to the Mexica. By depending on military conquest and constant collection of tribute, the Mexica failed to create among their subjects a belief that Mexican domination was, at some level, legitimate and equitable. The high level of discontent among subject peoples constituted the soft, vulnerable underbelly of the Mexican empire, a fact Spanish intruders exploited after AD 1492 to conquer the Mexica.

REVIEW Why were the Mexica able to build monumental cities and structures?

Conclusion: The World of Ancient Americans

Ancient Americans shaped the history of human beings in the New World for more than twelve thousand years. They established continuous human habitation in the Western Hemisphere from the time the first big-game hunters crossed Beringia until 1492 and beyond. Much of their history remains irretrievably lost because they relied on oral rather than written communication. But much can be pieced together from artifacts they left behind, like the Folsom points among the bones discovered by George McJunkin. Ancient Americans achieved their success through resourceful adaptation to the hemisphere's many and ever-changing natural environments. They also adapted to social and cultural changes caused by human beings—such as marriages, deaths, political struggles, and warfare—but the sparse evidence that has survived renders those adaptations almost entirely unknowable. Their creativity and artistry are unmistakably documented in the artifacts they left at kill sites, camps, and burial mounds. Those artifacts sketch the only likenesses of ancient Americans we will ever have—blurred, shadowy images that are indisputably human but forever silent.

In the five centuries after 1492—just 4 percent of the time human beings have inhabited the Western Hemisphere—Europeans and their descendants began to shape and eventually to dominate American history. Native American peoples continued to influence major developments of American history for centuries after 1492. But the new wave of strangers that at first trickled and then flooded into the New World from Europe and Africa forever transformed the peoples and places of ancient America.

Suggestions for Further Reading

Karen Olsen Bruhns and Karen R. Stothert, *Women in Ancient America* (1999). An informative account of ancient American women, who are often neglected in other books.

Colin G. Calloway, *One Vast Winter Count: The Native American West before Lewis and Clark* (2003). A fascinating overview of Native Americans in the West.

Michael D. Coe and Rex Koontz, *Mexico: From the Olmecs to the Aztecs* (5th ed., 2002). An authoritative survey of ancient Mexico.

Brian M. Fagan, *Ancient North America: The Archaeology of a Continent* (1991). The compelling story of the role of archaeological evidence in piecing together the history of ancient North America.

Tim Flannery, *The Eternal Frontier: An Ecological History of North America and Its Peoples* (2001). A sweeping ecological history of North American plants and animals covering millions of years.

▶ **FOR MORE BOOKS ABOUT TOPICS IN THIS CHAPTER**, see the Online Bibliography at **bedfordstmartins.com/roarkcompact**.

▶ **FOR ADDITIONAL FIRSTHAND ACCOUNTS OF THIS PERIOD**, see Chapter 1 in Michael Johnson, ed., *Reading the American Past*, Third Edition.

▶ **FOR WEB SITES AND DOCUMENTS RELATED TO TOPICS AND PLACES IN THIS CHAPTER**, see "HistoryLinks," "DocLinks," and "PlaceLinks" at **bedfordstmartins.com/roarkcompact**.

REVIEWING THE CHAPTER

Follow these steps to review and strengthen your understanding of the chapter.
STEP 1: *Study the **Key Terms** and **Timeline** to identify the significance of each item listed.*
STEP 2: *Answer the **Review Questions,** drawing on key terms and dates to support your answers.*
STEP 3: *Drawing on the Key Terms, Timeline, and Review Questions, answer the broader **Making Connections** questions.*

KEY TERMS

Who

George McJunkin (p. 3)
Carl Schwachheim (p. 3)
J. D. Figgins (p. 3)
Paleo-Indians (p. 7)
Folsom hunters (p. 12)
Great Basin peoples (p. 12)
California peoples (p. 12)
Chumash (p. 12)
Northwest peoples (p. 12)
Woodland peoples (p. 13)
Southwestern peoples (p. 14)
Mogollon (p. 15)
Hohokam (p. 15)
Anasazi (p. 15)
Adena (p. 17)
Hopewell peoples (p. 17)
Mississippian peoples (p. 18)
Algonquian peoples (p. 19)

Iroquoian peoples (p. 19)
Muskogean peoples (p. 20)
Great Plains peoples (p. 20)
Athapascans (p. 20)
Mexica (p. 21)

What

Wild Horse Arroyo (p. 3)
artifacts (p. 3)
Folsom points (p. 3)
Pangaea (p. 5)
continental drift (p. 5)
Homo erectus (p. 5)
Homo sapiens (p. 5)
Wisconsin glaciation (p. 6)
Beringia (p. 6)
Clovis points (p. 7)
Clovis culture (p. 10)
Archaic era (p. 10)

hunter-gatherer (p. 10)
Great Basin (p. 12)
agriculture (p. 13)
pottery (p. 13)
pueblo (p. 14)
kiva (p. 15)
agricultural settlements (p. 15)
burial mounds (p. 17)
chiefdoms (p. 17)
interregional trade (p. 18)
Cahokia (p. 18)
matrilineal rules of descent (p. 20)
League of Five Nations (p. 20)
Dalles site (p. 20)
Tenochtitlán (p. 21)
Huitzilopochtli (p. 21)
warriors (p. 21)
Mexican empire (p. 21)
tribute (p. 21)

TIMELINE

NOTE: Major events are depicted below in chronological order, but the time scale between events varies from millennia to centuries.

(*BP* is an abbreviation used by archaeologists for "years before the present.")

◄ **c. 80,000–**
10,000 BP • Wisconsin glaciation exposes Beringia.

c. 13,000 BP • First humans arrive in North America.

c. 11,500–11,000 BP • Paleo-Indians use Clovis points to hunt big game.

c. 11,000 BP • Mammoths become extinct.

c. 10,000–3000 BP • Archaic cultures dominate ancient America.

c. 4000 BP • Some Eastern Woodland peoples grow gourds and pumpkins and begin making pottery.

c. 3500 BP
• Southwestern cultures begin corn cultivation.
• Stone pipes for tobacco smoking appear in Eastern Woodland regions.

c. 2500 BP
• Eastern Woodland cultures start to build burial mounds.

REVIEW QUESTIONS

1. Why do historians rely on the work of archaeologists to write the history of ancient America? (pp. 4–5)

2. Why were humans able to migrate into North America after 15,000 BP? (pp. 5–10)

3. Why did post-Clovis Native Americans shift from big-game hunting to foraging and smaller-game hunting? (pp. 10–13)

4. How did the availability of food influence the distribution of Native American population across the continent? (pp. 14–18)

5. Why did some Native Americans set fire to the land? (pp. 18–21)

6. Why were the Mexica able to build monumental cities and structures? (pp. 21–22)

MAKING CONNECTIONS

1. Explain the different approaches historians and archaeologists bring to studying people in the past. How do the different sources they draw on shape their accounts of the human past? In your answer, cite specific examples from the history of ancient America.

2. Discuss Native Americans' strategies for surviving in the varied climates of North America. How did their different approaches to survival contribute to the diversity of Native American cultures?

3. For over twelve thousand years Native Americans successfully adapted to environmental changes in North America; they also produced significant changes in the environments around them. In your answer, discuss specific examples of how Native Americans changed the North American landscape.

4. Rich archaeological and manuscript sources have enabled historians to develop a detailed portrait of the Mexica on the eve of European contact. How did the Mexica establish and maintain their expansive empire?

► For practice quizzes, a customized study plan, and other study tools, see the Online Study Guide at bedfordstmartins.com/roarkcompact.

c. 2100 BP–AD 400 • Hopewell culture emerges in Mississippi and Ohio valleys.

c. AD 200–AD 900 • Mogollon culture emerges in New Mexico.

c. AD 500 • Bows and arrows appear in North America.
• Pacific Northwest cultures create elaborate wood carvings.

c. AD 500– • Hohokam culture develops
AD 1400   in Arizona.

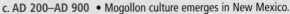

c. AD 800–AD 1500
• Mississippian culture flourishes in Southeast.

c. AD 1000–AD 1100 • Anasazi peoples build cliff dwellings.

c. AD 1325–AD 1500
• Mexica empire established.

AD 1492
• Christopher Columbus arrives in New World.

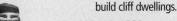

TAINO ZEMI BASKET
This basket is an example of the effigies Tainos made to represent *zemis,* their deities. The effigy illustrates the artistry of the basket maker, almost certainly a Taino woman. Crafted sometime between 1492 and about 1520, the effigy demonstrates that Tainos readily incorporated goods obtained through contacts with Europeans into their own traditional beliefs and practices. The basket maker used African ivory and European mirrors as well as Native American fibers, dyes, and designs.

Archìvio Fotogràfico del Museo Preistòrico Etnografico L. Pigorini, Roma.

Europeans Encounter the New World

1492–1600

A HALF HOUR BEFORE SUNRISE on August 3, 1492, Christopher Columbus commanded three ships to catch the tide out of a harbor in southern Spain and sail west. Just over two months later, in the predawn moonlight of October 12, 1492, Columbus glimpsed an island on the western horizon. At last, he believed, he had found what he had been looking for—the western end of a route across the Atlantic Ocean to Japan, China, and India. At daybreak, Columbus could see people on the shore who had spotted his ships. He rowed ashore and, as the curious islanders crowded around, he claimed possession of the land for Ferdinand and Isabella, king and queen of Spain, who had sponsored his voyage. He named the island San Salvador, in honor of the Savior, Jesus Christ.

A day or two afterward, Columbus described that first encounter with the inhabitants of San Salvador in an extensive diary he kept during his voyage. He called these people Indians, assuming that their island lay somewhere in the East Indies near Japan or China. The Indians were not dressed in the finery Columbus expected. "All of them go around as naked as their mothers bore them; and the women also," he observed. Their skin color was "neither black nor white." They were not familiar with the Spaniards' weapons. "I showed them swords," Columbus wrote, "and they took them by the edge and through ignorance cut themselves." This first encounter led Columbus to conclude, "They should be good and intelligent servants, for I see that they say very quickly everything that is said to them; and I believe that they would become Christians very easily, for it seemed to me that they had no religion."

The people Columbus called Indians called themselves Tainos, which to them meant "good" or "noble." They inhabited most of the Caribbean islands Columbus visited on his first voyage, as had their ancestors for more than two centuries. The Tainos were an agricultural people who grew cassava, a nutritious root, as well as sweet potatoes, corn, cotton, tobacco, and other crops. To fish and to travel from island to island, they built canoes from hollowed-out logs. The Tainos worshipped gods they called *zemis*, the spirits of ancestors and of natural objects like trees and stones. They made effigies of zemis and performed rituals to honor them. "It seemed to me that they were a people very poor in everything," Columbus wrote.

What the Tainos thought about Spaniards we can only surmise, since they left no written documents. At first, Columbus believed that the Tainos thought he and his men came from heaven. After six weeks of contact, Columbus

Cacique's Canoe

This sixteenth-century drawing of a large canoe carrying a cacique, or chief, and powered by twenty oarsmen probably resembles the canoes used by Tainos and the other Native Americans who paddled out to visit the ships of Columbus and other European explorers. The influence of such European contacts may be reflected in the flags flying from the corners of the leafy awning that shades the enthroned cacique and rowers.

The Pierpont Morgan Library / Art Resource, NY.

concluded that in fact he did not understand Tainos. Late in November 1492, he wrote that "the people of these lands do not understand me nor do I, nor anyone else that I have with me, them. And many times I understand one thing said by these Indians…for another, its contrary."

The confused communication between Europeans and Tainos suggests how different, how strange, each group seemed to the other. Columbus's perceptions of Tainos were shaped by European ideas, attitudes, and expectations, just as Tainos' perceptions of Europeans must have been colored by their own culture. Yet the word that Columbus coined for the Tainos— *Indians*, a word that originated in a colossal misunderstanding—hinted at the direction of the future. To Europeans, *Indians* came to mean all native inhabitants of the New World, the name they gave to the lands in the Western Hemisphere. After 1492, the perceptions, the cultures, and even the diseases of Europeans began to exert a transforming influence on the New World and its peoples.

Long before 1492, certain Europeans restlessly expanded the limits of the world known to them. Their efforts made possible Columbus's encounter with the Tainos. In turn, Columbus's landfall in the Caribbean changed the history not only of the Tainos, but also of Europe and the rest of the world. Beginning in 1492, the promise of the New World lured more and more Europeans to venture their lives and fortunes on the western shores of the Atlantic, a promise realized largely at the expense of New World peoples like the Tainos.

Europe in the Age of Exploration

Historically, the East—not the West—attracted Europeans. Around the year 1000, Norsemen ventured west across the North Atlantic and founded a small fishing village at L'Anse aux Meadows on the tip of Newfoundland that lasted only a decade or so. Viking sagas memorialized the Norse "discovery," but it had virtually no other impact in the New World or in Europe. Instead, wealthy Europeans developed a taste for luxury goods from Asia and Africa, and merchants competed to satisfy that taste. As Europeans traded with the East and with one another, they acquired new information about the world they inhabited. A few people—sailors, merchants, and aristocrats—

took the risks of exploring beyond the limits of the world known to Europeans. Those risks were genuine and could be deadly. But sometimes they paid off in new information, new opportunities, and eventually in the discovery of a world entirely new to Europeans.

Mediterranean Trade and European Expansion

From the twelfth through the fifteenth centuries, spices, silk, carpets, ivory, gold, and other exotic goods traveled overland from Persia, Asia Minor, India, and Africa and then were funneled into continental Europe through Mediterranean trade routes (Map 2.1). Dominated primarily by the Italian cities of Venice, Genoa, and Pisa, this lucrative trade enriched Italian merchants and bankers, who fiercely defended their near-**monopoly** of access to eastern goods. The vitality of the Mediterranean trade offered few incentives to look for alternatives. New routes to the East and the discovery of new lands were the stuff of fantasy.

Preconditions for turning fantasy into reality developed in fifteenth-century Europe. In the mid-fourteenth century, Europeans suffered a catastrophic epidemic of bubonic plague. The Black Death, as it was called, killed about a third of the European population. This devastating pestilence had major long-term consequences. By drastically reducing the population, it made Europe's limited supply of food more plentiful for survivors. Many survivors inherited property from plague victims, giving them new chances for advancement. The turmoil caused by the plague also prompted peasants to move away from their homes and seek opportunities elsewhere.

MAP 2.1   European Trade Routes and Portuguese Exploration in the Fifteenth Century
The strategic geographic position of Italian cities as a conduit for overland trade from Asia was slowly undermined during the fifteenth century by Portuguese explorers who hopscotched along the coast of Africa and eventually found a sea route that opened the rich trade of the East to Portuguese merchants.

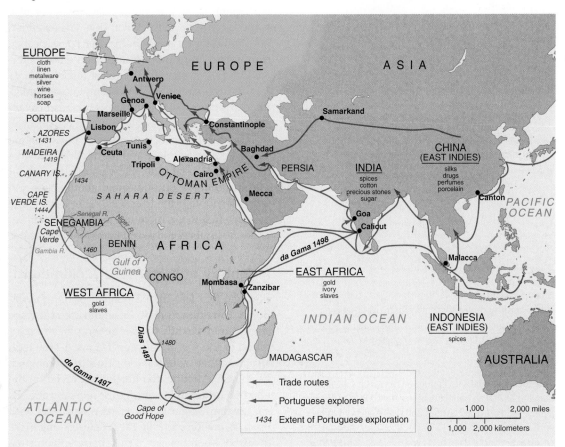

Ivory Saltcellar

This exquisitely carved sixteenth-century ivory saltcellar combines African materials, craftsmanship, and imagery in an artifact for Portuguese tables. Designed to hold table salt in the central globe, the saltcellar portrays a victim about to be beheaded by the armed man who has already beheaded five others. To Portuguese eyes, the saltcellar dramatized African brutality and quietly suggested the superiority of Portuguese virtues and their beneficial influence in Africa.

Archivio Fotogràfico del Museo Preistòrico Etnografico L. Pigorini, Roma.

Understandably, most Europeans perceived the world as a place of alarming risks where the delicate balance of health, harvests, and peace could quickly be tipped toward disaster by epidemics, famine, and violence. Most people protected themselves from the constant threat of calamity by worshipping the supernatural, by living amid kinfolk and friends, and by maintaining good relations with the rich and powerful. But the insecurity and uncertainty of fifteenth-century European life also encouraged a few people to take greater risks, such as embarking on dangerous sea voyages through uncharted waters to points unknown.

Exploration promised fame and fortune in European societies to those who succeeded, whether they were kings or commoners. Monarchs hoped to enlarge their realms and enrich their dynasties. More territory meant more subjects who could pay more taxes, provide more soldiers, and participate in more commerce, magnifying monarchs' power and prestige. Voyages of exploration also could stabilize monarchs' regimes by diverting unruly noblemen toward distant lands. Some explorers, like Columbus, were commoners who hoped to be elevated to the aristocracy as a reward for their daring achievements.

Scientific and technological advances also helped set the stage for exploration. The invention of movable type made printing easier and cheaper, stimulating diffusion of information among literate Europeans, including news of discoveries. By 1400, crucial navigational aids employed by maritime explorers like Columbus were already available: compasses; hourglasses, which allowed calculation of elapsed time, useful in estimating speed; and the astrolabe and the quadrant, devices for determining latitude. Many people throughout fifteenth-century Europe knew about these and other technological advances. The Portuguese were the first to use them in a campaign to sail beyond the limits of the world known to Europeans.

A Century of Portuguese Exploration

Portugal had less than 2 percent of the population of Christian Europe, but it devoted far more energy and wealth to the geographical exploration of the world between 1415 and 1460 than all the other countries of Europe combined. Facing the Atlantic, the Portuguese lived on the margins of the thriving Mediterranean trade. As a Christian kingdom, Portugal cooperated with Spain in the Reconquest, the centuries-long drive to expel Muslims from the Iberian Peninsula.

The religious zeal that propelled the Reconquest also justified expansion into what the Portuguese considered heathen lands. The key victory came in 1415 when Portuguese forces conquered Ceuta, the Muslim bastion at the mouth of the Strait of Gibraltar that had blocked Portugal's access to the Atlantic coast of Africa.

The most influential advocate of Portuguese exploration was Prince Henry the Navigator, son of the Portuguese king. From 1415 until his death in 1460, Henry collected the latest information about sailing techniques and geography, supported new crusades against the Muslims, encouraged fresh sources of trade to fatten Portuguese pocketbooks, and pushed explorers to go farther still.

Neither the Portuguese nor anybody else in Europe knew the immensity of Africa or the length or shape of its coastline, which, in reality, fronted the Atlantic for more than 7,000 miles—about five times the considerable distance from Genoa, Columbus's hometown, to Lisbon, the Portuguese capital. By 1434, Portuguese mariners had sailed along the north African coast to reach the northern edge of the Sahara Desert, where strong westerly currents swept them out to sea. They soon learned to ride those currents far away from the coast before catching favorable winds that turned them back toward land, a technique that allowed them to reach Cape Verde by 1444 (see Map 2.1). To stow the supplies necessary for long periods at sea and to withstand the battering of waves in the open ocean, the Portuguese developed the caravel, a sturdy ship that became explorers' vessel of choice. In caravels, Portuguese mariners sailed into and around the Gulf of Guinea and as far south as the Congo by 1480.

Fierce African resistance confined Portuguese expeditions to coastal trading posts, where they bartered successfully for gold, slaves, and ivory. Portuguese merchants learned that relatively peaceful trading posts on the coast were far more profitable than attempts at violent conquest and **colonization** of inland regions. In the 1460s, the Portuguese used African slaves to develop sugar plantations on the Cape Verde Islands, inaugurating an association between enslaved Africans and plantation labor that would be transplanted to the New World in the centuries to come.

About 1480, Portuguese explorers began a conscious search for a sea route to Asia. In 1488, Bartolomeu Dias sailed around the Cape

Benin Queen Mother
Early in the sixteenth century, as the Portuguese began their forays along the African coast, the Oba (king) of Benin, in present-day Nigeria, introduced the notion of a queen mother who possessed the ability to communicate with supernatural deities. Brass castings of Benin queen mothers like the one shown here appeared on altars in royal palaces. The distinctive headdress apparently signified the queen mother's semidivine status.
The National Museums, Liverpool.

of Good Hope at the southern tip of Africa and hurried back to Lisbon with the exciting news that it appeared to be possible to sail on to India and China. In 1498, after ten years of careful preparation, Vasco da Gama commanded the first Portuguese fleet to sail to India. Portugal quickly capitalized on the commercial potential of da Gama's new sea route. By the early sixteenth century, the Portuguese controlled a far-flung commercial empire in India, Indonesia, and China (collectively referred to as the East Indies). Their new sea route to the East eliminated overland travel and allowed Portuguese merchants to charge much lower prices for the eastern goods they imported.

Portugal's African explorations during the fifteenth century broke the monopoly of the old Mediterranean trade with the East, dramatically expanded the world known to Europeans, established a network of Portuguese outposts in Africa and Asia, and developed methods of sailing the high seas that Columbus employed on his revolutionary voyage west.

> **REVIEW** Why did European exploration expand dramatically in the fifteenth century?

A Surprising New World in the Western Atlantic

In retrospect, the Portuguese seemed ideally qualified to venture west across the Atlantic. They had pioneered the **frontiers** of seafaring, exploration, and geography for almost a century. However, the Portuguese and most other European experts believed that sailing west to landfall across the Atlantic was literally impossible. The European discovery of America required someone bold enough to believe that the experts were wrong. That person was Christopher Columbus. His explorations inaugurated a geographical revolution that forever altered Europeans' understanding of the world and its peoples, including themselves. Columbus's landfall in the Caribbean originated a thriving exchange between the people, ideas, cultures, and institutions of the Old and New Worlds that continues to this day.

Columbus's First Voyage to the New World, 1492–1493

The Explorations of Columbus

Born in 1451 into the family of an obscure master weaver in Genoa, Italy, Columbus went to sea when he was about fourteen. Sometime around 1476, he arrived in Lisbon and within a few years married Felipa Moniz. Felipa's father had been raised in the household of Prince Henry the Navigator, and her family retained close ties to the prince. Through Felipa, Columbus gained access to explorers' maps and papers crammed with information about the tricky currents and winds encountered in sailing the Atlantic. Columbus himself ventured into the Atlantic frequently and at least twice sailed all the way to the central coast of Africa.

Like other educated Europeans, Columbus believed that the earth was a sphere and that theoretically it was possible to reach the East Indies by sailing west. Most Europeans believed, however, that the earth was simply too big for anyone to sail west from Europe to Asia. Sailors would die of thirst and starvation long before they reached Asia.

Columbus rejected this conventional wisdom. With flawed calculations, he estimated that Asia was only about 2,500 miles from the westernmost boundary of the known world, a shorter distance than Portuguese ships routinely sailed between Lisbon and the Congo. In fact, the shortest distance to Japan from Europe's jumping-off point was nearly 11,000 miles. Convinced by his erroneous calculations, Columbus became obsessed with a scheme to prove he was right.

In 1492, after years of unsuccessful lobbying in Portugal, Spain, England, and France,

Columbus finally won financing for his journey from Spain's monarchs, Ferdinand and Isabella. The Spanish monarchs saw Columbus's venture as an inexpensive gamble: The potential loss was small while the potential gain was huge.

After scarcely three months of hurried preparation, Columbus and his small fleet—the *Niña* and *Pinta*, both caravels, and the *Santa María*, a larger merchant vessel—headed west. Six weeks after leaving the Canary Islands, where he stopped for supplies, Columbus landed on a tiny Caribbean island about three hundred miles north of the eastern tip of Cuba.

Columbus and his men understood that they had made a momentous discovery. Yet they found it frustrating. Although the Tainos proved friendly, they did not have the riches Columbus expected to find in the East Indies. For three months Columbus cruised from island to island, looking for the king of Japan and the Grand Khan of China. In mid-January 1493, he started back to Spain. When he reached Isabella and Ferdinand, they were overjoyed by his news. With a voyage that had lasted barely eight months, Columbus appeared to have catapulted Spain from a secondary position in the race for a sea route to Asia into that of a serious challenger to Portugal, whose explorers had not yet sailed to India or China. The Spanish monarchs elevated Columbus to the nobility and awarded him the title "Admiral of the Ocean Sea."

Soon after Columbus returned to Spain, the Portuguese and Spanish monarchs negotiated the Treaty of Tordesillas in 1494. The treaty drew an imaginary line eleven hundred miles west of the Canary Islands (Map 2.2). Land discovered west of the line belonged to Spain; Portugal claimed land to the east.

Before Columbus died in 1506, he returned to the New World three times without relinquishing his belief that the East Indies were there, someplace. Other explorers continued to search for a passage to the East or some other source of profit. Before long, however, prospects of beating the Portuguese to Asia began to dim along with the hope of finding vast hoards of gold. Nonetheless, Columbus's discoveries forced sixteenth-century Europeans to think about the world in new ways. He proved that it was possible to sail from Europe to the western rim of the Atlantic and return to

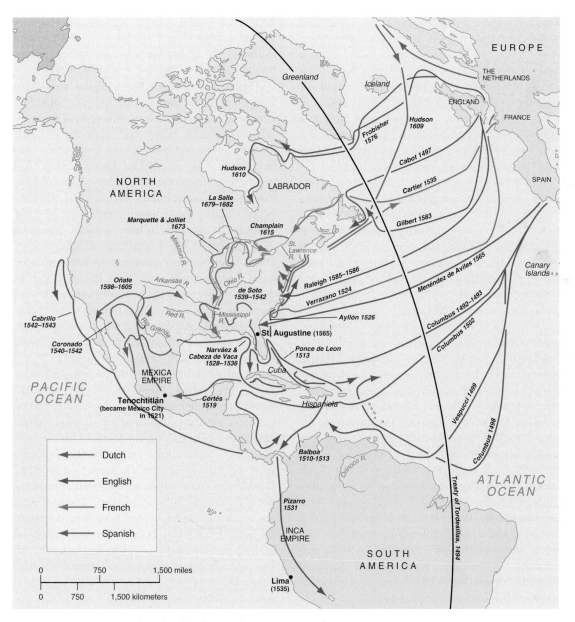

MAP 2.2   European Exploration in Sixteenth-Century America
This map illustrates the approximate routes of early European explorations of the New World.

Europe. Most important, Columbus made clear that beyond the western shores of the Atlantic lay lands entirely unknown to Europeans.

The Geographic Revolution and the Columbian Exchange

Within thirty years of Columbus's initial discovery, Europeans' understanding of world geography underwent a revolution. An elite of perhaps twenty thousand people with access to Europe's royal courts and trading centers learned the exciting news about global geography. But it took a generation of additional exploration before they could comprehend the larger contours of Columbus's discoveries.

European monarchs hurried to stake their claims to the newly discovered lands. In 1497, King Henry VII of England, who had spurned Columbus a decade earlier, sent John Cabot to look for a "Northwest Passage" to the Indies across the North Atlantic (see Map 2.2). Cabot reached the tip of Newfoundland, which he believed was part of Asia, and hurried back to

England, where he assembled a small fleet and sailed west again in 1498. But he was never heard from again. Three thousand miles to the south, a Spanish expedition landed on the northern coast of South America in 1499 accompanied by Amerigo Vespucci, an Italian businessman. In 1500, Pedro Álvars Cabral commanded a Portuguese fleet bound for the Indian Ocean that accidentally made landfall on the coast of Brazil as it looped westward into the Atlantic.

By 1500, European experts knew that several large chunks of land cluttered the western Atlantic. A few cartographers speculated that these chunks were connected to one another in a landmass that was not Asia. In 1507, Martin Waldseemüller, a German cartographer, published the first map that showed the New World separate from Asia; he named the land America, in honor of Amerigo Vespucci.

Two additional discoveries confirmed Waldseemüller's speculation. In 1513, Vasco Núñez de Balboa crossed the isthmus of Panama and reached the Pacific Ocean. Clearly, more water lay between the New World and Asia. How much water Ferdinand Magellan discovered when he led an expedition to circumnavigate the globe in 1519. Sponsored by King Charles I of Spain, Magellan's voyage took him first to the New World, around the southern tip of South America, and into the Pacific late in November 1520. Crossing the Pacific took almost four months. By the time he reached the Philippines, his crew had been decimated by starvation and thirst. Magellan himself was killed by Philippine tribesmen. A remnant of his expedition continued on to the Indian Ocean and managed to transport a cargo of spices back to Spain in 1522.

In most ways Magellan's voyage was a disaster. One ship and 18 men crawled back from an expedition that had begun with five ships and more than 250 men. But the geographic information it provided left no doubt that America was a continent separated from Asia by the enormous Pacific Ocean. The voyage made clear that Columbus was dead wrong about the identity of what he had discovered. It was possible to sail west to reach the East Indies, but that was a terrible way to go. After Magellan, most Europeans who sailed west set their sights on the New World, not on Asia.

Columbus's arrival in the Caribbean anchored the western end of what might be imagined as a sea bridge that spanned the Atlantic, connecting the Western Hemisphere to Europe.

That sea bridge ended the age-old separation of the hemispheres and initiated the **Columbian exchange**, a transatlantic exchange of goods, people, and ideas that has continued ever since.

Spaniards brought novelties to the New World that were commonplace in Europe, including Christianity, iron technology, sailing ships, firearms, wheeled vehicles, horses and other domesticated animals, and much else. Unknowingly, they also smuggled along many Old World viruses that caused epidemics of smallpox, measles, and other diseases that would kill the vast majority of Indian peoples during the sixteenth century and continue to decimate survivors in later centuries. European diseases made the Columbian exchange catastrophic for Native Americans. In the long term, these diseases were decisive in transforming the dominant peoples of the New World from descendants of Asians, who had inhabited the hemisphere for millennia, to descendants of Europeans and Africans, recent arrivals from the Old World by way of the newly formed sea bridge.

Ancient American goods, people, and ideas made the return trip across the Atlantic. Europeans were introduced to New World foods such as corn and potatoes as well as exotic fruits like pineapples, named for their resemblance to pinecones. Columbus's sailors became infected with syphilis in sexual encounters with New World women and then unwittingly carried the deadly parasite back to Europe, where it may already have had a foothold. New World tobacco created a European fashion for smoking that ignited quickly and has yet to be extinguished. But for almost a generation after 1492, this Columbian exchange did not reward Spaniards with the riches they yearned to find.

REVIEW   How did Columbus's landfall in the Caribbean help revolutionize Europeans' understanding of world geography?

Spanish Exploration and Conquest

During the sixteenth century, the New World helped Spain become the most powerful monarchy in both Europe and the Americas. Spaniards enslaved Caribbean islanders and put them to work growing crops and mining gold. But the profits from these early ventures barely covered

Columbian Exchange

The arrival of Columbus in the New World started an ongoing transatlantic exchange of goods, people, and ideas. Spaniards brought domesticated animals from the Old World, including horses, cattle, goats, chickens, cats, and sheep (left). The novelty of such animals is demonstrated by the Nahua words the Mexican people initially used to refer to these strange new beasts: for horses, they used the Nahua word for deer; a cow was "one with horns"; a goat was a "bearded one with horns"; a chicken was a "Spanish turkey hen"; a cat was a "little cougar"; a sheep was referred to with the word for cotton, linking the animal with its fibrous woolen coat. Spaniards brought many other alien items such as cannon, which the Mexica at first termed "fat fire trumpets," and guitars, which the Mexica called "rope drums." Spaniards also carried Old World microorganisms that caused devastating epidemics of smallpox, measles, and other diseases (center). Ancient American people, goods, and ideas made the return trip across the Atlantic. Columbus's sailors quickly learned to use Indian hammocks and became infected with syphilis in sexual encounters with Indian women; then they carried both hammocks and syphilis back to Europe. Smoking tobacco, like the cigar puffed by the ancient Mayan lord (right), became such a fashion in Europe that some came to believe, as a print of two men relaxing with their pipes was captioned, "Life Is Smoke." The strangeness of New World peoples and cultures also reinforced Europeans' notions of their own superiority. Although the Columbian exchange went in both directions, it was not a relationship of equality. Europeans seized and retained the upper hand.

University of California at Berkeley, The Bancroft Library; Arxiu Mas; Collection of Dr. Francis Robicsek.

the costs of maintaining the settlers. After almost thirty years of exploration, the promise of Columbus's discovery seemed illusory.

In 1519, however, that promise was fulfilled, spectacularly, by Hernán Cortés's march into the Mexican mainland. By about 1545, Spanish conquests extended from northern Mexico to southern Chile, and New World riches filled Spanish treasure chests. Cortés's expedition served as the model for Spaniards' and other Europeans' expectations that the New World could yield bonanza profits for its conquerors.

The Conquest of Mexico

Hernán Cortés, who became the richest and most famous conquistador (conqueror), arrived in the New World in 1504, an obscure nineteen-year-old Spaniard seeking adventure and the chance to make a name for himself. He fought in the conquest of Cuba and elsewhere in the Caribbean. In 1519, the governor of Cuba authorized Cortés to organize an expedition to investigate rumors of a fabulously wealthy kingdom somewhere in the interior of the mainland. A charming, charismatic

Cortés Arrives in Tenochtitlán

This portrayal of the arrrival of Cortés and his army in the Mexican capital illustrates the importance of Malinali, who stands at the front of the Spaniards' procession, serving as their translator and intermediary with Montezuma (not pictured), who has come out to greet the invaders. Painted by a Mexican artist after the conquest, the work contrasts Cortés—dressed as a Spanish gentleman, respectfully doffing his hat to Montezuma and accompanied by his horse and African groom—with his soldiers, who are armed and ready for battle. The painting displays the choices confronted by the Mexica: accepting the pacific overtures of Cortés or facing the lances, swords, and battle axes of the Spanish soldiers. Also notable is the importance of Indian porters who carried the Spaniards' food and other supplies. What do you think was the significance of the winged image on the flag?
Bibliothèque Nationale, Paris.

accompanied Cortés, "we would not have understood the language of New Spain and Mexico." With her help, Cortés talked and fought with Indians along the Gulf coast of Mexico, trying to discover the location of the fabled kingdom.

In the capital of the Mexican empire, Tenochtitlán, the emperor Montezuma heard rumors about some strange creatures sighted along the coast. (Montezuma and his people are often called Aztecs, but they called themselves Mexica.) Montezuma sent representatives to meet with the strangers and bring them gifts fit for gods. Before the Mexican messengers served food to the Spaniards, they sacrificed several hostages and soaked the food in their blood. This fare disgusted the Spaniards and might have been enough to turn them back to Cuba. But along with the food, the Mexica also brought the Spaniards another gift, a "disk in the shape of a sun, as big as a cartwheel and made of very fine gold," as one of the Mexica recalled. Here was conclusive evidence that the rumors of fabulous riches heard by Cortés had some basis in fact.

In August 1519, Cortés marched inland to find Montezuma. Leading about 350 men armed with swords, lances, and muskets and supported by ten cannons, four smaller guns, and sixteen horses, Cortés had to live off the land, establishing peaceful relations with indigenous tribes when he could and killing them when he thought necessary. On November 8, 1519, Cortés reached Tenochtitlán. Montezuma came out to welcome the Spaniards and showered them with lavish hospitality. Quickly, Cortés took Montezuma hostage and held him under house arrest, hoping to make him a puppet through which the Spaniards could rule the Mexican empire. This uneasy peace existed for several months until, after a brutal massacre of many Mexican nobles by one of Cortés's subordinates, the population of Tenochtitlán revolted, murdered Montezuma, and mounted a ferocious assault on the Spaniards. On June 30, 1520, Cortés and about a hundred other Spaniards fought their way out of Tenochtitlán and retreated toward the coast about one hundred miles to Tlaxcala, a stronghold of bitter enemies of the Mexica. The Tlaxcalans—who had long resented Mexican power—allowed Cortés to regroup, obtain reinforcements, and plan a strategy to conquer Tenochtitlán.

leader, Cortés quickly assembled a force of about six hundred men, loaded his ragtag army aboard eleven ships, and set out.

Cortés's confidence that he could talk his way out of most situations and fight his way out of the rest fortified the small band of Spaniards. But Cortés could not speak any Native American language. Landing first on the Yucatán peninsula, he had the good fortune to receive a gift from a chief of the Tobasco people: a fourteen-year-old girl named Malinali who spoke Mayan and Nahuatl, the language of the Mexica, the most powerful people in what is now Mexico and Central America (see chapter 1). Malinali, whom the Spaniards called Marina, soon learned Spanish and became Cortés's interpreter. "Without her help," wrote one of the Spaniards who

Cortés's Invasion of Tenochtitlán, 1519–1521

→ Cortés' original route, 1519
→ Cortés' retreat, 1520
→ Cortés' return route, 1520–1521

In the spring of 1521, Cortés mounted a complex campaign against the Mexican capital. The Spaniards and tens of thousands of Indian allies laid siege to the city. With a relentless, scorched-earth strategy, Cortés finally defeated the last Mexican defenders on August 13, 1521. The great capital of the Mexican empire "looked as if it had been ploughed up," one of Cortés's soldiers remembered. A defeated Mexica lamented, "The houses are roofless now, and their walls are red with blood."

The Search for Other Mexicos

Lured by their insatiable appetite for gold, conquistadors quickly fanned out from Tenochtitlán in search of other sources of treasure like Mexico. The most spectacular prize fell to Francisco Pizarro, who conquered the Incan empire in Peru. The Incas controlled a vast, complex region that contained more than nine million people and stretched along the western coast of South America for more than two thousand miles. In 1532, Pizarro and his army of fewer than two hundred men captured the Incan emperor Atahualpa and held him hostage. As ransom, the Incas gave Pizarro the largest treasure yet produced by the conquests: gold and silver equivalent to half a century's worth of precious-metal production in Europe. With the ransom in hand, the Spaniards executed Atahualpa. The Incan treasure spurred Spaniards to search for more.

Juan Ponce de León had sailed along the Florida coast in 1513. Encouraged by Cortés's success, he went back to Florida in 1521 to find riches, only to be killed in battle with Calusa Indians. A few years later, Lucas Vázquez de Ayllón explored the Atlantic coast north of Florida to present-day South Carolina. In 1526 he established a small, short-lived settlement on the Georgia coast that he named San Miguel de Gualdape, the first Spanish attempt to establish a foothold in what is now the United States. Pánfilo de Narváez surveyed the Gulf coast from Florida to Texas in 1528. The Narváez expedition ended disastrously with a shipwreck on the Texas coast near present-day Galveston.

In 1539, Hernando de Soto, a seasoned conquistador who had taken part in the conquest of Peru, set out to find another Peru in North America. Landing in Florida, de Soto literally slashed his way through much of southeastern North America for three years, searching for the rich, majestic civilizations he thought were there. After much brutality and hardship, de Soto died in

Mexican Warrior
Warriors held the most exalted status in Mexican society. This sixteenth-century Mexican painting of a warrior in full battle regalia illustrates the Mexica's careful attention to their magnificent, awe-inspiring costumes. The elaborate clothing and decorative adornments (notice the ornamental stone plug in the warrior's lower lip) expressed warriors' high status; they also were intended to intimidate enemies who dared oppose the fearsome Mexica. Spanish soldiers developed healthy respect for the military skills of the Mexica but were not intimidated by the costumes of Mexican warriors. They did not understand the meaning the costumes had for the Mexica—for example, the costumes' evocation of supernatural support. In addition, although Mexican wooden swords lined with sharp stones could inflict deadly wounds, they proved no match for Spanish body armor, steel swords, horses, and guns.
Bibliothèque Nationale, Paris.

1542. His men buried him in the Mississippi River before turning back to Mexico, disappointed.

Tales of the fabulous wealth of the mythical Seven Cities of Cíbola lured Francisco Vásquez de Coronado to search the Southwest and Great Plains of North America. In 1540, Coronado left

Zuñi Defend Pueblo against Coronado
This sixteenth-century drawing by a Mexican artist shows Zuñi bowmen fighting back against the arrows of Coronado's men and the entreaties of Christian missionaries. Intended to document the support some Mexican Indians gave to Spanish efforts to extend the conquest into North America, the drawing depicts the Zuñi defender at the bottom of the pueblo aiming his arrow at a Mexican missionary armed only with religious weaponry: a crucifix, a rosary, and a book—presumably the Bible.
Hunterian Museum Library, University of Glasgow. Glasgow University Library, Department of Special Collections.

northern Mexico with a large expedition and a priest who claimed to know the way to what he called "the greatest and best of the discoveries." Cíbola turned out to be a small Zuñi pueblo of about a hundred families. Convinced that the rich cities must lie somewhere over the horizon, Coronado kept moving all the way to central Kansas before deciding in 1542 that the rumors he had pursued were just that, nothing more.

Juan Rodríguez Cabrillo led a maritime expedition in 1542 that sailed along the coast of California. Cabrillo died on Santa Catalina Island, offshore from present-day Los Angeles, but his men sailed on to Oregon, where a ferocious storm forced them to turn back toward Mexico.

These probes into North America by de Soto, Coronado, and Cabrillo persuaded Spaniards

that enormous territories stretched northward, but their inhabitants had little to loot or exploit. After a generation of vigorous exploration, Spaniards concluded that there was only one Mexico and one Peru.

New Spain in the Sixteenth Century

For all practical purposes, Spain was the dominant European power in the Western Hemisphere during the sixteenth century (Map 2.3). Portugal claimed the giant territory of Brazil under the Tordesillas treaty but was far more concerned with exploiting its hard-won trade with the East Indies than with colonizing the New World. England and France were absorbed by domestic and diplomatic concerns in Europe and largely lost interest in America until late in the century. In the decades after 1519, Spaniards created the distinctive colonial society of New Spain that showed other Europeans how the New World could be made to serve the purposes of the Old.

The Spanish monarchy claimed ownership of most of the land in the Western Hemisphere and gave the conquistadors permission to explore and plunder. (See "Documenting the American Promise," page 40.) The crown took one-fifth, called the "royal fifth," of any loot confiscated and allowed the conquerors to divide the rest. In the end, most conquistadors received very little after the plunder was divided among leaders such as Cortés and his favorite officers. To compensate his disappointed, battle-hardened soldiers after the conquest of Tenochtitlán, Cortés gave them towns the Spaniards had subdued.

The distribution of conquered towns institutionalized the system of *encomienda*, which empowered conquistadors to rule the Indians and the lands in and around their towns. The concept of encomienda was familiar to the Spaniards, who had used it to govern regions recaptured from the Muslims during the Reconquest. In New Spain, encomienda allowed the Spanish *encomendero* (the man who "owned" the town) to collect the tribute goods that the town had previously paid to the Mexican empire.

In theory, encomienda involved a reciprocal relationship between the encomendero and "his" Indians. In return for the tribute and labor of the Indians, the encomendero was supposed to encourage the Indians to convert to Christianity, to be responsible for their material well-being, and to guarantee order and justice in the town. Catholic missionaries labored earnestly to convert Indians to Christianity. Missionaries fervently believed that

God expected them to save Indians' souls by convincing them to abandon their old, sinful beliefs and to embrace the one true Christian faith. After baptizing tens of thousands of Indians, the missionaries learned that many Indians continued to worship their own gods along with the Christian God. Most friars came to believe that the Indians were lesser beings inherently incapable of fully understanding the Christian faith.

In practice, encomenderos were far more interested in what the Indians could do for them than in what they or missionaries could do for the Indians. Encomenderos subjected Indians to chronic overwork, mistreatment, and abuse. As one Spaniard remarked, "Everything [the Indians] do is slowly done and by compulsion. They are malicious, lying, [and] thievish." Economically, however, encomienda recognized a fundamental reality of New Spain: The most important treasure the Spaniards could plunder from the New World was not gold but uncompensated Indian labor. To exploit that labor, New Spain's richest natural resource, encomienda gave encomenderos the right to force Indians to work when, where, and how the Spaniards pleased.

Encomienda engendered two groups of influential critics. A few of the missionaries were horrified at the brutal mistreatment of the Indians. "What will [the Indians] think about the God of the Christians," Father Bartolomé de Las Casas asked, when they see their friends "with their heads split, their hands amputated, their intestines torn open?…Would

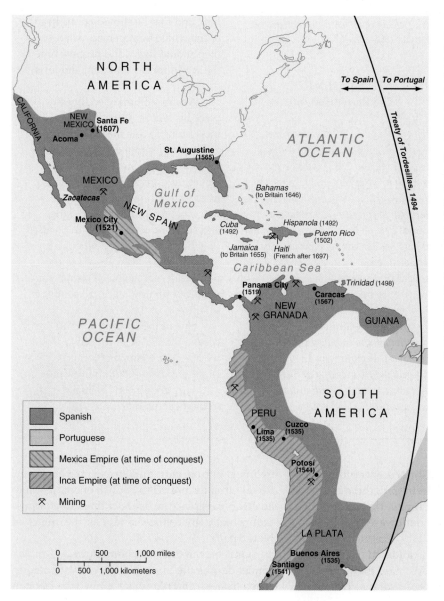

MAP 2.3   New Spain in the Sixteenth Century

Spanish control spread throughout Central and South America during the sixteenth century, with the important exception of Portuguese Brazil. North America, though claimed by Spain under the Treaty of Tordesillas, remained peripheral to Spain's New World empire.

READING THE MAP: Track Spain's efforts at colonization by date. How did political holdings, the physical layout of the land, and natural resources influence where the Spanish directed their energies?

CONNECTIONS: What was the purpose of the Treaty of Tordesillas? How might the location of silver and gold mines have affected Spain's desire to assert its claims over regions still held by Portugal after 1494, and Spain's interest in California, New Mexico, and Florida?

FOR MORE HELP ANALYZING THIS MAP, see the map activity for this chapter in the Online Study Guide at bedfordstmartins.com/roarkcompact.

Justifying Conquest

The immense riches Spain reaped from its New World empire came largely at the expense of Indians. A few individual Spaniards raised their voices against the brutal exploitation of Indians. Their criticisms prompted the Spanish monarchy to formulate an official justification of conquest that, in effect, blamed Indians for resisting Spanish dominion.

DOCUMENT 1
Montecino's 1511
Sermon

In 1511, a Dominican friar named Antón Montecino delivered a blistering sermon that astonished the Spaniards gathered in the church in Santo Domingo, headquarters of the Spanish Caribbean.

Your greed for gold is blind. Your pride, your lust, your anger, your envy, your sloth, all blind....You are in mortal sin. And you are heading for damnation....For you are destroying an innocent people. For they are God's people, these innocents, whom you destroyed. By what right do you make them die? Mining gold for you in your mines or working for you in your fields, by what right do you unleash enslaving wars upon them? They have lived in peace in this land before you came, in peace in their own homes. They did nothing to harm you to cause you to slaughter them wholesale.... Are you not under God's command to love them as you love yourselves? Are you out of your souls, out of your minds? Yes. And that will bring you to damnation.

SOURCE: Zvi Dor-Ner, *Columbus and the Age of Discovery* (New York: William Morrow, 1991), 220–21.

DOCUMENT 2
The Requerimiento

Montecino returned to Spain to bring the Indians' plight to the king's attention. In 1512 and 1513, King Ferdinand met with philosophers, theologians, and other advisers and concluded that the holy duty to spread the Christian faith justified conquest. To buttress this claim, the king had his advisers prepare the Requerimiento. According to the Requerimiento, Indians who failed to welcome Spanish conquest and all its blessings deserved to die. Conquistadors were commanded to read the Requerimiento to Indians before any act of conquest. Beginning in 1514, they routinely did so, speaking in Spanish while other Spaniards brandishing unsheathed swords stood nearby.

On the part of the King... [and] queen of [Spain], subduers of the barbarous nations, we their servants notify and make known to you, as best we can, that the Lord our God, living and eternal, created the heaven and the earth, and one man and one woman, of whom you and we, and all the men of the world, were and are descendants....

God our lord gave charge to one man called St. Peter, that he should be lord and superior to all the men in the world, that all should obey him, and that he should be the head of the whole human race, wherever men should live...and he gave him the world for his kingdom and jurisdiction.

And he commanded him to place his seat in Rome, as the spot most fitting to rule the world from.... This man was called Pope, as if to say, Admirable Great Father and Governor of men. The men who lived in that time obeyed that St. Peter and took him for lord, king, and superior of the universe. So also they have regarded the others who after him have been elected to the pontificate, and so has it been continued even till now, and will continue till the end of the world.

One of these pontiffs, who succeeded that St. Peter as lord of the world...made donation of these islands and mainland to the aforesaid king and queen [of Spain] and to their successors....

they want to come to Christ's sheepfold after their homes had been destroyed, their children imprisoned, their wives raped, their cities devastated, their maidens deflowered, and their provinces laid waste?" Las Casas and other outspoken missionaries softened few hearts among the encomenderos, but they did win some sympathy for the Indians from the Spanish monarchy and royal bureaucracy. Royal officials moved to abolish encomienda in an effort to replace swashbuckling old conquistadors with royal bureaucrats as the rulers of New Spain.

One of the most important blows to encomienda was the imposition in 1549 of a reform called the *repartimiento,* which limited the labor an

So their highnesses are kings and lords of these islands and mainland by virtue of this donation; and… almost all those to whom this has been notified, have received and served their highnesses, as lords and kings, in the way that subjects ought to do, with good will, without any resistance, immediately, without delay, when they were informed of the aforesaid facts. And also they received and obeyed the priests whom their highnesses sent to preach to them and to teach them our holy faith; and all these, of their own free will, without any reward or condition have become Christians, and are so, and the highnesses have joyfully and graciously received them, and they have also commanded them to be treated as their subjects and vassals; and you too are held and obliged to do the same. Wherefore, as best we can, we ask and require that you consider what we have said to you, and that you take the time that shall be necessary to understand and deliberate upon it, and that you acknowledge the Church as the ruler and superior of the whole world, and the high priest called Pope, and in his name the king and queen [of Spain] our lords, in his place, as superiors and lords and kings of these islands and this mainland by virtue of the said donation, and that you consent and permit that these religious fathers declare and preach to you.…

If you do so…we…shall receive you in all love and charity, and shall leave you your wives and your children and your lands free without servitude, that you may do with them and with yourselves freely what you like and think best, and they shall not compel you to turn to Christians unless you yourselves, when informed of the truth, should wish to be converted to our holy Catholic faith.…And besides this, their highnesses award you many privileges and exemptions and will grant you many benefits.

But if you do not do this or if you maliciously delay in doing it, I certify to you that with the help of God we shall forcefully enter into your country and shall make war against you in all ways and manners that we can, and shall subject you to the yoke and obedience of the Church and of their highnesses; we shall take you and your wives and your children and shall make slaves of them, and as such shall sell and dispose of them as their highnesses may command; and we shall take away your goods and shall do to you all the harm and damage that we can, as to vassals who do not obey and refuse to receive their lord and resist and contradict him; and we protest that the deaths and losses which shall accrue from this are your fault, and not that of their highnesses, or ours, or of these soldiers who come with us.

Indians who heard the Requerimiento could not understand Spanish, of course. No native documents survive to record the Indians' thoughts upon hearing the Spaniards' official justification for conquest, even when it was translated into a language they recognized. But one conquistador reported that when the Requerimiento was translated for two chiefs in Colombia, they responded that if the pope gave the king so much territory that belonged to other people, "the Pope must have been drunk."

Source: Adapted from A. Helps and M. Oppenheim, eds., *The Spanish Conquest in America and Its Relation to the History of Slavery and to the Government of the Colonies,* 4 vols. (London and New York, 1900–1904), 1:264–67.

QUESTIONS FOR ANALYSIS AND DEBATE

1. How did the Requerimiento answer the criticisms of Montecino? According to the Requerimiento, why was conquest justified? What was the source of Indians' resistance to conquest?

2. What arguments might a critic like Montecino have used to respond to the Requerimiento's justification of conquest? What arguments might the Mexican leader Montezuma have made against those of the Requerimiento?

3. Was the Requerimiento a faithful expression or a cynical violation of Spaniards' Christian faith?

encomendero could command from his Indians to forty-five days per year from each adult male. The repartimiento, however, did not challenge the principle of forced labor, nor did it prevent encomenderos from continuing to mistreat their Indians. However, as the old encomenderos died, repartimiento slowly replaced encomienda as the basic system of exploiting Indian labor.

The practice of coerced labor in New Spain grew directly out of the Spaniards' assumption that they were superior to the Indians. As one missionary put it, the Indians "are incapable of learning.…The Indians are more stupid than asses and refuse to improve in anything." Therefore, most Spaniards assumed, Indians' labor should be organized by and for their

Testerian Catechism

After conquest, Catholic missiionaries tried to teach the Mexica the basic doctrines of Christianity by using pictures (pictographs) that resembled the symbols in preconquest Mexican codices (books composed of pictographs). Missionaries hoped to appeal to the Mexica's respect for the authority of the ancient texts. These Testerian catechisms demonstrate the missionaries' awareness that the Mexica often retained their faith in their preconquest gods. The catechism shown here incorporates symbols of both Christian and Mexican belief. Try to puzzle out the identity of the various figures and the meanings Catholic missionaries intended them to convey to the Mexica.

conquerors. Spaniards seldom hesitated to use violence to coerce Indians to work.

From the viewpoint of Spain, the single most important economic activity in New Spain after 1540 was silver mining. In the early decades of the century, Spain imported more New World gold than silver, but that changed with the discovery of major silver deposits at Potosí, Bolivia, in 1545 and Zacatecas, Mexico, in 1546. As these mines swung into large-scale production, an ever-growing stream of silver flowed from New Spain to Spain (Figure 2.1). Overall, exports of precious metals from New Spain during the sixteenth century were worth about twenty-five times more than hides, the next most important export. The mines required large capital investments and many miners. Typically, a few Spaniards supervised large groups of Indian miners, who were supplemented by African slaves later in the sixteenth century.

For Spaniards, life in New Spain was relatively easy. Only a few thousand Spaniards actually fought during the conquests. Although the riches they won fell far short of their expectations, the benefits of encomienda gave them a comfortable, leisurely life that was the envy of many Spaniards back in Europe. As one colonist wrote to his brother in Spain, "Don't hesitate [to come]....This land [New Spain] is as good as ours [in Spain], for God has given us more here than there, and we shall be better off."

During the century after 1492, about 225,000 Spaniards settled in the colonies. Virtually all of them were poor young men of common (non-noble) lineage who came directly from Spain. Laborers and **artisans** made up the largest proportion, but soldiers and sailors were also numerous. Throughout the sixteenth century, men vastly outnumbered women, although the proportion of women grew from about one in twenty before 1519 to one in three by the 1580s. The gender and number of Spanish settlers shaped two fundamental features of the society of New Spain. First, Europeans never made up more than 1 or 2 percent of the total population. Although Spaniards ruled New Spain, the population was almost wholly Indian. Second, the shortage of Spanish women meant that Spanish men frequently married Indian women or used them as concubines.

The tiny number of Spaniards, the masses of Indians, and the frequency of intermarriage created a steep social hierarchy defined by perceptions of national origin and race. Natives of Spain—*peninsulares* (people born on the Iberian Peninsula)—enjoyed highest social status in New Spain. Below them but still within the white elite were creoles, children born in the New World to Spanish men and Spanish women. Together, peninsulares and creoles made up barely 1 or 2 percent of the population. Below them on the social pyramid was a larger group of mestizos, the offspring of Spanish men and Indian women, who comprised 4 or 5 percent of the population. So many of the mestizos were born to unmarried parents that the term *mestizo* (after the Spanish word for "mixed") became almost synonymous with bastard in the sixteenth century. Some mestizos worked as artisans and labor overseers and lived well, and a few rose into the ranks of the elite, especially if their Indian ancestry was not obvious from their skin color. Most mestizos, however, were lumped with Indians, the enormous bottom mass of the population.

The society of New Spain established the precedent for what would become a pronounced pattern in the European colonies of the New World: a society stratified sharply by social origin and race. All Europeans of whatever social origin considered themselves superior to Native Americans; in New Spain, they were a dominant minority in both power and status.

The Toll of Spanish Conquest and Colonization

By 1560, the major centers of the Indians' civilization had been conquered, their leaders overthrown, their religion held in contempt, and their people forced to work for the Spaniards.

FIGURE 2.1 New World Gold and Silver Imported into Spain during the Sixteenth Century, in Pesos
Spain imported more gold than silver during the first three decades of the sixteenth century, but the total value of this treasure was quickly eclipsed during the 1530s and 1540s when rich silver mines were developed. Silver accounted for most of the enormous growth in Spain's precious-metal imports from the New World.

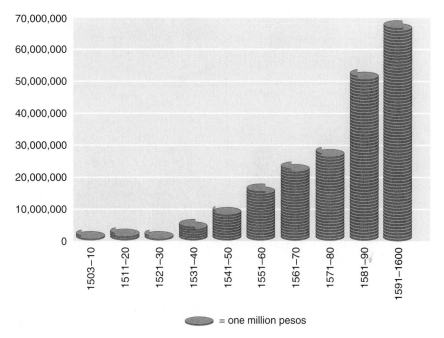

= one million pesos

Español con India,
Mestizo.

Mestizo con Española
Castizo.

Castizo con Española
Español.

Español con Mora
Mulato.

Mulato con Española
Morisco.

Morisco con Española
Chino.

Chino con India
Salta atras.

Salta atras con Mulata
Lobo.

Profound demoralization pervaded Indian society. As a Mexican poet wrote:

> Nothing but flowers and songs of sorrow
> are left in Mexico…
> where once we saw warriors and wise men.…
> We are crushed to the ground;
> we lie in ruins.
> There is nothing but grief and suffering
> in Mexico.

Adding to the culture shock of conquest and colonization was the deadly toll of European diseases. As conquest spread, Indians succumbed to virulent epidemics of measles, smallpox, and respiratory illnesses. Indians had built up no immunity to these diseases because they had not been exposed to them before the arrival of Europeans. By 1570, only a half century after Cortés entered Tenochtitlán, the Indian population of New Spain had fallen about 90 percent from what it was when Columbus arrived. The destruction of the Indian population was a catastrophe unequaled in human history. A Mayan Indian recalled that when sickness struck his village, "Great was the stench of the dead.…The dogs and vultures devoured the bodies. The mortality was terrible.…So it was that we became orphans.…We were born to die!" For most Indians, New Spain was a graveyard.

For Spaniards, Indian deaths meant that the most valuable resource of New Spain—Indian labor—dwindled. By the last quarter of the sixteenth century, Spanish colonists felt the pinch

Mixed Races

Residents of New Spain maintained a lively interest in each person's racial lineage. These eighteenth-century paintings illustrate forms of racial mixture common in the sixteenth century. In the first painting, a Spanish man and an Indian woman have a mestizo son; in the fourth, a Spanish man and a woman of African descent have a mulatto son; in the fifth, a Spanish woman and a mulatto man have a *morisco* daughter. The many racial permutations of parents led residents of New Spain to develop an elaborate vocabulary of ancestry. The child of a morisco and a Spaniard was a *chino;* the child of a chino and an Indian was a *salta abas;* the child of a salta abas and a mulatto was a *lobo;* and so on. Can you detect hints of some of the meanings of racial categories in the clothing depicted in these paintings?
Bob Schalkwijk / INAH.

FOR MORE HELP ANALYZING THIS IMAGE, see the visual activity for this chapter in the Online Study Guide at bedfordstmartins.com/roarkcompact.

of a labor shortage. To help redress the need for laborers, the colonists began to import African slaves. Some Africans had come to Mexico with the conquistadors. In the years before 1550 while Indian labor was still adequate, only 15,000 slaves were imported from Africa. Even after Indian labor began to decline, the relatively high cost of African slaves kept imports low, approximately 36,000 from 1550 to the end of the century. During the sixteenth century, New Spain continued to rely primarily on a diminishing number of Indians.

Spanish Outposts in Florida and New Mexico

After the explorations of de Soto, Coronado, and Cabrillo, officials in New Spain lost interest in America north of Mexico. The monarchy claimed that Spain owned all of North America and insisted that a few settlements be established in the northernmost borderlands of New Spain to give some tangible reality to its claims. Settlements in Florida would have the additional benefit of protecting Spanish ships from enemy ships that lurked along the southeastern coast to prey upon the Spanish treasure fleet sailing from Spanish colonies to Spain.

In 1565, the Spanish king sent Pedro Menéndez de Avilés to create settlements along the Atlantic coast of North America. In early September, Menéndez founded St. Augustine in Florida, the first permanent European settlement within what became the United States. By 1600, St. Augustine had a population of about five hundred, the remaining Spanish beachhead on the vast Atlantic shoreline of North America.

More than sixteen hundred miles west of St. Augustine, Spaniards founded another outpost in 1598. Juan de Oñate led an expedition of about five hundred people to settle northern Mexico, now called New Mexico, and claim the booty rumored to exist there. When Oñate and his companions reached pueblos near present-day Albuquerque and Santa Fe, he met with the pueblos' leaders and received their oath of loyalty to the Spanish king and the Christian God. Oñate sent out scouting parties to find the legendary treasures of the region and to locate the ocean, which he believed must be nearby. Meanwhile, relations with the Indians deteriorated. When the Acoma pueblo revolted against the Spaniards in 1599, Oñate ruthlessly suppressed the uprising, killing 800 Indians. Although

Catholic Feather Mosaic

In sixteenth-century Europe, Catholic churches conveyed religious messages in paintings, sculptures, and stained glass. The visual images both dramatized Christian stories and made religious doctrines accessible to the majority of Europeans who could not read. This feather mosaic produced by Mexican craftsmen in 1539 had a similar purpose. It follows European Christians' example of portraying a major event in Christian faith—Christ's resurrection after his death on the cross—in the distinctively Mexican medium of a mosaic of feathers collected from New World birds. Can you detect any other hints that the mosaic was designed to be understood by the Mexica?

The Mass of St. Gregory, 1539, feather mosaic, Auch, Musée des Jacobins, France (Gers).

Oñate reconfirmed the Spaniards' military superiority, he did not bring peace or stability to the region. After a second pueblo revolt occurred in 1599, many of Oñate's settlers returned to Mexico, leaving New Mexico as a small, dusty assertion of Spanish claims to the North American Southwest.

REVIEW   Why did New Spain develop a society highly stratified by race and national origin?

A Sign of Conquest

This skull of an Indian man in his fifties was recently excavated from the site of a Native American village in southwestern Georgia visited by de Soto's expedition in 1540. The skull shows that the man suffered a fatal sword wound above his right eye. Combined with slashed and severed arm and leg bones from the same site, the skull demonstrates the brutality de Soto employed against indigenous peoples on his voyage through the Southeast. No native weapons could have inflicted the wounds indelibly left on this skull and the other bones.

Robert L. Blakely.

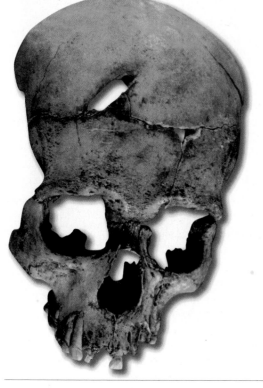

African Slaves Mining Gold

This sixteenth-century illustration depicts African slaves mining gold in New Spain. Spaniards imported African slaves in substantial numbers after the Native American population had been decimated by conquest and disease. Here, the two slaves on the right dig ore, from which the gold is separated by the slave in the center and then washed in hot water over the fire. The clean nuggets are then given to the Spaniard, who carefully weighs and saves them. How did the artist emphasize the differences between the Spaniard and the slaves? Is it possible to detect the artist's point of view about who was more "civilized"?

The Pierpont Morgan Library, New York. MA 3900, f.100.

The New World and Sixteenth-Century Europe

The riches of New Spain helped make the sixteenth century the Golden Age of Spain. After the deaths of Queen Isabella and King Ferdinand, their sixteen-year-old grandson became King Charles I of Spain in 1516. Three years later, just as Cortés ventured into Mexico, Charles I used judicious bribes to secure his selection as Holy Roman Emperor Charles V. His empire encompassed more than that of any other European monarch. He used the wealth of New Spain to protect his sprawling empire and to defend orthodox Christianity from the insurgent heresy of the **Protestant Reformation**. Spain's power in sixteenth-century Europe spread the message that a New World empire could bankroll Old World ambitions.

The Protestant Reformation and the European Order

In 1517, Martin Luther, an obscure Catholic priest in central Germany, initiated the Protestant Reformation by publicizing his criticisms of the Catholic Church. Luther's ideas won the sympathy of many Catholics, but they were considered extremely dangerous by church officials and monarchs like Charles V who believed with total conviction that, just as the church spoke for God, they ruled for God.

Luther preached a doctrine known as *justification by faith*: Individual Christians could obtain salvation and life everlasting only by having faith that God would save them. Giving offerings to the church, following the orders of priests, or participating in church rituals would not put believers one step closer to heaven. The only true source of information about God's will was the Bible, not the church. By reading the Bible, any Christian could learn as much about God's commandments as any priest. Indeed, Luther called for a "priesthood of all believers."

In effect, Luther charged that the Catholic Church was in many respects fraudulent. Luther insisted that priests were not necessary for salvation and that they encouraged Christians to violate God's will by promoting religious practices not specifically commanded by the Bible. The church, Luther declared, had neglected its true purpose of helping individual Christians understand the spiritual realm revealed in the Bible and had wasted its resources in worldly conflicts of politics and wars. Luther hoped his ideas would reform the Catholic Church, but instead they ruptured forever the unity of Christianity in western Europe.

Charles V pledged to exterminate Luther's **Protestant** heresies. The wealth pouring into Spain from the New World fueled his efforts to defend orthodox Catholic faith against Protestants as well as against Muslims in eastern Europe and any other nation bold enough to contest Spain's supremacy. As the wealthiest and most powerful monarch in Europe, Charles V, followed by his son and successor, Philip II, assumed responsibility for upholding the existing order of sixteenth-century Europe.

New World Treasure and Spanish Ambitions

Both Charles V and Philip II fought wars throughout the world during the sixteenth century. Mexican silver funneled through the royal treasury into the hands of military suppliers, soldiers, and sailors wherever Spain's forces fought. New World treasure was dissipated in military adventures that served the goals of the monarchy but did very little to benefit the average Spaniard.

In a sense, New World wealth made the Spanish monarchy too rich and too powerful among the states of Europe since it fueled grandiose Spanish ambitions. The ambitions of Charles V and Philip II were so great that the expenses of constant warfare far outstripped the revenues arriving from New Spain. To help meet military expenditures, both kings raised taxes in Spain more than fivefold during the sixteenth century. Since the nobility, by far the wealthiest class, was exempt from taxation, the burdensome new taxes fell mostly on poor peasants. The ambitions of the monarchy impoverished the vast majority of Spain's population and brought the nation to the brink of bankruptcy. When taxes proved insufficient, the monarchy borrowed heavily from European bankers. By the end of the sixteenth century, interest payments on royal debts swallowed two-thirds of the crown's annual revenues. In retrospect, the riches from New Spain proved a short-term blessing but a long-term curse.

But sixteenth-century Spaniards did not see it that way. As they looked at their accomplishments in the New World, they saw unmistakable signs of progress. They had added enormously to their knowledge and wealth. They had built mines, cities, Catholic churches, and even universities on the other side of the Atlantic. Their military, religious, and economic achievements gave them great pride and confidence.

Europe and the Spanish Example

The lessons of sixteenth-century Spain were not lost on Spain's European rivals. Spain proudly displayed the fruits of its New World conquests. In 1520, for example, Charles V exhibited some of the gifts Montezuma had given to Cortés. The objects astonished the German artist Albrecht Dürer, who wrote in his diary that he "marveled over the subtle ingenuity of the men in these distant lands" who created such "things which were brought to the King…[such as] a sun entirely of gold, a whole fathom [six feet] broad." But the most exciting news about "the men in these distant lands" was that they could serve the interests of Europeans as Spain had shown. With a few notable exceptions, Europeans saw the New World as a place for the expansion of European influence, a place where, as one Spaniard wrote, Europeans could "give to those strange lands the form of our own."

France and England tried to follow Spain's example. Both nations warred with Spain in Europe, preyed on Spanish treasure fleets, and ventured to the New World, where they too hoped to find an undiscovered passageway to the East Indies or another Mexico or Peru.

Algonquian Ceremonial Dance
When the English artist John White visited the coast of present-day North Carolina in 1585 as part of
Raleigh's expedition, he painted this watercolor portrait of an Algonquian ceremonial dance. This and
White's other portraits are the only surviving likenesses of sixteenth-century North American Indians
that were drawn from direct observation in the New World. White's portrait captures the individuality
of these Indians' appearances and gestures while depicting a ceremony that must have appeared
bizarre and alien to a sixteenth-century Englishman. The significance of this ceremonial dance is still a
mystery, although the portrait's obvious signs of order, organization, and collective understanding show
that the dancing Indians knew what it meant.

In 1524, France sent Giovanni da Verrazano to scout the Atlantic coast of North America from North Carolina to Canada, looking for a Northwest Passage (see Map 2.2). Eleven years later, France probed farther north with Jacques Cartier's voyage up the St. Lawrence River. Encouraged, Cartier returned to the region with a group of settlers in 1541, but the colony they established—like the search for a Northwest Passage—came to nothing.

English attempts to follow Spain's lead were slower but equally ill fated. Not until 1576, almost eighty years after John Cabot's voyages, did the English try again to find a Northwest Passage. This time Martin Frobisher sailed into the frigid waters of northern Canada. His sponsor was the Cathay Company, which hoped to open trade with China (see Map 2.2). Like many other explorers who preceded and followed him, Frobisher was mesmerized by the Spanish example and was sure he had found gold. But the tons of "ore" he hauled back to England proved worthless, the Cathay Company collapsed, and English interests shifted southward.

English explorers' attempts to establish North American settlements were no more fruitful than their search for a northern route to China. Sir Humphrey Gilbert led expeditions in 1578 and 1583 that made feeble efforts to found colonies in Newfoundland until Gilbert vanished at sea. Sir

Walter Raleigh organized an expedition in 1585 to settle Roanoke Island off the coast of present-day North Carolina. The first group of explorers left no colonists on the island, but two years later Raleigh sent a contingent of more than one hundred settlers to Roanoke under John White's leadership. White returned to England for supplies, and when he came back to Roanoke in 1590, the colonists had disappeared, leaving only the word *Croatoan* (whose meaning is unknown) carved on a tree. The Roanoke colonists most likely died from a combination of natural causes and unfriendly Indians. By the end of the century, England had failed to secure a New World beachhead.

Roanoke Settlement, 1585–1590

REVIEW   How did Spain's conquests in the New World shape Spanish influence in Europe?

Conclusion: The Promise of the New World for Europeans

The sixteenth century in the New World belonged to the Spaniards who employed Columbus and to the Indians who greeted him as he stepped ashore. Spaniards initiated the Columbian exchange between the New World and the Old that continues to this day. The exchange subjected Native Americans to the ravages of European diseases and Spanish conquest. Spanish explorers, conquistadors, and colonists forced Indians to serve the interests of Spanish settlers and the Spanish monarchy. The exchange illustrated one of the most important lessons of the sixteenth century: After millions of years, the Atlantic no longer was an impermeable barrier separating the Eastern and Western Hemispheres. After the voyages of Columbus, European sailing ships regularly bridged the Atlantic and carried people, products, diseases, and ideas from one shore to the other.

No European monarch could forget the seductive lesson taught by Spain's example: The New World could vastly enrich the Old.

Spain remained a New World power for almost four centuries, and its language, religion, culture, and institutions left a permanent imprint. By the end of the sixteenth century, however, other European monarchies had begun to contest Spain's dominion in Europe and to make forays into the northern fringes of Spain's New World preserve. To reap the benefits Spaniards enjoyed from their New World domain, other Europeans had to learn a difficult lesson: how to deviate from Spain's example. That discovery lay ahead.

Suggestions for Further Reading

Álvar Núñez Cabeza de Vaca, *Adventures in the Unknown Interior of America* (1993, and many other editions). A riveting account by a sixteenth-century Spaniard shipwrecked on the Gulf Coast who lived among Native Americans for years before returning to New Spain.

John L. Kessell, *Spain in the Southwest: A Narrative History of Colonial New Mexico, Arizona, Texas, and California* (2002). The story of the long legacy of New Spain in what is now the Southwest of the United States.

Diarmaid MacCulloch, *The Reformation: A History* (2004). A sweeping, authoritative overview of the historic rupture of Christianity.

Hugh Thomas, *Conquest: Montezuma, Cortés, and the Fall of Old Mexico* (2002). The amazing history of the conquest of Mexico.

Hugh Thomas, *Rivers of Gold: The Rise of the Spanish Empire from Columbus to Magellan* (2004). The fascinating history of the Spanish explorations that forged the connections between the Old and the New Worlds.

▶ FOR MORE BOOKS ABOUT TOPICS IN THIS CHAPTER, see the Online Bibliography at bedfordstmartins.com/roarkcompact.

▶ FOR ADDITIONAL FIRSTHAND ACCOUNTS OF THIS PERIOD, see Chapter 2 in Michael Johnson, ed., *Reading the American Past,* Third Edition.

▶ FOR WEB SITES AND DOCUMENTS RELATED TO TOPICS AND PLACES IN THIS CHAPTER, see "HistoryLinks," "DocLinks," and "PlaceLinks" at bedfordstmartins.com/roarkcompact.

REVIEWING THE CHAPTER

Follow these steps to review and strengthen your understanding of the chapter.

STEP 1: *Study the* **Key Terms** *and* **Timeline** *to identify the significance of each item listed.*

STEP 2: *Answer the* **Review Questions,** *drawing on key terms and dates to support your answers.*

STEP 3: *Drawing on the Key Terms, Timeline, and Review Questions, answer the broader* **Making Connections** *questions.*

KEY TERMS

Who

Christopher Columbus (p. 27)
Tainos (p. 27)
Prince Henry the Navigator (p. 31)
Vasco de Gama (p. 31)
John Cabot (p. 33)
Amerigo Vespucci (p. 34)
Martin Waldseemüller (p. 34)
Ferdinand Magellan (p. 34)
Hernán Cortés (p. 35)
Malinali (p. 36)
Montezuma (p. 36)
Mexica (p. 36)
Tlaxcalans (p. 36)
Francisco Pizarro (p. 37)
Atahualpa (p. 37)
Hernando de Soto (p. 37)
Francisco Vásquez de Coronado (p. 37)
Juan Rodríguez Cabrillo (p. 38)

Bartolomé de Las Casas (p. 39)
Juan de Oñate (p. 45)
Holy Roman Emperor Charles V (King Charles I of Spain) (p. 46)
Martin Luther (p. 46)
Philip II (p. 47)
Jacques Cartier (p. 48)
Martin Frobisher (p. 48)
Sir Walter Raleigh (p. 49)
John White (p. 49)

What

bubonic plague (p. 29)
the Reconquest (p. 30)
caravel (p. 31)
Treaty of Tordesillas (p. 32)
Northwest Passage (p. 33)
Columbian exchange (p. 34)
conquistador (p. 35)

conquest of Tenochtitlán (p. 36)
Incan empire (p. 37)
San Miguel de Gualdape (p. 37)
Seven Cities of Cíbola (p. 37)
New Spain (p. 38)
royal fifth (p. 38)
encomienda (p. 38)
repartimiento (p. 40)
Potosí, Bolivia (p. 42)
Zacatecas, Mexico (p. 42)
peninsulares (p. 43)
creoles (p. 43)
mestizos (p. 43)
St. Augustine (p. 45)
Acoma pueblo revolt (p. 45)
Protestant Reformation (p. 46)
justification by faith (p. 47)
Roanoke Island (p. 49)

TIMELINE

NOTE: Events are depicted chronologically, but the passage of time is not to exact scale.

◀ 1480 • Portuguese ships reach Congo.

1488 • Bartolomeu Dias rounds Cape of Good Hope.

1492 • Christopher Columbus lands on Caribbean island that he names San Salvador.

1493 • Columbus makes second voyage to New World.

1494 • Portugal and Spain negotiate Treaty of Tordesillas.

1497 • John Cabot searches for Northwest Passage.

1498 • Columbus makes third voyage to New World.
• Vasco da Gama sails to India.

1502 • Columbus makes fourth voyage to New World.

1513 • Vasco Núñez de Balboa crosses isthmus of Panama.

1517 • Protestant Reformation begins in Germany.

1519 • Hernán Cortés leads expedition to find wealth in Mexico.
• Ferdinand Magellan sets out to sail around the world.

1520 • Mexica in Tenochtitlán revolt against Spaniards.

1521 • Cortés conquers the Mexica at Tenochtitlán.

REVIEW QUESTIONS

1. Why did European exploration expand dramatically in the fifteenth century? (pp. 28–31)

2. How did Columbus's landfall in the Caribbean help revolutionize Europeans' understanding of world geography? (pp. 31–34)

3. Why did New Spain develop a society highly stratified by race and national origin? (pp. 34–45)

4. How did Spain's conquests in the New World shape Spanish influence in Europe? (pp. 46–49)

MAKING CONNECTIONS

1. The Columbian exchange exposed people on both sides of the Atlantic to surprising new people and goods. It also produced dramatic demographic and political transformations in the Old World and the New. How did the Columbian exchange lead to redistributions of power and population? Discuss these changes, being sure to cite examples from both contexts.

2. Despite inferior numbers, the Spaniards were able to conquer the Mexica and maintain control of the colonial hierarchy that followed. Why did the Spanish conquest of the Mexica succeed, and how did the Spaniards govern the conquered territory to maintain their dominance?

3. Spanish conquest in North America brought new peoples into constant contact. How did Spaniards' and Indians' perceptions of each other shape their interactions? In your answer, cite specific examples and consider how perceptions changed over time.

4. How did the astonishing wealth generated for the Spanish crown by its conquest of the New World influence European colonial exploration throughout the sixteenth century? In your answer, discuss the ways in which it both encouraged and limited interest in exploration.

▶ **FOR PRACTICE QUIZZES, A CUSTOMIZED STUDY PLAN, AND OTHER STUDY TOOLS,** see the Online Study Guide at bedfordstmartins.com/roarkcompact.

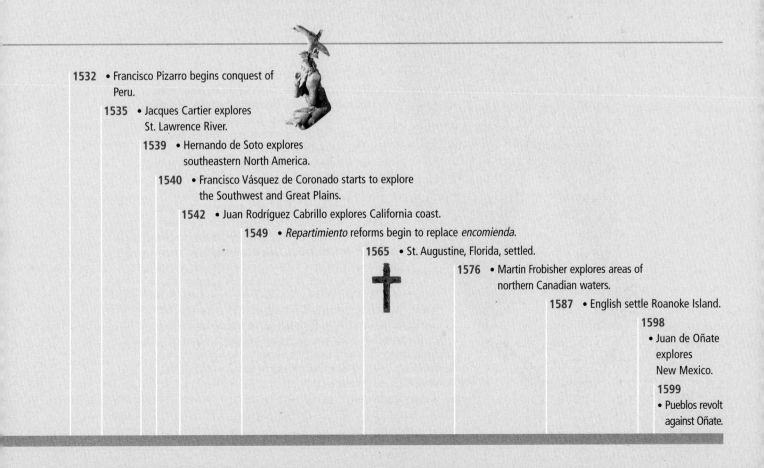

1532 • Francisco Pizarro begins conquest of Peru.

1535 • Jacques Cartier explores St. Lawrence River.

1539 • Hernando de Soto explores southeastern North America.

1540 • Francisco Vásquez de Coronado starts to explore the Southwest and Great Plains.

1542 • Juan Rodríguez Cabrillo explores California coast.

1549 • *Repartimiento* reforms begin to replace *encomienda*.

1565 • St. Augustine, Florida, settled.

1576 • Martin Frobisher explores areas of northern Canadian waters.

1587 • English settle Roanoke Island.

1598 • Juan de Oñate explores New Mexico.

1599 • Pueblos revolt against Oñate.

ALGONQUIAN POUCH

This pouch belonged to an important Algonquian Indian, possibly even the chief Powhatan, whose people inhabited the region first settled by the Virginia colonists. One or more Algonquian women probably made the pouch. Dangling from each end are two arrow-shaped pendants decorated with nearly 6,000 beads made from shells collected from Virginia's beaches. Algonquians—again, probably women—cut beads from the shells and punctured each bead, creating a tiny hole through which they threaded sinew interwoven with strips of deer hide to make the elaborate beaded design. Only a powerful Algonquian dignitary could command the labor and materials necessary to produce such a pouch. In turn, the pouch signaled the dignitary's importance when he wore it. The wearer draped the pouch over a belt that passed through the fold at the top. The opening to the pouch is on the inside of the fold and not visible here. The wearer probably used the pouch to carry tobacco and ritualistic objects that symbolized his authority. Most likely, however, the main function of the pouch was to dazzle ordinary Algonquians with the wearer's magnificence.

Ashmolean Museum, Oxford, England.

The Southern Colonies in the Seventeenth Century

1601–1700

I N DECEMBER 1607, barely six months after arriving at Jamestown with the first English colonists, Captain John Smith was captured by warriors of Powhatan, the supreme chief of about fourteen thousand Algonquian people who inhabited the coastal plain of present-day Virginia, near the Chesapeake Bay. According to Smith, Powhatan "feasted him after their best barbarous manner." Then, Smith recalled, "two great stones were brought before Powhatan: then as many [Indians] as could layd hands on [Smith], dragged him to [the stones], and thereon laid his head, and being ready with their clubs, to beate out his braines." At that moment, Pocahontas, Powhatan's eleven-year-old daughter, rushed forward and "got [Smith's] head in her armes, and laid her owne upon his to save him from death." Pocahontas, Smith wrote, "hazarded the beating out of her owne braines to save mine, and…so prevailed with her father, that I was safely conducted [back] to James towne."

This romantic story of an Indian maiden rescuing a white soldier and saving Jamestown and ultimately English colonization of North America has been enshrined in the writing of American history since 1624 when Smith published his *Generall Historie of Virginia*. Historians believe that this episode happened more or less as Smith described it. But Smith did not understand why Pocahontas acted as she did. Many commentators have claimed that her love for Smith caused her to rebel against her father's authority. Pocahontas herself left no document that explains her motives; most likely, she could not write. Everything known about her comes from the pens of Smith or other Englishmen. When their writings are considered in the context of what is known about the Algonquian society Pocahontas was born into, her actions appear in an entirely different light.

Most likely, what Smith interpreted as Pocahontas's saving him from certain death was instead a ceremonial enactment of Powhatan's willingness to incorporate Smith and the white strangers at Jamestown into Powhatan's empire. The ceremony displayed Powhatan's power of life or death over a subordinate chief—Smith—and Powhatan's willingness to give protection to those who acknowledged his supremacy—in this case, the interlopers at Jamestown. By appearing to save Smith, Pocahontas was probably acting out Smith's new status as an adopted member of Powhatan's extended family. Rather than a rebellious, love-struck girl, Pocahontas was almost certainly a dutiful daughter playing the part prescribed for her by her father and her culture.

Smith went back to England about two years after the adoption ritual. In the meantime, Pocahontas frequently visited the English settlement and often brought gifts of food to the colonists from her father. Powhatan routinely attached his sons and daughters to subordinate tribes as an expression of his protection and his dominance. It appears that Pocahontas's attachment to the English colonists grew out of Powhatan's attempt to treat the tribe of white strangers at Jamestown as he did other tribes in his empire, an attempt that failed.

Pocahontas in England

Shortly after Pocahontas and her husband John Rolfe arrived in England in 1616, an engraver made this portrait of her dressed in English clothing suitable for a princess. The portrait captures the dual novelty of England for Pocahontas and of Pocahontas for the English. Ornate, courtly clothing probably signified to English observers that Pocahontas was royalty and to Pocahontas that the English were accepting her as befitted the "Emperor" Powhatan's daughter. The mutability of Pocahontas's identity is displayed in the engraving's identification of her as "Matoaka" or "Rebecca."

Library of Congress.

In 1613, after relations between Powhatan and the English colonists had deteriorated into bloody raids by both parties, the colonists captured Pocahontas and held her hostage at Jamestown. Within a year she converted to Christianity and married one of the colonists, a widower named John Rolfe. After giving birth to a son named Thomas, Pocahontas, her husband, and the new baby sailed for England in the spring of 1616. When John Smith heard that Pocahontas was in London, he went to see her. According to Smith, Pocahontas said, "You did promise Powhatan what was yours should bee his, and he the like to you; you called him father, being in his land a stranger, and by the same reason so must I doe you." It seems likely that Pocahontas believed her incorporation into English society was a counterpart of the adoption ritual Powhatan had staged for John Smith in Virginia back in 1607.

Pocahontas died in England in 1617. Her son, Thomas, ultimately returned to Virginia, and by the time of the American Revolution his descendants numbered in the hundreds. But the world Thomas Rolfe and his descendants inhabited was shaped by a reversal of the power ritualized when his mother "saved" John Smith. By the end of the seventeenth century, Native Americans no longer dominated the newcomers who arrived in the Chesapeake with John Smith.

During the seventeenth century, English colonists learned how to deviate from the example of New Spain (see chapter 2) by growing tobacco, a crop Native Americans had cultivated in small quantities for centuries. The new settlers, however, grew enormous quantities of tobacco and exported most of it to England. Instead of incorporating Powhatan's people into their new society, the settlers encroached on Indian lands and they built new societies on the foundation of tobacco agriculture and transatlantic trade.

To produce large crop surpluses for export required hard labor and people who were willing—or could be forced—to do it. For the most part, Native Americans refused to be conscripted into the colonists' fields. Instead, the settlers depended on the labor of family members, **indentured servants**, and—by the last third of the seventeenth century—African slaves. By the end of the century, the southern colonies had become sharply different both from the world dominated by Powhatan when the Jamestown settlers first arrived and from contemporary English society. In ways unimaginable to Powhatan, Pocahontas, and John Smith, the colonists paid homage to the international market and the English monarch by working mightily to make a good living growing crops for sale to the Old World.

An English Colony on the Chesapeake

When James I became king of England in 1603, he eyed North America as a possible location for English colonies that could supply profits similar to those Spanish colonies sent to Spain. In 1606, London investors organized the Virginia Company, a joint stock company that received from King James a grant of over six million acres in North America. In effect, the king's **land grant** was a royal license to poach on both Spanish claims and Powhatan's chiefdom.

The Virginia Company investors hoped to found an empire that would strengthen England both overseas and at home. Richard Hakluyt, a strong proponent of **colonization**, claimed that a colony would provide work for swarms of poor "valiant youths rusting and hurtfull by lack of employment" in England. Colonists could buy English goods and make products that England now had to import from other nations. Enthusiastic reports from explorers claimed that in Virginia "the earth bringeth foorth all things in aboundance … without toile or labour." Maybe a valuable crop could be grown or perhaps rich lodes of gold and silver awaited discovery, as they had in New Spain. Such hopes failed to grapple with the difficulties of adapting European desires and expectations to the New World, already inhabited by Native Americans. Within two decades, the Jamestown settlement managed to survive, but royal government replaced the private Virginia Company, which never earned a penny for its investors.

The Fragile Jamestown Settlement

In December 1606, the ships *Susan Constant, Discovery,* and *Godspeed* carried 144 Englishmen toward Virginia. They arrived at the mouth of the Chesapeake Bay on April 26, 1607. That night while the colonists rested on shore, one of them later recalled, a band of Indians "creeping upon all foure, from the Hills like Beares, with their Bowes in their mouthes," attacked and dangerously wounded two men. The attack gave the colonists an early warning that the North American wilderness was not quite the paradise

Secotan Village

This engraving, published in 1612, was copied from an original drawing John White made in 1585 when he visited the village of Secotan on the coast of North Carolina. The drawing provides a schematic view of daily life in the village, which may have resembled one of Powhatan's settlements. White noted on the original that the fire burning behind the line of crouching men was "the place of solemne prayer." The large building in the lower left was a tomb where the bodies of important leaders were kept. Dwellings similar to those illustrated on John Smith's map of Virginia (see page 56) lined a central space, where men and women ate. Corn is growing in the fields along the right side of the village. The engraver included hunters shooting deer at the upper left. Hunting was probably never so convenient—no such hunters or deer appear in White's original drawing. This drawing conveys the message that Secotan was orderly, settled, religious, harmonious, and peaceful (notice the absence of fortifications), and very different from English villages.

Princeton University Libraries, Department of Rare Books and Special Collections.

FOR MORE HELP ANALYZING THIS IMAGE, see the visual activity for this chapter in the Online Study Guide at bedfordstmartins.com/roarkcompact.

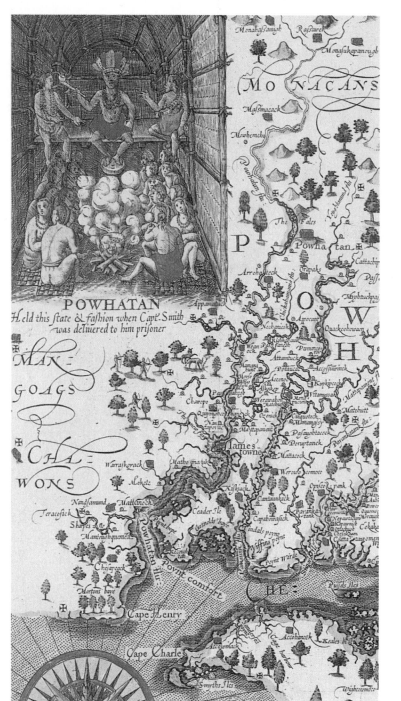

John Smith's Map of Virginia

In 1612, John Smith published a detailed map that showed not only geographic features of early Virginia but also the limits of exploration (indicated by small crosses), the locations of the houses of the Indian "kings" (indicated by red boxes), and "ordinary houses" of indigenous people (indicated by dots). The map shows the early settlers' intense interest in knowing where the Indians were — and were not. Notice the location of Jamestown (upriver from Point Comfort) and of Powhatan's residence at the falls (just to the right of the large *P* outside the hut on the upper left side). The drawing of Powhatan surrounded by some of his many wives was almost certainly made by an English artist who had never been to Virginia or seen Powhatan but tried to imagine the scene as described by John Smith.

Princeton University Libraries, Department of Rare Books and Special Collections.

described by the Virginia Company's publications in England. A few weeks later they went ashore on a small peninsula in the midst of Powhatan's chiefdom. With the memory of their first night in America fresh in their minds, they quickly built a fort, the first building in the settlement they named Jamestown.

The Jamestown fort showed the colonists' awareness that they needed to protect themselves from Indians and Spaniards. Spain employed spies to stay informed about the new English colony. Spain planned to wipe out Jamestown when the time was ripe, but that time never came. Powhatan's people defended Virginia as their own. The settlers and Powhatan's warriors skirmished repeatedly. English muskets and cannon repelled Indian attacks on Jamestown, but the Indians' superior numbers and knowledge of the Virginia wilderness made it risky for the settlers to venture far beyond the peninsula. Late in June 1607, Powhatan sensed a stalemate and made peace overtures.

The settlers soon confronted dangerous, invisible threats: disease and starvation. During the summer, many of the Englishmen lay "night and day groaning in every corner of the Fort most pittiful to heare," wrote George Percy, one of the settlers. The colonists increased their misery by bickering among themselves, leaving crops unplanted and food supplies shrinking. "For the most part [the settlers] died of meere famine," Percy wrote; "there were never Englishmen left in a forreigne Countrey in such miserie as wee were in this new discovered Virginia."

Powhatan's people came to the rescue of the weakened and demoralized Englishmen. Early in September 1607, they began to bring corn to the colony for barter. When that was insufficient to keep the colonists fed, the settlers sent Captain John Smith to trade (and plunder) for corn with Indians upriver from Jamestown. His efforts managed to keep 38 of the original settlers alive until a fresh supply of food and 120 more colonists arrived from England in January 1608.

It is difficult to exaggerate the fragility of the early Jamestown settlement. Although the Virginia Company sent hundreds of new settlers to Jamestown each year, few survived. During the "starving time" winter of 1609–10, food became so short that one or two famished settlers resorted to eating their recently deceased neighbors. The Virginia Company continued to pour people into the colony, promising in a 1609 pamphlet that "the place will make them rich." But most settlers went instead to an early grave.

Cooperation and Conflict between Natives and Newcomers

Powhatan's people stayed in contact with the English settlers but maintained their distance. The Virginia Company boasted that the settlers bought from the Indians "the pearles of earth [corn] and [sold] to them the pearles of heaven [Christianity]." In fact, few Indians converted to Christianity, and the English devoted scant effort to proselytizing. Marriage between Indian women and English men was also rare, despite the acute shortage of English women in Virginia in the early years.

Powhatan's people regarded the English with suspicion, for good reasons. While the settlers often made friendly overtures to the Indians, they did not hesitate to use their guns and swords to enforce English notions of proper Indian behavior. More than once the Indians refused to trade their corn to the settlers, evidently hoping to starve them out. Each time the English broke the boycott by attacking the uncooperative Indians, pillaging their villages, and confiscating their corn.

Powhatan's people retaliated against English violence, but for fifteen years they did not organize an all-out assault on the European intruders, probably for several reasons. Although Christianity held few attractions for the Indians, the power of the settlers' God impressed them. One chief told John Smith that "he did believe that our [English] God as much exceeded theirs as our guns did their bows and arrows." Powhatan probably concluded that these powerful strangers would make better allies than enemies. As allies, the English strengthened Powhatan's dominance over the tribes in the region. They also traded with his people, usually exchanging European goods for corn. Native Virginians had some copper weapons and tools before the English arrived, but they quickly recognized the superiority of the intruders' iron and steel knives, axes, and pots and traded eagerly to obtain them.

The trade that supplied Indians with European conveniences provided English settlers with a necessity: food. But why did the settlers prove unable to feed themselves for more than a decade? First, as the staggering death rate suggests, many settlers were too sick to be productive members of the colony. Second, very few farmers came to Virginia in the early years. Instead, most of the newcomers were gentlemen and their servants, men who, in John Smith's words, "never did know what a day's work was." Smith

Wolf Head Pendant
A Susquehanna man probably wore this pendant suspended from the deer hide necklace (dyed red) extending from the back of the wolf head. The Native American who made the pendant in the mid-seventeenth century took the jawbone and teeth of a wolf and skillfully stitched them into a head shaped from deer hide stuffed with deer hair, taking care to display the wolf's menacing teeth. Inside the wolf's jaws, the maker sewed a realistic tongue (not visible in the picture) made of blue cloth obtained in trade with European colonists. Whether a wolf's tongue crafted from a European textile conveyed Susquehanna interpretation of words spoken by Europeans is unknown.
Courtesy, Skokloster Castle, Uppland, Sweden.

declared repeatedly that in Virginia "there is no country to pillage [as in New Spain]…all you can expect from [Virginia] must be by labor." For years, however, colonists clung to English notions that gentlemen should not work with their hands and tradesmen should work only in trades for which they had been trained, ideas about labor that made more sense in labor-rich England than in labor-poor Virginia. In the meantime, the colonists depended on the Indians' corn for food.

Powhatan died in 1618, and his brother Opechancanough replaced him as supreme chief. In 1622, Opechancanough organized an all-out assault on the English settlers. Striking on March 22, the Indians killed nearly a third of the English population. But the attack failed to dislodge the colonists. In the aftermath, the settlers unleashed a murderous campaign of Indian extermination that in a few years pushed Indians beyond the small circumference of white settlement. Before 1622, the settlers knew that the Indians, though dangerous, were necessary to keep the colony alive. After 1622, most colonists considered Indians their perpetual enemies.

From Private Company to Royal Government

The 1622 uprising prompted a royal investigation of affairs in Virginia. The investigators discovered that the appalling mortality among the colonists was caused more by disease and mismanagement than by Indian raids. In 1624, King James revoked the charter of the Virginia Company and made Virginia a royal colony, subject to the direction of the royal government rather than to the company's private investors, an arrangement that lasted until 1776.

The king now appointed the governor of Virginia and his council, but most other features of local government established under the Virginia Company remained intact. In 1619, for example, the company had inaugurated the House of Burgesses, an assembly of representatives (called burgesses) elected by the colony's inhabitants. Under the new royal government, laws passed by the burgesses had to be approved by the king's bureaucrats in England rather than by the company. Otherwise, the House of Burgesses continued as before, acquiring distinction as the oldest representative legislative assembly in the British colonies.

The demise of the Virginia Company marked the end of the first phase of colonization of the Chesapeake region. From the first 105 adventurers in 1607, the population had grown to about 1,200 by 1624. Despite mortality rates higher than during the worst epidemics in London, new settlers still came. Their arrival and King James's willingness to take over the struggling colony reflected a fundamental change in Virginia. After years of fruitless experimentation, it was becoming clear that English settlers could make a fortune in Virginia by growing tobacco.

REVIEW Why did Powhatan pursue largely peaceful relations with the Jamestown settlement?

A Tobacco Society

Tobacco grew wild in the New World, and Native Americans used it for thousands of years before Europeans arrived. During the sixteenth century, Spanish colonists in the New World sent tobacco to Europe, where it was an expensive luxury used sparingly by a few. During the next century, English colonists in North America sent so much tobacco to European markets that it became an affordable indulgence used often by many people. (See "Beyond America's Borders," page 60.)

John Rolfe—Pocahontas's husband-to-be—planted West Indian tobacco seeds in 1612 and learned that they flourished in Virginia. By 1617, the colonists had grown enough tobacco to send the first commercial shipment to England, where it sold for a high price. After that, Virginia pivoted from a colony of rather aimless adventurers into a society of dedicated tobacco **planters**.

Dedicated they were. By 1700, nearly 100,000 colonists lived in the Chesapeake region (encompassing Virginia, Maryland, and northern North Carolina), and they exported over 35 million pounds of tobacco. Chesapeake colonists mastered the demands of tobacco agriculture, and the "Stinkinge Weede" (a seventeenth-century Marylander's term for tobacco) also mastered the

colonists. Settlers lived by the rhythms of tobacco agriculture, and their endless need for labor attracted droves of English indentured servants to work in Chesapeake tobacco fields (Map 3.1).

Tobacco Agriculture

A demanding crop, tobacco required close attention and a great deal of hand labor year-round. Primitive tools and methods made this intensive cycle of labor taxing. Like the Indians, colonists "cleared" fields by cutting a ring of bark from trees (a procedure known as girdling), thereby killing them. Girdling brought sunlight to clearings but left fields studded with tree stumps, making the use of plows impractical. Instead, colonists tilled their tobacco fields with heavy hoes. To plant, a visitor observed, colonists "just make holes [with a stick] into which they drop the seeds," much as the Indians did.

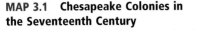

MAP 3.1 Chesapeake Colonies in the Seventeenth Century
The intimate association between land and water in the settlement of the Chesapeake in the seventeenth century is illustrated by this map. The fall line indicates the limit of navigable water, where rapids and falls prevented farther upstream travel. Although Delaware had excellent access to navigable water, it was claimed and defended by the Dutch colony at New Amsterdam (discussed in chapter 4) rather than by the English settlements in Virginia and Maryland shown on this map.

READING THE MAP: Using the notations on the map, create a chronology of the establishment of towns and settlements. What physical features correspond to the earliest habitation by English settlers?

CONNECTIONS: Why was access to navigable water so important? Given the settlers' need for defense against native tribes, what explains the distance between settlements?

FOR MORE HELP ANALYZING THIS MAP, see the map activity for this chapter in the Online Study Guide at bedfordstmartins.com/roarkcompact.

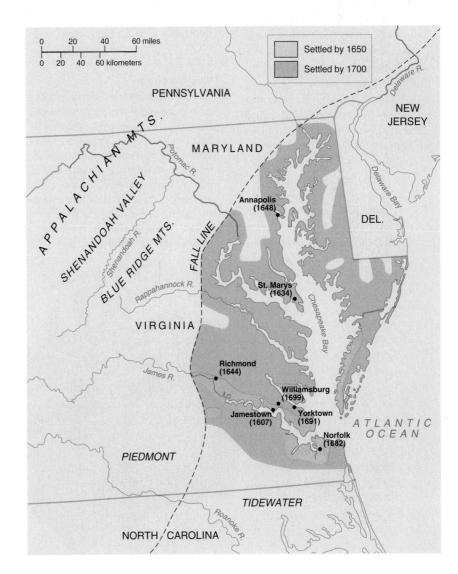

American Tobacco and European Consumers

English colonies in the Chesapeake were "wholly built upon smoke," King Charles I remarked. The king's shrewd comment highlighted the fundamental reason why the seventeenth-century Chesapeake colonies prospered by growing ever-increasing crops of tobacco: because people on the eastern side of the Atlantic were willing to buy ever-increasing quantities of tobacco to smoke—and to sniff, chew, and drink, and even to use for enemas. Europeans' desire for tobacco was the only reason it had commercial value. If Europeans had considered tobacco undesirable, the history of both the British North American colonies and the rest of the world would have been very different.

Some Europeans did hate tobacco, England's King James I foremost among them. In *A Counterblaste to Tobacco*, a pamphlet published in 1611, James declared that smoking was "A custome lothsome to the eye, hatefull to the Nose, harmefull to the braine, dangerous to the Lungs, and in the blacke stinking fume thereof, neerest resembling the horrible…smoke of the pit that is bottomelesse." James pulled out all the stops in attacking smoking. "What honour or policie can moove us to imitate the barbarous and beastly manners of the wilde, godlesse, and slavish Indians, especially in so vile and stinking a custome?" he asked. "Why doe we not as well imitate them in walking naked as

they doe? in preferring glasses, feathers, and such toyes, to golde and precious stones, as they do? yea why do we not denie God and adore the Devill, as they doe?" James reviled the "filthy smoke," the "stinking Suffumigation," the "spitting," the "lust," the "shameful imbecilitie," and the "sin" of tobacco. James's fulminations acknowledged that "the generall use of Tobacco" was "daily

Tobacco Cutter

Tobacconists in Europe used this machine to chop tobacco leaves into small pieces. Then they often flavored the chopped tobacco with oils, herbs, and spices much as coffeehouse baristas today add hazelnut, mocha, or vanilla flavors to lattes and cappucinos. The picture on the side of the cutter refers to the Native American origins of the tobacco processed by the cutter's screws, clamps, and blades.
Niemeyer Nederlands Tabacologisch Museum.

practiced…by all sorts and complexions of people." He noted, "The publike use [of tobacco], at all times, and in all places, hath now so farre prevailed that a man cannot heartily welcome his friend now, but straight they must bee in hand with Tobacco.…It is become…a point of good fellowship, and he that will refuse to take a pipe of Tobacco among his fellows…is accounted peevish and no good company." Clearly, James championed a lost cause.

When Spaniards first brought tobacco to Europe during the sixteenth century, physicians praised it as a wonder drug. One proclaimed that "to seek to tell the virtues and greatness of this holy herb, the ailments which can be cured by it, and have been, the evils from which it has saved thousands would be to go on to infinity…this precious herb is so general a human need [that it is] not only for the sick but for the healthy." Such strong recommendations from learned men were reinforced by everyday experiences of commoners. Sailors returning from the New World "suck in as much smoke as they can," one Spaniard observed, "[and] in this way they say that their hunger and thirst are allayed, their strength is restored and their spirits are refreshed; [and]… their brains are lulled by a joyous intoxication." That joyous intoxication—"a bewitching quality" King James called it—made tobacco irresistible to most Europeans. And, as we know all too well today, the bewitching intoxication of tobacco was highly addictive.

Feeding that habit was expensive at the beginning of the seventeenth century because tobacco was scarce. In 1603, for

Smoking Club

In Europe, tobacco smokers congregated in clubs to enjoy the intoxicating weed. This seventeenth-century print satirizes smokers' promiscuous gatherings of fashionable men, women, and children who indulged their taste for tobacco. Emblems of the tobacco trade adorn the wall; pipes, spittoons, and other smoking implements are close at hand; and the dog cleans up after those who cannot hold their smoke.

Koninklijke Bibliotheek, The Hague.

example, England imported only about 25,000 pounds of tobacco, all from New Spain. By 1700, England imported nearly 40 million pounds of tobacco, almost all from the Chesapeake colonies. The huge increase in tobacco supply caused prices to plummet. A quantity of tobacco that sold for a dollar in 1600 cost less than two and a half cents by 1700.

The low prices made possible by bumper crops harvested by planters in the Chesapeake transformed tobacco consumption in England and elsewhere in Europe. Per capita tobacco use in England grew over 200-fold during the seventeenth century, from less than a fifth of an ounce in the 1620s to 2.3 pounds by 1700.

American tobacco became the first colonial product of mass consumption by Europeans, blazing a trail followed by New World sugar, coffee, and chocolate.

Tobacco altered European culture. It spawned new industries, new habits, and new forms of social life. Smoking was the most common form of tobacco consumption in the seventeenth century, and smokers needed far more than tobacco to light up. They needed pipes, and hundreds of pipe makers supplied them with millions of ceramic pipes. They needed boxes or tins to hold their tobacco and a container to hold the embers they used to light the tobacco, or a flint and steel to strike

sparks; they needed pipe cleaners; they needed spittoons if they were smoking in a respectable place that disapproved of spitting on the floor. European merchants and manufacturers supplied all these needs, along with tobacco itself, which had to be graded, chopped, flavored, packaged, stored, advertised, and sold. Men and women smoked in taverns, in smoking clubs, around dinner tables, and in bed. A visitor to London noted that tobacco was not only in "frequent use…at every hour of the day but even at night [smokers] keep the pipe and steel at their pillows and gratify their longings."

The somewhat cumbersome paraphernalia of smoking caused many tobacco users to shift to snuff, which became common in the eighteenth century. Snuff use eliminated smoke, fire, and spitting with the more refined arts of taking a pinch of powdered, flavored tobacco from a snuffbox and sniffing it into one or both nostrils, which produced a fashionable sneeze followed by a genteel wipe with a dainty handkerchief. Sneezing induced by snuff was considered not only fashionable but healthful. One snuff taker explained that "by its gently pricking and stimulating the membranes, [snuff] causes Sneezing or Contractions, whereby the Glands like so many squeezed Sponges, dismiss their Seriosities and Filth."

Whether consumed by smoking, by sniffing, or in other ways, tobacco profoundly changed European habits, economies, and societies. It is no exaggeration to conclude that planters, servants, and eventually slaves in the Chesapeake made it possible for Europeans to become hooked on tobacco.

English settlers worked hard because their labor promised greater rewards in the Chesapeake region than in England. One colonist proclaimed that "the dirt of this Province affords as great a profit to the general Inhabitant, as the Gold of Peru doth to…the Spaniard." Although he exaggerated, it was true that a hired man could expect to earn two or three times more in Virginia tobacco fields than in England. Better still, in Virginia land was so abundant that it was extremely cheap, compared to land in England. By the mid-seventeenth century, common laborers could buy a hundred acres for less than their annual wages—an impossibility in England. New settlers who paid their own transportation to the Chesapeake received a grant of fifty acres of free land (termed a headright). The Virginia Company initiated the headright policy to encourage settlement, and the royal government continued it for the same reason.

A Servant Labor System

Headrights, cheap land, and high wages gave poor English folk powerful incentives to immigrate to the New World. Yet many potential immigrants could not scrape together the fare to cross the Atlantic. Their poverty and the colonists' crying need for labor formed the basic context for the creation of a servant labor system.

About 80 percent of the immigrants to the Chesapeake during the seventeenth century were indentured servants. Twenty Africans arrived in Virginia in 1619, and they probably were enslaved, although scanty records make it impossible to be certain. For the next fifty years, however, only a small number of slaves labored in Chesapeake tobacco fields. (Large numbers of slaves came in the eighteenth century, as chapter 5 explains.) Instead of a slave society, the seventeenth-century Chesapeake region was fundamentally a society of servants and ex-servants.

To buy passage aboard a ship bound for the Chesapeake, an English immigrant had to come up with about £5, roughly a year's wages for an English servant or laborer. Earning wages at all was difficult in England since job opportunities were shrinking. Unemployed people drifted into seaports like Bristol, Liverpool, and London, where they learned about the plentiful jobs in North America.

Unable to pay for their trip across the Atlantic, poor immigrants agreed to a contract called an indenture, which functioned as a form of credit. By signing an indenture, an immigrant borrowed the cost of transportation to the Chesapeake from a merchant or ship captain in England. To repay this loan, the indentured person agreed to work as a servant for four to seven years in North America. Once the indentured person arrived in the colonies, the merchant or ship captain sold his right to the immigrant's labor to a local tobacco planter. To obtain the servant's labor, the planter paid about twice the cost of transportation and agreed to provide the servant with food and shelter during the term of the indenture. When the indenture expired, the planter owed the former servant "freedom dues," usually a few barrels of corn and a suit of clothes.

Ideally, indentures allowed poor immigrants to trade their most valuable assets—their freedom and their ability to work—for a trip to the New World and a period of servitude followed by freedom in a land of opportunity. Planters reaped more immediate benefits. Servants meant more hands to grow more tobacco. A planter expected a servant to grow enough tobacco in one year to cover the price the planter paid for the indenture. Servants' labor during the remainder of the indenture promised a handsome profit for the planter. But roughly half of all servants became sick and died before serving out their indentures, reducing planters' gains. Planters also received a headright of fifty acres of land from the colonial government for every newly purchased servant.

About three out of four servants were men between the ages of fifteen and twenty-five when they arrived in the Chesapeake. Typically they shared the desperation of sixteen-year-old Francis Haires, who indentured himself for seven years because "his father and mother and All friends [are] dead and he [is] a miserable wandering boy." Like Francis, most servants had no special training or skills, although the majority had some experience with agricultural work. "Hunger and fear of prisons bring to us onely such servants as have been brought up to no Art or Trade," one Virginia planter complained. A skilled craftsman could obtain a shorter indenture, but few risked coming to the colonies since their prospects were better at home.

Women were almost as rare as skilled craftsmen in the Chesapeake and more ardently desired. In the early days of the tobacco boom, the Virginia Company shipped young single women servants to the colony as prospective wives for male settlers willing to pay "120 weight [pounds] of the best leaf tobacco for each of them," in effect getting both a wife and a servant. The company reasoned that, as one official wrote in 1622, "the plantation can never flourish till families be planted, and the respect of wives and children fix the people on the soil." The company's efforts as a marriage broker proved no more successful than its other ventures. Women remained a small minority of the Chesapeake population until late in the seventeenth century. The servant labor system perpetuated the gender imbalance. Although female servants cost about the same as males and generally served for the same length of time, only about one servant in four was a woman. Planters preferred male servants for fieldwork, although many servant women hoed and harvested tobacco fields. Most women servants also did household chores such as cooking, washing, cleaning, gardening, and milking.

Servant life was harsh by the standards of seventeenth-century England and even by the **frontier** standards of the Chesapeake. Unlike servants in England, Chesapeake servants had no control over who purchased their labor—and thus them—for the period of their indenture. Many servants were bought and sold several times before their indenture expired. A Virginia servant protested in 1623 that his master "hath sold me for £150 sterling like a damnd slave." But tobacco planters' need for labor muffled such complaints about treating servants as property.

Severe laws aimed to keep servants in their place. Punishments for petty crimes stretched servitude far beyond the original terms of indenture. Christopher Adams, for example, had to serve three extra years for running away for six months. Richard Higby received six extra years of servitude for killing three hogs. After midcentury, the Virginia legislature added three or more years to the indentures of most servants by requiring them to serve until they were twenty-four years old.

Women servants were subject to special restrictions and risks. They were prohibited from marrying until their servitude had expired. A servant woman, the law assumed, could not serve two masters at the same time: one who owned her indentured labor and another who was her husband. However, the predominance of men in the Chesapeake population inevitably pressured women to engage in sexual relations.

Indenture Contract
Indenture contracts were so common that forms were printed with blank spaces for details to be written in. In mid-November 1698, fifteen-year-old Matthew Evans, a friendless boy from Harfordshire, agreed to serve mariner Thomas Graves, or anybody to whom Graves sold his rights, for four years in Virginia. The contract specifies that Graves will carry Evans to Virginia and provide during the term of the indenture "all necessary Cloathes, Meat, Drink, Washing, Lodging and other necessaryes, fit and convenient for him according to the Custom of the said Plantation, as other Servants in such Cases are usually Provided for...."
The Library of Virginia.

As a rule, if a woman servant gave birth to a child, she had to serve two extra years and pay a fine. However, for some servant women, premarital pregnancy was a path out of servitude: The father of an unborn child sometimes purchased the indenture of the servant mother-to-be, freed, and married her.

Such punishments reflected four fundamental realities of the servant labor system. First, planters' hunger for labor caused them to demand as much labor as they could get from their servants, including devising legal ways to extend the period of servitude. Second, servants hoped to survive their servitude and use their freedom to obtain land and start a family. Third, servants' hopes frequently conflicted with planters' demands. Since servants saw themselves as free people in a temporary status of servitude, they often made grudging, half-hearted workers. Finally, both servants and planters put up with this contentious arrangement because the alternatives were less desirable.

Planters could not easily hire free men and women because land was readily available and free people preferred to work on their own land, for themselves. Nor could planters depend on much labor from family members. The preponderance of men in the population meant that families were few, were started late, and thus had few children. And, until the 1680s and 1690s, slaves were expensive and hard to come by. Before then, masters who wanted to expand their labor force and grow more tobacco had few alternatives to buying indentured servants.

Cultivating Land and Faith

Villages and small towns dotted the rural landscape of seventeenth-century England, but in the Chesapeake acres of wilderness were interrupted here and there by tobacco farms. Tobacco was such a labor-intensive crop that one fieldworker could tend only about two acres of the plants in a year (an acre is slightly smaller than a football field), plus a few more acres for food crops. A successful farmer needed a great deal more land, however, because tobacco quickly exhausted the fertility of the soil. Since each farmer cultivated only 5 or 10 percent of his land at any one time, a "settled" area comprised swatches of cultivated land surrounded by forest. Arrangements for marketing tobacco also contributed to the dispersion of settlements. Tobacco planters sought land that fronted a navigable river in order to minimize the work of transporting the heavy barrels of tobacco onto ships.

Most Chesapeake colonists were nominally **Protestants**. Attendance at Sunday services and conformity to the doctrines of the Church of England were required of all English men and women. Few clergymen migrated to the Chesapeake, however, and too few of those who did come were models of righteousness and piety. Certainly some colonists took their religion seriously. But on the whole, religion did not awaken the zeal of Chesapeake settlers, certainly not as it did the zeal of New England settlers in these same years (see chapter 4). The religion of the Chesapeake colonists was Anglican, but their faith lay in the turbulent, competitive, high-stakes gamble of survival as tobacco planters.

The situation was similar in the Catholic colony of Maryland. In 1632, England's King Charles I granted his Catholic friend Lord Baltimore about six and a half million acres in the northern Chesapeake region. In return, the king specified that Lord Baltimore pay him the token rent of "two Indian arrowheads" a year. Lord Baltimore intended to create a refuge for Catholics, who suffered severe discrimination in England. He fitted out two ships, the *Ark* and the *Dove*, gathered about 150 settlers, and sent them to the new colony, where they arrived on March 25, 1634. However, Maryland failed to live up to Baltimore's hopes. The colony's population grew very slowly for twenty years, and most settlers were Protestants rather than Catholics. The religious turmoil of the **Puritan** Revolution in England (discussed in chapter 4) spilled across the Atlantic, creating conflict between Maryland's few Catholics—most of them wealthy and prominent—and the Protestant majority, most of them neither wealthy nor prominent. During the 1660s, Maryland began to attract settlers as readily as Virginia, mostly Protestants. Although Catholics and the Catholic faith continued to exert influence in Maryland, the colony's society, economy, politics, and culture became nearly indistinguishable from Virginia's. Both colonies shared a devotion to tobacco, the true faith of the Chesapeake.

REVIEW   Why did the vast majority of European immigrants to the Chesapeake come as indentured servants?

Settlement Patterns along the James River

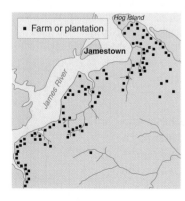

- Farm or plantation

Hog Island

Jamestown

James River

The Evolution of Chesapeake Society

The system of indentured servitude sharpened inequality in Chesapeake society by the mid-seventeenth century, propelling social and political polarization that culminated in 1676 with Bacon's Rebellion. The rebellion prompted reforms that stabilized relations between elite planters and their lesser neighbors and paved the way for a social hierarchy based less overtly on land and wealth than on race. Amid this social and political evolution, one thing did not change: the dedication of Chesapeake colonists to growing tobacco.

Social and Economic Polarization

The first half of the seventeenth century in the Chesapeake was the era of the **yeoman**—a farmer who owned a small plot of land sufficient to support a family and tilled largely by servants and a few family members. A small number of elite planters had larger estates and commanded ten or more servants. But for the first several decades, few men lived long enough to accumulate a fortune sufficient to set them much apart from their neighbors. Until midcentury, the principal division in Chesapeake society was less between rich and poor planters than between free farmers and unfree servants. While these two groups contrasted sharply in their legal and economic status, their daily lives had many similarities. Servants looked forward to the time when their indentures would expire and they would become free and eventually own land. On the whole, a rough, frontier equality characterized free families in the Chesapeake until about 1650.

Three major developments splintered that equality during the third quarter of the century. First, as planters grew more and more tobacco, the ample supply depressed tobacco prices in European markets. Cheap tobacco reduced planters' profits and made it more difficult for freed servants to save enough to become landowners. Second, because the mortality rate in the Chesapeake colonies declined, more and more servants survived their indentures, and landless freemen became more numerous and grew more discontented. Third, declining mortality also encouraged the formation of a planter elite. By living longer, the most successful planters compounded their success. The wealthiest planters also began to serve as merchants, marketing crops for their less successful neighbors, importing English goods for sale, and giving credit to hard-pressed customers.

By the 1670s, the society of the Chesapeake had become polarized. Landowners—the planter elite and the more numerous yeoman planters—clustered around one pole. Landless colonists, mainly freed servants, gathered at the other. Each group eyed the other with suspicion and mistrust. For the most part, planters saw landless freemen as a dangerous rabble rather than as fellow colonists with legitimate grievances. Governor William Berkeley feared the political threat to the governing elite posed by "six parts in seven [of Virginia colonists who]…are poor, indebted, discontented, and armed."

Tobacco Plantation
This print illustrates the processing of tobacco on a seventeenth-century plantation. Workers cut the mature plants and put the leaves in piles to wilt (left foreground and center background). After the leaves dry somewhat, they are suspended from poles in a drying barn (right foreground), where they are seasoned before being packed in casks for shipping. Sometimes, tobacco leaves are left to dry in the fields (center background). The print suggests the labor demands of tobacco by showing twenty-two individuals, all but two of them actively at work with the crop. The one woman, hand in hand with a man in the left foreground, may be on her way to work on the harvested leaves, but it is more likely that she and the man are overseeing the labor of their servants or employees.
From "About Tobacco," Lehman Brothers.

Government Policies and Political Conflict

In general, government and politics strengthened the distinctions in Chesapeake society. The most vital distinction separated servants and masters, and the colonial government enforced it with an iron fist. Poor men like William Tyler complained that "nether the Governor nor Counsell could or would doe any poore men right, but that they would shew favor to great men and wronge the poore." Most Chesapeake colonists, like most Europeans, assumed that "great men" should bear the responsibilities of government. Until 1670, all freemen could vote, and they routinely elected prosperous planters to the legislature. No former servant served in either the governor's council or the House of Burgesses after 1640. Yet Tyler and other poor Virginians believed that the "great men" used their government offices to promote their selfish personal interests, rather than governing impartially.

As discontent mounted among the poor during the 1660s and 1670s, colonial officials tried to keep political power in safe hands. Beginning in 1661, for example, Governor Berkeley did not call an election for the House of Burgesses for fifteen years. In 1670, the House of Burgesses outlawed voting by poor men, permitting only men who headed a household and were landowners to vote.

The king also began to tighten the royal government's control of trade and to collect substantial revenue from the Chesapeake. A series of navigation acts funneled the colonial trade exclusively into the hands of English merchants and shippers. Navigation Acts of 1650 and 1651 specified that colonial goods had to be transported in English ships with predominantly English crews. A 1660 act required all colonial products to be sent only to English ports, and a 1663 law stipulated further that all goods sent to the colonies must pass through English ports and be carried in English ships manned by English sailors. Taken together, these navigation acts reflected the English government's **mercantilist** assumptions about the colonies: What was good for England should determine colonial policy.

Assumptions about mercantilism also underlay the import duty on tobacco inaugurated by the 1660 Navigation Act. The law assessed an import tax of two pence on every pound of colonial tobacco brought into England, about the price a Chesapeake tobacco farmer received. The tax gave the king a major financial interest in the size of the tobacco crop. During the 1660s, these tobacco import taxes yielded about a quarter of all English customs revenues.

Bacon's Rebellion

Colonists, like residents of European monarchies, accepted social hierarchy and inequality as long as they believed government officials ruled for the general good. When rulers violated that precept, ordinary people felt justified in rebelling. In 1676, Bacon's Rebellion erupted as a dispute over Virginia's Indian policy. Before it was over, the rebellion convulsed Chesapeake politics and society, leaving in its wake death, destruction, and a legacy of hostility between the great planters and their poorer neighbors.

Opechancanough, the Algonquian chief who had led the Indian uprising of 1622 in Virginia, mounted another surprise attack in 1644 and killed about 500 Virginia colonists in two days. During the next two years of bitter fighting, the colonists eventually gained the upper hand, capturing and murdering the old chief. The treaty that concluded the war established policies toward the Indians that the government tried to maintain for the next thirty years. The Indians relinquished all claims to land already settled by the English. Wilderness land beyond the fringe of English settlement was supposed to be reserved exclusively for Indian use. The colonial government hoped to minimize contact between settlers and Indians and thereby maintain the peace.

Had the Chesapeake population remained constant, the policy might have worked. But the number of land-hungry colonists, especially poor, recently freed servants, continued to multiply. In their quest for land, they pushed beyond the treaty limits of English settlement and encroached steadily on Indian land. During the 1660s and 1670s, violence between colonists and Indians repeatedly flared along the advancing frontier. The government, headquartered in the tidewater region near the coast, far from the danger of Indian raids, took steps to calm the disputes and reestablish the peace. Frontier settlers thirsted for revenge against what their leader, Nathaniel Bacon, termed "the protected and Darling Indians." Indians were not the only enemies Bacon and his men singled out. Bacon charged that "Grandees," or elite planters, operated the government for their private gain, a charge that made sense to many colonists. Bacon crystallized the grievances of the small planters and poor farmers against both the Indians and the colonial rulers in Jamestown.

Hoping to maintain the fragile peace on the frontier in 1676, Governor Berkeley pronounced Bacon a rebel, threatened to punish him for treason, and called for new elections of burgesses who, Berkeley believed, would endorse his get-tough policy. To Berkeley's surprise, the elections backfired. Almost all the old burgesses were voted out of office, their places taken by local leaders, including Bacon. The legislature was now in the hands of minor grandees who, like Bacon, chafed at the rule of the elite planters.

In June 1676, the new legislature passed a series of reform measures known as Bacon's Laws. Among other changes, the laws gave local settlers a voice in setting tax levies, forbade officeholders from demanding bribes or other extra fees for carrying out their duties, placed limits on holding multiple offices, and restored the vote to all freemen. Under pressure, Berkeley pardoned Bacon and authorized his campaign of Indian warfare. But elite planters soon convinced Berkeley that Bacon and his men were a greater threat than Indians.

When Bacon learned that Berkeley had once again branded him a traitor, he declared war against Berkeley and the other grandees. For three months, Bacon's forces fought the Indians, sacked the grandees' plantations, and attacked Jamestown. Berkeley's loyalists retaliated by plundering the homes of Bacon's supporters. The fighting continued until late October, when Bacon unexpectedly died, most likely from dysentery, and several English ships arrived to bolster Berkeley's strength. With the rebellion crushed, Berkeley hanged several of Bacon's allies and destroyed farms that belonged to Bacon's supporters.

The rebellion did nothing to dislodge the grandees from their positions of power. If anything, it strengthened their position. When the king learned of the turmoil in the Chesapeake and its devastating effect on tobacco exports and customs duties, he ordered an investigation. Royal officials replaced Berkeley with a governor more attentive to the king's interests, nullified Bacon's Laws, and instituted an export tax on every hogshead of tobacco as a way of paying the expenses of government without having to

Inside a Poor Planter's House
The houses of seventeenth-century Chesapeake settlers were typically "earth-fast": The structural timbers that framed the house were simply placed in holes in the ground, and the floor was packed dirt. No seventeenth-century house was substantial enough to survive until today. This photo shows a carefully documented historical reconstruction of the interior of a poor planter's house at St. Mary's City, Maryland. The wall of this one-room dwelling with a loft features a window with a shutter but no glass; when the shutter was closed, the only source of light was a candle or a fire. Notice the rustic, unfinished bench, table, and walls. These meager furnishings were usually accompanied by a storage chest and some bedding but not a bed. If and when planters became more prosperous, a bed was likely to be their first acquisition, suggesting that the lack of a good night's sleep was one of their major discomforts.
Image courtesy of Historic St. Mary's City.

obtain the consent of the tightfisted House of Burgesses.

In the aftermath of Bacon's Rebellion, tensions between great planters and small farmers gradually lessened. Bacon's Rebellion showed, a governor of Virginia said, that it was necessary "to steer between…either an Indian or a civil war." The ruling elite concluded that it was safer for colonists to fight Indians rather than each other, and the government made little effort to restrict settlers' encroachment on Indian lands. Tax cuts were another policy welcomed by all freemen. The export duty on tobacco imposed by the king allowed the colonial government to reduce taxes by 75 percent between 1660 and 1700. In the long run, however, the most important contribution to political stability was the declining importance of the servant labor system. During the 1680s and 1690s, fewer servants arrived in the Chesapeake, partly because of improving economic conditions in England. Accordingly, the number of poor, newly freed servants also declined, reducing the size of the lowest stratum of free society. In 1700, as many as one-third of the free colonists still worked as tenants on land owned by others, but the social and political distance between them and the great planters did not seem as important as it had been in 1660. The main reason was that by 1700 the Chesapeake was in the midst of transition to a slave labor system that minimized the differences between poor farmers and rich planters and magnified the differences between whites and blacks.

> **REVIEW** Why did Chesapeake colonial society become increasingly polarized between 1650 and 1670?

Religion and Revolt in the Spanish Borderland

While English colonies in the Chesapeake grew and prospered with the tobacco trade, the northern outposts of the Spanish empire in New Mexico and Florida stagnated. Instead of attracting settlers and growing crops for export, New Mexico and Florida appealed to Spanish missionaries seeking to harvest Indian souls. The missionaries baptized thousands of Indians in Spanish North America during the seventeenth century, but they also planted the seeds of Indian uprisings against Spanish rule.

Few Spaniards came to New Spain's northern borderland during the seventeenth century. Only about 1,500 Spaniards lived in Florida and roughly twice as many inhabited New Mexico. One royal governor complained that "no [Spaniard] comes…to plow and sow [crops], but only to eat and loaf." In both colonies, Indians outnumbered Spaniards ten or twenty to one.

Royal officials seriously considered eliminating both colonies because their costs greatly exceeded their benefits. Every three years a caravan from Mexico brought wagons full of goods to outposts in New Mexico. Florida required even larger subsidies because it housed a garrison of soldiers as well as missionaries who persuaded the Spanish government that, instead of being losing propositions, the colonies represented golden opportunities to convert heathen Indians to Christianity. Stirrups adorned with Christian crosses on soldiers' saddles proclaimed the faith behind Spaniards' swords, and vice versa. Royal officials hoped that the missionaries' efforts would pacify Indians and be a relatively cheap way to preserve Spanish footholds in North America.

Dozens of missionaries came to Florida and New Mexico to teach Indians that their religious beliefs and rituals were idolatrous devil worship and that their way of life was barbaric. Missionaries followed royal instructions that Indians should be taught "to live in a civilized manner, clothed and wearing shoes…[and] given the use of…bread, linen, horses, cattle, tools, and weapons, and all the rest that Spain has had." In effect, missionaries sought to convert Indians not just into Christians but also into surrogate Spaniards.

Missionaries supervised the building of scores of Catholic churches across Florida and New Mexico. Typically, they conscripted Indian women and men to do the construction labor. Adopting practices common elsewhere in New Spain, missionaries forced Indians both to work and to pay tribute in the form of food, blankets, and other goods. While missionaries congratulated themselves on the many Indians they converted, their coercive methods subverted their goals. A missionary reported that an Indian in New Mexico asked him, "if we [missionaries] who are Christians caused so much harm and violence [to Indians], why should they [i.e., Indians] become Christians?"

Indians retaliated repeatedly against Spanish exploitation, but Spaniards suppressed the violent uprisings by taking advantage of the disunity among Indians much as Cortés did in the conquest of Mexico (see chapter 2). In 1680, however, Pueblo Indians organized a unified revolt under the leadership of Popé, who ordered his followers, as one recounted, to "break up and burn the images of the holy Christ, the Virgin Mary, and the other saints, the crosses, and everything pertaining to Christianity." During the Pueblo Revolt, Indians desecrated churches, killed two-thirds of Spanish missionaries, and drove Spaniards out of New Mexico to present-day El Paso, Texas. Spaniards managed to return to New Mexico by the end of the seventeenth century, but only by curtailing missionaries and reducing labor exploitation. Florida Indians never mounted a unified attack on Spanish rule, but they too organized sporadic uprisings and resisted conversion.

REVIEW Why did the Pueblo Indians revolt against Spanish missionaries in 1680?

Toward a Slave Labor System

During the sixteenth century, Spaniards and Portuguese supplemented Indian laborers in the New World with enslaved Africans. On this foundation, European colonizers built African slavery into the most important form of coerced labor in the New World. During the seventeenth century, British colonies in the West Indies followed the Spanish and Portuguese examples and developed sugar plantations with slave labor. In the British North American colonies, however, a slave labor system did not emerge until the last quarter of the seventeenth century. During the 1670s, settlers from Barbados brought slavery to the new English mainland colony of Carolina, where the imprint of the West Indies remained strong for decades. In

Sugar Mill

This seventeenth-century drawing of a Brazilian sugar mill highlights the heavy equipment needed to extract the juice from sugarcane. A vertical waterwheel turns a large horizontal gear that exerts force on the jaws of the press that squeezes the cane. Workers remove crushed cane from the press and replace it with freshly harvested cane as it is unloaded from an oxcart. Except for the overseer (just to the right of the waterwheel), all of the workers are black, presumably slaves from Africa, as suggested by their clothing. All of the mill workers appear to be men, a hint of the predominance of men among newly imported African slaves.

Musées Royaux des Beaux-Arts de Belgique.

Chesapeake tobacco fields at about the same time, slave labor began to replace servant labor, marking the transition toward a society of freedom for whites and slavery for Africans.

The West Indies: Sugar and Slavery

The most profitable part of the British New World empire in the seventeenth century lay in the Caribbean (Map 3.2). The tiny island of Barbados, colonized in the 1630s, was the jewel of the British West Indies. During the 1640s, Barbadian planters began to grow sugarcane with such success that a colonial official proclaimed Barbados "the most flourishing Island in all those American parts, and I verily beleive in all the world for the production of sugar." Sugar commanded high prices in England, and planters rushed to grow as much as they could. By midcentury, annual sugar exports from the British Caribbean totaled about 150,000 pounds; by 1700, exports reached nearly 50 million pounds.

Sugar transformed Barbados and other West Indian islands. Poor farmers could not afford the expensive machinery that extracted and refined sugarcane juice. Planters with the necessary capital to grow sugar got rich. By 1680, the wealthiest Barbadian sugar planters were, on average, four times richer than tobacco grandees in the Chesapeake. The sugar grandees differed from their Chesapeake counterparts in another crucial way: The average sugar baron in Barbados in 1680 owned 115 slaves.

African slaves planted, cultivated, and harvested the sugarcane that made West Indian planters wealthy. Beginning in the 1640s, Barbadian planters purchased thousands of slaves to work their plantations, and the African population on the island mushroomed. During the 1650s, when blacks made up only 3 percent of the Chesapeake population, they had already become the majority on Barbados. By 1700, slaves constituted more than three-fourths of the island's population.

For slaves, work on a sugar plantation was a life sentence to brutal, unremitting labor. Slaves suffered high death rates. Since slave men outnumbered slave women two to one, few slaves could form families and have children. These grim realities meant that in Barbados and elsewhere in the West Indies, the slave population did not grow by natural reproduction.

Instead, planters continually purchased enslaved Africans. Although sugar plantations did not gain a foothold in North America in the seventeenth century, the West Indies nonetheless exerted a powerful influence on the development of slavery in the mainland colonies.

Carolina: A West Indian Frontier

The early settlers of what became South Carolina were immigrants from Barbados. In 1663, a Barbadian planter named John Colleton and a group of seven other men obtained a charter from England's King Charles II to establish a colony south of the Chesapeake and north of the Spanish territories in Florida. The men, known as "proprietors," hoped to siphon settlers from Barbados and other colonies and encourage them to develop a profitable export crop comparable to West Indian sugar and Chesapeake tobacco. Following the Chesapeake example, the proprietors offered headrights of up to 150 acres of land for each settler. In 1670, they established the colony's first permanent English settlement, Charles Towne (later spelled Charleston) (see Map 3.2).

As the proprietors had planned, most of the early settlers were from Barbados. In fact, Carolina was the only seventeenth-century English colony to be settled principally by colonists from other colonies rather than from England. The Barbadian immigrants brought their slaves with them. More than a fourth of the early settlers were slaves, and as the colony continued to attract settlers from Barbados, the black population multiplied. By 1700, slaves made up about half the population of Carolina. The new colony's close association with Barbados caused English officials to refer routinely to "Carolina in ye West Indies."

The Carolinians experimented unsuccessfully to match their semitropical climate with profitable export crops of tobacco, cotton, indigo, and olives. In the mid-1690s, colonists identified a hardy strain of rice and took advantage of the knowledge of rice cultivation among their many African slaves to build rice plantations. Settlers also sold livestock and timber to the West Indies, as well as another "natural resource": They captured and enslaved several thousand local Indians and sold them to Caribbean planters. Both economically and socially, seventeenth-century Carolina was a frontier outpost of the West Indian sugar economy.

Slave Labor Emerges in the Chesapeake

By 1700, more than eight out of ten people in the southern colonies of British North America lived in the Chesapeake. Until the 1670s, almost all Chesapeake colonists were white people from England. By 1700, however, one out of eight people in the region was a black person from Africa. Between 1670 and 1700 hundreds of tobacco planters made the transition from servant to slave labor. For planters, slaves had several obvious advantages over servants. Although slaves cost three to five times more than servants, slaves never became free. Since the mortality rate had declined by the 1680s, planters could reasonably expect slaves to live longer than a servant's period of indenture. Slaves also promised to be a perpetual labor force, since children of slave mothers inherited the status of slavery.

For planters, slaves had another important advantage over servants: They could be con-trolled politically. Bacon's Rebellion had demonstrated how disruptive former servants could be when their expectations were not met. Slavery kept discontented laborers in permanent servitude, and their color was a badge of their bondage.

The slave labor system polarized Chesapeake society along lines of race and status: All slaves were black, and nearly all blacks were slaves; almost all free people were white, and all whites were free or only temporarily bound in indentured servitude. Unlike Barbados, however, the Chesapeake retained a vast white majority. Among whites, huge differences of wealth and status still existed. By 1700, more than three-quarters of white families had neither servants nor slaves. Nonetheless, poor white farmers enjoyed the privileges of free status. By emphasizing the privileges of freedom shared by all white people, the slave labor system reduced the tensions between poor folk and grandees that had plagued the Chesapeake region in the 1670s.

MAP 3.2   The West Indies and Carolina in the Seventeenth Century
Although Carolina was geographically close to the Chesapeake colonies, it was culturally closer to the West Indies in the seventeenth century because its early settlers—both blacks and whites—came from Barbados. South Carolina retained strong ties to the West Indies for more than a century, long after the arrival of many of its subsequent settlers from England, Ireland, France, and elsewhere.

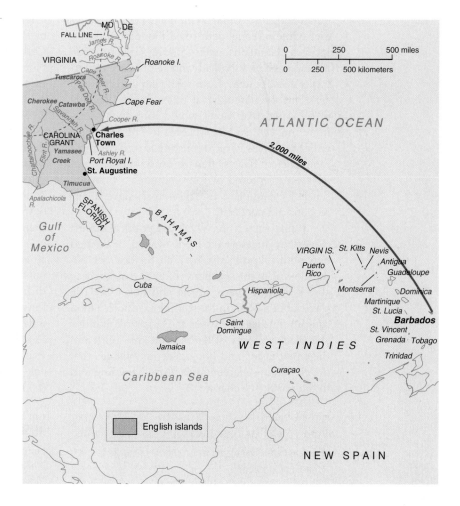

Bell of Slave Ship

The English slave ship *Henrietta Marie* sailed from England to the west African coast in 1699, loaded a cargo of slaves, made the **Middle Passage** to the West Indies, where the slaves were sold, then started back to England but sank with all aboard off the Florida Keys. Centuries later, this bronze bell was recovered from the wreckage.

© 1991 Mel Fisher Maritime Heritage Society, Key West, FL. Photo: Dylan Kibler.

In contrast to slaves in Barbados, most slaves in the seventeenth-century Chesapeake colonies had frequent and close contact with white people. Slaves and white servants performed the same tasks on tobacco plantations, often working side by side in the fields. Slaves took advantage of every opportunity to slip away from white supervision and seek out the company of other slaves. Planters often feared that slaves would turn such seemingly innocent social pleasures to political ends, either to run away or to conspire to strike against their masters. Slaves often ran away, but they usually were captured or returned after a brief absence. Despite planters' nightmares, slave insurrections did not occur.

While slavery resolved the political unrest caused by the servant labor system, it created new political problems. By 1700, the bedrock political issue in the southern colonies was keeping slaves in their place, at the end of a hoe. The slave labor system in the southern colonies stood roughly midway between the sugar plantations and black majority of Barbados to the south and the small farms and homogeneous villages that developed in seventeenth-century New England to the north (see chapter 4).

> **REVIEW**   Why had slave labor largely displaced indentured servant labor by 1700 in Chesapeake tobacco production?

Conclusion: The Growth of English Colonies Based on Export Crops and Slave Labor

By 1700, the colonies of Virginia, Maryland, and Carolina were firmly established. The staple crops they grew for export provided a livelihood for many, a fortune for a few, and valuable revenues for shippers, merchants, and the English monarchy. Their societies differed markedly from English society in most respects, yet the colonists considered themselves English people who happened to live in North America. They claimed the same rights and privileges as English men and women while they denied those rights and privileges to Native Americans and African slaves.

The English colonies also differed from the example of New Spain. Settlers and servants flocked to English colonies, in contrast to Spaniards who trickled into New Spain. Few English missionaries sought to convert Indians to Protestant Christianity, unlike the numerous Catholic missionaries in New Mexico and Florida. Large quantities of gold and silver never materialized in British North America. English colonists never adopted the system of *encomienda* (see chapter 2) because Indians were too few and too hostile and their communities too small and decentralized compared with those of the Mexica. Yet forms of coerced labor and racial distinction that developed in New Spain had North American counterparts, as English colonists employed servants and slaves and defined themselves as superior to Indians and Africans.

By 1700, the remnants of Powhatan's people still survived. As English settlement pushed north, west, and south of the Chesapeake Bay, Indians faced the new colonial world that Powhatan and Pocahontas had encountered when John Smith and the first colonists arrived at Jamestown. By 1700, the many descendants of Pocahontas's son, Thomas, as well as other colonists and Native Americans, understood that the English had come to stay.

Suggestions for Further Reading

James F. Brooks, *Captives and Cousins: Slavery, Kinship, and Community in the Southwest Borderlands* (2002). A detailed study of relationships among Native Americans in the Southwest Borderlands.

David Eltis, *The Rise of African Slavery in the Americas* (2001). An authoritative economic and cultural overview of the rise of slavery in the New World.

Jason Hughes, *Learning to Smoke: Tobacco Use in the West* (2003). The surprising history of how Europeans learned to consume tobacco by smoking.

Karen Kupperman, *Indians and English: Facing Off in Early America* (2002). An expert survey of encounters between Native Americans and English colonists.

Edmund S. Morgan, *American Slavery, American Freedom: The Ordeal of Colonial Virginia* (1975). Classic account of seventeenth-century Virginia by an eminent historian.

Helen C. Rountree, *Pocahontas, Powhatan, Opechancanough: Three Indian Lives Changed by Jamestown* (2005). The compelling story of how English settlement changed the lives of three important Native Americans.

▶ FOR MORE BOOKS ABOUT TOPICS IN THIS CHAPTER, see the Online Bibliography at bedfordstmartins.com/roarkcompact.

▶ FOR ADDITIONAL FIRSTHAND ACCOUNTS OF THIS PERIOD, see Chapter 3 in Michael Johnson, ed., *Reading the American Past*, Third Edition.

▶ FOR WEB SITES AND DOCUMENTS RELATED TO TOPICS AND PLACES IN THIS CHAPTER, see "HistoryLinks," "DocLinks," and "PlaceLinks" at bedfordstmartins.com/roarkcompact.

REVIEWING THE CHAPTER

Follow these steps to review and strengthen your understanding of the chapter.

STEP 1: *Study the* **Key Terms** *and* **Timeline** *to identify the significance of each item listed.*

STEP 2: *Answer the* **Review Questions**, *drawing on key terms and dates to support your answers.*

STEP 3: *Drawing on the Key Terms, Timeline, and Review Questions, answer the broader* **Making Connections** *questions.*

KEY TERMS

Who

Captain John Smith (p. 53)
Algonquian Indians (p. 53)
Powhatan (p. 53)
Pocahontas (p. 53)
John Rolfe (p. 54)
James I (p. 55)
Opechancanough (p. 57)
Charles I (p. 64)
Lord Baltimore (p. 64)
William Berkeley (p. 65)
Nathaniel Bacon (p. 66)
Pueblo Indians (p. 69)
Charles II (p. 70)

What

Virginia Company (p. 55)
joint stock company (p. 55)
colonization (p. 55)
Jamestown (p. 56)
royal colony (p. 57)
House of Burgesses (p. 58)
tobacco (p. 58)
headright (p. 62)
indentured servants (p. 62)
yeoman (p. 65)
Navigation Acts (p. 66)
mercantilism (p. 66)
Bacon's Rebellion (p. 66)

grandees (p. 67)
Bacon's Laws (p. 67)
Barbados (p. 70)

TIMELINE

NOTE: Events are depicted chronologically, but the passage of time is not to exact scale.

◀ **1588** • England defeats Spanish Armada.

1606 • Virginia Company receives royal charter.

1607 • English colonists found Jamestown settlement;
Pocahontas "rescues" John Smith.

1609 • Starvation plagues Jamestown.

1612 • John Rolfe begins to plant tobacco in Virginia.

1617 • First commercial tobacco shipment leaves Virginia for England.
• Pocahontas dies in England.

1618 • Powhatan dies; Opechancanough becomes
chief of the Algonquians.

1619 • First Africans arrive in Virginia.
• House of Burgesses begins to meet in Virginia.

1622 • Opechancanough leads Indian uprising
against Virginia colonists.

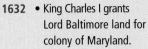

1624 • Virginia becomes royal colony.

1632 • King Charles I grants
Lord Baltimore land for
colony of Maryland.

REVIEW QUESTIONS

1. Why did Powhatan pursue largely peaceful relations with the Jamestown settlement? (pp. 55–58)

2. Why did the vast majority of European immigrants to the Chesapeake come as indentured servants? (pp. 58–64)

3. Why did Chesapeake colonial society become increasingly polarized between 1650 and 1670? (pp. 65–68)

4. Why did the Pueblo Indians revolt against Spanish missionaries in 1680? (pp. 68–69)

5. Why had slave labor largely displaced indentured servant labor by 1700 in Chesapeake tobacco production? (pp. 69–72)

MAKING CONNECTIONS

1. Given the extraordinary vulnerability of the Jamestown settlement in its first two decades, why did its sponsors and settlers not abandon it? In your answer, discuss the challenges the settlement faced and the benefits different participants in England and the New World hoped to derive from their efforts.

2. Tobacco dominated European settlement in the seventeenth-century Chesapeake. How did tobacco agriculture shape the region's development? In your answer, be sure to address the demographic and geographic features of the colony.

3. Bacon's Rebellion highlighted significant tensions within Chesapeake society. What provoked the rebellion, and what did it accomplish? In your answer, be sure to consider causes and results in the colonies and in England.

4. In addition to making crucial contributions to the economic success of seventeenth-century English colonies, Native Americans and enslaved Africans influenced colonial politics. Describe how European colonists' relations with these populations contributed to political friction and harmony within the colony.

> ▶ For practice quizzes, a customized study plan, and other study tools, see the Online Study Guide at bedfordstmartins.com/roarkcompact.

1634 • Colonists begin to arrive in Maryland.

1640s • Barbados colonists begin to grow sugarcane with labor of African slaves.

1644 • Opechancanough leads Indian uprising against Virginia colonists.

1660 • Navigation Act requires colonial tobacco to be shipped to English ports.

1663 • Royal charter is granted for Carolina colony.

1670
• Charles Towne, South Carolina, founded.

1670–1700
• Slave labor system emerges in Carolina and Chesapeake colonies.

1676
• Bacon's Rebellion.

1680
• Pueblo Revolt.

AMERICA'S FIRST BOOK

The first book printed in what is now the United States, this well-thumbed copy of *The Whole Booke of Psalmes Faithfully Translated into English Metre* was published in Cambridge, Massachusetts, in 1640. Puritan services banned musical instruments and other diversions from God's holy word. Worshippers used this book and others to sing psalms, celebrating with a chorus of voices the wonders of God's Truth. The famous Twenty-third Psalm begins near the bottom of the left-hand page and concludes on the facing page. Read the psalm aloud to re-create the experience of seventeenth-century New England Puritan congregations.

The Northern Colonies in the Seventeenth Century

1601–1700

ROGER WILLIAMS AND HIS WIFE MARY arrived in Massachusetts in February 1631. Fresh from a superb education at Cambridge University, the twenty-eight-year-old Williams was "a godly [Puritan] minister," noted Governor John Winthrop. Winthrop's Boston church asked Williams to become its minister, but he refused because the church had not openly rejected the corrupt Church of England. New England's premier Puritan church was not pure enough for Williams.

Williams and his wife moved to Plymouth colony for two years, where he spent a great deal of time among the Narragansett Indians. Williams believed that "Nature knows no difference between Europeans and Americans in blood, birth, [or] bodies...God having made of one blood all mankind." He sought to learn about their language, their religion, and their culture, without trying to convert them to Christianity. Williams insisted that Indians' religion and culture should be respected since all human beings should live according to their consciences as revealed to them by God. His respect for Indians led him to condemn English colonists for their "sin of unjust usurpation" of Indian lands.

Massachusetts officials defended colonists' settlement on Indian land. If land "lies common, and hath never been replenished or subdued, [it] is free to any that possess or improve it," Governor Winthrop explained. Besides, he said, "if we leave [the Indians] sufficient [land] for their use, we may lawfully take the rest, there being more than enough for them and us." Winthrop's arguments prevailed, but Williams refused to knuckle under. "God Land," he said, "[is] as great a God with us English as God Gold was with the Spaniards." Such views ultimately caused him to be banished from the colony.

Williams became the minister at Salem, Massachusetts, in 1633. Like other New England Puritans, the members of the Salem church had solemnly agreed to "**Covenant** with the Lord and one with another; and doe bynd our selves in the presence of God, to walke together in all his waies, according as he is pleased to reveale himself unto us in his Blessed word of truth [the Bible]." Most New England Puritans believed churches and governments should enforce both godly belief and behavior according to biblical rules. They claimed that "the Word of God is...clear." In contrast, Williams believed the

Bible shrouded the word of God in "mist and fog." Williams pointed out that devout and pious Christians could and did differ about what the Bible said. That observation led him to denounce the emerging New England order as impure, ungodly, and tyrannical.

Williams also disagreed with the New England government's requirement that everyone attend church service. He argued that forcing people who were not Christians to attend church was wrong in four major ways. First, Williams preached, it was akin to requiring "a dead child to suck the breast, or a dead man [to] feast." The only way for any person to become a true Christian was by God's gift of faith revealed to the person's conscience. Second, churches should separate "holy from unholy…[and] godly from ungodly." He said requiring everybody to attend church was "False Worshipping" that promoted "spiritual drunkenness and whoredom, a soul sleep and a soul sickness." Third, the government had no business ruling on spiritual matters. Williams termed New England's regulation of religious behavior "spiritual rape" that inevitably would lead governments to use coercion and violence to enforce the government's misguided way. Finally, Williams believed that governments should tolerate all religious beliefs because only God knows the truth; no person and no religion can understand God with absolute certainty. "I commend that man," Williams wrote, "that steers no otherwise than his conscience dares." In Williams's view, toleration of religious belief and liberty of conscience were the only paths to religious purity and political harmony.

New England's leaders denounced Williams's arguments. One minister wrote that Williams sought "liberty to enfranchise all false Religions," which was "the greatest impiety in the World." Genuine **liberty**, he said, was "to contend earnestly for the Truth; to preserve unity of Spirit, Faith, ordinances, to be all like minded, of one accord." Like-minded New Englanders banished Williams for his "extreme and dangerous" opinions. He escaped from an attempt to ship him back to England and in the winter of 1636 spent fourteen weeks walking south to Narragansett Bay. There he founded the colony of Rhode Island, which enshrined "Liberty of Conscience" as a fundamental ideal and became a refuge for other dissenters.

Although New England's leaders expelled Williams from their holy commonwealth, his dissenting ideas arose from orthodox Puritan doctrines. By urging believers to search for evidence of God's grace, **Puritanism** encouraged the faithful to listen for God's whisper of truth and faith. Puritanism combined rigid insistence on conformity to God's law and aching uncertainty about how to identify and act upon it. Despite the best efforts of New England's leaders to define their way as God's way, Puritanism inspired believers like Roger Williams to draw their own conclusions and stick to them.

During the seventeenth century, New England's Puritan zeal—exemplified by Roger Williams and his persecutors—cooled. The goal of founding a holy New England faded. Late in the century, new "middle" colonies—New York, New Jersey, and Pennsylvania—featuring greater religious and ethnic diversity than New England were founded. Religion remained important throughout all the colonies, but it competed with the growing faith that the promise of a better life required less focus on salvation and more attention to worldly concerns of family, work, and trade.

As settler populations increased throughout the British mainland colonies, settlements encroached on Indian lands, causing violent conflict to flare up repeatedly. Political conflict also arose among colonists, particularly in response to major political upheavals in England. By the end of the seventeenth century, the English monarchy exerted greater control over its North American empire. The lifeblood of the empire, however, remained the continual flow of products, people, and ideas that pulsed between England and the colonies, energizing both.

Puritan Origins: The English Reformation

The religious roots of the Puritans who founded New England reached back to the Protestant **Reformation**, which arose in Germany in 1517 (see chapter 2). The Reformation spread quickly to other countries, but the English church initially remained within the Catholic fold and continued its allegiance to the pope in Rome. King Henry VIII, who reigned from 1509 to 1547, understood that the Reformation offered him an opportunity to break with Rome and take control of the church in England. In 1534, Henry formally initiated the English Reformation. At his insistence, Parliament passed the Act of Supremacy, which outlawed the Catholic Church and proclaimed the king "the only supreme head on earth of the Church of England."

In the short run, the English Reformation allowed Henry VIII to achieve his political goal of controlling the church. In the long run, however, the Reformation brought to England the political and religious turmoil that Henry had hoped to avoid. Henry himself sought no more than a halfway Reformation. Protestant doctrines held no attraction for Henry; in almost all matters of religious belief and practice he remained an orthodox Catholic. Many English Catholics wanted to revoke the English Reformation; they hoped to return the Church of England to the pope and to restore Catholic doctrines and ceremonies. But many other English people insisted on a genuine, thoroughgoing Reformation; these people came to be called Puritans.

During the sixteenth century, Puritanism was less an organized movement than a set of ideas and religious principles that appealed strongly to many dissenting members of the Church of England. They sought to purify the Church of England by eliminating what they considered the offensive features of Catholicism. For example, they demanded that the church hierarchy be abolished and that ordinary Christians be given greater control over religious life. They wanted to do away with the rituals of Catholic worship and instead emphasize an individual's relationship with God developed through Bible study, prayer, and introspection. Although there were many varieties and degrees of Puritanism, all Puritans shared a desire to make the English church thoroughly Protestant.

The fate of **Protestantism** waxed and waned under the monarchs who succeeded Henry VIII. Elizabeth I assumed the throne in 1558 and tried to position the English church between the extremes of Catholicism and Puritanism. Like her father, she was less concerned with theology than with politics. Above all, she desired a church that would strengthen the monarchy and the nation. By the time Elizabeth died in 1603, many people in England looked on Protestantism as a defining feature of national identity.

When her successor, James I, became king, English Puritans petitioned for further reform of the Church of England. James authorized a new

Persecution of English Protestants
This sixteenth-century drawing shows Protestant prisoners being marched to London to be tried for heresy during the reign of Queen Mary I, a staunch Catholic. The artist emphasizes the severity of the Catholic persecutors by depicting the use of four well-armed guards, two on horseback, to escort some fifteen prisoners, including at least five women who are roped together but not because they appear menacing or likely to run away. The guards seem to be necessary less to maintain order among the prisoners than to discourage sympathetic citizens from rushing forward and freeing the prisoners. The artist seems to assume that most citizens opposed the queen's persecution of Protestants. The Bible verse from the book of Matthew underscores the Protestants' fealty to Christ rather than to mere "Princes and rulers" like Queen Mary.
Folger Shakespeare Library.

translation of the Bible, known ever since as the King James version. However, neither James I nor his son Charles I, who became king in 1625, was receptive to the ideas of Puritan reformers. James and Charles moved the Church of England away from Puritanism. They enforced conformity to the Church of England and punished dissenters, both ordinary Christians and ministers. In 1629, Charles I dissolved Parliament—where Puritans were well represented—and initiated aggressive anti-Puritan policies. Many Puritans despaired about continuing to defend their faith in England and began to make plans to emigrate. Some left for Europe, others for the West Indies. The largest number set out for America.

REVIEW Why did Henry VIII initiate the English Reformation?

Puritans and the Settlement of New England

Puritans who emigrated aspired to escape the turmoil and persecution of England and to build a new, orderly, Puritan version of England. Puritans established the first small settlement in New England in 1620, followed a few years later by additional settlements by the Massachusetts Bay Company. Allowed self-government through royal charter, these Puritans were in a unique position to direct the new colonies according to their faith. Their faith shaped the colonies they established in almost every way. Although many New England colonists were not Puritans, Puritanism remained a paramount influence in New England's religion, politics, and community life during the seventeenth century.

The Pilgrims and Plymouth Colony

One of the first Protestant groups to emigrate, later known as Pilgrims, espoused a heresy known as separatism. These Separatists sought to withdraw—separate—from the Church of England, which they considered hopelessly corrupt. In 1608, they moved to Holland; by 1620, they realized that they could not live and worship there as they had hoped. The Separatists formed a joint stock company and obtained permission to settle in the lands granted to the Virginia Company (see chapter 3). In August 1620, Pilgrim families boarded the *Mayflower* and, after eleven weeks at sea, all but one of the 102 migrants arrived at the outermost tip of Cape Cod, in present-day Massachusetts.

The Pilgrims realized immediately that they had landed far north of the Virginia grants and had no legal authority to settle in the area. To provide order and security as well as a claim to legitimacy, they drew up the Mayflower Compact on the day they arrived. They pledged to "covenant and combine ourselves together into a civil Body Politick, for our better Ordering and Preservation." The signers (all men) agreed to enact and obey necessary and just laws.

The Pilgrims settled at Plymouth and elected William Bradford their governor. That first winter "was most sad and lamentable," Bradford wrote later. "In two or three months' time half of [our] company died…being the depth of winter, and wanting houses and other comforts [and] being infected with scurvy and other diseases."

In the spring, Wampanoag Indians rescued the floundering Plymouth settlement. With the Indians' guidance in how to cultivate corn, the Pilgrims managed to harvest enough food to guarantee their survival through the coming winter, an occasion they celebrated in the fall of 1621 with a feast of thanksgiving attended by the Wampanoags.

The Plymouth colony remained precarious, but the Pilgrims lived quietly and simply, coexisting in relative peace with the Indians. They paid the Wampanoags when settlers gradually encroached on Indian lands. By 1630, Plymouth had become a permanent settlement, but it failed to attract many other English Puritans.

The Founding of Massachusetts Bay Colony

In 1629, shortly before Charles I dissolved Parliament, a group of Puritan merchants and country gentlemen obtained a royal charter for the Massachusetts Bay Company. The charter provided the usual privileges granted to joint stock companies, including land for **colonization**. In addition, a unique provision of the charter permitted the government of the Massachusetts Bay Company to be located in the colony rather than in England. This provision allowed Puritans to exchange their position as a harassed minority in England for self-government in Massachusetts.

To lead the emigrants, the stockholders of the Massachusetts Bay Company elected John Winthrop, a prosperous lawyer and landowner, to serve as governor. In March 1630, eleven ships crammed with seven hundred passengers sailed for Massachusetts; six more ships and another five hundred emigrants followed a few months later. Winthrop's fleet arrived in Massachusetts Bay in early June. Unlike the Separatists, Winthrop's Puritans aspired to reform the corrupt Church of England (rather than separate from it) by setting an example of godliness in the New World. Winthrop and a small group chose to settle on the peninsula that became Boston, and other settlers clustered at promising locations nearby.

In a sermon to his companions aboard the *Arbella* while they were still at sea—probably the most famous sermon in American history—Winthrop explained the cosmic significance of their journey. The Puritans had "entered into a covenant" with God to "work out our salvation under the power and purity of his holy ordinances," Winthrop proclaimed. This sanctified agreement with God meant that the Puritans had to make "extraordinary" efforts to "bring into familiar and constant practice" religious principles that most people in England merely preached. "We must be knit together in this work as one man," Winthrop declared. "We must delight in each other, make others' conditions our own, rejoice together, mourn together, labor and suffer together." The stakes could not be higher, Winthrop told his listeners: "We must consider that we shall be as a city upon a hill. The eyes of all people are upon us."

That belief shaped seventeenth-century New England as profoundly as tobacco shaped the Chesapeake. Winthrop's vision of a city on a hill fired the Puritans' fierce determination to keep their covenant and live according to God's laws, unlike the backsliders and compromisers who accommodated to the Church of England. Their determination to adhere strictly to God's plan charged nearly every feature of life in seventeenth-century New England with a distinctive, high-voltage piety.

The new colonists, as Winthrop's son John wrote later, had "all things to do, as in the beginning of the world." Unlike the early Chesapeake settlers, the first Massachusetts Bay colonists encountered few Indians because the local population had been almost entirely exterminated by an epidemic more than a decade earlier. Still, as in the Chesapeake, the colonists fell victim to deadly ailments. More than 200 settlers died during the first year, including one of Winthrop's sons and eleven of his servants. But each year from 1630 to 1640, ship after ship followed in the wake of

Winthrop's fleet. In all, more than 20,000 new settlers came, their eyes focused on the Puritans' city on a hill.

Often, when the Church of England cracked down on a Puritan minister in England, he and many of his followers uprooted and moved together to New England. By 1640, New England had one of the highest ratios of preachers to population in all of Christendom. A few ministers sought to carry the message of Christianity to Indians, accompanied by instructions replacing what missionary John Eliot termed Indians' "unfixed, confused, and ungoverned…life, uncivilized and unsubdued to labor and order." (See "Documenting the American Promise," page 82.) For the most part, however, the colonists focused on saving Indians' souls less than on saving their own.

The occupations of New England immigrants reflected the social origins of English Puritans. On the whole, the immigrants came from the middle ranks of English society. The vast majority of immigrants were either farmers or tradesmen, including carpenters, tailors, and textile workers. Servants, whose numbers dominated the Chesapeake settlers, accounted for only about a fifth of those headed for New England. Most New England immigrants paid their way to Massachusetts, even though the

Seal of Massachusetts Bay Colony
In 1629, the Massachusetts Bay Company designed this seal depicting an Indian man inviting English settlers to "Come Over And Help Us." Of course, such an invitation was never issued. The seal was an attempt to lend an aura of altruism to the Massachusetts Bay Company's colonization efforts. In English eyes, the Indian man obviously needed help. The only signs that he was more civilized than the pine trees flanking him were his girdle of leaves, his bow and arrow, and his miraculous use of English. In reality, colonists in Massachusetts and elsewhere were far less interested in helping Indians than in helping themselves. For the most part, that suited the Indians, who wanted no "help" from the colonists.
Courtesy of Massachusetts Archives.

FOR MORE HELP ANALYZING THIS IMAGE, see the visual activity for this chapter in the Online Study Guide at bedfordstmartins .com/roarkcompact.

King Philip Considers Christianity

Beginning in 1646, the Puritan minister John Eliot served as a missionary to New England's Indians, trying to teach the doctrines of Christianity and proper English behavior. During his half-century tenure as leader of the Puritan congregation in Roxbury, Massachusetts, Eliot studied the languages, customs, and beliefs of Native Americans, hoping to help them along the path to Christian piety and to strengthen them against colonists' unscrupulous encroachment on their lands. The efforts of Eliot and other missionaries convinced some Indians to leave their own communities and settle in "praying towns" populated by Native Americans who had agreed to live in conformity with English ways. Most Indians, however, did not move into praying towns or adopt the faith or manners of the colonists.

In Indian Dialogues, a book published in 1671, Eliot illustrated the challenge he and other missionaries confronted as they tried to convince Native Americans of the errors of their ways. Based on his decades of missionary experience, Eliot created imaginary conversations between converted Indians and those who resisted Christianity. Eliot's invented conversations echoed arguments he and other missionaries had encountered repeatedly. The following selection from an imaginary dialogue between two praying Indians, Anthony

and William, and King Philip (or Metacomet), the chief (or sachem) of the powerful Wampanoags, documents Eliot's perception of the attractions of Christianity and one Indian leader's doubts about it, doubts that ultimately prevailed when King Philip led the Wampanoags in an all-out attack against the settlers in 1675.

Anthony: Sachem, we salute you in the Lord, and we declare unto you, that we are sent by the church, in the name of our Lord Jesus Christ, to call you, and beseech you to turn from your vain conversation unto God, to pray unto God, and to believe in Jesus Christ for the pardon of your sins, and for the salvation of your soul.... So we are come this day unto you, in the name of Jesus Christ, to call you to come unto the Lord, and serve him.... We hear that many of your people do desire to pray to God, only they depend on you. We pray you to consider that your love to your people should oblige you to do them all the good you can.... You will not only yourself turn from sin unto God..., but all your people will turn to God with you, so that you may say unto the Lord, oh Lord Jesus, behold here am I, and all the people which thou hast given me. We all come unto thy service, and promise to pray unto God so long as

we live.... Oh how happy will all your people be.... It will be a joy to all the English magistrates, and ministers, and churches, and good people of the land, to hear that Philip and all his people are turned to God, and become praying Indians....

Philip: Often have I heard of this great matter of praying unto God, and hitherto I have refused.... Mr. Eliot himself did come unto me. He was in this town, and did persuade me. But we were then in our sports, wherein I have much delighted, and in that temptation, I confess, I did neglect and despise the offer, and lost that opportunity. Since that time God hath afflicted and chastised me, and my heart doth begin to break. And I have some serious thoughts of accepting the offer, and turning to God, to become a praying Indian, I myself and all my people. But I have some great objections, which I cannot tell how to get over, which are still like great rocks in my way, over which I cannot climb. And if I should, I fear I shall fall down the precipice on the further side, and be spoiled and undone. By venturing to climb, I shall catch a deadly fall to me and my posterity.

The first objection that I have is this, because you praying Indians do reject your sachems, and refuse to pay them tribute, in so much that if any of my people turn to pray unto God, I do reckon that I have lost him. He will no longer own me for his sachem, nor pay me any tribute. And hence it will come to pass, that if I should pray to God, and all my people with me, I must become as a common man among them, and so lose all my power and authority over them. This is such a temptation as… I, nor any of the other great sachems, can tell how to get over. Were this temptation removed, the way would be more easy and open for me to turn praying Indian. I begin to have some good likance of the way, but I am loth to buy it at so dear a rate.

William: …I say, if any of the praying Indians should be disobedient (in lawful things) and refuse to pay tribute unto their sachems, it is not their religion and praying to God that teaches them so to do, but their corruptions. …I am sure the word of God commandeth all to be subject to the higher powers, and pay them tribute.… And therefore, beloved sachem, let not your heart fear that praying to God will alienate your people from you…for the more beneficent you are unto them, the more obligation you lay upon them. And what greater beneficence can you do unto them than to further them in religion, whereby they may be converted, pardoned, sanctified, and saved?…

Philip: I have another objection stronger than this, and that is, if I pray to God, then all my men that are willing to pray to God will (as you say) stick to me, and be true to me. But all such as love not and care not to pray to God, especially such as hate praying to God, all these will forsake me, yea will go and adjoin themselves unto other sachems that pray not to God. And so it will come to pass, that if I be a praying sachem, I shall be a poor and weak one, and easily trod

upon by others, who are like to be more potent and numerous. And by this means my tribute will be small, and my people few, and I shall be a great loser by praying to God. In the way I am now, I am full and potent, but if I change my way and pray to God, I shall be empty and weak.…

William: …Suppose all your subjects that hate praying to God should leave you. What shall you lose by it? You are rid of such as by their sins vitiate others, and multiply transgression, and provoke the wrath of God against you and yours. But consider what you shall gain by praying to God.… All the praying Indians will rejoice at it, and be your friends, and they are not a few.… [And] you shall gain a more intimate love of the Governor, and Magistrates.… They will more honor, respect, and love you, than ever they did.… The Governor and Magistrates of the Massachusetts will own you, and be fatherly and friendly to you.… Yea more, the King of England, and the great peers who… yearly send over means to encourage and promote our praying to God, they will take notice of you.

Philip: I perceive that in your praying to God, and in your churches, all are brought to an equality. Sachems and people they are all fellow brethren in your churches. Poor and rich are equally privileged. The vote of the lowest of the people hath as much weight as the vote of the sachem. Now I doubt [worry] that this way will lift up the heart of the poor to too much boldness, and debase the

rulers to[o] low. This bringing all to an equality will bring all to a confusion.… [T]here is yet another thing that I am much afraid of, and that is your church admonitions and excommunications. I hear that your sachems are under that yoke. I am a sinful man as well as others, but if I must be admonished by the church, who are my subjects, I know not how I shall like that. I doubt [worry] it will be a bitter pill, too hard for me to get down and swallow.…I feel your words sink into my heart and stick there. You speak arrows.…I desire to ponder and consider of these things.…I am willing they should still lie soaking in my heart and mind.

SOURCE: John Eliot, *Indian Dialogues* (Cambridge, 1671), in Henry W. Bowden and James P. Ronda, eds., *John Eliot's Indian Dialogues: A Study in Cultural Interaction,* 120–31. Copyright © 1980. Reproduced with permission of Greenwood Publishing Group, Inc., Westport, CT.

QUESTIONS FOR ANALYSIS AND DEBATE

1. To what degree is Eliot's dialogue a reliable guide to Philip's doubts about the wisdom of becoming a praying Indian?

2. According to Eliot, was Philip's religion a stumbling block to his acceptance of Christianity? What made Philip fear that he would "fall down the precipice"?

3. If Philip had written a dialogue proposing that Eliot convert to the Wampanoag way of life, what arguments might he have made?

journey often took their life savings. In contrast to the Chesapeake newcomers, New England immigrants usually arrived as families. In fact, more Puritans came with family members than did any other group of immigrants in all of American history.

As Winthrop reminded the first settlers in his *Arbella* sermon, each family was a "little commonwealth" that mirrored the hierarchy among all God's creatures. Just as humankind was subordinate to God, so young people were subordinate to their elders, children to their parents, and wives to their husbands. The immi-

grants' family ties reinforced their religious beliefs with universally understood notions of hierarchy and mutual dependence. While immigrants to the Chesapeake were disciplined mostly by the coercions of servitude and the caprices of the tobacco market, immigrants to New England entered a social order defined by the interlocking institutions of family, church, and community.

REVIEW Why did the Puritans immigrate to North America?

New England Great Chair

This thronelike chair belonged to Michael Metcalf, a teacher in seventeenth-century Dedham, Massachusetts. The oldest known piece of New England furniture inscribed with a date, 1652, the chair was made in Dedham specifically for Metcalf (notice the initials flanking the date), who turned sixty-six in that year. Metcalf stored books, presumably including a Bible, in the enclosed compartment under the seat. No overstuffed recliner, the chair is suited less for a relaxing snooze than for alert concentration. The panels under the arms served to block chilly drafts. Otherwise, the chair shows few concessions to comfort or ease. The carved chair back—rigidly upright—displays motifs often found on Puritan tombstones. The grand austerity of the chair hints at the importance of serious Bible study and unflinching introspection in Puritan New England.

Dedham Historical Society/photo by Forrest Frazier.

European Throne Chair

In contrast to the New England great chair, this late-sixteenth-century European throne chair is embellished on every surface with elaborate carvings proclaiming the worldly magnificence of the chair's owner. This chair illustrates the ostentatious display of luxury and refinement that disgusted Puritans considered signs of the vanity and false pride that distracted people from seeking and following God's Truth.

Courtesy of Huntington Antiques Ltd., Gloucestershire, England.

MAP 4.1 New England Colonies in the Seventeenth Century

New Englanders spread across the landscape town by town during the seventeenth century. (For the sake of legibility, only a few of the more important towns are shown on the map.)

READING THE MAP: Using the notations on the map, create a chronology of the establishment of towns in New England. What physical features correspond to the earliest habitation by English settlers?

CONNECTIONS: Why were towns so much more a feature of seventeenth-century New England than of the Chesapeake (see also chapter 3)? How did Puritan dissent influence the settlement of New England colonies?

FOR MORE HELP ANALYZING THIS MAP, see the map activity for this chapter in the Online Study Guide at bedfordstmartins.com/roarkcompact.

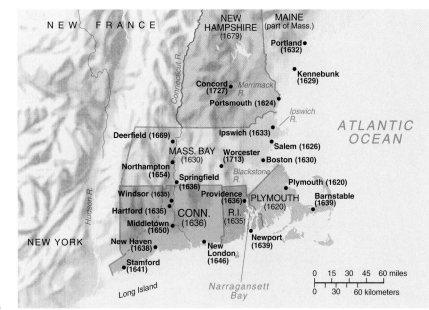

The Evolution of New England Society

The New England colonists, unlike their counterparts in the Chesapeake, settled in small towns, usually located on the coast or by a river (Map 4.1). Massachusetts Bay colonists founded 133 towns during the seventeenth century, each with one or more churches. Church members' fervent piety, buttressed by the institutions of local government, enforced remarkable religious and social conformity in the small New England settlements. During the century, tensions within the Puritan faith and changes in New England communities splintered religious orthodoxy and weakened Puritan zeal. By 1700, however, Puritanism still maintained a distinctive influence in New England.

Church, Covenant, and Conformity

Puritans believed that the church consisted of men and women who had entered a solemn covenant with one another and with God. Winthrop and three other men signed the original covenant of the first Boston church in 1630. Each new member of the covenant had to persuade existing members that she or he had fully experienced conversion. By 1635, the Boston church had added more than 250 names to the covenant.

Puritan views on religion and church membership derived from **Calvinism**, the doctrines of

John Calvin, a sixteenth-century Swiss Protestant theologian who insisted that Christians strictly discipline their behavior to conform to certain religious ideas. As followers of Calvin's ideas, the Puritans believed in **predestination**—the idea that all-powerful God, before the creation of the world, decided which few human souls would receive eternal life. Only God knows the identity of these fortunate, predestined individuals—the "elect" or "saints." Nothing a person did in his or her lifetime could alter God's inscrutable choice or provide assurance that the person was predestined for salvation with the elect or damned to hell with the doomed multitude.

Despite this looming uncertainty, Puritans believed that if a person lived a rigorously godly life—constantly winning the daily battle against sinful temptations—his or her behavior was likely to be a hint, a visible sign, that he or she was one of the elect. Puritans thought that "sainthood" would become visible in individuals' behavior, especially if they were privileged to know God's Word as revealed in the Bible.

The connection between sainthood and saintly behavior, however, was far from certain. Some members of the elect, Puritans believed, had not heard God's word as revealed in the Bible, and therefore their behavior did not necessarily signal their sainthood. One reason Puritans required all town residents to attend church services was to enlighten anyone who was ignorant of God's Truth. The slippery relationship between saintly behavior—observable by anybody—and God's

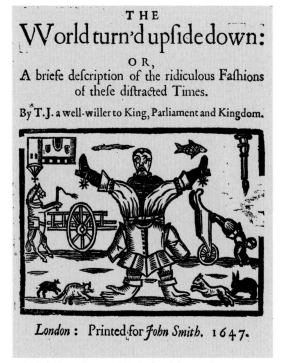

The Puritan Challenge to the Status Quo
This title page of "The World Turn'd Upside Down" satirizes the Puritan notion that the contemporary world was deeply flawed. Printed in London in 1647, the pamphlet refers to the "distracted Times" of the Puritan Revolution in England. The drawing ridicules criticisms of English society that were also common among New England Puritans. The drawing shows at least a dozen examples of the conventional world of seventeenth-century England turned upside down. Can you identify them? Puritans, of course, would claim that the artist had it wrong—that the conventional world turned God's order upside down. How might the drawing have been different if a devout Puritan had drawn it?
By permission of The British Library.

predestined election—invisible and unknowable to anyone—caused Puritans to worry constantly that individuals who acted like saints were fooling themselves and others. Nevertheless, Puritans thought that "visible saints"—persons who passed their demanding tests of conversion and church membership—probably, though not certainly, were among God's elect.

Members of Puritan churches ardently hoped that God had chosen them to receive eternal life and tried to demonstrate saintly behavior. Their covenant bound them to help each other attain salvation and to discipline the entire community by saintly standards. Church members kept an eye on the behavior of everybody in town. Infractions of morality, order, or propriety were reported to Puritan elders, who summoned the wayward to a church inquiry. By overseeing every aspect of life, the visible saints enforced a remarkable degree of righteous conformity in Puritan communities. Total conformity, however, was never achieved. Ardent Puritans differed among themselves; non-Puritans shirked orthodox rules. But Puritan doctrine spelled out the fiery punishment for failure to conform: A servant in Roxbury declared that "if hell were ten times hotter, [I] had rather be there than [I] would serve [my] master."

Despite the central importance of religion, churches played no direct role in the civil government of New England communities. Puritans did not want to mimic the Church of England, which they considered a puppet of the king rather than an independent body that served the Lord. They were determined to insulate New England churches from the contaminating influence of the civil state and its merely human laws. Although ministers were the most highly respected figures in New England towns, they were prohibited from holding government office.

Puritans had no qualms, however, about their religious beliefs influencing New England governments. As much as possible, the Puritans tried to bring public life into conformity with their view of God's law. For example, fines were issued for Sabbath-breaking activities such as working, traveling, playing a flute, smoking a pipe, and visiting neighbors.

Puritans mandated other purifications of what they considered corrupt English practices. They refused to celebrate Christmas or Easter because the Bible did not mention either one. They outlawed religious wedding ceremonies; couples were married by a magistrate in a civil ceremony. Cards, dice, shuffleboard, and other games of chance were banned, as were music and dancing. The distinguished minister Increase Mather insisted that "Mixt or Promiscuous Dancing…of Men and Women" could not be tolerated since "the unchaste Touches and Gesticulations used by Dancers have a palpable tendency to that which is evil."

Government by Puritans for Puritanism

It is only a slight exaggeration to say that seventeenth-century New England was governed by Puritans for Puritanism. The charter of the Massachusetts Bay Company empowered the company's stockholders, known as freemen, to meet as a body known as the General Court and make the laws needed to govern the company's affairs. The colonists transformed this arrangement for running a joint stock company into a structure for governing the colony. Hoping to ensure that godly men would decide government policies, the General Court expanded the number of freemen in 1631 to include all male church members. Only freemen had the right to vote for governor, deputy governor, and other colonial officials. As new settlers were recognized as freemen, the size of the General Court grew too large to meet conveniently. So in 1634, the freemen in each town agreed to send two deputies to the General Court to act as the colony's legislative assembly. All other men were classified as "inhabitants," and they had the right to vote, hold office, and participate fully in town government.

A "town meeting," composed of a town's inhabitants and freemen, chose the selectmen and other officials who administered local affairs. New England town meetings routinely practiced a level of popular participation in political life that was unprecedented elsewhere during the seventeenth century. Almost every adult man could speak out in town meetings and fortify his voice with a vote. However, all women—even church members—were prohibited from voting, and towns did not permit "contrary-minded" men to become or remain inhabitants. Although town meeting participants wrangled from time to time, widespread political participation tended to reinforce conformity to Puritan ideals.

One of the most important functions of New England government was land distribution. Settlers who desired to establish a new town entered a covenant and petitioned the General Court for a grant of land. The court granted town sites to suitably pious petitioners but did not allow settlement until the Indians who inhabited a grant agreed to relinquish their claim to the land, usually in exchange for manufactured goods.

Having obtained their grant, town founders apportioned land among themselves and any newcomers they permitted to join them. Normally, each family received a house lot large enough for an adjacent garden as well as one or more strips of agricultural land on the perimeter of the town. Although there was a considerable difference between the largest and smallest family plots, most clustered in the middle range—roughly fifty to one hundred acres—resulting in a more nearly equal distribution of land in New England than in the Chesapeake.

Sabbath Breakers

These seventeenth-century prints show some of the punishments to which Sabbath breakers could be subjected by man and God. In the upper illustration, a person who gathered sticks on the Sabbath is stoned to death as Puritans believed the Bible commanded. In the lower print, three women who broke the Sabbath by preparing flax to be spun and woven into linen suffer God's retribution when they are burned to death. New Englanders differed about exactly when the Sabbath began. Some thought it started at sunset on Saturday evening, but John Winthrop believed the Sabbath began about three o'clock Saturday afternoon. Given the extreme punishments inflicted on Sabbath breakers, New Englanders needed to be careful about what they did between Saturday afternoon and Monday morning.

Divine Examples of God's Severe Judgements upon Sabbath-Breakers (London, 1671).

Joseph Capen House

This substantial house was built in 1683 for Joseph Capen, a Harvard graduate who had recently arrived in Topsfield, Massachusetts, to serve as the local minister. The town granted Capen twelve acres for a homesite, and he probably paid for the house with the dowry of his new wife, Priscilla Appleton, the daughter of a wealthy colonist in nearby Ipswich, Massachusetts. The plain but imposing house suggests the sturdy ties between preachers and their congregations and, more generally, between families, faith, and communities. Capen lived in the house and preached to the Topsfield church for more than forty years until his death in 1725. Now, more than three centuries after Capen built the house, it still stands, a monument to New England colonists' convictions that they were building a society to endure for the ages. Picture Research Consultants & Archives.

The physical layout of New England towns encouraged settlers to look inward toward their neighbors, multiplying the opportunities for godly vigilance. Most people considered the forest that lay just beyond every settler's house an alien environment that was interrupted here and there by those oases of civilization, the towns. Footpaths connecting one town to another were so rudimentary that even John Winthrop once got lost within half a mile of his house and spent a sleepless night in the forest, circling the light of his small campfire and singing psalms.

The Splintering of Puritanism

Almost from the beginning, John Winthrop and other leaders had difficulty enforcing their views of Puritan orthodoxy. In England, persecution as a dissenting minority had unified Puritan voices in opposition to the Church of England. In New England, the promise of a godly society and the Puritans' emphasis on individual Bible study led New Englanders toward different visions of godliness. Puritan leaders, however, interpreted dissent as an error caused either by a misguided

believer or by the malevolent power of Satan. Whatever the cause, errors could not be tolerated. As one Puritan minister proclaimed, "The Scripture saith…there is no Truth but one."

Shortly after banishing Roger Williams, Winthrop confronted another dissenter, this time a devout Puritan woman steeped in Scripture and absorbed by religious questions: Anne Hutchinson. The mother of fourteen children, Hutchinson served her neighbors as a skilled midwife. After she settled into her new home in Boston in 1634, women gathered there to hear her weekly lectures on recent sermons. As one listener observed, she was a "Woman that Preaches better Gospell then any of your black-coates…[from] the Ninneversity." As the months passed, Hutchinson began to lecture twice a week, and crowds of sixty to eighty women and men gathered to listen to her.

Hutchinson expounded on the sermons of John Cotton, her favorite minister. Cotton stressed what he termed the "covenant of grace"—the idea that individuals could be saved only by God's grace in choosing them to be members of the elect. Cotton contrasted this familiar Puritan doctrine with the "covenant of works," the erroneous belief that a person's behavior—one's works—could win God's favor and ultimately earn a person salvation. Belief in the covenant of works and in the possibility of salvation for all was known as Arminianism. Cotton's sermons strongly hinted that many Puritans, including ministers, embraced Arminianism, which claimed—falsely, Cotton declared—that human beings could influence God's will. Anne Hutchinson agreed with Cotton. Her lectures emphasized her opinion that many of the colony's leaders affirmed the Arminian covenant of works. Like Cotton, she preached that only God's covenant of grace led to salvation.

The meetings at Hutchinson's house alarmed her nearest neighbor, John Winthrop, who believed that she was subverting the good order of the colony. In 1637, Winthrop had formal charges brought against Hutchinson and denounced her lectures as "not tolerable nor comely in the sight of God nor fitting for your sex." He told her, "You have stept out of your place, you have rather bine a Husband than a Wife and a preacher than a Hearer; and a Magistrate than a Subject."

In court, Winthrop interrogated Hutchinson, fishing for a heresy he could pin on her. Winthrop and other Puritan elders referred to Hutchinson and her followers as **antinomians**, people who believed that Christians could be saved by faith alone and did not need to act in accordance with God's law as set forth in the Bible and as interpreted by the colony's leaders. Hutchinson nimbly defended herself against the accusation of antinomianism. Yes, she acknowledged, she believed that men and women were saved by faith alone; but no, she did not deny the need to obey God's law. "The Lord hath let me see which was the clear ministry and which the wrong," she said. Finally, Winthrop had cornered her. How could she tell which ministry was which? "By an immediate revelation," she replied, "by the voice of [God's] own spirit to my soul." Winthrop spotted in this statement the heresy of prophecy, the view that God revealed his will directly to a believer instead of exclusively through the Bible, as every right-minded Puritan knew.

In 1638, the Boston church formally excommunicated Hutchinson. The minister decreed, "I doe cast you out and…deliver you up to Satan that you may learne no more to blaspheme to seduce and to lye." Banished, Hutchinson and her family moved first to Roger Williams's Rhode Island and then to present-day New York, where she and most of her family were killed by Indians.

The strains within Puritanism exemplified by Anne Hutchinson and Roger Williams caused it to splinter repeatedly during the seventeenth century. Thomas Hooker, a prominent minister, clashed with Winthrop and other leaders over the composition of the church. Hooker argued that men and women who lived godly lives should be admitted to church membership even if they had not experienced conversion. This issue, like most others in New England, had both religious and political dimensions, for only church members could vote in Massachusetts. In 1636, Hooker led an exodus of more than 800 colonists from Massachusetts to the Connecticut River valley, where they founded Hartford and neighboring towns. In 1639, the towns adopted the Fundamental Orders of Connecticut, a quasi-constitution that could be altered by the vote of freemen, who did not have to be church members, though nearly all of them were.

Other Puritan churches divided and subdivided throughout the seventeenth century as acrimony developed over doctrine and church government. Sometimes churches split over the appointment of a controversial minister. Sometimes families who had a long walk to the meetinghouse simply decided to form their own church nearer their houses. These schisms arose from ambiguities and tensions within Puritan belief. As the colonies matured, other tensions developed as well.

Religious Controversies and Economic Changes

A revolutionary transformation in the fortunes of Puritans in England had profound consequences in New England. Disputes between King Charles I and Parliament, dominated by Puritans, escalated in 1642 to civil war in England, a conflict known as the Puritan Revolution. Parliamentary forces led by the staunch Puritan Oliver Cromwell were victorious, executing Charles I in 1649 and proclaiming England a Puritan republic. From 1649 to 1660, England's rulers were not monarchs who suppressed Puritanism but believers who championed it. In a half century, English Puritans had risen from a harassed group of religious dissenters to a dominant power in English government.

When the Puritan Revolution began, the stream of immigrants to New England dwindled to a trickle, creating hard times for the colonists. They could no longer consider themselves a city on a hill setting a godly example for humankind.

David, Joanna, and Abigail Mason
This 1670 painting depicts the children of Joanna and Anthony Mason, a wealthy Boston baker. The artist lavished attention on the children's elaborate clothing. Fashionable slashed sleeves, fancy laces, silver-studded shoes, six-year-old Joanna's and four-year-old Abigail's necklaces, and nine-year-old David's silver-headed cane suggest not only the Masons' wealth but also their desire to display and memorialize their possessions and adornments. The painting hints that the children themselves were adornments, young sprouts of the Mason lineage, which could afford such finery. The portrait is unified not by signs of warm affection, innocent smiles, or familial solidarity but by trappings of wealth and sober self-importance. The painting expresses the growing respect for wealth and its worldly rewards in seventeenth-century New England.
Fine Arts Museums of San Francisco. Gift of Mr. and Mrs. John D. Rockefeller III.

English society was being reformed by Puritans in England, not New England. Furthermore, when immigrant ships became rare, the colonists faced sky-high prices for scarce English goods and few customers for their own colonial products. As they searched to find new products and markets, they established the enduring patterns of New England's economy.

New England's rocky soil and short growing season ruled out cultivating the southern colonies' crops of tobacco and rice that found a ready market in Atlantic ports. Exports that New Englanders could not get from the soil they took instead from the forest and the sea. During the first decade of settlement, colonists traded with Indians for animal pelts, which were in demand in Europe. By the 1640s, fur-bearing animals had become scarce unless traders ventured far beyond the **frontiers** of

English settlement. Trees from the seemingly limitless forests of New England proved a longer-lasting resource. Masts for ships and staves for barrels of Spanish wine and West Indian sugar were crafted from New England timber.

But the most important New England export was fish. Dried, salted codfish found markets in southern Europe and the West Indies. The fish trade also stimulated colonial shipbuilding and trained generations of fishermen, sailors, and merchants, creating a commercial network that endured for more than a century. But this export economy remained peripheral to most New England colonists. Their lives revolved around their farms, their churches, and their families.

Although immigration came to a standstill in the 1640s, the population continued to boom, doubling every twenty years. In New England, almost everyone married and women often had eight or nine children. Long, cold winters prevented the warm-weather ailments of the southern colonies and reduced New England mortality. The descendants of the immigrants of the 1630s multiplied and remultiplied, boosting the New England population to roughly equal that of the southern colonies (Figure 4.1).

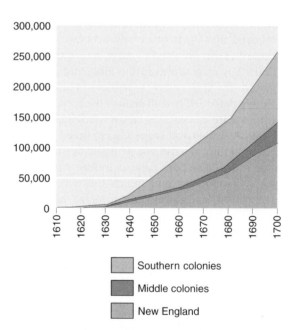

FIGURE 4.1   Population of the British North American Colonies in the Seventeenth Century
The colonial population grew at a steadily accelerating rate during the seventeenth century. New England and the southern colonies each composed about half the total colonial population until after 1680, when growth in Pennsylvania and New York contributed to a surge in the population of the middle colonies.

During the last half of the seventeenth century, under the pressures of steady population growth and integration into the Atlantic economy, the white-hot piety of the founders cooled. After 1640, the population grew faster than church membership. All residents attended sermons on pain of fines and punishment, but many could not find seats in the meetinghouses. By the 1680s, women were the majority of church members throughout New England. In some towns, only 15 percent of the adult men were members. A growing fraction of New Englanders, especially men, embraced what one historian has termed "horse-shed Christianity": They attended sermons but loitered outside near the horse shed, gossiping about the weather, fishing, their crops, or the scandalous behavior of neighbors. This slackening of piety led Puritan minister Michael Wigglesworth to ask, in verse,

> How is it that I find
>   In stead of holiness Carnality,
> In stead of heavenly frames an Earthly mind,
>   For burning zeal luke-warm Indifferency,
>   For flaming love, key-cold Dead-heartedness,
>   For temperance (in meat, and drinke, and cloaths) excess?
> Whence cometh it, that Pride, and Luxurie
>   Debate, Deceit, Contention, and Strife,
> False-dealing, Covetousness, Hypocrisie
>   (With such Crimes) amongst them are so rife,
> That one of them doth over-reach another?
>   And that an honest man can hardly trust his Brother?

Most alarming to Puritan leaders, many of the children of the visible saints of Winthrop's generation failed to experience conversion and attain full church membership. Puritans tended to assume that sainthood was inherited—that the children of visible saints were probably also among the elect. Acting on this premise, churches permitted saints  to baptize their infant sons and daughters, symbolically cleansing them of their contamination with original sin. As these children grew up during the 1640s and 1650s, however, they seldom experienced the inward transformation that signaled conversion and qualification for church membership. The problem of declining church membership and the watering-down of Puritan orthodoxy became urgent during the 1650s when the children of saints, who had grown to adulthood in New England but had not experienced conversion, began to have children

themselves. Their sons and daughters—the grandchildren of the founders of the colony—could not receive the protection that baptism afforded against the terrors of death because their parents had not experienced conversion.

Puritan churches debated what to do. To allow anyone, even the child of a saint, to become a church member without conversion was an unthinkable retreat from fundamental Puritan doctrine. In 1662, a synod of Massachusetts ministers reached a compromise known as the **Halfway Covenant**. Unconverted children of saints would be permitted to become "halfway" church members. Like regular church members, they could baptize their infants. But unlike full church members, they could not participate in communion or have the voting privileges of church membership. The Halfway Covenant generated a controversy that sputtered through Puritan churches for the remainder of the century. With the Halfway Covenant, Puritan churches came to terms with the lukewarm piety that had replaced the founders' burning zeal.

Nonetheless, New England communities continued to enforce piety with holy rigor. Beginning in 1656, small bands of Quakers—or members of the Society of Friends, as they called themselves—began to arrive in Massachusetts. Many of their beliefs were at odds with orthodox Puritanism. Quakers believed that God spoke directly to each individual through an "inner light," and that individuals needed neither a preacher nor the Bible in order to discover God's Word. Maintaining that all human beings were equal in God's eyes, Quakers refused to conform to mere temporal powers such as laws and governments unless God requested otherwise.

New England communities treated Quakers with ruthless severity. Some Quakers were branded on the face "with a red-hot iron with [an] H. for heresie." When Quakers refused to leave Massachusetts, Boston officials sentenced two men and a woman to be hanged in 1659.

New Englanders' partial success in realizing the promise of a godly society ultimately undermined the intense appeal of Puritanism. In the pious Puritan communities of New England, leaders tried to eliminate sin. In the process, they diminished the sense of utter human depravity that was the wellspring of Puritanism. By 1700, New Englanders did not doubt that human beings sinned, but they were more concerned with the sins of others than with their own.

Witches Show Their Love for Satan
Mocking pious Christians' humble obeisance to God, witches willingly debased themselves by standing in line to kneel and kiss Satan's buttocks—or so it was popularly believed. This seventeenth-century print portrays Satan with clawlike hands and feet, the tail of a rodent, the wings of a bat, and the head of a lustful ram attached to the torso of a man. Notice that women predominate among the witches eager to express their devotion to Satan and to do his bidding.
UCSF Library/Center for Knowledge Management.

Witch trials held in Salem, Massachusetts, were signs of the erosion of religious confidence and assurance. In 1692, the frenzied Salem proceedings accused more than 100 people of witchcraft, a capital crime. Most of the accused were middle-aged women who, according to their accusers, were in thrall to Satan, who tortured and bedeviled the accusers. Usually accusers had suffered a misfortune that they believed must have been caused by a witch. One woman claimed, for example, that her cow was bewitched because it gave discolored milk. Seventeenth-century New Englanders found such claims plausible since they believed supernatural power—whether God's or Satan's—influenced everything, even the color of a cow's milk. When something bad happened, an unhappy God may have caused it to show his displeasure, or a diabolical Satan acting through a witch might be to blame. If misfortunes could be pinned on a witch in thrall to Satan, then the accuser was absolved of responsibility and guilt. Witches helped New Englanders explain the disorder that crept into their communities: It was caused by Satan's minions, not by godly good folk. The Salem court executed 19 accused witches, signaling enduring belief in the supernatural origins of evil and gnawing doubt about the strength of Puritan New Englanders' faith.

REVIEW   Why did Massachusetts Puritans adopt the Halfway Covenant?

The Founding of the Middle Colonies

South of New England and north of the Chesapeake, a group of middle colonies were founded in the last third of the seventeenth century. Before the 1670s, few Europeans settled in the region. For the first two-thirds of the seventeenth century, the most important European outpost in the area was the relatively small Dutch colony of New Netherland. By 1700, however, the English monarchy had seized New Netherland, renamed it New York, and encouraged the creation of a Quaker colony led by William Penn. Unlike the New England colonies, the middle colonies of New York, New Jersey, and Pennsylvania originated as **land grants** by the English monarch to one or more proprietors, who then possessed both the land and the extensive, almost monarchical, powers of government (Map 4.2). These middle colonies attracted settlers of more diverse European origins and religious faiths than were found in New England.

From New Netherland to New York

In 1609, the Dutch East India Company dispatched Henry Hudson to search for a Northwest Passage to the Orient. Hudson sailed along the Atlantic coast and ventured up the large river that now bears his name until it dwindled to a stream that obviously did not lead to China. A decade later, the Dutch government granted the West India Company—a group of Dutch merchants and shippers—exclusive rights to trade with the Western Hemisphere.

In 1626, Peter Minuit, the resident director of the company, purchased Manhattan Island from the Manhate Indians for trade goods worth the equivalent of a dozen beaver pelts. New Amsterdam, the small settlement established at the southern tip of Manhattan Island, became the

MAP 4.2 The Middle Colonies in the Seventeenth Century

For the most part, the middle colonies in the seventeenth century were inhabited by settlers who clustered along the Hudson or Delaware rivers. The vast geographic extent of the colonies shown in this map reflects land grants authorized in England. Most of this area was inhabited by Native Americans rather than settled by colonists.

In 1664, New Netherland became New York. Charles II, who became king of England in 1660 when Parliament restored the monarchy, gave his brother James, the Duke of York, an enormous grant of land that included New Netherland. The duke quickly organized a small fleet of warships, which appeared off Manhattan Island in late summer 1664, and demanded that Stuyvesant surrender. With little choice, he did.

As the new proprietor of the colony, the Duke of York exercised almost the same unlimited authority over the colony as had the West India Company. The duke never set foot in New York, but his governors struggled to impose order on the unruly colonists. Like the Dutch, the duke permitted "all persons of what Religion soever, quietly to inhabit…provided they give no disturbance to the publique peace, nor doe molest or disquiet others in the free exercise of their religion." This policy of religious toleration was

principal trading center in New Netherland and the colony's headquarters.

Unlike the English colonies, New Netherland did not attract many European immigrants. Although few in number, New Netherlanders were remarkably diverse, especially compared with the homogeneous English settlers to the north and south. Religious dissenters and immigrants from Holland, Sweden, France, Germany, and elsewhere made their way to the colony. A minister of the Dutch Reformed Church complained to his superiors in Holland that several groups of Jews had recently arrived, adding to the religious mixture of "Papists, Mennonites and Lutherans among the Dutch [and] many Puritans…and many other atheists…who conceal themselves under the name of Christians."

The West India Company struggled to govern the motley colonists. Peter Stuyvesant, governor from 1647 to 1664, tried to enforce conformity to the Dutch Reformed Church, but the company declared that "the consciences of men should be free and unshackled," making a virtue of New Netherland necessity. The company never permitted the colony's settlers to form a representative government. Instead, the company appointed government officials who set policies, including taxes, which many colonists deeply resented.

New Amsterdam

In the background of this 1673 Dutch portrait of New Amsterdam appears the settlement on Manhattan Island—complete with a windmill. Wharves connect Manhattan residents to the seaborne commerce of the Atlantic world. In the foreground, the Dutch artist placed native inhabitants of the mainland, drawing them in such a way that they resemble Africans rather than Lenni Lenape (Delaware) Indians. Dutch merchants carried tens of thousands of African slaves to New World ports, New Amsterdam among them. Probably, the artist had never seen Indians, had never been to New Amsterdam, and depended on well-known artistic conventions about the appearance of Africans to create his Native Americans. The portrait contrasts orderly, efficient, businesslike New Amsterdam with the exotic natural environment of America, to which the native woman clings as if she is refusing to succumb to the culture represented by those neat rows of rectangular houses across the river.

less an affirmation of liberty of conscience than a recognition of the reality of the most heterogeneous colony in seventeenth-century North America.

New Jersey and Pennsylvania

The creation of New York led indirectly to the founding of two other middle colonies, New Jersey and Pennsylvania (see Map 4.2). In 1664, the Duke of York subdivided his grant and gave the portion between the Hudson and Delaware rivers to two of his friends. The proprietors of this new colony, New Jersey, quarreled, and called in a prominent English Quaker, William Penn, to arbitrate their dispute. Penn eventually worked out a settlement that continued New Jersey's proprietary government. In the process, Penn became intensely interested in what he

William Penn
This portrait was drawn about a decade after the founding of Pennsylvania. At a time when extravagant clothing and fancy wigs proclaimed that their wearer was an important person, Penn is portrayed informally, lacking even a coat, his natural hair neat but undressed — all a reflection of his Quaker faith. Penn's full face and double chin show that his faith did not make him a stranger to the pleasures of the table. No hollow-cheeked ascetic or wild-eyed enthusiast, Penn appears sober and observant, as if sizing up the viewer and reserving judgment. The portrait captures the calm determination — anchored in faith — that inspired Penn's hopes for his new colony.
Historical Society of Pennsylvania.

termed a "holy experiment" of establishing a genuinely Quaker colony in America.

Unlike most Quakers, William Penn came from an eminent family. His father had served both Cromwell and Charles II and had been knighted. Born in 1644, the younger Penn trained for a military career, but the ideas of dissenters from the reestablished Church of England appealed to him, and he became a devout Quaker.

The Quakers' concept of an open, generous God who made his love equally available to all people manifested itself in behavior that continually brought them into conflict with the English government. Quaker leaders were ordinary men and women, not specially trained preachers. Quakers allowed women to assume positions of religious leadership. "In souls there is no sex," they said. Since all people were equal in the spiritual realm, Quakers considered social hierarchy false and evil. They called everyone "friend" and shook hands instead of curtsying or removing their hats — even when meeting the king. These customs enraged many non-Quakers and provoked innumerable beatings and worse. Penn was jailed four times for such offenses, once for nine months.

Despite his many run-ins with the government, Penn remained on good terms with Charles II. Partly to rid England of the troublesome Quakers, Charles made Penn the proprietor in 1681 of a new colony called Pennsylvania.

Toleration and Diversity in Pennsylvania

Quakers flocked to Pennsylvania; between 1682 and 1685, nearly 8,000 immigrants arrived, most of them from England, Ireland, and Wales. They represented a cross section of the **artisans**, farmers, and laborers who predominated among English Quakers. Quaker missionaries also encouraged immigrants from the European continent, and many came, giving Pennsylvania greater ethnic diversity than any other English colony except New York. The Quaker colony prospered, and the capital city, Philadelphia, soon rivaled New York as a center of commerce. By 1700, the city's 5,000 inhabitants participated in a thriving trade exporting flour and other food products to the West Indies and importing English textiles and manufactured goods.

Penn was determined to live in peace with the Indians who inhabited the region. His Indian policy expressed his Quaker ideals and contrasted sharply with the hostile policies of the other English colonies. Penn instructed his agents to obtain the Indians' consent by purchasing their land, respecting their claims, and dealing with them fairly.

Penn declared that the first principle of government was that every settler would "enjoy the free possession of his or her faith and exercise of worship towards God." Accordingly, Pennsylvania tolerated Protestant sects of all kinds as well as Roman Catholics. All voters and officeholders had to be Christians, but the government did not compel settlers to attend religious services, as in Massachusetts, or to pay taxes to maintain a state-supported church, as in Virginia.

Despite its toleration and diversity, Pennsylvania was as much a Quaker colony as New England was a stronghold of Puritanism. Penn had no hesitation about using civil government to enforce religious morality. One of the colony's first laws provided severe punishment for "all such offenses against God, as swearing, cursing, lying, profane talking, drunkenness, drinking of healths, [and] obscene words... which excite the people to rudeness, cruelty, looseness, and irreligion."

As proprietor, Penn had extensive powers, subject only to review by the king. He appointed a governor who maintained the proprietor's power to veto any laws passed by the colonial council, which was elected by property owners who possessed at least one hundred acres of land or who paid taxes. The council had the power to originate laws and administer all the affairs of government. A popularly elected assembly served as a check on the council; its members had the authority to reject or approve laws framed by the council.

Penn stressed that the exact form of government mattered less than the men who served in it. In Penn's eyes, "good men" staffed Pennsylvania's government because Quakers dominated elective and appointive offices. Quakers, of course, differed among themselves. Members of the assembly struggled to win the right to debate and amend laws, especially tax laws. They finally won the battle in 1701 when a new Charter of Privileges gave the proprietor the power to appoint the council and in turn stripped the council of all its former powers and gave them to the assembly, which became the only single-house legislature in all the British colonies.

REVIEW How did Quaker ideals shape the colony of Pennsylvania?

The Colonies and the British Empire

Proprietary grants to faraway lands had been a cheap way for the king to reward friends. As the colonies grew, however, the grants became more valuable. After 1660, the king took initiatives to channel colonial trade through English hands and to consolidate royal authority over colonial governments. These initiatives defined the basic relationship between the colonies and England that endured until the American Revolution (Map 4.3).

Royal Regulation of Colonial Trade

English economic policies toward the colonies were designed to yield customs revenues for the monarchy and profitable business for English merchants and shippers. Also, the policies were intended to divert the colonies' trade from England's enemies, especially the Dutch and the French.

The Navigation Acts of 1650, 1651, 1660, and 1663 (see chapter 3) set forth two fundamental rules governing colonial trade. First, goods shipped to and from the colonies had to be transported in English ships using primarily English crews. Second, the Navigation Acts listed ("enumerated," in the language of the time) specific colonial products that could be shipped only to England or to other English colonies. While these regulations prevented Chesapeake **planters** from shipping their tobacco directly to the European continent, they interfered less with the commerce of New England and the middle colonies, whose principal exports—fish, lumber, and flour—were not enumerated and could legally be sent directly to their most important markets in the West Indies.

By the end of the seventeenth century, colonial commerce was defined by regulations that subjected merchants and shippers to royal supervision and gave them access to markets throughout the British empire. In addition, colonial commerce received protection from the British navy. By 1700, colonial goods (including those from the West Indies) accounted for onefifth of all British imports and for two-thirds of all goods reexported from England to the European continent. In turn, the colonies absorbed more than one-tenth of British exports. The commercial regulations gave economic value to England's proprietorship of American colonies.

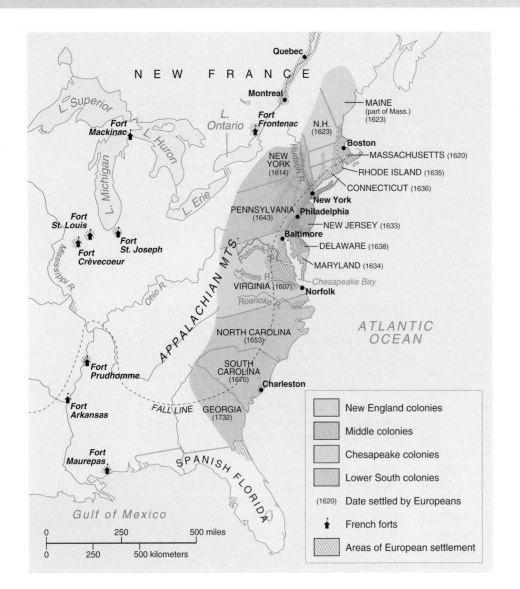

MAP 4.3   American Colonies at the End of the Seventeenth Century
By the end of the seventeenth century, settlers inhabited a narrow band of land that stretched more or less continuously from Boston to Norfolk, with pockets of settlement farther south. The colonies' claims to enormous tracts of land to the west were contested by Native Americans as well as by France and Spain.

Pine Tree Shilling

Currency was in short supply in the colonies. Since England prohibited the export of its coins, the precious currency circulating in the North American colonies tended to be Spanish, Dutch, French, or Portuguese. In violation of English rules that forbade colonies from issuing their own currency, John Hull, a wealthy Boston merchant and shipowner, began to mint coins in 1652. Shown here is one of his pine tree shillings, both sides boldly announcing its Massachusetts origins. A shilling was worth twelve pennies; twenty shillings equaled a pound sterling. Despite Hull's attempt to ease the currency shortage, the legal tender most colonists used consisted of such commonly available items as bushels of corn or wheat, skins of beaver or deer, and, following Native American practice, wampum.

Courtesy of the Museum of the American Numismatic Association.

King Philip's War and the Consolidation of Royal Authority

The monarchy also took steps to exercise greater control over colonial governments. Virginia had been a royal colony since 1624; Maryland, South Carolina, and the middle colonies were proprietary colonies with close ties to the crown. The New England colonies possessed royal charters, but they had developed their own distinctively Puritan governments. Charles II, whose father, Charles I, had been executed by Puritans in England, took a particular interest in harnessing the New England colonies more firmly to the British empire. The occasion was a royal investigation following King Philip's War.

In 1675, warfare between Indians and colonists erupted in the Chesapeake and New England. Massachusetts settlers had massacred hundreds of Pequot Indians in 1637, but they had established relatively peaceful relations with the more potent Wampanoags. In the decades that followed, New Englanders steadily encroached on Indian lands, and, in 1675, the Wampanoags struck back with attacks on settlements in western Massachusetts. Metacomet—whom the colonists called King Philip—probably neither planned the attacks nor masterminded a conspiracy with the Nipmucks and the Narragansetts, as the colonists feared. But when militias from Massachusetts and other New England colonies counterattacked all three tribes, a deadly sequence of battles killed over a thousand colonists and thousands more Indians. The Indians utterly destroyed thirteen English settlements and partially burned another half dozen. The colonists finally defeated the Indians, principally with a scorched-earth policy of burning their food supplies. King Philip's War left the New England colonists with an enduring hatred of Indians, a large war debt, and a devastated frontier. And in 1676, an agent of the king arrived to investigate whether New England was abiding by English laws.

Not surprisingly, the king's agent found all sorts of deviations from English rules, and the monarchy decided to govern New England more directly. In 1684, an English

King Philip (Metacomet)
No portrait of Metacomet, or King Philip, was made during his lifetime. The artist of this likeness imagines him as a proud warrior wrapped in a shawl and armed with a musket, which indicates both his adoption of this European weapon and his willingness to use it against English colonists.
Library of Congress.

court revoked the Massachusetts charter, the foundation of the distinctive Puritan government. Two years later, royal officials incorporated Massachusetts and the other colonies north of Maryland into the Dominion of New England. To govern the dominion, the English sent Sir Edmund Andros to Boston. Some New England merchants cooperated with Andros, but most colonists were offended by his flagrant disregard of such Puritan traditions as keeping the Sabbath. Worst of all, the Dominion of New England invalidated all land titles, confronting every landowner in

King Philip's War, 1675

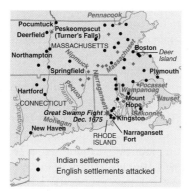

- ◆ Indian settlements
- ● English settlements attacked

King Philip's Sash
This woolen sash belonged to Wampanoag chief Metacomet, or King Philip. Small white glass beads, obtained through trade with Europeans, are stitched into the sash in the shape of a serpent.
Peabody Museum of Archaeology and Ethnology, Harvard University.

New England with the horrifying prospect of losing his or her land.

Events in England, however, permitted Massachusetts colonists to overthrow Andros and retain title to their property. When Charles II died in 1685, he was succeeded by his brother James II, a zealous Catholic. James's aggressive campaign to appoint Catholics to government posts engendered such unrest that in 1688 a group of Protestant noblemen in Parliament invited the Dutch ruler William III of Orange, James's son-in-law, to claim the English throne. When William III landed in England at the head of a large army, James fled to France and William III and his wife Mary II (James's daughter) became co-rulers in the relatively bloodless "Glorious Revolution," reasserting Protestant influence in England and its empire.

Rumors of the revolution raced across the Atlantic and emboldened colonial uprisings against royal authority in Massachusetts, New York, and Maryland. In Boston in 1689, rebels tossed Andros and other English officials in jail, destroyed the Dominion of New England, and reestablished the former charter government. New Yorkers followed the Massachusetts example. Under the leadership of Jacob Leisler, rebels seized the royal governor in 1689 and ruled the colony for more than a year. That same year in Maryland, the Protestant Association, led by John Coode, overthrew the colony's pro-Catholic government, fearing it would not recognize the new Protestant king.

But these rebel governments did not last. When King William III's governor of New York arrived in 1691, he executed Leisler for treason. Coode's men ruled Maryland until the new royal governor arrived in 1692 and ended both Coode's rebellion and Lord Baltimore's proprietary government. In Massachusetts, John Winthrop's city on a hill became another royal colony in 1691. The new charter said that the governor of the colony would be appointed by the king rather than elected by the colonists' representatives. But perhaps the most unsettling change was the new qualification for voting. Possession of property replaced church membership as a prerequisite for voting in colony-wide elections. Wealth replaced God's grace as the defining characteristic of Massachusetts citizenship.

Much as colonists chafed under increasing royal control, they still valued English protection from hostile neighbors. While the northern colonies were distracted by the Glorious Revolution, French forces from the fur-trading regions along the Great Lakes and in Canada attacked villages in New England and New York. Known as King William's War, the conflict with the French was a colonial outgrowth of William's war against France in Europe. The war dragged on until 1697 and ended inconclusively in both Europe and the colonies. But it made clear to many colonists that along with English royal government came a welcome measure of military security.

> **REVIEW** Why did the "Glorious Revolution" in England lead to uprisings in the American colonies?

Conclusion: An English Model of Colonization in North America

By 1700, the diverse English colonies in North America had developed along lines quite different from the example New Spain had set in 1600. In the North American colonies, English immigrants and their descendants created societies of settlers unlike the largely Indian societies in New Spain ruled by a tiny group of Spaniards. Although many settlers came to North America from other parts of Europe and a growing number of Africans arrived in bondage, English laws, habits, ideas, and language dominated all the colonies.

Economically, the English colonies thrived on agriculture and trade instead of mining silver and exploiting Indian labor as in New Spain. Southern colonies grew huge crops of tobacco and rice with the labor of indentured servants and slaves, while farmers in the middle colonies planted wheat and New England fishermen harvested the sea. Although servants and slaves could be found throughout the North American colonies, many settlers depended principally on the labor of family members. Relations between settlers and Native Americans often exploded in bloody warfare, but Indians seldom served as an important source of labor for settlers, as they did in New Spain.

Protestantism prevailed in the North American settlements, relaxed in some colonies and straitlaced in others. The convictions of Puritanism that motivated John Winthrop and others to build a new England in the colonies became muted as the New England colonies matured and dissenters like Roger Williams multiplied. Catholics, Quakers, Anglicans (members of the Church of England), Jews, and others settled in the middle and southern colonies, creating considerable religious toleration, especially in Pennsylvania and New York.

Politics and government differed from colony to colony, although the imprint of English institutions and practices existed everywhere. And everywhere, local settlers who were free adult white men had an extraordinary degree of political influence, far beyond that of colonists in New Spain or ordinary citizens in England. A new world of settlers that Columbus could not have imagined, that Powhatan only glimpsed, had been firmly established in English North America by 1700. During the next half century, that English colonial world would undergo surprising new developments built on the achievements of the seventeenth century.

Suggestions for Further Reading

Virginia DeJohn Anderson, *Creatures of Empire: How Domestic Animals Transformed Early America* (2004). An innovative study of the influence of domestic animals on humans and the natural environment in early America.

Colin G. Calloway, *New Worlds for All: Indians, Europeans, and the Remaking of Early America* (1998). A sweeping overview of encounters between European settlers and Native Americans.

David D. Hall, *Worlds of Wonder, Days of Judgment: Popular Religious Belief in Early New England* (1989). A fascinating survey of popular religious belief in the context of Puritan New England.

Eve LaPlante, *American Jezebel: The Uncommon Life of Anne Hutchinson, the Woman Who Defied the Puritans* (2005). A compelling biography of the Puritan woman who challenged early New England orthodoxy.

Mary Beth Norton, *In the Devil's Snare: The Salem Witchcraft Crisis of 1692* (2002). An authoritative analysis of the cultural cross-currents that influenced the Salem witchcraft crisis.

Russell Shorto, *The Island at the Center of the World: The Epic Story of Dutch Manhattan and the Forgotten Colony That Shaped America* (2004). A vivid account of the Dutch colony that became New York.

▶ For more books about topics in this chapter, see the Online Bibliography at bedfordstmartins.com/roarkcompact.

▶ For additional firsthand accounts of this period, see Chapter 4 in Michael Johnson, ed., *Reading the American Past*, Third Edition.

▶ For web sites and documents related to topics and places in this chapter, see "HistoryLinks," "DocLinks," and "PlaceLinks" at bedfordstmartins.com/roarkcompact.

REVIEWING THE CHAPTER

Follow these steps to review and strengthen your understanding of the chapter.

STEP 1: *Study the* **Key Terms** *and* **Timeline** *to identify the significance of each item listed.*

STEP 2: *Answer the* **Review Questions,** *drawing on key terms and dates to support your answers.*

STEP 3: *Drawing on the Key Terms, Timeline, and Review Questions, answer the broader* **Making Connections** *questions.*

KEY TERMS

Who

Roger Williams (p. 77)
Henry VIII (p. 78)
Elizabeth I (p. 79)
James I (p. 79)
Charles I (p. 79)
Pilgrims (p. 80)
William Bradford (p. 80)
Wampanoag Indians (p. 80, 97)
John Winthrop (p. 80)
John Calvin (p. 85)
"visible saints" (p. 86)
Anne Hutchinson (p. 88)
John Cotton (p. 88)
antinomians (p. 89)
Thomas Hooker (p. 89)
Oliver Cromwell (p. 89)
Quakers (p. 91)
Peter Minuit (p. 92)
Manhate Indians (p. 92)
Peter Stuyvesant (p. 93)
Charles II (p. 93)
Duke of York (p. 93)

William Penn (p. 94)
Pequot Indians (p. 97)
Metacomet (p. 97)
Edmund Andros (p. 97)
James II (p. 98)
William III of Orange (p. 98)
Mary II (p. 98)
Jacob Leisler (p. 98)
John Coode (p. 98)

What

Rhode Island (p. 78)
English Reformation (p. 79)
Act of Supremacy (p. 79)
Church of England (p. 79)
Puritanism (p. 79)
separatism (p. 80)
Mayflower Compact (p. 80)
Plymouth (p. 80)
royal charter (p. 80)
Massachusetts Bay Company (p. 80)
Boston (p. 80)
Arbella (p. 80)

Calvinism (p. 85)
predestination (p. 85)
General Court (p. 87)
town meeting (p. 87)
covenant of grace (p. 88)
covenant of works (p. 89)
Arminianism (p. 89)
Fundamental Orders of Connecticut
  (p. 89)
Puritan Revolution (p. 89)
Halfway Covenant (p. 91)
Dutch East India Company
  (p. 92)
Manhattan Island (p. 92)
Philadelphia (p. 94)
Charter of Privileges (p. 95)
Navigation Acts (p. 95)
King Philip's War (p. 97)
Dominion of New England
  (p. 97)
Glorious Revolution (p. 98)
Protestant Association (p. 98)
King William's War (p. 98)

TIMELINE

◄ **1534** • King Henry VIII breaks with Roman Catholic Church.

1609 • Henry Hudson searches for Northwest Passage.

1620 • Plymouth colony is founded.

1626 • Manhattan Island is purchased and New Amsterdam founded.

1629 • Massachusetts Bay Company receives royal charter.

1630 • John Winthrop leads Puritan settlers to Massachusetts Bay.

1636 • Rhode Island colony is established.
       • Connecticut colony is founded.

1638 • Anne Hutchinson is excommunicated.

1642 • Puritan Revolution inflames England.

1649
       • English Puritans win civil war and execute Charles I.

REVIEW QUESTIONS

1. Why did Henry VIII initiate the English Reformation? (pp. 78–79)

2. Why did the Puritans immigrate to North America? (pp. 80–84)

3. Why did Massachusetts Puritans adopt the Halfway Covenant? (pp. 85–92)

4. How did Quaker ideals shape the colony of Pennsylvania? (pp. 92–95)

5. Why did the "Glorious Revolution" in England lead to uprisings in the American colonies? (pp. 95–98)

MAKING CONNECTIONS

1. How did the religious dissenters who flooded into the northern colonies address the question of religious dissent in their new homes? Comparing two colonies, discuss their different approaches and the implications of those approaches for colonial development.

2. In his sermon aboard the *Arbella*, John Winthrop spoke of the Massachusetts Bay Colony as "a city upon a hill." What did he mean? How did this expectation influence life in New England during the seventeenth century? In your answer, be sure to consider the relationship between religious and political life in the colony.

3. Religious conflict and political turmoil battered England in the seventeenth century. How did political developments in England affect life in the colonies? In your answer, consider the establishment of the colonies and the crown's attempts to exercise authority over them.

4. Although both were settled by the English, colonial New England was dramatically different from the colonial Chesapeake. How did they differ and why? In your answer, consider the economies, systems of governance, and patterns of settlement in each colony.

▶ FOR PRACTICE QUIZZES, A CUSTOMIZED STUDY PLAN, AND OTHER STUDY TOOLS, see the Online Study Guide at bedfordstmartins.com/roarkcompact.

1656 • Quakers arrive in Massachusetts and are persecuted there.

1660 • Monarchy restored in England; Charles II becomes king.
• Navigation Act.

1662 • Many Puritan congregations adopt Halfway Covenant.

1663 • Staple Act.

1664 • English seize Dutch colony, rename it New York.
• Colony of New Jersey created.

1675 • King Philip's War.

1681 • William Penn receives a charter for colony of Pennsylvania.

1686 • Dominion of New England created.

1688 • England's "Glorious Revolution"; William III and Mary II become the new rulers.

1692 • Salem witch trials.

COLONIAL SLAVE DRUM

An African in Virginia made this drum sometime around the beginning of the eighteenth century. The maker of the drum was probably a man who had been enslaved in Africa, transported across the Atlantic in the hold of a slave ship, and sold to a tobacco planter in the Chesapeake. The drum combines deerskin and cedar wood from North America with African skills and designs the maker had mastered before enslavement. The drum signifies the millions of enslaved African men, women, and children who were among the many goods bought and sold in the booming transatlantic trade of the eighteenth century. At a time when Benjamin Franklin and other whites—both native-born and immigrants from Europe—were finding opportunities to better their lives in America, tens of thousands of Africans were arriving in the British North American colonies in hereditary, lifetime bondage. The drum embodies slaves' use of African cultural resources in the alien and oppressive environment of New World slavery. During moments of respite from work, slaves played drums to accompany dances learned in Africa. They also drummed out messages from plantation to plantation. Whites knew slaves used drums for communication, but they could not decipher the meanings of the rhythms and sounds. Fearful that drums signaled rebellious uprisings, whites outlawed drumming but could not eliminate it. Most likely, the messages expressed by the hands that struck this drumhead included lamentations about a life of bondage in America.

Colonial America in the Eighteenth Century
1701–1770

EARLY ON A SUNDAY MORNING in October 1723, young Benjamin Franklin stepped from a wharf along the Delaware River onto the streets of Philadelphia. As he recalled in his autobiography, "I was dirty from my Journey; my Pockets were stuff'd out with Shirts and Stockings; I knew no Soul, nor where to look for Lodging. I was fatigu'd with Travelling, Rowing and Want of Rest. I was very hungry."

Born in 1706, Benjamin Franklin grew up in Boston, where his father, Josiah, worked making soap and candles. At the age of twelve, Benjamin signed a contract to serve for nine years as an apprentice to his brother James, a printer. In James's shop, Benjamin learned the printer's trade and had access to the latest books and pamphlets, which he read avidly. In 1721, James inaugurated the *New England Courant*, avowing to "expose the Vice and Follies of Persons of all Ranks and Degrees" with articles written "so that the meanest ploughman…may understand them."

Benjamin's responsibilities in the print shop grew quickly, but "My Brother was passionate and had often beaten me," he remembered. Benjamin resolved to escape from his apprenticeship "to assert my Freedom" and to run away to New York, nearly three hundred miles from anyone he knew. When he could not find work there, he talked his way aboard a small boat heading toward Philadelphia. After rowing half the night, Franklin arrived in the city and went straight to a bakery where he purchased "three great Puffy Rolls." Then he set off for the wharf, "with a Roll under each Arm," to wash down the bread with "a Draught of the River Water." After quenching his thirst, Franklin followed "many clean dress'd People…to the great Meeting House of the Quakers.…I sat down among them, and…I fell fast asleep, and continu'd so till the Meeting broke up."

Franklin's account of his life in Boston and his arrival in Philadelphia illustrates everyday experiences shared by many other colonists: long hours of labor subject to the authority of a parent, relative, or employer; and a restless quest for escape from the ties that bound, for freedom. Franklin's account hints at other, less tangible trends: ambition to make something of oneself in this world rather than worry too much about the hereafter; eagerness to subvert orthodox opinion by publishing dissenting views expressed in simple, clear language understandable by "the meanest ploughman"; confidence that, with a valued skill and a few coins, a young man could make his way in the world; and a slackening of religious fervor displayed, for example, in Franklin's quiet snooze during the Quaker meeting he wandered into on his first day in Philadelphia.

Mrs. Charles Willing

This portrait of Mrs. Charles Willing of Philadelphia illustrates the prosperity achieved by numerous women and men in the eighteenth-century colonies. Painted by the Philadelphia artist Robert Feke in 1746, the portrait depicts the close connections between Europe and the North American colonies made possible by thriving transatlantic commerce. Scholars have discovered that Anna Maria Garthwaite, an established textile designer in Spitalfields—a silk-weaving center near London—designed the silk used to make Mrs. Willing's dress in 1743. A Spitalfields weaver, Simeon Julins, then wove the fabric in the months between the fall of 1743 and the spring of 1744 and sold it to a merchant who exported it to Philadelphia in 1744. Mrs. Willing must have spotted the silk in a shop much like the one Benjamin Franklin eventually ran with his wife Deborah after he had become more established in Philadelphia. Mrs. Willing would have purchased enough to have this fashionable gown sewn and fitted for her portrait, only three years after Anna Garthwaite first sketched the design in Spitalfields. The portrait demonstrates that, like other prosperous colonists, Mrs. Willing kept abreast of the latest London fashions available in the shops of colonial merchants.

Courtesy, Winterthur Museum, gift of Mrs. George P. Bissell Jr.

Franklin's story introduces some of the major changes that affected all the British colonies in eighteenth-century North America. Social and economic changes tended to reinforce the differences among New England, the middle colonies, and the southern colonies, while important cultural and political developments tugged in the opposite direction, creating common experiences, aspirations, and identities. In 1776, when *E Pluribus Unum* (Latin meaning "From Many, One") was adopted as the motto for the Great Seal of the United States, the changes in eighteenth-century America that strengthened *Pluribus* also planted the seeds of *Unum*.

In contrast to the British colonies' economic growth and political maturation, the Spanish and French colonies in North America remained thinly populated outposts of European empires interested principally in maintaining a toehold in the vast North American territories they claimed. The social, cultural, and religious developments that tended to unify the British North American colonies were unique to what would soon become the United States of America.

A Growing Population and Expanding Economy in British North America

The most important fact about eighteenth-century British America is its phenomenal population growth: In 1700, colonists numbered about 250,000; by 1770, they tallied well over 2 million. An index of the emerging significance of colonial America is that in 1700 there were 19 people in England for every American colonist, but by 1770 there were only 3. The eightfold growth of the colonial population signaled the maturation of a distinctive colonial society. That society was by no means homogeneous. Colonists of different ethnic groups, races, and religions lived in varied environments under thirteen different colonial governments, all of them part of the British empire.

In general, the growth and diversity of the eighteenth-century colonial population derived from two sources: immigration and natural increase (growth through reproduction). Natural increase contributed about three-fourths of the population growth, immigration about one-fourth. Immigration shifted the ethnic and racial balance among the colonists, making them by

1770 less English and less white than ever before. Fewer than 10 percent of eighteenth-century immigrants came from England; about 36 percent were Scots-Irish, mostly from northern Ireland; 33 percent arrived from Africa, almost all of them slaves; nearly 15 percent had left the many German-language principalities (the nation of Germany did not exist until 1871); and almost 10 percent came from Scotland. In 1670, more than 9 out of 10 colonists were of English ancestry, and only 1 out of 25 was of African ancestry. By 1770, only about half the colonists were of English descent, while more than 20 percent descended from Africans. By 1770, the people of the colonies had a distinctive colonial—rather than English—profile (Map 5.1).

The booming population of the colonies hints at a second major feature of eighteenth-century colonial society: an expanding economy. In 1700, after almost a century of settlement, nearly all the colonists lived within fifty miles of the Atlantic coast. The almost limitless wilderness stretching westward made land relatively cheap. Land in the colonies commonly sold for a fraction of its price in the Old World. The abundance of land in the colonies made labor precious, and the colonists always needed more. The colonists' insatiable demand for labor was the fundamental economic environment that sustained the mushrooming population. Economic historians estimate that free colonists (those who were not **indentured servants** or slaves) had a higher standard of living than the majority of people elsewhere in the Atlantic world. The unique achievement of the eighteenth-century colonial economy was the modest economic welfare of the vast bulk of the free population.

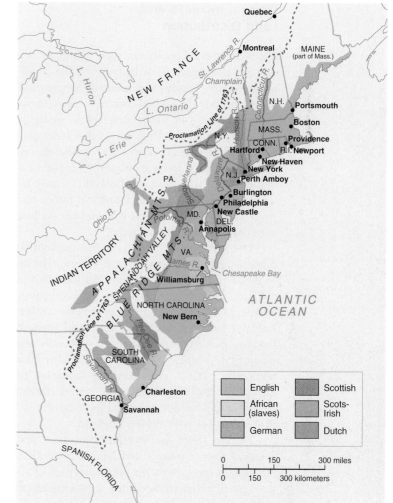

MAP 5.1   Europeans and Africans in the Eighteenth Century
This map illustrates regions where Africans and certain immigrant groups clustered. It is important to avoid misreading the map. Predominantly English and German regions, for example, also contained colonists from other places. Likewise, regions where African slaves resided in large numbers also included many whites, slave masters among them. The map suggests the polyglot diversity of eighteenth-century colonial society.

> **REVIEW**   How did the North American colonies achieve the remarkable population growth of the eighteenth century?

New England: From Puritan Settlers to Yankee Traders

The New England population grew sixfold during the eighteenth century but lagged behind the growth in the other colonies. Why did New England fail to keep pace? Most immigrants chose other destinations because of New England's relatively densely settled land and because Puritan orthodoxy made these colonies comparatively inhospitable to religious dissenters and those indifferent to religion. As the population grew, many settlers in search of farmland dispersed from towns, and Puritan communities lost much of their cohesion. Nonetheless, networks of economic exchange laced New Englanders to their neighbors, to Boston merchants, and to the broad currents of Atlantic commerce. In many ways, trade became a faith that competed strongly with the traditions of **Puritanism**.

Natural Increase and Land Distribution

The New England population grew mostly by natural increase, much as it had during the seventeenth century. Nearly every adult woman married. Most married women had children—often many children, thanks to the relatively low mortality rate in New England. The perils of childbirth gave wives a shorter life expectancy than husbands, but wives often lived to have six, seven, or eight babies. When a wife died, her husband usually remarried quickly. Benjamin Franklin's father had seven children with his first wife and ten (including Benjamin) with his second.

The burgeoning New England population pressed against a limited amount of land. The interior of New England was smaller than that of colonies farther south (see Map 5.1). Moreover, as the northernmost group of colonies, New England had a contested northern and western frontier. Powerful Indian tribes, especially the Iroquois and Mahicans, jealously guarded their territories. When provoked by colonial or European disputes, the French (and Catholic) colony of Quebec also menaced the English (and **Protestant**) colonies of New England.

During the seventeenth century, New England towns parceled out land to individual families. In most cases, the original settlers practiced partible inheritance (they subdivided land more or less equally among sons). By the eighteenth century, the original land allotments had to be further subdivided to accommodate grandsons and great-grandsons, and many plots of land became too small for subsistence. Sons who could not hope to inherit sufficient land to farm had to move away from the town where they were born.

During the eighteenth century, colonial governments in New England abandoned the seventeenth-century policy of granting land to towns. Needing revenue, the governments of both Connecticut and Massachusetts sold land directly to individuals, including speculators. Now money, rather than membership in a community bound by a church **covenant**, determined whether a person could obtain land. The new land policy eroded the seventeenth-century pattern of settlement. As colonists moved, they tended to settle on individual farms rather than in the towns and villages that characterized the seventeenth century. New Englanders still depended on their relatives and neighbors for help in clearing land, raising a house, worshipping God, and having a good time. But far more than in the seventeenth century, they regulated their behavior in newly settled areas by their own individual dictates.

Farms, Fish, and Trade

A New England farm was a place to get by, not to get rich. New England farmers did not produce a huge marketable surplus. Instead of one big crop, farmers grew many small ones. If they had extra, they sold to or traded with neighbors. Poor roads made travel difficult, time-consuming, and expensive, especially with bulky and heavy agricultural goods. The one major agricultural product the New England colonies exported—livestock—walked to market on its own legs. By 1770, New Englanders had only one-fourth as much wealth as free colonists in the southern colonies.

As consumers, New England farmers were the foundation of a diversified commercial economy that linked remote farms to markets throughout the world. Merchants large and small stocked imported goods—English textiles, ceramics, and metal goods; Chinese tea; West Indian sugar; and Chesapeake tobacco. Larger towns, especially Boston, housed skilled tradesmen such as cabinetmakers and silversmiths, along with printers like Benjamin Franklin's brother. Shipbuilders tended to do better than other **artisans** because they served the most dynamic sector of the New England economy.

Many New Englanders made their fortunes at sea, as they had since the seventeenth century. Fish accounted for more than a third of New England's eighteenth-century exports; livestock and timber made up another third. The West Indies absorbed two-thirds of all New England's exports. Slaves on Caribbean sugar plantations ate dried, salted codfish caught by New England fishermen, filled barrels crafted from New England timber with molasses and refined sugar, and loaded those barrels aboard ships bound ultimately for Europeans with a sweet tooth (Map 5.2). Almost all the rest of New England's exports went to England and continental Europe.

Merchants dominated this Atlantic commerce. The largest and most successful merchants lived in Boston, where they not only bought and sold imported goods but also owned and insured the ships that carried the merchandise. The luxurious homes of Boston's merchants

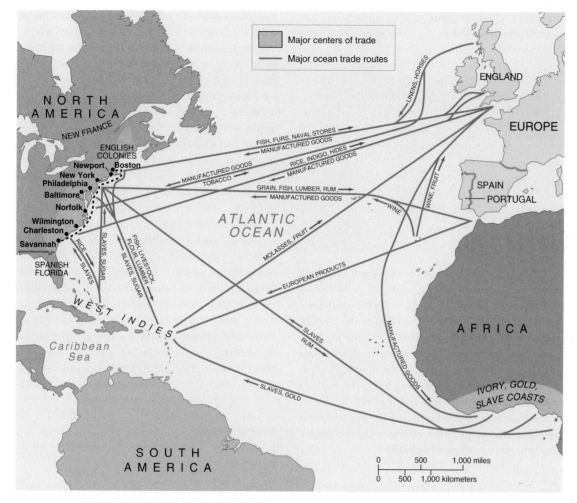

MAP 5.2 Atlantic Trade in the Eighteenth Century
This map illustrates the economic outlook of the colonies in the eighteenth century—east toward the Atlantic world rather than west toward the interior of North America. The long distances involved in the Atlantic trade and the uncertainties of seaborne travel suggest the difficulties Britain experienced governing the colonies and regulating colonial commerce.

contrasted with the modest dwellings of other New Englanders, an indication of the polarization of wealth that occurred in Boston and other seaports during the eighteenth century. By 1770, the richest 5 percent of Bostonians owned about half the city's wealth; the poorest two-thirds of the population owned less than one-tenth.

Although the rich got richer and everybody else had a smaller share of the total wealth, the incidence of genuine poverty did not change much. Overall, colonists were better off than most people in England. A Connecticut traveler wrote from England in 1764, "We in New England know nothing of poverty and want, we have no idea of the thing, how much better do our poor people live than 7/8 of the people on this much famed island."

The contrast with English poverty had meaning because the overwhelming majority of New Englanders traced their ancestry to England; New England was more homogeneous than any other region. People of African ancestry (almost all of them slaves) barely diluted the region's 97 percent white majority. New Englanders had no hesitation about acquiring slaves, and many Puritan ministers owned one or two. But New England's family farms were unsuited for slave labor. Instead, slaves concentrated in towns, especially Boston, where most of them worked as domestic servants and laborers.

By 1770, the population, wealth, and commercial activity of New England differed from what they had been in 1700. Ministers still enjoyed high status, but Yankee traders had replaced Puritan saints as the symbolic New Englanders.

> **REVIEW** Why did settlement patterns in New England change from the seventeenth to the eighteenth century?

The Middle Colonies: Immigrants, Wheat, and Work

In 1700, almost twice as many people lived in New England as in the middle colonies of Pennsylvania, New York, New Jersey, and Delaware. But by 1770, the population of the middle colonies had multiplied tenfold—mainly from an influx of German, Irish, Scottish, and other immigrants—and nearly equaled the population of New England. Immigrants made the middle colonies a uniquely diverse society. By 1800, barely one-third of Pennsylvanians and less than half the total population of the middle colonies traced their ancestry to England.

German and Scots-Irish Immigrants

Germans made up the largest contingent of migrants from the European continent to the middle colonies. By 1770, about 85,000 Germans had arrived in the colonies. Their fellow colonists often referred to them as "Pennsylvania Dutch," an English corruption of *Deutsch,* the word the immigrants used to describe themselves.

Most German immigrants came from what is now southwestern Germany, where, one observer noted, peasants were "not as well off as cattle elsewhere." Devastating French invasions of Germany during Queen Anne's War (1702–1713) made bad conditions worse and triggered the first large-scale migration. German immigrants included numerous artisans and a few merchants, but the great majority were farmers and laborers. Economically, they represented "middling" folk, neither the poorest (who could

not afford the trip) nor the better off (who did not want to leave).

By the 1720s, Germans who had established themselves in the colonies wrote back to their friends and relatives, as one reported, "of the civil and religious liberties [and] privileges, and of all the goodness I have heard and seen." Such letters prompted still more Germans to pull up stakes and embark for America, to exchange the miserable certainties of their lives in Europe for the uncertain attractions of life in the colonies.

Similar motives propelled the Scots-Irish, who considerably outnumbered German immigrants. The term *Scots-Irish* was another misleading label coined in the colonies. Immigrants labeled "Scots-Irish" actually hailed from the north of Ireland, Scotland, and northern England. Like the Germans, the Scots-Irish were Protestants, but with a difference. Most German immigrants worshipped in Lutheran or German Reformed churches; many others belonged to dissenting sects such as the Mennonites, Moravians, and Amish, whose adherents sought

German Hymnal
This manuscript hymnal contains words and music created by Johann Conrad Beissel, the founder of the Seventh-Day Baptists and among the earliest musical composers in the colonies. A German sect that migrated to Pennsylvania in 1732, the Seventh-Day Baptists, like many other German immigrants, continued to worship in their native German long after arriving in the British colonies. Once owned by Benjamin Franklin, this book expresses on its title page the hymns' evocation of the Seventh-Day Baptists' vision of this world and the next: "The Bitter good, or the song of the turtledove, the Christian church here on earth, in the valley of sadness, where it bemoans its 'widowhood'; and at the same time sings of another future reunion [with God]."
Roger Foley/Library of Congress.

relief from persecution they had suffered in Europe for their refusal to bear arms and to swear oaths, practices they shared with Quakers. In contrast, the Scots-Irish tended to be militant Presbyterians who seldom hesitated to bear arms or swear oaths. Like German settlers, however, Scots-Irish immigrants were clannish, residing when they could among relatives or neighbors from the old country.

In the eighteenth century, wave after wave of Scots-Irish immigrants arrived, beginning in 1717, cresting every twelve or fifteen years thereafter, and culminating in a flood of immigration in the years just before the American Revolution. Deteriorating economic conditions in northern Ireland, Scotland, and England pushed many toward America. Most of the immigrants were farm laborers or tenant farmers fleeing droughts, crop failures, high food prices, or rising rents. They came, they told British officials, because of "poverty," "tyranny of landlords," and the desire to "do better in America."

Both Scots-Irish and Germans probably heard the common saying that "Pennsylvania is heaven for farmers [and] paradise for artisans," but they almost certainly did not fully understand the risks of their decision to leave their native lands. Ship captains, aware of the hunger for labor in the colonies, eagerly signed up the penniless emigrants as "redemptioners," a variant of indentured servants. A captain would agree to provide transportation to Philadelphia, where redemptioners would obtain the money to pay for their passage by borrowing it from a friend or relative who was already in the colonies or, as most did, by selling themselves as servants. Impoverished Scots-Irish emigrants, especially the majority who traveled alone rather than with families, typically paid for their passage by contracting as indentured servants before they sailed to the colonies.

Redemptioners and indentured servants were packed aboard ships "as closely as herring," one migrant observed. Seasickness compounded by exhaustion, poverty, poor food, bad water, inadequate sanitation, and tight quarters encouraged the spread of disease. On the sixteen immigrant ships arriving in Philadelphia in 1738, over half the passengers died en route. When one ship finally approached land, a traveler wrote, "everyone crawls from below to the deck…and people cry for joy, pray, and sing praises and thanks to God." Unfortunately, their troubles were far from over. Redemptioners and indentured servants had to stay on board until somebody came to purchase their labor. Unlike indentured servants, redemptioners negotiated independently with their purchasers about their period of servitude. Typically, a healthy adult redemptioner agreed to four years of labor. Indentured servants commonly served five, six, or seven years.

Pennsylvania: "The Best Poor [White] Man's Country"

New settlers, whether free or in servitude, poured into the middle colonies because they perceived unparalleled opportunities, particularly in Pennsylvania, "the best poor Man's Country in the World," as an indentured servant wrote in 1743. Although the servant reported that "the Condition of bought Servants is very hard" and masters often failed to live up to their promise to provide decent food and clothing, opportunity abounded because there was more work to be done than workers to do it.

Most servants toiled in Philadelphia, New York City, or one of the smaller towns or villages. Artisans, small manufacturers, and shopkeepers prized the labor of male servants. Female servants made valuable additions to households, where nearly all of them cleaned, washed, cooked, or minded children. From the masters' viewpoint, servants were a bargain. A master could purchase five or six years of a servant's labor for approximately the wages a common laborer would earn in four months.

Since a slave cost at least three times as much as a servant, only affluent colonists could afford the long-term investment in slave labor. After Benjamin Franklin became prosperous, he purchased five slaves. But most farmers in the middle colonies used family labor, not slaves. Consequently, the population of African ancestry (almost all slaves) comprised only about 7 percent of the total population.

Enough slaves arrived to prompt colonial assemblies to pass laws that punished slaves much more severely than servants for the same transgressions. "For the least trespass," servant Moraley reported, slaves "undergo the severest Punishment." In practice, both servants and slaves were governed more by their masters than by the laws. But in cases of abuse, servants could and did charge masters with violating the terms of their indenture contracts. The terms of a slave's bondage were set forth in a master's commands, not in a written contract.

Small numbers of slaves managed to obtain their freedom, but free African Americans did not escape whites' firm convictions about black inferiority and white supremacy. Whites' racism and blacks' lowly social status made African Americans scapegoats for European Americans' suspicions and anxieties. In 1741, when arson and several unexplained thefts plagued New York City, officials suspected a murderous slave conspiracy. On the basis of little more than evidence of slaves' "insolence" (refusal to conform fully to whites' expectations of servile behavior), city authorities had thirteen slaves burned at the stake and eighteen others hanged. Although slaves were certifiably poor, they were not included among the poor for whom the middle colonies were reputed to be the best country in the world.

Immigrants swarmed to the middle colonies because of the availability of land. The Penn family encouraged immigration to bring in potential buyers for their enormous tracts of land in Pennsylvania. From the beginning, Pennsylvania followed a policy of negotiating with Indian tribes to purchase additional land. This policy reduced the violent frontier clashes more common elsewhere in the colonies.

The price of farmland depended on soil quality, access to water, distance from a market town, and the extent of improvements. One hundred acres of improved land that had been cleared, plowed, fenced, and ditched, and perhaps had a house and barn built on it, cost three or four times more than the same acreage of uncleared, unimproved land. Since the cheapest land always lay at the margin of settlement, would-be farmers tended to migrate to promising areas just beyond already improved farms. By mid-century, settlement had reached the eastern slopes of the Appalachian Mountains, and newcomers spilled south down the fertile valley of the Shenandoah River into western Virginia and the Carolinas. Thousands of settlers migrated from the middle colonies through this back door to the South.

Farmers made the middle colonies the breadbasket of North America. They planted a wide variety of crops to feed their families, but they grew wheat in abundance. Flour milling was the number-one industry and flour the number-one export, constituting nearly three-fourths of all exports from the middle colonies. Pennsylvania flour fed residents in other colonies, in southern Europe, and, above all, in the West Indies (see Map 5.2).

The standard of living in rural Pennsylvania was probably higher than in any other agricultural region of the eighteenth-century world. The comparatively widespread prosperity of all the middle colonies permitted residents to indulge in a half-century shopping spree for English imports. The middle colonies' per capita consumption of imported goods from England more than doubled between 1720 and 1770, far outstripping the per capita consumption of English goods in New England and the southern colonies.

At the crossroads of trade in wheat exports and English imports stood Philadelphia. By 1776, Philadelphia had a larger population than any other city in the entire British empire except London. Merchants occupied the top stratum of Philadelphia society. In a city where only 2 percent of the residents owned enough property to qualify to vote, merchants built grand homes and dominated local government. Many of Philadelphia's wealthiest merchants were Quakers. Quaker traits of industry, thrift, honesty, and sobriety encouraged the accumulation of wealth. A colonist complained that a Quaker "prays for his neighbor on First Days [the Sabbath] and then preys on him the other six."

The ranks of merchants reached downward to aspiring tradesmen like Benjamin Franklin. After he started to publish the *Pennsylvania Gazette* in 1728, Franklin opened a shop, run mostly by his wife, Deborah, that sold a little bit of everything: cheese, codfish, coffee, goose feathers, sealing wax, soap, and now and then a slave. In 1733, Franklin began to publish *Poor Richard's Almanack*, which preached the likelihood of long-term rewards for tireless labor. The *Almanack* sold thousands of copies, quickly becoming Franklin's most profitable product.

The popularity of *Poor Richard's Almanack* suggests that many Pennsylvanians thought less about the pearly gates than about their pocketbooks. Poor Richard's advice that "God

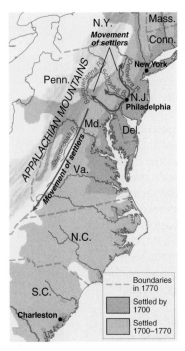

Patterns of Settlement, 1700–1770

Bethlehem, Pennsylvania

This view of the small community of Bethlehem, Pennsylvania, in 1757 dramatizes the profound transformation of the natural landscape wrought in the eighteenth century by highly motivated human labor. Founded
by Moravian immigrants in 1740, Bethlehem must have appeared at first like the dense woods on the upper
left horizon. In fewer than twenty years, precisely laid-out orchards and fields replaced forests and glades. By
carefully penning their livestock (lower center right) and fencing their fields (lower left), farmers safeguarded
their livelihoods from the risks and disorders of untamed nature. Individual farmsteads (lower center) and impressive multistory brick town buildings (upper center) integrated the bounty of the land with the delights of
community life. Few eighteenth-century communities were as orderly as Bethlehem, but many effected a comparable transformation of the environment.

Print Collection, Miriam and Ira D. Wallack Division of Art, Prints and Photographs, The New York Public Library. Astor, Lenox, and Tilden
Foundations.

FOR MORE HELP ANALYZING THIS IMAGE, see the visual activity for this chapter in the Online Study Guide at
bedfordstmartins.com/roarkcompact.

---

gives all Things to Industry" might be considered the motto for the middle colonies. The
promise of a worldly payoff made work a secular faith. Poor Richard advised, "Work as if you
were to live 100 years, Pray as if you were to die
Tomorrow."

William Penn's Quaker utopia became a
center of worldly affluence whose most famous
citizen, Franklin, was neither a Quaker nor a
utopian. Quakers remained influential, but
Franklin spoke for most colonists with his

aphorisms of work, discipline, and thrift that
echoed Quaker rules for outward behavior.
Franklin's maxims did not look to the Quakers'
divine inner light for guidance. They depended
instead on the spark of ambition and the glow
of gain.

> **REVIEW**   Why did German immigrants flood into
> Pennsylvania during the eighteenth century?

The Southern Colonies: Land of Slavery

Between 1700 and 1770, the population of the southern colonies of Virginia, Maryland, North Carolina, South Carolina, and Georgia grew almost ninefold. By 1770, about twice as many people lived in the South as in either the middle colonies or New England. As elsewhere, natural increase and immigration accounted for the rapid population growth. Many Scots-Irish and German immigrants funneled from the middle colonies into the southern backcountry. Other immigrants were indentured servants (mostly English and Scots-Irish) who followed their seventeenth-century predecessors. But slaves made the most striking contribution to the booming southern colonies, transforming the racial composition of the population. Slavery became the defining characteristic of the southern colonies during the eighteenth century, shaping the region's economy, society, and politics.

The Atlantic Slave Trade and the Growth of Slavery

The number of southerners of African ancestry (nearly all of them slaves) rocketed from just over 20,000 in 1700 to well over 400,000 in 1770. The black population increased nearly three times faster than the South's briskly growing white population. Consequently, the proportion of southerners who were black grew from 20 percent in 1700 to 40 percent in 1770.

Southern colonists clustered into two distinct geographic and agricultural zones. The colonies in the upper South, surrounding the Chesapeake Bay, specialized in growing tobacco, as they had since the early seventeenth century. Throughout the eighteenth century, nine out of ten southern whites and eight out of ten southern blacks lived in the Chesapeake region. The upper South retained a white majority during the eighteenth century.

In the lower South, a much smaller cluster of colonists inhabited the coastal region and specialized in the production of rice and indigo (a plant used to make blue dye). Lower South colonists made up only 5 percent of the total population of the southern colonies in 1700 but inched upward to 15 percent by 1770. South Carolina was the sole British colony along the southern Atlantic coast until 1732, when Georgia

was founded. (North Carolina, founded in 1711, was largely an extension of the Chesapeake region.) Blacks in South Carolina, in contrast to every other British mainland colony, outnumbered whites almost two to one; in some low-country districts, the ratio of blacks to whites exceeded ten to one.

The enormous growth in the South's slave population occurred through natural increase and the flourishing Atlantic slave trade (Map 5.3 and Table 5.1). Slave ships brought almost 300,000 Africans to British North America between 1619 and 1780. Of these Africans, 95 percent arrived in the South and 96 percent arrived during the eighteenth century. Unlike indentured servants or redemptioners, these Africans did not choose to come to the colonies. Most of them had been born into free families in villages located within a few hundred miles of the West African coast. Although they shared African origins, they came from many different African cultures, including Akan, Angolan, Asante, Bambara, Gambian, Igbo, Mandinga, and others.

The most important experience they had in common was enslavement. Captured in war, kidnapped, or sold into slavery by other Africans, they were brought to the coast, sold to African traders who assembled slaves for resale, and sold again to European or colonial slave traders or ship captains, who packed two to three hundred or more aboard ships that carried them on the **Middle Passage** across the Atlantic and then sold them yet again to a colonial slave merchant or a southern **planter**.

In 1789, Olaudah Equiano published an account of his own enslavement that hints at the stories that might have been told by the millions of other Africans swept up in the slave trade. Equiano was born in 1745 in the interior of what is now Nigeria. "I had never heard of white men or Europeans, nor of the sea," he recalled. One

TABLE 5.1	SLAVE IMPORTS, 1451–1870
Estimated Slave Imports to the Western Hemisphere	
1451–1600	275,000
1601–1700	1,341,000
1701–1810	6,100,000
1811–1870	1,900,000

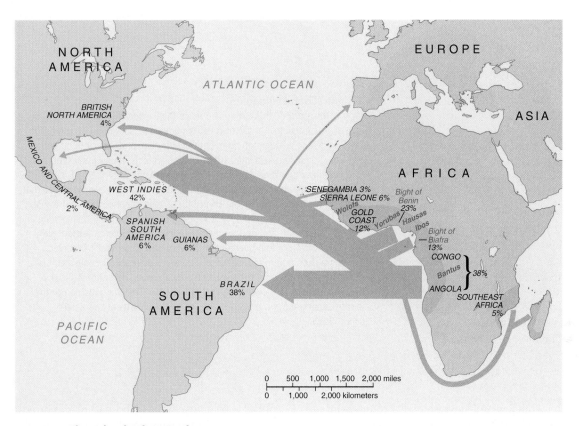

MAP 5.3   The Atlantic Slave Trade

Although the Atlantic slave trade lasted from about 1450 to 1870, its peak occurred during the eighteenth century, when more than six million African slaves were imported to the New World. Only a small fraction of the African slaves imported to the Western Hemisphere were taken to British North America; most went to sugar plantations in Brazil and the Caribbean.

READING THE MAP: From where in Africa did most slaves originate? Approximately how far was the trip from the busiest ports of origin to the two most common New World destinations?

CONNECTIONS: Why were so many more African slaves sent to the West Indies and Brazil than to British North America?

FOR MORE HELP ANALYZING THIS MAP, see the map activity for this chapter in the Online Study Guide at bedfordstmartins.com/roarkcompact.

day when Equiano was eleven years old, he was kidnapped by Africans, who sold him to other Africans, who in turn eventually sold him to a slave ship on the coast. Equiano feared he would be "eaten by those white men with horrible looks." Once the ship set sail, many slaves died from sickness, crowded together in suffocating heat fouled by filth of all descriptions. "The shrieks of the women and the groans of the dying rendered the whole a scene of horror almost inconceivable," Equiano recalled. Most of the slaves on the ship were sold in Barbados, but Equiano and other leftovers were shipped off to Virginia, where Equiano "saw few or none of our native Africans and not one soul who could talk to me."

Only about 15 percent of the slaves brought into the southern colonies came as Equiano did, aboard ships from the West Indies. All the other slaves brought into the southern colonies came directly from Africa, and almost all the ships that brought them (roughly 90 percent) belonged to British merchants. Most slaves on board were young adults, men usually outnumbering women two to one. Children under the age of fourteen, like Equiano, were typically no more than 10 or 15 percent of a cargo.

Mortality during the Middle Passage varied considerably from ship to ship. On average, about 15 percent of the slaves died, but sometimes half or more perished. The average mortality among

Olaudah Equiano
This portrait shows Equiano more than a decade after he had bought his freedom. The portrait evokes Equiano's successful acculturation to the customs of eighteenth-century England. His clothing and hairstyle reflect the fashions of respectable young Englishmen. In his *Interesting Narrative,* Equiano explained that he had learned to speak and understand English while he was a slave. He wrote that he "looked upon [the English]…as men superior to us [Africans], and therefore I had the stronger desire to resemble them, to imbibe their spirit and imitate their manners; I therefore embraced every occasion of improvement, and every new thing that I observed I treasured up in my memory." Equiano's embrace of English culture did not cause him to forsake his African roots. He honored his dual identity by campaigning against slavery. His *Narrative* was one of the most important and powerful antislavery documents of the time.
Library of Congress.

the white crew of slave ships was often nearly as bad. In general, the longer the voyage lasted, the larger was the number of deaths.

Normally an individual planter purchased at any one time a relatively small number of newly arrived Africans, or "new Negroes," as they were called. Planters preferred to purchase small groups of slaves to permit their other slaves—either those born into slavery in the colonies (often called "country-born" or "creole" slaves) or Africans who had arrived earlier—to help new Negroes become accustomed to their strange new surroundings.

Planters' preferences for slaves from specific regions of Africa aided slaves' acculturation (or "seasoning," as it was called) to the routines of bondage in the southern colonies. Chesapeake planters preferred slaves from Senegambia, the Gold Coast, or—like Equiano—the Bight of Biafra, the origin of 40 percent of all Africans imported to the Chesapeake. South Carolina planters favored slaves from the central African Congo and Angola regions, the origin of about 40 percent of the African slaves they imported (see Map 5.3). Although slaves within each of these regions spoke many different languages, enough linguistic and cultural similarities existed that they could usually communicate with other Africans from the same region.

Seasoning acclimated new Africans to the physical as well as the cultural environment of the

southern colonies. Slaves who had just endured the Middle Passage were poorly nourished, weak, and sick. In this vulnerable state they encountered the alien diseases of North America without having developed a biological arsenal of acquired immunities. As many as 10 or 15 percent of newly arrived Africans, sometimes more, died during their first year in the southern colonies.

While newly enslaved Africans poured into the southern colonies, slave mothers birthed babies who caused the slave population in the South to grow rapidly. Slave owners encouraged these births. Thomas Jefferson explained, "I consider the labor of a breeding [slave] woman as no object, that a [slave] child raised every 2 years is of more profit than the crop of the best laboring [slave] man." The growing number of slave babies set the southern colonies apart from other New World slave societies, which experienced a natural decrease of the slave population (slave deaths exceeded births). The high rate of natural increase in the southern colonies meant that by the 1740s the majority of southern slaves were country-born.

Slave Labor and African American Culture

Southern planters expected slaves to work from sunup to sundown and beyond. George Washington wrote that his slaves should "be at their work as soon as it is light, work til it is dark,

The African Slave Trade

The African slave trade existed to satisfy the New World's demand for labor and Europe's voracious appetite for such New World products as sugar, tobacco, and rice. African men, women, and children were kidnapped or captured in wars—typically by other Africans—and enslaved. Uprooted from their homes and kin, they were usually taken to coastal enclaves where African traders and European ship captains negotiated prices, made deals, and often branded the newly enslaved people. The collaboration between Europeans and their African trading partners is evident in the seventeenth-century Benin bronze box in the shape of a royal palace in Nigeria guarded by massive predatory birds and two Portuguese soldiers. Jammed into the holds of slave ships, enslaved Africans made the dreaded Middle Passage to the New World. The model of a slave ship shown here was used in parliamentary debates by antislavery leaders in Britain to demonstrate the inhumanity of shipping people as if they were just so much tightly packed cargo. The model does not show another typical feature of slave ships: weapons. Slaves vastly outnumbered the crews aboard the ships, and crew members justifiably feared slave uprisings.

Benin bronze box: Staatliche Museen Zu Berlin, Preussischer Kulturbesitz; slave ship model: Wilberforce House, Hull City Museums and Art Galleries, UK/Bridgeman Art Library.

and be diligent while they are at it." The conflict between the masters' desire for maximum labor and the slaves' reluctance to do more than necessary made the threat of physical punishment a constant for eighteenth-century slaves. Masters preferred black slaves to white indentured servants, not just because slaves served for life but also because colonial laws did not limit the force masters could use against slaves. As a traveler observed in 1740, "A new negro…[will] let a hundred men show him how to hoe, or drive a wheelbarrow; he'll still take the one by the bottom and the other by the wheel and…often die before [he] can be conquered." Slaves, the traveler noted, resisted their masters' demands because of their "greatness of soul," their stubborn unwillingness to conform to their masters' definition of them as merely slaves.

Some slaves escalated their acts of resistance to direct physical confrontation with the master,

the mistress, or an overseer. But a hoe raised in anger, a punch in the face, or a desperate swipe with a knife led to swift and predictable retaliation by whites. Throughout the southern colonies, the balance of physical power rested securely in the hands of whites.

Rebellion occurred, however, at Stono, South Carolina, in 1739. Before dawn on a September Sunday, a group of about twenty slaves attacked a country store, killed the two storekeepers, and confiscated the store's guns, ammunition, and powder. Enticing other rebel slaves to join, the group plundered and burned more than a half dozen plantations and killed more than twenty white men, women, and children. A mounted force of whites quickly suppressed the rebellion. The Stono rebellion illustrated that eighteenth-century slaves had no chance of overturning slavery and very little chance of defending themselves in any bold strike for freedom.

Slaves maneuvered constantly to protect themselves and to gain a measure of autonomy within the boundaries of slavery. In Chesapeake tobacco fields, most slaves were subject to close supervision by whites. In the lower South, the task system gave slaves some control over the pace of their work and some discretion in the use of the rest of their time. A "task" was typically defined as a certain area of ground to be cultivated or a specific job to be completed. A slave who completed the assigned task might use the remainder of the day, if any, to work in a garden, fish, hunt, spin, weave, sew, or cook.

Eighteenth-century slaves also planted the roots of African American lineages that branch out to the present. Slaves valued family ties and, as in West African societies, kinship structured slaves' relations with one another. Newly imported African slaves usually arrived alone, like Equiano, without kin. Often slaves who had traversed the Middle Passage on the same ship adopted one another as "brothers" and "sisters." Likewise, as new Negroes were seasoned and incorporated into existing slave communities, established families often adopted them as "fictive" kin.

When possible, slaves expressed many other features of their West African origins in their lives on New World plantations. They gave their children traditional dolls and African names such as Cudjo or Quash, Minda or Fuladi. They grew food crops they had known in Africa, such as yams and okra. They constructed huts with mud walls and thatched roofs similar to African residences. They fashioned banjos, drums, and other musical instruments, held dances, and observed funeral rites that echoed African practices. In these and many other ways, slaves drew upon their African heritages as much as the oppressive circumstances of slavery permitted.

Tobacco, Rice, and Prosperity

Slaves' labor bestowed prosperity on their masters, British merchants, and the monarchy. The southern colonies supplied 90 percent of all North American exports to England. Rice exports from the lower South exploded from less than half a million pounds in 1700 to eighty million pounds in 1770, nearly all of it grown by slaves. Exports of indigo also boomed. Together, rice and indigo made up three-fourths of lower South exports, nearly two-thirds of them going

to England and most of the rest to the West Indies, where sugar-growing slaves ate slave-grown rice. Tobacco was by far the most important export from British North America; by 1770, it represented almost one-third of all colonial exports and three-fourths of all Chesapeake exports. And under the provisions of the Navigation Acts (see chapter 4), nearly all of it went to England, where the monarchy collected a lucrative tax on each pound. British merchants then reexported more than 80 percent of the tobacco to the European continent, pocketing a nice markup for their troubles.

These products of slave labor made the southern colonies by far the richest in North America. The per capita wealth of free whites in the South was four times greater than that in New England and three times that in the middle colonies. At the top of the wealth pyramid stood the rice grandees of the lower South and the tobacco gentry of the Chesapeake. These elite families commonly resided on large estates in handsome mansions adorned by luxurious gardens, maintained and supported by slaves.

The vast differences in wealth among white southerners engendered envy and occasional tension between rich and poor, but remarkably little open hostility. In private, the planter elite spoke disparagingly of humble whites but in public acknowledged their lesser neighbors as equals, at least in belonging to the superior — in their minds — white race. Looking upward, white **yeomen** and tenants (who owned neither land nor slaves) sensed the gentry's condescension and veiled contempt. But they also appreciated the gentry for granting favors, upholding white supremacy, and keeping slaves in their place. While racial slavery made a few whites much richer than others, it also gave those who did not get rich a powerful reason to feel similar (in race) to those who were so different (in wealth).

The slaveholding gentry dominated the politics and economy of the southern colonies. In Virginia, only adult white men who owned at least one hundred acres of unimproved land or twenty-five acres of land with a house could vote. This property-holding requirement prevented about 40 percent of white men in Virginia from voting for representatives to the House of Burgesses. In South Carolina, only fifty acres of land were required to vote, and most adult white men qualified. But in both colonies, voters elected members of the gentry to serve in the colonial legislature. The gentry passed elected political offices from generation to generation, almost as if they were hereditary. Politically, the gentry built a self-perpetuating oligarchy—rule by the elite few—with the votes of their many humble neighbors.

The gentry also set the cultural standard in the southern colonies. They entertained lavishly, gambled regularly, and attended Anglican (Church of England) services more for social than for religious reasons. Above all, they cultivated the leisurely pursuit of happiness. They did not condone idleness, however. Their many pleasures and responsibilities as plantation owners kept them busy. Thomas Jefferson, a phenomenally productive member of the gentry, recalled that his earliest childhood memory was of being carried on a pillow by a family slave—a powerful image of the slave hands supporting the gentry's leisure and achievement.

REVIEW Why did the Stono rebellion fail?

Unifying Experiences

While the societies of New England, the middle colonies, and the southern colonies became more sharply differentiated during the eighteenth century, colonists throughout British North America shared certain unifying experiences that eluded settlers in Spanish and French colonies. The first was economic. Colonists sold their distinctive products in markets that, in turn, offered to consumers throughout British North America a more or less uniform array of goods. A second unifying experience was a decline in the importance of religion. Some settlers called for a revival of religious intensity, but most people focused less on religion and more on the affairs of the world than they had in the seventeenth century. Third, white inhabitants throughout British North America became aware that they shared a distinctive identity as British colonists. Royal officials who expected loyalty from the colonists often had difficulty obtaining obedience. The British colonists asserted their prerogatives as British subjects to defend their special colonial interests.

Commerce and Consumption

Eighteenth-century commerce whetted the appetite to consume. Colonial products spurred the development of mass markets throughout the Atlantic world (Figure 5.1). Huge increases in the supply of colonial tobacco and sugar brought the price of these small luxuries within reach of most free whites. Colonial goods brought into focus an important lesson of eighteenth-century commerce: Ordinary people, not just the wealthy elite, would buy the things that they desired in addition to what they absolutely needed. Even news, formerly restricted mostly to a few people through face-to-face conversations or private letters, became an object of public consumption through the innovation of newspapers. With the appropriate stimulus, market demand seemed unlimited.

The Atlantic commerce that took colonial goods to markets in England brought objects of consumer desire back to the colonies. English merchants and manufacturers recognized that colonists made excellent customers, and the Navigation Acts gave English exporters privileged access to the colonial market. Most English exports went to the vast European market, where potential customers outnumbered those in the colonies by more than one hundred to one. But as European competition stiffened, colonial markets became increasingly important. English exports to North America multiplied eightfold between 1700 and 1770, outpacing the rate of population growth after midcentury (see Figure 5.1). When the colonists' eagerness to consume exceeded their ability to pay, English exporters willingly extended credit, and colonial debts soared.

Imported mirrors, silver plate, spices, bed and table linens, clocks, tea services, wigs, books, and more infiltrated parlors, kitchens, and bedrooms throughout the colonies. Despite the many differences among the colonists, the consumption of English exports built a certain material uniformity across region, religion, class, and status. Consumption of English exports made the colonists look and feel more British even though they lived at the edge of a wilderness an ocean away from England.

The rising tide of colonial consumption had other less visible but no less important consequences. Consumption presented women and men with a novel array of choices. In many respects, the choices might appear trivial: whether to buy knives and forks, teacups, or a clock. But such small choices confronted eighteenth-century consumers with a big question: "What do you want?" As colonial consumers defined and expressed their desires with greater frequency during the eighteenth century, they became accustomed to thinking of themselves as individuals who had the power to make decisions that influenced the quality of their lives—attitudes

FIGURE 5.1
Colonial Exports, 1768–1772

These pie charts provide an overview of the colonial export economy in the 1760s. The first two show that almost two-thirds of colonial exports came from the South and that the majority of the colonies' exports went to Great Britain. The remaining charts illustrate the distinctive patterns of exports in each colonial region. Fish, livestock, and wood products were New England's most important exports; they were sent primarily to the West Indies, only a small fraction going to Great Britain. From the colonial breadbasket in the middle colonies, grain products made up three-fourths of all exports, most of which went to the West Indies or to southern Europe. The Chesapeake also exported some grain, but tobacco accounted for three-fourths of the region's export trade, nearly all of it bound for Great Britain as mandated by the Navigation Acts. Rice and indigo comprised three-fourths of the exports from the lower South, the bulk of which was sent to Great Britain. Taken together, these charts reveal Britain's economic interest in the exports of the North American colonies.

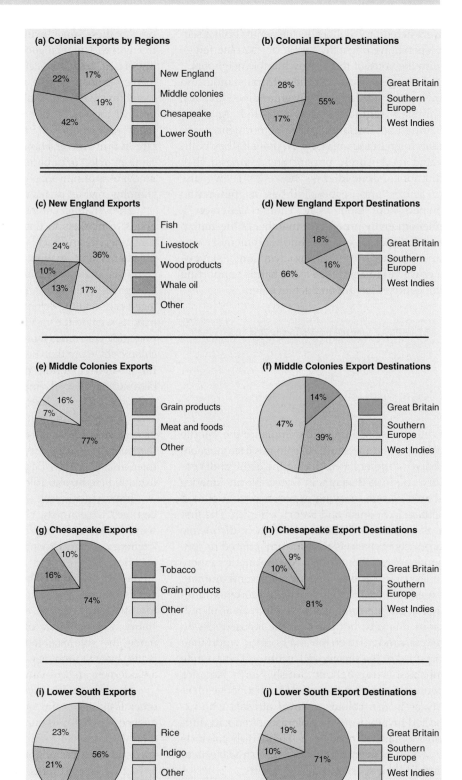

(a) Colonial Exports by Regions
- 17% — New England
- 19% — Middle colonies
- 22%
- 42% — Lower South
- Chesapeake

(b) Colonial Export Destinations
- 55% — Great Britain
- 28%
- 17% — Southern Europe
- West Indies

(c) New England Exports
- 36% — Fish
- 17%
- 13%
- 10%
- 24% — Livestock, Wood products, Whale oil, Other

(d) New England Export Destinations
- 18% — Great Britain
- 16% — Southern Europe
- 66% — West Indies

(e) Middle Colonies Exports
- 16%
- 7%
- 77% — Grain products, Meat and foods, Other

(f) Middle Colonies Export Destinations
- 14% — Great Britain
- 39% — Southern Europe
- 47% — West Indies

(g) Chesapeake Exports
- 10%
- 16%
- 74% — Tobacco, Grain products, Other

(h) Chesapeake Export Destinations
- 9%
- 10%
- 81% — Great Britain, Southern Europe, West Indies

(i) Lower South Exports
- 23%
- 21%
- 56% — Rice, Indigo, Other

(j) Lower South Export Destinations
- 19%
- 10%
- 71% — Great Britain, Southern Europe, West Indies

of significance in the hierarchical world of eighteenth-century British North America.

Religion, Enlightenment, and Revival

Eighteenth-century colonists could choose from almost as many religions as consumer goods. Virtually all of the bewildering variety of religious denominations represented some form of Christianity, almost all of them Protestant. Slaves made up the largest group of non-Christians. A few slaves converted to Christianity in Africa or after they arrived in North America, but most continued to embrace elements of indigenous African religions. Roman Catholics concentrated in Maryland as they had since the seventeenth century, but even there they were outnumbered by Protestants.

The varieties of Protestant faith and practice ranged across a broad spectrum. The middle colonies and the southern backcountry included militant Baptists and Presbyterians. In New England, old-style Puritanism splintered into strands of Congregationalism that differed over fine points of theological doctrine. The Congregational Church was the official established church in New England, and all residents paid taxes for its support. Throughout the plantation South and in urban centers like Charleston, New York, and Philadelphia, prominent colonists belonged to the Anglican Church, which received tax support in the South. But dissenting faiths grew everywhere, and in most colonies their adherents won the right to worship publicly, although the established churches retained official support.

Many educated colonists became deists, looking for God's plan in nature more than in the Bible. Deists shared the ideas of eighteenth-century European **Enlightenment** thinkers who tended to agree that science and reason could disclose God's laws in the natural order. In the colonies as well as in Europe, Enlightenment ideas encouraged people to study the world around them, to think for themselves, and to ask whether the disorderly appearance of things masked the principles of a deeper, more profound natural order. The American Philosophical Society, founded in 1769, fostered communication among leading colonial thinkers; Benjamin Franklin was its first president. Franklin's interest in electricity, stoves, and eyeglasses exemplified the shift of focus among many eighteenth-century colonists from heaven to the here and now.

Most eighteenth-century colonists went to church seldom or not at all, although they probably considered themselves Christians. In the leading colonial cities, church members were a small minority of eligible adults, no more than 10 to 15 percent. Anglican parishes in the South rarely claimed more than one-fifth of eligible adults as members. In some regions of rural New England and the middle colonies, church membership embraced two-thirds of eligible adults, while in other areas only one-quarter of the residents belonged to a church. As a late-eighteenth-century traveler observed, "Religious indifference is imperceptibly disseminated from one end of the continent to the other."

The spread of religious indifference, of deism, of denominational rivalry, and of comfortable backsliding profoundly concerned many Christians. A few despaired that, as one wrote, "religion…lay a-dying and ready to expire its last breath of life." Some ministers set out to convert nonbelievers and to revive the piety of the faithful with a new style of preaching that appealed more to the heart than to the head. Historians have termed this wave of revivals the **Great Awakening**. In Massachusetts during the mid-1730s, the fiery Puritan minister Jonathan Edwards reaped a harvest of souls by reemphasizing traditional Puritan doctrines of humanity's utter depravity and God's vengeful omnipotence. The title of Edwards's most famous sermon, "Sinners in the Hands of an Angry God," conveys the flavor of his message. In Pennsylvania and New Jersey, William Tennent led revivals that dramatized spiritual rebirth with accounts of God's miraculous powers, such as raising Tennent's son from the dead.

The most famous revivalist in the eighteenth-century Atlantic world was George Whitefield. An Anglican, Whitefield preached well-worn messages of sin and salvation to large audiences in England using his spellbinding, unforgettable voice. Whitefield visited the North American colonies seven times, staying for more than three years during the mid-1740s and attracting tens of thousands to his sermons, including Benjamin Franklin. Whitefield's preaching transported many in his audience to emotion-choked states of religious ecstasy.

The revivals awakened and refreshed the spiritual energies of thousands of colonists struggling with the uncertainties and anxieties of eighteenth-century America. The revivals communicated that every soul mattered, that men and women could choose to be saved, that individuals had

George Whitefield

An anonymous artist portrayed George Whitefield preaching, emphasizing the power of his sermons to transport his audience to a revived awareness of divine spirituality. Light from above gleams off Whitefield's forehead. His crossed eyes and faraway gaze suggest that he spoke in a semihypnotic trance. Notice the absence of a Bible at the pulpit. Rather than elaborating on God's word as revealed in Scripture, Whitefield speaks from his own inner awareness. The young woman bathed in light below his hands appears transfixed, her focus not on Whitefield but on some inner realm illuminated by his words. Her eyes and Whitefield's do not meet, yet the artist's use of light suggests that she and Whitefield see the same core of holy Truth. The other people in Whitefield's audience appear not to have achieved this state. They remain intent on Whitefield's words, failing so far to be ignited by the divine spark.

National Portrait Gallery, London.

revivalists as "Pedlars in divinity." Like consumption, revivals contributed to a set of common experiences that bridged colonial divides of faith, region, class, and status.

> **REVIEW** Why did religious revivals flourish during the 1730s and 1740s?

Bonds of the British Empire

The plurality of peoples, faiths, and communities that characterized the North American colonies arose from the somewhat haphazard policies of the eighteenth-century British empire. Since the mid-seventeenth century, British monarchs had valued the colonies' contributions to trade and encouraged their growth and development. Unlike Spain and France—whose policies of excluding Protestants and foreigners kept the population of their North American colonial territories tiny—Britain kept the door to its colonies open to anyone, and tens of thousands of non-British immigrants settled in the North American colonies and raised families. The open door did not extend to trade, however, as the seventeenth-century Navigation Acts restricted colonial trade to British ships and traders. These policies evolved because they served the interests of the monarchy and of influential groups in England and the colonies. The policies also gave the colonists a common framework of political expectations and experiences.

At a minimum, British power defended the colonists from foreign enemies. Each colony organized a militia, but the British navy and army bore responsibility for colonial defense. Royal officials warily eyed the small North American settlements of New France and New Spain for signs of threats to the colonies. Alone, neither New France nor New Spain jeopardized British North America, but with Indian allies they could become a potent force that kept colonists on their guard.

the power to make a decision for everlasting life or death. Colonial revivals expressed in religious terms many of the same democratic and egalitarian values expressed in economic terms by colonists' patterns of consumption. One colonist noted the analogy by referring to itinerant

Defending the Borderlands of Empire: Indians and French and Spanish Outposts

All along the ragged edge of settlement, colonists encountered Indians. Native Americans' impulse to defend their territory from colonial incursions warred with their desire for trade, which tugged them toward the settlers. As a colonial official observed in 1761, "A modern Indian cannot subsist without Europeans…[the European goods that were] only conveniency at first [are] now become necessity." To obtain such necessities as guns, ammunition, clothing, sewing utensils, and much more that was manufactured largely by the British, Indians trapped beaver, deer, and other fur-bearing animals throughout the interior.

Colonial traders and their respective empires competed to control the fur trade (Map 5.4). British, French, Spanish, and Dutch officials monitored the trade to prevent their competitors from deflecting the flow of furs toward their own markets. Indians took advantage of this competition to improve their own prospects, playing one trader and empire off against another. Indian tribes and confederacies also competed among themselves for favored trading rights with one colony or another, a competition colonists encouraged.

The shifting alliances and complex dynamics of the fur trade struck a fragile balance along the frontier. The threat of violence from all sides was ever present, and the threat became reality often enough for all parties to be prepared for the worst. In the Yamasee War of 1715, Yamasee and Creek Indians—with French encouragement—mounted a coordinated attack against colonial settlements in South Carolina and inflicted heavy casualties. The Cherokees, traditional enemies of the Creeks, refused to join the attack. Instead, they protected their access to British trade goods by allying with the colonists and turning the tide of battle, thus triggering a murderous rampage of revenge by the colonists against the Creeks and Yamasees.

Relations between Indians and the colonists differed from colony to colony and from year to year. But the colonists' nagging perceptions of menace on the frontier kept them continually hoping for help from the British in keeping the Indians at bay and in maintaining the essential flow of trade. In 1754, the colonists' endemic competition with the French flared into the Seven Years' War (also known as the French and Indian War), which would inflame the frontier for years (see chapter 6). Before the 1760s, neither the colonists nor the British developed a coherent policy toward Indians. But both agreed that Indians made deadly enemies, profitable trading partners, and powerful allies. As a result, the British and the colonists kept an eye on the Spanish empire to the west and relations with the Indians there.

Indians' potential as allies prompted officials in New Spain to mount a campaign to block Russian access to present-day California by building forts (called *presidios*) and missions. Russian hunters in search of seals and sea otters ventured along the California coast and threatened to become a permanent presence on New Spain's northern frontier.

In 1769, an expedition headed by a military man, Gaspar de Portolá, and a Catholic priest, Junípero Serra, traveled north from Mexico to present-day San Diego, where they founded the first California mission, San Diego de Alcalá. They soon journeyed all the way to Monterey, which became the capital of Spanish California. There Portolá established a presidio in 1770 "to defend us from attacks by the Russians," he wrote. By 1772, Serra had founded other missions along the path from San Diego to Monterey.

For Indians, the Spaniards' California missions had horrendous consequences, as they had elsewhere in the Spanish borderlands. European diseases decimated Indian populations, Spanish soldiers raped Indian women, and missionaries beat Indians and subjected them to near slavery. Indian uprisings against the Spaniards occurred repeatedly (see "Documenting the American Promise," page 124), but the presidios and missions endured as feeble projections of the Spanish empire along the Pacific coast.

Spanish Missions in California

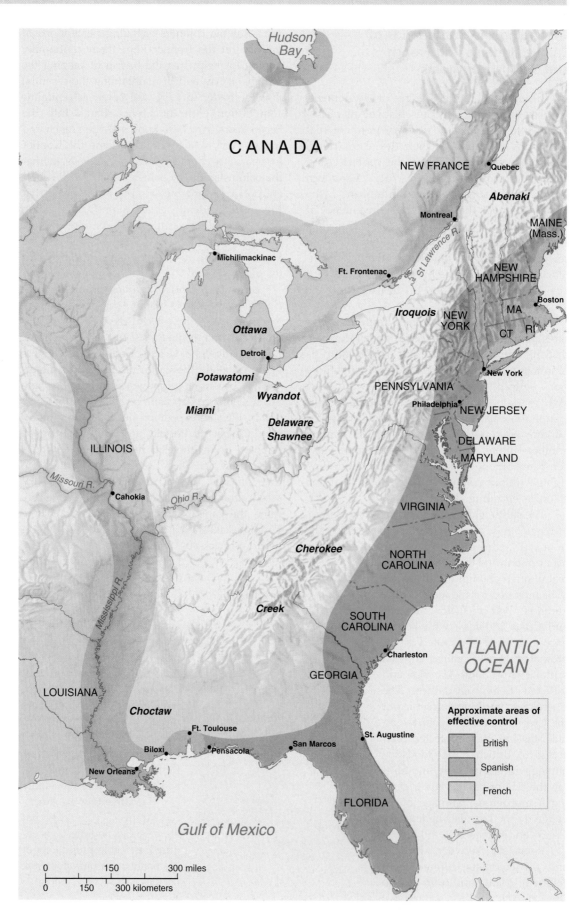

Monterey Presidio

This eighteenth-century portrait of the Monterey Presidio illustrates the military significance of the Spanish outposts in California. The walled enclosure and proximity to the bay (in the background) served defensive purposes, principally against Russian expansion but also against British and French interlopers. The Indian men and women working in the fields and hanging out laundry served to support the soldiers in the presidio. Notice that no Spaniard is pictured at work. At Monterey and elsewhere in Spanish California, the presidios and missions focused on maintaining outposts of empire rather than on developing booming settlements or producing goods for export.
University of California at Berkeley, Bancroft Library.

Colonial Politics in the British Empire

British attempts to exercise political power in their colonial governments met with success so long as British officials were on or very near the sea. Colonists acknowledged—although they did not always readily comply with—British authority to collect customs duties, inspect cargoes, and enforce trade regulations. But when royal officials tried to wield their authority on land, in the internal affairs of colonies, they invariably encountered colonial resistance. A governor appointed by the king in each of the nine royal colonies (Rhode Island and Connecticut selected their own governors) or by the proprietors in Maryland and Pennsylvania headed the government of each colony. The British envisioned colonial governors as mini-monarchs able to exert influence in the colonies much as the king did in England. But colonial governors were not kings, and the colonies were not England.

◀ **MAP 5.4   Zones of Empire in Eastern North America**
British colonies extending westward from the Atlantic coast were much more densely settled than the zones under French, Spanish, or Indian control. The comparatively large number of settlers made British colonists more secure than the relatively few colonists in the vast regions claimed by France and Spain or settlers among the many Indian peoples in the huge area between the Mississippi River and the Appalachian Mountains. Yet British colonists were not powerful enough to dominate the French, Spanish, or Indians. Instead, British colonists had to guard against powerful Indian groups who allied with either the French or the Spanish, since such alliances threatened settlers in the region under British control.

Missionaries Report on California Missions

Catholic missionaries sent regular reports to their superiors in Mexico City, New Spain's capital city. The reports described what the missionaries considered their successes in converting pagan Indians—whom they called gentiles—as well as the difficulties caused by the behavior of both Spaniards and Indians.

DOCUMENT 1
Father Luis Jayme
Describes Conditions
at Mission San Diego
de Alcalá, 1772

Father Luis Jayme, a Franciscan missionary, reported on the deplorable behavior of some of the Spanish soldiers at Mission San Diego, who frequently raped Indian women, causing many Indians to resist the efforts of the missionaries.

With reference to the Indians, I wish to say that great progress [in converting Indians] would be made if there was anything to eat and the soldiers would set a good example. We cannot give them anything to eat because what Don Pedro [the governor] has given is not enough to last half a year for the Indians from the Californias who are here. Thus little progress will be made under present conditions. As for the example set by the soldiers, no doubt some of them are good exemplars and deserve to be treated accordingly, but very many of them deserve to be hanged on account of the continuous outrages which they are committing in seizing and raping the women. There is not a single mission where all the gentiles have not been scandalized, and even on the roads, so I have been told. Surely, as the gentiles themselves state, they [the soldiers] are committing a thousand evils, particularly of a sexual nature....

At one of these Indian villages near this mission of San Diego, which said village is very large, and which is on the road to Monterey, the gentiles therein many times have been on the point of coming here to kill us all, and the reason for this is that some soldiers went there and raped their women, and other soldiers who were carrying the mail to Monterey turned their animals into their fields and they ate up their crops. Three other Indian villages...[near] here have reported the same thing to me several times. For this reason on several occasions when...I have gone to see these Indian villages, as soon as they saw us they fled from their villages and fled to the woods or other remote places....They do this so that the soldiers will not rape their women as they have already done so many times in the past.

No wonder the Indians here were bad when the mission was first founded. To begin with, they did not know why [the Spaniards] had come, unless they wanted to take their lands away from them. Now they all want to be Christians because they know that there is a God who created the heavens and earth and all things, that there is a Hell and Glory, that they have souls, etc., but when the mission was first founded...they thought they were like animals, and ...they were very loath to pray, and they did not want to be Christians at all....[Now] they all know the natural law, which, so I am informed, they have observed as well or better than many Christians elsewhere. They do not have idols; they do not go on drinking sprees; they do not marry relatives; and they have but one wife. The married men sleep with their wives only....Some of the first adults whom we baptized, when we pointed out to them that it was wrong to have sexual intercourse with a woman to whom they were not married, told me that they already knew that, and that among them it was considered to be very bad, and so they do not do so at all. "The soldiers," they told me, "are Christians and, although they know that God will punish them in Hell, do so, having sexual intercourse

Eighty percent of colonial governors had been born in England, not in the colonies. Some governors stayed in England, close to the source of royal patronage, and delegated the grubby details of colonial affairs to subordinates. Even the best-intentioned colonial governors had difficulty developing relations of trust and respect with influential colonists because their terms of office averaged just five years and could be terminated at any time. In obedience to England, colonial with our wives." "We," they said, "although we did not know that God would punish us for that in Hell, considered it to be very bad, and we did not do it, and even less now that we know that God will punish us if we do so." When I heard this, I burst into tears to see how these gentiles were setting an example for us Christians.

DOCUMENT 2
Father Junípero Serra Describes the Indian Revolt at Mission San Diego de Alcalá, 1775

Father Junípero Serra, the founder of many of the California missions, reported to his superiors in Mexico City that an Indian uprising had destroyed Mission San Diego. He recommended rebuilding and urged officials to provide additional soldiers to defend the missions, but not to punish the rebellious Indians.

As we are in the vale of tears, not all the news I have to relate can be pleasant. And so I make no excuses for announcing…the tragic news that I have just received of the total destruction of the San Diego Mission, and of the death of the senior of its two religious ministers, called Father Luis Jayme, at the hand of the rebellious gentiles and of the Christian neophytes [Indians who lived in the mission]. All this happened, November 5th, about one or two o'clock at night. The gentiles came together from forty rancherías, according to information given me,

and set fire to the church, after sacking it. They then went to the storehouse, the house where the Fathers lived, the soldiers' barracks, and all the rest of the buildings. They killed a carpenter…and a blacksmith…. They wounded with their arrows the four soldiers, who alone were on guard at the…mission….

And now, after the Father has been killed, the Mission burned, its many and valuable furnishings destroyed, together with the sacred vessels, its paintings, its baptismal, marriage, and funeral records, and all the furnishings for the sacristy, the house, and the farm implements—now the forces [of soldiers] of both presidios [nearby] come together to set things right…. What happened was that before they set about reestablishing the Mission, they wanted to…lay hands on the guilty ones who were responsible for the burning of the Mission, and the death of the Fathers, and chastise them. The harassed Indians rebelled anew and became more enraged….And so the soldiers there are gathered together in their presidios, and the Indians in their state of heathenism….

While the missionary is alive, let the soldiers guard him, and watch over him, like the pupils of God's very eyes. That is as it should be…. But after the missionary has been killed, what can be gained by campaigns [against the rebellious Indians]? Some will say to frighten them and prevent them from killing others. What I say is that, in order to

prevent them from killing others, keep better guard over them than they did over the one who has been killed; and, as to the murderer, let him live, in order that he should be saved—which is the very purpose of our coming here, and the reason which justifies it.

SOURCES: Maynard Geiger, trans. and ed., *Letter of Luís Jayme, O.F.M.: San Diego, October 17, 1772* (Los Angeles, 1970), 38–42. Antonine Tibesar, O.F.M., ed., *The Writings of Junípero Serra.* © 1956. Reprinted by permission of the American Academy of Franciscan History.

QUESTIONS FOR ANALYSIS AND DEBATE

1. In what ways did Jayme and Serra agree about the motivations of Indians in and around Mission San Diego? In what ways did they disagree? How would Serra's recommendations for rebuilding the mission address the problems identified by Jayme that caused the revolt?

2. How did the goals and activities of the Spanish soldiers compare with those of the Catholic missionaries? What accounts for the differences and similarities?

3. How did the religious convictions of Jayme and Serra influence their reports? What might Spanish soldiers or Indians have said about these events? What might they have said about missionaries like Jayme and Serra?

governors fought incessantly with the colonial assemblies. They battled over governors' vetoes of colonial legislation, removal of colonial judges, creation of new courts, dismissal of the representative assemblies, and other local issues. Some

governors developed a working relationship with the assemblies. But during the eighteenth century, the assemblies gained the upper hand.

Since British policies did not clearly define the powers of colonial assemblies, they made

Ambush of Spanish Expedition
This detail from a remarkable hide painting depicts an ambush of a Spanish expedition by French soldiers and their Pawnee and Oto allies in August 1720. Two and a half months earlier, the governor of New Mexico had sent forty-three Spanish soldiers along with sixty Pueblo Indian allies to expel French intruders from the northern borderlands of New Spain. When the expedition reached the confluence of the Platte and Loup rivers in present-day Nebraska, they were surprised by an attack by French, Pawnees, and Otos, who killed thirty-three Spaniards and twelve Pueblos and drove the expedition back to New Mexico. Shortly afterward, an artist—whether Indian or Spanish is unknown—recorded the disastrous ambush of the Spaniards in this painting. The priest in the center of the detail shown here was Father Juan Minguez, the first priest assigned to Albuquerque; he was killed in the ambush. The Indian directly in front of the priest was Joseph Naranjo, who was also killed; he came from the Santa Clara Pueblo. He was the leader of the Spaniards' Pueblo allies and was the son of Domingo Naranjo, a leader of the Pueblo Revolt against the Spaniards in 1680.
Courtesy of the Museum of New Mexico, Neg. No. 149804.

many of their own rules and established a strong tradition of representative government analogous, in their eyes, to the English Parliament. Voters often returned the same representatives to the assemblies year after year, building continuity in power and leadership that far exceeded that of the governor. By 1720, colonial assemblies had won the power to initiate legislation, including tax laws and authorizations to spend public funds. Although all laws passed by the assemblies (except in Maryland, Rhode Island, and Connecticut) had to be approved by the governor and then by the Board of Trade in England, the difficulties in communication about complex subjects over long distances effectively ratified the assemblies' decisions.

The heated political struggles between royal governors and colonial assemblies that occurred throughout the eighteenth century taught colonists a common set of political lessons. They learned to employ traditionally British ideas of representative government to defend their own interests. They learned that power in the British colonies rarely belonged to the British government.

> **REVIEW** Why did the Spanish expand and fortify their presence in California in the eighteenth century?

Conclusion: The Dual Identity of British North American Colonists

During the eighteenth century, a society that was both distinctively colonial and distinctively British emerged in British North America. Tens of thousands of immigrants and slaves gave the colonies an unmistakably colonial complexion and contributed to the colonies' growing population and expanding economy. People of different ethnicities and faiths sought their fortunes in the colonies, where land was cheap, labor was dear, and—as Benjamin Franklin preached—work promised to be rewarding. Indentured servants and redemptioners risked a temporary period of bondage for the potential reward of better opportunities than on the Atlantic's eastern shore. Slaves endured lifetime servitude that they neither chose nor desired but from which their masters greatly benefited.

Identifiably colonial products from New England, the middle colonies, and the southern colonies flowed across the Atlantic. Back came unquestionably British consumer goods along with fashions in ideas, faith, and politics. The bonds of the British empire required colonists to think of themselves as British subjects and, at the same time, encouraged them to consider their status as colonists.

People of European origin in the North American colonies of Spain and France did not share in the emerging political identity of the British colonists. They also did not participate in the cultural, economic, social, and religious changes experienced by their counterparts in British North America. Unlike the much more numerous colonists in British North America, North American Spanish and French colonists did not develop societies that began to rival the European empires that sponsored and supported them.

By 1750, British colonists in North America could not imagine that their distinctively dual identity—as British and as colonists—would soon become a source of intense conflict. But by 1776, colonists in British North America had to choose whether they were British or American.

Suggestions for Further Reading

Ira Berlin, *Generations of Captivity: A History of African-American Slaves* (2003). An expert overview of the rise of slavery in British North America.

George M. Marsden, *Jonathan Edwards: A Life* (2003). A thoughtful biography of the leading minister of the Great Awakening.

Kerby A. Miller, et al., eds., *Irish Immigrants in the Land of Canaan: Letters and Memoirs from Colonial and Revolutionary America* (2003). A rich treasury of contemporary accounts of eighteenth-century American through the eyes of Irish immigrants.

Simon P. Newman, *Embodied History: The Lives of the Poor in Early Philadelphia* (2003). A revealing look at the poor in the "best poor man's country."

Randy J. Sparks, *Two Princes of Calabar: An Eighteenth-Century Odyssey* (2004). The amazing saga of two brothers, both Africans involved in the slave trade, who become enslaved and, like Equiano, eventually freed, but unlike Equiano, they return to Africa and continue slave trading.

David Waldstreicher, *Runaway America: Benjamin Franklin, Slavery, and the American Revolution* (2004). A fascinating study of Benjamin Franklin and slavery.

▶ **FOR MORE BOOKS ABOUT TOPICS IN THIS CHAPTER,** see the Online Study Guide at bedfordstmartins.com/roarkcompact.

▶ **FOR ADDITIONAL FIRSTHAND ACCOUNTS OF THIS PERIOD,** see Chapter 5 in Michael Johnson, ed., *Reading the American Past,* Third Edition.

▶ **FOR WEB SITES AND DOCUMENTS RELATED TO TOPICS AND PLACES IN THIS CHAPTER,** see "HistoryLinks," "DocLinks," and "PlaceLinks" at bedfordstmartins.com/roarkcompact.

REVIEWING THE CHAPTER

Follow these steps to review and strengthen your understanding of the chapter.

STEP 1: *Study the* **Key Terms** *and* **Timeline** *to identify the significance of each item listed.*

STEP 2: *Answer the* **Review Questions,** *drawing on key terms and dates to support your answers.*

STEP 3: *Drawing on the Key Terms, Timeline, and Review Questions, answer the broader* **Making Connections** *questions.*

KEY TERMS

Who

Benjamin Franklin (p. 103)
Iroquois (p. 106)
Mahican Indians (p. 106)
Pennsylvania Dutch (p. 108)
middling folk (p. 108)
Scots-Irish (p. 108)
redemptioners (p. 109)
Olaudah Equiano (p. 112)
"new Negroes" (p. 114)
Jonathan Edwards (p. 119)
George Whitefield (p. 119)
Yamasee (p. 121)
Creek Indians (p. 121)
Cherokee (p. 121)
Gaspar de Portolá (p. 121)
Junípero Serra (p. 121)

What

natural increase (p. 104)
partible inheritance (p. 106)
Queen Anne's War (p. 108)
Poor Richard's Almanack (p. 110)
Middle Passage (p. 112)
creole (p. 114)
"seasoning" (p. 114)
Senegambia (Gold Coast) (p. 114)
Bight of Biafra (p. 114)
African Congo (p. 114)
Angola (p. 114)
Stono rebellion (p. 115)
task system (p. 116)
gentry (p. 116)
property-holding requirement (p. 116)
mass markets (p. 117)

Congregational Church (p. 119)
deism (p. 119)
Enlightenment (p. 119)
American Philosophical Society (p. 119)
Great Awakening (p. 119)
fur trade (p. 121)
Yamasee War of 1715 (p. 121)
Seven Years' War (p. 121)
presidios (p. 121)
San Diego de Alcalá (p. 121)

TIMELINE

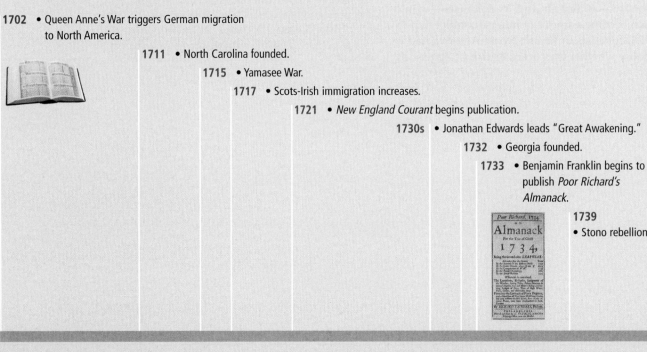

1702 • Queen Anne's War triggers German migration to North America.

1711 • North Carolina founded.

1715 • Yamasee War.

1717 • Scots-Irish immigration increases.

1721 • *New England Courant* begins publication.

1730s • Jonathan Edwards leads "Great Awakening."

1732 • Georgia founded.

1733 • Benjamin Franklin begins to publish *Poor Richard's Almanack.*

1739 • Stono rebellion.

REVIEW QUESTIONS

1. How did the North American colonies achieve the remarkable population growth of the eighteenth century? (pp. 104–05)

2. Why did settlement patterns in New England change from the seventeenth to the eighteenth century? (pp. 105–08)

3. Why did German immigrants flood into Pennsylvania during the eighteenth century? (pp. 108–11)

4. Why did the Stono rebellion fail? (pp. 112–17)

5. Why did religious revivals flourish during the 1730s and 1740s? (pp. 117–20)

6. Why did the Spanish expand and fortify their presence in California in the eighteenth century? (pp. 120–26)

MAKING CONNECTIONS

1. Colonial products such as tobacco and sugar transformed consumption patterns on both sides of the Atlantic in the eighteenth century. How did consumption influence the relationship between the American colonies and Britain? In your answer, consider how it might have strengthened and weakened connections.

2. Why did the importance of religion decline throughout the colonies from the seventeenth to the eighteenth century? How did American colonists respond to these changes?

3. Surging population expanded British colonial frontiers and the potential for conflict with Indians and other Europeans in the eighteenth century. How did different colonies attempt to manage relations with Indians? How did Indians attempt to manage relationships with Europeans? In your answer, consider disputes over territory *and* trade.

4. Varied immigration patterns contributed to important differences between the British colonies. Compare and contrast patterns of immigration to the middle and southern colonies. Who came and how did they get there? How did they shape the economic, cultural, and political character of each colony?

▶ **FOR PRACTICE QUIZZES, A CUSTOMIZED STUDY PLAN, AND OTHER STUDY TOOLS**, see the Online Study Guide at bedfordstmartins.com/roarkcompact.

1740s • George Whitefield preaches religious revival.
     • Majority of southern slaves are colonial-born.

  1741 • New York slave conspiracy trials.

      1745 • Olaudah Equiano born.

        1750s • Colonists begin to move down Shenandoah Valley.

          1754 • Seven Years' War begins.

            1769 • American Philosophical Society founded.

            1770 • Mission and presidio established at Monterey, California.
               • British North American colonists number over 2 million.

               1775 • Indians destroy San Diego mission.

PATRICK HENRY'S MAP DESK

Like many of the leading gentry of 1760s Virginia, Patrick Henry pursued land speculation as a way to gain wealth. From 1767 to 1773, he engaged in a half-dozen land ventures, buying up thousands of acres of frontier land in regions now part of Kentucky—purchases that would soon figure in the emerging crisis of empire. This odd little table was Henry's map desk. Its fold-out extensions provided support for the large maps required to represent Virginia's vast western land claims, and its light weight allowed Henry to position it near the best light source in his law office. As is often the case with speculative purchases, Henry's land deals entailed risk: Many of his properties were occupied by the Cherokee, who did not recognize his claim of ownership. The British government, fearing war between Indians and settlers, tried to choke off risky land speculation in 1763 by establishing an imaginary line along the crest of the Appalachian Mountains beyond which settlement was prohibited. But men like Henry continued to buy land cheap in the hopes of selling dear at a later time. As a leading planter and powerful orator, Patrick Henry quickly became a spokesman in the growing imperial struggle with Britain. When he gained election to the Virginia House of Burgesses in 1765, he skillfully maneuvered that assembly into the startling repudiation of British power known as the Virginia Resolves. By 1775 he favored independence from England, a position that eventually would unleash settlers looking to buy land in the West. In 1776, he was elected the first governor of the Commonwealth of Virginia. Patrick Henry ultimately had seventeen children, fourteen of whom survived to adulthood. Through astute land purchases, he managed to establish each with a landed estate.

Courtesy of Scotchtown, photo by Katherine Wetzel.

6

The British Empire and the Colonial Crisis
1754–1775

I N 1771, THOMAS HUTCHINSON became the royal governor of the colony of Massachusetts. Unlike most royal governors, who were British aristocrats sent over by the king for short tours of duty, Hutchinson was a fifth-generation American. A Harvard-educated member of the Massachusetts elite, from a family of successful merchants, Hutchinson had served two decades in the Massachusetts general assembly. In 1758 he was appointed lieutenant governor, and in 1760 he also became chief justice of the colony's highest court. He lived in the finest mansion in Boston. Wealth, power, and influence were his in abundance. He was proud of his connection to the British empire and loyal to his king.

Hutchinson had the misfortune to be a loyal colonial leader during the two very tumultuous decades leading up to the American Revolution. He worked hard to keep the British and colonists aligned in interests, even promoting a plan to unify the colonies into a single defensive unit (the Albany Plan of Union) to ward off Indian wars. The plan of union failed, and a major war ensued—the Seven Years' War, pitting the British and colonists against the French and their Indian allies in the backcountry of the American colonies. When the war ended and the British government began to think about taxing colonists to pay for it, Hutchinson had no doubt that the new British policies were legitimate. Unwise, perhaps, in their specific formulation, but certainly legitimate.

Not everyone in Boston shared his opinion. Fervent, enthusiastic crowds protested against a succession of British taxation policies enacted after 1763—the Sugar Act, the Stamp Act, the Townshend duties, the Tea Act, all landmark events on the road to the American Revolution. But Hutchinson maintained his steadfast loyalty to England. His love of order and tradition inclined him to unconditional support of the British empire, and he was, by nature, a measured and cautious man. "My temper does not incline to enthusiasm," he once wrote.

Privately, he lamented the stupidity of the British acts that provoked trouble, but his sense of duty required him to defend the king's policies, however misguided. Quickly, he became an inspiring villain to the emerging revolutionary movement. Governor Hutchinson came to personify all that was wrong with British and colonial relations. The man not inclined to enthusiasm unleashed popular enthusiasm all around him. He never appreciated that irony.

In another irony, Thomas Hutchinson was actually one of the first Americans to recognize the difficulties of maintaining full rights and privileges for colonists so far from their supreme government, the king and

Thomas Hutchinson
The only formal portrait of Thomas Hutchinson still in existence shows an assured young man in ruffles and hair ribbons. Decades of turmoil in Boston failed to puncture his self-confidence. Doubtless he sat for several portraits, as did all the Boston leaders in the 1760s to 1780s, but no other likeness has survived. One portrait hung in his summer house outside Boston, but a revolutionary crowd mutilated it and stabbed out the eyes. In 1775, Hutchinson fled to England, the country he had regarded as his cultural home, only to realize how very American he was.
Courtesy of the Massachusetts Historical Society.

the course of that decade, colonists insistently raised serious questions about American liberties and rights, especially over the issues of taxation and representation. Many came to believe what Thomas Hutchinson could never credit, that a tyrannical Britain had embarked on a course to enslave the colonists by depriving them of their traditional English liberties.

The opposite of **liberty** was slavery, a condition of nonfreedom and of coercion. Political rhetoric about liberty, tyranny, and slavery heated up emotions of white colonists during the many crises of the 1760s and 1770s. But this rhetoric turned out to be a two-edged sword. The call for an end to tyrannical slavery meant one thing when sounded by Boston merchants whose commercial shipping rights had been revoked; the same call meant something quite different in 1775 when sounded by black Americans locked in the bondage of slavery.

All of this was set in motion by the Seven Years' War. The British victory at first fortified loyalty to England, but its aftermath, taxation, stirred up discussions of rights, fueled white colonists' fear of enslavement by king and Parliament, and produced a potent political vocabulary with unexpected consequences.

The Seven Years' War, 1754–1763

For the first fifty years of the eighteenth century, England was at war intermittently with France or Spain. Often the colonists in America experienced reverberations from these conflicts, most acutely along the French **frontier** in northern New England. In the 1750s, international tensions mounted again, but this time over events originating in America. The conflict centered on contested land in the Ohio Valley, variously claimed by Virginians, Pennsylvanians, the French in Canada, and the Indians already living on the land. The result was the costly Seven Years' War, which spread in 1756 to encompass much of Europe, the Caribbean, and even India. Many thousands of British and American soldiers shared the hardships of battle and the glory of victory over the French and their Indian allies. But the immense costs of the war—in money, death, and desires for revenge by losers and even winners—laid the groundwork for the imperial crisis of the 1760s between the British and Americans.

Parliament in England. In 1769, when British troops occupied Boston in an effort to provide civil order, he wrote privately to a friend in England, "There must be an abridgement of what are called English liberties.... I doubt whether it is possible to project a system of government in which a colony three thousand miles distant from the parent state shall enjoy all the liberty of the parent state." What he could not imagine was the possibility of giving up the parent state and creating an independent government closer to home.

Thomas Hutchinson was a loyalist; in the 1750s, most English-speaking colonists were affectionately loyal to England. But the Seven Years' War, which England and its colonies fought together as allies, shook that affection, and imperial policies in the decade following the war (1763–1773) shattered it completely. Over

French-British Rivalry in the Ohio Country

For several decades, French traders had culti-vated alliances with the Indian tribes in the Ohio Country, a frontier region encompassing pres-ent day western Pennsylvania and eastern Ohio. Cementing their relationships with gifts, they es-tablished a profitable trade of manufactured goods for beaver furs. But in the 1740s, aggres-sive Pennsylvanians began to poach on their business, underselling French goods and threat-ening to reorient Indian loyalties. Virginians too advanced on the same land, obtaining a charter to settle it from the British king in 1747. A group of enterprising Virginians, includ-ing the brothers Lawrence and Augustine Washington, formed the Ohio Company; their hope for profit lay not in the fur trade but in land speculation, fueled by the ex-ploding English-American population.

In response to these incursions, the French sent soldiers to build a series of mili-tary forts to secure their trade routes and to create a western barrier to British-American population expansion. In 1753, the royal governor of Virginia, Robert Dinwiddie, himself a shareholder in the Ohio Company, sent a messenger to warn the French that they were trespassing on Virginia land.

The messenger on this dangerous mission was George Washington, younger half-brother of the Ohio Company leaders. Although only twenty-one, Washington was an ambitious youth whose imposing height (six feet two) and air of silent com-petence convinced the governor he could do the job. The middle child in a family of eight, Washington did not stand to inherit great wealth, so he sought to gain public repu-tation and impress the Virginia elite by volunteering for this per-ilous duty.

Washington returned from his mission with crucial intelli-gence about French military plans. Impressed, Dinwiddie appointed the youth to lead a small military expedition west to assert and, if need be, def-end Virginia's claim. Imperial officials in London, concerned by the French fortifications, had authorized the governor "to repel force by force," but only if the French attacked first. By

early 1754, the French had built Fort Duquesne at the forks of the Ohio River; Washington's assign-ment was to chase the French away without being the aggressor.

In spring of 1754, Washington set out with 160 Virginians along with Indian allies of the Mingo tribe. The first engagement with the French occurred early one May morning when the Mingo chief Tanaghrisson led a detachment of Washington's sol-diers to a small French encamp-ment in the woods. A brief skir-mish left fourteen Frenchmen wounded. While Washington struggled to communicate with the injured French commander, Tanaghrisson and his men inter-vened to kill and then scalp the wounded soldiers, including the commander, probably with the aim of enflaming hostilities be-tween the French and colonists.

This sudden massacre vio-lated Washington's instructions to avoid being the aggressor and

Washington's Journal, 1754

When George Washington returned from his first mis-sion to the French, Gover-nor Dinwiddie asked him to write a full report of what he had seen of the western countryside, of the Indians, and of French troop strength. Washington obliged, writing about 7,000 words in less than two days (about equivalent to a 25-page double-spaced paper). He coolly narrated scenes of per-sonal danger: of traveling in deep snow, of falling off a raft into an icy river, of being shot at by a lone Indian. Dinwiddie printed Washing-ton's report, along with his own letter and the French commander's defiant answer, in a 32-page pam-phlet; shortly thereafter it was re-printed in London. The governor's aim was to inform Virginians and British leaders about the French threat to the west. But the pamphlet suited Washington's aims as well: At age twenty-two, he became known on both sides of the Atlantic for resolute and rugged courage.

The Huntington Library and Art Collections, San Marino, California.

Ohio River Valley, 1753

The brave old Hendrick, the great SACHEM or Chief of the Mohawk Indians, one of the Six Nations now in Alliance with, & Subject to the King of Great Britain.
Sold by Eliz. Bakewell opposite Birchin Lane in Cornhill.

Chief Hendrick and John Caldwell

What might it mean when a Mohawk chief dresses in English clothes and a British soldier goes native? Dress is a symbol system that conveys status and self-presentation to viewers. Might it also change the way the dresser thinks about himself or herself? Chief Hendrick (top) worked closely with the British in New York to maintain the trade alliance known as the Covenant Chain. At age sixty, he traveled to England and sat for this portrait. His red coat, ruffled shirt, and three-cornered hat are all signs of the well-dressed British gentleman; but he holds a tomahawk in one hand and wampum in the other, and his long white hair is conspicuously uncurled, unlike an eighteenth-century gent's wig. John Caldwell (bottom) holds a tomahawk and sports Indian garb: feather headdress, blankets, leggings, and moccasins. During the Revolutionary War, Caldwell was stationed at Fort Detroit, a British garrison that provided aid to tribes in the Ohio Valley battling Americans. Caldwell acquired this Indian outfit for a diplomatic mission to the Shawnee in 1780; he took the clothes back to England and wore them for this portrait. Do you think these instances of imitation indicate a willingness to cross cultural boundaries and try to be like, think like, or experience the other culture? Is the co-opting just play or a sign of something deeper?

Hendrick: Courtesy of the John Carter Brown Library at Brown University; Caldwell: The Board of Trustees of the National Museums & Galleries on Merseyside (King's Regiment Collection).

---

raised the stakes considerably. Fearing retaliation, Washington ordered his men to fortify their position; the flimsy "Fort Necessity" was the result. Reinforcements amounting to several hundred more Virginians arrived; but the Mingos, sensing disaster and displeased by Washington's style of command, fled. (Tanaghrisson later said: "The Colonel was a good-natured man, but had no experience; he took upon him to command the Indians as his slaves, [and] would by no means take advice from the Indians.") In early July, over 600 French soldiers aided by Indians attacked Fort Necessity, killing or wounding a third of Washington's men. The message was clear: The French would not depart from the disputed territory.

The Albany Congress and Intercolonial Defense

Even as Virginians, Frenchmen, and Indians fought and died in the Ohio Country, British imperial leaders hoped to prevent a larger war. One obvious strategy was to strengthen British alliances with seemingly neutral Indian tribes. To this end, British authorities directed the governor of New York to convene a colonial conference.

In June and July of 1754, twenty-four delegates from seven colonies met in Albany, New York. Also attending were Iroquois Indians of the Six Nations, a confederacy of tribes inhabiting the central and western parts of present-day New York. Albany was the traditional meeting place of the Covenant Chain, a trade alliance first created in 1692 between New York leaders and Mohawk Indians, the most easterly of the Six Nations. In 1753, the aged Mohawk leader, Hendrick, accused the English of breaking the Covenant Chain, so a prime goal of the Albany Congress was to repair trade relations with the Mohawk and secure their help—or at least their neutrality—against the French threat.

Two delegates at the congress had more ambitious plans. Benjamin Franklin of Pennsylvania and Thomas Hutchinson of Massachusetts, both rising political stars in their home colonies, coauthored the Albany Plan of Union, a proposal for a government unifying the colonies but limited to war and defense policies. In the course of the meeting, the Albany delegates learned of Washington's defeat at Fort Necessity and understood instantly the escalating risk of war with France; they approved the plan. Key features included a president general appointed by the crown and a grand council, meeting annually to consider questions of war, peace, and trade with the Indians. The writers of the Albany Plan humbly reaffirmed Parliament's authority; this was no bid for enlarged autonomy of the colonies.

To Franklin's surprise, not a single colony approved the Albany Plan. The Massachusetts assembly feared it was "a Design of gaining power over the Colonies," especially the power of taxation. Others objected that it would be impossible to agree on unified policies toward scores of quite different Indian tribes. The British government never backed the Albany Plan either, and soon after it appointed two superintendents of Indian affairs, one for the northern and another for the southern colonies, each with exclusive powers to negotiate with tribes.

The Indians at the Albany Congress were not impressed with the Albany Plan either. The Covenant Chain alliance with the Mohawk tribe was reaffirmed, but the other nations left without pledging to help the British battle the French. At this very early point in the Seven Years' War, the Iroquois figured that the French military presence around the Great Lakes would discourage the westward push of American colonists and therefore better serve their interests.

The War and Its Consequences

By 1755, Washington's frontier skirmish had turned into a major mobilization of British and American troops against the French. At first, the British hoped for quick victory on three fronts. General Edward Braddock, recently arrived from England, marched his army toward Fort Duquesne in western Pennsylvania. In Massachusetts, Governor William Shirley aimed his soldiers at Fort Niagara, critically located between Lakes Erie and Ontario. And William Johnson, a New Yorker recently appointed superintendent of Indian affairs, led forces north toward Lake Champlain, intending to push the French back to Canada (Map 6.1).

Unfortunately for the British, the French had cemented respectful alliances with many Indian tribes. In July 1755, General Braddock's force of 2,000 British and Virginia troops was aided by just eight Oneida Indians. One day short of Fort Duquesne, they were ambushed by 250 French soldiers and 640 Indian warriors, including Ottawas, Ojibwas, Potawatomis, Shawnees, and Delawares. In the bloody battle nearly a thousand on the British side were killed or wounded. Washington was unhurt, though two horses in succession were shot out from under him; General Braddock was killed.

News of Braddock's defeat caused the other two British armies, then hacking their way through the dense forests of northern New York, to retreat from action. For the next two years, the British stumbled badly on the American front. What finally turned the war around was the rise to power in 1757 of William Pitt, England's prime minister, a man willing to commit massive resources to fight France and its ally Spain worldwide. In America, British and American troops captured Forts Duquesne, Niagara, and Ticonderoga and then the French cities of Quebec and Montreal, all from 1758 to 1760.

American colonists rejoiced, but the worldwide war was not over yet. Battles continued in the Caribbean, where the French sugar islands Martinique and Guadeloupe fell to the British, as did Spain's Cuba. After further fighting in Europe and India, France and Spain capitulated, and the Treaty of Paris was signed in 1763.

The triumph of victory was sweet but short-lived. The complex peace negotiations reorganized the map of North America but stopped short of providing England with the

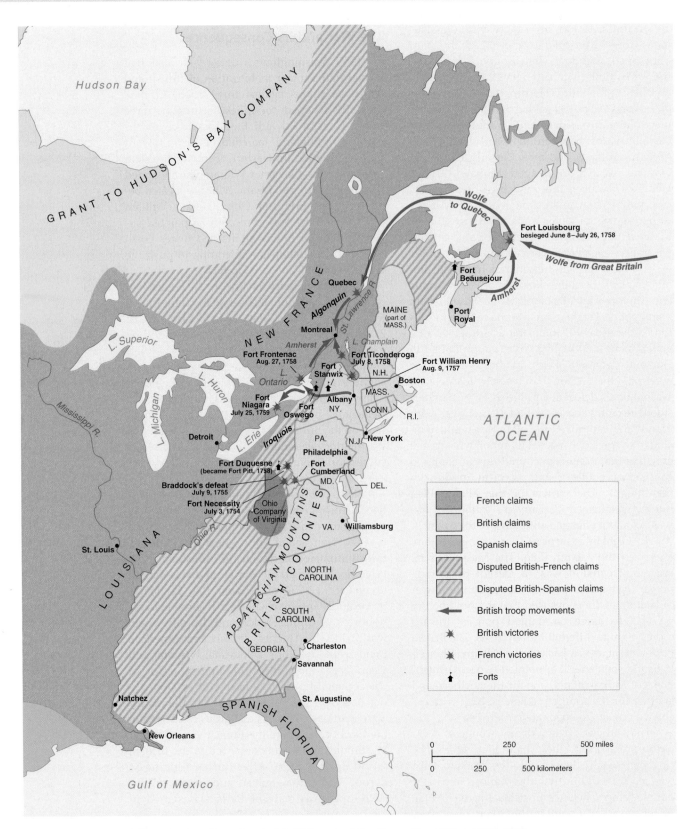

MAP 6.1   European Areas of Influence and the Seven Years' War, 1754–1763
In the mid-eighteenth century, France, England, and Spain claimed vast areas of North America, many of them already inhabited by various Indian peoples. The early flash points of the Seven Years' War were in regions of disputed claims where the French had allied with powerful native groups—the Iroquois and the Algonquian—to put pressure on the westward-moving English.

1763
- British claims
- French claims
- Spanish claims
- Russian claims

RUSSIAN AMERICA

Hudson Bay

HUDSON'S BAY COMPANY

QUEBEC

French fishing rights

St. Pierre & Miquelon (Fr.)

Louisbourg

Great Lakes

St. Lawrence R.

Missouri R.

BRITISH COLONIES

ATLANTIC OCEAN

Proclamation Line of 1763

LOUISIANA

Ohio R.

PACIFIC OCEAN

SPANISH FLORIDA

Guadeloupe (Fr.)

Mississippi R.

Rio Grande

New Orleans

NEW SPAIN

BAHAMAS (Br.)

Puerto Rico (Sp.)

Dominica (Br.)

Gulf of Mexico

Cuba

Jamaica

St. Domingue

Martinique (Fr.)
St. Lucia (Fr.)
Barbados (Br.)

Caribbean Sea

0   500   1000 miles
0   500   1000 kilometers

MAP 6.2   North America after the Seven Years' War
In the peace treaty of 1763, France ceded its interior lands but retained fishing rights and islands in the far north and several sugar islands in the Caribbean. Much of France's claim to the area called Louisiana went not to England but to Spain.

full spoils of victory. England gained control of Canada, eliminating the French threat from the north and west. English and American title to the eastern half of North America, precisely what England had claimed before the war, was confirmed. But all French territory west of the Mississippi River, including New Orleans, was transferred to Spain as compensation for Spain's assistance to France during the war. Stranger still, Cuba was returned to Spain, and Martinique and Guadeloupe were returned to France (Map 6.2).

In truth, the French islands in the Caribbean were hardly a threat to Americans, for they provided a profitable trade in smuggled molasses. The main threat to the safety of colonists came instead from Indians, ignored by the Treaty of Paris. With the French gone, the Indians lost the advantage of having two opponents to play off against each other, and they now had to cope with the westward-moving Americans. Indian policy would soon become a serious point of contention between the British government and the colonists.

England's version of the victory of 1763 awarded all credit to the mighty British army, inadequately supported by ungrateful colonists. Worse still, the colonists had engaged in smug-gling—notably a lively trade in beaver pelts with French fur traders and an illegal molasses trade in the Caribbean. American traders, grumbled the British leaders, were really traitors. William Pitt was convinced that the illegal trade "principally, if not alone, enabled France to sustain and protract this long and expensive war."

Colonists read the lessons of the war differently. American colonial soldiers had turned out in force, they claimed, but had been relegated to grunt work by arrogant British leaders and subjected to unexpectedly harsh military discipline, ranging from floggings to executions. General Braddock had foolishly bragged to Benjamin Franklin that "these savages may, indeed, be a formidable enemy to your raw American militia, but upon the king's regular and disciplined troops, sir, it is impossible they should make any impression." Braddock's defeat "gave us Americans," Franklin wrote, "the first suspicion that our exalted ideas of the prowess of British regulars had not been well founded."

The human costs of the war were etched especially sharply in the minds of New England colonists. About one-third of all Massachusetts men between fifteen and thirty had seen service. Many families lost loved ones, a cost not soon forgotten. The enormous expense of the war caused

Silver Medal to Present to Indians

After Pontiac's uprising ended, the British attempted to mend relations with Indian tribes by honoring them with gifts. This silver medal, minted in 1766, displays a profile of King George III on the front and a cozy depiction on the back of an Indian and Briton sharing a smoking peace pipe. The Latin words on the front announce George's name, title, and kingly dominions; the English words on the back would have been equally unintelligible to the recipients of the gift. Imagine a conversation between an Indian chief and an English translator who tries to explain what the slogan "happy while united" might mean. The scene depicted—two men with relaxed, friendly body language—illustrates "happy" and "united." The "while," rooted in a sense of time, temporariness, and contingency, might be tricky to explain. Why?

The American Numismatic Society.

by Pitt's no-holds-barred military strategy cast another huge shadow over the victory. By 1763, England's national debt, double what it had been when Pitt took office, posed a formidable challenge to the next decade of leadership in England.

British Leadership, Indians, and the Proclamation of 1763

In 1760, in the middle of the Seven Years' War, twenty-two-year-old George III came to the British throne. Timid and insecure, the new king trusted only his Scottish tutor, the Earl of Bute, an outsider to power circles in London, and made him head of his cabinet of ministers. Bute made blunders and did not last long, but he made one significant decision—to keep a standing army in the colonies after the last battle was over in 1760. In both financial and political terms, this was a costly move.

The ostensible reason for stationing British troops in America was to maintain the peace between the colonists and the Indians. This was not a misplaced concern. The defeat and withdrawal of the French from North America had left their Indian allies—who did not accept defeat—in a state of alarm. Just three months after the Treaty of Paris was signed in 1763, Pontiac, chief of the Ottawa tribe in the northern Ohio region, attacked the British garrison near Detroit. Six more attacks on forts quickly followed, and frontier settlements were also raided by nearly a dozen tribes from western New York, the Ohio Valley, and the Great Lakes region.

By fall, more than 400 British soldiers were dead and another 2,000 colonists killed or taken captive. Pontiac's uprising was quelled in December 1763 by the combined efforts of British and colonial soldiers, but tensions remained high. (See "Historical Question," page 140.)

To minimize violence, the British government issued the Proclamation of 1763, forbidding colonists to settle west of the Appalachian Mountains. The Proclamation chiefly aimed to separate Indians and settlers, but it also limited trade with Indians to traders licensed by colonial governors, and it forbade private sales of Indian land. The Proclamation's language took care not to identify western lands as belonging to the Indians. Instead, it spoke of Indians "who live under our protection" on "such parts of our Dominions and Territories as, not having been ceded to or purchased by Us, are reserved to them, as their Hunting Grounds." Other parts of the Proclamation of 1763 referred to American and even French colonists in Canada as "our loving subjects" entitled to English rights and privileges. The Indians were not described as British subjects.

The 1763 boundary proved impossible to enforce. Surging population growth had already sent many hundreds of settlers west of the Appalachians, and land speculators, such as those of Virginia's Ohio Company, had no desire to lose opportunities for profitable resale of their land grants. Bute's decision to post a standing army in the colonies was thus a cause for concern for western settlers, eastern speculators, and Indian tribes alike.

REVIEW   How did the Seven Years' War erode relations between colonists and Britain?

Pontiac's Uprising, 1763

Lake Ontario
Fort Niagara
Lake Michigan
Bloody Run July 1763
Ft. Detroit May 1763
Point Pelee May 1763
Fort St. Joseph
Fort Presqu'Isle
Fort Le Boeuf
Lake Erie
Fort Venango
Maumee R.
Fort Sandusky
Fort Pitt
Fort Ligonier
Bushy Run Aug. 1763
Fort Miami
Scioto R.
Miami R.
Ohio R.
Wabash R.
Fort Ouiatenon

✳ Attacks by Indians
■ Battle sites

The Sugar and Stamp Acts, 1763–1765

Lord Bute lost power in 1763, and the young King George turned to a succession of leaders throughout the 1760s, searching for a prime minister he could trust. A half dozen ministers in seven years took turns dealing with one basic, underlying British reality: A huge war debt, amounting to £123 million and growing due to interest, needed to be serviced, and the colonists, as British subjects, should help to pay it off. To many Americans, however, that proposition seemed in deep violation of what they perceived to be their rights and liberties as British subjects, and it created resentment that eventually erupted in rebellion. The first provocative revenue acts were the work of Sir George Grenville, prime minister from 1763 to 1765.

Grenville's Sugar Act

To find revenue, George Grenville scrutinized the customs service, which collected all import and export duties. Grenville found that the salaries of customs officers cost the government four times what was collected in revenue. The shortfall was due in part to bribery and smuggling, so Grenville began to insist on rigorous attention to paperwork and a strict accounting of collected duties.

The hardest duty to enforce was the one imposed by the Molasses Act of 1733—a stiff tax of six pence per gallon on any molasses purchased from non-British sources. The purpose of the tax was to discourage trade with French Caribbean islands and redirect the molasses trade to British sugar islands. But it did not work: French molasses remained cheap and abundant because French **planters** on Martinique and Guadeloupe had no use for it. A by-product of sugar production, molasses was a key ingredient in rum, a drink the French scorned. Rum-loving Americans were eager to buy French molasses, and they had ignored the tax law for decades.

Grenville's ingenious solution was the Revenue Act of 1764, popularly dubbed the "Sugar Act." It lowered the duty on French molasses to three pence, making it more attractive for shippers to obey the law, and at the same time raised penalties for smuggling. The act appeared to be in the tradition of navigation acts meant to regulate trade, but Grenville's actual intent was

Paper Currency of the 1750s to 1770s
Colonists generally used coins of valued metal for money (British shillings, Spanish doubloons) or else engaged in barter. But during the upheaval of the Seven Years' War, several colonies printed paper money. The currency shown here is laden with words stipulating the legality and value of the money. To discourage counterfeiting, each paper had an elaborate design, a unique handwritten number, and the signature of some authority who vouched for its authenticity. London merchants did not like accepting colonial paper money and prevailed on Parliament to pass a Currency Act in 1764 prohibiting the colonies from printing any, which put a crimp in the colonial economy, always short of coinage. In 1775, the newly established Continental Congress began printing paper money to finance the war. Notice the three-dollar paper at the lower left.
Courtesy of the Decorative & Industrial Arts Collection of the Chicago Historical Society.

to raise revenue. He was using an established form of law for new ends and accomplishing his goal by the novel means of lowering a duty.

The Sugar Act toughened enforcement policies. From now on, all British naval crews could act as impromptu customs officers, boarding suspicious ships and seizing cargoes found to be in violation. Smugglers caught without proper paperwork would be prosecuted, not in a friendly civil court with a local jury but in a vice-admiralty court located in Halifax, Nova Scotia, where a single judge presided. The implication was that justice would be sure and severe.

Grenville hoped that the new Sugar Act would reform American smugglers into law-abiding shippers and in turn generate income for

How Long Did the Seven Years' War Last in Indian Country?

France was defeated on the North American continent in 1760, and the Treaty of Paris officially ended the global war between France and England in 1763. But there was no lasting peace for the Indian nations of the Ohio Valley and Great Lakes region. In 1761, a Chippewa chief named Minavavana clearly explained why in an ominous speech delivered to a British trader at Fort Michilimackinac, a British outpost guarding the straits of Mackinaw where Lakes Huron and Michigan meet: "Englishman, although you have conquered the French, you have not yet conquered us! We are not your slaves. These lakes, these woods and mountains were left to us by our ancestors. They are our inheritance; and we will part with them to none." Furthermore, Minavavana pointedly noted, "your king has never sent us any presents, nor entered into any treaty with us, wherefore he and we are still at war; and until he does these things we must consider that we have no other father, nor friend, among the white men than the King of France."

Minavavana and other Indians of the region had cause to be alarmed. With the exit of the French, British regiments took over the French-built forts all over the Northwest. Fort Duquesne, renamed Fort Pitt in honor of the British leader who authorized the war-winning strategy, underwent two years of fortification. No one could mistake the new walls—sixty feet

thick at their base, ten at the top—for the external facade of a friendly fur trading post. Nonmilitary Americans were moving into Fort Pitt's neighborhood too, just as Indians had feared they would, crowding out native inhabitants and relying on the military protection of the fort.

Minavavana's complaint about the lack of British presents was a far more serious problem than the British military leaders figured. Gifts exchanged in Indian culture cemented social relationships; they symbolized honor and established obligation. The French over many decades had mastered the subtleties of gift exchange, distributing clothing, textiles, and hats, and receiving calumets (ornamented ceremonial pipe stems) as symbols of friendship. New to the practice, British military leaders often discarded the calumets as trivial trinkets, thereby insulting the givers. Major General Jeffrey Amherst was sometimes willing to offer gifts to particular Indian leaders, positioning the "gift" as a bribe in the British frame of reference. But Amherst saw extensive gift exchange as demeaning to the British, forcing them to pay tribute to people whom he considered inferior. "It is not my intention ever to attempt to gain the friendship of Indians by presents," Amherst declared. The Indian view was the opposite: Generous givers expressed dominance and protection, not subordination, in the act of giving. William Johnson, superintendent of northern Indian affairs, warned

Amherst that he was insulting the Indians, but the imperious Amherst did not listen.

A religious revival in 1760–1761, fueled by the prophetic visions of an Indian leader named Neolin, greatly enhanced the prospects of frontier war in the Northwest. Neolin, of the Delaware tribe, predicted a swift decline for all tribes unless they altered their ways, gave up quarreling with each other, shunned trade in guns, alcohol, and other trade goods, and curbed their overkill of animals for the pelt trade. His preachings spread quickly, gaining credence as the British bungled diplomacy and American settlers continued to penetrate western lands.

A renewal of commitment to Indian ways and the formation of tribal alliances led to open warfare in 1763, called (by the British) Pontiac's War. (The Indians would not have credited Pontiac with sole leadership; the coordination of the uprising was the work of many men.) Jeffrey Amherst, never a shrewd observer of Indian relations, flatly declared in April 1763 that reports of impending attack were "Meer Bugbears." But by mid-May, the British commander at Detroit knew the threat was real. Pontiac, chief of the Ottawa, along with Potawatomi and Huron warriors, attacked Fort Detroit and laid siege for two months. In late May, within two weeks of Pontiac's first move, Indians captured four more forts in Ohio, through ruses in which Indians pretending to have peaceful business gained entry to the garrisons. A fifth fort, at Michilimackinac, fell to Ojibwas who seemed to be playing a game of lacrosse near the fort. After several hours of strenuous play, the ball landed near the fort's open gate, and the enthralled British spectators realized too late that the convergence of players on the ball was really a rush

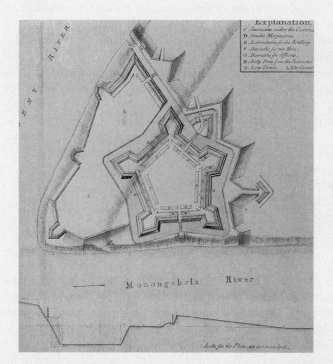

Plan of the New Fort at Pittsburgh
The French Fort Duquesne sat at the strategic forks of the Ohio River on a triangle of land formed by the Allegheny and Monongahela rivers rushing together to create the mighty Ohio. Built in 1754, Fort Duquesne provided a supply depot and a meeting place for the Indian allies of the French. It was the intended target of General Braddock's English army in 1755, but Braddock was forced into battle and soundly defeated a day before his planned attack. In 1758, the British captured an English-speaking man named Johnson along with some Indians taken prisoner. Johnson, an apparent traitor, saved his life by yielding information that Fort Duquesne was greatly undermanned and an easy hit. British and colonial troops sped to attack it; once taken, the fort was blown into rubble. In 1759, this plan for a new fort, named for Prime Minister William Pitt, showed a grand and imposing stronghold with room enough to house 1,000 soldiers inside the thick protective walls. By 1762, the fort was finished, fulfilling Pitt's mandate to "maintain His Majesty's subjects in undisputed possession of the Ohio."

of warriors into the fort. The players seized tomahawks that had been hidden under blankets worn by Indian women on the sidelines. The Ojibwas took the fort.

By the end of June, thirteen British garrisons had either fallen or been evacuated under threat of attack. Yet the British managed to hold on to the three most important forts—Detroit, Niagara, and Pitt—besieged by Indians. At Fort Pitt, two ostensibly friendly Delaware Indians showed up at the end of May to suggest that the British leave to avoid attack. Pitt's commander thanked them but declined their suggestion and sent them on their way with his idea of a gift: two blankets and a handkerchief used by British smallpox patients in the fort. "We hope it will have the desired effect," wrote a militiaman in his diary. Two months later, Jeffrey Amherst suggested to a subordinate that spreading smallpox—a practice akin to later germ warfare—should be considered as a method of war: "We must use Every Stratagem in our Power to Reduce them." There is no evidence that the infected blankets actually propagated smallpox or that Amherst's war strategem was put into greater practice.

From late summer of 1763 into the early months of 1764, Indian country was the scene of tremendous bloodshed. Indians targeted British supply routes and civilian settlements, resulting in several thousand deaths. Two thousand British troops were moved west from points in upper New York and Canada to join the fray. In December, Pennsylvania civilians went on the offensive. Some fifty vigilantes known as the Paxton Boys decided to make war on any Indians they could find. They descended on a peaceful village of friendly Conestoga Indians and murdered and scalped twenty of them. The vigilantes, numbers swelling to 500, next marched on Philadelphia to try to capture and murder some Christian Indians held in protective custody. British troops prevented that, but the unruly Paxton Boys escaped all punishment for their murderous attack on the Conestoga.

In 1764, the rebellion faded. The Indians were short on ammunition; the British were tired and broke. Amherst's superiors in Britain blamed him for mishandling the conflict, and when he was recalled home, his own soldiers toasted his leaving. Thomas Gage took command and soon distributed gifts profusely among the Indians.

Was the Seven Years' War finally over for the Indians, ten years after it started? If 1764 represents an end, it was only a brief one. Periodic raids and killings punctuated the rest of the 1760s and early 1770s, climaxing in the late 1770s as Indians joined the British to fight the Americans in the Revolutionary War. Warfare and massacres occurred in New England and New York, down to South Carolina and Georgia, and especially in the Ohio Country. The American Revolution eventually ended as well, but the frontier war between Americans and Indians continued on and off—mostly on—until 1815, the end of the War of 1812. Perhaps the Seven Years' War could be called the Sixty-One Years' War, from the Indian point of view.

the empire. Unfortunately, the decrease in duty was not sufficient to offset the attractions of smuggling. The vigilant customs officers made bribery harder to accomplish, and several ugly confrontations occurred in port cities. Reaction to the Sugar Act foreshadowed questions about England's right to tax Americans, but in 1764 objections to the act came principally from Americans in the shipping trades inconvenienced by the law.

From the British point of view, the Proclamation of 1763 and the Sugar Act seemed to be reasonable efforts to administer the colonies. To the Americans, however, the British supervision appeared to be a disturbing intrusion into colonial practices.

The Stamp Act

By his second year in office, Grenville had made almost no dent in the national debt. So in February 1765, he escalated his revenue program with the Stamp Act, precipitating a major conflict between England and the colonies over Parliament's right  to tax. The Stamp Act imposed a tax on all paper used for official documents—newspapers, pamphlets, court documents, licenses, wills, ships' cargo lists—and required an affixed stamp as proof the tax had been paid. Unlike the Sugar Act, which regulated trade, the Stamp Act was designed plainly and simply to raise money. It affected nearly everyone who used any taxed paper, but most of all those in the business and legal communities, heavily reliant on official documents.

Grenville was no fool. Anticipating that the stamp tax would be unpopular—Thomas Hutchinson had forewarned him—he delegated the administration of the act to Americans, to avoid the problem of hostility to British enforcers. In each colony, local stamp distributors would be hired at a handsome salary of 8 percent of the revenue collected.

British tradition held that taxes were a gift of the people to their monarch, granted by the people's representatives. This view of taxes as a freely given gift preserved an essential concept of English political theory: the idea that citizens have the liberty to enjoy and use their property without fear of confiscation. The king could not demand money; only the House of Commons could grant it. Grenville quite agreed with the notion of taxation by consent, but he argued that the colonists were

already "virtually" represented in Parliament. The House of Commons, he insisted, represented all British subjects, wherever they were.

Colonial leaders emphatically rejected this view, arguing that **virtual representation** could not withstand the stretch across the Atlantic. The stamp tax itself, levied by a distant Parliament on unwilling colonies, illustrated the problem. "The MINISTER'S virtual representation in Support of the TAX on us is fantastical and frivolous," Maryland inhabitants complained.

Resistance Strategies and Crowd Politics

News of the Stamp Act arrived in the colonies in April 1765, seven months before it was to take effect on November 1. There was time therefore to object. Governors were unlikely to challenge the law, for most of them owed their office to the king. Instead, the colonial assemblies took the lead; eight of them held discussions on the Stamp Act.

Virginia's assembly, the House of Burgesses, was the first. At the end of its May session, after two-thirds of the members had left, Patrick Henry, a young political newcomer, presented a series of resolutions on the Stamp Act that were debated and passed, one by one. They became known as the Virginia Resolves.

Henry's resolutions inched the assembly toward radical opposition to the Stamp Act. The first three stated the obvious: that Virginians were British citizens, that they enjoyed the same rights and privileges as Britons, and that self-taxation was one of those rights. The fourth resolution noted that Virginians had always taxed themselves, through their representatives in the House of Burgesses. The fifth took a radical leap by pushing the other four unexceptional statements to one logical conclusion—that the Virginia assembly alone had the right to tax Virginians.

Two more fiery resolutions were debated as Henry pressed the logic of his case to the extreme. The sixth resolution denied legitimacy to any tax law originating outside Virginia, and a seventh boldly called anyone who disagreed with these propositions an enemy of Virginia. This was too much for the other representatives. They voted down resolutions six and seven and later rescinded their vote on number five as well.

Their caution hardly mattered, however, because newspapers in other colonies printed all seven Virginia Resolves, creating the impression that a daring first challenge to the Stamp Act had occurred. Consequently, other assemblies were willing to consider even more radical questions, such as: By what authority could Parliament legislate for the colonies without also taxing them? No one disagreed, in 1765, that Parliament had legislative power over the colonists, who were, after all, British subjects. Several assemblies advanced the argument that there was a distinction between *external* taxes, imposed to regulate trade, and *internal* taxes, such as a stamp tax or a property tax, which could only be self-imposed.

Reaction to the Stamp Act ran far deeper than political debate in assemblies. Every person whose livelihood required official paper had to decide whether to comply with the act. Local communities strategized their responses. Should they boycott all paper use? A boycott would keep noncompliance within the law but would be highly inconvenient, crippling newspapers as well as legal and business paperwork. Should communities defy the law and conduct business as usual on unstamped paper, running the risk of fines or jail? A third strategy promised the surest success: preventing distribution of the stamps at the source, before the law took effect, thus ensuring universal noncompliance.

The first organized resistance to the Stamp Act began in Boston, under the leadership of Samuel Adams, a town politician with a history of opposition to Lieutenant Governor Thomas Hutchinson. Unlike Hutchinson, Adams cared nothing for status, high office, or fine material goods. He was the Harvard-educated son of a Boston brewer, a man with shrewd political instincts and a gift for organizing. He mobilized shopkeepers, master craftsmen, dockworkers, and laborers into a group of protesters who called themselves the Sons of Liberty.

The plan hatched by the Boston Sons of Liberty called for a large street demonstration highlighting a ritualized mock execution, designed to convince Andrew Oliver, the stamp distributor, to resign. On August 14, 1765, a crowd of two to three thousand demonstrators hung an effigy of Oliver in a tree and then paraded it around town before finally beheading and burning it. The flesh-and-blood Oliver stayed in hiding; the next day he resigned his office in a well-publicized announcement.

The demonstration provided lessons for everyone. Oliver learned that stamp distributors would be very unpopular people. Francis Bernard, the royal governor, learned the limitations of his power to govern, with no police to call on. The demonstration's leaders learned that street action was effective. And hundreds of laborers, sailors,

Andrew Oliver
This portrait shows Bostonian Andrew Oliver at age twenty-two, just a few years after his graduation from Harvard College. The powdered wig and stern look add years to his face; the blousy clothing adds substance to his body. He was fifty-nine and probably even more imposing in appearance when he ran afoul of the Stamp Act rioters in Boston in 1765.
Collection of the Oliver Family, photo by Clive Russ.

and apprentices not only learned what the Stamp Act was all about but also gained pride in their ability to have a decisive impact on politics.

Twelve days later, another crowd action showed how well these lessons had been learned. On August 26, a crowd visited the houses of three detested customs and court officials, breaking windows and raiding wine cellars. A fourth target was the finest dwelling in Massachusetts, owned by the stiff-necked Thomas Hutchinson. Rumors abounded that Hutchinson had urged Grenville to adopt the Stamp Act. Although he had done the opposite, Hutchinson refused to set the record straight, saying curtly, "I am not obliged to give an answer to all the questions that may be put me by every lawless person." The crowd attacked his house, and by daybreak only the exterior walls were standing.

The destruction of Hutchinson's house brought a temporary halt to crowd activities in

Boston. The Boston town meeting issued a statement of sympathy, but a large reward for the arrest and conviction of rioters failed to produce a single lead. The Sons of Liberty denied involvement. Essentially, the opponents of the Stamp Act in Boston had triumphed; no one volunteered to replace Oliver as distributor. When the Stamp Act took effect on November 1, customs officers were unable to prevent ships lacking properly stamped clearance papers from passing through the harbor.

Liberty and Property

Boston's crowd actions of August sparked similar eruptions by groups calling themselves Sons of Liberty in nearly fifty towns throughout the colonies, and stamp distributors everywhere hastened to resign. One Connecticut distributor was forced by a crowd to throw his hat and powdered wig in the air while shouting a cheer for "Liberty and property!" This man fared better than another Connecticut stamp agent, who was nearly buried alive by Sons of Liberty. Only when the thuds of dirt sounded on his coffin did he have a sudden change of heart, shouting out his resignation to the crowd above. Luckily, he was heard. In Charleston, South Carolina, the stamp distributor resigned after crowds burned effigies and chanted "Liberty! Liberty!"

Some colonial leaders, disturbed by the riots, sought a more moderate challenge to parliamentary authority. Twenty-seven delegates representing nine colonial assemblies met in New York City in October 1765 as the Stamp Act Congress. For two weeks, the men hammered out a petition about taxation addressed to the king and Parliament. Their statement closely resembled the first five Virginia Resolves, claiming taxes were "free gifts of the people" that only the people's representatives could give. They dismissed virtual representation: "The people of these colonies are not, and from their local circumstances, cannot be represented in the House of Commons." But the delegates carefully affirmed their subordination to Parliament and monarch in deferential language. Nevertheless, the Stamp Act Congress, by the mere fact of its meeting, advanced a radical potential, the notion of intercolonial political action.

The rallying cry of "Liberty and property" made perfect sense to many white Americans of all social ranks, who feared that the Stamp Act threatened their traditional right to liberty as British subjects. In this case the liberty in question was the right to be taxed only by representative government. "Liberty and property" came from a trinity of concepts—"life, liberty, property"—that had come to be regarded as the birthright of freeborn British subjects since at least the seventeenth century. A powerful tradition of British political thought invested representative government with the duty to protect individual lives, liberties, and property (possessions or money) against potential abuse by royal authority. Up to 1765, Americans consented to accept Parliament as a body that in some way represented them. But now, in this matter of taxation via stamps, Parliament seemed a distant body that had failed to protect Americans' liberty and property against royal authority.

Alarmed, some Americans began to speak and write about a plot by British leaders to enslave them. The opposite of liberty was slavery, the condition of being under the control of someone else. A Maryland writer warned that if the colonies lost "the right of exemption from all taxes without their consent," that loss would "deprive them of every privilege distinguishing freemen from slaves." The opposite meanings of liberty and slavery were utterly clear to white Americans, but they stopped short of applying similar logic to the half million black Americans they held in bondage. Many blacks, however, could see the contradiction. When a crowd of Charleston blacks paraded with shouts of "Liberty!" just a few months after white Sons of Liberty had done the same, the town militia turned out to break up the demonstration.

Politicians and merchants in England reacted with alarm to the American demonstrations and petitions. Merchants particularly feared trade disruptions and pressured Parliament to repeal the Stamp Act. By late 1765, yet another new minister, the Marquess of Rockingham, headed the king's cabinet and sought a way to repeal the act without losing face. The solution came in March 1766: The Stamp Act was repealed, but with it came the Declaratory Act, which asserted Parliament's right to legislate for the colonies "in all cases whatsoever." Perhaps the stamp tax had been inexpedient, but the power to tax—one prime case of a legislative power—was stoutly upheld.

REVIEW Why did the Sugar and Stamp acts draw fierce opposition from colonists?

The Townshend Acts and Economic Retaliation, 1767–1770

Rockingham was soon out of government, replaced by William Pitt, who then appointed Charles Townshend to be chancellor of the exchequer, the chief financial minister. Facing both the old war debt and the continuing cost of stationing British troops in America, Townshend turned again to taxation. But his simple yet naive idea to raise revenue touched off a year of coordinated boycotts of British goods in the colonies. Even women were politicized as self-styled "Daughters of Liberty." Boston led the uproar, causing the British to send peacekeeping soldiers to assist the royal governor. The stage was thus set for the first fatalities in the brewing revolution.

The Townshend Duties

Townshend proposed new taxes in the old form of a navigation act. Officially called the Revenue Act of 1767, it established new duties on tea, glass, lead, paper, and painters' colors imported into the colonies, to be paid by the importer but passed on to consumers in the retail price. A year before, the duty on French molasses had been reduced from three pence to one pence per gallon, and finally the Sugar Act was pulling in a tidy revenue of about £45,000 annually. So it was not unreasonable to suppose that duties on additional trade goods might also improve the cash flow. Townshend assumed that external taxes on transatlantic trade would be more acceptable to Americans than internal taxes, such as the stamp tax.

The Townshend duties were not especially burdensome, but the principle they embodied—taxation through trade duties—looked different to the colonists in the wake of the Stamp Act crisis. Although Americans once distinguished between external and internal taxes, that distinction was wiped out by an external tax meant only to raise money. John Dickinson, a Philadelphia lawyer, articulated this view in a series of articles titled *Letters from a Farmer in Pennsylvania*, widely reprinted in the winter of 1767–68. "We are taxed without our consent....We are therefore—SLAVES," Dickinson wrote, calling for "a total denial of the power of Parliament to lay upon these colonies any 'tax' whatever."

A controversial provision of the Townshend duties directed that some of the revenue generated would pay the salaries of royal governors. Before 1767, local assemblies set the salaries of their own officials, giving them significant influence over crown-appointed officeholders. Townshend wanted to strengthen the governors' position as well as to curb the growing independence of the assemblies.

The Massachusetts assembly took the lead in protesting the Townshend duties. Samuel Adams, a member from Boston, argued that any form of parliamentary taxation was unjust because Americans were not represented in Parliament. Further, he argued that the new way to pay governors' salaries subverted the proper relationship between the people and their rulers. The assembly circulated a letter with Adams's arguments to other colonial assemblies for their endorsement. As with the Stamp Act Congress of 1765, colonial assemblies were starting to coordinate their protests.

In response to Adams's letter, the new man in charge of colonial affairs in Britain, Lord Hillsborough, instructed the Massachusetts governor, Francis Bernard, to dissolve the assembly if it refused to repudiate the letter. The assembly refused and Governor Bernard carried out his instruction. In the summer of 1768, Boston was in an uproar.

Nonconsumption and the Daughters of Liberty

The Boston town meeting had already passed resolutions, termed "nonconsumption agreements," calling for a boycott of all British-made goods. Dozens of other towns passed similar resolutions in 1767 and 1768. For example, prohibited purchases in the town of New Haven, Connecticut, included carriages, furniture, hats, clothing, lace, clocks, and textiles. The idea was to encourage home manufacture and to hurt trade, causing London merchants to pressure Parliament for repeal of the duties.

Nonconsumption agreements were very hard to enforce. With the Stamp Act, there was one hated item, a stamp, and a limited number of official distributors. In contrast, an agreement to boycott all British goods required serious personal sacrifice. Some merchants were wary of nonconsumption because it hurt their pocketbooks, and a few continued to import in readiness for the end of nonconsumption (or to sell on the side to people choosing to ignore noncon-sumption). In Boston, such merchants found themselves blacklisted in newspapers and broadsides.

A more direct blow to trade came from non-importation agreements, but it proved more diffi-cult to get merchants to agree to these. There was always the risk that merchants in other colonies might continue to trade and thus receive hand-some profits if neighboring colonies prohibited trade. Not until late 1768 could Boston merchants agree to suspend trade through a nonimportation agreement lasting one year starting January 1, 1769. Sixty signed the agreement. New York mer-chants soon followed suit, as did Philadelphia and Charleston merchants in 1769.

Doing without British products, whether luxury goods, tea, or textiles, no doubt was a hardship. But it also presented an opportunity, for many of the British products specified in nonconsumption agreements were household goods traditionally under the control of the "ladies." By 1769, male leaders in the patriot cause clearly understood that women's coopera-tion in nonconsumption and home manufacture was beneficial to their cause. The Townshend duties thus provided an unparalleled opportu-nity for encouraging female patriotism. During the Stamp Act crisis, Sons of Liberty took to the streets in protest. During the difficulties of 1768–69, the concept of "Daughters of Liberty" emerged to give shape to a new idea—that women might play a role in public affairs.

Any woman could express affiliation with the colonial protest through conspicuous boycotts of British-made goods. In Boston, over three hun-dred women signed a petition to abstain from tea, "sickness excepted," in order to "save this abused Country from Ruin and Slavery." A nine-year-old girl visiting the royal governor's house in New Jersey took the tea she was offered, curtsied, and tossed the beverage out a nearby window.

Homespun cloth became a prominent sym-bol of patriotism. A young Boston girl learning to spin called herself "a daughter of liberty," noting that "I chuse to wear as much of our own manu-factory as pocible." In the boycott period of 1768–1770, newspapers reported on spinning matches or bees in some sixty New England towns, in which women came together in public to make yarn. Nearly always, the bee was held at the local minister's house, and the yarn produced was charitably handed over to him for distribu-tion to the poor. Newspaper accounts variously called the spinners "Daughters of Liberty" or "Daughters of Industry."

This surge of public spinning was related to the politics of the boycott, which infused tradi-tional women's work with new political purpose. But the women spinners were not equivalents of the Sons of Liberty. The Sons marched in streets, burned effigies, threatened hated officials, and celebrated anniversaries of their successes with raucous drinking and feasting in taverns. The Daughters manifested their patriotism quietly, in

Spinning Wheel

A lot of skill was needed to spin high-quality thread and yarn. This wheel was used for spinning flax (a plant with a long fibrous stem) into linen thread; it is likely the type used in the politicized 1769 spinning bees in which "Daughters of Liberty" proclaimed their boycott of British textiles. A foot treadle controls the turning of the wheel, and a spindle holds the thread produced. The art of spinning was all in the spinster's hand, which controlled the tension on the thread and the speed of the twisting. The spinning Daughters of Liberty were praised for their virtuous industry. Responding to such praise, one young woman complained, in a Rhode Island newspaper, that young male patriots were defi-cient in virtue: "Alas! We hear nothing of their working matches, nothing of their concern for the honor of their King or for the safety or liberties of their country"; instead the news is of "nocturnal Carousals and Exploits; of their drinking, gaming & whoring matches; and how they disturb the quiet of honest people." Smithsonian Institution, Washington, D.C.

ways marked by piety, industry, and charity. The difference was due in part to cultural ideals of gender, which prized masculine self-assertion but feminine selflessness. It also was due to class: The Sons were a cross-class alliance, with leaders from the middling orders reliant on men and boys of the lower ranks to fuel their crowds. The Daughters, dusting off spinning wheels and shelving their teapots, were genteel ladies used to buying British goods. The difference between the Sons and Daughters also speaks to two views of how best to challenge authority. Was resistance to British policy most effectively communicated through violent threats and street actions? Or were self-discipline and self-sacrifice the better strategies?

On the whole, the anti-British boycotts were a success. Imports fell by more than 40 percent; British merchants felt the pinch and let Parliament know it. In Boston, the Hutchinson family also endured losses, but even more alarming to the rigid and orderly lieutenant governor, Boston seemed overrun with anti-British sentiment. The Sons of Liberty staged annual rollicking celebrations of the Stamp Act riot, and Hutchinson along with Governor Bernard concluded that British troops were necessary to restore order.

Military Occupation and "Massacre" in Boston

In the fall of 1768, three thousand uniformed troops arrived to occupy Boston. The soldiers drilled conspicuously on the Common, played loud music on the Sabbath, and in general grated on the nerves of Bostonians. Although the situation was frequently tense, no major troubles occurred during that winter and through most of 1769. But as January 1, 1770, approached, marking the end of the nonimportation agreement, it was clear that some merchants—the Hutchinsons, for example—would no longer engage in the boycott.

Trouble began in January, when the door of the Hutchinson brothers' shop was defaced by "Hillsborough paint," a potent mixture of human excrement and urine. In February, a crowd surrounded the house of customs official Ebenezer Richardson, who panicked and fired a musket, accidentally killing a young boy passing on the street. The Sons of Liberty mounted a massive funeral procession to mark this first instance of violent death in the struggle with England.

For the next week, tension gripped Boston. The climax came on Monday evening, March 5,

1770, when a crowd taunted eight British soldiers guarding the customs house, throwing snowballs and rocks and daring the soldiers to fire; finally one did. After a short pause, during which someone yelled "Fire!" the other soldiers shot into the crowd, hitting eleven men, five of them fatally.

The Boston Massacre, as the event quickly became called, was over in minutes. In the immediate aftermath, Hutchinson (now acting governor after Bernard's recall to England) showed courage in addressing the crowd from the balcony of the statehouse. He quickly removed the regiments to an island in the harbor to prevent further bloodshed, and he jailed Captain Thomas Preston and his eight soldiers, a protective move, promising they would be held for trial.

The Sons of Liberty staged elaborate martyrs' funerals for the five victims. Significantly, the one nonwhite victim shared equally in the public's veneration: Crispus Attucks, a sailor and ropemaker in his forties, son of an African man and a Natick Indian woman, a slave in his youth but at the time of his death a free laborer at the Boston docks. Attucks was possibly the first American partisan to die in the American Revolution, and certainly the first African American.

The trial of the eight soldiers came in the fall of 1770. They were defended by two young Boston attorneys, Samuel Adams's cousin John Adams and Josiah Quincy. Because Adams and Quincy had direct ties to the leadership of the Sons of Liberty, their decision to defend the British soldiers at first seems odd. But John Adams was deeply committed to the idea that even unpopular defendants deserve a fair trial. Samuel Adams respected his cousin's decision to take the case, for there was a tactical benefit as well. It showed that the Boston leadership was not lawless but could be seen as defenders of British liberty and law.

The five-day trial, with dozens of witnesses, resulted in acquittal for Preston and for all but two of the soldiers, who were convicted of manslaughter, branded on the thumbs, and released. Nothing materialized in the trial to indicate a conspiracy or concerted plan to provoke trouble, either by the British or by the Sons of Liberty. To this day, the question of responsibility for the Boston Massacre remains obscure.

REVIEW   Why did Britain send troops to occupy Boston in the fall of 1768?

The Tea Party and the Coercive Acts, 1770–1774

In the same week as the Boston Massacre, a new British prime minister, Frederick North, recommended repeal of the Townshend duties. A skillful politician, Lord North took office in 1770 and kept it for twelve years; at last King George had stability at the helm. Seeking peace with the colonies and prosperity for British merchants, North persuaded Parliament to remove all the duties except the tax on tea, kept as a symbol of Parliament's power.

The renewal of trade and the return of cooperation between England and the colonies gave men like Thomas Hutchinson hope that the worst of the crisis was behind them. For nearly two years, peace seemed possible, but tense incidents in 1772 followed by a renewed struggle over the tea tax in 1773 precipitated a full-scale crisis that by 1775 resulted in war.

The Calm before the Storm

Repeal of the Townshend duties brought an end to nonimportation, despite the tax on tea. Trade boomed in 1770 and 1771. Moreover, the leaders of the popular movement seemed to be losing their power. Samuel Adams, for example, ran for a minor local office in Boston and lost to a conservative merchant.

Then in 1772, several incidents again brought the conflict with England into sharp focus. One was the burning of the *Gaspée*, a Royal Navy ship pursuing suspected smugglers off the coast of Rhode Island. A British investigating commission failed to arrest anyone but announced that it would send suspects, if any were found, to England for trial on charges of high treason. This ruling seemed to fly in the face of the traditional English right to trial by a jury of one's peers.

When news of the *Gaspée* investigation spread, it was greeted with disbelief in other colonies. Patrick Henry, Thomas Jefferson, and Richard Henry Lee in the Virginia House of Burgesses proposed that a network of standing committees be established to link the colonies and pass along alarming news. By mid-1773, every colonial assembly except Pennsylvania's had a "committee of correspondence."

Another British action in 1772 further spread the communications network. Lord North proposed to pay the salaries of superior court justices out of the tea revenue, similar to Townshend's plan for paying royal governors.

The Bloody Massacre Perpetrated in King Street, Boston, on March 5, 1770

This mass-produced engraving by Paul Revere sold for six pence a copy. In this patriot version of events, British soldiers fire on an unarmed crowd under orders of their captain. The tranquil dog is an artistic device to signal the crowd's peaceful intent. Crispus Attucks, a black sailor, was among the five killed, but Revere shows only whites among the casualties.

Anne S. K. Brown Military Collection, Brown University Library.

FOR MORE HELP ANALYZING THIS IMAGE, see the visual activity for this chapter in the Online Study Guide at bedfordstmartins.com/roarkcompact.

Tossing the Tea
This colored engraving appeared in an English book published in 1789, recounting the history of
North America from its earliest settlement to "becoming united, free, and independent states."
Men on the ship break into the chests and dump the contents; a few are depicted in Indian dis-
guise, with feathers on their heads or topknots of hair. A large crowd on the shore looks on. The
red rowboat is clearly stacked with tea chests, suggesting that some of the raiders were stealing
rather than destroying the tea. However, the artist, perhaps careless, shows the rowboat heading
toward the ship instead of away. This event was not dubbed the "Tea Party" until the 1830s,
when a later generation celebrated the illegal destruction of the tea and made heroes out of the
few surviving participants, by then men in their eighties and nineties.
Library of Congress.

The Boston town meeting, fearful that judges
would now be in the pockets of their new pay-
masters, urged all Massachusetts towns to establish a committee of correspondence. The first
vital message, circulated in December 1772, attacked the judges' salary policy as the latest proof
of a British plot to undermine traditional "liberties": unjust taxation, military occupation, massacre, now capped by the subversion of justice.
By spring 1773, half the towns in Massachusetts
had set up committees of correspondence, providing local forums for debate. These committees
politicized ordinary townspeople and bypassed
the official flow of power and information
through the colony's royal government.

The final incident shattering the relative
calm of the early 1770s was the Tea Act of 1773.
Americans had resumed buying the taxed British
tea, but they were also smuggling large quantities of Dutch tea, cutting into the sales of Britain's
East India Company. So Lord North proposed
legislation giving favored status to the East India
Company, allowing it to sell tea directly to government agents rather than through public auction to independent merchants. The hope was to
lower the price of the East India tea, including the
duty, below that of the smuggled Dutch tea, mo-
tivating Americans to obey the law.

Tea in Boston Harbor

In the fall of 1773, news of the Tea Act reached the
colonies. Parliamentary legislation to make tea inexpensive struck many colonists as an insidious
plot to trick Americans into buying large quantities of the duties tea. The real goal, some argued,
was the increased revenue, which would be used
to pay the royal governors and judges. The Tea Act
was thus a painful reminder of Parliament's claim
to the power to tax and legislate for the colonies.

But how to resist the Tea Act? Nonimportation
was not viable, because the tea trade was too

lucrative to expect all merchants to give it up willingly. Consumer boycotts were ineffective, because it was impossible to distinguish between dutied tea (the object of the boycott) and smuggled tea (illegal but politically clean) once it was in the teapot. The appointment of tea agents, parallel to the stamp act distributors, suggested one solution. In every port city, revived Sons of Liberty pressured tea agents to resign, and tea cargoes either landed without paperwork or were sent on their way home.

But Boston under Hutchinson was different. Three ships bearing tea arrived in November 1773. They cleared customs and unloaded their other cargoes but not the tea. Sensing the town's extreme tension, the captains wished to return to England, but Hutchinson would not grant them clearance to leave without paying the tea duty. Also, there was a time limit on the stay allowed in the harbor. After twenty days, the duty had to be paid or local authorities would confiscate the tea. Hutchinson refused to bend any rules.

For the full twenty days, pressure built in Boston. Daily mass meetings energized citizens from Boston and surrounding towns, alerted by the committees of correspondence. On the final day, December 16, a large crowd gathered at Old South Church to hear Samuel Adams declare, "This meeting can do nothing more to save the country." This was a signal to adjourn to the harbor, where between 100 and 150 men, thinly disguised as Indians, boarded the ships and dumped thousands of pounds of tea into the water while a crowd of 2,000 watched.

The Coercive Acts

Lord North's response was swift and stern; he persuaded Parliament to issue the Coercive Acts, four laws meant to punish Massachusetts. In America those laws, along with a fifth one, the Quebec Act, were soon known as the Intolerable Acts.

The Boston Port Act closed Boston harbor to all shipping as of June 1, 1774, until the destroyed tea was paid for. England's objective was to halt the commercial life of the city. The second act, called the Massachusetts Government Act, altered the colony's charter, underscoring Parliament's claim to supremacy over Massachusetts. The royal governor's powers were greatly augmented, and the council became an appointive, not elective, body. No town meeting beyond the annual spring election of town selectmen could be held unless the governor expressly permitted it.

Not only Boston but every Massachusetts town felt the punitive sting.

The third Coercive Act, the Impartial Administration of Justice Act, stipulated that any royal official accused of a capital crime—for example, Captain Preston and his soldiers at the Boston Massacre—would be tried in a court in England. It did not matter that Preston got a fair trial in Boston. What this act ominously suggested was that down the road more Captain Prestons and soldiers might be firing into unruly crowds.

The fourth act amended the 1765 Quartering Act and permitted military commanders to lodge soldiers wherever necessary, even in private households. In a related move, Lord North appointed General Thomas Gage, commander of the Royal Army in New York, governor of Massachusetts. Thomas Hutchinson was out, relieved at long last of his duties. Military rule, including soldiers, returned once more to Boston.

Ill-timed, the fifth act—the Quebec Act—had nothing to do with the four Coercive Acts, but it fed American fears. It confirmed the continuation of French civil law, government form, and Catholicism for Quebec—all an affront to **Protestant** New Englanders denied their own representative government. The act also gave Quebec control of disputed lands (and control of the lucrative fur trade) throughout the Ohio Valley, lands also claimed by Virginia, Pennsylvania, and a number of Indian tribes.

The five Intolerable Acts spread alarm in all the colonies. If England could squelch Massachusetts—change its charter, suspend government, inaugurate military rule, and on top of that give Ohio to Catholic Quebec—then what liberties were secure? Fearful royal governors in a half-dozen colonies suspended the sitting assemblies, adding to the sense of urgency; some suspended assemblies defiantly continued to meet in new locations. Through the committees of correspondence, colonial leaders arranged to meet in Philadelphia in the fall of 1774 to respond to the crisis.

The First Continental Congress

Every colony except Georgia sent delegates to Philadelphia to the First Continental Congress in September 1774. The gathering included notables such as Samuel Adams and John Adams from Massachusetts and George Washington and Patrick Henry from Virginia. A few colonies purposely sent men who opposed provoking a crisis with England, such as Pennsylvania's

Joseph Galloway, to keep the congress from becoming too radical.

Delegates sought to identify their liberties as British subjects and the powers Parliament held over them, and they debated possible responses to the Coercive Acts. Some wanted a total ban on trade with England to force repeal, while others, especially southerners dependent on tobacco and rice exports, opposed halting trade. Samuel Adams and Patrick Henry were eager for a ringing denunciation of all parliamentary control. The conservative Joseph Galloway proposed a plan (quickly defeated) to create a secondary parliament in America to assist the British Parliament in ruling the colonies.

The congress met for seven weeks and produced a declaration of rights couched in traditional language: "We ask only for peace, liberty and security. We wish no diminution of royal prerogatives, we demand no new rights." But, from England's point of view, the rights assumed already to exist were radical. Chief among them was the claim that Americans were not represented in Parliament and so each colonial government had the sole right to govern and tax its own people. The one slight concession to England was a carefully worded agreement that the colonists would "cheerfully consent" to trade regulations for the larger good of the empire—so long as trade regulation was not a covert means of raising revenue.

To put pressure on England, the delegates agreed to a staggered and limited boycott of trade—imports prohibited this year, exports the following, and rice totally exempted (to keep South Carolinians happy). To enforce the boycott, they called for a Continental Association, with chapters in each town variously called committees of public safety or of inspection, to monitor all commerce and punish suspected violators of the boycott (sometimes with a bucket of tar and a bag of feathers). Its work done, the congress disbanded in October 1774, with agreement to reconvene the following May.

The committees of public safety, the committees of correspondence, the regrouped and defiant colonial assemblies, and the Continental Congress were all political bodies functioning without any constitutional authority. British officials did not recognize them as legitimate, but many Americans who supported the patriot cause instantly accepted them. A key reason for the stability of such unauthorized governing bodies was that they were composed of generally the same men who had held elective office before.

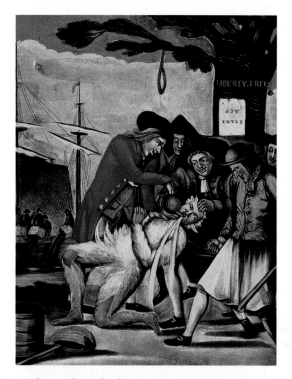

Tarring and Feathering Cartoon
In 1774, a Boston crowd tarred and feathered customs collector John Malcolm as punishment for extorting money from shippers. This ritualized humiliation involved stripping a man, painting him with hot tar, and dipping him in chicken feathers. Local committees of public safety often used threats of this treatment as a weapon to enforce boycotts; actual tarring and feathering was not a common occurrence. This cartoon, of British origin, is hostile to Americans, who are shown with cruelly gleeful faces, forcing tea down Malcolm's throat. The Liberty Tree has become a gallows; posted to it is the Stamp Act, upside down. The dumping of tea in the harbor is shown in the background.
Courtesy of the John Carter Brown Library at Brown University.

England's severe reaction to Boston's destruction of the tea finally succeeded in making many colonists from New Hampshire to Georgia realize that the problems of British rule went far beyond questions of taxation. The Coercive Acts infringed on liberty and denied self-government; they could not be ignored. With one colony already subordinated to military rule and a British army at the ready in Boston, the threat of a general war was at the doorstep.

REVIEW   Why did Parliament pass the Coercive Acts in 1774?

Domestic Insurrections, 1774–1775

Before the Second Continental Congress could meet, war broke out in Massachusetts. General Thomas Gage, military commander and the new royal governor, at first thought he faced a domestic insurrection that could be quieted with only a show of force. But the rebels saw things differently: They were defending their homes and liberties against an intrusive power bent on enslaving them. To the south, a different and inverted version of the same story began to unfold, as thousands of enslaved black men and women seized an unprecedented opportunity to mount a different kind of insurrection—against planter-patriots who looked over their shoulders uneasily whenever they called out for liberty from the British.

Lexington and Concord

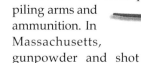

Over the winter of 1774–75 Americans pressed on with boycotts. Optimists hoped to effect a repeal of the Coercive Acts; pessimists started stockpiling arms and ammunition. In Massachusetts, gunpowder and shot were secretly stored, and militia units known as minutemen prepared to respond on a minute's notice to any threat from the British troops in Boston.

Thomas Gage soon realized how desperate the British position was. The people, Gage wrote Lord North, were "numerous, worked up to a fury, and not a Boston rabble but the freeholders and farmers of the country." Gage requested twenty thousand reinforcements. He also

---

British Troops in Concord Center

In this contemporary engraving by Amos Doolittle, based on a painting done on the spot by Ralph Earl, two British officers seek the high ground of the cemetery in Concord, Massachusetts, to orient themselves to the unfamiliar town at around 9 A.M. on April 19, 1775. Their troops march in formation, fresh from the skirmish at Lexington. American militiamen had amassed at the Old North Bridge, off to the right about a mile from the town center. The officer with the telescope is undoubtedly scanning for them.

Miriam and Ira D. Wallah Division of Art, Prints and Photographs, The New York Public Library. Astor, Lenox and Tilden Foundations.

strongly advised repeal of the Coercive Acts, but leaders in England could not admit failure. Instead, they ordered Gage in mid-April 1775 to arrest the trouble-makers immediately, before the Americans got better organized.

Gage quickly planned a surprise attack on a suspected ammunition storage site at Concord, a village eighteen miles west of Boston (Map 6.3). Near midnight on April 18, 1775, British soldiers moved west across the Charles River. Boston silversmith Paul Revere and William Dawes, a tanner, raced ahead to alert the minutemen. When the soldiers got to Lexington, a village five miles east of Concord, they were met by some seventy armed men assembled on the village green. The British commander barked out, "Lay down your arms, you damned rebels, and disperse." The militiamen hesitated and began to comply, turning to leave the green, but then someone—unknown—fired. In the next two minutes, more firing left eight Americans dead and ten wounded.

The British units continued their march to Concord, any pretense of surprise gone. Three companies of minutemen nervously occupied the town center but offered no challenge to the British as they searched in vain for the ammunition. Finally, at Old North Bridge in Concord, troops and minutemen exchanged shots, killing two Americans and three British soldiers.

By now both sides were very apprehensive. The British had failed to find the expected arms storage, and the Americans had failed to stop their raid. As the British returned to Boston along a narrow road, militia units in hiding attacked from the sides of the road in the bloodiest fighting of the day. In the end, 273 British soldiers were wounded or dead; the toll for the Americans stood at about 95. It was April 19, 1775, and the war had begun.

Rebelling against Slavery

News of the battles of Lexington and Concord spread rapidly. Within eight days, Virginians had heard of the fighting, and, as Thomas Jefferson reflected, "A phrenzy of revenge seems to have seized all ranks of people." The royal governor of Virginia, Lord Dunmore, removed a large quantity of gunpowder from the Williams-

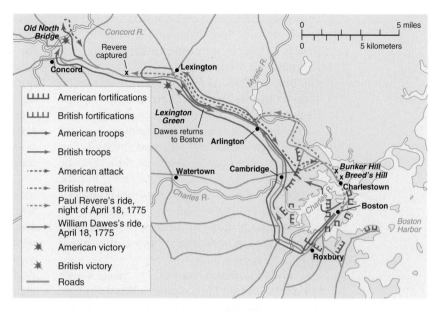

MAP 6.3 Lexington and Concord, April 1775
Under pressure from England, some 900 British forces at Boston staged a raid on a suspected rebel arms supply in Concord, Massachusetts, starting the first battle of the Revolutionary War. The routes of two early warning scouts are marked. Paul Revere went by boat from Boston to Charlestown and then continued by horse through Medford to Lexington, while William Dawes casually passed British sentries guarding the only land route out of Boston, a land bridge called the Neck, and then rode his horse full speed to Lexington. Re-vere and Dawes reached Samuel Adams and John Hancock, guests in a Lexington home, and urged them to flee to avoid capture. The two then went on to Concord, to warn residents of the impending attack.

READING THE MAP: William Dawes was, like Paul Revere, a messenger who raced ahead of British troops to warn the minutemen of British plans for raiding their supply of weapons. How did Dawes's route differ from Revere's? What kinds of terrain and potential dangers did each man face during his ride, according to the map?

CONNECTIONS: Why might it matter who shot first on the Lexington Green? What is at stake for each side in claiming the other shot first?

FOR MORE HELP ANALYZING THIS MAP, see the map activity for this chapter in the Online Study Guide at bedfordstmartins.com/roarkcompact.

burg powder house and put it on a ship in the dead of night, out of reach of any frenzied Virginians. Next, he threatened to arm slaves, if necessary, to ward off attacks by colonists.

This was an effective threat; Dunmore understood full well how to produce panic among the planters. He did not act on his warning until November 1775, when he issued an official proclamation promising freedom to defecting able-bodied slaves who would fight for the British. Although Dunmore wanted to scare the planters, he had no intention of liberating all slaves or of starting a real slave rebellion. Female, young, and elderly slaves were not welcome behind British lines, and many were sent back to face irate masters. Astute blacks noticed that Dunmore neglected to free his own slaves. A Virginia barber named Caesar declared that "he did not know any one foolish enough to believe him [Dunmore], for if he intended to do so, he ought first to set his own free."

By December 1775, around 1,500 slaves in Virginia had fled to Lord Dunmore, who armed them and called them his "Ethiopian Regiment." Camp diseases quickly set in: dysentery, typhoid fever, and worst of all, smallpox. When Dunmore sailed for England in mid-1776, he took just 300 black survivors with him. But the association of freedom with the British authorities had been established, and throughout the war, thousands more southern slaves made bold to run away as soon as they heard the British army was approaching.

In the northern colonies as well, slaves clearly recognized the evolving political struggle with England as an ideal moment to bid for freedom. A twenty-one-year-old Boston domestic slave employed biting sarcasm in a 1774 newspaper essay to call attention to the hypocrisy of local slave owners:  "How well the Cry for Liberty, and the reverse Disposition for exercise of oppressive Power over others agree,—I humbly think it does not require the Penetration of a Philosopher to Determine." This extraordinary young woman, Phillis Wheatley, had already gained international recognition through a book of poems, endorsed by Governor Thomas Hutchinson and Boston merchant John Hancock and published in London in 1773. Possibly neither man fully appreciated the irony of his endorsement, however, for Wheatley's poems spoke of "Fair Freedom" as the "Goddess long desir'd" by Africans enslaved in America. At the urging of his wife, Wheatley's master freed the young poet in 1775.

Wheatley's poetic ideas about freedom found concrete expression among other discontented groups. Some slaves in Boston petitioned Thomas Gage, promising to fight for the British if he would liberate them. Gage turned them down. In Ulster County, New York, along the Hudson River, two blacks were overheard discussing gunpowder, and thus a plot unraveled that involved at least twenty slaves in four villages discovered to have ammunition stashed away.

In Maryland, soon after the news of the Lexington battle arrived, blacks exhibited impatience with their status as slaves, causing one Maryland planter to report that "the insolence of the Negroes in this county is come to such a height, that we are under a necessity of disarming them.…We took about eighty guns, some bayonets, swords, etc." In North Carolina, a planned uprising was uncovered and scores of slaves were arrested; ironically, it was the revolutionary committee of public safety that ordered the whippings to punish this quest for liberty.

By 1783, when the Revolutionary War ended, as many as 20,000 blacks had voted against slavery with their feet by seeking refuge with the British army. Most failed to achieve the liberation they were seeking. The British generally used them for menial labor; and disease, especially smallpox, devastated encampments of runaways. But some eight to ten thousand persisted through the war and later, under the protection of the British army, left America to start new lives of freedom in Canada's Nova Scotia or Africa's Sierra Leone.

REVIEW How did enslaved people in the colonies react to the stirrings of revolution?

Conclusion: How Far Does Liberty Go?

The Seven Years' War set the stage for the imperial crisis of the 1760s and 1770s by creating distrust between England and its colonies and by running up a huge deficit in the British treasury. The years from 1763 to 1775 brought repeated attempts by the British government to subordinate the colonies into taxpaying partners in the larger scheme of empire.

American resistance grew slowly but steadily over those years. In 1765, loyalist Thomas Hutchinson shared with patriot Samuel Adams the belief that it was exceedingly unwise for England to assert a right to taxation, because Parliament did not adequately represent Americans. But by temperament and office, Hutchinson had to uphold British policy; Adams, in contrast, protested the policy and made political activists out of thousands in the process.

By 1775, events propelled many Americans to the conclusion that a concerted effort was afoot to deprive them of all their liberties, the most important of which were the right to self-taxation, the right to live free of an occupying army, and the right to self-rule. Hundreds of minutemen converged on Concord, prepared to die for these American liberties. April 19 marked the start of their rebellion.

Another rebellion under way in 1775 was doomed to be short-circuited. Black Americans who had experienced actual slavery listened to shouts of "Liberty!" from white crowds and appropriated the language of revolution swirling around them that spoke to their deepest needs and hopes. Defiance of authority was indeed contagious.

The emerging leaders of the patriot cause were mindful of a delicate balance they felt they had to strike. To energize the American public about the crisis with England, they had to politicize masses of men—and eventually women too—and infuse them with a keen sense of their rights and liberties. But in so doing, they became fearful of the unintended consequences of teaching a vocabulary of rights and liberties. They worried that the rhetoric of enslavement might go too far.

The question of how far the crisis could be stretched before something snapped was largely unexamined in 1765. Patriot leaders in that year wanted a correction, a restoration of an ancient liberty of self-taxation that Parliament seemed to be ignoring. But events from 1765 to 1775 convinced many that a return to the old ways was impossible. Challenging Parliament's right to tax had led, step by step, to challenging Parliament's right to legislate over the colonies in any matter. If Parliament's sovereignty was set aside, then who actually had authority over the American colonies? By 1775, with the outbreak of fighting and the specter of slave rebellions, American leaders turned to the king for the answer to that question.

Suggestions for Further Reading

Fred Anderson, *Crucible of War: The Seven Years' War and the Fate of Empire in British North America, 1754–1766* (2000). A gripping and richly detailed account of the world war that precipitated the American Revolution.

Bernard Bailyn, *The Ordeal of Thomas Hutchinson* (1974). A sympathetic portrait of an unyielding man caught in a revolution he could not countenance.

Robert A. Gross, *The Minutemen and Their World* (25th anniversary ed., 2001). The American Revolution in microcosm, built on a social history of the sleepy village of Concord, Massachusetts.

Woody Holton, *Forced Founders: Indians, Debtors, Slaves, and the Making of the American Revolution in Virginia* (1999). An account of how debt crisis, land speculation, and fears of Indian raids and slave rebellions shaped the political actions of the Virginia gentry on the eve of the Revolution.

Robert Middlekauff, *The Glorious Cause: The American Revolution, 1763–1789* (rev. ed., 2005). A classic panoramic history of the American Revolution.

Alfred F. Young, *The Shoemaker and the Tea Party: Memory and the American Revolution* (1999). An exploration of the life of the last surviving participant in the Boston Tea Party.

▶ For more books about topics in this chapter, see the Online Study Guide at bedfordstmartins.com/roarkcompact.

▶ For additional firsthand accounts of this period, see Chapter 6 in Michael Johnson, ed., *Reading the American Past,* Third Edition.

▶ For Web sites and documents related to topics and places in this chapter, see "HistoryLinks," "DocLinks," and "PlaceLinks" at bedfordstmartins.com/roarkcompact.

REVIEWING THE CHAPTER

Follow these steps to review and strengthen your understanding of the chapter.

STEP 1: *Study the **Key Terms** and **Timeline** to identify the significance of each item listed.*

STEP 2: *Answer the **Review Questions**, drawing on key terms and dates to support your answers.*

STEP 3: *Drawing on the Key Terms, Timeline, and Review Questions, answer the broader **Making Connections** questions.*

KEY TERMS

Who

Thomas Hutchinson (p. 131)
Robert Dinwiddie (p. 133)
George Washington (p. 133)
Tanaghrisson (p. 133)
Benjamin Franklin (p. 135)
Edward Braddock (p. 135)
William Pitt (p. 135)
George III (p. 138)
Pontiac (p. 138)
George Grenville (p. 139)
Patrick Henry (p. 142)
Samuel Adams (p. 143)
Andrew Oliver (p. 143)
Charles Townshend (p. 145)
Thomas Preston (p. 147)
Frederick North (p. 148)
Thomas Gage (p. 152)

minutemen (p. 152)
Paul Revere (p. 153)
Lord Dunmore (p. 153)
Phillis Wheatley (p. 154)

What

Seven Years' War (p. 132)
Ohio Company (p. 133)
Fort Duquesne (p. 133)
"Fort Necessity" (p. 134)
Covenant Chain (p. 135)
Albany Plan of Union (p. 135)
Treaty of Paris (p. 135)
Proclamation of 1763 (p. 138)
Molasses Act of 1733 (p. 139)
Sugar Act (Revenue Act of 1764) (p. 139)
Stamp Act (p. 142)
virtual representation (p. 142)

Virginia Resolves (p. 142)
Sons of Liberty (p. 143)
Stamp Act Congress (p. 144)
Declaratory Act (p. 144)
Revenue Act of 1767 (p. 145)
nonconsumption agreements (p. 145)
nonimportation agreements (p. 146)
Daughters of Liberty (p. 146)
Boston Massacre (p. 147)
Gaspée (p. 148)
committees of correspondence (p. 149)
Tea Act of 1773 (p. 149)
Coercive Acts (p. 150)
First Continental Congress (p. 150)
Continental Association (p. 151)
committees of public safety (p. 151)

TIMELINE

◄ **1747** • Ohio Company of Virginia formed.

1754 • Seven Years' War begins in North America.
• Albany Congress proposes Plan of Union (never implemented).

1755 • Braddock's defeat in western Pennsylvania.

1757 • William Pitt fully commits England to war effort.

1759 • Quebec falls to British.

1760 • Montreal falls to British.
• George III becomes British king.

1763 • Treaty of Paris ends Seven Years' War.
• Pontiac's uprising.
• Paxton Boys massacre friendly Indians in Pennsylvania.
• Proclamation of 1763.

1764 • Parliament enacts Revenue (Sugar) Act.

1765 • Parliament enacts Stamp Act.
• Virginia Resolves challenge Stamp Act.
• Dozens of crowd actions by Sons of Liberty.
• Stamp Act Congress meets.

REVIEW QUESTIONS

1. How did the Seven Years' War erode relations between colonists and Britain? (pp. 132–38)

2. Why did the Sugar and Stamp acts draw fierce opposition from colonists? (pp. 139–44)

3. Why did Britain send troops to occupy Boston in the fall of 1768? (pp. 145–47)

4. Why did Parliament pass the Coercive Acts in 1774? (pp. 148–51)

5. How did enslaved people in the colonies react to the stirrings of revolution? (pp. 152–54)

MAKING CONNECTIONS

1. In the mid-eighteenth century, how did Native Americans influence relations between European nations? Between Britain and the colonists?

2. Why did disputes over taxation figure so prominently in the deteriorating relations between Britain and the colonies? In your answer, refer to specific disputed British attempts to raise revenue and the colonial response.

3. How did the colonists organize to oppose British power so effectively? In your answer, discuss the role of communications in facilitating the colonial resistance, being sure to cite specific examples.

▶ **FOR PRACTICE QUIZZES, A CUSTOMIZED STUDY PLAN, AND OTHER STUDY TOOLS,** see the Online Study Guide at bedfordstmartins.com/roarkcompact.

1766 • Parliament repeals Stamp Act and passes Declaratory Act.

1767 • Parliament enacts Townshend duties.

1768 • British station troops in Boston.

1769 • Merchants sign nonimportation agreements.

1770 • Boston Massacre.
     • Parliament repeals Townshend duties.

1772 • British navy ship *Gaspée* burned.
     • Committees of correspondence formed.

1773 • Parliament passes Tea Act.
     • Dumping of tea in Boston Harbor.

1774 • Parliament passes Coercive Acts (Intolerable Acts).
     • First Continental Congress meets; Continental Association formed.

1775 • Battles of Lexington and Concord.
     • Lord Dunmore promises freedom to defecting slaves.

CONTINENTAL ARMY UNIFORM WORN AT THE SIEGE OF FORT STANWIX, 1777

In 1775, the Continental Congress faced the daunting prospect of fielding an army to fight the largest military force in the world. Money was scarce, soldiers were hastily trained and short of equipment, and uniforms were hard to come by. (Many were purchased from France.) At the start of the war, ordinary enlisted men often wore brown work clothes, and while this outfit gave them a unified look, it did not allow for easy categorization of soldiers by their units. When General Washington finally issued dress specifications, he chose the color already preferred by many officers—dark blue—and then specified the variety of colors to be used for the facings and linings of the coat to establish the rank and the unit of each soldier. Officers especially needed distinctive clothing to distinguish them from ordinary soldiers and from other officers, so that the military hierarchy could be maintained at all times. The coat pictured here belonged to a brigadier general, Peter Gansevoort, who was twenty-eight in 1777 and in command of Fort Stanwix in the Mohawk Valley of New York. The coat has a buff-colored lining (seen inside the coattails) and bright red facings on the collar, the lapel, and the cuffs, marking him as a New York soldier. The color of the shoulder ribbons reveals Gansevoort's rank; the ribbons could be easily replaced with a new color, enabling a man to ascend in rank without having to get a new coat. Young Gansevoort became a celebrated hero when he successfully defended Fort Stanwix against an attack by British and Indians; his grandson, the author Herman Melville, named his second son Stanwix to honor the event.

National Museum of American History, Smithsonian Institution, Washington, D.C.

7

The War for America
1775–1783

ABIGAIL ADAMS WAS IMPATIENT for American independence. While her husband, John, was away in Philadelphia as a member of the Second Continental Congress, Abigail tended house and farm in Braintree, Massachusetts, just south of British-occupied Boston. She had four young children to look after, and in addition to her feminine duties, such as cooking, sewing, and making soap, she also had to shoulder masculine duties in her husband's absence—hiring farm help, managing rental property, selling the crop. John wrote to her often, approving of the fine "Farmeress" who was conducting his business so well. She replied, conveying news of the family along with shrewd commentary on revolutionary politics. In December 1775, she chastised the congress for being too timid and urged that independence be declared. A few months later, she astutely observed to John that southern slave owners might shrink from a war in the name of **liberty**: "I have sometimes been ready to think that the passion for Liberty cannot be Equally strong in the Breasts of those who have been accustomed to deprive their fellow Creatures of theirs."

"I long to hear that you have declared an independency," she wrote in March 1776. "And by the way in the new Code of Laws which I suppose it will be necessary for you to make I desire you would Remember the Ladies, and be more generous and favourable to them than your ancestors." If Abigail was politically precocious in favoring independence and questioning slave owners' devotion to liberty, she was positively visionary in this extraordinary plea to her husband to "Remember the Ladies." "Do not put such unlimited power into the hands of the Husbands," she advised. "Remember all Men would be tyrants if they could." Abigail had put her finger on another form of tyranny that was rarely remarked on in her society: that of men over women. "If particular care and attention is not paid to the Ladies," she jokingly threatened, "we are determined to foment a Rebellion, and will not hold ourselves bound by any Laws in which we have no voice, or Representation."

John Adams dismissed his wife's provocative idea as a "saucy" suggestion: "As to your extraordinary Code of Laws, I cannot but Laugh." The Revolution had perhaps unleashed discontent among other dependent groups, he allowed; children, apprentices, students, Indians, and blacks had grown "disobedient" and "insolent." "But your Letter was the first Intimation that another Tribe more numerous and powerful than all the rest were grown discontented." Men were too smart to repeal their "Masculine Systems," John assured her, for otherwise they would find themselves living under a "despotism of the petticoat."

This clever exchange between husband and wife in 1776 says much about the cautious, limited radicalism of the American Revolution. Both John and Abigail Adams understood (Abigail probably far more than John) that ungluing the hierarchical bond between the king and his subjects potentially unglued

Abigail Adams

Abigail Smith Adams was twenty-two when she sat for this pastel portrait in 1766. A wife for two years and a mother for one, Adams exhibits a steady, intelligent gaze. Pearls and a lace collar anchor her femininity, while her facial expression projects a confidence and maturity not often credited to young women of the 1760s.

Courtesy of the Massachusetts Historical Society ©.

other kinds of social inequalities. John was surely joking in listing the groups made unruly in the spirit of a challenge to authority, for children, apprentices, and students were hardly rebellious in the 1770s. But it would soon prove to be an uncomfortable joke, because Indians and blacks did strike for their own liberty during the Revolution, and the great majority of them saw their liberty best served by joining the British side in the war.

Though Abigail Adams was impatient for independence, many other Americans feared separation from Britain. What kind of civilized country had no king? Who, if not Britain, would protect Americans from the French and Spanish? How could the colonies possibly win a war against the most powerful military machine on the globe? Reconciliation, not independence, was favored by many.

Members of the Continental Congress, whether they were pro-independence like John Adams or more cautiously hoping for reconcilia-

tion, had their hands full in 1775 and 1776. The war had already begun, and the congress had to raise an army, finance it, and explore diplomatic alliances with foreign countries. In part a classic war with professional armies and textbook battles, the Revolutionary War was also a civil war in America, at times even a brutal **guerrilla war**, of committed rebels versus loyalists.

In one glorious moment, the congress issued a ringing statement about how social hierarchy would be rearranged in America after submission to the king was undone. That was on July 4, 1776, when the Declaration of Independence asserted that "all men are created equal." But this striking phrase went completely unremarked in the two days of congressional debate spent tinkering with the language of the Declaration. The solvent to dissolve social inequalities in America was created at that moment, but none of the men at the congress, or even Abigail Adams up in Braintree, fully realized it at the time.

The Second Continental Congress

On May 10, 1775, nearly one month after the fighting at Lexington and Concord, the Second Continental Congress assembled in Philadelphia. The congress immediately set to work on two crucial and seemingly contradictory tasks: to raise and supply an army and to explore reconciliation with England. To do the former, they needed soldiers and a commander to come to the aid of the Massachusetts militiamen, they needed money, and they needed to work out a declaration of war. To do the latter, however, they needed diplomacy to approach the king. But the king was not receptive, and by 1776, as the war progressed and hopes of reconciliation faded, delegates at the congress began to ponder the treasonous act of declaring independence—said by some to be plain common sense.

Assuming Political and Military Authority

Like members of the First Continental Congress (see chapter 6), the delegates to the second were well-established figures in their home colonies, but they still had to learn to know and trust each other; they did not always agree. The Adams cousins John and Samuel defined the radical end of the spectrum, favoring independence. John

Dickinson of Pennsylvania, no longer the eager revolutionary who had dashed off *Letters from a Farmer* back in 1767, was now a moderate, seeking reconciliation with England. Benjamin Franklin, fresh off a ship from an eleven-year residence in England, was feared by some to be a British spy. Mutual suspicions flourished easily when the undertaking was so dangerous, opinions were so varied, and a misstep could spell disaster.

Most of the delegates were not yet prepared to break with England. Several legislatures instructed their delegates to oppose independence. Some felt that government without a king was unworkable, while others feared it might be suicidal to lose England's protection against the traditional enemies, France and Spain. Colonies that traded actively with England feared undermining their economies. Probably the vast majority of ordinary Americans were unable to envision independence. From the Stamp Act of 1765 to the Coercive Acts of 1774 (see chapter 6), the constitutional struggle with England had turned on the issue of parliamentary power. During that decade, almost no one had questioned the legitimacy of the monarchy.

The few men at the Continental Congress who did think that independence was desirable were, not surprisingly, from Massachusetts. Their colony had been stripped of civil government under the Coercive Acts, and their capital was occupied by the British army. Even so, those men knew that it was premature to push for a break with England. John Adams wrote to Abigail in June 1775: "America is a great, unwieldy body. Its progress must be slow. It is like a large fleet sailing under convoy. The fleetest sailors must wait for the dullest and slowest."

As slow as the American colonies were in sailing toward political independence, they needed to take swift action to coordinate a military defense, for the Massachusetts countryside was under threat of further attack. Even the hesitant moderates in the congress agreed that a military buildup was necessary. Around the country, militia units from New York to Georgia collected arms and drilled on village greens in anticipation. (See "The Promise of Technology," page 162.) On June 14, the congress voted to create the Continental army. Choosing the commander in chief offered an opportunity to demonstrate that this was no local war of a single rebellious colony. The congress bypassed Artemas Ward from Massachusetts, a veteran of the Seven Years' War, then already commanding the soldiers massed around Boston, and instead chose a southerner, George Washington.

Washington's appointment sent the clear message to England that there was widespread commitment to war beyond New England.

Next the congress drew up a document titled "A Declaration on the Causes and Necessity of Taking Up Arms," which rehearsed familiar arguments about the tyranny of Parliament and the need to defend English liberties. This declaration was first drafted by a young Virginia **planter**, Thomas Jefferson, a newcomer to the congress and a radical on the question of independence. The moderate John Dickinson, fearing that the declaration would offend England and rule out reconciliation, was allowed to rewrite it; however, he still left much of Jefferson's highly charged language about choosing "to die freemen rather than to live slaves." Even a man as reluctant for independence as Dickinson acknowledged the necessity of military defense against an invading army.

To pay for the military buildup, the congress authorized a currency issue of $2 million. The Continental dollars were merely paper; they did not represent gold or silver, for the congress owned no precious metals. The delegates somewhat naively expected that the currency would be accepted as valuable on trust as it spread in the population through the hands of soldiers, farmers, munitions suppliers, and beyond.

In just two months, the Second Continental Congress had created an army, declared war, and issued its own currency. It had taken on the major functions of a legitimate government, both military and financial, without any legal basis for its authority, for it had not—and would not for a full year—declare independence from the authority of the king.

Pursuing Both War and Peace

Three days after the congress approved a Continental army, one of the bloodiest battles of the Revolution occurred. The British commander in Boston, Thomas Gage, had recently received troop reinforcements, three talented generals (William Howe, John Burgoyne, and Henry Clinton), and new instructions to root out the rebels around Boston. But before Gage could take the offensive, the Americans fortified the hilly terrain of Charlestown, a peninsula just north of Boston, on the night of June 16, 1775.

The British generals could have nipped off the peninsula where it met the mainland, to box in the Americans. But General Howe insisted on a bold frontal assault, sending his 2,500 soldiers across the water and up the hill in an intimidating but

Arming the Soldiers: Muskets and Rifles

How combat-ready was the American side in the Revolutionary War? Were there adequate numbers of firearms along with men trained in their use? These lively and important questions have recently generated sharp debate among historians. A book published in 2000 argued that gun ownership was surprisingly rare in the 1770s, occurring in only one out of seven households. This finding did not square with historians' largely untested assumption that a militia-based defense system implied that nearly all households contained a gun. The ensuing controversy quickly became a firestorm, involving activists on both sides of the modern gun-control debate as well as historians. In consequence, the examination of evidence and methods to evaluate gun ownership has been considerably sharpened.

What were eighteenth-century guns like? Guns called fowling pieces fired shot (small pellets) and were useful for hunting ducks and wild turkeys and small game such as raccoons and squirrels. For larger game and for warfare, muskets, a sixteenth-century invention, were the preferred weapon. By the mid-eighteenth century, the musket had an improved flintlock ignition system: The trigger released a spring-held cock that caused a hammer to strike a flint, creating sparks; the sparks set off a small charge in a priming pan, producing a larger explosion in the gun barrel. To load a musket, the shooter first put the hammer on half cock to prevent an accidental firing. He next put a small quantity of gunpowder (carried in a powder horn) in the priming pan and closed it, poured more gunpowder down the smooth gun barrel, dropped in the projectile—usually a one-ounce lead ball—and with a ramrod wadded paper down the gun barrel to hold the loose ball in place. He then raised the gun to firing position, put the hammer on full cock, and fired. The whole procedure took highly experienced shooters from 45 to 90 seconds.

The range of muskets extended only about 50 to 100 yards. They were notoriously inaccurate because of the poor fit between ball and barrel and the considerable kick produced by firing, which interfered with aiming. Far more accurate were the longer-barreled rifles, used in frontier regions where big-game hunting was more common. Spiral grooves inside the rifle barrel imparted spin to the lead ball as it traversed the barrel, stabilizing and lengthening its flight and enabling expert marksmen to hit small targets at 150 or 200 yards. Yet militiamen preferred muskets. Rifles took twice as long to load and fire, and their longer barrels made them unwieldy for soldiers on the march. Inaccurate muskets were quite deadly enough when fired by a group of soldiers in unison at targets 50 yards away.

How many American men actually owned fowling pieces, muskets, or rifles? A partial answer can be gleaned from probate inventories, many thousands of which exist in state archives. Inventories listed a decedent's possessions to facilitate settling the estate and to make sure creditors were paid off. Yet these sources are fraught with thorny problems. For one thing, many inventories are not complete: If few of them itemized clothing, can we conclude the decedents went nude? If no firearm is listed, can we conclude the decedent *never* owned a gun? Clearly not. Probate inventories were made for only a subset of dead property owners, primarily for the use of creditors and heirs, so they are biased by age (older), sex (male), and wealth (more).

Despite complexities, scholars have worked with probate inventories to establish a baseline figure for gun ownership. It takes sophistication with statistical sampling technique as well as ability to read old handwriting to use the evidence, since the thousands of inventories cannot all be tallied. Recent careful studies based on this source yield estimates on overall gun ownership that range from 40 to 50 percent of all probated estates in the 1770s.

A second way to assess gun ownership is to look at the arms procurement experiences of state legislatures and the Continental Congress as they geared up for war. In the early months of 1775, New England patriot leaders had a keen interest to know how many armed soldiers could be mobilized in the event of war. One scholar has located militia returns from thirty towns in Massachusetts, New Hampshire, and Rhode Island. Scattered returns from other states exist in archives. At their most complete, these records form a census of soldiers and equipment taken on a militia training day. A particularly detailed list from Salem, Massachusetts, notes against each man's name his ownership of a fire-lock, a bayonet, a sword, a pouch, a cartouche box, a cartridge, a flint, lead balls, gunpowder, a knapsack, and priming wires. Salem's list appears to support the conclusion that 100 percent of adult men owned guns, yet the scholar seeking to calculate gun ownership must ask: Who is not on this list? Who failed to report to the muster exercise? This careful study concludes that in 1775, probably three-quarters of all men ages sixteen to sixty in New England owned guns.

These high rates of ownership, however, are not matched by a final kind of evidence: reports from militia officers to state legislatures complaining of being underarmed. A New Hampshire captain complained of his unit's plight in June 1775: "We are in want of both arms and ammunition. There is but very little, nor none worth mentioning—perhaps one pound of powder to twenty men, and not one-half our men have arms." A militia officer in Pennsylvania noted that men who owned high-quality muskets and rifles were often reluctant to report for active duty with them unless assured they would be reimbursed in the event of loss of the valuable possession. A Prussian general who volunteered his expertise to the Continental army arrived at Valley Forge in 1778 and was shocked to find "muskets, carbines, fowling pieces, and rifles" all in the same company of troops. Lack of unifor-mity in guns posed considerable problems for supplying appropriate ammunition. While this evidence seems to point to an underarmed soldiery, the opposite evidence—militia captains who failed to register complaints—did not leave a corresponding paper trail for historians. Historians must take care not to be misled by stray documents or quotations that may be atypical.

The Continental Congress knew more guns were needed, certainly. Before 1774, American artisans imported British-made gunlocks, the central firing mechanism, and added the wooden stock and iron barrel to produce muskets. But in October 1774, the British Parliament, anticipating trouble, prohibited all gunlock and firearm exports to the colonies. Congress then turned to French and Dutch suppliers to purchase gunlocks, gunpowder, and finished muskets.

Muskets and even fowling pieces worked well enough for the Revolutionary War, where similarly armed combatants engaged in massed, synchronized firing at close range. In individual use, however, muskets were clumsy, inaccurate, and not highly lethal. High rates of musket ownership did not translate to high rates of successful homicide or accidental deaths by shooting. Sixty years after the Revolution, all that changed with the advent of machine-tooled firearms such as the Colt revolver and the Remington rifle. Those new repeat-fire weapons were cheaper, more accurate, and far more deadly. Comparing ownership rates of muskets and of revolvers—or assault weapons—across time may not be the most meaningful path to understanding this country's historic relationship with guns.

Powder Horn

James Pike, a twenty-three-year-old New England militiaman, made and then personalized this powder horn, a hollow cow's horn capped on both ends with leather. The stopper was designed to be pulled off by the teeth so the hands of the user would be free to hold the musket barrel and pour the powder. Pike's carvings suggest his motivation for fighting. Above his name he depicts a scene dated April 19, 1775, in which British soldiers, labeled "the Aggressors," fire through the Liberty Tree at "Provincials, Defending." Pike was not at Lexington or Concord; his first combat experience came two months later at the battle of Bunker Hill, where he saw his brother killed and was himself wounded in the shoulder.
Chicago Historical Society.

Committee of Safety Musket

This gun was one of the small number of American-made muskets produced in 1775 in a German region of Pennsylvania where blacksmith shops were numerous. The smithy forged and fashioned the gun barrel and attached it to an imported gunlock, the mechanism over the trigger. A wooden stock completed the design.
York County Historical Society.

potentially costly attack. The American troops, 1,400 strong, listened to the British drummers pacing the uphill march and held their fire until the British were about twenty yards away. At that distance, the musket volley was sure and deadly, and the British turned back. Twice more General Howe sent his men up the hill and received the same blast of firepower; each time they had to step around the bodies of men felled in the previous attempts.

Battle of Bunker Hill, 1775

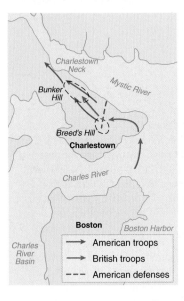

On the third assault, the British took the hill, mainly because the American ammunition supply gave out, and the defenders quickly retreated. The battle of Bunker Hill was thus a British victory, but an expensive one. The dead numbered 226 on the British side, with more than 800 wounded; the Americans suffered 140 dead, 271 wounded, and 30 captured. As General Clinton later remarked, "It was a dear bought victory; another such would have ruined us."

Instead of pursuing the fleeing Americans, Howe pulled his army back to Boston, unwilling to risk more raids into the countryside. If the British had had any grasp of the basic instability of the American units gathered around Boston, they might have pushed westward and perhaps decisively defeated the Americans. Instead they lingered in Boston, abandoning it without a fight nine months later. Howe used the time in Boston to inoculate his army against smallpox, because a new epidemic of the deadly disease was spreading in port cities along the Atlantic. Inoculation worked by producing a light but real (and therefore risky) case of smallpox, followed by lifelong immunity. Howe's instinct here was right: From 1775 to 1782, the years coinciding with the American Revolution, some 130,000 people on the American continent, most of them Indians, died of smallpox.

A week after Bunker Hill, when General Washington arrived to take charge of the new Continental army, he found enthusiastic but undisciplined troops. Sanitation was an unknown concept, drunkenness on duty was common, and soldiers came and went at will. The amazed general attributed the disarray to the New England custom of letting militia units elect their own officers, a custom he felt undermined deference. Washington quickly imposed more hierarchy and authority.

While military plans moved forward, the Second Continental Congress pursued its second,

contradictory objective, reconciliation with England. Delegates from the middle colonies (Pennsylvania, Delaware, and New York), whose merchants depended on trade with England, urged that channels for negotiation remain open. In July 1775, congressional moderates led by John Dickinson engineered an appeal to the king called the Olive Branch Petition. The petition affirmed loyalty to the monarchy and blamed all the troubles on the king's ministers and on Parliament. It proposed that the American colonial assemblies be recognized as individual parliaments, under the umbrella of the monarchy. By late fall 1775, however, reconciliation was out of the question. King George III rejected the Olive Branch Petition and heatedly condemned the Americans, calling them rebels and traitors. Thereafter it was hard to blame only ministers and not the king himself for the conflict.

Thomas Paine and the Case for Independence

Pressure for independence started to mount in January 1776, when a pamphlet titled *Common Sense* appeared in Philadelphia. Thomas Paine, its author, was an English **artisan** and coffeehouse intellectual who had come to America in the fall of 1774. He landed a job with the *Pennsylvania Magazine* and soon met delegates from the Second Continental Congress. With their encouragement, he wrote *Common Sense* to lay out a lively and compelling case for complete independence.

In simple yet forceful language, Paine elaborated on the absurdities of the British monarchy. Why should one man, by accident of birth, claim extensive power over others? he asked. A king might be foolish or wicked. "One of the strongest natural proofs of the folly of hereditary right in kings," Paine wrote, "is that nature disapproves it; otherwise she would not so frequently turn it into ridicule by giving mankind *an ass for a lion*." Calling the king of England an ass broke through the automatic deference most Americans still had for the monarchy. To replace monarchy, he advocated **republican** government, based on the consent of the people. Rulers, according to Paine, were only representatives of the people, and the best form of government relied on frequent elections to achieve the most direct **democracy** possible.

Paine's pamphlet sold more than 150,000 copies in a matter of weeks. Newspapers reprinted it; men read it aloud in taverns and coffeehouses; John Adams sent a copy to Abigail Adams, who passed it around to neighbors. New

An Exact View of the Late Battle at Charlestown, June 17th 1775

This dramatic panorama is the earliest visual representation of the battle of Bunker Hill. On sale to the public six weeks after the battle, the engraving shows Charlestown in flames (center back) and British and American soldiers in fixed formation firing muskets at each other. The Americans, to the left, are dug in along the crest of the hill; British casualties have begun to mount up. The artist, Bernard Romans, was a noted cartographer, military engineer, linguist, and mathematician. Born in the Netherlands, he came to America as a British-paid surveyor, but he took the American side in the Revolution. His maps of war zones were bought by Americans eager to track the geography of war. His large depiction of Bunker Hill, produced in multiple copies, some of them hand-colored like this one, likely decorated many a patriot's wall. It was advertised for sale in newspapers in Philadelphia and Virginia, and a half-size copy was engraved and inserted in an issue of *The Pennsylvania Magazine,* a monthly periodical edited by Thomas Paine. One ad for the picture promised that "Every well-wisher to this country cannot but delight in seeing a plan of the ground on which our brave American Army conquered the British Ministerial Forces." Technically the British won the battle by taking the hill, but that was not the story told by this picture.

Colonial Williamsburg Foundation.

George Washington's Camp Chest

This portable camp chest (or mess kit) belonged to George Washington during the Revolutionary War. The wooden box, covered in leather and lined with wool fabric, held an elaborate setup neatly collapsed into a small space: four tin pots with detached handles, five tin plates, three tin platters, two tin boxes, two knives, three forks, eight glass bottles with cork stoppers, salt and pepper shakers, and a woolen sack with six compartments. The chest also contained a tinder box, which held kindling and a flint for starting a fire, and a gridiron (or grate) with collapsed legs for cooking over the fire. Washington—or, more likely, a subordinate preparing his food—would have used this chest when the army was on the move. It was an officer's chest, presented to the general by a Philadelphia merchant in 1776; enlisted men would have had something much more basic, if anything. Washington saved the chest for two decades after the war. After his death it was auctioned off and donated to the federal government by the new owner. It is now owned by the Smithsonian Institution in Washington, D.C.

National Museum of American History, Smithsonian Institution, Behring Center.

Englanders desired independence, but other colonies, under no immediate threat of violence, remained cautious. But by May, all but four colonies favored independence. Two of the holdouts were Pennsylvania and South Carolina, both with large loyalist populations.

In early June, the Virginia delegation introduced a resolution calling for independence. The moderates still commanded enough support to postpone a vote on the measure until July, so they could go home and consult about this extreme step. In the meantime, the congress appointed a committee, with Thomas Jefferson and others, to draft a longer document setting out the case for independence.

On July 2, after intense politicking, all but one state voted for independence; New York abstained. The congress then turned to the document drafted by Jefferson and his committee. Jefferson began with a preamble that articulated philosophical principles about natural rights, equality, the right of revolution, and the consent of the governed as the only true basis for government. He then listed more than two dozen grievances against King George. The congress merely glanced at the political philosophy, finding nothing exceptional in it; the ideas about natural rights and the consent of the governed were seen as "self-evident truths," just as the document claimed. In itself, this absence of comment showed a remarkable transformation in political thinking since the end of the Seven Years' War. The single phrase declaring the natural equality of "all men" was also passed over without comment; no one elaborated on its radical implications.

For two days, the congress wrangled over the list of grievances, especially the issue of slavery. Jefferson had included an impassioned statement blaming the king for slavery, which delegates from Georgia and South Carolina struck out. They had no intention of denouncing their labor system as an evil practice. But the congress let stand another of Jefferson's fervent grievances, blaming the king for mobilizing "the merciless Indian Savages" into bloody **frontier** warfare, a reference to Pontiac's uprising (see chapter 6).

On July 4, the amendments to Jefferson's text were complete and the congress formally adopted the document. (See appendix I, page A-1.) A month later, the delegates gathered to sign the official parchment copy, handwritten by an exacting scribe. Four men, including John Dickinson, declined to sign; several others "signed with regret…and with many doubts," according to John Adams. The document was then printed, widely distributed, and read aloud in celebrations everywhere. A crowd in New York listened to a public reading of it and then toppled a lead statue of George III on horseback to melt it down for bullets. On July 15, the New York delegation switched from abstention to endorsement, making the vote on independence unanimous.

> **REVIEW** Why were many Americans reluctant to pursue independence from Britain?

The First Year of War, 1775–1776

Both sides approached the war for America with uneasiness. The Americans, with inexperienced militias, opposed the mightiest military power in the world. Also, their country was not unified; many remained loyal to Britain. The British faced serious obstacles as well. Their disdain for the fighting abilities of the Americans required reassessment in light of the Bunker Hill battle. The logistics of supplying an army with food across three thousand miles of water were daunting. And since the British goal was to regain allegiance, not to destroy and conquer, the army was often constrained in its actions. These patterns—undertrained American troops, British troops strangely unwilling to press their advantage—played out repeatedly in the first year of war when the Americans invaded Canada, the British invaded New York, and the two sides chased each other up and down the length of New Jersey.

The American Military Forces

Americans claimed that the initial months of war were purely defensive, triggered by the British army's invasion. But quickly the war also became a rebellion, an overthrowing of long-established authority. As both defenders and rebels, Americans were generally highly motivated to fight, and the potential manpower that could be mobilized was in theory very great.

Local defense in the colonies had long rested with a militia requiring participation from able-bodied men over age sixteen. When the main threat to public safety was the occasional Indian attack, the local militia made sense. But such attacks were now mostly limited to the frontier. Southern militias trained with potential slave rebellions in mind, but these too were rare. The annual muster day in most communities had evolved into a holiday of drinking, marching, and shooting practice with small fowling guns or muskets.

Militias were best suited to limited engagements and not for extended wars requiring military campaigns far from home. In forming the Continental army, the congress set enlistment at one year, but army leaders soon learned that was inadequate time to train soldiers and carry out campaigns. A three-year enlistment earned a new soldier a $20 bonus, while men who committed for the duration of the war were promised a postwar **land grant** of one hundred acres. For this inducement to be effective, of course, recruits had to believe that the Americans would win.

Women also served in the Continental army, cooking, washing, and nursing the wounded. The British army established a ratio of one woman to every ten men; in the Continental army, the ratio was set at one woman to fifteen men. Close to 20,000 women served during the war, probably most of them wives of men in service. Children tagged along as well, and babies were born in the camps and on the road.

Black Americans were at first excluded from the Continental army, by George Washington's orders. But as manpower needs increased, the northern states welcomed free blacks into service; slaves in some states could serve, with their masters' permission. About 5,000 black men served in the Revolutionary War on the rebel side, nearly all from the northern states. Black Continental soldiers sometimes were segregated into separate units; two battalions from Rhode Island were entirely black. Just under three hundred blacks joined regiments from Connecticut. While some of these were **draftees**, others were clearly inspired by the ideals of freedom being voiced in a war against tyranny. For example, twenty-three blacks gave "Liberty," "Freedom," or "Freeman" as their surname at the time of enlistment.

Military service helped to politicize Americans during the early stages of the war. In early 1776, independence was a risky idea, potentially treasonous. But as the war heated up and recruiters demanded commitment, some Americans discovered that apathy had its dangers as well. Anyone who refused to serve ran the risk of being called a traitor to the cause. Military service became a prime way of defining and demonstrating political allegiance.

The American army was at times raw and inexperienced and much of the time woefully undermanned. It never had the precision and discipline of European professional armies. But it was never as bad as the British continually

Black Revolutionary War Sailor
From the beginning of the war, the fledgling American navy recruited blacks from the pool of experienced free black sailors in northern maritime cities. Most were hired as ordinary seamen, but a few served as ship pilots. The names of these men are preserved in crew lists; rarely, however, were their likenesses preserved. This 1780 portrait by an unknown artist shows an unnamed man in dress uniform, sword and scabbard at hand, with a ship in view to establish his naval connection.
Collection of A. A. McBurney.

assumed. The British were to learn that it was a serious mistake to underrate the enemy.

The British Strategy

The American strategy was straightforward—to repulse and defeat an invading army. The British strategy was not nearly so clear. England wanted to put down a rebellion and restore monarchical power in the colonies, but the question was how to accomplish this. A decisive defeat of the Continental army was essential but not sufficient to end the rebellion, for the British would still have to contend with an armed and motivated insurgent population.

Furthermore, there was no single political nerve center whose capture would spell certain victory. The Continental Congress moved from place to place, staying just out of reach of the

British. During the course of the war, the British captured and occupied every major port city, but that brought no serious loss to the Americans, 95 percent of whom lived in the countryside.

England's delicate task was to restore the old governments, not to destroy an enemy country. Hence, the British generals were reluctant to ravage the countryside, confiscate food, or burn villages and towns. There were thirteen distinct political entities to capture, pacify, and then restore to the crown, and they stretched in a long line from New Hampshire to Georgia. Clearly a large land army was required for the job. Without the willingness to seize food from the locals, the British needed hundreds of supply ships bringing food for storage. The British strategy also assumed that many Americans remained loyal to the king and would come to their aid. Without substantial numbers of loyal subjects, the plan to restore old royal governments made no sense.

The overall British plan was a divide-and-conquer approach, focusing first on New York, the state judged to harbor the greatest number of loyal subjects. New York offered a geographic advantage as well: Control of the Hudson River would allow the British to isolate those troublesome New Englanders. British armies could descend from Canada and move up from New York City along the Hudson River into western Massachusetts. Squeezed between a naval blockade on the eastern coast and army raids in the west, Massachusetts could be driven to surrender. New Jersey and Pennsylvania would fall in line, the British thought, due to loyalist strength. Virginia was a problem, like Massachusetts, but the British were confident that the Carolinas would help them isolate and subdue Virginia.

Quebec, New York, and New Jersey

In late 1775, an American expedition was swiftly launched to capture the British cities Montreal and Quebec before British reinforcements could arrive. This offensive was a clear sign that the war was not purely a reaction to the invasion of Massachusetts. A force of New York Continentals commanded by General Richard Montgomery took Montreal easily in September 1775 and then advanced on Quebec. Meanwhile, a second contingent of Continentals led by Colonel Benedict Arnold moved north through Maine to Quebec, a punishing trek through freezing rain with woefully inadequate supplies; many men died. Arnold's determination to get to Quebec was heroic, but in human costs the campaign was a tragedy. Arnold and Montgomery jointly attacked Quebec in December but failed to take the city (Map 7.1). Worse yet, they encountered smallpox, which killed more men than had been felled by the British.

The main action of the first year of war came not in Canada, however, but in New York, so crucial to England. In August 1776, some 45,000 British troops (including 8,000 German mercenaries, called Hessians) landed south of New York City, under the command of General Howe. General Washington had anticipated that New York would be Howe's target and had moved his army, numbering about 20,000, south from Massachusetts. The battle of Long Island, in late August 1776, pitted the well-trained British "redcoats" (common slang referring to the red British uniforms) against a very green Continental army. Howe attacked, inflicting many casualties (1,500 dead and wounded) and spreading panic among the American soldiers, who fled to the eastern edge of Long Island. Howe failed to press forward, however, perhaps remembering the costly victory of Bunker Hill, and Washington evacuated his troops to Manhattan Island in the dead of a foggy night.

Washington knew it would be hard to hold Manhattan, so he further withdrew north to two forts on either side of the Hudson River. For two months, the armies engaged in limited skirmishing, but in November, Howe finally captured Fort Washington and Fort Lee, taking thousands of prisoners. Washington retreated quickly across New Jersey into Pennsylvania. Yet again Howe unaccountably failed to press his advantage. Had

MAP 7.1 The War in the North, 1775–1778 ▶
After the early battles in Massachusetts in 1775, rebel forces invaded Canada but failed to capture Quebec. A large British army landed in New York in August 1776, turning New Jersey into a continual site of battle in 1777 and 1778. Burgoyne arrived to secure Canada and made his attempt to pinch off New England along the Hudson River line, but he was stopped at Saratoga in 1777 in the key battle of the early war years.

Reading the map: Which general's troops traveled the farthest in each of these years: 1775, 1776, and 1777? How did the availability of water routes affect British and American strategy?

Connections: Why did the French wait until early 1778 to join American forces against the British? What did they hope to gain from participating in the war?

For more help analyzing this map, see the map activity for this chapter in the Online Study Guide at bedfordstmartins.com/roarkcompact.

he attacked Washington's army at Philadelphia, he probably would have taken the city. Instead he parked his German troops in winter quarters along the Delaware River. Perhaps he knew that many of the Continental soldiers' enlistment periods ended on December 31, so he felt confident that the Americans would not attack him. But he was wrong. On December 25 near midnight, as a

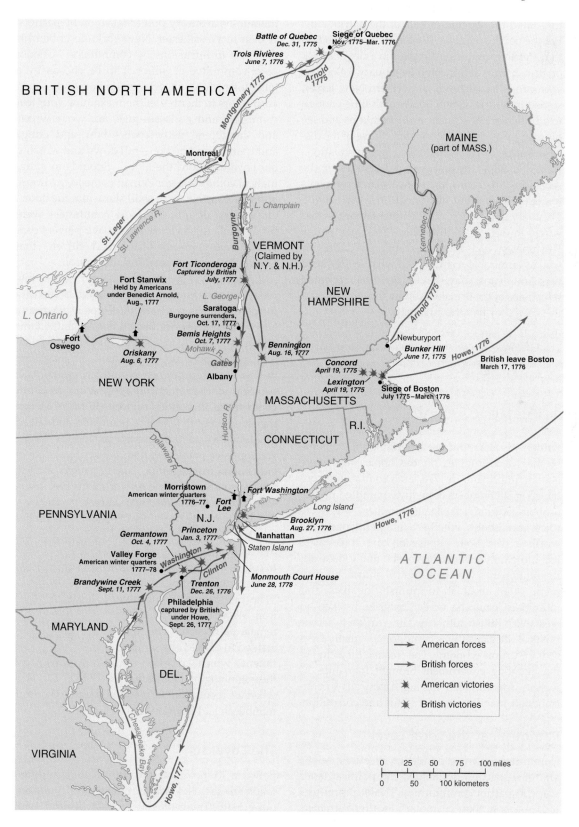

BRITISH NORTH AMERICA

Battle of Quebec
Dec. 31, 1775

Siege of Quebec
Nov. 1775–Mar. 1776

Trois Rivières
June 7, 1776

Montgomery 1775

Arnold 1775

Montreal

L. Champlain

St. Leger

St. Lawrence R.

Burgoyne

MAINE
(part of MASS.)

Kennebec R.

VERMONT
(Claimed by
N.Y. & N.H.)

NEW
HAMPSHIRE

Fort Ticonderoga
Captured by British
July, 1777

Fort Stanwix
Held by Americans
under Benedict Arnold,
Aug., 1777

L. George

Saratoga
Burgoyne surrenders,
Oct. 17, 1777

L. Ontario

Bemis Heights
Oct. 7, 1777

Arnold 1775

Newburyport

Fort
Oswego

Oriskany
Aug. 6, 1777

Mohawk R.

Bennington
Aug. 16, 1777

Bunker Hill
June 17, 1775

Howe, 1776

NEW YORK

Gates

Concord
April 19, 1775

British leave Boston
March 17, 1776

Albany

Lexington
April 19, 1775

Siege of Boston
July 1775–March 1776

MASSACHUSETTS

Hudson R.

CONNECTICUT

R.I.

Delaware R.

Morristown
American winter quarters
1776–77

Fort Washington

Fort
Lee

Long Island

PENNSYLVANIA

N.J.

Brooklyn
Aug. 27, 1776

Howe, 1776

Germantown
Oct. 4, 1777

Princeton
Jan. 3, 1777

Manhattan

Staten Island

Valley Forge
American winter quarters
1777–78

Washington

Clinton

Monmouth Court House
June 28, 1778

ATLANTIC
OCEAN

Brandywine Creek
Sept. 11, 1777

Trenton
Dec. 26, 1776

Philadelphia
captured by British
under Howe,
Sept. 26, 1777

MARYLAND

DEL.

VIRGINIA

Chesapeake Bay

Howe, 1777

→ American forces

→ British forces

✳ American victories

✳ British victories

0   25   50   75   100 miles

0   50   100 kilometers

storm of sleet and hail rained down, Washington stealthily moved his large army across the icy Delaware River and in the early morning made a quick capture of the unsuspecting German soldiers encamped at Trenton. This impressive victory lifted the sagging morale of the patriot side. For the next two weeks, Washington remained on the offensive, capturing supplies in a clever attack on British units at Princeton on January 3. Soon he was safe in Morristown, in northern New Jersey, settled in for the winter, finally with time enough to administer mass smallpox inoculations and see his men through the abbreviated course of the disease. Future recruits would also face inoculation.

All in all, in the first year of declared war, the rebellious Americans had a few isolated moments to feel proud of but also much to worry about. The very inexperienced Continental army had barely hung on in the New York campaign. Washington had shown exceptional daring as well as admirable restraint, but what really saved the Americans may have been the repeated reluctance of the British to follow through militarily when they had the advantage.

> **REVIEW**   Why did the British exercise restraint in their efforts to recapture the colonies?

The Home Front

Battlefields alone did not determine the outcome of the war. Struggles on the home front were equally important. In 1776, each community contained small numbers of highly committed people on both sides and far larger numbers who were uncertain about whether independence was worth a war. Both persuasion and force were used to gain the allegiance of the many neutrals. Revolutionaries who took control of local government often used it to punish loyalists and intimidate neutrals, while loyalists worked to reestablish British authority. The struggle to secure political allegiance was complicated greatly by a shaky wartime economy. The creative financing of the fledgling government brought hardships as well as opportunities, forcing Americans to confront new manifestations of virtue and corruption.

Patriotism at the Local Level

Committees of correspondence, of public safety, and of inspection dominated the political landscape in patriot communities. These committees took on more than customary local governance;

they enforced boycotts, picked army draftees, and policed suspected traitors. They sometimes invaded homes to search for contraband goods such as British tea or textiles.

Loyalists were dismayed by what seemed to them to be arbitrary power taken on by patriots. A man in Westchester, New York, described his response to intrusions by committees: "Choose your committee or suffer it to be chosen by a half dozen fools in your neighborhood—open your doors to them—let them examine your tea-cannisters and molasses-jugs, and your wives' and daughters' petty coats—bow and cringe and tremble and quake—fall down and worship our sovereign lord the mob....Should any pragmatical committee-gentleman come to my house and give himself airs, I shall show him the door." Oppressive or not, the local committees were rarely challenged. Their persuasive powers convinced many middle-of-the-road citizens that neutrality was not a comfortable option.

Another group new to political life—white women—increasingly demonstrated a capacity for patriotism as wartime hardships dramatically altered their work routines. Like Abigail Adams on her farm, many wives with husbands away on military or political service took on masculine duties. Their competence to tend farms and make business decisions encouraged some to assert competence in politics as well. Eliza Wilkinson managed a South Carolina plantation and talked revolutionary politics with women friends. "None were greater politicians than the several knots of ladies who met together," she remarked, alert to the unusual turn female conversations had taken. "We commenced perfect statesmen."

Women from prominent Philadelphia families took more direct action, forming the Ladies Association in 1780 to collect money for Continental soldiers. A published broadside, "The Sentiments of an American Woman," defended their female patriotism. "The time is arrived to display the same sentiments which animated us at the beginning of the Revolution, when we renounced the use of teas [and] when our republican and laborious hands spun the flax."

The Loyalists

Between 20 and 30 percent of the American population remained loyal to the crown in 1776, and another 20 to 40 percent were probably neutral. With proper cultivation, this large base might have sustained the British empire in America (Map 7.2). In general, loyalists had strong cultural and economic ties to England; they thought that social stability depended on a government anchored by monarchy and aristocracy. Perhaps most of all, they feared democratic tyranny. Like Abigail Adams, they understood that dissolving the automatic respect that subjects had for their king could lead to a society in which hierarchy came unglued. Adams welcomed this chance to identify tyranny in unequal power relations, as between men and women; loyalists feared it. Patriots seemed to them to be unscrupulous, violent, self-interested men who simply wanted power for themselves.

The most visible loyalists (called Tories by their enemies) were royal officials, not only governors like Thomas Hutchinson but also local judges and customs officers. Wealthy merchants gravitated toward loyalism to maintain the trade protections of navigation acts and the British navy. Conservative urban lawyers admired the stability of British law and order. Some colonists chose loyalism simply to oppose traditional adversaries. For example, backcountry farmers in the Carolinas tended to be loyalists out of resentment over the political and economic power of the lowlands gentry. And of course southern slaves had their own resentments against the white slave-owning class and looked to Britain for hope of freedom.

Many Indian tribes hoped to remain neutral at the war's start, seeing the conflict as a civil war between English and American brothers. But eventually most were drawn in, many taking the British side. The powerful Iroquois confederacy divided: Mohawk, Cayuga, Seneca, and Onondaga peoples lined up with the British; the Oneida and Tuscarora aided Americans. One young Mohawk leader, Thayendanegea (known also by his English name, Joseph Brant), traveled to England in 1775 to complain to King George about American settlers cheating his people of land. "It is very hard when we have let the King's subjects have so much of our lands for so little value," he wrote, "they should want to cheat us in this manner of the small spots we have left for our women and children to live on. We are tired out in making complaints & getting no redress." Brant pledged Indian support for the king in exchange for protection from encroaching settlers. In the Ohio Country, parts of the Shawnee and Delaware tribes started out pro-American but shifted to the British side by 1779 in the face of repeated betrayals by American settlers and soldiers.

Pockets of loyalism thus existed everywhere—in the middle colonies, in the backcountry of

Joseph Brant
The Mohawk leader Thayendanegea, called Joseph Brant by Americans, had been educated in English ways at Eleazar Wheelock's New England school (which became Dartmouth College in 1769). In 1775, the thirty-four-year-old Brant traveled to England with another warrior to negotiate Mohawk support for the British. While there, he had his portrait painted by the English artist George Romney. Notice that Brant wears a metal gorget around his neck over his English shirt, along with Indian armbands, sash, and headdress. A gorget was a symbolic piece of armor, a shrunken version of a throatpiece from the feudal days of metal-clad knights. Many military men, both white and Indian, wore gorgets when they dressed formally for portraits—or for war.
National Gallery of Canada.

the southern colonies, and out beyond the Appalachian Mountains in Indian country. Even New England towns at the heart of turmoil, like Concord, Massachusetts, had a small and increasingly silenced core of loyalists who refused to countenance armed revolution.

Loyalists were most vocal between 1774 and 1776, when the possibility of a full-scale rebellion against England was still uncertain. Loyalists challenged the emerging patriot side in pamphlets and newspapers. In New York City, some loyalists circulated a broadside titled "A Declaration of Dependence," in rebuttal to the congress's July 4 declaration, denouncing this

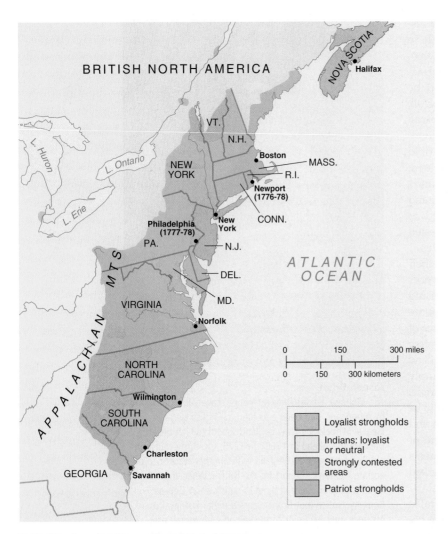

MAP 7.2   Loyalist Strength and Rebel Support
The exact number of loyalists can never be known. No one could have made an accurate count at the time; in addition, political allegiance often shifted with the winds. This map shows the regions of loyalist strength on which the British relied—most significantly the lower Hudson River Valley and the Carolina piedmont.

"most unnatural, unprovoked Rebellion that ever disgraced the annals of Time."

Who Is a Traitor?

In June 1775, the First Continental Congress declared loyalists to be traitors. Over the next year, state laws defined as treason acts such as joining or provisioning the British army, saying or printing anything that undermined patriot morale, or discouraging men from enlisting in the Continental army. Punishments ranged from house arrest and suspension of voting privileges to confiscation of property and deportation. And sometimes self-appointed committees of Tory-hunters bypassed the judicial niceties and terror-

ized loyalists, raiding their houses or tarring and feathering them.

Were wives of loyalists also traitors? When loyalist families fled the country, property controlled by the husband was typically confiscated. But if the wife stayed, courts usually allowed her to keep one-third of the property, the amount due her if widowed, and confiscated the rest. A wife who fled with her husband might have little choice in the matter. After the Revolution, descendants of refugee loyalists filed several lawsuits to regain property that had entered the family through the mother's inheritance. In one well-publicized Massachusetts case in 1805, the outcome confirmed the traditional view of women as political blank slates. The American son of loyalist refugee Anna Martin recovered her property on the grounds that she had no independent will to be a loyalist.

Tarring and feathering, property confiscation, deportation, terrorism—to the loyalists, such denials of liberty of conscience and of freedom to own private property proved that democratic tyranny was more to be feared than the monarchical variety. A Boston loyalist, Mather Byles, aptly expressed this point: "They call me a brainless Tory, but tell me… which is better—to be ruled by one tyrant three thousand miles away, or by three thousand tyrants not a mile away?" Byles was soon sentenced to deportation.

Throughout the war, probably 7,000 to 8,000 loyalists fled to England, and 28,000 found closer haven in Canada. But many chose to remain in the new United States and tried to swing with the changing political winds. In some instances, that proved difficult. In New Jersey, for example, 3,000 Jerseyites felt protected (or scared) enough by the occupying British army in 1776 to swear an oath of allegiance to the king. But then General Howe drew back to New York City, leaving them to the mercy of local patriot committees. British strategy depended on using loyalists to hold occupied territory, but the New Jersey experience showed how poorly that strategy was carried out.

Financial Instability and Corruption

Wars cost money—for arms and ammunition, for food and uniforms, for soldiers' pay. The Continental Congress printed money, but its value quickly deteriorated because the congress held no reserves of gold or silver to back the currency. In practice, it was worth only what buyers and sellers agreed it was worth; the dollar eventually bottomed out at one-fortieth  of its face value. States too were printing paper money to pay for wartime expenses, further complicating the economy.

As the currency depreciated, the congress turned to other means to procure supplies and labor. One method was to borrow **hard money** (gold or silver coins) from wealthy men in exchange for certificates of debt (public securities) promising repayment with interest. The certificates of debt were similar to present-day **government bonds**. To pay soldiers, the congress issued land grant certificates, written promises of acreage usually located in frontier areas such as central Maine or eastern Ohio. Both the public securities and the land grant certificates quickly became forms of negotiable currency. A soldier with no cash, for example, could sell his land grant certificate to get food for his family. These certificates soon depreciated too.

Depreciating currency inevitably led to rising prices, as sellers compensated for the falling value of the money. The wartime economy of the late 1770s, with its unreliable currency and price inflation, was extremely demoralizing to Americans everywhere. In 1778, in an effort to impose stability, local committees of public safety began to fix prices on essential goods like flour. Inevitably, some turned this unstable situation to their advantage. Money that fell fast in value needed to be spent quickly; being in debt was suddenly advantageous because the debt could be repaid in devalued currency. A brisk black market sprang up in prohibited luxury imports, such as tea, sugar, textiles, and wines, even though these items came from Britain. A New Hampshire delegate to the congress denounced the violation of the homespun association agreements of just a few years before: "We are a crooked and perverse generation, longing for the fineries and follies of those Egyptian task masters from whom we have so lately freed ourselves."

REVIEW How did the patriots promote support for their cause in the colonies?

The Campaigns of 1777–1779: The North and West

In early 1777, the Continental army faced bleak choices. General Washington had skillfully avoided outright defeat, but the minor victories in New Jersey lent only faint optimism to the American side. Meanwhile, British troops moved south from Quebec, aiming to isolate New England from the rest of the colonies by taking control of the Hudson River. Their presence drew the Continental army up into central New York, polarizing Indian tribes of the Iroquois nation and turning the Mohawk Valley into a bloody war zone. By 1779, tribes in western New York and in Indian country in the Ohio Valley were fully involved in the Revolutionary War; most sided with the British and against the Americans. The Americans had some success in this period, such as the victory at Saratoga, but the involvement of Indians and the continuing strength of the British forced the American government to look toward France for help.

Burgoyne's Army and the Battle of Saratoga

In 1777, British general John Burgoyne assumed command of an army of 7,800 soldiers in Canada and began the northern squeeze on the Hudson River valley. His goal was to capture Albany, near the intersection of the Hudson and Mohawk rivers (see Map 7.1). Accompanied by a thousand "camp followers" (cooks, laundresses, musicians) and some 400 Indian warriors, Burgoyne's army did not travel light. In addition to food and supplies for 9,200 people, the army carried food for the 400 horses hauling heavy artillery. Burgoyne also carted thirty trunks of personal belongings, including fine wines and elegant clothing.

In July, Burgoyne captured Fort Ticonderoga with ease. Some 3,000 American troops stationed there spotted the approaching British and abandoned the fort without a fight. The British continued to move south, but the large army moved slowly on primitive roads through heavily forested land.

The logical second step in isolating New England should have been to advance troops up the Hudson from New York City to meet Burgoyne. American surveillance indicated that General Howe in Manhattan was readying his men for a major move in August 1777. George Washington, watching from New Jersey, was astonished to see Howe's men sail south; Howe had decided to try to capture Philadelphia.

The third prong of the British strategy involved troops moving east from the Great Lakes and down the Mohawk River, aided by Mohawks and Senecas of the Iroquois confederacy. The British counted on help from Palatine Germans living in the Mohawk Valley, assumed to be loyalist. But a hundred miles west of Albany, they encountered American Continental soldiers at Fort Stanwix, reinforced by Palatine German militiamen and Oneida Indians. Led by the Mohawk Joseph Brant, the Senecas and Mohawks ambushed the Germans and the Oneidas in a narrow ravine called Oriskany and inflicted heavy losses, killing 500 out of 800 of them. On Brant's side, some 90 warriors were killed. But Fort Stanwix repelled the British and Seneca and forced them to retreat (see Map 7.1). The Oriskany and Fort Stanwix battles were very deadly; they were also complexly multiethnic, pitting Indians against Indians, German Americans against German mercenaries, New York patriots against neighboring New York loyalists, and English Americans against the British.

The British retreat at Fort Stanwix deprived General Burgoyne of the additional troops he expected. Camped at a small village called Saratoga, he was isolated with food supplies dwindling and men deserting. His adversary at Albany, General Horatio Gates, began moving 7,000 Continental soldiers toward him. Burgoyne decided to attack first because every day his army weakened. In this first attack, the British prevailed, but at the great cost of 600 dead or wounded redcoats. Three weeks later, an American attack on Burgoyne's forces at Saratoga cost the British another 600 men and most of their cannons. Burgoyne finally surrendered to the American forces at Saratoga on October 17, 1777.

General Howe, meanwhile, had succeeded in occupying Philadelphia in September 1777. Figuring that the Saratoga loss was balanced by the capture of Philadelphia, the British government proposed a negotiated settlement—not including independence—to end the war. The American side refused.

Battle of Saratoga, 1777

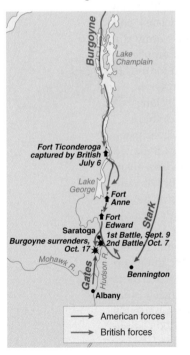

American forces
British forces

Patriot optimism was not well founded. Spirits ran high, but supplies of arms and food ran precariously low. Washington moved his troops into winter quarters at Valley Forge, just west of Philadelphia. Quartered in drafty huts, the men lacked blankets, boots, stockings, and food. Some 2,000 men at Valley Forge died of disease; another 2,000 deserted over the bitter six-month encampment.

Washington blamed the citizenry for lack of support, and indeed, evidence of corruption and profiteering was abundant. Army suppliers too often provided defective food, clothing, and gunpowder. A shipment of blankets turned out to be a quarter of their customary size. Preserved meat in barrels arrived rotten because brine had been drained to ease transport costs. Selfishness and greed seemed to infect the American side. As one Continental officer said, "The people at home are destroying the Army by their conduct much faster than Howe and all his army can possibly do by fighting us."

The War in the West: Indian Country

Burgoyne's defeat in the fall of 1777 and Washington's long stay at Valley Forge up to June 1778 might suggest that the war paused for a time; and it did, on the Atlantic coast. But in the interior western areas—the Mohawk Valley, the Ohio Valley, and Kentucky—the war was heating up. For native tribes, the struggle was not about taxation, representation, or monarchical rule; it was about independence, freedom, and land.

The ambush and slaughter at Oriskany in August 1777 marked the beginning of three years of terror for the inhabitants of the Mohawk Valley. Loyalists and Indians together engaged in many raids on farms throughout 1778, capturing or killing the residents. In retaliation, American militiamen destroyed Joseph Brant's home village, Onaquaga. A month later, Brant's warriors attacked the town of Cherry Valley, killing 32 townspeople and 16 soldiers and taking 71 people captive.

The following summer, General Washington authorized a campaign to wreak "total destruction and devastation" on all the Iroquoian villages of central New York. Some 4,500 troops commanded by General John Sullivan carried out a deliberate campaign of terror in the fall of 1779. Forty Indian towns met with total obliteration; the soldiers looted and torched the dwellings, then burned cornfields and orchards. In a few towns, women and children were slaughtered; but in most, the inhabitants managed to escape, fleeing to the British at Fort Niagara. Thousands of Indian refugees, sick and starving, camped around the fort in one of the most miserable winters on record.

Much farther to the west, beyond Fort Pitt, another complex story unfolded, of alliances and betrayals between American militiamen and Indians. Some 150,000 native peoples lived between the Appalachian Mountains and the Mississippi River, and by 1779, neutrality was no longer an option. Most sided with the British, who maintained a major garrison at Fort Detroit, but a portion of the Shawnee and Delaware tribes at first sought peace with the Americans. In mid-1778, the Delaware chief White Eyes negotiated a treaty at Fort Pitt, pledging Indian support in the war in exchange for supplies and trade goods. But escalating violence undermined the agreement. That fall, when American soldiers killed two friendly Shawnee chiefs, Cornstalk and Red Hawk, the Continental Congress hastened to apologize, as did the governors of Pennsylvania and Virginia, but the soldiers who stood trial for the murders were acquitted. Two months later, White Eyes, still nominally an ally and informant for the Americans, died under mysterious circumstances, almost certainly murdered by militiamen, who repeatedly had trouble honoring distinctions between allied and enemy Indians.

In Tennessee, the frontier war zone in the South, militias attacked Cherokee settlements, destroying thirty-six villages and burning fields and livestock. Indian raiders from north of the Ohio River in alliance with the British repeatedly attacked white settlements like Boonesborough in Kentucky (Map 7.3). In retaliation, a young Virginian, George Rogers Clark, led Kentucky militiamen into what is now Illinois, his men attacking and taking the British fort at Kaskaskia. Clark's men wore hunting shirts and breech cloths, native clothing, but their native dress was not a sign of solidarity with Indians. When they attacked British-held Fort Vincennes in 1779, Clark's troops tomahawked Indian captives and threw their still-live bodies in the river in a gory spectacle witnessed by the redcoats. "To excel them in barbarity is the only way to make war upon Indians," Clark announced. And, he might have added, a good way to terrorize the British soldiers as well.

By 1780, very few Indians remained neutral. Violent raids by Americans drove Indians into the arms of the British at Detroit and Niagara, or

A Soldier's Canteen
This wooden canteen belonged to Noah Allen, whose name and regiment number are carved into the side. Allen was from the Sixth Continental Regiment from Massachusetts. Almost no piece of equipment surpassed in importance the soldier's canteen.
Fort Ticonderoga Museum.

into the arms of the Spanish, who still held much of the land west of the Mississippi River. Said one officer on the Sullivan campaign, "Their nests are destroyed but the birds are still on the wing." For those who stayed near their native lands, chaos and confusion prevailed. Rare as it was, Indian support for the American side occasionally emerged out of a strategic sense that the Americans were unstoppable in their westward pressure and that it was better to work out an alliance than to lose in a war. But American treatment of even friendly Indians showed that for the Indians there was no winning strategy.

The French Alliance

On their own, the Americans could not have defeated Britain, and the western pressure from hostile Indians magnified their task. Essential help arrived as a result of the victory at Saratoga, which convinced the French to enter the war; a formal alliance was signed in February 1778. France recognized the United States as an independent nation and promised full military and commercial support throughout the war. Most crucial was the French navy, which could challenge England's transatlantic shipment of supplies and troops.

Although France had been waiting for a promising American victory to justify a formal declaration of war, since 1776 the French had been providing aid to the Americans in the form of cannons, muskets, gunpowder, and highly trained military advisers. Still, monarchical France was understandably cautious about endorsing a democratic revolution attacking the principles of kingship. For France, the main attraction of an alliance was the opportunity it provided to defeat archrival Britain. A victory would also open pathways to trade and perhaps result in France acquiring the coveted British West Indies. Even American defeat would not be

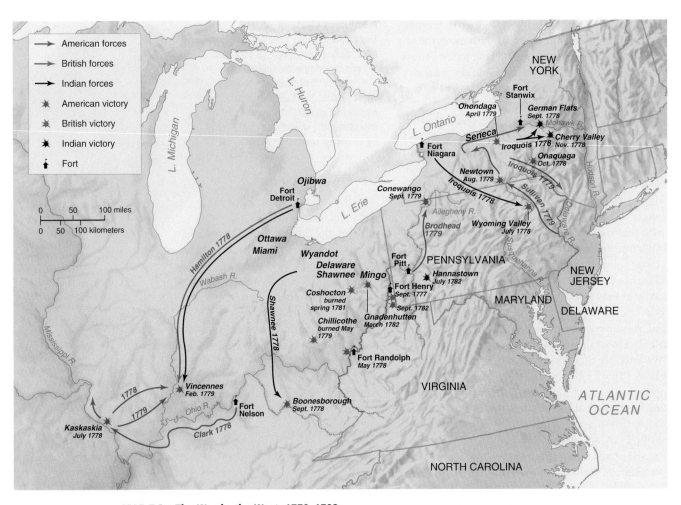

MAP 7.3 The War in the West, 1778–1782
The American Revolution involved many Indian tribes, most of them supporting the British side. Iroquois with British aid attacked American towns in New York's Mohawk Valley throughout 1778. In 1779 the Continental army marched on 40 Iroquois villages in central New York and destroyed them. The Shawnee and Delaware to the west of Fort Pitt tangled with American militia units in 1779, while tribes supported by the British at Fort Detroit conducted raids on Kentucky settlers who hit back with raids of their own. George Rogers Clark led Kentucky militiamen against Indians in the Illinois region. Sporadic fighting continued in the West through 1782, ending with Indian attacks on Hannastown, Pennsylvania, and Fort Henry on the Ohio River. By the late 1780s, occasional fighting resumed, sparked by American settlers pressing west onto Indian lands.

a full disaster for France if the war lasted many years and drained England of men and money.

French support materialized slowly. The navy arrived off the Virginia coast in July 1778 but then sailed south to the West Indies to defend the French sugar-producing islands. French help would prove indispensable to the American victory, but the alliance's first months brought no dramatic victories, and some Americans grumbled that the partnership would prove worthless.

> **REVIEW** Why did the Americans need assistance from the French to ensure victory?

The Southern Strategy and the End of the War

When France joined the war, some British officials wondered whether the fight was worth continuing. A troop commander, arguing for an immediate negotiated settlement, shrewdly observed that "we are far from an anticipated peace, because the bitterness of the rebels is too widespread, and in regions where we are masters the rebellious spirit is still in them. The land is too large, and there are too many people. The more land we win, the weaker our army gets in the field." The commander of the British navy argued for abandoning the war, and even Lord North, the prime minister, agreed. But the king was determined to crush the rebellion, and he encouraged a new strategy for victory focusing on the southern colonies, thought to be more persuadably loyalist. It was a brilliant but desperate plan, and ultimately unsuccessful. Southern colonists were not all that loyal and in fact were willing to engage in guerrilla warfare against the British. The southern strategy thus led to a British defeat at Yorktown and the end of the war.

Georgia and South Carolina

The new strategy called for British forces to abandon New England and focus on the South, with its valuable crops— tobacco, rice, and indigo—and its large slave population, potentially a powerful destabilizing factor that might keep rebellious white southerners in line. Georgia and the Carolinas appeared to hold large numbers of loyalists, providing a base for the British to recapture the southern colonies one by one, moving north to the more problematic middle colonies and saving prickly New England for last.

Georgia, the first target, fell at the end of December 1778 (Map 7.4). A small army of British soldiers occupied Savannah and Augusta, and a new royal governor and loyalist assembly were quickly installed. Taking Georgia was easy because the bulk of the Continental army was in New York and New Jersey, keeping an eye on General Henry Clinton, Howe's replacement as commander in chief, and the French were in the West Indies. The British in Georgia quickly organized twenty loyal militia units, and 1,400 Georgians swore an oath of allegiance to the king. So far, the southern strategy looked as if it might work.

Next came South Carolina. The Continental army put ten regiments into the port city of Charleston to defend it from attack by British troops shipped south from New York under the command of General Clinton. For five weeks in early 1780, the British laid siege to the city and took it in May 1780, sending 3,300 American soldiers, a tremendous loss, into British captivity. Again, the king's new strategy seemed to be on target.

Clinton returned to New York, leaving the pacification of South Carolina to General Charles Cornwallis and 4,000 troops. A bold commander, Lord Cornwallis quickly chased out the remaining Continentals and established military rule of South Carolina by midsummer. He purged rebels from government office and disarmed rebel militias. The export of South Carolina's main crop, rice, resumed, and as in Georgia, pardons were offered to Carolinians who swore loyalty oaths to the crown and took up arms for the British.

By August, American troops arrived from the North to strike back at Cornwallis. General Gates, the hero of the battle of Saratoga, led 3,000

MAP 7.4 The War in the South, 1780–1781

After taking Charleston in May 1780, the British advanced into South Carolina and the foothill region of North Carolina, leaving a bloody civil war in their wake. When the American general Horatio Gates and his men fumbled and fled from the humiliating battle of Camden, Gates was replaced by General Nathanael Greene and General Daniel Morgan, who pulled off major successes at King's Mountain and Cowpens. The British general Cornwallis then moved north and invaded Virginia but was bottled up and finally overpowered at Yorktown in the fall of 1781.

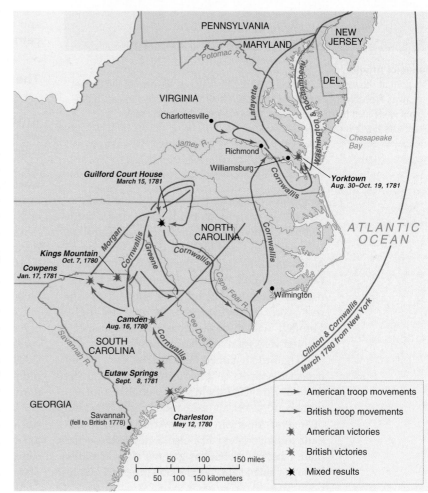

Benedict Arnold
This portrait shows Benedict Arnold in 1776, when he was the hero of the Quebec campaign. Probably the final straw for Arnold came when he failed to earn a promotion while men he considered inferior were elevated to higher rank.
Anne S. K. Brown Military Collection, Providence, R.I.

men, some of them experienced soldiers and others newly recruited militiamen, into battle against Cornwallis at Camden, South Carolina, on August 16 (see Map 7.4). Gates's militiamen panicked at the sight of the approaching enemy cavalry and fled. When regiment leaders tried to regroup the next day, only 700 showed up; the rest were dead, captured, or still in flight. Camden was a devastating defeat; prospects seemed very grim for the Americans.

The British gained help in 1780 from an unexpected source: An American general, Benedict Arnold, furnished them with valuable information about American troop movements. The hero of several American battles, Arnold was a brilliant military talent but also a deeply insecure man who never felt he got his due in either honor or financial reward. Sometime in 1779, he

opened secret negotiations with General Clinton in New York, trading information for money and hinting that he could deliver far more of value. When General Washington made him commander of West Point, a new fort sixty miles north of New York City on the Hudson River, Arnold's plan crystallized. West Point controlled the Hudson; its easy capture by the British might well have meant victory in the war.

Arnold's plot to sell a West Point victory to the British was foiled when Americans captured the man carrying plans of the fort's defense from Arnold to Clinton. News of Arnold's treason created shock waves. Arnold represented all of the patriots' worst fears about themselves: greedy self-interest like that of the war profiteers, the unprincipled abandonment of war aims like that of turncoat southern Tories, panic like that of the terrified soldiers at Camden. But instead of symbolizing all that was troubling about the American side of the war, the treachery of Arnold was publicly and ritually denounced in a kind of displacement of the anxieties of the moment. Vilifying Arnold allowed Americans to stake out a wide distance between themselves and dastardly conduct. It inspired a renewal of patriotism at a particularly low moment.

The Other Southern War: Guerrillas

Shock over Gates's defeat at Camden and Arnold's treason revitalized rebel support in western South Carolina, an area that Cornwallis believed to be pacified and loyal. The backcountry of the South soon became the site of guerrilla warfare. In hit-and-run attacks, both sides burned and ravaged not only opponents' property but the property of anyone claiming to be neutral. Loyalist militia units organized by the British were met by fierce rebel militia units who figured they had little to lose. In South Carolina, some six thousand rebels met loyalist units in bloody engagements. Some were classic battles, but on other occasions the fighters were more like bandits than soldiers. Guerrilla warfare soon spread to Georgia and North Carolina. Both sides committed murders and atrocities and plundered property, clear deviations from standard military practice.

The British southern strategy depended on sufficient loyalist strength to hold reconquered territory as the army moved north. The backcountry civil war proved this assumption false. The Americans won few major battles in the

South, but they ultimately succeeded by harassing the British forces and preventing them from foraging for food. Cornwallis moved the war into North Carolina in the fall of 1780, not because he thought South Carolina was secure—it was not—but because the North Carolinians were supplying the South Carolina rebels with arms and men (see Map 7.4). Then news of a brutal massacre of loyalist units in western South Carolina at King's Mountain, at the hands of 1,400 frontier riflemen, sent him hurrying back. The British were stretched too thin to hold on to even two of their onetime colonies.

Surrender at Yorktown

In 1781, Cornwallis moved back to North Carolina again and thence to Virginia, where he captured Williamsburg in June. A raiding party proceeded to Charlottesville, the seat of government, capturing members of the Virginia assembly but not Governor Thomas Jefferson, who escaped the soldiers by a mere ten minutes. (More than a dozen of Jefferson's slaves chose this moment to seek refuge with the British.) These minor victories allowed Cornwallis to imagine that he was gaining the upper hand in Virginia. He next marched to Yorktown, near Chesapeake Bay, to await arrival of back-up troops by ship from New York City, still held by the British.

At this juncture, the French-American alliance came into play. Already French regiments commanded by the Comte de Rochambeau had joined General Washington in Rhode Island in mid-1780, and now in 1781 warships under the Comte de Grasse sailed from France. Washington, Rochambeau, and de Grasse fixed their attention on the Chesapeake Bay in Virginia. The French fleet got there ahead of the British troop ships from New York; a five-day naval battle left the French navy in clear control of the Virginia coast. This proved to be the decisive factor in ending the war, because it eliminated the possibility of reinforcements for Cornwallis's army, dug in at Yorktown, and made rescue by the British navy impossible.

On land, General Cornwallis and his 7,500 troops faced a combined French and American army numbering over 16,000. For twelve days, the Americans and French bombarded the British fortifications at Yorktown; Cornwallis ran low on food and ammunition. An American observer keeping a diary noted that "the enemy, from want of forage, are killing off their horses in

great numbers. Six or seven hundred of these valuable animals have been killed, and their carcasses are almost continually floating down the river." Realizing escape was impossible, Cornwallis signaled his intention to surrender. On October 19, 1781, he formally capitulated.

What began as a promising southern strategy in 1778 turned into a discouraging defeat by 1781. British attacks in the South had energized American resistance, as did the timely exposure of Benedict Arnold's treason. The arrival of the French fleet sealed the fate of Cornwallis at Yorktown, and the military war quickly came to a halt.

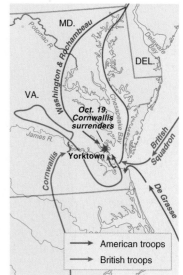

Siege of Yorktown, 1781

The Losers and the Winners

The surrender at Yorktown proved to be the end of the war with England, but it took some time for the principals to realize that. Frontier areas in Kentucky, Ohio, and Illinois still blazed with Indian warfare. The British army still occupied three coastal cities, and the Continental army remained in the field, in case the treaty process failed.

The peace treaty was two years in the making. Commissioners from America, Britain, and France met in Paris and worked out eighty-two articles of peace. The first article went to the heart of the matter: "His Britannic Majesty acknowledges the said United States to be free Sovereign and independent States." Other articles set the western boundary of the new country at the Mississippi River and guaranteed that creditors on both sides could collect debts owed them in sterling money, a provision especially important to British merchants. England agreed to withdraw its troops quickly; more than a decade later, this promise still had not been fully kept. The Treaty of Paris was signed on September 2, 1783.

Like the treaty ending the Seven Years' War, this treaty failed to recognize the Indians as players in the conflict. As one American told the Shawnee people, "Your Fathers the English have made Peace with us for themselves, but forgot you their Children, who Fought with them, and neglected you like Bastards." Indian lands were assigned to the victors as though they were uninhabited. Some Indian refugees fled west

"The Ballance of Power," 1780

This cartoon was published in England soon after Spain and the Netherlands declared an alliance with France to support the war in America. On the left, Britannia, a female figure representing Great Britain, cannot be moved by all the lightweights combined on the right side of the scale. France wears a ruffled shirt, Spain has a feather in his hat, and a Dutch boy has just hopped on, saying, "I'll do anything for money." The forlorn Indian maiden, the standard icon representing America in the eighteenth century, sits on the scale, head in hand, wailing, "My Ingratitude is Justly Punished." The poem printed below the cartoon predicts that "The Americans too will with Britons unite." This fanciful prediction was punctured nine months after it appeared, when the British surrendered to the Americans and the French at Yorktown in 1781.

Print Collection, Miriam and Ira D. Wallach Division of Art, Prints, and Photographs, the New York Public Library. Astor, Lenox and Tilden Foundations.

FOR MORE HELP ANALYZING THIS IMAGE, see the visual activity for this chapter in the Online Study Guide at bedfordstmartins.com/roarkcompact.

into present-day Missouri and Arkansas, and others, such as Joseph Brant's Mohawks, relocated to Canada. But significant numbers remained within the new United States, occupying their traditional homelands in areas west and north of the Ohio River. For them, the Treaty of 1783 brought no peace at all; their longer war against the Americans would extend at least until 1795 and for some to 1813. Their ally, Britain, conceded defeat, but the Indians did not.

With the treaty finally signed, the British began their evacuation of New York, Charleston, and Savannah, a process complicated by the sheer numbers involved—soldiers, fearful loyalists, and runaway slaves by the thousands. In New York City, more than 27,000 soldiers and 30,000 loyalists sailed on hundreds of ships for England in late fall 1783. In a final act of mischief, on the November day when the last ships left, the losing side raised the British flag at the southern tip of Manhattan, cut away the ropes used to hoist it, and greased the flagpole.

REVIEW   Why did the British southern strategy ultimately fail?

Conclusion: Why the British Lost

The British began the war for America convinced that they could not lose. They had the best-trained army and navy in the world; they were familiar with the landscape from the Seven Years' War; they had the willing warrior-power of most of the native tribes of the backcountry; and they easily captured every port city of consequence in America. Probably one-fifth of the population was loyalist, and another two-fifths were undecided. Why, then, did the British lose?

One continuing problem the British faced was the uncertainty of supplies. Unwilling to ravage the countryside, the army depended on supply ships from England. Insecurity about food helps explain their reluctance to pursue the Continental army aggressively. A further obstacle was their continual misuse of loyalist energies. Any plan to repacify the colonies required the cooperation of the loyalists, but repeatedly, the British left them to the mercy of vengeful rebels.

French aid looms large in any explanation of the British defeat. Even before the formal alliance, French artillery and ammunition proved vital for the underarmed Continental army. After 1780, the French army brought a new infusion of troops to a war-weary America, and the French navy made the Yorktown victory possible. Finally, the British abdicated civil power in the colonies in 1775 and 1776, when royal officials fled to safety, and they never really regained it. For seven years, the Americans created their own government structures, from the Continental Congress to local committees and militias. Staffed by many who before 1775 had been the political elites, these new government agencies had remarkably little trouble establishing their authority to rule. The basic British goal—to turn back the clock to imperial rule—receded into impossibility as the war dragged on.

The war for America had lasted just over five years, from Lexington to Yorktown; negotiations and the evacuation took two more. It profoundly disrupted the lives of Americans everywhere. It was a war for independence from England, but it was more. It was a war that required men and women to think about politics and the legitimacy of authority. The precise disagreement with England about representation and political participation had profound implications for the kinds of governance the Americans would adopt, both in the moment of emergency and in the longer run of the late 1770s and early 1780s when states began to write their constitutions. The rhetoric employed to justify the revolution against England put words such as *liberty, tyranny, slavery, independence,* and *equality* into common usage. These words carried far deeper meanings than a mere complaint over taxation without representation. As Abigail Adams and others saw, the Revolution unleashed a dynamic of equality and liberty. That it was largely unintended and unwanted by the revolutionary leaders of 1776 made it all the more potent a force in American life in the decades to come.

Suggestions for Further Reading

Carol Berkin, *Revolutionary Mothers: Women in the Struggle for America's Independence* (2005). A lively account of the many ways women participated in the war for independence, including camp followers, generals' wives, loyalists, slaves, and Indians.

Clare Brandt, *The Man in the Mirror: A Life of Benedict Arnold* (1994). A highly readable account of a man whose very name became synonymous with treachery.

Piers Mackesy, *The War for America, 1775–1783* (1964). A classic that presents the Revolution from the point of view of the British.

Pauline Maier, *American Scripture: Making the Declaration of Independence* (1997). Meticulous and fascinating scholarship showing the context and precursors to the famous document of 1776.

Ray Raphael, *A People's History of the American Revolution: How Common People Shaped the Fight for Independence* (2001). A look at the Revolution from the bottom up.

Charles Royster, *A Revolutionary People at War: The Continental Army and American Character, 1775–1783* (1979). A prize-winning social history exploring how the long war tested the ideals and beliefs of the American soldiers.

▶ **For more books about topics in this chapter,** see the Online Study Guide at bedfordstmartins.com/roarkcompact.

▶ **For additional firsthand accounts of this period,** see Chapter 7 in Michael Johnson, ed., *Reading the American Past,* Third Edition.

▶ **For Web sites and documents related to topics and places in this chapter,** see "HistoryLinks," "DocLinks," and "PlaceLinks" at bedfordstmartins.com/roarkcompact.

REVIEWING THE CHAPTER

Follow these steps to review and strengthen your understanding of the chapter.

STEP 1: *Study the* **Key Terms** *and* **Timeline** *to identify the significance of each item listed.*

STEP 2: *Answer the* **Review Questions***, drawing on key terms and dates to support your answers.*

STEP 3: *Drawing on the Key Terms, Timeline, and Review Questions, answer the broader* **Making Connections** *questions.*

KEY TERMS

Who

Abigail Adams (p. 159)
John Dickinson (p. 161)
George Washington (p. 161)
Thomas Jefferson (p. 161)
Thomas Gage (p. 161)
William Howe (p. 161)
George III (p. 164)
Thomas Paine (p. 164)
Richard Montgomery (p. 168)
Benedict Arnold (pp. 168, 178)
Hessians (p. 168)
redcoats (p. 168)
Tories (p. 171)
Joseph Brant (Thayendanegea) (p. 171)

John Burgoyne (p. 173)
Horatio Gates (p. 174)
John Sullivan (p. 174)
White Eyes (p. 175)
Henry Clinton (p. 177)
Charles Cornwallis (p. 177)
Comte de Rochambeau (p. 179)

What

Second Continental Congress (p. 160)
Continental army (p. 161)
battle of Bunker Hill (p. 164)
smallpox (p. 164)
Olive Branch Petition (p. 164)
Common Sense (p. 164)

battle of Long Island (p. 168)
Ladies Association (p. 170)
Fort Ticonderoga (p. 173)
Fort Stanwix (p. 174)
battle of Oriskany (p. 174)
battle of Saratoga (p. 174)
Valley Forge (p. 174)
Mohawk Valley (p. 174)
Fort Niagara (p. 175)
Fort Pitt (p. 175)
southern strategy (p. 177)
battle of Camden (p. 178)
battle of King's Mountain (p. 179)
battle of Yorktown (p. 179)
Treaty of Paris (p. 179)

TIMELINE

1775 • Second Continental Congress convenes.
• British win battle of Bunker Hill.
• King George rejects Olive Branch Petition.

1776 • Americans lose battle of Quebec.
• *Common Sense* published.
• British evacuate Boston.
• **July 4.** Congress adopts Declaration of Independence.
• British forces take Manhattan.

1777 • British take Fort Ticonderoga.
• Ambush at Oriskany.
• Americans hold Fort Stanwix.
• British occupy Philadelphia.
• British surrender at Saratoga.
• Continental army endures winter in Valley Forge.

1778 • France enters war on American side.
• American militiamen destroy Mohawk Joseph Brant's village.
• White Eyes negotiates a treaty with Americans; later mysteriously dies.

REVIEW QUESTIONS

1. Why were many Americans reluctant to pursue independence from Britain? (pp. 160–66)

2. Why did the British exercise restraint in their efforts to recapture the colonies? (pp. 166–70)

3. How did the patriots promote support for their cause in the colonies? (pp. 170–73)

4. Why did the Americans need assistance from the French to ensure victory? (pp. 173–76)

5. Why did the British southern strategy ultimately fail? (pp. 176–80)

MAKING CONNECTIONS

1. Even before the colonies had committed to independence, they faced the likelihood of serious military conflict. How did they mobilize for war? In your answer, discuss specific challenges they faced, noting any unintended consequences of their solutions.

2. Congress's adoption of the Declaration of Independence confirmed a decisive shift in the conflict between the colonies and Britain. Why did the colonies make this decisive break in 1776? In your answer, discuss some of the arguments for and against independence.

3. The question of whether colonists' loyalty would be to the new government or to the old king was pivotal during the Revolutionary War. Discuss the importance of loyalty to the outcome of the conflict. In your answer, consider both military and political strategy.

4. American colonists and British soldiers were not the only participants in the Revolutionary War. Discuss the role of Native Americans in the war. How did they shape the conflict? What benefits did they hope to gain? Did they succeed?

▶ FOR PRACTICE QUIZZES, A CUSTOMIZED STUDY PLAN, AND OTHER STUDY TOOLS, see the Online Study Guide at bedfordstmartins.com/roarkcompact.

1779
- Militias attack Cherokee settlements in North Carolina and Tennessee.
- Americans destroy 40 Indian towns in New York.
- Americans take Forts Kaskaskia and Vincennes.

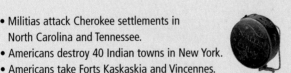

    1780
- Philadelphia Ladies Association raises money for soldiers.
- British take Charleston, South Carolina.
- French army arrives at Newport.
- British win battle of Camden.
- Benedict Arnold exposed as traitor.
- Americans win battle of King's Mountain.

        1781
- British forces invade Virginia.
- French fleet blockades Chesapeake Bay.
- Cornwallis surrenders at Yorktown; concedes British defeat.

           1783
- Treaty of Paris ends war; United States gains all land to the Mississippi River.

ARTICLES OF CONFEDERATION

The first written frame of government that bound together the thirteen rebelling colonies was called the Articles of Confederation. Delegates to the Second Continental Congress hammered out the plan over many months in 1776 and 1777, working on it when there was time free from the more pressing problems of pursuing the war. Once the congress agreed on it, the plan was printed and distributed to state legislatures for ratification, a process that took nearly five years because it required the assent of all thirteen. After ratification, in February 1781, this parchment copy became the official original version. As was often done with significant manuscript documents, a professional scribe wrote the opening words of the Articles in very large print, to proclaim the news. How does "To all to whom" compare with such famous opening words as "In Congress, July 4, 1776" (the start of the Declaration of Independence) and "We the people" (the start of the U.S. Constitution, which replaced the Articles in 1788)? Do you think "To all to whom" would have become a slogan or catchphrase had the Articles persisted as the country's sacred text? Why or why not?

National Archives.

Building a Republic
1775–1789

JAMES MADISON GRADUATED from Princeton College in New Jersey in 1771, not knowing what to do next with his life. Certainly the twenty-year-old had an easy fallback position. As the firstborn son of a wealthy plantation owner, he could return home to the foothills of Virginia and wait to inherit substantial land and a large force of slaves. But James was an intensely studious young man, uninterested in farming and reluctant to leave the collegiate environment. Five years at boarding school had given him fluency in Greek, Latin, French, and mathematics, and three years at Princeton acquainted him with the great thinkers, both ancient and modern. Driven by a thirst for learning, young Madison slept only five hours a night, perhaps undermining his health. Protesting that he was too ill to travel, he hung around Princeton six months after graduation.

In 1772, he returned home, still adrift. He tried studying law, but his unimpressive oratorical talents discouraged him. Instead he swapped reading lists and ideas about political theory by letter with a Princeton classmate, prolonging his student life. While Madison struggled for direction, the powerful winds before the storm of the American Revolution swirled through the colonies; the youth's drifting would abruptly end. In May 1774, Madison traveled north to deliver his brother to boarding school and was in Philadelphia when the startling news broke that Britain had closed the port of Boston in retaliation for the destruction of the tea. Turbulent protests over the Coercive Acts turned him into a committed revolutionary.

Back in Virginia, Madison joined his father on the newly formed committee of public safety. For a few days in early 1775, the twenty-four-year-old took up musket practice, but his continued poor health ruled out the soldier's life. His special talent lay in the science of politics, and in the spring of 1776, he gained election to the Virginia Convention, a revolutionary assembly replacing the defunct royal government. The convention's main task was to hammer out a state constitution with innovations like frequent elections and a limited executive power. Shy, self-effacing, and still learning the ropes, Madison mostly stayed on the sidelines, but Virginia's elder statesmen noted the young man's logical, thoughtful contributions. When his county failed to return him to the assembly in the next election, he was appointed to the governor's council, where he spent two years gaining experience in a wartime government.

In early 1780, Madison represented Virginia in the Continental Congress. Not quite twenty-nine, unmarried, and supported by his father's money, Madison was free of the burdens that made distant political service difficult for so many others. He stayed in the North for three years, working with men such as Alexander Hamilton of New York and Robert Morris of Pennsylvania as the congress wrestled with the chaotic economy and the ever-precarious war effort. In one crisis Madison's negotiating skills proved crucial: He broke the deadlock over the ratification of the Articles of Confederation by arranging for the cession of Virginia's vast western lands. Those lands would soon appear on maps as the Northwest Territory, calling forth a series of western land ordinances planned out by Madison's friend Thomas Jefferson that were the shining example of promise and high hopes for the future of the new confederation government. But more often, service in the congress proved frustrating to Madison because the confederation government seemed to lack essential powers, chief among them the power to tax.

Madison resumed a seat in the Virginia state assembly in 1784. But he did not retreat to a local point of view as so many other state politicians of the decade did. The difficult economic hardships created by heavy state taxation programs—which in Massachusetts led to a full-fledged rebellion against state government—spurred Madison to pursue means to strengthen the government of the thirteen new states. He worked hard to bring about an all-state convention in Philadelphia in the late spring of 1787, where he took the lead in steering the delegates to a complete rewrite of the structure of the national government, investing it with considerably greater powers. True to form,

Madison spent the months before the convention in feverish study of the great thinkers he had read in college, searching out the best way to constitute a government on **republican** principles. His lifelong passion for scholarly study, seasoned by a dozen years of energetic political experience, paid off handsomely. The United States Constitution was the result.

By the end of the 1780s, James Madison had had his finger in every kind of political pie, on the local, state, confederation, and finally national level. He had transformed himself from a directionless and solitary youth into one of the leading political thinkers of the Revolutionary period. His personal history over the 1780s was deeply entwined with the path of the emerging United States.

The Articles of Confederation

For five years after declaring independence, the Second Continental Congress continued to meet in Philadelphia and other cities without any formal constitutional basis. Delegates first had to work out a plan of government that embodied Revolutionary principles. With monarchy gone, where would sovereignty lie? What would be the nature of representation? Who would hold the power of taxation? Who should vote; who

James Madison, by Charles Willson Peale

A short and slight man, James Madison appeared younger than he was. This miniature portrait, made in 1783 when he was thirty-two, shows him with natural hair (no wig) and a boyishly smooth face. Madison commissioned the portrait on the occasion of his first serious romance. The Philadelphia artist Charles Willson Peale painted matching miniatures of Madison and his fiancée, Kitty Floyd, the sixteen-year-old daughter of a New York delegate to the Continental Congress. Madison and his Virginia friend Thomas Jefferson both boarded with the Floyd family while the congress met in Philadelphia. Jefferson, a very recent widower, encouraged the shy Madison and assured him that Kitty "will render you happier than you can possibly be in a single state." Madison's portrait was mounted in a brooch (note the pin sticking out on the right) so that his lady love might wear it on her person; the back of the brooch held a neatly plaited lock of Madison's hair. The companion miniature of Kitty no longer holds a lock of her hair, if it ever did, for Kitty soon jilted Madison for a suave younger man and returned the Madison miniature to the grieving bachelor. Eleven years later, Madison tried romance again when New York congressman Aaron Burr introduced him to a Virginia widow named Dolley Payne Todd, seventeen years his junior. Madison was forty-three and Dolley was twenty-six; they married four months after meeting. Library of Congress.

should rule? The resulting plan, called the Articles of Confederation, proved to be surprisingly difficult to implement, mainly because the thirteen states had serious disagreements about how to manage lands to the west whose political ownership was contested. Once the Articles were finally ratified and the confederation was formally constituted, that arena of government seemed to many to be far less relevant or interesting than the state governments.

Congress, Confederation, and the Problem of Western Lands

Only after declaring independence did the Continental Congress turn its attention to creating a written document that would specify what powers the congress had and by what authority it existed. There was widespread agreement on key government powers: pursuing war and peace, conducting foreign relations, regulating trade, and running a postal service. But there was serious disagreement about the powers of the congress over the western boundaries of the states. Virginia and Connecticut, for example, had old colonial charters that located their western boundaries at the Mississippi River. States without extensive land claims insisted on redrawing those colonial boundaries.

For over a year, the congress tinkered with drafts of the Articles of Confederation, reaching agreement only in November 1777. The Articles defined the union as a loose confederation of states, characterized as "a firm league of friendship" existing mainly to foster a common defense. The structure of the government paralleled that of the existing Continental Congress. There was no national executive (that is, no president) and no national judiciary. The congress was composed of two to seven delegates from each state, selected annually by the state legislatures and prohibited from serving more than three years out of any six. The actual number of delegates was not critical, since each state delegation cast a single vote.

Routine decisions in the congress required a simple majority of seven states; for momentous decisions, such as declaring war, nine states needed to agree. To approve or amend the Articles required the unanimous consent both of the thirteen state delegations and of the thirteen state legislatures. The congressional delegates undoubtedly thought they were guaranteeing

that no individual state could be railroaded by the other twelve in fundamental constitutional matters. But what this requirement really did was to hamstring the government. One state could—and did—hold the rest of the country hostage to its demands.

On the delicate question of taxes, needed to finance the war, the Articles provided an ingenious but ultimately troublesome solution. Each state was to contribute in proportion to the property value of the state's land. Large and populous states would give more than small or sparsely populated states. The actual taxes would be levied by the state legislatures, not by the congress, to preserve the Revolution's principle of taxation only by direct representation. However, no mechanism was created to compel states to contribute their fair share.

The lack of centralized authority in the confederation government was exactly what many state leaders wanted in the late 1770s. A league of states with rotating personnel, no executive branch, no power of taxation, and a requirement of unanimity for any major change seemed to be a good way to avoid the potential tyranny of government. But right away, the inherent weaknesses of these features became apparent.

The requirement for unanimous approval, for example, stalled the acceptance of the Articles for five years. The key dispute involved the problem of lands west of the existing states. Five states, all lacking land claims, insisted that the congress control western lands as a national domain that would eventually constitute new states. The other eight states refused to yield their colonial-era claims and opposed giving the congress power to alter boundaries (Map 8.1). In all the heated debate, few seemed to remember that those same western lands were inhabited by many thousands of Indians not party to the disputes.

The eight land-claiming states were ready to sign the Articles of Confederation in 1777. Three states without claims, Rhode Island, Pennsylvania, and New Jersey, eventually capitulated and signed, "not from a Conviction of the Equality and Justness of it," said a New Jersey delegate, "but merely from an absolute Necessity there was of complying to save the Continent." But Delaware and Maryland continued to hold out, insisting on a national domain policy. In 1779, the disputants finally compromised: Any land a state volunteered to

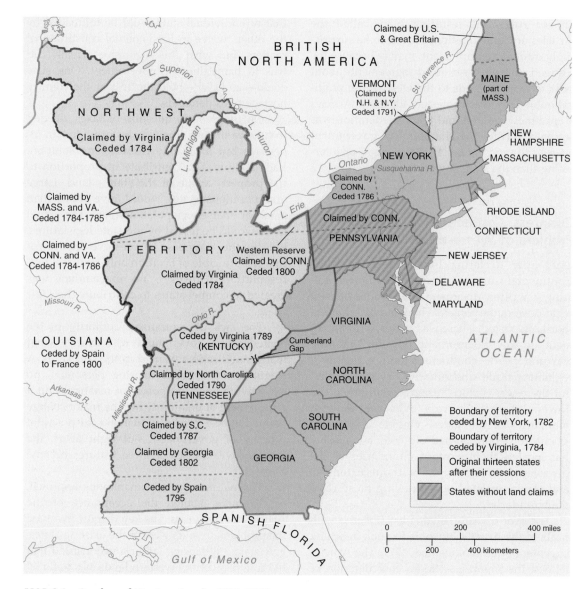

MAP 8.1 Cession of Western Lands, 1782–1802
The thirteen new states found it hard to ratify the Articles of Confederation without settling their conflicting land claims in the West, an area larger than the original states and occupied by Indian tribes. The five states objecting to the Articles' silence over western lands policy were Maryland, Delaware, New Jersey, Rhode Island, and Pennsylvania.

relinquish would become the national domain. When James Madison and Thomas Jefferson ceded Virginia's huge land claim in 1781, the Articles were at last unanimously approved.

The western lands issue demonstrated that powerful interests divided the thirteen new states. The apparent unity of purpose inspired by fighting the war against England papered over sizable cracks in the new confederation.

Running the New Government

No fanfare greeted the long-awaited inauguration of the new government. The congress continued to sputter along, its problems far from solved by the signing of the Articles. Lack of a quorum often hampered day-to-day activities. The Articles required representation from seven states to conduct business, and a minimum of two men from each state's delegation.

But some days, fewer than fourteen men in total showed up. State legislatures were slow to select delegates, and many of those appointed were reluctant to attend, especially if they had wives and children at home. Consequently, some of the most committed delegates were young bachelors like James Madison and men in their fifties and sixties whose families were grown, like Samuel Adams. Many politicians preferred to devote their energies to state governments, especially during the creative burst of state constitution writing in the late 1770s. Often the Continental Congress seemed deadlocked or, worse, irrelevant.

It also did not help that the congress had no permanent home. During the war, when the British army threatened Philadelphia, the congress relocated to small Pennsylvania towns such as Lancaster and York and then to Baltimore. After hostilities ceased, the congress moved from Trenton to Princeton to Annapolis to New York City.

To address the difficulties of an inefficient congress, executive departments of war, finance, and foreign affairs were created to handle purely administrative functions. When the department heads were ambitious—as was Robert Morris, a wealthy Philadelphia merchant who served as superintendent of finance—they could exercise considerable executive power. The Articles of Confederation had deliberately refrained from setting up an executive branch, but a modest one was being invented by necessity.

> **REVIEW** Why was the confederation government's authority so limited?

The Sovereign States

In the first decade of independence, the states were sovereign and all-powerful. Relatively few functions, like that of declaring war and peace, had been transferred to the confederation government. As Americans discarded their British identity, they thought of themselves instead as Virginians or New Yorkers or Rhode Islanders. Familiar and close to home, state government claimed the allegiance of citizens and became the arena in which the Revolution's innovations would first be tried. States defined who was a voter, and they also defined who would be free.

The question of slavery quickly became a front-burner issue, as all the states were forced to grapple with squaring revolutionary ideals with lifelong bondage for African Americans. Northern states had more success with this than did the southern, where slavery was deeply entrenched in the economy.

The State Constitutions

In May 1776, the congress recommended that all states draw up constitutions based on "the authority of the people." By 1778, ten had done so, and three more (Connecticut, Massachusetts, and Rhode Island) adopted and updated their original colonial charters. Having been denied unwritten British **liberties**, Americans wanted written contracts that guaranteed basic principles.

A shared feature of all the state constitutions was the conviction that government ultimately rests on the consent of the governed. Political writers in the late 1770s embraced the concept of republicanism as the underpinning of the new governments. Republicanism meant more than popular elections and representative institutions. For some, republicanism invoked a way of thinking about who leaders should be: autonomous, virtuous citizens who placed civic values above private interests. For others, it suggested direct **democracy**, with nothing standing in the way of the will of the people. For all, it meant government that promoted the people's welfare.

Widespread agreement about the virtues of republicanism went hand in hand with the idea that republics could succeed only in relatively small units, so the people could make sure their interests were being served. Nearly every state continued the colonial practice of a two-chamber assembly but greatly augmented the powers of the lower house. Two states, Pennsylvania and Georgia, abolished the more elite upper house altogether, and most states severely limited the powers and terms of the governor. Instead, real power resided with the lower houses, constituted to be very responsive to popular majorities, with annual elections and guaranteed rotation in office. If a representative displeased his constituents, he could be out of office in a matter of months.

Six of the state constitutions included bills of rights, lists of basic individual liberties that governments could not abridge. Virginia debated and passed the first bill of rights in June 1776, and many of the other states borrowed from it. Its language bears a close resemblance to the wording of the Declaration of Independence, which Thomas Jefferson was drafting that same June in Philadelphia: "That all men are by nature equally free and independent, and have certain inherent rights, of which, when they enter into a state of society, they cannot by any compact deprive or divest their posterity; namely, the enjoyment of life and liberty, with the means of acquiring and possessing property, and pursuing and obtaining happiness and safety." Along with these inherent rights went more specific rights to freedom of speech, freedom of the press, and trial by jury.

Who Are "the People"?

When the Continental Congress called for state constitutions based on "the authority of the people," and when the Virginia bill of rights granted "all men" certain rights, who was meant by "the people"? Who exactly were the citizens of this new country, and how far would the principle of democratic government extend? Different people answered these questions differently, but in the 1770s certain limits to full political participation by all Americans were widely agreed upon.

One limit was defined by property. In nearly every state, candidates for the highest offices had to meet substantial property qualifications. In Maryland, a candidate for governor had to be worth £5,000, a large sum of money. Voters in Maryland had to own fifty acres of land or £30, a barrier to one-third of adult white males. In the most democratic state, Pennsylvania, voters and candidates needed to be taxpayers, owning enough property to owe taxes. Only property owners were presumed to possess the necessary independence of mind to make wise political choices. Are not propertyless men, asked John Adams, "too little acquainted with public affairs to form a right judgment, and too dependent upon other men to have a will of their own?"

Property qualifications probably disfranchised from one-quarter to one-half of adult white males in all the states. Not all of them took their nonvoter status quietly. One Maryland man wondered what was so special about being worth £30: "Every poor man has a life, a personal liberty, and a right to his earnings; and is in danger of being injured by government in a variety

of ways." Why then restrict such a man from voting? Others pointed out that propertyless men were fighting and dying in the Revolutionary War; surely they were expressing an active concern about politics. Finally, a few radical voices challenged the notion that owning property transformed men into good citizens. Perhaps it did the opposite: The richest men might well be greedy and selfish and therefore bad citizens. But ideas like this were clearly outside the mainstream. The writers of the new constitutions, themselves men of property, viewed the right to own and preserve property as a central principle of the Revolution.

Another exclusion from voting—women—was so ingrained that few stopped to question it. Yet the logic of allowing propertied females to vote did occur to at least two well-placed women. Abigail Adams wrote to John in 1782 that "Even in the freest countrys our property is subject to the controul and disposal of our partners, to whom the Laws have given a sovereign Authority. Deprived of a voice in Legislation, obliged to submit to those Laws which are imposed upon us, is it not sufficient to make us indifferent to the publick Welfare?" A wealthy Virginia widow named Hannah Corbin wrote to her brother, Richard Henry Lee, to complain of her taxation without the corresponding representation. Her letter no longer exists, but his reply does: "You complain that widows are not represented, and that being temporary possessors of the estates, ought not to be liable to the tax." Yet, he continued, women would be "out of character... to press into those tumultuous assemblies of men where the business of choosing representatives is conducted."

Only three states specified that voters had to be male, so powerful was the unspoken assumption that only men could vote. Still, in one state, small numbers of women began to turn out at the polls in the 1780s. New Jersey's constitution of 1776 enfranchised all free inhabitants worth over £50, language that in theory opened the door to free blacks as well as unmarried women, if propertied. (Married women owned no property, for by law their husbands held title to everything.) Little fanfare accompanied this radical shift, and some historians have inferred that the inclusion of unmarried women and blacks was an oversight. Yet other parts of the **suffrage** clause pertaining to residency and property were extensively debated when it was put in the state constitution, and no objections were raised at that time to its gender- and race-free language. Thus other historians have concluded that the law was intentionally inclusive. In 1790, a revised election law used the words *he* or *she* in reference to voters, making woman suffrage explicit. As one New Jersey legislator declared, "Our Constitution gives this right to maids or widows *black* or *white*."

In 1790, only about 1,000 free black adults of both sexes lived in New Jersey, a state with a population of 184,000. The number of unmarried adult white women was probably also small, mainly widows. In view of the property requirement, the voter bloc enfranchised under this law could not have been decisive in elections. Still, this highly unusual situation lasted until 1807, when a new state law specifically disfranchised both blacks and women. Henceforth, independence of mind, that essential precondition of voting, was redefined to be sex- and race-specific.

In the 1780s, voting everywhere was class-specific, due to the property restrictions. John Adams urged the framers of the Massachusetts constitution not even to discuss the scope of suffrage but simply to adopt the traditional colonial property qualifications. If suffrage is brought up for debate, he warned, "there will be no end of it. New claims will arise; women will demand a vote; lads from twelve to twenty-one will think their rights not enough attended to; and every man who has not a farthing, will demand an equal voice with any other." Adams was astute enough to anticipate complaints about excluding women, youth, and poor men from political life, but it did not even occur to him to worry about another group: slaves.

Equality and Slavery

Restrictions on political participation did not mean that propertyless people enjoyed no civil rights and liberties. The various state bills of rights applied to all individuals who had, as the Virginia bill so carefully phrased it, "enter[ed] into a state of society." No matter how poor, a free person was entitled to life, liberty, property, and freedom of conscience. Unfree people, however, were another matter.

The author of the Virginia bill of rights was George Mason, a plantation owner with 118 slaves. When he penned the sentence "all men are

A Possible Voter in Essex County, New Jersey
Mrs. Elizabeth Alexander Stevens was married to John Stevens, a New Jersey delegate to the Continental Congress in 1783. Widowed in 1792, she would have then been eligible to vote in state elections according to New Jersey's unique enfranchisement of property-holding women. Mrs. Stevens's family was a prominent one. Her father had been surveyor general of New Jersey and New York; her husband was active in politics and was secretary to the governor of New York. Her son, John Stevens, was the inventor of steamboat and locomotive innovations; her daughter Mary married Robert R. Livingston of New York, also a delegate to the Continental Congress and a man who later built a fortune in steamboating. Essex County, where Elizabeth Stevens lived, was said to be the place where female suffrage was exercised most actively. This portrait, done around 1793–1794, represents the most likely face of that rare bird, the eighteenth-century female voter. The widow Stevens died in 1799, before suffrage was redefined to be the exclusive right of males.
New Jersey Historical Society.

by nature equally free and independent," he did not have slaves in mind; he meant that Americans were the equals of the British and could not be denied the liberties of British citizens. Other Virginia legislators, worried about misinterpretations, added the phrase specifying that rights belonged only to people who had entered civil society. As one wrote, with relief, "Slaves, not being constituent members of our society, could never pretend to any benefit from such a maxim."

One month later, the Declaration of Independence used essentially the same phrase about equality, this time without the modifying clause about entering society. Two state constitutions, for Pennsylvania and Massachusetts, also picked it up. In Massachusetts, one town suggested rewording the draft constitution to read "All men, whites and blacks, are born free and equal." The suggestion fell on deaf ears.

Nevertheless, after 1776 the ideals of the Revolution about natural equality and liberty began to erode the institution of slavery. Sometimes enslaved blacks led the challenge. (See "Documenting the American Promise," page 194.) In 1777, several Massachusetts slaves petitioned the state legislature, claiming a "natural & unalienable right to that freedom which the great Parent of the Universe hath bestowed equally on all mankind." They modestly asked for freedom for their children at age twenty-one and were turned down. In 1779, similar petitions in Connecticut and New Hampshire met with no success. Seven Massachusetts freemen, including the mariner brothers Paul and John Cuffe, refused to pay taxes for three years on the grounds that they could not vote and so were not represented. The Cuffe brothers landed in jail in 1780 for tax evasion, but their petition to the state legislature soon spurred the extension of suffrage to taxpaying free blacks in that state.

Another way to bring the issue before lawmakers was to sue in court. In 1781, a Massachusetts slave named Quok Walker charged his master with assault and battery, arguing that he was a free man under the state constitution's assertion that "all men are born free and equal." Walker won and was set free, a decision confirmed in an appeal to the state's superior court in 1783. Several similar cases followed, and by 1789 slavery had been effectively abolished by judicial decision in Massachusetts.

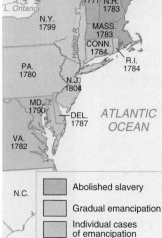

Legal Changes to Slavery, 1777–1804

In other northern states, untold numbers of blacks simply ran away from owners and claimed their freedom, sometimes with the help of sympathetic whites. One estimate holds that more than half of young slave men in Philadelphia took flight in the 1780s and joined the ranks of free blacks. By 1790, free blacks outnumbered slaves in Pennsylvania by nearly a factor of two.

Pennsylvania ended slavery by a gradual **emancipation** law in 1780. Only infants born to a slave mother on or after March 1, 1780, would be freed, but not until age twenty-eight. Thus no current slave in Pennsylvania would gain freedom until 1808; well into the nineteenth century those blacks born before 1780 would still be slaves. (Not until 1847 did Pennsylvania fully abolish slavery.) Rhode Island and Connecticut adopted gradual emancipation laws in 1784. In 1785, New York expanded the terms under which individual owners could free slaves, but only in 1799 did the state adopt a gradual emancipation law; New Jersey followed suit in 1804. These were the two northern states with the largest number of slaves: New York in 1800 with 20,000, New Jersey with more than 12,000. In contrast, slaves in Pennsylvania numbered just 1,700. Gradual emancipation illustrates the tension between radical and conservative implications of republican ideology. Republican government protected people's liberties and property, yet slaves were both people and property. Gradual emancipation balanced the civil rights of blacks and the property rights of their owners by delaying the promise of freedom.

South of Pennsylvania, in Delaware, Maryland, and Virginia, where slavery was so important to the economy, emancipation bills were rejected. All three states, however, eased legal restrictions and allowed individual acts of emancipation for adult slaves below the age of forty-five, under new manumission laws passed in 1782 (Virginia), 1787 (Delaware), and 1790 (Maryland). By 1790, close to 10,000 newly freed Virginia slaves had formed local free black communities complete with schools and churches.

In the deep South—the Carolinas and Georgia—freedom for slaves was unthinkable for whites. Yet several thousands had defected to the British during the war, and between three and four thousand shipped out of Savannah and Charleston, destined for freedom. Adding northern blacks evacuated from New York City in 1783, the probable total of emancipated blacks who left the United States was between eight and ten thousand. Some went to Canada, some to England, and some to Sierra Leone, on the west coast of Africa. Many hundreds took refuge with Seminole and Creek Indians, becoming permanent members of their communities in Spanish Florida and western Georgia.

Although all these instances of emancipation were gradual, small, and certainly incomplete, their symbolic importance was enormous. Every state from Pennsylvania northward acknowledged that slavery was fundamentally inconsistent with Revolutionary ideology; "all men are created equal" was beginning to acquire real force as a basic principle.

REVIEW How did states determine who would be allowed to vote?

The Critical Period

From 1781 to 1786, a sense of crisis gripped some of the Revolutionary leaders who feared the Articles of Confederation were too weak. But others defended the Articles as the best guarantee of individual liberty, because real governance occurred at the state level, closer to the people. Political theorizing about the proper relation among citizen, state, and confederation remained active and controversial throughout the decade as Americans confronted questions of finance, territorial expansion, and civil disorder.

Financial Chaos and Paper Money

Seven years of war produced a chaotic economy in the 1780s. The confederation and the individual states had run up huge war debts, financed

Black Loyalists in Canada
This rare sketch from 1788 shows an ordinary day laborer: a black woodcutter who came to Nova Scotia in the migration of black loyalists. Over 3,000 black refugees from the American Revolution arrived in northeastern Canada between 1783 and 1785. Very few were able to acquire land, and after 1786 the British authorities stopped provisioning them. Most, like the man pictured here, were forced to become servants or day laborers for whites. Low wages created dissatisfaction, and racial tensions broke loose in a riot. In 1791–1792, nearly a third of the black refugees in Nova Scotia left for Sierra Leone in West Africa, where British officials promised them landownership and opportunities for self-rule. In 1798, a refugee from South Carolina named Boston King published a memoir of his experiences joining the British during the Revolution, living in Nova Scotia, and traveling on to Sierra Leone; his rich account is one of the few existing personal narratives of black loyalism.
William Booth, National Archives of Canada C-401621.

by printing paper money and borrowing from private sources. Some $400 to $500 million in paper currency had been injected into the economy, and prices and wages fluctuated wildly. Private

debt and rapid expenditure flourished, and jails became crowded with debtors. A serious postwar

Blacks Petition for Freedom and Rights

In the 1780s, a language of rights and liberty was in the air and on many lips. Extraordinary times encouraged extraordinary actions, and enslaved as well as newly freed African Americans everywhere felt emboldened to make bids to enlarge their own liberty. Brand-new state governments held out the potential for revolutionary change in legal and social relations, encouraging some blacks to petition for various freedoms. To be effective, petitions generally needed to beg or persuade rather than assert. Notice the kinds of arguments made by these petitioners, the ways they describe themselves, and the promises they make about how they will use their hoped-for freedom.

DOCUMENT 1
Four Men Petition the Massachusetts Assembly for Their Freedom, 1773

Massachusetts law in the 1770s allowed even slaves to present petitions to the government. These four enslaved men printed their petition and sent a copy to each representative instead of submitting a single petition to the assembly, a shrewd strategy to maximize its impact.

Boston, April 20th, 1773
Sir, The efforts made by the legislative of this province in their last sessions to free themselves from slavery, gave us, who are in that deplorable state, a high degree of satisfaction. We expect great things from men who have made such a noble stand against the designs of their fellow-men to enslave them. We cannot but wish and hope Sir, that you will have the same grand object, we mean civil and religious liberty, in view in your next session. The divine spirit of freedom, seems to fire every humane breast on this continent, except such as are bribed to assist in executing the execrable plan.

We are very sensible that it would be highly detrimental to our present masters, if we were allowed to demand all that of right belongs to us for past services; this we disclaim. Even the Spaniards, who have not those sublime ideas of freedom that English men have, are conscious that they have no right to all the services of their fellow-men, we mean the Africans, whom they have purchased with their money; therefore they allow them one day in a week to work for themselves, to enable them to earn money to purchase the residue of their time.... We acknowledge our obligations to you for what you have already done, but as the people of this province seem to be actuated by the principles of equity and justice, we cannot but expect your house will again take our deplorable case into serious consideration, and give us that ample relief which, as men, we have a natural right to.

But since the wise and righteous governor of the universe, has permitted our fellow men to make us slaves, we bow in submission to him, and determine to behave in such a manner as that we may have reason to expect the divine approbation of, and assistance in, our peaceable and lawful attempts to gain our freedom.

We are willing to submit to such regulations and laws, as may be made relative to us, until we leave the province, which we determine to do as soon as we can, from our joynt labours procure money to transport ourselves to some part of the Coast of Africa, where we propose a settlement. We are very desirous that you should have instructions relative to us, from your town, therefore we pray you to communicate this letter to them, and ask this favor for us.

In behalf of our fellow slaves in this province, and by order of their Committee.

Peter Bestes,   Felix Holbrook,
Sambo Freeman,   Chester Joie.

SOURCE: Herbert Aptheker, ed., *A Documentary History of the Negro People in the United States* (New York: Citadel Press, 1968), 1:7–8. Copyright © by Citadel Press. Reprinted with permission.

DOCUMENT 2
Paul and John Cuffe Protest Taxation in Massachusetts, 1780

After judicial emancipation in Massachusetts, Paul and John Cuffe, together with five other freed men from the town of Dartmouth, sent this petition to the Massachusetts legislature.

To the Honourable Councel and House of Representatives in General Court assembled for the State of the Massachusetts Bay in New England—March 14th AD 1780—
The petition of several poor Negroes & molattoes who are Inhabitant of the Town of Dartmouth

Humbly Sheweth—That we being Chiefly of the African Extract and by Reason of Long Bondag and hard Slavery we have been deprived of Injoying the Profits of our Labouer or the advantage of Inheriting Estates from our Parents as our Neighbouers the white peopel do haveing some of us not long Injoyed our own freedom & yet of late, Contrary to the invariable Custom & Practice of the Country we have been & now are Taxed both in our Polls and that small Pittance of Estate which through much hard Labour & Industry we have got together to Sustain our selves & families withal—We apprehand it therefore to be hard usag and will doubtless if Continued will Reduce us to a State of Beggary whereby we shall become a Berthan to others if not timely prevented by the Interposition of your Justice & power & yor Petitioners farther sheweth that we apprehand ourselves to be Aggreeved, in that while we are not allowed the Privilage of freemen of the State having no vote or Influence in the Election of those that Tax us yet many of our Colour (as is well known) have cheerfully Entered the field of Battle in the defence of the Common Cause and that (as we conceive) against a similar Exertion of Power (in Regard to taxation) too well Known to need a recital in this place—

That these the Most honouerable Court we Humbley Beseech they would take this into Considerration and Let us aside from Paying tax or taxes or cause us to Be Cleaired for we ever have Been a people that was fair from all these thing ever since the days of our four fathers and therefore we take it as aheard ship that we should be so delt By now in these Difficulty times for there is not to exceed more then five or six that hath a

cow in this town and theirfore in our Distress we send unto the peaceableness of thee people and the mercy of God that we may be Releaved for we are not alowed in voating in the town meating in nur to chuse an oficer Neither their was not one ever heard in the active Court of the General Asembly the poor Dispised miserable Black people, & we have not an equal chance with white people neither by Sear nur by Land therefore we take it as a heard ship that poor old Negroes should be Rated which have been in Bondage some thirty some forty and some fifty years and now just got their Liberty some by going into the serviese and some by going to Sea and others by good fortan and also poor Distressed mungrels which have no larning and no land.... Neither where to put their head but some shelter them selves into an old rotten hut which thy dogs would not lay in.

Therefore we pray that these may give no offence at all...therefore we Humbley Beg and pray thee to plead our Case for us with thy people O God; that those who have the rule in their hands may be mercyfull unto the poor and needy give unto those who ask of thee and he that would Borrow of thee turn not away empty.... Neither with lieing Lips therefore we think that we may be clear from being called tories tho some few of our Colour hath Rebelled and Done Wickedly however we think that there is more of our Collour gone into the wars according to the Number of them into the Respepiktive towns then any other nation here.... We most humbley Request therefore that you would take our unhappy Case into your serious Consideration and in your wisdom and Power grant us Relief from Taxation while under

our Present depressed Circumstances and your poor Petioners as in duty bound shall ever pray &c.

Source: Herbert Aptheker, ed., *A Documentary History of the Negro People in the United States* (New York: Citadel Press, 1968), 1:15–16. Copyright © 1968 by Citadel Press. Reprinted with permission.

Questions for Analysis and Debate

1. What do the four Massachusetts petitioners mean when they congratulate the state legislators for their recent efforts "to free themselves from slavery"? Are they contradictory when they claim a natural right "as men" to relief from slavery but then also "bow in submission" to the "governor of the universe" who has allowed their slavery? What is it they "disclaim" out of consideration to their present masters? Why do they raise the case of a Spanish version of slavery?

2. Is the Cuffe petition essentially a call for "no taxation without representation"? Does it differ from the Revolutionaries' stand on taxation in relation to Britain? Do the petitioners want representation or relief from taxation? Why do they mention their military service?

3. What can you conclude about the options available to northern blacks to secure freedom or rights under law? Are the petitioners confident about their rights or about the outcome they expect? How have they had to shape their petitions to appeal to an all-white legislature? Do you see instances of subtle irony or sarcasm?

Scale of Depreciation

This chart shows the monthly value of U.S. Continental dollars from January 1777 to February 1781 as stipulated by the government of Massachusetts. For example, in March 1780, 3,736 Continental dollars equaled the buying power of $100 in gold or silver based on values of the dollar in January 1777. By April 1780, the same value of hard money required $4,000 Continentals. Such a chart was needed when debtors and creditors settled accounts contracted at one time and paid off later in greatly depreciated dollars. How easy would you find it to keep your head above water in an economy with such fast currency depreciation? What level of arithmetic and chart-reading skills were required? Notice the handwritten figuring at the bottom of the chart. Do these arithmetic operations look familiar to you?

Courtesy, American Antiquarian Society.

depression settled in by the mid-1780s and did not lift until the 1790s.

The confederation government itself was in a terrible financial fix. Continental dollars had lost almost all value: It took 146 of them to buy what one dollar had bought in 1775. Desperate times required desperate measures. The congress chose Robert Morris, Philadelphia merchant and newly reelected delegate, to be superintendent of finance. Morris had a gift for financial dealings but had resigned from the congress in 1778 amid accusations of enriching his firm while engaged in public service. Now his talents were again needed, and from 1781 to 1784 he took charge of the confederation's economic problems.

To augment the government's revenue, Morris first proposed a 5 percent impost (an import tax). Since the Articles of Confederation did not authorize taxation, an amendment was needed; but unanimous agreement proved impossible. Rhode Island and New York, whose bustling ports provided ample state revenue, preferred to keep their money and simply refused to agree to a national impost.

Morris's next idea was the creation of the Bank of North America. This private bank would enjoy a special relationship with the confederation, holding the government's **hard money** as well as private deposits, and providing it with short-term loans. The bank's contribution to economic stability came in the form of banknotes, pieces of paper inscribed with a dollar value. Unlike paper money, banknotes were backed by hard money in the bank's vaults and thus would not depreciate. Morris hoped this form of money would retain value; Congress agreed and voted to approve the bank in 1781. But the bank had limited success curing the confederation's economic woes because it issued very little currency; its charter was allowed to expire in 1786.

If Morris could not resuscitate the economy in the 1780s, probably no one could have done it. Because the Articles of Confederation reserved most economic functions to the states, the congress was helpless to tax trade, control inflation, curb the flow of state-issued paper money, or pay the mounting public debt. But the confederation had acquired one source of enormous potential wealth: the huge territory ceded by Virginia, which in 1784 became the national domain.

Land Ordinances and the Northwest Territory

The Continental Congress appointed Thomas Jefferson to draft a national domain policy. Jefferson proposed dividing the territory north of the Ohio River and east of the Mississippi—called the Northwest Territory—into ten new states consisting of townships ten miles square. He at first advocated giving the land to settlers, rather than selling it, arguing that future property taxes on the improved lands would be payment enough. Jefferson's aim was to encourage rapid and democratic settlement, to build a nation of freeholders (as opposed to renters), and to avoid land speculation. Jefferson also insisted on representative governments in the new states; they would not become colonies of the older states. Finally, Jefferson's draft prohibited slavery in the ten new states.

The congress adopted parts of Jefferson's plan in the Ordinance of 1784: the rectangular grid, the ten states, and the guarantee of self-government and eventual statehood. What the congress found too radical was the proposal to give away the land; the national domain was the confederation's only source of independent wealth. The slavery prohibition also failed, by a vote of seven to six states.

A year later, the congress revised the legislation with procedures for mapping and selling the land. The Ordinance of 1785 called for three to five states divided into townships six miles square, further divided into thirty-six sections of 640 acres, each section enough for four family farms. Property was thus reduced to easily mappable squares. Land would be sold by public auction, at a minimum price of one dollar an acre, with highly desirable land bid up for more. Two further restrictions applied: The minimum purchase was 640 acres, and payment must be in hard money or in certificates of debt from Revolutionary days. This effectively meant that the land's first owners would be prosperous speculators. The grid of invariant squares further enhanced speculation, allowing buyers and sellers to operate without ever setting foot on the acreage. The commodification of land had been taken to a new level.

Speculators usually held the land for resale rather than inhabiting it. Thus they avoided direct contact with the most serious obstacle to settlement: the dozens of Indian tribes that

Thomas Jefferson, by John Trumbull

This miniature shows Thomas Jefferson at age forty-five, during his years as a diplomat in Paris. The American artist John Trumbull visited France in 1788 and painted Jefferson's likeness in this five-by-four-inch format so he could later copy it into his planned large canvas depicting the signing of the Declaration of Independence. Jefferson requested three replicas of the miniature to bestow as gifts. One went to his daughter Martha, another to an American woman in London, and the third to Maria Cosway, a British artist with whom Jefferson shared an intense infatuation during his stay in France. A widower, Jefferson never remarried, but a scandal over his private life erupted in 1802, when a journalist charged that he had fathered several children by his slave Sally Hemings. In 1998, a careful DNA study concluded that uniquely marked Jefferson Y-chromosomes were common to male descendants in both the Hemings and Jefferson lines. The DNA evidence, when combined with historical evidence about Jefferson's whereabouts at the start of each of Hemings's six pregnancies, makes it nearly certain that Jefferson fathered some or perhaps all of her children. What cannot be known is the nature of the relationship between the two. Was it coerced or voluntary, or somewhere in between? In all his voluminous writings, Jefferson left no comment about Sally Hemings, and the record on her side is entirely mute.

Monticello / Thomas Jefferson Memorial Foundation, Inc.

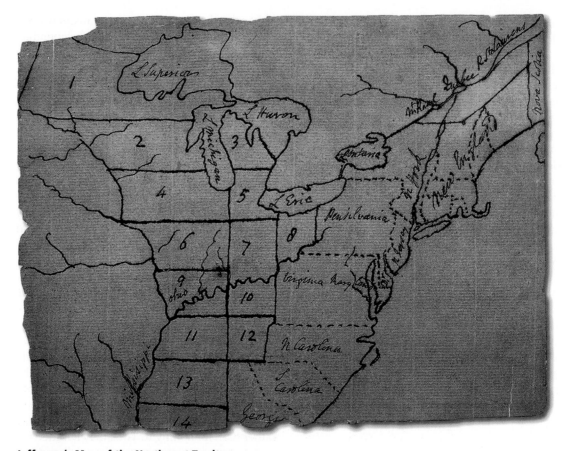

Jefferson's Map of the Northwest Territory

Thomas Jefferson sketched out borders for ten new states in his initial plan for the Northwest Territory in 1784. Straight lines and right angles held a strong appeal for him. But such regularity ignored inconvenient geographic features such as rivers and even more inconvenient political features such as Indian territorial claims, most unlikely to be ceded by treaty in orderly blocks. Jefferson also submitted ten distinctive names for the states. Number 9, for example, was Polypotamia, "land of many rivers" in Greek.

William L. Clements Library.

FOR MORE HELP ANALYZING THIS IMAGE, see the visual activity for this chapter in the Online Study Guide at **bedfordstmartins.com/roarkcompact**.

claimed the land as their own. Treaties signed at Fort Stanwix in 1784 and Fort McIntosh in 1785 coerced partial cessions of land from Iroquois, Delaware, Huron, and Miami tribes. Then in 1786, a united Indian meeting near Detroit issued an ultimatum: No cession would be valid without unanimous consent. The Indians advised the United States to "prevent your surveyors and other people from coming upon our side of the Ohio river." For two more decades, violent Indian wars in Ohio and Indiana would continue to impede white settlement (see chapter 9).

In 1787, a third land act, called the Northwest Ordinance, set forth a three-stage process by which settled territories would advance to statehood. First, congress would appoint officials for a sparsely populated territory who would adopt a legal code and appoint local magistrates to administer justice. When the free male population of voting age and landowning status (fifty acres) reached 5,000, the territory could elect its own legislature and send a nonvoting delegate to the congress. When the population of voting citizens reached 60,000, they could write a state constitution and apply for full admission to the Union. At all three territorial stages, the inhabitants were subject to taxation to support the Union, in the same manner as were the original states.

The Northwest Ordinance of 1787 was perhaps the most important legislation passed by the confederation government. It ensured that the new United States, so recently released from colonial dependency, would not itself become a colonial power—at least not with respect to white citizens. The mechanism it established allowed for the successful and orderly expansion of the United States across the continent in the next century.

Nonwhites were not forgotten or neglected in the 1787 ordinance. The brief document acknowledged the Indian presence in the Northwest Territory and promised that "the utmost good faith shall always be observed towards the Indians; their lands and property shall never be taken from them without their consent; and, in their property, rights, and liberty, they shall never be invaded or disturbed, unless in just and lawful wars authorized by Congress." The 1787 ordinance further pledged that "laws founded in justice and humanity, shall from time to time be made for preventing wrongs being done to them, and for preserving peace and friendship with them." These promises were full of noble intentions, but they were not generally honored in the decades to come.

Jefferson's original and remarkable suggestion to prohibit slavery in the Northwest Territory resurfaced in the 1787 ordinance, passing this time without any debate. Probably the addition of a fugitive slave provision in the act set southern congressmen at ease: Escaped slaves caught north of the Ohio River would be returned south. The ordinance thus acknowledged and supported slavery. Further, abundant territory south of the Ohio was still available for the spread of slavery. Still, the prohibition of slavery in the Northwest Territory perpetuated the dynamic of gradual emancipation in the North: North-South sectionalism based on slavery was slowly taking shape.

Shays's Rebellion, 1786–1787

Without an impost amendment, and with public land sales projected but not yet realized, the confederation turned to the states in the 1780s to contribute revenue voluntarily. Struggling with their own war debts, most state legislatures were reluctant to tax their constituents too heavily. Massachusetts, however, had a fiscally conservative legislature, dominated by the coastal commercial centers. For four years, the legislature passed tough tax laws that called for payment in hard money, not cheap paper. Farmers in the western two-thirds of the state found it increasingly difficult to comply and repeatedly petitioned against what they called oppressive taxation. In July 1786, when the legislature adjourned having yet again ignored their complaints, dissidents held a series of conventions and called for revisions to the state constitution to promote democracy, eliminate the elite upper house, and move the capital farther west in the state.

Still unheard in Boston, the dissidents targeted the county courts, the local symbol of state authority. In the fall of 1786, several thousand armed men marched on courthouses in six Massachusetts counties and forced bewildered judges to close their courts until the state constitution was revised. Sympathetic local militias did not intervene. The insurgents were not predominantly poor or debt-ridden farmers; they included veteran soldiers and officers in the Continental army as well as town leaders. One was a farmer and one-time army captain, Daniel Shays, from the town of Pelham.

The governor of Massachusetts, James Bowdoin, who had once organized protests against British taxes, now characterized the western dissidents as illegal rebels. He vilified Shays as the chief leader, and a Boston newspaper claimed Shays planned to burn Boston to the ground and overthrow the government, clearly an overreaction. Another former radical, Samuel Adams, took the extreme position that "the man who dares rebel against the laws of a republic ought to suffer death." Those aging revolutionaries had given little thought to the possibility that popular majorities, embodied in a state legislature, could seem to be just as oppressive as monarchs. The dissidents challenged the assumption that popularly elected governments would always be fair and just.

Members of the Continental Congress worried that the Massachusetts insurgency was spinning out of control. In October, the congress attempted to triple the size of the federal army, calling for 660 new recruits from Massachusetts and another 560 from New England; but fewer than 100 enlisted in the troubled state. So Governor Bowdoin raised a

Silver Bowl for an Anti-Shays General
Members of the militia of Springfield in western Massachusetts presented their leader, General William Shepard, with this silver bowl to honor his victory over the insurgents in Shays's Rebellion. Presentational silver conveyed a double message. It announced gratitude and praise in engraved words, and it transmitted considerable monetary value in the silver itself. General Shepard could display his trophy on a shelf, use it as a punch bowl, will it to descendants to keep his famous moment alive in memory, or melt it down in hard times. Shepard's is not the only name commemorated on the bowl; Shays's name appears in the last line, there for the ages to remember.
Yale University Art Gallery, Mabel Brady Garvan Collection.

Some 4,000 men gained leniency by confessing their misconduct and swearing an oath of allegiance to the state. A special Disqualification Act prohibited the penitent rebels from voting, holding public office, serving on juries, working as schoolmasters, or operating taverns for up to three years.

Shays's Rebellion caused leaders throughout the country to worry about the confederation's ability to handle civil disorder. Inflammatory Massachusetts newspapers wrote about bloody mob rule; perhaps, some feared, similar "combustibles" in other states were awaiting the spark that would set off a dreadful political conflagration. New York lawyer John Jay wrote to George Washington, "Our affairs seem to lead to some crisis, some revolution—something I cannot foresee or conjecture. I am uneasy and apprehensive; more so than during the war." Benjamin Franklin, in his eighties, shrewdly observed that in 1776 Americans had feared "an excess of power in the rulers" but now the problem was "a defect of obedience" in the subjects. Among such leaders, the sense of crisis in the confederation had greatly deepened.

REVIEW   Why did farmers in western Massachusetts revolt against the state legislature?

private army, gaining the services of some 3,000 by paying them bounties provided by wealthy and fearful Boston merchants (and later repaid by the state).

In January 1787, the insurgents learned of the private army marching their way, and 1,500 of them moved swiftly to capture a federal armory in Springfield to gain weapons. But a militia band loyal to the state government beat them to the weapons facility and met their attack with gunfire; four rebels were killed and another twenty wounded. The final and bloodless encounter came at Petersham, where Bowdoin's army surprised the rebels on a freezing February morning and took 150 prisoners; the others fled into the woods. Shays took off for Canada and other leaders left the state, but more than 1,000 dissidents were rounded up and jailed.

In the end, two men were executed for rebellion; sixteen more sentenced to hang were reprieved at the last moment on the gallows.

Shays's Rebellion, 1786–1787

⁂ Attacks by Shays's followers

⁂ Encounters between Shays's and government forces

The United States Constitution

Shays's Rebellion provoked an odd mixture of fear and hope that the government under the Articles of Confederation was losing its grip on power. A small circle of Virginians decided to try one last time to augment the powers granted to the government by the Articles. Their call for a meeting to discuss trade regulation led, more quickly than they could have imagined in 1786, to a total reworking of the national government.

From Annapolis to Philadelphia

The Virginians, led by James Madison, convinced the congress to allow a meeting of delegates at Annapolis, Maryland, in September

1786, to try again to revise the trade regulation powers of the Articles. But only five states participated, and they rescheduled the meeting for Philadelphia in May 1787. The congress reluctantly endorsed the Philadelphia meeting and limited its scope to "the sole and express purpose of revising the Articles of Confederation." But at least one representative at the Annapolis meeting had more ambitious plans. Alexander Hamilton of New York hoped the Philadelphia meeting would do whatever was necessary to strengthen the federal government. Hamilton got his wish as the meeting soon turned into a constitutional convention.

Alexander Hamilton by character was suited for such bold steps. The illegitimate son of a poor mother in the West Indies, at age sixteen the bright lad greatly impressed an American trader, who sent him to New York City for a college education. Hamilton soon got swept up in the military enthusiasm of 1776 and by 1777 had joined George Washington's staff, serving at the general's side through much of the Revolution. After the war, he studied law, married into a New York merchant family, and sat in the Continental Congress for two years. Despite his stigmatized and impoverished childhood, the aspiring Hamilton identified with the elite classes and their fear of democratic disorder.

The fifty-five men who assembled at Philadelphia in May 1787 were generally those most concerned about weaknesses in the Articles of Confederation. Few attended who were opposed to revising the Articles. Patrick Henry, author of the Virginia Resolves in 1765 and more recently state governor, refused to go, saying he "smelled a rat." Rhode Island refused to send delegates. Two New York representatives left in dismay in the middle of the convention, leaving Hamilton as the sole New York delegate.

This gathering of white men included no **artisans** or day laborers or even farmers of middling wealth. Two-thirds of the delegates were lawyers. The majority had served in the confederation congress and knew its strengths and weaknesses; half had been officers in the Continental army. Seven men had been governors of their states and knew firsthand the frustrations of thwarted executive power. A few elder statesmen attended, such as Benjamin Franklin and George Washington, but on the whole, the delegates were young, like Madison and Hamilton.

The Virginia and New Jersey Plans

The convention worked in secrecy, so the men could freely explore alternatives without fear that their honest opinions would come back to haunt them. The Virginia delegation first laid out a fifteen-point plan for a complete restructuring of the government. This Virginia Plan

City Tavern

Philadelphia's City Tavern, built in 1773, became a favorite gathering place for members of the Continental Congress. Taverns provided important public meeting spaces for business and social functions; they were critical nodes on the information network of the day, the place to learn news from travelers, newspapers, or local gossip. John Adams called the City Tavern "the most genteel one in America." In the Long Room on the second floor, delegates toasted each other on the anniversary of the Declaration of Independence on July 4, 1777. The men who wrote the Constitution in the summer of 1787 took meals and drinks there. This engraving and others like it aided in the complete reconstruction of the tavern on its original site in the 1970s; today it is open to the public as a period restaurant, complete with staff in costume.

Rare Book Department, The Free Library of Philadelphia.

was a total repudiation of the principle of a confederation of states. Largely the work of Madison, the plan set out a three-branch government composed of a two-chamber legislature, a powerful executive, and a judiciary. It practically eliminated the voices of the smaller states by pegging representation in both houses of the congress to population. The theory was that government operated directly on people, not on states. Among the breathtaking powers assigned to the congress were the rights to veto state legislation and to coerce states militarily to obey national laws. To prevent the congress from having absolute power, the executive and judiciary could jointly veto its actions.

In mid-June, delegates from New Jersey, Connecticut, Delaware, and New Hampshire—all small states—unveiled an alternative proposal.

The Pennsylvania Statehouse

The constitutional convention assembled at the Pennsylvania statehouse to sweat out the summer of 1787. Despite the heat, the delegates nailed the windows shut to eliminate the chance of being heard by eavesdroppers, so intent were they on secrecy. The statehouse, built in the 1740s to house the colony's assembly, accommodated the Continental Congresses at various times in the 1770s and 1780s. The building is now called Independence Hall, in honor of the signing of the Declaration of Independence within its walls in 1776.

Historical Society of Pennsylvania.

The New Jersey Plan, as it was called, maintained the existing single-house congress of the Articles of Confederation in which each state had one vote. Acknowledging the need for an executive, it created a plural presidency to be shared by three men elected by the congress from among its membership. Where it sharply departed from the existing government was in the sweeping powers it gave to the congress: the right to tax, to regulate trade, and to use force on unruly state governments. In favoring national power over **states' rights**, it aligned itself with the Virginia Plan. But the New Jersey Plan retained the confederation principle that the national government was to be an assembly of states, not of people.

For two weeks, delegates debated the two plans, focusing on the key issue of representation. The small-state delegates conceded that one house in a two-house legislature could be apportioned by population, but they would never agree that both houses could be. Madison was equally vehement about bypassing representation by state, which he viewed as the fundamental flaw in the Articles.

The debate seemed deadlocked, and for a while the convention was "on the verge of dissolution, scarce held together by the strength of a hair," according to one delegate. Only in mid-July did the so-called Great Compromise break the stalemate and produce the basic structural features of the emerging United States Constitution. Proponents of the competing plans agreed on a bicameral legislature. Representation in the lower house, the House of Representatives, would be apportioned by population, and representation in the upper house, the Senate, would come from all the states equally. Instead of one vote per state in the upper house, as in the New Jersey Plan, the compromise provided two senators who voted independently.

Representation by population turned out to be an ambiguous concept once it was subjected to rigorous discussion. Who counted? Were slaves, for example, people or property? As people, they would add weight to the southern delegations in the House of Representatives, but as property they would add to the tax burdens of those states. What emerged was the compromise known as the three-fifths clause: All free persons plus "three-fifths of all other Persons" constituted the numerical base for the apportionment of representatives. Using "all other Persons" as a substitute for "slaves" indicates the discomfort delegates felt in acknowledging in the Constitution the existence of slavery. But though slavery was nowhere named, nonetheless it was recognized, guaranteed, and thereby perpetuated by the U.S. Constitution.

Democracy versus Republicanism

The delegates in Philadelphia made a distinction between *democracy* and *republicanism* new to American political vocabulary. Pure democracy was now taken to be a dangerous thing. As a Massachusetts delegate put it, "the evils we experience flow from the excess of democracy." The delegates still favored republican institutions, but they created a government that gave direct voice to the people only in the House and that granted a check on that voice to the Senate, a body of men elected not by direct popular vote but by the state legislatures. Senators served for six years, with no limit on reelection; they were protected from the whims of democratic majorities, and their long terms fostered experience and maturity in office.

Similarly, the presidency evolved into a powerful office out of the reach of direct democracy. The delegates devised an electoral college whose only function was to elect the president and vice president. Each state's legislature would choose the electors, whose number was the sum of representatives and senators for the state, an interesting melding of the two principles of representation. The president thus would owe his office not to the Congress, the states, or the people, but to a temporary assemblage of distinguished citizens who could vote their own judgment on the candidates.

The framers had developed a far more complex form of federal government than that provided by the Articles of Confederation. To curb the excesses of democracy, they devised a government with limits and checks on all three branches of government. They set forth a powerful president who could veto Congress, but they gave Congress power to override presidential vetoes. They set up a national judiciary to settle disputes between states and citizens of different states. They separated branches of government not only by functions and by reciprocal checks but by deliberately basing the election of each branch on different universes of voters—voting citizens (the House), state legis-

lators (the Senate), and the electoral college (the presidency).

The convention carefully listed the powers of Congress and of the president. The president could initiate policy, propose legislation, and veto acts of Congress; he could command the military and direct foreign policy; and he could appoint the entire judiciary, subject to Senate approval. Congress held the purse strings: the power to levy taxes, to regulate trade, and to coin money and control the currency. States were expressly forbidden to issue paper money. Two more powers of Congress—to "provide for the common defence and general Welfare" of the country and "to make all laws which shall be necessary and proper" for carrying out its powers—provided elastic language that came closest to Madison's wish to grant sweeping powers to the new government.

While no one was entirely satisfied with every line of the Constitution, only three dissenters refused to sign the document. The Constitution specified a mechanism for ratification that avoided the dilemma faced earlier by the confederation government: Nine states, not all thirteen, had to ratify it, and special ratifying conventions elected only for that purpose, not state legislatures, would make the crucial decision.

> **REVIEW** Why did the government proposed by the constitutional convention employ multiple checks on each branch?

Ratification of the Constitution

Had a popular vote been taken on the Constitution in the fall of 1787, it would probably have been rejected. In the three most populous states—Virginia, Massachusetts, and New York—substantial majorities opposed a powerful new national government. North Carolina and Rhode Island refused to call ratifying conventions. Seven of the eight remaining states were easy victories for the Constitution, but securing the approval of the ninth proved difficult. Pro-Constitution forces, called Federalists, had to strategize very shrewdly to defeat anti-Constitution forces, who were called Antifederalists.

The Federalists

Proponents of the Constitution moved into action swiftly. To silence the criticism that they had gone beyond their charge (which indeed they had), they sent the document to the congress. Congress withheld explicit approval but resolved to send the Constitution to the states for their consideration. The pro-Constitution forces shrewdly secured another advantage by calling themselves "Federalists." By all logic, this label was more suitable for the backers of the confederation concept, because the Latin root of the word *federal* means "league." Their opponents became known as "Antifederalists," a label that made them sound defensive and negative, lacking a program of their own.

To gain momentum, the Federalists targeted the states most likely to ratify quickly. Delaware provided unanimous ratification by early December, before the Antifederalists had even begun to campaign. Pennsylvania, New Jersey, and Georgia followed within a month (Map 8.2). Delaware and New Jersey were small states surrounded by more powerful neighbors; a government that would regulate trade and set taxes according to population was an attractive proposition. Georgia sought the protection that a stronger national government would afford against hostile Indians and Spanish Florida to the south.

Another three easy victories came in Connecticut, Maryland, and South Carolina. As in Pennsylvania, merchants, lawyers, and urban artisans in general favored the new Constitution, as did large landowners and slaveholders. This tendency for the established political elite to be Federalist enhanced the prospects of victory, for Federalists already had power disproportionate to their numbers. Antifederalists in these states tended to be rural, western, and noncommercial, men whose access to news was limited and whose participation in state government was tenuous.

Massachusetts was the only early state that gave the Federalists difficulty. The vote to select the ratification delegates decidedly favored the Antifederalists, whose strength lay in the western areas of the state, home to Shays's Rebellion. One rural delegate from Worcester County voiced widely shared suspicions: "These lawyers and men of learning and money men that talk so finely, and gloss over matters so smoothly, to make us poor illiterate people swallow down the pill, expect to get into Congress themselves; they expect to be the managers of the Constitution and get all the power and all the money into their own hands, and then they will swallow up all us little folks." Nevertheless, the Antifederalist lead was slowly eroded by a vigorous newspaper campaign. In the end, the Federalists won by a very slim margin and only with promises that amendments to the Constitution would be taken up in the first Congress.

By May 1788, eight states had ratified; only one more was needed. North Carolina and Rhode Island were hopeless for the Federalist cause, and New Hampshire seemed nearly as bleak. More worrisome was the failure to win over the largest and most important states, Virginia and New York.

The Antifederalists

Antifederalists were a composite group, united mainly in their desire to block the Constitution. Although much Antifederalist strength came from backcountry areas long suspicious of eastern elites, many Antifederalist leaders came from the same social background as Federalist leaders; economic class alone did not differentiate them. Antifederalism also drew strength in states already on sure economic footing, like New York, that could afford to remain independent. Probably the biggest appeal of antifederalism lay in the long-nurtured fear that distant power might infringe on people's liberties. The language of the earlier revolutionary movement was not easily forgotten.

For example, in the proposed House of Representatives, the only directly democratic element of the Constitution, one member represented some 30,000 people. How could that member really know or communicate with his whole constituency, the Antifederalists wondered. In contrast, one wrote, "The members of our state legislatures are annually elected—they are subject to instructions—they are chosen within small circles—they are sent but a small distance from their respective homes. Their conduct is constantly known to their constituents. They frequently see, and are seen, by the men whose servants they are."

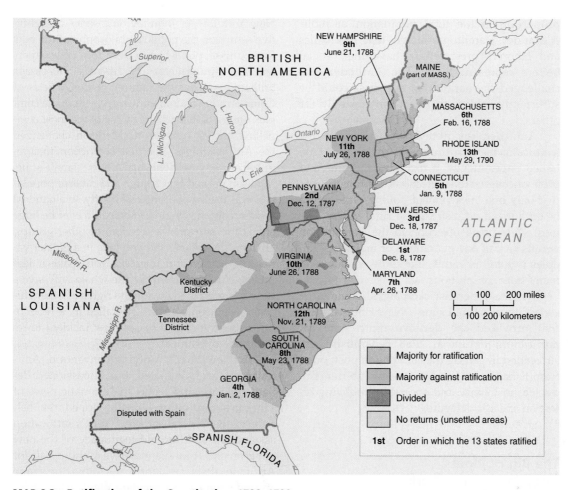

MAP 8.2   Ratification of the Constitution, 1788–1790
Populated areas cast votes for delegates to state ratification conventions. This map shows Antifederalist strength generally concentrated in backcountry, noncoastal, and nonurban areas, but with significant exceptions (for example, Rhode Island).

READING THE MAP: Where was Federalist opinion concentrated? How did the distribution of Federalist and Antifederalist sentiment affect the order of state ratifications of the Constitution?
CONNECTIONS: What objections did Antifederalists have to the new United States Constitution? How did their locations affect their view of the Federalist argument?

FOR MORE HELP ANALYZING THIS MAP, see the map activity for this chapter in the Online Study Guide at
bedfordstmartins.com/roarkcompact.

The Antifederalists also worried that elected representatives would always be members of the elite. Such men "will be ignorant of the sentiments of the middling and much more of the lower class of citizens, strangers to their ability, unacquainted with their wants, difficulties, and distress," worried a Maryland man. None of this would be a problem under a confederation system, according to the Antifederalists, because real power would continue to reside in the state governments.

The Federalists generally agreed that the elite would be favored for election to the House of Representatives, not to mention the Senate and the presidency. That was precisely what they hoped. Federalists wanted power to flow to intelligent, virtuous, public-spirited leaders like themselves. They did not envision a government constituted of every class of people. "Fools and knaves have voice enough in government already," argued a New York Federalist, without being guaranteed representation in proportion to the total population of fools. Alexander Hamilton claimed that mechanics and laborers preferred to have their social betters represent them. The Antifederalists challenged the notion that any class could be sufficiently selfless to rule disinterestedly for others.

Antifederalists fretted over many specific features of the Constitution. It prohibited state-issued paper money. It regulated the time and place of congressional elections, leading to fears that only one inconvenient polling place might be authorized, to disfranchise rural voters. The most widespread objection to the Constitution was its lack of any guarantees of individual liberties in a bill of rights, like those contained in many state constitutions.

Despite Federalist campaigns in the large states, it was a small state—New Hampshire—that provided the decisive ninth vote for ratification, on June 21, 1788. Federalists there succeeded in getting the convention postponed from February to June and in the interim conducted an intense and successful lobbying effort on specific delegates.

The Big Holdouts: Virginia and New York

Four states still remained outside the new union, and a glance at a map demonstrated the necessity of pressing the Federalist case in the two largest, Virginia and New York. Though Virginia was home to Madison and Washington, an influential Antifederalist group led by Patrick Henry and George Mason made the outcome uncertain. The Federalists finally but barely won ratification by proposing twenty specific amendments that the new government would promise to consider.

New York voters tilted toward Antifederalism out of a sense that a state so large and powerful need not relinquish so much authority to the new federal government. But New York was also home to some of the most persuasive Federalists. Starting in October 1787, Alexander Hamilton collaborated with James Madison and New York lawyer John Jay on a series of eighty-five essays on the political philosophy of the new Constitution, published in New York newspapers and later republished as *The Federalist*. The essays brilliantly set out the failures of the Articles of Confederation and offered an analysis of the complex nature of federalism. In one of the most compelling essays, number 10, Madison challenged the Antifederalists' heartfelt conviction that republican government had to be small-scale. Madison argued that a large and diverse population was itself a guarantee of liberty. In a national government, no single faction could ever be large enough to subvert the freedom of other groups. "Extend the sphere, and you take in a greater variety of parties and interests; you make it less probable that a majority of the whole will have a common motive to invade the rights of other citizens," Madison asserted. He called it "a republican remedy for the diseases most incident to republican government."

At New York's ratifying convention, Antifederalists predominated, but impassioned debate and lobbying—plus the dramatic news of Virginia's ratification—finally tipped the balance to the Federalists. New York's ratification assured the solidity and legitimacy of the new government. It took another year and a half for Antifederalists in North Carolina to come around. Fiercely independent Rhode Island held out until May 1790, and even then it ratified by only a two-vote margin.

In less than twelve months, the U.S. Constitution was both written and ratified. (See appendix I, page A-3.) An amazingly short time by twentieth-century standards, it is even more remarkable for the late eighteenth century, with its horse-powered transportation and hand-printed communications. The Federalists had faced a formidable task, but by building momentum and assuring consideration of a **Bill of Rights**, they did indeed carry the day.

REVIEW   Why did Antifederalists oppose the Constitution?

Conclusion: The "Republican Remedy"

Thus ended one of the most intellectually tumultuous and creative decades in American history. American leaders experimented with ideas and drew up plans to embody their evolving and conflicting notions of how a society and a government ought to be formulated. There was widespread agreement that government should derive its power and authority from the people, but there was fierce disagreement over the degree of democracy—the amount of direct control of government by the people—that would be workable in American society.

The decade began in 1776 with a confederation government that could barely be ratified because of its requirement of unanimity, but there was no reaching unanimity on the western lands, on the impost amendment, or on the proper way to respond to unfair taxation in a republican state. The new Constitution offered a different approach to these problems by loosening the grip of impossible unanimity and by embracing the ideas of a heterogeneous public life and a carefully balanced government that together would prevent any one part of the public from tyrannizing another. The genius of James Madison was to anticipate that diversity of opinion was not only an unavoidable reality but a hidden strength of the new society beginning to take shape. This is what he meant in his tenth *Federalist* essay when he spoke of the "republican remedy" for the troubles most likely to befall a government where the people are the source of authority.

Despite Madison's optimism, political differences remained keen and worrisome to many. The Federalists still hoped for a society in which leaders of exceptional wisdom would discern the best path for public policy. They looked backward to a society of hierarchy, rank, and benevolent rule by an aristocracy of talent, but they created a government with forward-looking **checks and balances** as a guard against corruption, which they figured would most likely emanate from the people. The Antifederalists also looked backward, but to an old order of small-scale direct democracy and local control, where virtuous people kept a close eye on potentially corruptible rulers. Antifederalists feared a national government led by distant, self-interested leaders who needed to be held in check. In the 1790s, these two conceptions of republicanism and of leadership would be tested in real life.

Suggestions for Further Reading

Lance Banning, *The Sacred Fire of Liberty: James Madison and the Founding of the Federal Republic* (1995). An eloquent biography detailing Madison's passionate involvement in the politics of the 1780s.

Saul Cornell, *The Other Founders: Anti-Federalism and the Dissenting Tradition in America, 1788–1828* (1999). Nuances of Antifederalism illuminated by the fascinating histories of those who opposed the Constitution.

Joanne Pope Melish, *Disowning Slavery: Gradual Emancipation and "Race" in New England, 1780–1860* (1998). A fine-grained study of gradual emancipation in New England.

Jack N. Rakove, *Original Meanings: Politics and Ideas in the Making of the Constitution* (1996). A prize-winning book on the political theory of the framers in Philadelphia.

Leonard L. Richards, *Shays's Rebellion: The American Revolution's Final Battle* (2002). A new interpretation of the Massachusetts insurgency based on a social profile of the arrested men.

Rosemarie Zagarri, *A Woman's Dilemma: Mercy Otis Warren and the American Revolution* (1995). A short, highly readable account of the life of the foremost political woman of the 1780s.

▶ **FOR MORE BOOKS ABOUT TOPICS IN THIS CHAPTER,** see the Online Study Guide at bedfordstmartins.com/roarkcompact.

▶ **FOR ADDITIONAL FIRSTHAND ACCOUNTS OF THIS PERIOD,** see Chapter 8 in Michael Johnson, ed., *Reading the American Past,* Third Edition.

▶ **FOR WEB SITES AND DOCUMENTS RELATED TO TOPICS AND PLACES IN THIS CHAPTER,** see "HistoryLinks," "DocLinks," and "PlaceLinks" at bedfordstmartins.com/roarkcompact.

REVIEWING THE CHAPTER

Follow these steps to review and strengthen your understanding of the chapter.

STEP 1: *Study the **Key Terms** and **Timeline** to identify the significance of each item listed.*

STEP 2: *Answer the **Review Questions**, drawing on key terms and dates to support your answers.*

STEP 3: *Drawing on the Key Terms, Timeline, and Review Questions, answer the broader **Making Connections** questions.*

KEY TERMS

Who

James Madison (p. 185)
Abigail Adams (p. 190)
John Adams (p. 191)
George Mason (p. 191)
Paul and John Cuffe (p. 192)
Quok Walker (p. 192)
Robert Morris (p. 196)
Iroquois (p. 198)
Delaware (p. 198)
Huron (p. 198)
Miami (p. 198)
Daniel Shays (p. 199)
James Bowdoin (p. 199)
Federalists (p. 204)
Antifederalists (p. 204)

What

Virginia Convention (p. 185)
Continental Congress (p. 186)
Articles of Confederation (p. 187)
republicanism (p. 189)
bills of rights (p. 189)
manumission law (p. 192)
gradual emancipation (p. 193)
impost (p. 196)
Bank of North America (p. 196)
Northwest Territory (p. 197)
Ordinance of 1784 (p. 197)
Ordinance of 1785 (p. 197)
Fort Stanwix (p. 198)
Fort McIntosh (p. 198)
Northwest Ordinance (p. 198)

Disqualification Act (p. 200)
U.S. Constitution (p. 200)
constitutional convention
  (p. 201)
Virginia Plan (p. 201)
New Jersey Plan (p. 202)
Great Compromise (p. 202)
three-fifths clause (p. 202)
The Federalist (p. 206)

TIMELINE

NOTE: Events are depicted chronologically, but the passage of time is not to exact scale.

1775 • Second Continental Congress meets.

1776 • Virginia adopts state bill of rights.

1777 • Articles of Confederation sent to states.

1778 • State constitutions completed.

1780 • Pennsylvania institutes gradual emancipation.
     • Massachusetts extends suffrage to taxpaying free blacks.

1781 • Articles of Confederation ratified.
     • Creation of executive departments.
     • Bank of North America chartered.
     • Slave Quok Walker successfully sues for freedom.

1782 • Virginia relaxes state manumission law.

1783 • Treaty of Paris signed, ending the Revolutionary War.

1784 • Gradual emancipation laws passed in Rhode Island and Connecticut.
     • Treaty of Fort Stanwix.

REVIEW QUESTIONS

1. Why was the confederation government's authority so limited? (pp. 186–89)

2. How did states determine who would be allowed to vote? (pp. 189–93)

3. Why did farmers in western Massachusetts revolt against the state legislature? (pp. 193–200)

4. Why did the government proposed by the constitutional convention employ multiple checks on each branch? (pp. 200–03)

5. Why did Antifederalists oppose the Constitution? (pp. 203–06)

MAKING CONNECTIONS

1. Leaders in the new nation held that voting should be restricted to citizens who possessed independence of mind. Why? What did they mean by independence of mind? How did this principle limit voters in the early republic?

2. Why did many Revolutionary leaders shaping the government of the new nation begin to find the principle of democracy troubling? How did they attempt to balance democracy with other concerns in the new government?

3. Twenty-first-century Americans see a profound tension between the revolutionary ideals of liberty and equality, and the persistence of American slavery. Did

Americans in the late eighteenth century see a tension? In your answer, be sure to discuss factors that might have shaped varied responses, such as region, race, and class.

4. The Northwest Territory was the confederation's greatest asset. Discuss the proposals to manage settlement of the new territory. How did they shape the nation's expansion? Which proposals succeeded and which failed?

▶ FOR PRACTICE QUIZZES, A CUSTOMIZED STUDY PLAN, AND OTHER STUDY TOOLS, see the Online Study Guide at bedfordstmartins.com/roarkcompact.

1786 • Virginia adopts Statute of Religious Freedom.
   • Shays's Rebellion begins.
   1787 • Shays's Rebellion crushed.
      • Northwest Ordinance.
      • Delaware provides manumission law.
      • Constitutional convention meets in Philadelphia.
      1788 • U.S. Constitution ratified.
         1790 • Maryland provides manumission law.
            1799 • Gradual emancipation law passed in New York.
               1804 • Gradual emancipation law passed in New Jersey.

WASHINGTON STANDS OUTSIDE OF TIME
A French clockmaker and artist produced this piece of Washington memorabilia after the death of the president. Washington's trim figure, rendered in gilt bronze, sports a spiffy uniform complete with fringed epaulets. One gloved hand rests on a sword; the other holds a rolled parchment, offered up in front of an eagle, the symbol of America's strength. Below the eagle a familiar motto is inscribed: "E Pluribus Unum" — "Out of many, one" — a reference to the political unity of the sovereign states. Below the clock is a motto about Washington that was first uttered in his funeral eulogy: "First in War, First in Peace, and First in the Hearts of his Countrymen." Death elevated Washington to celebrity status, and Americans immortalized him in many souvenirs.

The Warner Collection of Gulf States Paper Corporation.

The New Nation Takes Form

1789–1800

ALEXANDER HAMILTON, the first secretary of the United States Treasury, faced a challenge in June 1790. The new Constitution, with its power to raise taxes, explicitly promised to honor the Revolutionary War debt, and it fell to Hamilton to propose an implementation plan. Hamilton's controversial solution was to roll over the nearly worthless federal debt certificates of the 1770s and 1780s into new certificates having the same dollar amount with interest payments guaranteed by the new government. Hamilton also proposed adding to the federal debt all the states' still-outstanding debts. This large-scale debt consolidation (called *assumption* at the time) struck critics as expensive, unnecessary, unfair, and, worse, a power grab by the new government to subordinate the states. Hamilton's bold plan became deadlocked in Congress.

Hamilton's chief opponent on the debt question was James Madison, now a member of the first federal Congress sitting in New York City. Together, these former allies had written *The Federalist* essays during ratification, brilliantly creating the intellectual underpinnings of federalism. But the trust between them had eroded. Madison feared that Virginians, who had responsibly paid down their state's debt, would be taxed to pay the debts of other states. He also objected to the windfall profits to be realized by speculators who bought old debt certificates at a fraction of their face value. Greedy speculators, Madison claimed, "are still exploring the interior & distant parts of the Union in order to take advantage of the holders." Through strenuous politicking, Madison had stalled out Hamilton's plan.

At this first crisis point—one of many to come in the 1790s—a solution arrived thanks to the hospitality of Thomas Jefferson, the secretary of state. Deeply worried about the stability of the Union, Jefferson invited Hamilton and Madison to dinner at his New York residence. Over good food and candlelight, Hamilton secured the reluctant Madison's promise to restrain his opposition. In return, Hamilton pledged to back efforts to locate the nation's new capital city in the South, along the Potomac River, an outcome that was sure to please Virginians. In early July, Congress voted for the Potomac site, and in late July, Congress passed the debt package, assumption and all.

This tense political transaction both revealed and perpetuated the fragility of the new government in its first years of existence. Jefferson and Madison feared that Hamilton's funding plan would not only reward the wrong sort of men but dangerously bind them by financial ties to the government. Jefferson

***Alexander Hamilton*, by John Trumbull**
Hamilton was brash, confident, handsome, and audacious. Through force of personality, he overcame what was for his era and culture a double obstacle in life, being born in obscurity and bastardy on the small West Indies island of Nevis. His mother died when he was thirteen, and five years later he made his way to the mainland colony of New York and managed to charm his way into elite circles. He attended college, served in the Continental army, earned George Washington's uncommon admiration, and helped to write and ratify the Constitution. Along the way, he married Betsey Schuyler, whose father was one of the richest men in New York. He posed for this portrait in 1792, at the age of thirty-seven and at the height of his power.
Yale University Art Gallery.

later wrote that the deal "was unjust, and was acquiesced in merely from a fear of disunion, while our government was still in its infant state." They feared "disunion" when fellow Virginians compared Hamilton's assumption plan to the parlia-

mentary taxation that had sparked the Revolution. Their solution was to do what it took to get the capital city situated in their own region, the better to watch and influence it.

From 1790 to 1800, the "Founding Fathers" of the Revolution and Constitution era became competitors and even bitter rivals. Personalities clashed: Hamilton's charm no longer worked with Madison, and it had never worked with John Adams, the new vice president, who privately called Hamilton "the bastard brat of a Scotch pedlar" motivated by "disappointed Ambition and unbridled malice and revenge." Abigail Adams thought Hamilton a second Napoleon Bonaparte, an uncomplimentary reference to the belligerent leader of war-torn France. Years later, when asked why he deserted Hamilton, Madison replied, "Colonel Hamilton deserted me."

Rivalry also sprang from serious differences in political philosophy. Hamilton assumed that government was safest when in the hands of "the rich, the wise, and the good"—in other words, America's commercial elite. For Hamilton, economic and political power naturally belonged together, creating an energetic force for economic growth. In contrast, Jefferson and Madison trusted most those whose livelihood was tied to the land. Agrarian values ran deep with them, and they were suspicious of get-rich-quick speculators and financiers.

And finally, the 1780s Federalist alliance broke up over differing views of and policies toward European powers. Hamilton was an unabashed admirer of everything British, while Jefferson was enchanted by France, where he had lived in the 1780s. These loyalties governed foreign relations in the late 1790s, when the United States was in a war or near war with both of these overseas rivals.

The personal and political antagonisms of this first generation of American leaders left their marks on the young country. No one was prepared for the intense and passionate polarization that emerged over economic and foreign policy. The disagreements were articulated around particular events and policies: taxation and the public debt, a new farmers' rebellion in a western region, policies favoring commercial development, a treaty with England, a rebellion in Haiti, and a quasi-war with France that led to severe strictures on ideas of sedition and free speech. But at their heart, these disagreements arose out of opposing ideological stances on the value of **democracy**, the nature of leadership, and the limits of federal power. About the only major policy development that did not replicate or intensify these antagonisms among political leaders was Indian policy in the new republic.

By 1800, the oppositional politics ripening between Hamiltonian and Jeffersonian politicians would begin to crystallize into political parties, the Federalists and the Republicans. To the men of that day, this appeared to be an unhappy development.

The Search for Stability

Political parties were not part of the Constitution's plan for government. James Madison had argued in *The Federalist* in 1788 that a superior feature of the national government was precisely that the country's extensive size would prevent small, selfish factions from becoming dangerously dominant. Parties were thought of as destructive political forces, and their development was unanticipated and unwelcome. Only in future decades would American politicians come to realize that parties serve to organize conflict, legitimize disagreement, and mediate among competing political strategies.

Leaders in the early 1790s instead sought ways to heal divisions of the 1780s and maximize unity. Widespread veneration for President Washington promoted political stability. People trusted him to exercise the untested and perhaps elastic powers of the presidency. Congress quickly agreed on a **Bill of Rights**, which answered concerns of many Antifederalists. And the private virtue of women was mobilized to bolster the public virtue of male citizens; **republicanism** was forcing a rethinking of women's relation to the state.

Washington Inaugurates the Government

The election of George Washington in February 1789 was quick work, the tallying of the unanimous votes by the electoral college a mere formality. Everyone's first choice, Washington, perfectly embodied the republican ideal of disinterested, public-spirited leadership. Indeed, he cultivated that image through astute ceremonies such as the dramatic surrender of his sword to the Continental Congress at the end of the war, symbolizing the subservience of military power to the law.

Once in office, Washington calculated his moves, knowing that every step set a precedent and any misstep could be dangerous for the fragile government. How kingly should a president be? Congress debated a range of titles, such as "His Highness, the President of the United States of America and Protector of Their Liberties" and "His Majesty, the President"; Washington was known to favor "His High Mightiness." But in the end, republican simplicity prevailed. The final title was simply "President of the United States of America," and the established form of address became "Mr. President," a subdued yet dignified title in a society where only property-owning adult white males could presume to be called "Mister."

Washington's genius in establishing the presidency lay in his capacity for implanting his own reputation for integrity into the office itself.

Liverpool Souvenir Pitcher, 1789
A British pottery manufacturer produced this commemorative pitcher for the American market to capture sales at the time of George Washington's inauguration in 1789. The design shows Liberty as a woman dressed in a golden gown, her liberty cap on a pole, holding a laurel wreath (signifying classical honors) over Washington's head. Fifteen labeled links encircle the scene, representing the states, although in 1789, Rhode Island and North Carolina had not yet ratified the Constitution, and two more—Vermont and Kentucky—were merely anticipated states. The Liverpool manufacturer was looking ahead. Commemorative pitchers, jugs, and mugs were commonplace articles of consumer culture produced in Britain for specialized markets.
Smithsonian Institution, Washington, D.C.

He was not a brilliant thinker or a shrewd political strategist. He was not even a particularly congenial man. In the political language of the day, he was *virtuous*, meaning that he took pains to elevate the public good over private interest and projected honesty and honor over ambition. He remained aloof, resolute, and dignified, to the point of appearing wooden at times. He encouraged pomp and ceremony to create respect for the office, traveling with six horses to pull his coach, hosting formal balls, and surrounding himself with uniformed servants. He even held weekly levees, as European monarchs did, hourlong audiences granted to distinguished visitors (and including women), at which Washington appeared attired in black velvet, with a feathered hat and a polished sword. The president and his guests bowed, avoiding the egalitarian familiarity of handshakes. But he always managed, perhaps just barely, to avoid the extreme of royal splendor.

Washington chose talented and experienced men to preside over the newly created departments of war, treasury, and state. Yet deep philosophical differences separated key appointees. For the Department of War, Washington chose General Henry Knox, former secretary of war in the confederation government. For the Treasury—an especially tough job in view of revenue conflicts during the confederation (see chapter 8)—the president picked Alexander Hamilton, known for his general brilliance and financial astuteness. To lead the Department of State, the foreign policy arm of the executive branch, Washington chose Thomas Jefferson, a master of diplomatic relations and the current minister to France. For attorney general, Washington picked Edmund Randolph, a Virginian who had attended the Constitutional Convention but had turned Antifederalist during ratification. For chief justice of the Supreme Court, Washington designated John Jay, a New York lawyer who, along with Madison and Hamilton, had vigorously defended the Constitution in *The Federalist*.

Soon Washington began to hold regular meetings with these men, thereby establishing the precedent of a presidential cabinet. (Vice President John Adams was not included; his only official duty, to preside over the Senate, he found "a punishment" because he could not participate in legislative debates. To his wife he complained, "My country has in its wisdom contrived for me the most insignificant office.") No one anticipated that two decades of party turbulence would emerge from the brilliant but explosive mix of Washington's first cabinet.

The Bill of Rights

An early order of business in the First Congress was the passage of a Bill of Rights. Seven states had ratified the Constitution on the condition that guarantees of individual liberties and limitations to federal power be swiftly incorporated. Federalists of 1787 had thought an enumeration of rights unnecessary, but in 1789 Congressman James Madison understood that healing the divisions of the 1780s was of prime importance. "It will be a desirable thing to extinguish from the bosom of every member of the community, any apprehensions that there are those among his countrymen who wish to deprive them of the liberty for which they valiantly fought and honorably bled."

Madison pulled much of his wording of rights directly from various state constitutions with bills of rights. He enumerated guarantees of freedom of speech, press, and religion, the right to petition and assemble, the right to be free from unwarranted searches and seizures. One amendment asserted the right to keep and bear arms in support of a "well-regulated militia," to which Madison added, "but no person religiously scrupulous of bearing arms, shall be compelled to render military service in person." That provision for what a later century would call "conscientious objector" status failed to gain acceptance in Congress.

In September 1789, Congress approved a set of twelve amendments and sent them to the states for approval; ten were eventually ratified. Amendments One through Eight dealt with individual liberties, and Nine and Ten concerned the boundary between federal and state authority. (See the amendments to the U.S. Constitution in appendix I, page A-8.) One proposal that failed of passage suggested a formula for finetuning the ratio of representation as population grew; the other required that any congressional pay raise voted in would not take effect until after the next election (not until 1992 did this amendment—the Twenty-seventh—pass). The process of state ratification took another two years, but there was no serious doubt about the outcome.

Still, not everyone was entirely satisfied. State ratifying conventions had submitted some eighty proposed amendments. Congress never considered proposals to change structural features of the new government, and Madison had no intention of reopening debates about the length of the president's term or the power to levy excise taxes.

Significantly, no one complained about one striking omission in the Bill of Rights: the right to vote. Only much later was voting seen as a fundamental **liberty** requiring protection by constitutional amendment—indeed, by four amendments. The Constitution deliberately left the definition of voters to the states, because of the existing wide variation in local voting practices, most based on property qualifications but some touching on religion and, in one unusual case, New Jersey, on sex and race (see chapter 8, page 190).

The Republican Wife and Mother

The exclusion of women from political activity did not mean they had no civic role or responsibility. A flood of periodical articles in the 1790s by both male and female writers reevaluated courtship, marriage, and motherhood in light of republican ideals. Tyrannical power in the ruler, whether king or husband, was now declared a thing of the past. Affection, not duty, bound wives to their husbands and citizens to their government. In republican marriages, the writers claimed, women had the capacity to reform the morals and manners of men. One male author promised women that "the solidity and stability of the liberties of your country rest with you; since Liberty is never sure, 'till Virtue reigns triumphant.... While you thus keep our country virtuous, you maintain its independence."

Until the 1790s, public virtue was strictly a masculine quality. But another sort of virtue loomed in importance: sexual chastity, a private asset prized as a feminine quality. Essayists of the 1790s explicitly advised young women to use sexual virtue to increase public virtue in men. "Love and courtship...invest a lady with more authority than in any other situation that falls to the lot of human beings," one male essayist proclaimed. If women spurned selfish suitors, they could promote good morals more than any social institution could, essayists promised.

Republican ideals also cast motherhood in a new light. Throughout the 1790s, advocates for female education, still a controversial proposition, argued that education would produce better mothers, who in turn would produce better

Republican Womanhood: Judith Sargent Murray
The twenty-one-year-old in this portrait became known eighteen years later as America's foremost public spokeswoman for the idea of woman's equality to man. Judith Sargent Murray frequently wrote essays for *Massachusetts Magazine* under the pen name "Constantia." In "On the Equality of the Sexes," published in 1790, she confidently asserted that women had "natural powers" of mind fully the equal of men's. Murray, the wife of a Universalist minister, also wrote plays that were performed on the Boston stage. In 1798 she published her collected "Constantia" essays in a book titled *The Gleaner;* George Washington and John Adams each bought a copy. Her indexed letter book contains copies of nearly two thousand letters that she wrote during her lifetime.

John Singleton Copley, *Portrait of Mrs. John Stevens* (Judith Sargent, later Mrs. John Murray), 1770–1772, oil on canvas, 50 × 40 inches, Terra Foundation for the Arts, Daniel J. Terra Art Acquisition Endowment Fund, 2000.6; photograph courtesy of Terra Foundation for the Arts, Chicago.

citizens. Benjamin Rush, a Pennsylvania physician and educator, called for female education because "our ladies should be qualified...in instructing their sons in the principles of liberty and government." A series of published essays by Judith Sargent Murray of Massachusetts favored education that would remake women into self-confident, rational beings, poised to become the equals of men. But even Murray had to dress her advanced ideas in the cloak of republican motherhood, justifying female education in the context of family duty.

Although women's obligations as wives and mothers were now infused with political meaning, traditional gender relations remained unaltered. (For the relatively few American voices that raised questions about what rights women might have, see "Beyond America's Borders," page 218.) The analogy between marriage and civil society worked precisely because of the self-subordination inherent in the term *virtue*. Men should put the public good first, before selfish desires, just as women must put their husbands and families first, before themselves. Women might gain literacy and knowledge, but only in the service of improved domestic duty. In Federalist America, wives and citizens alike should feel affection for their rulers; neither should ever rebel.

> **REVIEW**   How did political leaders in the 1790s attempt to overcome the divisions of the 1780s?

Hamilton's Economic Policies

The new government had the lucky break to be launched in flush economic times. Compared to the severe financial instability of the 1780s, the 1790s brimmed with opportunity and prosperity, as seen in increased agricultural trade, transportation, and banking improvements. In 1790, the federal government moved from New York City to Philadelphia, a more central location with a substantial mercantile class. There, Alexander Hamilton, secretary of the treasury, embarked on his innovative and controversial plan to solidify the government's economic base.

Agriculture, Transportation, and Banking

Dramatic increases in international grain prices motivated American farmers to boost agricultural production for the export trade. Europe's rising population needed grain, and the French Revolutionary and Napoleonic Wars that engulfed Europe for a dozen years after 1793 severely compromised production there. From the Connecticut River valley to the Chesapeake, farmers planted more wheat,

generating new jobs for millers, coopers, dockworkers, and ship and wagon builders.

Cotton production also underwent a boom, spurred by market demand and a mechanical invention. Limited amounts of smooth-seed cotton had long been grown in the coastal areas of the South, but this variety of cotton did not prosper in the drier, inland regions. Green-seed cotton grew well inland, but its rough seeds stuck to the cotton fibers and were difficult to remove. In 1793, Yale graduate Eli Whitney visited Georgia and devised a machine called a gin that separated out the seeds. Cotton planting soared, the cleaned cotton shipped to English factories to be made into textiles.

A surge of road building stimulated the economy. Before 1790, a series of bumpy Post Roads connected the miles from Maine to Georgia, but with the establishment of the U.S. Post Office in 1792, six times as many miles of road were quickly constructed to facilitate the transport of mail. Privately chartered companies also built roads; the first toll road in the nation was the Lancaster Turnpike of 1794, connecting Philadelphia with Lancaster, Pennsylvania. Another turnpike linked Boston with Albany, New York. Farther inland, a major road extended southwest down the Shenandoah Valley, while another joined Richmond, Virginia, with the Tennessee towns of Knoxville and Nashville.

By 1800, a dense network of dirt, gravel, or plank roadways connected cities and towns in southern New England and the Middle Atlantic states, spurring commercial stage companies to regularize and speed up passenger traffic. A trip from New York to Boston took four days; from New York to Philadelphia, less than two (Map 9.1). In 1790, Boston had only three stagecoach companies; by 1800 there were twenty-four. Transport of goods by road was still expensive per mile compared to water transport on navigable rivers or along the coast, but at least it was possible.

A third development signaling economic resurgence was the growth of commercial bank-

Major Roads in the 1790s

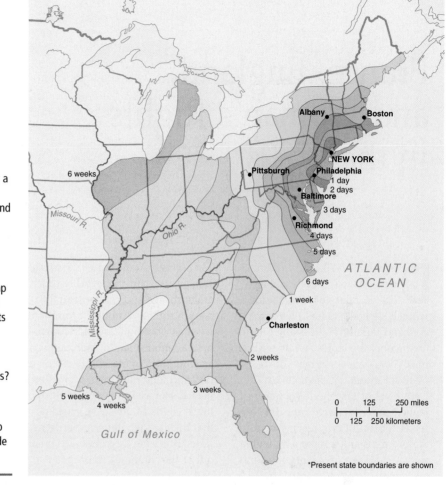

MAP 9.1   Travel Times from New York City in 1800
Notice that travel out of New York extends over a much greater distance in the first week than in subsequent weeks. River corridors in the West and East speeded up travel—but only if one were going downriver. Also notice that travel by sea (north and south along the coast) was much faster than land travel.

READING THE MAP: Compare this map to the map of "Major Roads in the 1790s" (page 216) and to Map 9.2. What physical and cultural elements account for the slower travel times west of Pittsburgh?

CONNECTIONS: Why did Americans in the 1790s become so interested in traveling long distances? How did travel times affect the American economy?

FOR MORE HELP ANALYZING THIS MAP, see the map activity for this chapter in the Online Study Guide at bedfordstmartins.com/roarkcompact.

ing. During the 1790s, the number of banks nationwide multiplied tenfold, from three to twenty-nine in 1800. Banks drew in money chiefly through the sale of stock. They then made loans in the form of banknotes, paper currency backed by the gold and silver that stockholders paid in. Because banks issued two or three times as much money in banknotes as they held in **hard money**, they were creating new money for the economy.

The Public Debt and Taxes

The upturn in the economy suggested that the government might soon repay its wartime debts, amounting to some $52 million owed to foreign and domestic creditors. But Hamilton had a different plan. He issued a *Report on Public Credit* in January 1790, recommending that the debt be funded—but not repaid immediately—at full value. This meant that old certificates of debt would be rolled over into new bonds, which would earn interest until they were retired several years later. There would still be a

public debt, but it would be secure, supported by citizens' presumed confidence in the new government. The bonds would circulate, injecting new valuable money into the economy. "A national debt if not excessive will be to us a national blessing; it will be a powerfull cement of our union," Hamilton wrote to a financier.

A large part of the old debt had been bought up cheaply by speculators in the late 1780s. (Hamilton himself held no certificates, but his father-in-law had certificates with a face value of $60,000.) These investors would have a direct financial stake in the new government, support that Hamilton regarded as essential to the country's stability. They would also own some $40 million in secured bonds, ready for new investment.

This funding plan was controversial, but Hamilton further proposed adding to the federal debt another $25 million that some state governments still owed to individuals. During the war, all the states had obtained supplies by issuing IOUs to farmers, merchants, and moneylenders. Some states, such as Virginia and New

France, England, and Woman's Rights in the 1790s

During the 1770s and 1780s in America, only rarely did anyone wonder about rights for women. Abigail Adams's letter to husband John in 1776, asking him to "remember the ladies" when writing new laws, stayed a private document for a century. Boycotts by Daughters of Liberty did not challenge gender hierarchy, nor did New Jersey's handful of women voters. Simply replacing a monarchy with a republic did not, in America, lead to an immediate or substantial challenge to women's subordinate status. It was influence from abroad, not at home, that initially sparked Americans' ideas about women's place in society.

In France between 1789 and 1793, the revolution against monarchy enlarged ideas about citizenship and led some women to argue for the concept of the *citoyenne*, the female citizen. Women's political clubs such as the Society of Republican Revolutionary Women in Paris sent petitions and gave speeches to the National Assembly, demanding education, voting rights, and a curbing of the paternal and marital powers of men over women. In 1791, Frenchwoman Olympe de Gouges rewrote the male revolutionaries' document

The Rights of Man into *The Rights of Woman,* asserting that "All women are born free and remain equal to men in rights." Another prominent woman, Théroigne de Méricourt, held a feminist salon, marched around Paris in masculine riding attire, and took part in an attack on a palace. Her vision went beyond political rights to the social customs that dictated women's subordination: "It is time for women to break out of the shameful incompetence in which men's ignorance, pride, and injustice have so long held us captive."

While voting rights for French women never passed in that era, the male National Assembly reformed French civil and family law in the early 1790s. Marriage was removed from the control of the church, divorce was legalized, and the age of majority for women was lowered. A far-reaching advance in inheritance law required division of a patriarch's estate among all his children, regardless of age, sex, and even legitimacy. Henceforth daughters could inherit along with sons; no longer did a woman from a family of means need to marry money—or indeed, to marry at all. In contrast, most American states imported traditional English family

law virtually unchanged into their lawbooks.

French **feminism** traveled across the channel to England and directly inspired a talented woman named Mary Wollstonecraft. In 1792 she published *A Vindication of the Rights of Woman,* arguing for the intellectual equality of the sexes, economic independence for women, and participation in representative government. Most radically, she called marriage legalized prostitution.

Wollstonecraft's book created a sensation in America. Excerpts appeared immediately in Philadelphia and Boston periodicals, bookstores stocked the London edition, and by 1795 there were three American reprints. Some women readers were cautious. A sixty-year-old Philadelphian, Elizabeth Drinker, reflected in her diary that "In very many of her sentiments, she, as some of our friends say, speaks my mind; in some others, I do not altogether coincide with her. I am not for quite so much independence." Other women embraced Wollstonecraft's ideas. A woman much younger than Drinker, Priscilla Mason, gave a biting commencement address at the new Young Ladies' Academy in Philadelphia in 1794 and took Wollstonecraft as her departure for a rousing speech condemning "the high and mighty lords"—men—who had denied women education and professional opportunities in church, law, and politics. "Happily, a more liberal way of thinking begins to prevail....Let us by suitable education, qualify ourselves for those high departments," and, she concluded with unwarranted optimism, "they will open before us." Many women's letters report lively debates stimulated by *A Vindication of the Rights of Woman.*

Male readers' responses were varied as well. Aaron Burr, a senator from New York, called the book "a work of genius." A Fourth of July speaker in New Jersey in 1793 proclaimed that "the Rights of Woman are no longer strange sounds to an American ear," and he hoped they would soon be embedded in state law codes. A more negative orator on that same holiday in New York argued that woman's rights really meant a woman's duty "to submit to the control of that government she has voluntarily chosen," namely the government of a husband. And a New Hampshire July Fourth orator advanced this tart joke: "Every man, by the Constitution, is born with an equal right to be elected to the highest office. And every woman is born with an equal right to be the wife of the most eminent man." For some, it was clearly hard to think seriously about gender equality.

The notion of equal rights for women had a long incubation period in the United States. In the 1790s, ideas of equality were too closely associated with the radicalism of the French Revolution, a divisive topic in America; and soon revelations of Wollstonecraft's unconventional personal life as an unwed mother dampened enthusiasm for her pioneering book. Not until the 1830s and 1840s would there be a new generation of women, led by Sarah Grimké, raising questions of sex equality anew (see chapter 11, page 272, and chapter 12, page 308). Most Americans of the 1790s preferred a moderate stance, praising women's contribution to civil society through their influence on family—the "Republican motherhood" concept, historians have called it. While this fell far short of an egalitarian claim to rights, it did justify—and this was no small gain—women's formal education. A young woman speaker at a Fourth of July picnic in Connecticut in 1799 summed it up perfectly to her all-female audience: "As mothers, wives, sisters, and daughters, we may all be important, [and] teach our little boys, the inestimable value of Freedom, how to blend and harmonize the natural and social rights of man, and as early impressions are indelible, thus assist our dear country, to be as glorious in maintaining, as it was great in gaining her immortal independence."

FRONTISPIECE.

Published at Philadⁿ. Decʳ. 1ˢᵗ 1792.

Woman's Rights in the *Lady's Magazine* of 1792

This frontispiece, appearing in the first volume of the Philadelphia periodical the *Lady's Magazine and Repository of Entertaining Knowledge*, accompanied excerpts from Mary Wollstonecraft's *Vindication*. (The editor was a literary man, Charles Brockden Brown.) The caption identified the kneeling figure as "the Genius of the *Lady's Magazine*," accompanied by "the Genius of Emulation" carrying a trumpet and a laurel wreath. (*Genius* here meant a spirit; *emulation* meant ambition to excel, now an obsolete usage. Thus the genius of emulation was the spirit of ambition—women's ambition in this case.) The spirit representing the *Lady's Magazine* kneels before Liberty, identified by her liberty cap on a pole, and presents a paper titled "rights of woman." Study the objects arranged below Liberty: two books, a musical instrument, artist's paints, a globe, and a page of geometrical shapes. The kneeling figure seems to gesture toward them. What do they suggest about the nature of the "rights of woman" that this picture endorses?
Library Company of Philadelphia.

RATE OF TOLL

	Cts
Each foot passenger	3
Horse & rider	8
Two wheeled Pleasure carriage	20
Four wheeled do. do.	30
Curricle	30
Cart or waggon by one beast	10
Drawn by two beasts	15
Loaded do.	25
By three do. empty	20
Loaded do.	30
By four do. empty	25
Loaded do.	37½
Each additional beast	3
Sleigh drawn by one beast	10
By two do.	15
Sled by one do.	6½
By two do.	12½
By four do.	25
Each additional beast	6
Horse jack or mule	4
Neat cattle	3
Sheep & swine each	1

Bridge Toll Sign, 1796
This sign lists an amazing variety of tolls charged for crossing a bridge over the Connecticut River between Cornish, New Hampshire, and Windsor, Vermont, in 1796. Owners of bridges and toll roads collected fees from users of their privately built rights-of-way. Can you deduce any principle of pricing in this list? Is the list exhaustive? What if a boy with a dog attempted to cross the bridge? Do you imagine there were traffic jams at the tollgate?
New Hampshire Historical Society.

York, had paid off these debts entirely. Others, like Massachusetts, had partially paid them through heavy taxation of the inhabitants. About half the states had made little headway. Hamilton called for the federal government to assume these state debts and combine them with the federal debt, in effect consolidating federal power over the states.

Congressman James Madison objected to putting windfall profits in the pockets of speculators. He proposed instead a complex scheme to pay both the original holders of the federal debt and the speculators, each at fair fractions of the face value. He also strenuously objected to assumption of all the states' debts. A large debt was dangerous, Madison warned, especially because it would lead to high taxation. Secretary of State Jefferson also was fearful of Hamilton's

proposals. "No man is more ardently intent to see the public debt soon and sacredly paid off than I am. This exactly marks the difference between Colonel Hamilton's views and mine, that I would wish the debt paid tomorrow; he wishes it never to be paid, but always to be a thing where with to corrupt and manage the legislature." Eventually, Madison, Jefferson, and Hamilton worked out a compromise at that fateful dinner party in June 1790 (see chapter opening). Hamilton got his way on the federal assumption of state debts, and in exchange, a decision favoring Virginians was reached to locate the nation's capital on the banks of the Potomac River, on the border shared by Virginia and Maryland.

The First Bank of the United States and the *Report on Manufactures*

The second and third major elements of Hamilton's economic plan were his proposal to create a national Bank of the United States and his program to encourage domestic manufacturing. Believing that banks were the "nurseries of national wealth," Hamilton modeled his bank plan on the Bank of England, a private corporation that worked primarily for the public good. According to Hamilton's plan, the federal government would buy 20 percent of the bank's stock. In effect, the bank would become the government's fiscal agent, holding its revenues derived from import duties, land sales, and various other taxes. The other 80 percent of the bank's capital would come from private investors, who could buy stock in the bank with either hard money (silver or gold) or federal securities. Because of its size and the privilege of being the only national bank, the bank would help stabilize the economy by exerting prudent control over credit, interest rates, and the value of the currency.

Concerned that a few rich bankers might have undue influence over the economy, Madison tried but failed to stop the plan in Congress. Jefferson advised President Washington that the Constitution did not permit Congress to charter banks. Hamilton, however, pointed out that the Constitution gave Congress specific powers to regulate commerce and a broad right "to make all laws which shall be necessary and proper for carrying into execution the foregoing powers." Washington sided with Hamilton and signed the Bank of the United States into law in February 1791, with a charter allowing it to operate for twenty years.

When the bank's privately held stock went on sale in New York City in July, it sold out in a few hours, touching off an immediate mania of speculation in resale. A discouraged Madison reported that "the Coffee House is an eternal buzz with the gamblers," some of them self-interested congressmen intent on "public plunder."

The third component of Hamilton's plan was issued in December of 1791 in the *Report on Manufactures*, a proposal to encourage the production of American-made goods. Domestic manufacturing (chiefly iron products) was in its infancy, the result of years of dependence on British imports. Hamilton aimed to mobilize the new powers of the federal government to grant subsidies to manufactures and to impose moderate tariffs on those same products from overseas. This would protect the nascent industries at home and give them extra incentive to get established. Because the treasury secretary was cautious about tariff hikes, not wanting to undercut his important merchant allies, the proposed protective tariffs only covered goods in competition with domestic production. The *Report on Manufactures*, however, was not approved by Congress.

The Whiskey Rebellion

Hamilton's plan to restore public credit required new taxation to pay the interest on the large national debt. Hamilton did not propose a general increase in import duties, in deference to the merchant class, nor did he propose land taxes, which would have fallen hardest on the nation's wealthiest landowners. Instead, he convinced Congress in 1791 to pass a 25 percent excise tax on whiskey, to be paid by farmers when they brought their grain to the distillery, then passed on to individual whiskey consumers in the form of higher prices. Members of Congress from eastern areas favored the tax—especially those from New England, where the favorite drink was rum. A New Hampshire representative observed that the country would be "drinking down the national debt," an idea he evidently found acceptable.

Not surprisingly, the new excise tax proved unpopular with cash-short grain farmers in the western regions and whiskey drinkers everywhere. In 1791, farmers in the western parts of Pennsylvania, Virginia, Maryland, and the Carolinas and throughout Kentucky forcefully conveyed to Congress their resentment of Hamilton's tax. Congress responded with modest modifications to the tax in 1792; but even so, dis-

content was rampant, and the tax proved hard to collect. Simple evasion of the law was the most common response. In some places, crowds threatened to tar and feather federal tax collectors, and some distilleries underreported their production. With embarrassment, Hamilton admitted to Congress that the revenue was far less than anticipated, but instead of abandoning the law, he tightened up the prosecution of tax evaders.

In western Pennsylvania, Hamilton had one ally, a stubborn tax collector named John Neville, who refused to quit even after a group of spirited farmers burned him in effigy. In May 1794, Neville filed charges against seventy-five farmers and distillers for tax evasion. In July, he and a federal marshal were ambushed in Allegheny County by a group of forty men; then Neville's house was burned to the ground by a crowd estimated at five hundred, and one man in the crowd was killed. At the end of July, 7,000 Pennsylvania farmers planned a march—or perhaps an attack, some thought—on Pittsburgh to protest the hated tax.

In response, President Washington nationalized the Pennsylvania militia and set out, with Hamilton at his side urging him on, at the head of 13,000 soldiers. A worried Philadelphia newspaper criticized the show of force: "Shall Pennsylvania be converted into a human slaughter house because the dignity of the United States will not admit of conciliatory measures? Shall torrents of blood be spilled to support an odious excise system?" But in the end, no blood was spilled. By the time the army arrived in late September, the demonstrators had dispersed. No battles were fought, and no shots were exchanged. Twenty men were rounded up as rebels and charged with high treason, but only two were convicted, and both were soon pardoned by Washington.

Had the federal government overreacted? Thomas Jefferson thought so; he saw the event as a replay of Shays's Rebellion of 1786, when a protest against government taxation had been met with unreasonable government force (see chapter 8). The rebel farmers agreed; they felt entitled to protest oppressive taxation. Hamilton and Washington, however, thought laws passed by a republican government must be obeyed. The Whiskey Rebellion presented an opportunity for the new federal government to flex its muscles and stand up to civil disorder.

REVIEW   Why were Hamilton's economic policies controversial?

Conflicts West, East, and South

While the whiskey rebels challenged federal leadership from within the country, disorder threatened the United States from external sources as well. From 1790 onward, serious trouble brewed in three directions. To the west, a powerful confederation of Indian tribes in the Ohio Country resisted white encroachment, resulting in a brutal war. At the same time, conflicts between the major European powers forced Americans to take sides and nearly thrust the country into another war, this time across the Atlantic. And to the south, a Caribbean slave rebellion raised fears that racial war would be imported to the United States. Despite these conflicts, and the grave threats they posed to the young country, Washington won reelection to the presidency unanimously in the fall of 1792.

To the West: The Indians

By the Treaty of Paris of 1783, England had given up all land east of the Mississippi River to the United States—but without consulting its onetime allies, the Indian tribes who inhabited 25,000 square miles of that territory. When the Indians learned of the treaty terms, they expressed astonishment. "They told me they never could believe that our king could pretend to cede to America what was not his own to give," the British commander at Fort Niagara wrote of the Iroquois. In Ohio, British Indian agents assured the Shawnee and Delaware peoples that England had relinquished only political control to the United States and the Indians still had the right to occupy the land. Also, British troops still occupied a half dozen forts in the northwest. Such confusion and misrepresentation aggravated an already volatile situation.

The doubling of the American population from two million in 1770 to nearly four million in 1790 greatly intensified the pressure for western land. Several thousand settlers a year moved down the Ohio River in the mid-1780s. Most headed for Kentucky on the south bank of the river, but some eyed the forests to the north, in Indian country. By the late 1780s, government land sales in eastern Ohio had commenced (Map 9.2), though actual settlement lagged.

Meanwhile, the U.S. army entered the western half of Ohio, where white settlers did not dare to go. Fort Washington, built on the Ohio River in 1789 at the site of present-day Cincinnati, became the command post for three major invasions of Indian country. General Josiah Harmar, under orders to subdue the Indians of western Ohio, marched with 1,400 men into Ohio's northwest region in the fall of 1790, burning Indian villages. His inexperienced troops were ambushed by Miami and Shawnee Indians led by their chiefs Little Turtle and Blue Jacket, and one in eight of Harmar's men was killed.

Harmar's defeat—so humiliating that Harmar was court-martialed—spurred efforts to clear Ohio for permanent American settlement. General Arthur St. Clair, the military gov-

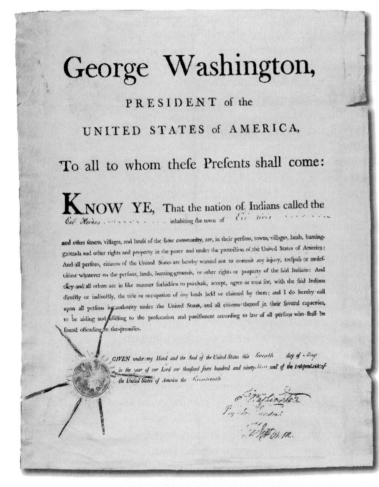

Washington's Proclamation Protecting Indian Territory
The president's name, in bold print, prefaces a warning that American citizens were forbidden to injure Indians or trespass on their lands in the Northwest Territory. When the federal government signed treaties with tribes ceding land, it often guaranteed protections for land not ceded. This poster of 1793, designed to be tacked up on trees, announced federal protection for Indians around the Eel River in Ohio. Such warnings were not very effective. Washington wrote in 1796, "I believe scarcely any thing short of a Chinese Wall, or line of Troops will restrain Land Jobbers, and the Incroachment of Settlers, upon Indian Territory."
The Huntington Library and Art Collections, San Marino, California.

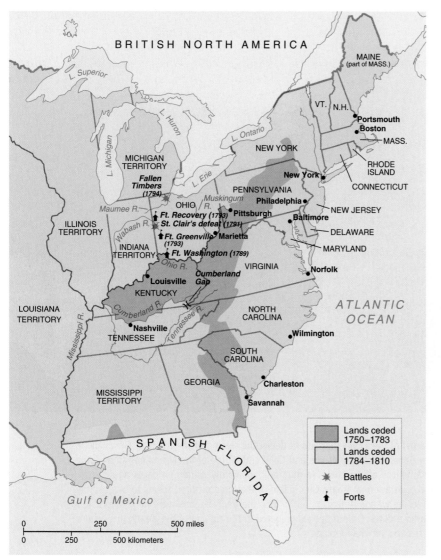

MAP 9.2 Western Expansion and Indian Land Cessions to 1810 By the first decade of the nineteenth century, intense Indian wars had resulted in significant cessions of land to the U.S. government by treaty.

ernor of the Northwest Territory, had pursued peaceful tactics in the 1780s, signing treaties with Indians for land in eastern Ohio—dubious treaties, as it happened, since the Indian negotiators were not authorized to yield land. In the wake of Harmar's bungled operation, St. Clair geared up for military action, and in the fall of 1791 he led 2,000 men (accompanied by 200 women camp followers) north from Fort Washington to engage in battle with the Miami and Shawnee. The Indians attacked at daybreak on November 4, at the headwaters of the Wabash River. Before noon, 55 percent of the Americans were dead or wounded; only three of the women escaped alive. The Indians scalped and dismembered the dying and pursued fleeing survivors for miles. With more than 900 lives lost, this was the most stunning American loss in the entire history of the U.S.-Indian wars.

Grisly tales of St. Clair's defeat became instantly infamous, increasing the level of sheer terror that Americans brought to their confrontations with the Indians.

President Washington doubled the U.S. military presence in Ohio and appointed a new commander, General Anthony Wayne of Pennsylvania, nicknamed "Mad Anthony" for his headstrong, hard-drinking style of leadership. About the Ohio natives Wayne wrote, "I have always been of the opinion that we never should have a permanent peace with those Indians until they were made to experience our superiority." With some 3,500 men, Wayne established two new military camps, Fort Greenville and Fort Recovery, deep in Indian territory in western Ohio.

Throughout 1794 Wayne's army engaged in skirmishes with Shawnee, Delaware, and Miami Indians. Chief Little Turtle of the Miami tribe

Treaty of Greenville, 1795
This painting by an unknown artist of the 1790s purports to depict the signing of the Treaty of Greenville in 1795. The treaty was signed by General Anthony Wayne and Chief Little Turtle of the Miami and Chief Tarhe the Crane of the Wyandot. An American officer kneels in the front, apparently writing on paper on his knee—not a likely posture in which to draft a formal treaty. One Indian of the three pictured seems to be gesturing with emphasis, as if to dictate to the writing American, but in fact, the treaty's terms were most favorable to the Americans. Many Indians from a dozen Ohio tribes congregated at the signing of the treaty; this picture shows unrealistically open spaces and very few Indians.
Chicago Historical Society.

advised negotiation; in his view, Wayne's large army looked overpowering. But Blue Jacket of the Shawnees counseled continued warfare, and his view prevailed. The decisive action came in August 1794 at the battle of Fallen Timbers, near the Maumee River where a recent tornado had felled many trees. The confederated Indians—mainly Ottawa, Potawatomi, Shawnee, and Delaware, numbering around 800—ambushed the Americans but were underarmed, and Wayne's troops made effective use of their guns and bayonets. The Indians withdrew and sought refuge at nearby Fort Miami, still held by the British. Their former allies, however, locked the gate and refused protection. Surviving Indians fled to the woods, their ranks decimated.

Fallen Timbers was a major defeat for the Indians. The Americans had destroyed corn-fields and villages on the march north, and with winter approaching, the Indians' confidence was sapped. They reentered negotiations in a much less powerful bargaining position. In 1795, about a thousand Indians representing nearly a dozen tribes met with Wayne and other American emissaries to work out the Treaty of Greenville.

The Americans offered treaty goods (calico shirts, axes, knives, blankets, kettles, mirrors, ribbons, thimbles, and abundant wine and liquor casks) worth $25,000 and promised additional shipments every year. The government's idea was to create a dependency on American goods to keep the Indians friendly. In exchange, the Indians ceded most of Ohio to the Americans; only the northwest part of the territory was reserved solely for the Indians.

The treaty brought temporary peace to the region, but it did not restore a peaceful life to the Indians. The annual allowance from the United States too often came in the form of liquor. "More of us have died since the Treaty of Greenville than we lost by the years of war before, and it is all owing to the introduction of liquor among us," said Chief Little Turtle in 1800. "This liquor that they introduce into our country is more to be feared than the gun and tomahawk."

Across the Atlantic: France and England

While Indian battles engaged the American military, another war overseas had to be closely watched. Since 1789, revolution had been raging in France. At first, the general American reaction was positive, for it was flattering to think that the American Revolution had inspired imitation in France. Monarchy and privilege were overthrown in the name of republicanism; towns throughout America celebrated the victory of the French people with civic feasts and public festivities.

But news of the beheading of King Louis XVI quickly dampened the uncritical enthusiasm for everything French. Those who fondly remembered the excitement and risk of the American Revolution were still likely to regard France with optimism. However, the reluctant revolutionaries of the 1770s and 1780s, who had worried about excessive democracy and social upheaval in America, deplored the far greater violence occurring in the name of republicanism as France in 1793 moved into the Reign of Terror, with its surge of executions.

Support for the French Revolution could remain a matter of personal conviction until 1793, when England and France went to war and French versus British loyalty became a critical foreign policy question. France had helped America substantially during the American Revolution, and the confederation government had signed an alliance in 1778 promising aid if France were ever under attack. Americans optimistic about the eventual outcome of the French Revolution wanted to deliver on that promise. But others, including those shaken by the guillotining of thousands of French people as well as those with strong commercial ties to England, sought ways to stay neutral.

In May 1793, President Washington issued a Neutrality Proclamation with friendly assurances to both sides. But tensions at home flared in response to official neutrality. "The cause of France is the cause of man, and neutrality is de-sertion," wrote H. H. Brackenridge, a western Pennsylvanian, voicing the sentiments of thousands. Dozens of pro-French political clubs called Democratic or Republican Societies sprang up around the country. The societies mobilized farmers and mechanics, issued circular letters, injected pro-French and anti-British feelings into local elections, and in general heightened popular participation and public interest in foreign policy. The activities of these societies disturbed Washington and Hamilton intensely, for they encouraged opposition to the policies of the president.

The Neutrality Proclamation fit Washington's goal of staying out of European wars. Yet American ships continued to trade between the French West Indies and France, and in late 1793 and early 1794, the British expressed their displeasure by capturing more than three hundred of these vessels near the West Indies. Clearly, something had to be done to assert American power.

President Washington sent John Jay, the chief justice of the Supreme Court and a man of strong pro-British sentiments, to England to negotiate commercial relations in the British West Indies and secure compensation for the seizure of American ships. In addition, Jay was supposed to resolve several long-standing problems. Southern **planters** wanted reimbursement for the slaves lured away by the British army during the war, and western settlers wanted England to vacate the frontier forts still occupied because of their proximity to the Indian fur trade.

Jay returned from his diplomatic mission in 1795 with a treaty that no one could love. First, the treaty failed to address the captured cargoes or the lost property in slaves. Second, it granted the British eighteen months to withdraw from the frontier forts along with continued rights in the fur trade. (Even with the delay, the provision disheartened the Indians just then negotiating the Treaty of Greenville out in Ohio; it was a significant factor in their decision to make peace.) Finally, the Jay Treaty called for repayment with interest of the debts that some American planters still owed to British firms dating from the Revolutionary War. In exchange for such generous terms, Jay secured limited trading rights in the West Indies and agreement that some issues—boundary disputes with Canada, the damage and loss claims of the shipowners—would be decided later by arbitration commissions.

When newspapers published the terms of the treaty, powerful opposition emerged from Maine to Georgia. In Massachusetts, graffiti read: "Damn John Jay!…Damn everyone who won't stay up all night damning John Jay!" Nevertheless, the treaty passed the Senate in 1795 by a vote of twenty to ten. Some representatives in the House, led by Madison, tried to undermine the Senate's approval by insisting on a separate vote on the funding provisions of the treaty, on the grounds that the House controlled all money bills. Finally, in 1796, the House approved funds to implement the various commissions mandated by the treaty, but by only a three-vote margin. The cleavage of votes in both houses of Congress divided along the same lines as the Hamilton-Jefferson split on economic policy.

To the South: The Haitian Revolution

In addition to the Indian wars in Ohio and the European wars across the Atlantic, a third bloody conflict to the south polarized and even terrorized many Americans in the 1790s. The western third of the large Caribbean island of Hispaniola, just to the east of Cuba, became engulfed in revolution starting in 1791. The eastern portion of the island was a Spanish colony called Santo Domingo; the western part, in bloody conflagration, was the French Saint Domingue. War raged in Saint Domingue for over a decade, resulting in the birth of the Republic of Haiti in 1804, distinguished as the first and only independent black state to arise out of a successful slave revolution.

The Haitian Revolution was a complex event involving many participants, including the diverse local population and, eventually, three European countries. Some 30,000 whites ruled the island in 1790, running sugar and coffee plantations with close to half a million slaves, two-thirds of them of African birth. The white French colonists were not the only plantation owners, however. About 28,000 free coloreds (*gens de couleur*) of mixed race also lived in Saint Domingue; they owned one-third of the island's plantations and nearly a quarter of the slave

Haitian Revolution, 1790–1804

Caribbean Sea

■ Beginning of slave revolt, 1791
— Border of Saint Domingue/ Santo Domingo, 1790
— Border of Haiti/ Santo Domingo, 1820

labor force. Despite their economic status, the free coloreds were barred from political power, but they aspired to it.

The French Revolution of 1789 was the immediate catalyst for rebellion in this already tense society. First, white colonists challenged the white royalist government in an effort to link Saint Domingue with the new revolutionary government in France. Next the free coloreds rebelled in 1791, demanding equal civil rights with the whites. No sooner was this revolt viciously suppressed than another part of the island exploded as thousands of slaves armed with machetes and torches wreaked devastation and slaughter. In 1793, the civil war escalated to include French, Spanish, and British troops fighting the inhabitants and also each other. Slaves led by Toussaint L'Ouverture in alliance with Spain occupied the northern regions of the island, leaving a thousand plantations in ruins and tens of thousands of people dead. Thousands of whites and free coloreds, along with some of their slaves, fled to Spanish Louisiana and southern cities of the United States.

White Americans followed the revolution in fascinated horror through newspapers and refugees' accounts. A few sympathized with the impulse for liberty, but many more shuddered at the violent atrocities. Many black American slaves also followed the revolution, for the amazing news of the success of a first-ever, massive revolution by slaves traveled quickly in this oral culture. Whites complained of behaviors that might prefigure plots and conspiracies, such as increased insolence and higher runaway rates among slaves.

The Haitian Revolution provoked naked fear in white Americans. Jefferson, agonizing over the contagion of liberty in 1797, wrote another Virginia slaveholder that "if something is not done, and soon done, we shall be the murderers of our own children…; the revolutionary storm, now sweeping the globe, will be upon us, and happy if we make timely provision to give it an easy passage over our land. From the present state of things in Europe and America, the day which brings our combustion must be near at hand; and only a single spark is wanting to make that day tomorrow."

REVIEW Why did the United States feel vulnerable to international threats in the 1790s?

Federalists and Republicans

By the mid-1790s, polarization over the French Revolution, Haiti, the Jay Treaty, and Hamilton's economic plans had led to two distinct and consistent rival political groups: Federalists and Republicans. Politicians and newspapers adopted these labels, words that summarized conflicting ideologies and principles; they did not yet describe full-fledged political parties. Washington's decision not to seek a third term led to serious partisan electioneering in the presidential and congressional elections of 1796. Federalist John Adams won the presidency, but party strife accelerated over failed diplomacy in France, bringing the United States to the brink of war. Pro-war and antiwar antagonism created a major crisis over political free speech, militarism, and fears of sedition and treason.

The Election of 1796

Washington struggled to appear to be above party politics, and in his farewell address he stressed the need to maintain a "unity of government" reflecting a unified body politic. He also urged the country to "steer clear of permanent alliances with any portion of the foreign world." The leading contenders for his position, John Adams of Massachusetts and Thomas Jefferson of Virginia, in theory agreed with him, but around them raged a party contest split along pro-English versus pro-French lines.

The leading Federalists informally caucused and chose Adams as their candidate, with Thomas Pinckney of South Carolina to run with him; the Republicans settled on Aaron Burr of New York to pair with Jefferson. The Constitution did not anticipate parties and tickets. Instead, each electoral college voter could cast two votes for any two candidates, but on only one ballot. The top vote-getter became president and the next highest assumed the vice presidency. (This procedural flaw was corrected by the Twelfth Amendment, adopted in 1804.) With only one ballot, careful maneuvering was required to make sure the chief rivals for the presidency did not land in the top two spots.

Into that maneuverable moment stepped Alexander Hamilton. No longer in the cabinet, Hamilton had returned to his law practice in

Washington's Farewell Address Printed on a Textile, 1806
This small square of fabric, suitable for framing or tacking to the wall, was one of many items that served to immortalize Washington as the benevolent savior of the young Republic. Known well by close associates as a man with ordinary human failings—one Federalist member of his last cabinet complained that he was "vain and weak and ignorant"—Washington in death became a demigod, a genius of inspired leadership and faultless integrity. This 1806 textile features the final paragraph of Washington's 1796 farewell address, one highlighting his modesty and self-deprecation. At the bottom, the American eagle and the British lion flank two sailing ships (one close, one far off) under the words "Commercial Union." The textile picture, then, was an implicit criticism of the new president, Thomas Jefferson, whose leadership was producing deteriorating relations with Britain that would finally result in the War of 1812.
Collection of Janice L. and David J. Frent.

1795, but he kept a firm hand on political developments. Hamilton did not trust Adams; he preferred Pinckney, and he tried to influence electors to throw their support to the South Carolinian. But his plan backfired: Adams was elected president with 71 electoral votes, and Jefferson came in second with 68 and thus became vice president. Pinckney got 59 votes, while Burr trailed with 30.

Adams's inaugural speech pledged neutrality in foreign affairs and respect for the French people, which made Republicans hopeful. To please Federalists, Adams retained three

***John Adams*, by John Trumbull**

In 1793, a year after painting a portrait of the youthful secretary of the treasury Alexander Hamilton (see page 212), Trumbull painted Vice President John Adams, then age fifty-eight. A friend once listed Adams's shortcomings as a politician: "He can't dance, drink, game, flatter, promise, dress, swear with gentlemen, and small talk and flirt with the ladies."

National Portrait Gallery, Smithsonian Institution / Art Resources, NY.

cabinet members from Washington's administration—the secretaries of state, treasury, and war. But the three were Hamilton loyalists, passing on Hamilton's judgments and advice as their own to the unwitting Adams. Vice President Jefferson expected to work closely with Adams, but the Hamiltonian cabinet ruined the honeymoon. Jefferson's advice was spurned, and he withdrew from active counsel of the president.

The XYZ Affair

From the start, Adams's presidency was in crisis. France retaliated for the British-friendly Jay Treaty by abandoning its 1778 alliance with the United States. French privateers—armed private vessels—started detaining American ships carrying British goods; by March 1797, more than 300 American vessels had been seized. To avenge these insults, Federalists started murmuring openly about war with France. Adams preferred negotiations and dispatched a three-man commis-

sion to France in the fall of 1797. When the three commissioners arrived in Paris, French officials would not receive them. Finally the French minister of foreign affairs, Talleyrand, sent three French agents, unnamed and later known to the American public as X, Y, and Z, to the American commissioners with the information that $250,000 might grease the wheels of diplomacy and a $12 million loan to the French government would be the price of a peace treaty. Incensed, the commissioners brought news of the bribery attempt to the president.

Americans reacted to the XYZ affair with shock and anger. Even staunch pro-French Republicans began to reevaluate their allegiance. The Federalist-dominated Congress appropriated money for an army of 10,000 soldiers and repealed all prior treaties with France. In 1798 twenty naval warships launched the United States into its first undeclared war, called the Quasi-War by historians to underscore its uncertain legal status. The main scene of action was the Caribbean, where over 100 French ships were captured.

There was no home-front unity in this time of undeclared war; antagonism only intensified between Federalists and Republicans. Republican newspapers heaped abuse on Adams. Pro-French mobs roamed the capital city, and Adams, fearing for his personal safety, stocked weapons in his presidential quarters. Federalists too went on the offensive. In Newburyport, Massachusetts, they lit a huge bonfire and burned issues of the state's Republican newspapers. One Federalist editor ominously declared that "he who is not for us is against us."

The Alien and Sedition Acts

With tempers so dangerously high, and fears that political dissent was perhaps akin to treason, Federalist leaders moved to muffle the opposition. In mid-1798, Congress hammered out a Sedition Act that made not only conspiracy and revolt illegal, but also penalized speaking or writing anything that defamed the president or Congress. Criticisms of government leaders became criminal utterances. In all, twenty-five men, almost all Republican newspaper editors, were charged with sedition; twelve were convicted.

Congress also passed two Alien Acts. The first extended the waiting period for an alien to achieve citizenship from five to fourteen years and required all aliens to register with the federal government. The second empowered the presi-

Cartoon of the Matthew Lyon Fight in Congress
The political tensions of 1798 were not merely intellectual. A February session in Congress degenerated from name-calling to a brawl. Roger Griswold, a Connecticut Federalist, called Matthew Lyon, a Vermont Republican, a coward. Lyon responded with some well-aimed spit, the first departure from the gentleman's code of honor. Griswold responded by raising his cane to Lyon, whereupon Lyon grabbed nearby fire tongs to beat back his assailant. Madison wrote to Jefferson that the two should have dueled: "No man ought to reproach another with cowardice, who is not ready to give proof of his own courage" by negotiating a duel, the honorable way to avenge insults in Virginia's planter class. But Lyon, a Scots-Irish immigrant, did not come from a class or culture that cultivated the art of the duel; rough-and-tumble fighting was his first response to insult. What is the picture on the back wall?
Library of Congress.

FOR MORE HELP ANALYZING THIS IMAGE, see the visual activity for this chapter in the Online Study Guide at **bedfordstmartins.com/roarkcompact**.

dent in time of war to deport or imprison without trial any foreigner suspected of being a danger to the United States. The clear intent of the alien laws was to harass French immigrants already in the United States and discourage others from coming.

Republicans strongly opposed the Alien and Sedition Acts on the grounds that they were in conflict with the Bill of Rights, but they did not have the votes to revoke the acts in Congress, nor could the federal judiciary, dominated by Federalist judges, be counted on to challenge them. Jefferson and Madison turned to the state legislatures, the only other competing political arena, to press their opposition. Each man drafted a set of resolutions condemning the acts and had the legislatures of Virginia and Kentucky present them to the federal government in late fall 1798. The Virginia and Kentucky Resolutions tested the novel argument that state legislatures have the right to judge the constitutionality of federal laws and to **nullify** laws that infringe on the liberties of the people as defined in the Bill of Rights. The resolutions made little dent in the Alien and Sedition Acts, but the idea of a state's right to nullify federal law did not disappear. It surfaced several times in decades to come, most notably in a major tariff dispute in

1832 and in the sectional arguments that led to the Civil War.

Amid all the war hysteria and sedition fears in 1798, President Adams regained his balance. He was uncharacteristically restrained in pursuing opponents under the Sedition Act, and he finally refused to declare war on France, as extreme Federalists wished. No doubt he was beginning to realize how much he had been the dupe of Hamilton. He also shrewdly realized that France was not in fact eager for war and that a peaceful settlement might be close at hand. In January 1799, a peace initiative from France arrived in the form of a letter assuring Adams that diplomatic channels were open again and that new commissioners would be welcomed in France. Adams accepted this overture and appointed new negotiators. By late 1799, the Quasi-War with France had subsided, and in 1800 the negotiations resulted in a treaty declaring "a true and sincere friendship" between the United States and France. But Federalists were not pleased; Adams lost the support of a significant part of his own party and sealed his fate as the first one-term president of the United States.

The election of 1800 was openly organized along party lines. The self-designated national leaders of each group met to handpick their candidates for president and vice president. Adams's chief opponent was Thomas Jefferson. When the election was finally over, President Jefferson mounted the inaugural platform to announce, "We are all republicans, we are all federalists," an appealing rhetoric of harmony appropriate to an inaugural address. But his formulation perpetuated a denial of the validity of party politics, a denial that ran deep in the founding generation of political leaders.

> **REVIEW** Why did Congress pass the Alien and Sedition Acts in 1798?

Conclusion: Parties Nonetheless

American political leaders began operating the new government in 1789 with great hopes to unify the country and to overcome selfish factionalism. The enormous trust in President Washington was the central foundation for that hope, and Washington did not disappoint, becoming a model

Mr. President with a blend of integrity and authority. Stability was further aided by easy passage of the Bill of Rights (to appease Antifederalists) and by attention to cultivating a virtuous citizenry of upright men supported and rewarded by republican womanhood. Yet the hopes of the honeymoon period soon turned to worries and then fears as major political disagreements flared up.

At the core of the conflict was a group of talented men—Hamilton, Madison, Jefferson, and Adams—so recently allies but now opponents. They diverged over Hamilton's economic program, over relations with the British and the Jay Treaty, over the French and Haitian revolutions, and over preparedness for war abroad and free speech rights at home. Hamilton was perhaps the driving force in these conflicts, but the antagonism was not about mere personality. Parties were taking shape, not around individuals but around principles, such as ideas about what constitutes enlightened leadership, how powerful should the federal government be, who is the best ally in Europe, and when does oppositional political speech turn into treason. The Federalists were pro-British, pro-commerce, and ever alarmed about the potential excesses of democracy. The Republicans celebrated, up to a point, the radical republicanism of France and opposed the Sedition Act as an alarming example of an overbearing government cutting off freedom of speech.

When Jefferson, then, in his inaugural address of 1800 offered his conciliatory assurance that Americans were at the same time "all republicans" and "all federalists," he probably mystified some listeners. Possibly he meant to suggest that both groups shared two basic ideas—the value of republican government, in which power derived from the people, and the value of the unique federal system of shared governance structured by the Constitution. But by 1800, these two words defined competing philosophies of government. To at least some of his listeners, Jefferson's assertion of harmony across party lines could only have seemed bizarre. For the next two decades, these two parties would battle each other, each fearing that the success of the other might bring the demise of the country. And for the next two decades, leaders continued to worry that party spirit itself was a bad thing.

Suggestions for Further Reading

Susan Branson, *These Fiery Frenchified Dames: Women and Political Culture in Early National Philadelphia* (2001). A study of 1790s women in the capital city and their developing relationship to print culture, literacy, and political thought.

Ron Chernow, *Alexander Hamilton* (2004). An intimate biography of the financial genius of the 1790s.

Stanley Elkins and Eric McKitrick, *The Age of Federalism: The Early American Republic, 1788–1800* (1993). The authoritative and exhaustive account of the 1790s.

Joseph J. Ellis, *Founding Brothers: The Revolutionary Generation* (2000). Captivating chapters illuminate the complex rivalries of the 1790s leaders.

David McCullough, *John Adams* (2001). John Adams glorified *and* humanized by a superb storyteller.

Henry Wiencek, *An Imperfect God: George Washington, His Slaves, and the Creation of America* (2003). A close exploration of Washington's words and personal actions regarding slavery.

▶ **For more books about topics in this chapter**, see the Online Study Guide at bedfordstmartins.com/roarkcompact.

▶ **For additional firsthand accounts of this period**, see Chapter 9 in Michael Johnson, ed., *Reading the American Past*, Third Edition.

▶ **For Web sites and documents related to topics and places in this chapter**, see "HistoryLinks," "DocLinks," and "PlaceLinks" at bedfordstmartins.com/roarkcompact.

REVIEWING THE CHAPTER

Follow these steps to review and strengthen your understanding of the chapter.

STEP 1: *Study the* **Key Terms** *and* **Timeline** *to identify the significance of each item listed.*

STEP 2: *Answer the* **Review Questions**, *drawing on key terms and dates to support your answers.*

STEP 3: *Drawing on the Key Terms, Timeline, and Review Questions, answer the broader* **Making Connections** *questions.*

KEY TERMS

Who

Alexander Hamilton (pp. 211, 214, 217)
James Madison (pp. 211, 214, 220)
Thomas Jefferson (pp. 211, 214)
George Washington (p. 213)
John Jay (pp. 214, 225)
Judith Sargent Murray (p. 215)
Eli Whitney (p. 216)
Josiah Harmar (p. 222)
Arthur St. Clair (p. 222)
Anthony Wayne (p. 223)
Little Turtle (p. 223)
Blue Jacket (p. 224)
Toussaint L'Ouverture (p. 226)

What

Revolutionary War debt (p. 211)
Bill of Rights (p. 214)
Report on Public Credit (p. 217)
Bank of the United States (p. 220)
Report on Manufactures (p. 221)
Whiskey Rebellion (p. 221)
Fort Washington (p. 222)
Fort Greenville (p. 223)
Fort Recovery (p. 223)
battle of Fallen Timbers (p. 224)
Treaty of Greenville (p. 224)

Neutrality Proclamation (p. 225)
Jay Treaty (p. 225)
Haitian Revolution (p. 226)
Federalists (p. 227)
Republicans (p. 227)
XYZ affair (p. 228)
Quasi-War (p. 228)
Sedition Act (p. 228)
Alien Acts (p. 228)
Virginia and Kentucky Resolutions
   (p. 229)

TIMELINE

1789 • George Washington inaugurated first president.
• French Revolution begins.
• First Congress meets.
• Fort Washington erected in western Ohio.

1790 • Congress approves Hamilton's debt plan.
• Judith Sargent Murray publishes "On the Equality of the Sexes."
• Shawnee and Miami Indians in Ohio defeat General Josiah Harmar.

1791 • States ratify Bill of Rights.
• Congress charters Bank of the United States.
• Ohio Indians defeat General Arthur St. Clair.
• Congress passes whiskey tax.
• Haitian Revolution begins.
• Hamilton issues *Report on Manufactures*.

1793 • Napoleonic Wars break out between France and England.
• Washington issues Neutrality Proclamation.
• Eli Whitney invents cotton gin.

REVIEW QUESTIONS

1. How did political leaders in the 1790s attempt to overcome the divisions of the 1780s? (pp. 213–16)

2. Why were Hamilton's economic policies controversial? (pp. 216–21)

3. Why did the United States feel vulnerable to international threats in the 1790s? (pp. 222–26)

4. Why did Congress pass the Alien and Sedition Acts in 1798? (pp. 227–30)

MAKING CONNECTIONS

1. Why did the Federalist alliance fracture in the 1790s? Why was this development troubling to the nation? In your answer, cite specific ideological and political developments that compromised cooperation.

2. What provoked the Whiskey Rebellion? How did the government respond? In your answer, discuss the foundations and precedents of the conflict as well as the significance of the government's response.

3. Americans held that virtue was pivotal to the success of their new nation. What did they mean by virtue? How did they hope to ensure that their citizens and their leaders possessed virtue?

4. The domestic politics of the new nation were profoundly influenced by conflicts beyond the nation's borders. Discuss how conflicts abroad contributed to domestic political developments in the 1790s.

▶ FOR PRACTICE QUIZZES, A CUSTOMIZED STUDY PLAN, AND OTHER STUDY TOOLS, see the Online Study Guide at bedfordstmartins.com/roarkcompact.

1794 • Whiskey Rebellion.
• Battle of Fallen Timbers.

    1795 • Treaty of Greenville.
        • Jay Treaty.

        1796 • Federalist John Adams elected second president, Thomas Jefferson vice president.

           1797 • XYZ affair.

                1798 • Quasi-War with France erupts.
                        • Alien and Sedition Acts.
                        • Virginia and Kentucky Resolutions.

                    1800 • Republican Thomas Jefferson elected third president.

A JEFFERSON FAN

Ladies' fans became increasingly popular fashion accessories in the late eighteenth and early nineteenth centuries, equally useful for communication and cooling. This folding fan of vellum and carved ivory, made in the early 1800s, features a medallion portrait of President Thomas Jefferson. Carried by the ribbon on a woman's wrist, the fan could be flicked open to announce a partisan political statement. Fans and other handheld articles such as parasols and handkerchiefs expanded the repertoire of nonverbal expression for women, who by the custom and training of the time were expected to be less assertive than men in mixed-sex conversation. Many emotions and messages—from modesty, coyness, and flirtatiousness to anger, irritability, and boredom—could be communicated by the expert deployment of this delicate emblem of femininity. Women learned the conventions of fluttering the fan by close observation and perhaps by explicit training.

Collection of David J. and Janice L. Frent.

10

Republicans in Power

1800–1824

THE NAME TECUMSEH translates to "Shooting Star," a fitting name for the Shawnee chief who reached meteoric heights of fame among Indians during Thomas Jefferson's presidency. From Canada to Georgia and west to the Mississippi, Tecumseh was accounted a charismatic leader of Indians, for which white Americans praised (and feared) him. Graceful, eloquent, compelling, astute: Tecumseh was all these and more, a gifted natural commander, equal parts politician and warrior.

The Ohio Country, where Tecumseh was born in 1768, was home to some dozen Indian tribes, including the Shawnee, recently displaced from the South. During the Revolutionary War, the region became a battleground with the Big Knives, as the Shawnee people called the Americans. Tecumseh's childhood was marked by repeated violence and the loss of his father and two brothers in battle. The Revolution's end in 1783 brought no peace to the Indians' country; American settlers pushed west, and the youthful Tecumseh honed his warrior skills by ambushing pioneers flatboating down the Ohio River. He fought at the battle of Fallen Timbers, a major Indian defeat, but avoided the 1795 negotiations of the Treaty of Greenville, in which a half dozen dispirited tribes ceded much of Ohio to the Big Knives. With frustration he watched as seven additional treaties between 1802 and 1805 whittled away more Indian land.

Some Indians, resigned and tired, looked for ways to accommodate to new realities, taking up farming, trade, and even intermarriage with the Big Knives. Others spent their treaty payments on deadly alcohol. Tecumseh's younger brother Tenskwatawa led an embittered life of idleness and drink. But Tecumseh rejected assimilation and inebriation and instead campaigned for a return to ancient ways. Donning traditional animal-skin garb, he traveled around the Great Lakes area in the years after 1805, persuading tribes to join his pan-Indian confederacy. The American territorial governor of Indiana, William Henry Harrison, reported, "For four years he has been in constant motion. You see him today on the Wabash, and in a short time hear of him on the shores of Lake Erie or Michigan, or on the banks of the Mississippi, and wherever he goes he makes an impression favorable to his purpose." In 1811, the leader named Shooting Star traveled among tribes in the South, while an especially brilliant comet illuminated the night sky.

Even his once-dissolute brother was born anew. After a near-death experience in 1805, Tenskwatawa revived and recounted a startling vision of meeting the Master of Life. Renaming himself the Prophet, Tenskwatawa urged Indians everywhere to regard the white Americans as children of the Evil Spirit, destined to be destroyed. Tecumseh and the Prophet established a new village called Prophetstown, located in present-day Indiana, offering a potent blend of spiritual regeneration and political unity that attracted thousands of

Tecumseh
Several portraits of Tecumseh exist, but they all present a different visage, and none of them enjoys verified authenticity. This one perhaps comes closest: It is an 1848 engraving adapted from an earlier drawing that no longer exists, sketched by a French trader in Indiana named Pierre Le Dru in a live sitting with the Indian leader in 1808. The engraver has given Tecumseh a British army officer's uniform, showing that he fought on the British side in the War of 1812. Notice the head covering and the medallion around the neck, marking Tecumseh's Indian identity.
Library of Congress.

followers. Governor Harrison admired and feared Tecumseh, calling him "one of those uncommon geniuses which spring up occasionally to produce revolutions." President Jefferson had great reason to worry about an organized Indian opposition, and more, its potential for a renewed Indian alliance with the British in Canada.

Those worries became a reality in Jefferson's second term in office. Although his first term brought notable successes, such as the Louisiana Purchase and the Lewis and Clark expedition, his second term was consumed by the threat of war with either Britain or France, in a replay of the late-1790s tensions. When war came, in 1812, the enemy was Britain, bolstered by a reenergized Indian-British alliance. Among the causes of the war were insults over international shipping rights, the capture of American vessels, and

the impressment of American sailors, but the war also derived compelling strength from Tecumseh's confederacy, now pledged to help the British in Canada. Significant battles pitted American soldiers against Indians in the Great Lakes, Tennessee, and Florida.

In the end, the War of 1812 settled little between the Americans and the British, but it was tragically conclusive for the Indians. Eight hundred warriors led by Tecumseh helped defend Canada against American attacks, but the British did not reciprocate when Indians were under threat. Tecumseh died on Canadian soil at the battle of the Thames in the fall of 1813. No Indian leader with the star power of Tecumseh would emerge again east of the Mississippi.

The briefly unified Indian confederacy under Tecumseh had no counterpart in the young Republic's confederation of states, where widespread unity and enthusiasm behind a single leader proved impossible to achieve. Republicans did battle with Federalists during the Jefferson and Madison administrations, but then Federalists doomed their party by opposing the War of 1812 and after 1815 ceased to be a major force in political life. The next two presidents, James Monroe and John Quincy Adams, congratulated themselves on the Federalists' demise and Republican unity, but in fact divisions within their own party were extensive. Wives of politicians increasingly inserted themselves into this dissonant mix, managing men's politicking and jockeying for power in the Capitol, enabling their husbands to appear above the fray and maintain the fiction of a nonfactionalized state. That it was a fiction became sharply apparent in the most serious political crisis of this period, the Missouri Compromise of 1820.

Jefferson's Presidency

The nerve-wracking election of 1800, decided in the House of Representatives, enhanced fears that party divisions would ruin the country. A panicky Federalist newspaper in Connecticut predicted that Jefferson's victory would produce bloody civil war and usher in an immoral reign of "murder, robbery, rape, adultery and incest." Similar fears were expressed in the South, where a frightful slave uprising seemed a possible outcome of Jefferson's victory. But nothing nearly so drastic occurred. Jefferson later called his election the "revolution of 1800," referring to his repudiation of monarchical practices, his undoing of Federalist judicial appointments, and his cutbacks in military spending and taxes.

Jefferson indeed did radically transform the presidency, away from the Federalists' vision of a powerful executive branch to **republican** simplicity and limited government. Yet even Jefferson found that circumstances sometimes required him to draw on the expansive powers of the presidency. The rise of Napoleon to power in France brought France and England into open warfare again in 1803, creating unexpected opportunities and challenges for Jefferson's administration. One major opportunity arrived in the spectacular purchase from France of the Louisiana Territory; on the challenge side, British and French naval forces nipped at American ships—and American honor—in the Atlantic Ocean.

Turbulent Times: Election and Rebellion

The result of the election of 1800 remained uncertain from polling time in November to repeated roll-call votes in the House of Representatives in February 1801. Federalist John Adams, never secure in his leadership of the Federalist Party, was no longer in the presidential race once it got to the House. Instead, the contest was between Jefferson and his own running mate, Senator Aaron Burr of New York. Republican voters in the electoral college slipped up, giving Jefferson and Burr equal numbers of votes, an outcome possible because of the single balloting to choose both president and vice president. (The Twelfth Amendment to the Constitution, adopted four years later, provided for distinct ballots for the two offices to fix this problem.) The vain and ambitious Burr declined to concede, so the sitting Federalist-dominated House of Representatives got to choose the president.

Each state delegation commanded one vote, and the winner needed nine votes. Some Federalists preferred Burr, believing his character flaws made him especially susceptible to Federalist pressure. But the influential Alexander Hamilton, though no friend to Jefferson, recognized that the high-strung Burr would be more dangerous than Jefferson in the presidency. Jefferson was a "contemptible hypocrite" in Hamilton's opinion, but at least he was not corrupt. (In 1804, Burr shot and killed Hamilton in a formal but illegal dual, bearing out Hamilton's intuition that Burr was a dangerous man.) Jefferson got the votes of eight states on the first ballot. Thirty-six ballots and six days later he got the critical ninth vote (and also a tenth). This election demonstrated a remarkable

feature of the new constitutional government: No matter how hard fought the campaign, the leadership of the nation could shift from one group to a distinctly different group in a peaceful transfer of power effected by ballots, not bullets.

As the country struggled over its white leadership crisis, news of a plotted rebellion of slaves surfaced in Virginia. A twenty-four-year-old blacksmith named Gabriel, the slave of Thomas Prossor, was said to be organizing a thousand slaves to march on the state capital at Richmond and take the governor, James Monroe, hostage. On the appointed day, however, a few nervous slaves went to the authorities, and within days, scores of implicated conspirators were jailed and brought to trial.

One of the jailed rebels compared himself to the most venerated icon of the early Republic: "I have nothing more to offer than what General Washington would have had to offer, had he been taken by the British and put to trial by them." Such talk invoking the specter of a black George Washington worried white Virginians, and in September and October 1801, 27 black men were hanged for contemplating rebellion. Finally, President Jefferson advised Governor Monroe that the hangings had gone far enough: "The world at large will forever condemn us if we indulge a principle of revenge," Jefferson wrote.

The Jeffersonian Vision of Republican Simplicity

Jefferson sidestepped the problem of slavery and turned his attention to establishing his administration in clear contrast to the Federalists. For his inauguration, held in the village optimistically called Washington City, he dressed in everyday clothing, to strike a tone of republican simplicity, and he walked to the Capitol building for the modest swearing-in ceremony. Once in office, he continued to emphasize unfussy frugality. He scaled back on Federalist building plans for Washington and cut the government budget. He wore plain clothes, appearing "neglected but not slovenly," according to one onlooker. He cultivated a casual style, wearing slippers to greet important guests, avoiding the formality of state parties and liveried servants. Jefferson's studied carelessness was very deliberate.

Martha Washington and Abigail Adams had received the wives of government figures at weekly teas, thereby creating and cementing social relations in the governing class. But Jefferson, a long-term widower, disdained female gatherings

Jefferson's Red Waistcoat

During his presidency, Jefferson often wore this red silk waistcoat as informal daywear. The garment had a velvet collar, woolen sleeves, and a thick lining made from recycled cotton and wool stockings. The thrifty Jefferson preferred to conserve firewood by wearing layers of warm clothes. A senator visiting in 1802 reported in dismay that the president was "dressed, or rather undressed, with an old brown coat, red waistcoat, old corduroy small clothes, much soiled, woolen hose, and slippers without heels." Another guest in 1804 found him wearing the red waistcoat, green velveteen breeches with pearl buttons, and "slippers down at the heels" that made him look like an ordinary farmer. Such colorful clothing in silk and velveteen carries dressy or feminine connotations in the twenty-first century, but it did not in 1800. Jefferson put on silk stockings and clean linen for fancy dinner parties; and when he lived in Paris in the 1780s, he wore an elaborately embroidered silk waistcoat under a greatcoat trimmed with gold lace. But in the 1800s, he used simple, colorful clothes to make a point about republican manners.

Courtesy of Monticello. Photo by Colonial Williamsburg.

and avoided the women of Washington City. He abandoned George Washington's practice of weekly formal receptions, scaling back these drop-in gatherings to just two a year. His preferred social event was the small dinner party with carefully chosen politicos, either all Republicans or all Federalists (and all male). At these intimate dinners, the president demonstrated his version of statecraft, exercising influence and strengthening informal relationships that would help him to govern.

Jefferson's paramount goal was to scale back federal power. Jefferson was no Antifederalist. He had supported the Constitution in 1788, although he had qualms about the unrestricted reelection allowed to the president. But events of the 1790s had caused him to worry about the stretching of powers in the executive branch. Jefferson had watched with distrust as Hamiltonian policies refinanced the public debt, established a national bank, and secured commercial ties with England (see chapter 9). These policies seemed to Jefferson to promote the interests of greedy speculators at the expense of the rest of the country. Jefferson was not at all anticommerce. But financial schemes that seemed merely to allow rich men to become richer were corrupt and worthless, he believed, and their promotion by the federal government was not authorized by the Constitution. In Jefferson's vision, the source of true **liberty** in America was the independent farmer, someone who owned and worked his land both for himself and for the market.

Jefferson set out to dismantle Federalist innovations. He reduced the size of the army by a third, leaving only three thousand soldiers, and he cut back the navy from twenty-five to seven ships. Peacetime defense, he felt, should rest with "a well-disciplined militia," not a standing army. With the consent of Congress, he abolished all federal internal taxes based on population or on whiskey. A national tax on population had been tried just once, in 1798, and proved as burdensome and expensive as taking a census. Government revenue would now derive solely from customs duties and from the sale of western lands. This strategy was of particular benefit to the South, because the three-fifths clause of the Constitution counted slaves for both representation and taxation. The South could exercise its extra influence in the House of Representatives without the threat of extra taxes. By the end of his first term, Jefferson had deeply reduced Hamilton's cherished national debt.

A properly limited federal government, according to Jefferson, was responsible merely for running a postal system, maintaining the federal courts, staffing lighthouses, collecting customs duties, and conducting a census once every ten years. Government jobs were kept to a minimum. The president had just one private secretary, a young man named Meriwether Lewis, to help with his correspondence, and Jefferson paid him out of his own pocket. The Department of State employed only 8 people: Secretary James Madison, 6 clerks, and a messenger. The Treasury Department was by far the largest unit, with 73 revenue commissioners, auditors, and clerks, plus 2 watchmen. The entire payroll of the executive branch amounted to a mere 130 people in 1801.

The Judiciary and the Midnight Judges

There was one set of government workers not under Jefferson's control to appoint. His predecessor, John Adams, seized the few weeks between his election defeat and Jefferson's inauguration to appoint 217 Federalist men to various judicial, diplomatic, and military posts.

Most of this windfall of appointments came to Adams as a result of the Judiciary Act of 1801, passed in the final month of his presidency. Its predecessor, the Judiciary Act of 1789, had established a six-man Supreme Court and six circuit courts. The new law authorized sixteen circuit courts, each headed by a new judge. If he acted quickly, Adams could appoint sixteen circuit court judges with lifetime tenure, plus dozens more attorneys, marshals, and clerks for each court. The 1801 act also reduced the Supreme Court from six to five justices. Prior to its passage, however, Adams appointed solidly Federalist Virginian John Marshall to a vacant sixth seat. After the 1801 act became law, a future president would not be able to fill the next empty seat.

In the last weeks of February 1801, Adams and Marshall worked feverishly to secure agreements from the new appointees. In view of the slowness of mail, achieving 217 acceptances was astonishing. The two men were at work until 9 p.m. on the last night Adams was president, signing and delivering commissions (appointment papers) to the new officeholders.

The appointment of the "midnight judges" infuriated the Republicans. Jefferson, upon taking office, immediately canceled the appointments of the nontenured men and refused to honor the few appointments that had not yet been delivered. One of them was addressed to William Marbury, who soon decided to sue the new secretary of state, James Madison, for failure to make good on the appointment. This action gave rise to a landmark Supreme Court case, *Marbury v. Madison*, decided in 1803. The Court, presided over by John Marshall, ruled that although Marbury's commission was valid and the new president should have delivered it, the Court could not compel him to do so. What made the case significant was little noted at the time: The Court found that the grounds of Marbury's suit, resting in the Judiciary Act of 1789, were in conflict with the Constitution. For the first time, the Court acted to disallow a law on the grounds that it was unconstitutional. John Marshall quietly established the concept of judicial review; the Supreme Court in effect assumed the legal authority to **nullify** acts judged in conflict with the Constitution.

The Promise of the West: The Louisiana Purchase and the Lewis and Clark Expedition

The reach of the *Marbury* decision went largely unnoticed in 1803 because the president and Congress were preoccupied with other major issues, among them the acquisition of the Louisiana Territory. Up through the Seven Years' War (see chapter 6), France claimed but only lightly settled a large expanse of land west of the Mississippi River, only to lose it to Spain in the 1763 Treaty of Paris. Spain never sent adequate forces to control or settle the land, and Spanish power in North America remained precarious everywhere outside New Orleans. Meanwhile, American farming families were settling Kentucky and Tennessee, along rivers emptying into the upper Mississippi, and for a time, the Spanish allowed them to ship their agricultural produce downriver and even encouraged American settlements across the river, in an effort to augment the population. By 1801, Americans made up a sizable minority of the population around the lower Mississippi.

In 1802, rumors reached Jefferson that Spain had struck a secret bargain with France to hand over a large part of Spain's trans-Mississippi territory to Napoleon in exchange for some land in Italy. Spain had proved a weak western neighbor, but France was another story. Jefferson was so alarmed that he instructed Robert R. Livingston, America's minister in France, to try to buy New Orleans. At first the French denied they owned the city, but when Livingston hinted that the United States might simply seize it if buying was not an option, the French negotiator suddenly asked him to name his price for the entire Louisiana Territory, from the Gulf of Mexico north to Canada. Livingston stalled, and the Frenchman made suggestions: $125 million? $60 million? Livingston shrewdly stalled some more, and within days the French sold the entire territory for the bargain price of $15 million (Map 10.1).

Jefferson and most of Congress were delighted with the outcome of the diplomatic mission. Still, Jefferson had some qualms about the Louisiana Purchase. The price was right, and the enormous territory fulfilled Jefferson's dream of abundant farmland for future generations. But by what authority expressed in the Constitution could he justify the purchase? His frequent criticism of Hamilton's stretching of the Constitution came back to haunt him. His legal reasoning told him he needed a constitutional amendment to

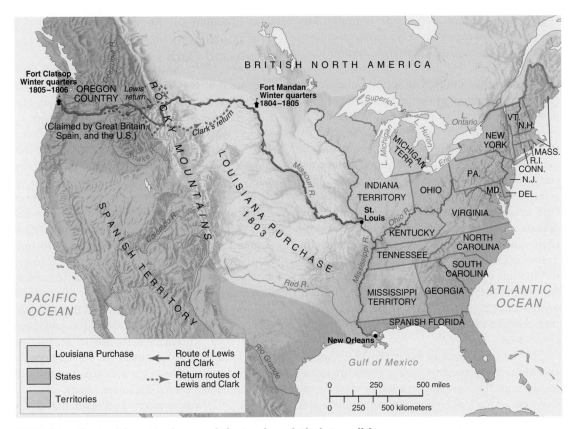

MAP 10.1   The Louisiana Purchase and the Lewis and Clark Expedition
Robert Livingston's bargain buy of 1803 far exceeded his initial assignment, to acquire the city of New Orleans. New England Federalists, worried that their geographically based power in the federal government would someday be eclipsed by the West, voted against the purchase. The Indians who inhabited the vast region, unaware that their land had been claimed by either the French or the Americans, got their first look at Anglo-American and African American men when the Lewis and Clark expedition came exploring in 1804–1806.

READING THE MAP: What natural boundaries defined the Louisiana Purchase? How did the size of the newly acquired territory compare to the existing land area of American states and territories?
CONNECTIONS: What political events in Europe created the opportunity for the Jefferson administration to purchase Louisiana? What constitutional obstacles to expansion did Jefferson have to contend with? How did the American acquisition of the Louisiana territory affect Spain's hold on North America?

FOR MORE HELP ANALYZING THIS MAP, see the map activity for this chapter in the Online Study Guide at
bedfordstmartins.com/roarkcompact.

---

authorize the addition of territory; more expedient minds told him the treaty-making powers of the president were sufficient. Expediency won out. In late 1803, the American army took formal control of the Louisiana Territory, and the United States grew by 828,000 square miles.

Even before the Louisiana Purchase, Jefferson had eyed the trans-Mississippi West with intense curiosity. In early 1803, he had arranged congressional funding for a secret scientific and military mission into Spanish and Indian territory. Jefferson appointed twenty-eight-year-old Meriwether Lewis, his personal secretary, to head the expedition, instructing him to investigate Indian cultures, to collect plant and animal specimens, and to chart the geography of the West. Congress had more traditional goals in mind: The expedition was to scout locations for military posts, open commercial agreements for the fur trade, and locate any possible waterway between the east and west coasts.

For his co-leader, Lewis chose Kentuckian William Clark, a veteran of the 1790s Indian wars. Together they handpicked a crew of forty-five, including expert rivermen, gunsmiths, hunters, interpreters, a cook, and a slave named York,

Grizzly Bear Claw Necklace

Lewis and Clark collected hundreds of Indian artifacts on their expedition, but until December 2003 only six were known to still exist. Then this grizzly bear claw necklace unexpectedly turned up at Harvard University's Peabody Museum of Archaeology and Ethnology, stored by mistake in a South Pacific collection. Curators instantly recognized it as a necklace missing since 1899 that had been part of a Lewis and Clark museum exhibit in the mid-nineteenth century. In their expedition journal, the famed explorers noted seeing bear claw necklaces on Shoshone warriors in the Rocky Mountains; possibly one of these warriors gave his necklace to the travelers. The 38 impressive claws, each 3 to 4 inches long, are strung together by rawhide thongs; the necklace required at least two four-pawed grizzly bears. Male grizzlies are large—6 to 7 feet tall, 500 to 900 pounds—and aggressive. What would it be like to wear this necklace? Whether spiritual or physical, it seems certain that a sense of power was bestowed on the wearer.

Peabody Museum of Archaeology and Ethnology, Harvard University.

who belonged to Clark. The explorers left St. Louis in the spring of 1804, working their way northwest up the Missouri River. They camped for the winter at a Mandan village in what is now central North Dakota.

The following spring, the explorers headed west, aided by a French trapper accompanied by a sixteen-year-old Indian woman named Sacajawea and their baby. Sacajawea's presence was to prove unexpectedly helpful, and not only for her translating abilities. Indian tribes encountered en route withdrew their suspicion that the Americans were hostile because, as Lewis wrote in his journal, "no woman ever accompanies a war party of Indians in this quarter."

The Lewis and Clark expedition reached the Pacific Ocean at the mouth of the Columbia River in November 1805. When Lewis and Clark returned home the following year, they were greeted as national heroes. They had established favorable relations with dozens of Indian tribes; they had collected invaluable information on the peoples, soils, plants, animals, and geography of the West; and they had inspired a nation of restless explorers and solitary imitators.

Transatlantic Troubles: Impressment and Embargo

The excitement of the Lewis and Clark expedition was balanced by dismaying and escalating tensions with France and England. Each European rival, embroiled in war, repeatedly warned America not to aid the other. Britain acted on these threats in 1806,

stopping American ships, inspecting cargoes for military aid to France, and seizing suspected deserters from the British navy, along with not a few Americans. Ultimately, 2,500 sailors were swept up—impressed—by the British. In retaliation, Jefferson convinced Congress to pass nonimportation laws banning a select list of British-made goods.

One incident made the usually cautious Jefferson nearly belligerent. In June 1807, an American ship, the *Chesapeake*, harboring some British deserters, was ordered to stop by a British frigate, the *Leopard*. The *Chesapeake* refused, and the *Leopard* opened fire, killing three Americans—right at the mouth of Chesapeake Bay, well within U.S. territory. In response Congress passed a total embargo in December 1807, banning all importation of British goods into the country. Though surely a drastic measure, the embargo was meant to forestall war. The goal was to make Britain suffer, and all foreign ports were declared off-limits, to discourage illegal trading through secondary ports. Jefferson was convinced that England needed America's agricultural products far more than America needed British goods. He also was wary of Federalist shipowners who might circumvent the ban.

The Embargo Act of 1807 was a total disaster. From 1790 to 1807, U.S. exports had increased

The *Chesapeake* Incident, June 22, 1807

fivefold; the embargo brought commerce to a standstill. In New England, the heart of the shipping industry, unemployment rose. Grain plummeted in value, river traffic halted, tobacco rotted in the South, and cotton went unpicked. Protest petitions flooded Washington. The federal government suffered too, for import duties were a significant source of revenue. Jefferson paid political costs as well. The Federalist Party, in danger of fading away after its weak showing in the elections of 1804, began to revive.

> **REVIEW**   How did Jefferson attempt to undo the Federalist innovations of earlier administrations?

The Madisons in the White House

In mid-1808, Jefferson indicated that he would not run for a third term. Secretary of State James Madison got the nod from Republican caucuses — informal political groups that orchestrated the selection of candidates for state and local elections. Federalist caucuses chose Charles Cotesworth Pinckney, their candidate also in 1804. Madison won, but Pinckney received 47 electoral votes, nearly half Madison's total. Support for the Federalists remained centered in New England, but Republicans still held the balance of power nationwide.

As president, Madison continued Jefferson's policy of economic pressure on Britain and France with a modified embargo, but he broke new ground in the domestic management of the executive office, with the aid of his astute and talented wife, Dolley Madison. Under her leadership, the president's house was designated the White House — something close to a palace, but a palace many Americans were welcome to visit. Under his leadership, the country went to war in 1812 with Britain and with Tecumseh's warrior confederacy. In 1814, British forces burned the White House and Capitol building nearly to the ground.

Women in Washington City

During in her first eight years in Washington, as wife of the highest-ranking cabinet officer, Dolley Madison developed elaborate social networks that, in the absence of any Mrs. Jefferson, constituted the top level of female politicking in the highly political city. Though women could not vote and

supposedly left politics to men, the women of Washington took on several overtly political functions that greased the wheels of the affairs of state. They networked through dinners, balls, receptions, and the intricate custom of "calling," in which men and women paid brief visits and left calling cards at each other's houses. Webs of friendship and influence in turn facilitated female political lobbying. It was not uncommon for women in this social set to write letters of recommendation for men seeking government work. Hostessing was therefore no trivial or leisured business: It influenced the patronage system of the federal government.

When James Madison became president, Dolley Madison, called by some the "presidentress," struck a balance between queenliness and republican openness. She dressed the part in resplendent clothes, choosing a plumed velvet turban for her headdress at her husband's inaugura-

Dolley Madison, **by Gilbert Stuart**
The "presidentress" of the Madison administration sat for this official portrait in 1804. Mrs. Madison here wears an empire-style dress, at the height of French fashion in 1804 and worn by many women at the coronation of the emperor Napoleon in Paris. The hallmarks of an empire dress were light fabric in muslin or chiffon, short sleeves, a high waistline from which the fabric fell straight to the ground, and usually a low open neckline as shown here. The artist made a companion likeness of James Madison, and the two portraits hung in the drawing room of Madison's Virginia estate, Montpelier.
Courtesy of the Pennsylvania Academy of the Fine Arts, Philadelphia.

tion. She opened three large and newly elegant rooms in the executive mansion to evening parties once a week. George and Martha Washington's receptions had been stiff, brief affairs with few guests accomplishing little more than bows and curtsies. In contrast, the Madisons' parties went on for hours with scores and even hundreds of guests milling about, talking, and eating. Attendance at the weekly party, nicknamed "Mrs. Madison's crush" or "squeeze," required an invitation or letter of introduction if one did not already know the Madisons. Evidently invitations were not difficult to obtain. Members of Congress, cabinet officers, distinguished guests, envoys from foreign countries, all these and their womenfolk attended with regularity. Even people who hated parties—or these gatherings in particular—attended. Mrs. Madison's "squeeze" was an essential event for gaining political access and establishing informal channels that would smooth the governing process.

In 1810–1811, Dolley Madison's house acquired its present name, the "White House," probably a reference to its light sandstone exterior. The many guests at the weekly parties experienced simultaneously the splendor of the executive mansion and the atmosphere of republicanism that made it accessible to so many. Dolley Madison, ever an enormous political asset to her rather shy husband, understood well the symbolic function of inventing this new White House to enhance the power and legitimacy of the presidency.

Indian Troubles in the West

While the Madisons cemented alliances at home, difficulties with Britain and France overseas and with Indians in the old Northwest continued to increase. The Shawnee chief Tecumseh actively solidified his confederacy, while far northern tribes renewed ties with supportive British agents and fur traders in Canada, a potential source of food and weapons. If the United States went to war with Britain, there would clearly be serious repercussions on the **frontier**.

Shifting demographics raised the stakes for both sides. The 1810 census counted some 230,000 Americans living in Ohio, only seven years after statehood. Another 40,000 Americans inhabited the territories of Indiana, Illinois, and Michigan. The Indian population of the entire region (the old Northwest Territory) was much smaller, probably about 70,000, a number unknown (because uncounted) to the Americans but certainly gauged by Tecumseh during his extensive travels.

***Tenskwatawa*, by George Catlin**
Tenskwatawa, the Shawnee Prophet, and his brother Tecumseh led the spiritual and political efforts of a number of Indian tribes to resist land-hungry Americans moving west in the decade before the War of 1812. George Catlin portrays the Prophet wearing beaded necklaces, metal arm- and wristbands, and earrings. Compare the metal gorget here with the one worn by Joseph Brant (page 171).
National Museum of American Art, Washington, D.C. / Art Resource, NY.

Up to 1805, Indiana's territorial governor, William Henry Harrison, had negotiated a series of treaties in a divide-and-conquer strategy extracting Indian lands for paltry payments. But with the rise to power of Tecumseh and his brother Tenskwatawa, the Prophet, Harrison's strategy faltered. A fundamental part of Tecumseh's message was the assertion that all Indian lands were held in common by all the tribes: "No tribe has the right to sell, even to each other, much less to strangers.... Sell a country! Why not sell the air, the great sea, as well as the earth? Didn't the Great Spirit make them all for the use of his children?" Taking advantage of Tecumseh's absence on a recruiting trip, Harrison assembled leaders of the Potawatomi, Miami, and Delaware tribes to negotiate the Treaty of Fort Wayne in 1809. After promising (falsely) that this was the last cession of land the United States would seek, Harrison secured three million acres at about two cents per acre.

When he returned, Tecumseh was furious with both Harrison and the tribal leaders. Leaving his

Battle of Tippecanoe, 1811

brother in charge at Prophetstown on Tippecanoe Creek, the Shawnee chief left on a trip to seek alliances in the South. Harrison then decided to attack Prophetstown with one thousand men. The two-hour battle resulted in the deaths of 62 Americans and 40 Indians before the Prophet's forces fled the town, which Harrison's men set on fire. The November 1811 battle of Tippecanoe was heralded as a glorious victory for the Americans. But Tecumseh was now more ready than ever to make war on the Americans.

The War of 1812

The Indian conflicts in the Northwest Territory in 1811 soon merged into the wider conflict with England now known as the War of 1812. Between 1809 and 1812, President Madison teetered between declaring England or France the prime enemy, as attacks by both countries on American ships continued. In 1809, Congress had replaced Jefferson's stringent embargo with the Non-Intercourse Act, which prohibited trade only with England and France and their colonies, thus opening up other trade routes to diminish somewhat the anguish of shippers, farmers, and **planters**. By 1811, the country was seriously divided and in a deep quandary. To some, the United States seemed, appropriately, on the verge of war—though with France or England was not clear. To others, war with either meant disaster for commerce.

A new Congress arrived in Washington in March 1811. Several dozen of the younger Republican members were eager to avenge the insults from abroad. Henry Clay, thirty-four, from Kentucky, and John C. Calhoun, twenty-nine, from South Carolina, became the center of a group informally known as the **War Hawks**. They saluted Harrison's Tippecanoe victory and urged the country to war. Mostly lawyers by profession, they came from the West and South, and they welcomed a war with England both to legitimize attacks on the Indians and to bring an end to impressment. Many were also expansionists, looking to occupy Florida and threaten Canada. Clay was elected Speaker of the House, an extraordinary honor for a young newcomer; Calhoun won a seat on the Foreign Relations Committee. The War Hawks approved major defense expenditures, and the army soon quadrupled in size.

In June 1812, Congress declared war on Great Britain in a vote divided on sectional lines: New England and some Middle Atlantic states opposed the war, while the South and West were strongly for it. Ironically, Great Britain had just announced it would stop the search and seizure of American ships, but the war momentum would not be slowed. The Foreign Relations Committee issued an elaborate justification titled *Report on the Causes and Reasons for War*, written mainly by Calhoun and containing extravagant language about Britain's "lust for power," "unbounded tyranny," and "mad ambition." These were fighting words in a war that was in large measure about insult and honor.

The War Hawks proposed an invasion of Canada, confidently predicting victory in four weeks. Instead, the war lasted two and a half years, and Canada never fell. The northern invasion turned out to be a series of blunders that revealed the grave unpreparedness of the United States for war. The combined British and Indian forces were unexpectedly powerful, and the United States made no attempt at the outset to create a naval presence on the Great Lakes. Detroit quickly fell, as did Fort Dearborn (site of the future Chicago). By the fall of 1812, the outlook was grim.

Worse, the New England states dragged their feet in raising troops, and some New England merchants carried on illegal trade with Great Britain. President Madison fumed in Washington about Federalist disloyalty while Bostonians drank India tea in Liverpool cups. The fall presidential election pitted Madison against DeWitt Clinton of New York, nominally a Republican but able to attract the Federalist vote. Clinton picked up all of New England's electoral votes, with the exception of Vermont's, and also took New York, New Jersey, and part of Maryland. Madison won in the electoral college, 128 to 89, but his margin of victory was considerably smaller than in 1808.

In late 1812 and early 1813, the tide began to turn in the Americans' favor. First came some reassuring victories at sea. Then Americans attacked York (now Toronto), the capital of Upper Canada, and burned it in April 1813. A few months later, Commodore Oliver Hazard Perry defeated the British fleet at the western end of Lake Erie. Emboldened, General Harrison drove an army into Canada from Detroit and in October 1813 defeated the British and Indians at the battle of the Thames, where Tecumseh met his death (Map 10.2).

Indians in the South who had allied with Tecumseh's confederacy were also plunged into

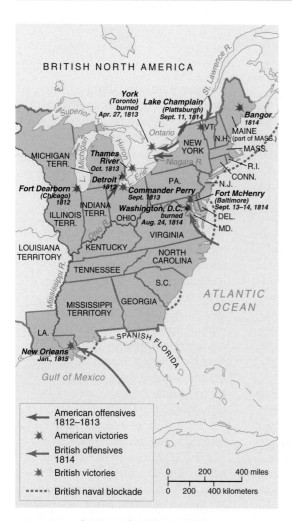

MAP 10.2 The War of 1812
During the War of 1812, battles were fought along the border of Canada and in the Chesapeake region. The most important American victory came in New Orleans two weeks after peace had been agreed to in England.

all-out war. Some fifty villages containing around 10,000 Creek Indians in the southern region of Mississippi Territory put up a spirited fight against American militia troops for ten months in 1813–1814. Even without Tecumseh's recruitment trip of 1811 or the War of 1812, the Creeks had grievances aplenty, sparked by American settlers moving into their territory. Using guns obtained in the panhandle of Spanish Florida, the Creeks mounted a strong defense. But the Creek War was suddenly over in March 1814, when a general named Andrew Jackson led 2,500 Tennessee militiamen in a bloody attack called the Battle of Horseshoe Bend. More than 550 Indians were killed, and several hundred more died trying to escape across a river. Later that year, General Jackson extracted from the defeated Creeks a treaty relinquishing thousands of square miles of their land to the United States.

Washington City Burns: The British Offensive

In August 1814, British ships sailed into Chesapeake Bay, throwing the capital into a panic. Families evacuated, banks hid their money, and government clerks carted away boxes of important papers. Dolley Madison, with dinner for guests cooking on the fire (see "The Promise of Technology," page 246), fled with her husband's papers and a portrait of George Washington. Five thousand British troops entered the city and burned the White House, the Capitol, a newspaper office, and a well-stocked arsenal. Instead of trying to hold the city, the British headed north and attacked Baltimore, but a fierce defense by the Maryland militia thwarted that effort.

In another powerful offensive, British troops marched from Canada into New York State, but a series of mistakes cost them a naval skirmish at Plattsburgh on Lake Champlain and also cost them their nerve, and they retreated to Canada. The withdrawal was a decisive military event, for British leaders in England, hearing of the retreat, concluded that incursions by land into the United States would be expensive and difficult.

This point was confirmed when a large British army landed in lower Louisiana and encountered General Andrew Jackson and his militia just outside New Orleans in early January 1815. Jackson's forces dramatically carried the day. The British suffered between 2,000 and 3,000 casualties, the Americans fewer than 80. Jackson became an instant hero. The battle of New Orleans was the most glorious victory the Americans had experienced, allowing some Americans to boast that the United States had won a second war of independence from England. No one in the United States knew that negotiators in Europe had signed a peace agreement two weeks earlier.

The Treaty of Ghent, signed in December 1814, settled few of the surface issues that had led to war. Neither country could claim victory, and no land changed hands. Instead, the treaty reflected a mutual agreement to give up certain goals. The Americans yielded on impressment and gave up any claim to Canada; and the British agreed to abandon aid to Indians. Nothing was said about shipping rights. The most concrete result was a plan for a commission to determine the exact boundary between the United States and Canada.

Stoves Transform Cooking

The cookstove, one of the most underrated achievements of the technology of daily life, fundamentally changed the way men and women labored to put food on the table. Its slow development can be traced in the nearly one thousand patents registered between 1815 and 1850 by inventors tinkering to control heat, devise convenient cooking surfaces, and improve fuel efficiency.

Before 1815, nearly all household cooking was accomplished in wood-burning fireplaces. Daily fires used for cooking and heating consumed immense amounts of wood; in cold climates, a household might require 40 cords of wood per year. Supplying each cord (a pile measuring 4-by-4-by-8 feet) was laborious men's work; the difficult and dangerous tasks of cooking and maintaining the fire fell to women. Great skill was needed to time the peak heat to coordinate with the varying temperature needs of baking, stewing, and roasting. Muscles and stamina were required to hoist 20-pound iron pots and cauldrons onto the hooks that suspended them over the fire. Cooks worked dangerously close to open flames when tending a roasting joint of meat on a spit or raking smaller fires out of the large one to heat frying skillets set on trivets on the hearth. Women wearing long skirts risked clothing fires, and children running about sometimes collided with hot pots and burning logs at floor level. The heavy lifting and exposure to the blasting heat, especially uncomfortable on hot summer days, exacted a toll on every cook.

In 1744, Benjamin Franklin developed a heating stove that enclosed a wood fire on three sides in a small cast-iron box, which radiated heat to the room. (The open fourth side allowed a pleasing view of the dancing flames.) The Franklin stove cut fuel costs, but it did not catch on for another half century as an alternative to heating by fireplace. Its inadequate venting of smoke was one problem, not fixed until the 1790s. Further, cast iron was expensive and wood was cheap, and the Franklin stove offered no provision for cooking. As long as wood remained affordable, Americans preferred the look of a log fire and the taste of food cooked over one.

Then, between 1800 and 1815, a serious fuel shortage driven by the depletion of forests caused wood prices to double along the eastern coast. At the same time, domestic iron manufacturing started to flourish, encouraged by Jefferson's shipping embargo and the War of 1812. With wood rising and iron falling in price, the conditions were right for the start of serious cookstove manufacture. Many inventors got to work.

The cast iron contraptions advertised around 1815 were larger than the Franklin stove and had a flat surface on top where pots and pans could be heated by the fire burning below. One challenge was to find a simple way to modulate the fire by varying the amount of air feeding it, through better design of the damper system. Dampers were valves or movable plates that controlled the draft of air to the fire and hence the rate of combustion. A related challenge was to manage the temperatures of the cooking spaces and surfaces. This could be done by moving pots around, by raising and lowering the grate that held the logs inside the firebox, or even by using cranks to rotate the fire.

Most of the new stoves raised the cooking surface nearly to waist level, offering relief from the backbreaking labor required by fireplace cookery. They fully enclosed the fire, minimizing the risk of clothing fires; they prevented sparks from jumping on floors and carpets; and they piped sooty air with combustion pollutants out of the house. For all these reasons, stove cooking was a great advance in safety.

New stoves changed not only the way people cooked but the way they ate. On a hearth, separate dishes required separate fires, so cooks generally limited meals to one-pot stews. Using the new stoves, cooks could prepare several different dishes with

---

Antiwar New England Federalists could not gloat over the war's ambiguous conclusion, because of an ill-timed and seemingly unpatriotic move on their part. The region's leaders had convened a secret meeting in Hartford, Connecticut, in December 1814, to discuss dramatic measures to curb the South's power. They proposed amending the Constitution to abolish the three-fifths clause as a basis of representation; to specify that congressional powers to pass embargoes, admit states, or declare war should require a two-thirds vote instead of a simple majority; and to limit the president to one term and prohibit the election of successive presidents

An Early Cookstove

A stove of the 1820s, patented by W. T. James, sits in this reconstructed historical site adjacent to the fireplace it has replaced. A stovepipe vents combustion fumes out the old chimney; a large flat surface over the fire provides a cooktop, shown here with a copper pot and a teakettle whose extremely large base speeds water to a boil. The round container on the lower ledge of the stove is a reflector oven, called a "tin kitchen," first used with fireplaces and then adapted for cookstoves. A spit inside held meat, and a crank (visible on the end) was used to turn the food. Put against the fire, the tin oven cooked its contents by direct and reflected heat, while the round bottom preserved the meat juices. In this scene, the old fireplace is bricked up and used for storing wood for the stove. Householders of the 1820s would have seen this setup as a highly modern convenience offering improvements in safety, fuel efficiency, and heat control.
Old Sturbridge Village.

The cookstove changed home labor for both men and women. It shrank men's role in meal preparation by curtailing the work of procuring wood. No such reduction occurred for women. Replacing the hours of careful fire-tending that women had once done were hours spent maintaining and cleaning stoves—removing ashes, cleaning soot from flues and dampers, and blacking the entire stove weekly with a thick paste to keep it from rusting.

From 1815 to the mid-nineteenth century, the cookstove was a work in progress; the many imperfections in the initial designs sent inventors back to the workbench again and again to try to perfect this new cooking system. Nonetheless, women wanted stoves for their safety and convenience, and men liked them for their fuel efficiency. In the late 1840s, the widespread popularity of cookstoves became evident along wagon trails heading west. Many families had packed up their stoves for the trip—evidence they embraced the new style of cooking—but had to abandon them along the way when forced to lighten their loads. One traveling teenager wrote that "we heard great talk of things being thrown away on the road but we saw little that was any good excepting stoves and there were plenty of them." Cookstoves had become America's first popular "consumer durable."

just one fire, and meals became more varied. However, not everyone was pleased. Many complained that the convenience of stoves came at the price of food quality. Oven-baked meat was nearly universally regarded as less savory than meat roasted over a fire, and in flavor and crustiness oven-baked bread did not measure up to bread baked in the brick chamber of a fireplace wall. Nonetheless, convenience triumphed.

from the same state. The cumulative effect of these proposals would have been to reduce the South's political power and break the lock of the Virginia dynasty on national office. New England wanted to assure that no one sectional party could again lead the country into war against the clear interests of another. The Federalists at Hartford even discussed secession from the Union but rejected that path. Coming just as peace was achieved, however, the Hartford Convention suddenly looked very unpatriotic. The Federalist Party never recovered its grip, and within a few years its presence even in New England was reduced to a shadow.

No one really won the War of 1812. Americans celebrated as though they had, however, with parades and fireworks. The war gave rise to a new spirit of **nationalism**. The paranoia over British tyranny evident in the 1812 declaration of war was laid to rest, replaced by pride in a more equal relationship with the old mother country. Indeed, in 1817 the two countries signed the Rush-Bagot disarmament treaty (named after its two negotiators), which limited each country to a total of four naval vessels, each with just a single cannon, to patrol the vast watery border between them. The Rush-Bagot treaty was perhaps the most successful disarmament treaty for a century to come.

The biggest winners in the War of 1812 were the young men, once called War Hawks, who took up the banner of the Republican Party and carried it in new, expansive directions. These young politicians favored trade, western expansion, internal improvements, and the energetic development of new economic markets. The biggest losers of the war were the Indians. Tecumseh was dead, the Prophet discredited, the prospects of an Indian confederacy dashed, the Creeks' large homeland seized, and the British protectors gone.

> **REVIEW**   Why did Congress declare war on Great Britain in 1812?

Women's Status in the Early Republic

With the model of "presidentress" Dolley Madison before the public, and the 1790s debate over education for motherhood still fresh (see chapter 9), it might be expected that the early nineteenth century would post advances in the status of women. And in one area, female education, marked improvement did occur: Both boys and girls profited from the spread of basic public schooling, seen as vital to the production of citizens in a **democratic** state. By 1830, female literacy and numeracy were rapidly rising. Adolescent girls from genteel families could pursue higher learning at any of the 400 new female academies founded between 1790 and 1830. But other arenas and institutions central to the shaping of women's lives—laws, marriage, and church—showed either no change or only incremental change. State legislatures and the courts grappled with the legal dependency of married white women in a country whose defining characteristic was independence, while religious organizations struggled to redefine the role of women in church governance. If, in the end, there was no giant step forward for women in these decades, it is still significant that these questions were raised at all.

Women and the Law

The Anglo-American view of women, implanted in British common law, was that wives had no independent legal or political personhood. The legal doctrine of *feme covert* (covered woman) held that a wife's civic life was completely subsumed by her husband's. A wife was obligated to obey her husband; her property was his, her domestic and sexual services were his, and even their children were legally his. Women had no right to keep their wages, to make contracts, or to sue or be sued. State legislatures generally passed up the opportunity to rewrite the laws of domestic relations even though they redrafted other British laws in light of republican principles. Lawyers never paused to defend, much less to challenge, the assumption that unequal power relations lay at the heart of marriage.

The one aspect of family law that changed in the early Republic was divorce. Before the Revolution, only New England jurisdictions recognized a limited right to divorce; by 1820, every state except South Carolina did so. However, divorce was uncommon and difficult and in many states could be obtained only by petition to the state's legislature, a daunting obstacle for many ordinary people. A mutual wish to terminate a marriage was never sufficient grounds for legal divorce. A New York judge affirmed that "it would be aiming a deadly blow at public morals to decree a dissolution of the marriage contract merely because the parties requested it. Divorces should never be allowed, except for the protection of the innocent party, and for the punishment of the guilty." States upheld the institution of marriage both to protect persons they thought of as naturally dependent (women and children) and to regulate the use and inheritance of property. (Unofficial self-divorce, desertion, and bigamy were remedies that ordinary people sometimes chose to get around the strictness of marriage law. But powerful social sanctions against such behavior usually prevailed.) Legal enforcement of marriage as an unequal relationship played a major role in maintaining gender inequality in the nineteenth century.

Single adult women could own and convey property, make contracts, initiate lawsuits, and pay taxes. They could not vote (except in New Jersey before 1807), serve on juries, or practice law, so their civil status was limited. Single women's economic status was often limited as well, by custom as much as by law. Unless they had inherited adequate property or could live with married siblings, single adult women in the early Republic were very often poor.

None of the legal institutions that structured white gender relations applied to black slaves. As property themselves, slaves could not freely consent to any contractual obligations, including marriage. The protective features of state-sponsored unions were thus denied to black men and women in slavery, who were controlled by a more powerful authority: the slave owner. But this also meant that slave unions did not establish unequal power relations between partners, backed by the force of law, as did marriages among the free.

Women and Church Governance

In most **Protestant** denominations around 1800, white women made up the majority of congregants, as they had for some time. Yet the church hierarchy—ordained ministers and elders—was exclusively male, and the governance of most denominations rested in men's hands.

There were some exceptions, however. In Baptist congregations in New England, women served along with men on church governance committees, deciding on admissions of new members, voting on hiring ministers, and even debating doctrinal points. Quakers, too, had a history of recognizing women's spiritual talents. Quaker women who felt a special call were accorded the status of minister, which meant they were capable of leading and speaking in Quaker meetings.

Between 1790 and 1820, a small and highly unusual set of women emerged who actively engaged in open preaching. Most were from Freewill Baptist groups centered in New England and upstate New York. Others came from small Methodist sects, and yet others rejected any formal religious affiliation. Probably fewer than a hundred such women existed, but several dozen traveled beyond their local communities, creating converts and controversy. They spoke from the heart, without prepared speeches, often exhibiting trances and claiming to exhort (counsel or warn) rather than to preach. None of these women were ordained ministers with official credentials to preach or perform baptisms.

Perhaps the most well-known exhorting woman was Jemima Wilkinson, who called herself the "Publick Universal Friend." After a near-death experience from high fever in 1776, Wilkinson proclaimed her body no longer female or male but the incarnation of the "Spirit of Light." She dressed in men's clothes, wore her hair in a masculine style, shunned gender-specific pronouns, and preached openly in Rhode Island and Philadelphia. In the early nineteenth century, Wilkinson withdrew to a settlement called New Jerusalem in western New York with some 250 followers.

The decades from 1790 to the 1820s marked a period of unusual confusion, ferment, and creativity in American religion. New denominations blossomed, new styles of religiosity gripped adherents, and an extensive periodical press devoted to religion popularized all manner of theological

Women and the Church: Jemima Wilkinson
Jemima Wilkinson, the "Publick Universal Friend," in an early woodcut, wears a clerical collar and body-obscuring robe, in keeping with the claim that the former Jemima was now a person without sex or gender. Her hair is pulled back tight on her head and curled at the neck in a masculine style of the 1790s. Did she become masculinized, or did she truly transcend gender?
Rhode Island Historical Society.

and institutional innovations. Congregations increasingly attracted vibrant female participation, often eclipsing the percentage of male congregants. In such a climate, the age-old tradition of gender subordination came into question here and there among the most radically democratic of the churches. But the presumption of male authority over women was deeply entrenched in American culture. Even denominations that had allowed women to participate in church governance began to pull back, and most churches reinstated patterns of hierarchy along gender lines.

> **REVIEW**   How did the civil status of American women and men differ in the decades of the early Republic?

Monroe and Adams

With the elections of 1816 and 1820, Virginians continued their long hold on the presidency. In 1816, James Monroe beat Federalist Rufus King of New York by 183 electoral votes to 34. In 1820, Monroe was reelected with all but one electoral vote, but that near unanimity did not necessarily reflect voter satisfaction, for barely one-quarter of eligible voters went to the polls.

After Monroe's first victory, the collapse of the Federalist Party led one over-optimistic newspaper to proclaim the arrival of an "Era of Good Feelings," as though a period of one-party government was destined to be harmonious. The harmony did not last long. Monroe and his aloof wife Elizabeth sharply curtailed social gatherings in the White House, driving the hard work of social networking into different and competing channels. Ill feelings were stirred by a sectional crisis over the admission of Missouri to the Union, and foreign policy questions animated sharp disagreements as well. The election of 1824 brought forth an abundance of candidates, all claiming to be Republicans. The winner was John Quincy Adams, in an election decided by the House of Representatives and, many believed, by a backroom bargain. Put to the test of practical circumstances, the one-party political system failed and then fractured.

The Missouri Compromise

In February 1819, Missouri applied for statehood. Since 1815, four other states had joined the Union (Indiana, Mississippi, Illinois, and Alabama),

following the blueprint laid out by the Northwest Ordinance of 1787. But Missouri posed a problem. Although much of its area was on the same latitude as the free state of Illinois, its territorial population included 10,000 slaves brought there by southern white planters.

Missouri's unusual combination of geography and demography led a New York congressman, James Tallmadge Jr., to propose two amendments to the statehood bill. The first stipulated that slaves born in Missouri after statehood would be free at age twenty-five, and the second declared that no new slaves could be imported into the state. Tallmadge modeled the first amendment on New York's gradual **emancipation** law of 1799. It did not strip slave owners of their current property, and it allowed them full use of the labor of newborn slaves well into their prime productive years. Still, Southerners in Congress objected, because in the long run the amendments would make Missouri a free state, and presumably one no longer allied with southern economic and political interests. Just as southern economic power rested on slave labor, southern political power drew extra strength from the slave population because of the three-fifths rule. In 1820, the South owed seventeen of the region's seats in the House of Representatives to its slave population.

Tallmadge's amendments passed in the House by a close and sharply sectional vote of North against South. The ferocious debate led a Georgia representative to observe that the question had started "a fire which all the waters of the ocean could not extinguish. It can be extinguished only in blood." The Senate voted down the amendments, and Missouri statehood was postponed for the next congressional term.

In 1820, a compromise emerged. Maine, once a part of Massachusetts, applied for statehood as a free state, balancing against Missouri as a slave state. The Senate further agreed that the southern boundary of Missouri—latitude 36°30'—extended west, would become the permanent line dividing slave from free states, guaranteeing the North a large area where slavery was banned (Map 10.3). The House also approved the compromise, thanks to expert deal brokering by Kentucky's Henry Clay, who earned the nickname the "Great Pacificator" for his superb negotiating skills. The whole package passed because seventeen northern congressmen decided that minimizing sectional conflict was the best course and voted with the South.

President Monroe and former president Jefferson at first worried that the Missouri crisis

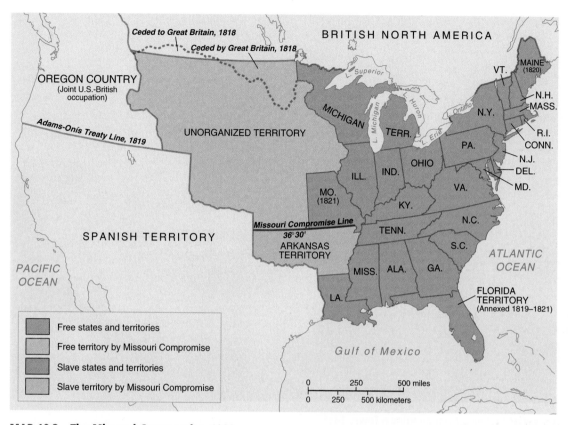

MAP 10.3 The Missouri Compromise, 1820
After a difficult battle in Congress, Missouri entered the Union in 1821 as part of a package of compromises. Maine was admitted as a free state to balance slavery in Missouri, and a line drawn at latitude 36°30′ put most of the rest of the Louisiana Territory off limits to slavery in the future.

would reinvigorate the Federalist Party as the party of the North. But even ex-Federalists agreed that the split between free and slave states was too dangerous a fault line to be permitted to become a shaper of national politics. When new parties did develop in the 1830s, they took pains to bridge geography, each party developing a presence in both North and South. Monroe and Jefferson also worried about the future of slavery. Each understood slavery to be deeply problematic, but, as Jefferson said, "We have the wolf by the ears, and we can neither hold him, nor safely let him go. Justice is in one scale, and self-preservation in the other."

The Monroe Doctrine

New foreign policy challenges arose even as Congress struggled with the slavery issue. In 1816, American troops led by General Andrew Jackson invaded Spanish Florida in search of Seminole Indians harboring escaped slaves. Once there, Jackson declared himself the commander of northern Florida, demonstrating his power in 1818 by executing two British men who he claimed were dangerous enemies. In asserting rule over the territory, and surely in executing the two British subjects on Spanish land, Jackson had gone too far. Privately, President Monroe was distressed and pondered court-martialing Jackson, prevented only by Jackson's immense popularity as the hero of the battle of New Orleans. Instead, John Quincy Adams, the secretary of state, negotiated with Spain the Adams-Onís Treaty, which delivered Florida to the United States in 1819. In exchange, the Americans agreed to abandon any claim to Texas or Cuba.

Spain at that moment was preoccupied with its colonies in South America. One after another— Chile, Colombia, Peru, and finally Mexico— declared itself independent in the early 1820s. To discourage Spain or France from reconquering these colonies, Monroe formulated a declaration of principles on South America. Incorporated into his annual message to Congress in December 1823, the declaration became known in later years as the **Monroe Doctrine**. The president warned that

A View of St. Louis from an Illinois Town, 1835
Just fifteen years after the Missouri Compromise, St. Louis was already a booming city, having gotten its start in the eighteenth century as a French fur-trading village. It was incorporated as a town in 1809 and chartered as a city in 1822. In this 1835 view, commercial buildings and steamships line the riverfront; a ferry on the Illinois shore prepares to transport travelers across the Mississippi River. Black laborers (in the foreground) handle loading tasks. The Illinois side is a free state; Missouri, where the ferry lands, is a slave state.
A View of St. Louis from an Illinois Town, 1835: Private collection.

FOR MORE HELP ANALYZING THIS IMAGE, see the visual activity for this chapter in the Online Study Guide at bedfordstmartins.com/roarkcompact.

"the American Continents, by the free and independent condition which they have assumed and maintain, are henceforth not to be considered as subjects for future colonization by any European power." Any attempt to interfere in the Western Hemisphere would be regarded as "the manifestation of an unfriendly disposition towards the United States." In exchange for noninterference by Europeans, Monroe pledged that the United States would stay out of European struggles.

The Election of 1824

Monroe's nonpartisan administration was the last of its kind, a throwback to eighteenth-century ideals, led by the last president to wear a powdered wig and knee breeches. Monroe's cabinet contained men of sharply different philosophies. Secretary of State John Quincy Adams repre-

sented the urban Northeast; South Carolinian John C. Calhoun spoke for the planter aristocracy as secretary of war; and William H. Crawford of Georgia, secretary of the treasury, was a proponent of Jeffersonian **states' rights** and limited federal power. Even before the end of Monroe's first term, these men and others began to maneuver for the election of 1824.

Crucially helping them to maneuver were their wives, who accomplished some of the work of modern campaign managers by courting of men—and women—of influence. The parties not thrown by Mrs. Monroe were now given all over town by women whose husbands were jockeying for political favor. Louisa Catherine Adams remodeled her house and had parties every Tuesday night for guests numbering in the hundreds. The somber Adams lacked charm—"I am a man of reserved, cold, austere, and forbidding manners" he once wrote—but his abundantly charming (and hardworking) wife made up for that. She attended to the etiquette of social calls, sometimes making two dozen in a morning, and counted sixty-eight members of Congress as her regular Tuesday guests.

Since 1800, the congressional caucus of each party had met to identify and lend its considerable but still informal support to its party's leading candidate. In 1824, with only one party alive—and alive with five serious candidates—the caucus system splintered. Since such a large number of candidates reduced the chance of anyone securing a majority in the electoral college, many expected that the final election would be decided by the House of Representatives. Having sixty-eight members of Congress on one's regular guest list was thus smart politics.

John Quincy Adams (and Louisa Catherine) very much wanted the presidency, an ambition fed by John's sense of rising to his father's accomplishment. Henry Clay, Speaker of the House, declared his candidacy; a man of vast congressional experience, he had engaged in high-level diplomacy in negotiating the Treaty of Ghent in 1814 with Britain. Clay promoted his "American System," a package of protective tariffs to encourage manufacturing and federal expenditures for extensive internal improvements such as roads and canals. Treasurer William Crawford was a favorite of Republicans from Virginia and New York; despite suffering an incapacitating stroke in mid-1824, he remained their favorite. Calhoun was another serious contender, having served in Congress and in several cabinets. Like Clay, he favored internal improvements and protective tariffs, which gained him support in northern states.

The final candidate was an outsider and a late-comer: General Andrew Jackson of Tennessee. Jackson had much less national political experience than the others, having served one year in the House and two in the Senate. His fame derived from his reputation as a military leader. In 1824, on the anniversary of the battle of New Orleans, the Adamses threw a spectacular ball with five hundred guests in honor of General Jackson. No doubt Adams hoped that some of Jackson's charisma would rub off on him; he was not yet thinking of Jackson as a rival for office. But later in 1824, Jackson supporters put his name in play, and voters in the West and South reacted with enthusiasm. Calhoun soon dropped out of the race and shifted his attention to winning the vice presidency.

The 1824 election was the first presidential contest in which candidates' popularity with

Election Sewing Box from 1824
The female owner of this sewing box displayed her presidential preference for John Quincy Adams. His picture adorns the interior surface of the lid; the top of the box, not visible here, carries a velvet pincushion emblazoned with the slogan "BE FIRM FOR ADAMS." Thousand of souvenir campaign boxes were manufactured for the leading candidates using a new lithographic process just coming into wide use in the 1820s.
Collection of Janice L. and David J. Frent.

ordinary voters could be measured. Recent changes in state constitutions gave voters in all but six states the power to choose electors for the electoral college. (Before, state legislatures had held this power.) Jackson was by far the most popular candidate with voters, winning 153,000 votes. Adams was second with 109,000, Clay won 47,000 votes, and the debilitated Crawford garnered 46,600. This was not a large voter turnout, probably amounting to only a quarter of adult white males. Many more voters participated regularly in local and state elections, where the real political action generally lay.

In the electoral college, Jackson received 99 votes, Adams 84, Crawford 41, and Clay 37 (Map 10.4). Jackson did not have a majority, so the election went to the House of Representatives, for the second (and last) time in American history. Each state delegation had one vote; according to the Twelfth Amendment to the Constitution, passed in 1804, only the top three candidates could enter the runoff. Thus Henry Clay was out of the race and in a position to bestow his support on another candidate.

Jackson's supporters later characterized the election of 1824 as the "corrupt bargain." Clay backed Adams, and Adams won by one vote in the House, in a vote in February 1825. Clay's support made sense on several levels. Despite strong mutual dislike, he and Adams agreed on issues such as federal support to build roads and canals, and Clay was uneasy with Jackson's volatile temperament and unstated political views and with Crawford's diminished capacity. What made Clay's decision look "corrupt" was that immediately after the election, Adams offered to appoint Clay secretary of state—and Clay accepted.

In the weeks before the vote in the House, rumors of such a deal had been denied by Adams and Clay supporters, confident that the two archenemies could never cooperate. There probably was no concrete bargain; Adams's subsequent cabinet appointments demonstrated his lack of political astuteness. But Andrew Jackson felt that the election had been stolen from him, and he wrote bitterly that "the Judas of the West has closed the contract and will receive the thirty pieces of silver."

The Adams Administration

John Quincy Adams, like his father, was a one-term president. His career had been built on diplomacy, not electoral politics, and, despite his wife's deft experience in the art of political influence, his own political horse sense was not well developed. His cabinet choices welcomed his opposition into his inner circle. He asked Crawford to stay on in the Treasury. He retained an openly pro-Jackson postmaster general even though that position controlled thousands of nationwide patronage appointments. He even asked Jackson to become secretary of war. With Calhoun as vice president (elected without opposition by the electoral college) and Clay at the State Department, the whole argumentative crew would have been thrust into the executive branch. Crawford and Jackson had the good sense to decline the appointments.

Adams had lofty ideas for federal action during his presidency, and the plan he put before Congress was so sweeping that it took Henry Clay aback. Adams called for federally built roads, canals, and harbors. He proposed a national university in Washington as well as government-sponsored scientific research. He wanted to build observatories to advance astronomical knowledge and to promote precision in timekeeping, and he backed a

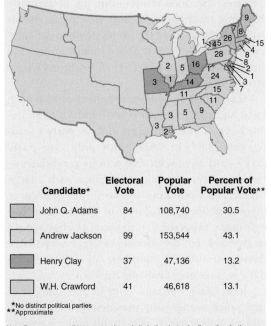

Candidate*	Electoral Vote	Popular Vote	Percent of Popular Vote**
John Q. Adams	84	108,740	30.5
Andrew Jackson	99	153,544	43.1
Henry Clay	37	47,136	13.2
W.H. Crawford	41	46,618	13.1

*No distinct political parties
**Approximate

Note: Because no candidate garnered a majority in the electoral college, the election was decided in the House of Representatives. Although Clay was eliminated from the running, as Speaker of the House he influenced the final decision in favor of Adams.

MAP 10.4   The Election of 1824

decimal-based system of weights and measures. In all these endeavors, Adams believed he was continuing the Jefferson and Madison legacy, using the powers of government to advance knowledge. But his opponents feared he was too Hamiltonian, using federal power inappropriately to advance commercial interests.

Whether he was more truly Federalist or Republican was a moot point, however. Lacking the give-and-take political skills required to gain congressional support, Adams was unable to implement much of his program. He scorned the idea of courting voters to gain support and using the patronage system to enhance his power. He often made appointments (to posts such as customs collectors) to placate enemies rather than reward friends. A story of a toast offered to the president may well have been mythical, but as humorous folklore it made the rounds during his term and came to summarize Adams's precarious hold on leadership. A dignitary raised a glass and said, "May he strike confusion to his foes…," to which another voice scornfully chimed in, "as he has already done to his friends."

REVIEW   How did the collapse of the Federalist Party influence the administrations of James Monroe and John Quincy Adams?

Conclusion: Republican Simplicity Becomes Complex

Jeffersonian Republicans tried at first to undo much of what Federalists had created in the 1790s, but their promise of a simpler government gave way to the complexities of domestic and foreign issues. The sudden acquisition of the Louisiana Purchase promised land and opportunity to settlers but also complicated the country's political future with the issues central to the Missouri Compromise. Antagonism from both foreign and Indian nations led to complex and costly policies such as embargoes, treaties, and military action, culminating in the War of 1812, a war motivated less by concrete economic or political issues than by questions of honor. Its conclusion at the battle of New Orleans allowed Americans the illusion that they had fought a second war of independence.

The War of 1812 was the Indians' second *lost* war for independence. Tecumseh's vision of an unprecedentedly large confederacy of Indian tribes that would halt western expansion by white Americans was cut short by the war and by his death. Without British support, the Indians probably could not have successfully challenged for long the westward dynamic of American settlement. But British support came at a time when Canada was under attack, and the British valued their own defense more than they valued their promises to help the Indians.

The war elevated to national prominence General Andrew Jackson, whose sudden popularity with voters in the 1824 election surprised traditional politicians—and their politically astute wives—and threw the one-party rule of Republicans into a tailspin. John Quincy Adams had barely occupied his office in 1825 before the election campaign of 1828 was off and running. Appeals to the people—the mass of white male voters—would be the hallmark of all elections after 1824. It was a game Adams could not easily play.

Politics in this entire period was a game that women could not play either. Except for the political wives of Washington, women, whether white or free black, had no place in government. Male legislatures maintained women's *feme covert* status, keeping wives dependent on husbands. A few women found a pathway to greater personal autonomy through religion. Meanwhile, the routine inclusion of girls in public schools and the steady spread of female academies planted seeds that would blossom into a major transformation of gender in the 1830s and 1840s.

The War of 1812 started another chain of events that would prove momentous in later decades. Jefferson's long embargo and Madison's wartime trade stoppages gave strong encouragement to American manufacturing, momentarily protected from competition with British factories. When peace returned in 1815, the years of independent development burst forth into a period of sustained economic growth that continued nearly unabated into the mid-nineteenth century.

Suggestions for Further Reading

Catherine Allgor, *Parlor Politics: In Which the Ladies of Washington Help Build a City and a Government* (2000). A subtle study of the capital's female culture that supported and shaped national politics from Jefferson to Jackson.

George Dangerfield, *The Era of Good Feelings* (1952). An unmatched classic that takes the reader deep into politics from the Treaty of Ghent to the inauguration of Jackson.

David Edmunds, *Tecumseh and the Quest for Indian Leadership* (1984). An interesting, short biography of the great Shawnee leader.

Joseph J. Ellis, *American Sphinx: The Character of Thomas Jefferson* (1997). An astute psychological portrait of the sentimental third president.

Joanne B. Freeman, *Affairs of Honor: National Politics in the New Republic* (2001). A study of honor in the new nation that situates slander and dueling in the culture of politics.

Jon Kukla, *A Wilderness So Immense: The Louisiana Purchase and the Destiny of America* (2003). A gripping story of the country's greatest real estate purchase.

▶ **For more books about topics in this chapter,** see the Online Study Guide at bedfordstmartins.com/roarkcompact.

▶ **For additional firsthand accounts of this period,** see Chapter 10 in Michael Johnson, ed., *Reading the American Past*, Third Edition.

▶ **For Web sites and documents related to topics and places in this chapter,** see "HistoryLinks," "DocLinks," and "PlaceLinks" at bedfordstmartins.com/roarkcompact.

REVIEWING THE CHAPTER

Follow these steps to review and strengthen your understanding of the chapter.

STEP 1: *Study the* **Key Terms** *and* **Timeline** *to identify the significance of each item listed.*

STEP 2: *Answer the* **Review Questions**, *drawing on key terms and dates to support your answers.*

STEP 3: *Drawing on the Key Terms, Timeline, and Review Questions, answer the broader* **Making Connections** *questions.*

KEY TERMS

Who

Tecumseh (p. 235)
Tenskwatawa (the Prophet) (p. 235)
Thomas Jefferson (p. 236)
Aaron Burr (p. 237)
John Marshall (p. 239)
James Madison (pp. 239, 242)
Meriwether Lewis (p. 240)
William Clark (p. 240)
Sacajawea (p. 241)
Dolley Madison (p. 242)
William Henry Harrison (p. 243)
Henry Clay (pp. 244, 250)
John C. Calhoun (p. 244)

Andrew Jackson (p. 245)
Jemima Wilkinson (p. 249)
James Monroe (p. 250)
James Tallmadge Jr. (p. 250)
John Quincy Adams (p. 254)

What

Treaty of Greenville (p. 235)
Gabriel's rebellion (p. 237)
Judiciary Act of 1801 (p. 239)
Marbury v. Madison (p. 239)
Louisiana Purchase (p. 239)
impressment (p. 241)
the *Chesapeake* (p. 241)

Embargo Act of 1807 (p. 241)
Treaty of Fort Wayne (p. 243)
battle of Tippecanoe (p. 244)
War of 1812 (p. 244)
Creek War (p. 245)
battle of New Orleans (p. 245)
Treaty of Ghent (p. 245)
Hartford Convention (p. 247)
Rush-Bagot disarmament treaty (p. 248)
feme covert (p. 248)
"Era of Good Feelings" (p. 250)
Missouri Compromise (p. 250)
Adams-Onís Treaty (p. 251)
Monroe Doctrine (p. 251)

TIMELINE

◀ **1789** • Judiciary Act establishes six Supreme Court justices.

1800 • Republicans Thomas Jefferson and Aaron Burr tie in electoral college.
• Fears of slave rebellion led by Gabriel in Virginia lead to 27 executions.

1801 • Judiciary Act reduces Supreme Court justices to five, increases circuit courts.
• House of Representatives elects Jefferson president after 36 ballots.

1803 • *Marbury v. Madison.*
• England and France place embargoes on American shipping.
• United States purchases Louisiana Territory.

1804–1806 • Lewis and Clark expedition goes to the Pacific.

1807 • British attack and search *Chesapeake.*
• Embargo Act.

1808 • Republican James Madison elected president; Dolley Madison soon dubbed "presidentress."

1809 • Treaty of Fort Wayne.
• Non-Intercourse Act.

1811 • Battle of Tippecanoe.

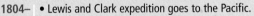

REVIEW QUESTIONS

1. How did Jefferson attempt to undo the Federalist innovations of earlier administrations? (pp. 236–42)

2. Why did Congress declare war on Great Britain in 1812? (pp. 242–48)

3. How did the civil status of American women and men differ in the decades of the early Republic? (pp. 248–50)

4. How did the collapse of the Federalist Party influence the administrations of James Monroe and John Quincy Adams? (pp. 250–54)

MAKING CONNECTIONS

1. When Jefferson assumed the presidency following the election of 1800, he expected to transform the national government. Describe his Republican vision and his successes and failures in implementing it. Did subsequent Republican presidents advance the same objectives?

2. How did the United States expand and strengthen its control of territory in North America in the early nineteenth century? In your answer, discuss the roles of diplomacy, military action, and political leadership in contributing to this development.

3. Regional tensions emerged as a serious danger to the American political system in the early nineteenth century. Discuss specific conflicts that had regional dimensions. How did Americans resolve, or fail to resolve, these tensions?

4. Although the United States denied its female citizens equality in public life, some women were able to exert considerable influence. How did they do so? In your answer, discuss the legal and political status of women in the Republic.

> ▶ For practice quizzes, a customized study plan, and other study tools, see the Online Study Guide at bedfordstmartins.com/roarkcompact.

1812 • United States declares war on Great Britain.

   1813 • Tecumseh dies at battle of the Thames.

      1814 • British attack Washington, D.C.
            • Treaty of Ghent.
            • New England Federalists meet at Hartford Convention.

        1815 • Battle of New Orleans.

           1816 • Republican James Monroe elected president.

              1819 • Adams-Onís Treaty.

               1820 • Missouri Compromise.

                   1823 • Monroe Doctrine asserted.

                     1825 • John Quincy Adams elected president by House of Representatives.

SHIP'S FIGUREHEAD OF ANDREW JACKSON

Carved in 1834 and affixed to the bow of the revered navy frigate *Constitution,* this figurehead of Andrew Jackson symbolized national pride by putting "the image of the most popular man of the West upon the favorite ship of the East," according to the commodore who commissioned it. But when Jackson introduced a new, strict banking policy, his popularity in the urban East quickly plummeted. In Boston, where the *Constitution* was docked, protesters complained that the figurehead of a tyrant corrupted their ship. On the night of July 3, 1834, the eve of the national holiday, a twenty-seven-year-old mariner and ardent Whig stole on board and decapitated the figurehead, sawing it through just below the ears. Jackson deflected the insult with humor, declaring, "I never did like that image! Give the man a postmaster's job." The commodore, himself alert to symbolic actions, wrapped the headless statue in a flag and sent it to New York City, where woodworkers fashioned a new head in 1835. The figurehead was reattached to the ship in another port: Jackson's banking policies still rankled in urban financial centers, and naval authorities did not want to risk a second mutilation of the president's image. In 1990, the original head was recovered from a private collector in France and restored to view in the museum that now owns the figurehead.

Museum of the City of New York, Gift of the Seawanhaka Corinthian Yacht Club.

The Expanding Republic

1815–1840

PRESIDENT ANDREW JACKSON was the dominant figure of his age, yet his precarious childhood little foretold the fame, fortune, and influence he would enjoy in the years after 1815. Jackson was born in the Carolina backcountry in 1767. His Scots-Irish father had recently died, leaving a poor, struggling mother to support three small boys. During the Revolution, Andrew followed his brothers into the militia, where both died of disease, as did his mother. Orphaned at fourteen, Jackson drifted around, drinking, gambling, and brawling.

Then at seventeen, his prospects began to improve. He studied under a lawyer for three years and moved to Nashville, a **frontier** community full of opportunities for a young man with legal training and an aggressive temperament. He became a public prosecutor, married into a leading family, and acquired land and slaves. When Tennessee became a state in 1796, Jackson, then twenty-nine, was elected to Congress and served a single term. In 1802, he became major-general of the Tennessee militia, cultivating a fierce style of military leadership.

Jackson captured national attention in 1815 by leading the victory at the battle of New Orleans. With little else to celebrate about the War of 1812, many Americans seized on the Tennessee general as the champion of the day. Songs, broadsides, and an admiring biography set him up as the original self-made man, the parentless child magically responsible for his own destiny. Jackson seemed to have created himself, a gritty, forceful personality extracting opportunities from the dynamic, turbulent frontier.

Jackson was more than a man of action, however. He was also strong-willed, reckless, and quick to anger, impulsively challenging men to duels, sometimes on slight pretexts. In one legendary fight in 1806, Jackson deliberately let his opponent, an expert marksman, shoot first. The bullet hit him in a rib, but Jackson masked all sign of injury under a loose cloak and immobile face. He then took careful aim at the astonished man and killed him. Such steely courage chilled his political opponents.

Jackson's image as a tough frontier hero set him apart from the learned and privileged gentlemen from Virginia and Massachusetts who had occupied the presidency up to 1828. When he lost the 1824 election to John Quincy Adams, an infuriated Jackson vowed to fight a rematch. He won in 1828 and again in 1832, capturing large majorities. His appeal stretched across the urban working classes of the East, frontier voters of the West, and slaveholders in the South, who all saw something of themselves in Jackson. Once elected, he brought a combative style to politics and enlarged the powers of the presidency.

The confidence and even recklessness of Jackson's personality mirrored the new confidence of American society in the years after 1815. An entrepreneurial spirit gripped the country, producing a market revolution of unprecedented scale. Old social hierarchies eroded; ordinary men dreamed of moving high on the ladder of success, just as Jackson had done. Stunning advances in transportation and economic productivity fueled such dreams and propelled thousands to move west or to cities. Urban growth and technological change fostered the diffusion of a distinctive and vibrant public culture, spread mainly through increased circulation of newspapers, which allowed popular opinions to coalesce and intensify; Jackson's sudden nationwide celebrity was a case in point.

Expanded communication transformed politics dramatically. Sharp disagreements over the best way to promote individual **liberty**, economic opportunity, and national prosperity in the new market economy defined key differences between Jackson and Adams and the parties they gave rise to in the 1830s. The process of party formation brought new habits of political participation and party loyalty to many thousands more adult white males. Religion became democratized as well: A nationwide **evangelical** revival brought its adherents the certainty that salvation and perfection were now available to all.

As president from 1829 to 1837, Jackson presided over all these changes, fighting some and supporting others in his vigorous and volatile way. As with his own stubborn personality, there was a dark underside to the confidence and expansiveness of American society. Steamboats blew up, banks and businesses periodically collapsed, alcoholism rates soared, Indians were killed or relocated farther west, and slavery continued to expand. The brash confidence that turned some people into rugged, self-promoting, Jackson-like individuals inspired others to think about the human costs of rapid economic expansion and thus about reforming society in dramatic ways. The common denominator was a faith that people and societies could shape their own destinies.

The Market Revolution

The return of peace in 1815 unleashed powerful forces that revolutionized the organization of the economy. Spectacular changes in transportation facilitated the movement of commodities, information, and people, while textile mills and other factories created many new jobs, especially for young unmarried women. Innovations in banking, legal practices, and tariff policies promoted swift economic growth.

This was not yet an industrial revolution, as was beginning in Britain, but a market revolution, fueled by traditional sources—water, wood, beasts of burden, and human muscle. What was new was the accelerated pace of economic activity and the scale of distribution of goods. Men and women were drawn out of old patterns of rural self-sufficiency into the wider realm of national market relations. At the same time, the nation's money supply enlarged considerably, leading to speculative investments in commerce, manufacturing, transportation, and land. The new nature and scale of production and consumption changed Americans' economic behavior, attitudes, and expectations.

Improvements in Transportation

Before 1815, transportation in the United States was slow and expensive; it cost as much to ship a crate over thirty miles of domestic roads as it did to send it across the Atlantic Ocean. The fastest stagecoach trip from Boston to New York took four days. But between 1815 and 1840, networks of roads, canals, steamboats, and finally railroads dramatically raised the speed and lowered the cost of travel (Map 11.1). Andrew Jackson spent weeks riding to Nashville in the 1790s along old Indian trails, but in 1829, it took only days for the new president to get to Washington, D.C., by steamboat and turnpike.

Improved transportation moved goods into wider markets. It moved passengers too, broadening their horizons and allowing youth as well as adults to take up new employment in cities or factory towns. Transportation also facilitated the flow of political information through heavy traffic in newspapers, periodicals, books, and the U.S. mail.

Enhanced public transport was expensive and produced uneven economic benefits, so administrations from Jefferson to Monroe were reluctant to fund it with federal dollars. Only the National Road, begun in 1806, was government sponsored. By 1818, it linked Baltimore with Wheeling, in western Virginia. Instead, private investors pooled resources and chartered transport companies, receiving significant subsidies and **monopoly** rights from state governments.

MAP 11.1 Routes of Transportation in 1840

By the 1830s, transportation advances had cut travel times significantly. Goods and people could move from New York City to Buffalo, New York, in four days by way of the Erie Canal, a trip that took two weeks by road in 1800. A trip from New York to New Orleans that took four weeks in 1800 could be accomplished in less than half that time on steamboats in the western rivers.

READING THE MAP: In what parts of the country were canals built most extensively? Were most of them within a single state's borders, or did they encourage interstate travel and shipping? **CONNECTIONS:** What impact did the Erie Canal have on the development of New York City? How did improvements in transportation affect urbanization in other parts of the country?

FOR MORE HELP ANALYZING THIS MAP, see the map activity for this chapter in the Online Study Guide at bedfordstmartins.com/roarkcompact.

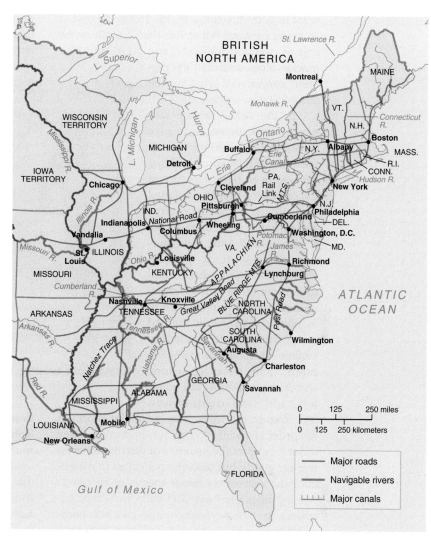

Turnpike and roadway mileage dramatically increased after 1815, reducing shipping costs. Stagecoach companies proliferated, and travel time on main routes was cut in half.

Water travel was similarly transformed. In 1807, Robert Fulton's steam-propelled boat, the *Clermont*, churned up the Hudson River from New York City to Albany, touching off a steamboat craze. In 1820, a dozen boats left New York City daily, and scores more operated on midwestern rivers and the Great Lakes. A voyager on one of the first steamboats to go down the Mississippi reported that the Chickasaw Indians called the vessel a "fire canoe" and considered it "an omen of evil." By the early 1830s, more than seven hundred steamboats were in operation on the Ohio and Mississippi rivers.

Steamboats were not benign advances, however. The urgency to cut travel time led to overstoked furnaces, sudden boiler explosions, and terrible mass fatalities. Another huge cost, to the environment, was the deforestation brought by steamboats, which had to load fuel—"wood up"—every twenty miles or so. By the 1830s the banks of main rivers were denuded of trees, and forests miles in from the rivers fell to the ax. Steamboats burned large amounts of wood,

transferring the carbon stored in trees into the atmosphere, creating America's first significant air pollution.

Canals were another major innovation of the transportation revolution. These shallow highways of water allowed passage for barges and boats pulled by horses or mules trudging on a towpath. Travel speed was slow, under five miles per hour; the economy came from increased loads. The low-friction water allowed one horse to pull a fifty-ton barge. Pennsylvania in 1815 and New York in 1817 commenced major state-sponsored canal enterprises. Pennsylvania's Schuylkill Canal stretched 108 miles west from Philadelphia when it was completed in 1826. Much more impressive was the Erie Canal, finished in 1825, covering 350 miles between Albany and Buffalo and linking the port of New York City with the entire Great Lakes region. Wheat and flour moved east, household goods and tools moved west, and passengers went in both directions. By the 1830s, the cost of shipping by canal fell to less than a tenth of the cost of overland transport, and New York City quickly blossomed into the premier commercial city in the United States.

In the 1830s, private railroad companies began to give canals stiff competition, and by the mid-1840s the canal-building era was over. (However, use of the canals for freight continued well into the twentieth century.) The nation's first railroad, the Baltimore and Ohio, laid thirteen miles of track in 1829. During the 1830s, three thousand more miles of track materialized nationwide, the result of a speculative fever in railroad construction masterminded by bankers, locomotive manufacturers, and state legislators, who provided subsidies, charters, and land rights-of-way. Rail lines in the 1830s were generally short, on the order of twenty to one hundred miles. They did not yet provide an efficient distribution system for goods, but passengers flocked to experience the marvelous travel speeds of fifteen to twenty miles per hour. Railroads and other advances in transportation made possible enormous change by unifying the country culturally and economically.

Factories, Workingwomen, and Wage Labor

Transportation advances promoted expansion of manufacturing after 1815, creating a larger market for goods. The two leading industries, newly altering methods of production and labor relations, were textiles and shoes. Textile production was greatly spurred by the development of water-driven machinery, built near fast-coursing rivers. Shoe manufacturing, still using the power and skill of human hands, involved only a reorganization of production. Both mechanized and manual manufacturing pulled young women into the labor market for the first time.

The earliest factory, built by British immigrant Samuel Slater in Pawtucket, Rhode Island, in the 1790s, featured a mechanical spinning machine that produced thread and yarn. By 1815,

Cotton Textile Industry, 1839

nearly 170 spinning mills dotted lower New England. In British manufacturing cities, entire families worked in low-wage, health-threatening factories. American factories, in contrast, targeted young women as employees, cheap to hire because of their limited employment options. Mill girls would retire to marriage, replaced by fresh recruits earning a beginner's wage.

In 1821, a group of Boston entrepreneurs founded the town of Lowell, on the Merrimack River, centralizing all aspects of cloth production: combing, shrinking, spinning, weaving, and dyeing. By 1830, the eight mills in Lowell employed more than 5,000 young women, who lived in closely supervised company-owned boardinghouses. Corporation rules required church attendance and prohibited drinking and unsupervised courtship; dorm lockdown came at 10 p.m. Typical mill workers averaged $2 to $3 for a seventy-hour workweek, more than a seamstress or domestic servant could earn but less than a young man's wages. The job consisted of tending noisy power looms in rooms kept hot and humid, ideal for thread but not for people.

Despite the discomforts, young women left farms and flocked to factory towns in the hope of gaining more autonomy. They welcomed the unprecedented if still limited personal freedom of living in an all-female social space, away from parents and domestic tasks and with pay in their pockets. In evenings, the women could engage in self-improvement activities, such as attending lectures or writing for the company's periodical, *The Lowell Offering*.

In the mid-1830s, worldwide changes in the cotton market impelled mill owners to speed up work and lower wages. The workers protested, emboldened by their communal living arrangements and by their relative independence from the job as temporary employees. In 1834 and again in 1836, hundreds of women at Lowell went out on strike. All over New England, female mill workers led strikes and formed unions. Women at a mill in Dover, New Hampshire, in 1834 denounced their owners for trying to turn them into "slaves": "However freely the epithet of 'factory slaves' may be bestowed upon us, we

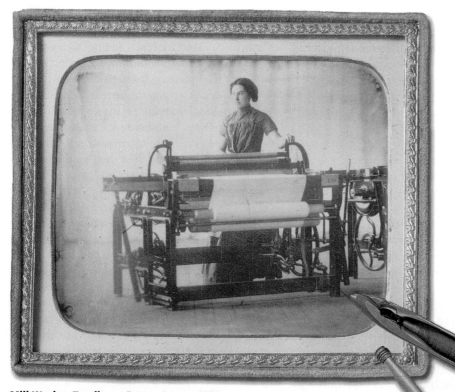

Mill Worker Tending a Power Loom, 1850

This daguerreotype—the earliest form of photograph—shows a young woman tending a power loom in a textile mill. Her main task was to replace the spindle when it ran out of thread, loading a new spindle into the shuttle. The close-up shows spindles of pink and blue thread next to a shuttle. The factory operative had to be constantly alert for sudden breaks in the warp yarn, which required a fast shutdown of the loom and a quick repair of the thread. In the 1830s, women weavers generally tended two machines at a time; in the 1840s, some companies increased the workload to four.

Mill worker: American Textile History Museum; shuttle with spindles: Picture Research Consultants & Archives.

will never deserve it by a base and cringing submission to proud wealth or haughty insolence." Their assertiveness surprised many; but ultimately their easy replaceability undermined their bargaining power, and owners in the 1840s began to shift to immigrant families as their labor source.

Other manufacturing enterprises of the 1820s and 1830s, such as shoemaking, employed women in ever larger numbers. New modes of organizing the work allowed the manufacturers to step up production, control wastage and quality, and lower wages by subdividing the tasks and by hiring women, including wives. Male workers cut leather and made soles. The stitching of the upper part of the shoe, called shoebinding, became women's work, performed at home so that it could mesh with domestic chores. Although their wages were lower than

men's, shoebinder wives contributed earned cash to family income.

In the economically turbulent 1830s, shoebinder wages fell. Unlike the mill workers, women shoebinders worked in isolation, a serious hindrance to organized protest. In Lynn, Massachusetts, a major shoemaking center, women used female church networks to organize resistance, communicating via religious newspapers. The Lynn shoebinders who demanded higher wages in 1834 built on a collective sense of themselves as women even though they did not share daily work lives. "Equal rights should be extended to all—to the weaker sex as well as the stronger," they wrote in a document forming the Female Society of Lynn.

In the end, the Lynn shoebinders' protests failed to achieve wage increases. Isolated workers all over New England continued to accept low wages, and even in Lynn, many women shied away from organized protest, preferring to situate their work in the context of family duty (helping their menfolk to finish shoes) instead of market relations.

Bankers and Lawyers

Entrepreneurs like the Lowell factory owners relied on innovations in the banking system to finance their ventures. The number of state-chartered banks in the United States more than doubled in the boom years 1814–1816, from fewer than 90 to 208. By 1830, there were 330; by 1840, hundreds more. Banks stimulated the economy by making loans to merchants and manufacturers and by enlarging the money supply. Borrowers were issued loans in the form of banknotes—certificates unique to each bank—which were used as money for all transactions. Neither federal nor state governments issued paper money, so banknotes became the currency of the country.

In theory, a note could always be traded in at a bank for its **hard-money** equivalent in gold or silver (in a transaction known as "specie payment"). A note from a solid local bank might be worth exactly what it was written for, but the face value of a note from a distant or questionable bank would be discounted by a fraction. Buying and selling banknotes in Jacksonian America required knowledge and caution. Not surprisingly, counterfeiting flourished.

Bankers exercised great power over the economy, deciding who would get loans and what the discount rates would be. The most powerful bankers sat on the board of directors for the second Bank of the United States, headquartered in Philadelphia. The twenty-year charter of the first Bank of the United States had expired in 1811. The second Bank of the United States, with eighteen branches throughout the country, opened for business in 1816 under another twenty-year charter. The rechartering of this bank would be a major issue in Andrew Jackson's reelection campaign in 1832.

Accompanying the market revolution was a revolution in commercial law, fashioned by politicians to enhance the prospects of private investment. In 1811, states started to rewrite laws of incorporation (allowing the chartering of businesses by states), and the number of corporations expanded rapidly, from about twenty in 1800 to eighteen hundred by 1817. Incorporation protected individual investors from being held liable for corporate financial debts. State lawmakers also wrote laws of eminent domain, empowering states to buy land for roads and canals, even from unwilling sellers. They drafted legislation on contributory negligence, relieving employers from responsibility for workplace injuries. In such ways, entrepreneurial lawyers of the 1820s and 1830s created the legal foundation for an economy that would give priority to ambitious individuals interested in maximizing their own wealth.

Not everyone applauded these developments. Andrew Jackson, himself a skillful lawyer-turned-politician, spoke for a large and mistrustful segment of the population when he warned about the abuses of power "which the moneyed interest derives from a paper currency which they are able to control, from the multitude of corporations with exclusive privileges which they have succeeded in obtaining in the different states, and which are employed altogether for their benefit." Jacksonians believed that ending government-granted privileges was the way to maximize individual liberty and economic opportunity.

Booms and Busts

One aspect of the economy that the lawyer-politicians could not control was the threat of financial collapse. The boom years from 1815 to 1818 exhibited a volatility that resulted in the first sharp, large-scale economic downturn in U.S. history, a depression that Americans called a "panic"; the pattern was repeated in the 1830s. Rapidly rising consumer demand stimulated price increases for goods, and speculative investment opportunities offering the possibility of high payoffs abounded—in bank stocks, western land sales, urban real estate, and commodities markets. High inflation made some people wealthy but created hardships for workers on fixed incomes.

When the bubble burst in 1819, the overnight rich suddenly became the overnight poor. Some blamed the panic of 1819 on the second Bank of the United States. The national bank had failed to exercise control over state banks, and many of them had suspended specie payments—the exchange of gold or silver for banknotes—in their eagerness to expand the economic bubble. In mid-1818, when the Bank of the United States started to call in its loans and insisted that state banks do likewise, the contracting of the money supply created tremors throughout the economy. The crunch was made worse by a financial crisis in Europe in the spring of 1819. Overseas, prices for

American cotton, tobacco, and wheat plummeted by more than 50 percent. Thus when the Bank of the United States and the state banks called in their outstanding loans, American debtors involved in the commodities trade could not come up with the money. The number of business and personal bankruptcies skyrocketed. The intricate web of credit and debt relationships meant that almost everyone with even a toehold in the new commercial economy was affected by the panic of 1819. Thousands of Americans lost their savings and property, and unemployment estimates suggest that a half million people lost their jobs.

Recovery took several years. Unemployment rates fell, but bitterness lingered, ready to be stirred up by politicians in the decades to come. The dangers of a system dependent on extensive credit were now clear: In one folksy formulation that circulated around 1820, a farmer compared credit to "a man pissing in his breeches on a cold day to keep his arse warm—very comfortable at first but I dare say…you know how it feels afterwards."

By the mid-1820s, the booming economy was back on track, driven by increases in productivity and consumer demand for goods, accelerating international trade, and a restless and calculating people moving goods, human labor, and investment capital in expanding circles of commerce. But an undercurrent of anxiety about rapid economic change continued to shape the political views of many Americans.

> **REVIEW** Why did the United States experience a market revolution after 1815?

The Spread of Democracy

Just as the market revolution held out the promise, if not the reality, of economic opportunity for all who worked, the political transformation of the 1830s held out the promise of political opportunity for all who voted. During Andrew Jackson's presidency, 1829 to 1837, the second American party system took shape, although not until 1836 would the parties have distinct names and consistent programs that transcended the particular personalities running for office. Over those years, more men could and did vote, responding to new methods of arousing voter interest. In 1828, Jackson's charismatic personality

defined his party, and his election over John Quincy Adams turned on questions of character. Once in office, Jackson championed ordinary citizens against the power elite—**democracy** versus aristocracy in Jackson's terminology. A lasting contribution of the Jackson years was the notion that politicians needed to have the common touch in their dealings with voters.

Popular Politics and Partisan Identity

The election of 1828 was the first presidential contest in which popular votes determined the outcome. In twenty-two out of twenty-four states, voters—not state legislatures—now designated electors committed to a particular candidate. More than a million voters participated, three times the number in 1824 and nearly half the free male population, reflecting the high stakes that voters perceived in the Adams-Jackson rematch. Throughout the 1830s, voter turnout continued to rise, up to 70 percent in some localities, partly due to the disappearance of property qualifications in all but three states and partly due to heightened political interest.

The 1828 election inaugurated new campaign styles. State-level candidates routinely gave speeches at rallies, picnics, and banquets. Adams and Jackson still declined such activities as undignified; but Henry Clay of Kentucky, campaigning for Adams, earned the nickname "Barbecue Orator." Campaign rhetoric, under the necessity to create popular appeal, became more informal and even blunt. The Jackson camp established many Hickory Clubs, trading on Jackson's popular nickname, "Old Hickory," from a common Tennessee tree suggesting resilience and toughness. (Jackson was the first presidential candidate to have an affectionate and widely used nickname.)

Partisan newspapers in ever larger numbers defined issues and publicized political personalities as never before. Improved printing technology and rising literacy rates were fueling a great expansion of newspapers of all kinds (see Table 11.1).

TABLE 11.1	**THE GROWTH OF NEWSPAPERS, 1820–1840**			
	1820	*1830*	*1835*	*1840*
U.S. population (in millions)	9.6	12.8	15.0	17.1
Number of newspapers published	500	800	1,200	1,400
Daily newspapers	42	65	—	138

Party leaders dispensed subsidies and other favors to secure the loyalties of papers, even in remote towns and villages. In New York State, where party development was most advanced, a pro-Jackson group called the Bucktails controlled fifty weekly publications. Stories from the leading Jacksonian paper in Washington, D.C., were reprinted two days later in a Boston or Cincinnati paper, as fast as the mail stage could carry them. Presidential campaigns were now coordinated in a national arena.

Politicians at first identified themselves as Jackson or Adams men, honoring the fiction of Republican Party unity. By 1832 the terminology had evolved to National Republicans, favoring federal action to promote commercial development, and Democratic Republicans, who promised to be responsive to the will of the majority. Between 1834 and 1836, National Republicans shifted to the term Whig, while Jackson's party became simply the Democrats.

The Election of 1828 and the Character Issue

The campaign of 1828 was the first national election in which scandal and character questions reigned supreme. They became central issues because voters used them to comprehend the kind of public officer each man would make. Character issues conveyed in shorthand larger questions about morality, honor, and discipline. Jackson and Adams presented two radically different styles of masculinity.

John Quincy Adams was vilified by his opponents as an elitist, bookish academic, perhaps even a monarchist. Critics pointed to Adams's White House billiard table and ivory chess set as symbols of his aristocratic degeneracy along with the "corrupt bargain" of 1824, the alleged election deal between Adams and Henry Clay (see chapter 10). Adams's supporters returned fire with fire. They played on Jackson's fatherless childhood to portray him as the bastard son of a prostitute. Worse, the cloudy circumstances around his marriage to Rachel Donelson Robards in 1791 gave rise to the story that Jackson was a seducer and an adulterer, having married a woman whose divorce from her first husband was not entirely legal. Pro-Adams newspapers howled that Jackson was sinful and impulsive, while portraying Adams as pious, learned, and virtuous.

Editors in favor of Adams played up Jackson's notorious violent temper, evidenced by the many duels, brawls, and canings they could recount. Jackson's supporters used the same stories to project Old Hickory as a tough frontier hero who knew how to command obedience. As for learning, Jackson's rough frontier education gave him a "natural sense," wrote a Boston editor, that "can never be acquired by reading books—it can only be acquired, in perfection, by reading men."

Jackson won a sweeping victory, 56 percent of the popular vote and 178 electoral votes to Adams's 83. Old Hickory took most of the South and West and carried Pennsylvania and New York as well; the loser carried the remainder in the East. Jackson's vice president was John C. Calhoun, who had just served as vice president under Adams but had broken with Adams's policies.

After 1828, national politicians no longer deplored the existence of political parties. They were coming to see that parties mobilized and delivered voters, sharpened candidates' differences, and created party loyalty that surpassed loyalty to individual candidates and elections. Adams and Jackson clearly symbolized and defined for voters the competing ideas of the emerging parties: Whigs—a moralistic, top-down party ready to make major decisions to promote economic growth; Democrats—a contentious, energetic party ready to embrace liberty-loving individualism.

Jackson's Democratic Agenda

Before the inauguration in March 1829, Rachel Jackson died. Certain that the ugly campaign had hastened her death, the president went into deep mourning, his depression worsened by constant pain from the 1806 bullet still lodged in his chest and by mercury poisoning from the medicines he took. Sixty-two years old, Jackson carried only 140 pounds on his six-foot-one frame. His adversaries doubted he would make it to a second term. His supporters, however, went wild at the inauguration. Thousands cheered his ten-minute inaugural address, the shortest in history. An open reception at the White House turned into a near riot as well-wishers jammed the premises, used windows as doors, stood on furniture for a better view of the great man, and broke thousands of dollars' worth of china and glasses.

 During his presidency, Jackson continued to offer unprecedented hospitality to the public. Twenty spittoons newly installed in the East Room of the White House accommodated the

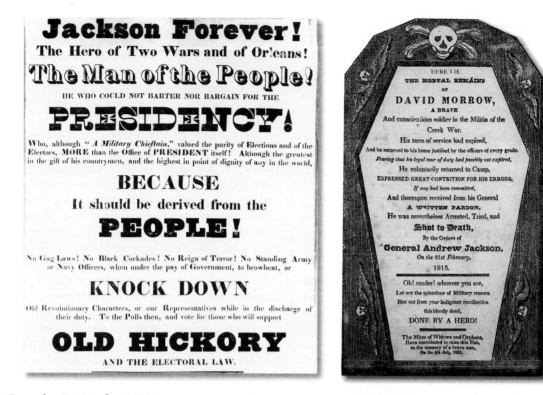

Campaign Posters from 1828

The poster on the left praises Andrew Jackson as a war hero and "man of the people" and reminds readers that Jackson, who won the largest popular vote in 1824, did not stoop to bargain for the presidency, as presumably John Quincy Adams had done in his dealings with Henry Clay. (What "two wars" does this poster refer to?) The poster with ominous tombstone and coffin graphics accuses Jackson of the unjustified killing of a Kentucky militiaman (one of six executed) during the Creek War in 1815. The text implores readers to think of the "hero" as a man capable of "bloody deeds."

Pro-Jackson broadside: © Collection of the New-York Historical Society; anti-Jackson broadside: Smithsonian Institute, Washington, D.C.

tobacco-chewers among the throngs that arrived daily to see the president. The courteous Jackson, committed to his image as president of the "common man," held audiences with unannounced visitors throughout his two terms.

Jackson's appointments marked a departure. Past presidents had tried to lessen party conflict by including men of different factions in their cabinets, but Jackson would have only Jackson loyalists. For secretary of state, the key job, he tapped New Yorker Martin Van Buren, one of the shrewdest politicians of the day. Throughout the federal government, from postal clerks to ambassadors, Jackson removed competent civil servants and installed party loyalists. "To the victor belong the spoils," said a Democratic senator from New York, expressing approval of patronage-driven appointments. Jackson's approach to civil service employment got tagged the **spoils system**; it was a concept the president strenuously defended.

Jackson's agenda quickly emerged. He favored a Jeffersonian limited federal government, fearing that intervention in the economy inevitably favored some groups at the expense of others. He therefore opposed federal support of transportation and grants of monopolies and charters that privileged wealthy investors. Like Jefferson, he anticipated rapid settlement of the country's interior, where land sales would spread economic democracy to settlers. Thus, establishing a federal policy to remove the Indians had high priority. Unlike Jefferson, however, Jackson exercised presidential veto powers over Congress. In 1830, he vetoed a highway project in Maysville, Kentucky— Henry Clay's home state—that Congress had voted to support with federal dollars. The Maysville Road veto articulated Jackson's principled stand that citizens' federal tax dollars could be spent only on projects of a "general, not local" character. In all, Jackson used the veto twelve times; all previous presidents had exercised that right a total of nine times.

REVIEW   Why did Jackson defeat John Quincy Adams so dramatically in the 1828 election?

Cultural Shifts, Religion, and Reform

Despite their differences about the best way to enhance commercial development, Jackson's Democratic Republicans and Henry Clay's National Republicans shared enthusiasm for the outcome—a growing, booming economy. For increasing numbers of families, especially in the commercialized Northeast, standards of living rose, consumption patterns changed, and the nature and location of work altered. All of these changes had a direct impact on the duties of men and women and on the training of youth for the economy of the future.

Along with economic change came an unprecedented revival of evangelical religion known as the **Second Great Awakening**. Just as universal male **suffrage** allowed all white men to vote, democratized religion offered salvation to all who chose to embrace it. Among the most serious adherents of evangelical **Protestantism** were men and women of the new merchant classes whose self-discipline in pursuing market ambitions meshed well with the message of self-discipline in pursuit of spiritual perfection. Not content with individual perfection, many of these men and women sought to perfect society as well, by defining excessive alcohol consumption, nonmarital sex, and slavery as three major evils of modern life in need of correction.

The Family and Separate Spheres

The centerpiece of new ideas about gender relations was the notion that husbands found their status and authority in the new world of work, leaving wives to tend the hearth and home. Sermons, advice books, periodicals, and novels reinforced the idea that men and women inhabited **separate spheres** and had separate duties. "To woman it belongs…to elevate the intellectual character of her household [and] to kindle the fires of mental activity in childhood," wrote Mrs. A. J. Graves in a popular book titled *Advice to American Women*. For men, in contrast, "the absorbing passion for gain, and the pressing demands of business, engross their whole attention." In particular, the home, now the exclusive domain of women, was sentimentalized as the source of intimacy, love, and safety, a refuge from the cruel and competitive world of market relations.

Some new aspects of society gave substance to this formulation of separate spheres. Men's work was undergoing profound change after 1815 and increasingly brought cash to the household, especially in the manufacturing and urban Northeast. Farmers and tradesmen sold products in a market, and bankers, bookkeepers, shoemakers, and canal diggers got pay envelopes. Furthermore, many men performed jobs outside of the home, at an office or store. For men who were not farmers, work indeed seemed newly disconnected from life at home.

A woman's domestic role was more complicated than the cultural prescriptions indicated. Although the vast majority of married white women did not hold paying jobs, the home continued to be a site of time-consuming labor. But the advice books treated household tasks as loving familial duties; housework as work was thereby rendered invisible in an economy that evaluated work by how much cash it generated. In reality, wives directly contributed to family income in many ways. Some took in boarders, while others engaged in outwork, earning pay for shoebinding, hatmaking, or needlework done at home. Wives in the poorer classes of society, including most free black wives, did not have the luxury of husbands earning adequate wages; for them, work as servants or laundresses helped augment family income.

The Education and Training of Youth

The market economy with its new expectations for men and women required fresh methods of training youth of both sexes. The generation that came of age in the 1820s and 1830s had opportunities for education and work unparalleled in previous eras, at least for white children in the middling classes and above. Northern states adopted public schooling between 1790 and the 1820s, and in the 1820s and 1830s southern states followed suit. The curriculum produced pupils who were able, by age twelve or fourteen, to read, write, and participate in marketplace calculations. Remarkably, girls usually received the same basic education as boys. Literacy rates for white females climbed dramatically, rivaling the rates for white males for the first time.

The fact that taxpayers paid for children's education created an incentive to seek an inexpensive teaching force. By the 1830s, school districts began replacing male teachers with young females. Like mill workers, teachers were in their late teens and regarded the work as temporary. Some were trained in private female academies, now numbering in the hundreds, while others attended teacher training schools ("normal" schools) for women students. With the exception of Oberlin College in Ohio, no colleges admitted women until after the Civil War, but a handful of private "female seminaries" established a rigorous curriculum that rivaled that of the best men's colleges. Two of the most prominent were the Troy Seminary in New York, founded by Emma Willard in 1821, and Mount Holyoke in Massachusetts, founded by Mary Lyon in 1837.

Male youths leaving public school faced two paths. A small percentage continued at private boys' academies, and a far smaller number entered the country's two dozen colleges. More typically, boys left school at fourteen to apprentice in a specific trade or to seek business careers in entry-level clerkships, abundant in the growing urban centers. Young girls also headed for mill towns or for the cities in unprecedented numbers, seeking work in the expanding service sector as seamstresses and domestic servants.

Changes in patterns of youth employment meant that large numbers of youngsters in the 1830s and later escaped the watchful eyes of their families. Moralists fretted about the dangers of

Women Graduates of Oberlin College, Class of 1855

Oberlin College, founded in Ohio by evangelical and abolitionist activists in the 1830s, admitted men and women, both white and black. In the early years, the black students were all male, and the women students were all white. Instruction was not coeducational. The women attended classes in a separate Ladies' Department. By 1855, as this daguerreotype shows, black women had integrated the Ladies' Department. The two older women wearing bonnets were the principal and a member of the board. The students wear the latest fashion: dark taffeta dresses with sloping shoulders and a tight bodice topped by detachable white lace collars. Hair fashions were similarly uniform for women of all ages throughout the 1850s: a central part, hair dressed with oil and lustrously coiled over the ears. Compare these women with the mill woman pictured on page 263. What differences do you see? Oberlin College Archives, Oberlin, Ohio.

unsupervised youth, and, following the lead of the Lowell mill owners, some established apprentices' libraries and uplifting lecture series to keep young people honorably occupied. Advice books published by the hundreds instructed youth in the virtues of hard work and delayed gratification.

The Second Great Awakening

A newly invigorated version of Protestantism gained huge momentum in the 1820s and 1830s as the economy reshaped gender and age relations. The earliest manifestations of this fervent piety appeared in 1801 in Kentucky, when a crowd of ten thousand people camped out on a hillside at Cane Ridge for a revival meeting that lasted several weeks. By the 1810s and 1820s, "camp meetings" had spread to the Atlantic seaboard states, finding especially enthusiastic audiences in western New York and Pennsylvania. The outdoor settings permitted huge attendance, which itself intensified the emotional impact of the experience. "For more than a half mile, I could see people on their knees before God in humble prayer," recalled one Cane Ridge worshipper.

The gatherings attracted women and men hungry for a more immediate access to spiritual peace, one not requiring years of soul-searching. One eyewitness at a revival reported that "some of the people were singing, others praying, some crying for mercy....At one time I saw at least five hundred swept down in a moment as if a battery of a thousand guns had been opened upon them, and then immediately followed shrieks and shouts that rent the very heavens."

From 1800 to 1820, church membership doubled in the United States, much of it among the evangelical groups. Methodists, Baptists, and Presbyterians formed the core of the new movement; Episcopalians, Congregationalists, Unitarians, Dutch Reformed, Lutherans, and Catholics maintained strong skepticism about the emotional enthusiasm. Women more than men were attracted to the evangelical movement, and wives and mothers typically recruited husbands and sons to join them.

The leading exemplar of the Second Great Awakening was a lawyer-turned-minister. Charles Grandison Finney lived in western New York, where the completion of the Erie Canal in 1825 fundamentally altered the social and economic landscape overnight. Towns swelled with new inhabitants who brought in remarkable prosperity along with other, less admirable side effects, such as prostitution, drinking, and gaming. Finney saw New York canal towns as especially ripe for evangelical awakening. In Rochester, New York, he sustained a six-month revival through the winter of 1830, generating thousands of new converts.

Finney's message was directed primarily at women and men of the business classes. He argued that a reign of Christian perfection loomed, one that required public-spirited outreach to the less than perfect to foster their salvation. Evangelicals promoted Sunday schools to bring piety to children; they battled to end mail delivery, to stop public transport, and to close shops on Sundays to honor the Sabbath. Many women formed missionary societies, which distributed millions of Bibles and religious tracts. Through such avenues, evangelical religion offered women expanded spheres of influence. Finney adopted tactics of Jacksonian-era politicians—publicity, argumentation, rallies, and speeches—to sell his cause. His object, he said, was to get Americans to "vote in the Lord Jesus Christ as the governor of the Universe."

The Temperance Movement and the Campaign for Moral Reform

The evangelical disposition—a combination of faith, energy, self-discipline, and righteousness—animated vigorous campaigns to eliminate alcohol abuse and eradicate sexual sin. Millions of Americans took the temperance pledge to abstain from strong drink, and thousands became involved in efforts to end prostitution.

Alcohol consumption had risen steadily in the decades up to 1830, when the average person over age thirteen annually consumed an astonishing 9 gallons of hard liquor plus 30 gallons of hard cider, beer, and wine. All classes imbibed. A lively saloon culture fostered masculine camaraderie along with extensive alcohol consumption among laborers, while in elite homes, the after-dinner whiskey or sherry was commonplace. Colleges before 1820 routinely served students a pint of ale with meals, and the army and navy included rum in the standard daily ration.

Organized opposition to drinking first surfaced in the 1810s among health and religious reformers. In 1826, Lyman Beecher, a Connecticut minister of an "awakened" church, founded the American Temperance Society, which warned that drinking led to poverty, idleness, crime, and family violence. Adopting the methods of evangelical ministers, temperance lecturers traveled the country expounding the damage of drink; by 1833, some six thousand local affiliates of the

Charles G. Finney and His Broadway Tabernacle
The Reverend Charles G. Finney (shown here in a portrait done in 1834) took his evangelical movement to New York City in the early 1830s, operating first out of a renovated theater. In 1836, the Broadway Tabernacle was built for his pastorate. In its use of space, the tabernacle resembled a theater more than a traditional church, but in one respect it departed radically from one very theaterlike tradition of churches—the custom of charging pew rents. In effect, most churches required worshippers to purchase their seats. Finney, in contrast, insisted that all seats in his house were free, unreserved, and open to all.
Oberlin College Archives, Oberlin, Ohio.

FOR MORE HELP ANALYZING THIS IMAGE, see the visual activity for this chapter in the Online Study Guide at bedfordstmartins.com/roarkcompact.

American Temperance Society boasted more than a million members. Middle-class drinking began a steep decline.

In 1836, leaders of the **temperance movement** regrouped into a new society, the American Temperance Union, which demanded total abstinence of its adherents. The intensified war against alcohol moved beyond individual moral suasion into the realm of politics, as reformers sought to deny taverns liquor licenses. By 1845, temperance advocates had put an impressive dent in alcohol consumption, which diminished to one-quarter of the per capita consumption of 1830. In 1851, Maine became the first state to ban entirely the manufacture and sale of all alcoholic beverages.

More controversial than temperance was a social movement called "moral reform," which first aimed at public morals in general but quickly narrowed to a campaign to eradicate sexual sin, especially prostitution. In 1833, a group of Finneyite women started the New York Female Moral Reform Society. Its members insisted that uncontrolled male sexual expression posed a serious threat to society in general and to women in particular. The society's nationally distributed newspaper, the *Advocate of Moral Reform,* was the first major paper in the country that was written, edited, and typeset by women. In it they condemned men who visited brothels or who seduced innocent victims. Within five years, more than four thousand auxiliary groups of women members had sprung up, mostly in New England, New York, Pennsylvania, and Ohio.

In its analysis of the causes of licentiousness and its conviction that women had a duty to speak out about unspeakable things, the Moral Reform Society pushed the limits of what even the men in the evangelical movement could tolerate. Yet these women did not regard themselves as radicals. They were simply pursuing the logic of a gender system that defined home protection and morality as women's special sphere and a religious conviction that called for the eradication of sin.

Organizing against Slavery

More radical still was the movement in the 1830s to abolish the sin of slavery. The only previous antislavery organization, the American Colonization Society, had been founded in 1817 by some Maryland and Virginia **planters** to promote gradual individual **emancipation** of slaves followed by **colonization** in Africa. By the early 1820s, several thousand ex-slaves had been transported to Liberia on the West African coast. But not surprisingly, newly freed men and women were often not eager to emigrate; their African roots were three or more generations in the past. Colonization was too gradual (and expensive) to have much impact on American slavery.

Around 1830, northern challenges to slavery surfaced with increasing frequency and resolve, beginning in free black communities. In 1829, a Boston printer named David Walker published *An Appeal…to the Coloured Citizens of the World,* which condemned racism, invoked the egalitarian language of the Declaration of Independence, and hinted at racial violence if whites did not change their prejudiced ways. In 1830, at the inaugural National Negro Convention meeting in Philadelphia, forty blacks from nine states discussed the racism of American society and proposed emigration to Canada. In 1832, a twenty-eight-year-old black woman, Maria Stewart, delivered public lectures for black audiences in Boston on slavery and racial prejudice. While her arguments against slavery were welcomed, her voice—that of a woman—created problems even among her sympathetic audiences. Few American-born women had yet engaged in public speaking beyond theatrical performances or religious prophesizing; Stewart was breaking a social taboo. She retired from the platform in 1833 but took up writing and published her lectures in a national publication called the *Liberator,* giving them much wider circulation.

The *Liberator,* founded in 1831 in Boston, took antislavery agitation to new heights. Its founder and editor, an uncompromising twenty-six-year-old white printer named William Lloyd Garrison, advocated immediate abolition: "On this subject, I do not wish to think, or speak, or write, with moderation. No! No! Tell a man whose house is on fire to give a moderate alarm; tell him to moderately rescue his wife from the hands of the ravisher; tell the mother to gradually extricate her babe from the fire into which it has fallen;—but urge me not to use moderation in a cause like the present."

In 1832, Garrison supporters started the New England Anti-Slavery Society; similar groups were organized in Philadelphia and New York in 1833. Soon a dozen antislavery newspapers and scores of antislavery lecturers were spreading the word and inspiring the formation of new local societies, which numbered 1,300 by 1837. Entirely confined to the North, their membership totaled a quarter of a million men and women.

Many white Northerners were not prepared to embrace the abolitionist call for emancipation, immediate or gradual. They might oppose slavery as a blot on the country's ideals or as a rival to the **free-labor** system of the North, but at the same time most white Northerners remained antiblack and therefore antiabolition. From 1834 to 1838, there were more than a hundred eruptions of serious mob violence against abolitionists or free blacks. On one occasion, antislavery headquarters in Philadelphia and a black church and orphanage were burned to the ground; in another incident, Illinois abolitionist editor Elijah Lovejoy was killed by a rioting crowd attempting to destroy his printing press.

Women played a prominent role in abolition, just as they did in moral reform and evangelical religion. (See "Beyond America's Borders," page 274.) They formed women's auxiliaries and engaged in fund-raising to support lecturers in the field. They circulated antislavery petitions, presented to the U.S. Congress with tens of thousands of signatures. Garrison particularly welcomed women's activity. When a southern plantation daughter named Angelina Grimké wrote to him about her personal repugnance for slavery, Garrison published the letter in the *Liberator* and brought her overnight fame. In 1837, Grimké and her older sister Sarah became antislavery lecturers targeting women, but their powerful eyewitness speeches attracted men as well, causing leaders of the Congregational Church in Massachusetts to warn all ministers not to let the Grimké sisters use their pulpits. Like Maria Stewart, the Grimkés had violated a gender norm by presuming to instruct men.

In the late 1830s, the cause of abolition divided the nation as no other issue did. Even among the abolitionists, significant divisions emerged. The Grimké sisters, radicalized by the public reaction to their speaking tour, began to write and speak about woman's rights. They were opposed by moderate abolitionists who were unwilling to mix a new and controversial issue about women with their first cause, the rights of blacks. A few radical men, like Garrison, embraced women's rights fully, working to get women leadership positions in the national antislavery group.

The many men and women active in reform movements in the 1830s found their initial inspiration in evangelical Protestantism's dual message: Salvation was open to all, and society needed to be perfected. Their activist mentality squared well with the interventionist tendencies of the party forming in opposition to Andrew Jackson's Democrats. Generally, reformers gravitated to the Whig Party, the males as voters and the females as rallying supporters in the 1830s campaigns.

REVIEW   How did evangelical Protestantism contribute to the social reform movements of the 1830s?

Jackson Defines the Democratic Party

As president, Andrew Jackson worked to implement his vision of a politics of opportunity for all white men. To open land for white settlement, he favored relocation of all eastern Indian peoples. He dramatically confronted John C. Calhoun and South Carolina when that state tried to nullify the tariff of 1828. Disapproving of all government-granted privilege, Jackson challenged what he called the "monster" Bank of the United States and took it down to defeat. Jackson's legacy to his successor, Martin Van Buren, was a Democratic Party strong enough to withstand the passing of Old Hickory. But another of his legacies was the most severe economic contraction yet to hit the U.S. economy. Although the panic of 1837 was not solely Jackson's doing, it was a fitting end to a decade of rambunctious speculation and expansion.

Indian Policy and the Trail of Tears

Probably nothing defined Jackson's presidency more than his efforts to "solve" what he saw as the Indian problem. Thousands of Indians lived in the South and the old Northwest, and some remained in New England and New York. Jackson, who rose to fame fighting the Creek and

Abolitionist Purses
Female antislavery societies raised many thousands of dollars to support the abolitionist cause by selling handcrafted items at giant antislavery fairs. Toys, infant clothes, quilts, caps and collars, purses, needlebooks, wax flowers, inlaid boxes: The list was endless. Items were often emblazoned with abolitionist mottoes, such as "Let My People Go," "Liberty," and "Loose the Bonds of Wickedness." These pink silk drawstring bags were decorated with pictures of the hapless slave woman, an object of compassion. Dollars raised at antislavery fairs supported the travels of abolitionist speakers as well as the publication and distribution of many antislavery books and articles.
The Daughters of the American Revolution Museum, Washington, D.C. Gift of Mrs. Erwin L. Broecker.

the Seminole tribes in the 1810s, declared in 1829 in his first message to Congress that removing Indians to territory west of the Mississippi was the only way to save them. White civilization destroyed Indian resources and thus doomed the Indians: "That this fate surely awaits them if they remain within the limits of the states does not admit of a doubt. Humanity and national honor demand that every effort should be made to avert so great a calamity." Jackson never publicly wavered from this seemingly noble theme, returning to it in his next seven annual messages.

Prior administrations had tried different policies. Starting in 1819, Congress granted $10,000 a year to various missionary associations eager to "civilize" native peoples by converting them to Christianity and encouraging English literacy and agricultural practices. Missionaries also promoted white gender customs, but Indian women were reluctant to embrace practices that accorded them less power than their tribal system did. The federal government had also pursued aggressive treaty making with many tribes, dealing with the Indians as if they were foreign nations. (See chapter 10, page 243.)

Transatlantic Abolition

Abolitionism blossomed in the United States in the 1830s, but its roots stretched back to the 1780s, both in the northern states and in Europe. Developments on both sides of the Atlantic reinforced each other, leading to a transatlantic antislavery movement with shared ideas and strategies, shared activists, shared songs, and, eventually, shared victories.

An important source of antislavery sentiment derived from the Quaker religion, with its deep convictions of human equality, so, not surprisingly, antislavery activism first spread along established Quaker networks in England, Ireland, and the United States, propelled by traveling ministers and religious pamphlet literature. In Pennsylvania, Quakers launched the Pennsylvania Society for Promoting the Abolition of Slavery, which non-Quakers Benjamin Franklin and Thomas Paine also joined. Founded in 1784, the Society worked to end slavery in that state and also petitioned the confederation congress—unsuccessfully—to put an end to American participation in the international slave trade. Quaker counterparts in the British cities of London and Plymouth formed antislavery societies that same year and embarked on a drive to ban Britain's transatlantic traffic in humans. A French group, the Société des Amis des Noirs (Society of the Friends of Blacks) sprang up in Paris in 1788. All three groups agreed that ending the overseas commerce was the critical first step in ending slavery.

The English Quakers were initially the most successful in mounting a public campaign. From 1787 to 1791, the Society for Effecting the Abolition of the Slave Trade amassed thousands of signatures on petitions and organized a boycott of slave-produced sugar from the British West Indies, a boycott said to have involved 300,000 Britons. Women, the traditional cooks of English families, were essential to that effort. In 1789, the Society scored a publicity coup by publishing two chilling illustrations of cross-sectioned slaving ships stacked with human cargo, the dark, near-naked bodies packed like sardines in each ship's hold. These images, reprinted by the thousands, created a sensation. The Reverend Thomas Clarkson of the Society distributed them in Paris and in northern U.S. cities along with a book he wrote detailing the shipboard tortures inflicted on slaves by the use of shackles, handcuffs, whips, and branding irons. The Society mobilized the resulting groundswell of antislavery sentiment to pressure Parliament. A sympathetic member of that body, the Methodist William Wilburforce, brought the anti–slave trade issue to a debate and vote in 1791; it lost.

American Quakers approached the first federal Congress, meeting in New York in 1790, with petitions requesting an immediate end to the slave trade. This action caused some puzzlement at first, because the U.S. Constitution contained a clause prohibiting the federal government from banning the "Importation of Such Persons as any of the States now existing shall think proper to admit" (that is, slaves) before the year 1808. Congressmen banished the Quaker petitions to a committee. The next day, a bolder Quaker petition, endorsed by the venerated Benjamin Franklin, arrived requesting an end to slavery as well as to the slave trade and suggesting how to accomplish it. The petitioners urged Congress to invoke the constitutional provision that empowered the government to make all laws "necessary and proper" to ensure the "general welfare" of the country, arguing that "Liberty for all Negroes" was crucial to the general welfare. This petition triggered the first debate in the new government on slavery. As in Britain's Parliament, the outcome did not bode well for slaves: By a close vote (29 to 25), Congress not only rejected this move for emancipation but also clarified its view—in a precedent-setting resolution—that slavery was under the sole regulation of the states where it existed.

Over the next three decades, the antislavery cause in Britain and in America moved forward in piecemeal fashion. Efforts to ban the slave trade in England came to parliamentary votes in 1805 and again in 1807, when a law forbidding British ships to carry Africans into slavery finally passed. (The British law was not perfect, however; it levied a fine of £100 per slave on any British captain caught with illegal cargo, creating a grim incentive for captains to shove people overboard if they faced challenge by the British navy.) A year later, in 1808, the United States also banned the slave trade, meeting the constitutional time limit. What made passage relatively easy at this time was the burgeoning natural increase of the African American population. Older slave states supported the international ban because it increased the value of their native-born slaves, who could be sold and transported to points west in the interstate slave trade.

British antislavery opinion took a new tack in the 1820s, when women became active and pushed beyond the ban on trade. Quaker widow Elizabeth Heyrick authored *Immediate not Gradual Abolition* in 1824, triggering the formation of scores of all-women societies. A massive petition campaign again bombarded Parliament, and of the 1.3 million signatures submitted in 1833, 30 percent were women's. In 1833, Parliament finally passed the Abolition of Slavery Act, which freed all slave children under age six and gradually phased out slavery for everyone older during a four-year apprenticeship. The act also provided financial compensation for owners (£20 million), a key proviso made possible by the relatively small number of slave owners in the British slaveholding colonies.

American abolitionists were also heating up the struggle in the 1830s, and as in Britain, women's involvement was accelerating. The Grimké sisters were only the most visible part of women's new activism. Many hundreds of women joined female antislavery organizations and held fairs where they sold handmade goods to raise money to promote the abolitionist cause. Both women and men abolitionists from both sides of the Atlantic traveled overseas to meet their counterparts abroad. In one worrisome moment, a Boston crowd threatened to lynch British abolitionist George Thompson and his host, William Lloyd Garrison, the editor of the *Liberator*.

British and American abolitionists came together in full force at the World Antislavery Convention, held in London in 1840. Among the 409 delegates were Clarkson, who presided; Garrison; and Philadelphia Quaker Lucretia Mott, a lifelong antislavery activist. A half dozen French delegates attended; 53 others were Americans, and the rest were from Britain and the West Indies. Only about a quarter of the attendees were Quakers. Ten days of meetings produced speeches and fact-finding reports on slavery worldwide, captured in a 600-page book detailing the proceedings. Economic and religious strategies were debated, and a plan was hatched to inform America about how British emancipation had worked. Memorials were sent to governments, and each governor of a southern U.S. state was targeted with a letter condemning the interstate slave trade. The delegates closed their meeting, exhilarated by the idea of their international congress to move toward international solutions to an international problem.

Description of a Slave Ship
This powerful and often-reprinted image combined a precise technical rendering of a British ship (normally evoking pride in Britons) with the horrors of a crowded mass of dark human flesh.

Peabody Essex Museum, Salem, MA.

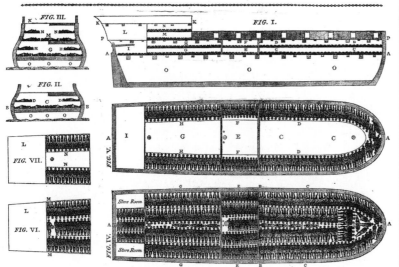

Privately, Andrew Jackson thought it was "absurd" to treat the Indians as foreigners; he saw them as subjects of the United States. Jackson also did not approve of assimilation; that way lay extinction, he said. In his 1833 annual message to Congress he wrote, "They have neither the intelligence, the industry, the moral habits, nor the desire of improvement which are essential.... Established in the midst of a superior race... they must necessarily yield to the force of circumstances and ere long disappear." Congress backed Jackson's goal and passed the Indian Removal Act of 1830, appropriating $500,000 to relocate eastern tribes west of the Mississippi. About 100 million acres of eastern land would be vacated for eventual white settlement under this act authorizing ethnic expulsion (Map 11.2).

For northern tribes, their numbers diminished by years of war, gradual removal was already well under way. But not all the Indians went quietly. In 1832 in western Illinois, Black Hawk, a leader of the Sauk and Fox Indians who

had fought with Tecumseh in the War of 1812 (see chapter 10, pages 244–45), resisted. Volunteer militias attacked and chased the Indians into southern Wisconsin, where, after several skirmishes and a deadly battle (later called the Black Hawk War), Black Hawk was captured and some 400 of his people were massacred.

Southern tribes proved even more resistant to removal. The powerful Creek, Chickasaw, Choctaw, and Cherokee tribes refused to relocate. A second Seminole War in Florida broke out as the Indians there—a mixture of Seminoles and escaped black slaves who had intermarried with the tribe—took up arms against relocation in 1836–1837.

The Cherokee of Georgia responded with a unique legal challenge to being treated as subjects. More than any other southern tribe, the 17,000 Cherokee had incorporated white political and economic practices into their tribal life. Spurred by dedicated missionaries, they had adopted written laws, including a constitution of 1827 modeled on

MAP 11.2   Indian Removal and the Trail of Tears

The federal government under President Andrew Jackson pursued a vigorous policy of Indian removal in the 1830s. Tribes were forcibly moved west to land known as Indian Territory (in present-day Oklahoma). As many as a quarter of the Cherokee Indians died in 1838 on the route known as the Trail of Tears.

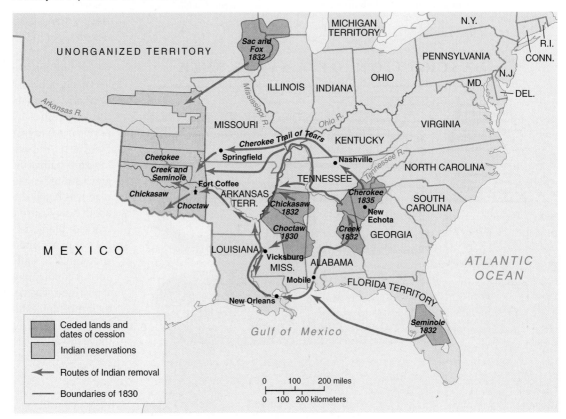

the U.S. Constitution. Two hundred of the wealthiest Cherokees had intermarried with whites and had adopted white styles of housing, dress, and cotton agriculture, including the ownership of a thousand slaves. They had developed a written alphabet and published a newspaper as well as Christian prayerbooks in their language.

In 1831, after Georgia announced it would subject the Indians to state law and seize their property, the Cherokee tribe appealed to the U.S. Supreme Court to restrain Georgia. Chief Justice John Marshall found for Georgia on the grounds that the Cherokee did not have standing to sue. When Georgia jailed two missionaries under an 1830 state law forbidding missionary aid to Indians without permission, the Cherokee brought suit again, fronting one of the missionaries as plaintiff. In the 1832 case, *Worcester v. Georgia,* the Supreme Court upheld the territorial sovereignty of the Cherokee, recognizing their existence as "a distinct community, occupying its own territory, in which the laws of Georgia can have no force." Ignoring the Supreme Court's decision, an angry President Jackson pressed the Cherokee for removal west. "If they now refuse to accept the liberal terms offered, they can only be liable for whatever evils and difficulties may arise. I feel conscious of having done my duty to my red children."

The Cherokee tribe remained in Georgia for two more years without significant violence. Then in 1835, a small, unauthorized part of the tribe signed a treaty selling all the tribal lands to the state, and Georgia rapidly resold the land to whites. But most Cherokees refused to move, so in May 1838, the deadline for voluntary evacuation, federal troops sent by Jackson's successor, Martin Van Buren, arrived to deport them. Under armed guard, the Cherokees embarked on a 1,200-mile journey west that came to be called the Trail of Tears. Nearly a quarter of the Cherokees died en route from the hardship. Survivors joined the fifteen thousand Creek, twelve thousand Choctaw, five thousand Chickasaw, and several thousand Seminole Indians also forcibly relocated to "Indian Territory" (which became, in 1907, the state of Oklahoma).

In his farewell address to the nation in 1837, Jackson again professed his belief about the benefit of Indian removal: "This unhappy race… are now placed in a situation where we may well hope that they will share in the blessings of civilization and be saved from the degradation and destruction to which they were rapidly hastening while they remained in the states." Possibly Jackson genuinely believed that exile to the West was necessary to save Indian cultures from destruction. But for the forcibly removed tribes, the costs of relocation were high.

The Tariff of Abominations and Nullification

Jackson's Indian policy happened to harmonize with the principle of **states' rights**: The president supported Georgia's right to ignore the Supreme

Cherokee Phoenix
Around 1820, Sequoyah, about forty-five years old and nephew of a Cherokee chief, invented written symbols to convey the Cherokee language. Each symbol represented a syllable of sound. In 1828, the Cherokees in New Echota, Georgia, ordered custom-made type embodying the new symbols and began printing a newspaper, the *Cherokee Phoenix,* the first newspaper published by Native Americans, printed in both English and Cherokee.
Special Collections Division, Georgetown University Library, Washington, D.C.

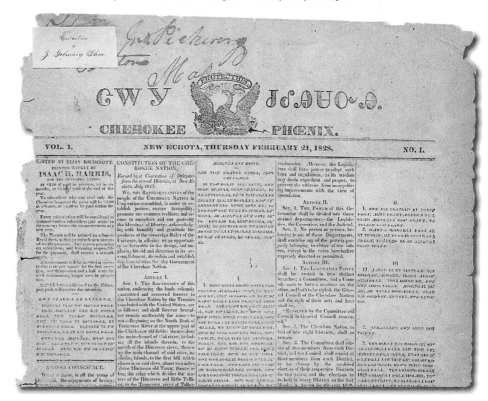

Court decision in *Worcester v. Georgia*. But in another pressing question of states' rights, Jackson contested South Carolina's attempt to ignore federal tariff policy.

Federal tariffs as high as 33 percent on imports such as textiles and iron goods had been passed in 1816 and again in 1824, in an effort to favor new American manufactures and shelter them from foreign competition as well as to raise federal revenue. Some southern congressmen opposed the steep tariffs, fearing they would decrease overseas shipping and hurt cotton exports. During John Quincy Adams's administration (1825–1829), tariff policy generated heated debate. In 1828, Congress passed a revised tariff that came to be known as the Tariff of Abominations. A bundle of conflicting duties— some as high as 50 percent—the legislation had provisions that pleased and angered every economic and sectional interest. Assembled mostly by southern congressmen, who loaded it with duties on raw materials needed by New England, it also contained protectionist elements favored by northern manufacturers.

South Carolina in particular suffered from the Tariff of Abominations. Worldwide prices for cotton had declined in the late 1820s, and the falloff in shipping caused by the high tariffs further hurt the South. In 1828, a group of South Carolina politicians headed by John C. Calhoun advanced a doctrine called **nullification**. The Union, they argued, was a confederation of states that had yielded some but not all power to the federal government. When Congress overstepped its powers, states had the right to nullify Congress's acts; as precedents they pointed to the Virginia and Kentucky Resolutions of 1798, which had attempted to invalidate the Alien and Sedition Acts (see chapter 9). Congress had erred in using tariff policy as an instrument to benefit specific industries, the South Carolinians claimed; tariffs should be used only to raise revenue.

On assuming the presidency in 1829, Jackson ignored the South Carolina statement of nullification and shut out Calhoun, his new vice president, from influence or power. Tariff revisions in early 1832 brought little relief to the South. Sensing futility, Calhoun resigned from the vice presidency in 1832 and accepted election by the South Carolina legislature to a seat in the U.S. Senate, where he could better argue his state's antitariff stance. Strained to their limit, the South Carolina leaders took the radical step of declaring the federal tariffs to be null and void in their state as of February 1,

1833. Finally, the constitutional crisis was out in the open.

Opting for a dramatic confrontation, Jackson sent armed ships to Charleston's harbor and threatened to invade the state. He pushed through Congress a bill, called the Force Bill, defining the Carolina stance as treason and authorizing military action to collect federal tariffs. At the same time, Congress moved quickly to pass a revised tariff more acceptable to the South. The conciliating Senator Henry Clay rallied support for a moderate bill that gradually reduced tariffs down to the 1816 level. On March 1, 1833, Congress passed both the new tariff and the Force Bill. South Carolina responded by withdrawing its nullification of the old tariff—and then nullifying the Force Bill. It was a symbolic gesture, since Jackson's show of muscle was no longer necessary. Both sides were satisfied with the immediate outcome. Federal power had prevailed over a dangerous assertion of states' rights, and South Carolina got the lower tariff it wanted.

Yet the question of federal power versus states' rights was far from settled. The implied threat behind nullification was secession, a position articulated in 1832 by some South Carolinians whose concerns went beyond tariff policy. The growing voice of antislavery activism in the North threatened the South's economic system. If and when a northern-dominated federal government decided to end slavery, the South Carolinians thought, the South must have the right to remove itself from the Union.

The Bank War and the Panic of 1837

Along with the tariff and nullification, President Jackson fought another political battle over the Bank of the United States. After riding out the panic of 1819, the bank finally prospered. It handled the federal government's deposits, extended credit and loans, and issued banknotes—by 1830 the most stable currency in the country. Now having twenty-nine branches, it benefited the whole nation. Jackson, however, did not find the bank's functions sufficiently valuable to offset his criticism of the concept of a national bank. In his first two annual messages to Congress, in 1829 and 1830, Jackson claimed that the bank concentrated undue economic power in the hands of a few.

National Republican (Whig) senators Daniel Webster and Henry Clay decided to force the issue. They convinced the bank to apply for charter renewal in 1832, well before the fall election, even though the existing charter ran until 1836. They fully expected that Congress's renewal would force Jackson to follow through on his rhetoric with a veto, that the unpopular veto would cause Jackson to lose the election, and that the bank would survive on an override vote from a new Congress swept into power on the anti-Jackson tide.

At first the plan seemed to work. The bank applied for rechartering, Congress voted to renew, and Jackson, angry over being manipulated, issued his veto. But it was a brilliantly written veto, full of fierce language about the privileges of the moneyed elite who oppress the democratic masses in order to enrich themselves. "Many of our rich men have not been content with equal protection and equal benefits, but have besought us to make them richer by act of Congress," Jackson wrote.

Clay and his supporters found Jackson's economic ideas so absurd and his language of class antagonism so shocking that they distributed thousands of copies of the bank veto as campaign material for their own party. A confident Henry Clay headed his party's ticket for the presidency. But the plan backfired. Jackson's translation of the bank controversy into a language of class antagonism and egalitarian ideals strongly resonated with many Americans. Old Hickory won the election easily, gaining 55 percent of the popular vote and a lopsided electoral college vote of 219 to 49. The Jackson party still controlled Congress, so no override was possible. The second Bank of the United States would cease to exist after 1836.

Jackson, however, wanted to destroy the bank sooner. Calling it a "monster," he ordered the sizable federal deposits to be removed from its vaults and redeposited into Democratic-inclined state banks. In retaliation, the Bank of the United States raised interest rates and called in loans. This action caused a brief decline in the economy in 1833 and actually enhanced Jackson's claim that the bank was too powerful for the good of the country.

Unleashed and unregulated, the economy in 1834 went into high gear. Perhaps only a small part of the problem arose from irresponsible banking practices. Just at this moment, an excess of silver from Mexican mines made its way into American banks, giving bankers license to print ever more banknotes. Inflation soared from 1834 to 1837; prices of basic goods rose more than 50 percent. States quickly chartered many hundreds of new private banks. Each bank issued its own banknotes and set interest rates as high as the market would bear. Entrepreneurs borrowed and invested money, much of it funneled into privately financed railroads and canals.

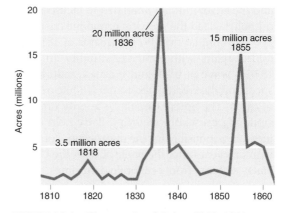

FIGURE 11.1 Western Land Sales, 1810–1860
Land sales peaked in the 1810s, 1830s, and 1850s as Americans rushed to speculate in western lands sold by the federal government. The surges in 1818 and 1836 demonstrate the volatile, speculative economy that suddenly collapsed in the panics of 1819 and 1837.

The market in western land sales heated up. In 1834, about 4.5 million acres of the public domain had been sold, the highest annual volume since the peak year 1819; by 1836, the total reached an astonishing 20 million acres (Figure 11.1). Some of this was southern land in Mississippi and Louisiana, which slave owners rushed to bring under cultivation, but much more was in the North, where land offices were deluged with buyers. The Jackson administration worried that the purchasers were overwhelmingly eastern capitalists, land speculators instead of self-reliant **yeoman** farmers who intended to settle on the land.

In one respect, the economy attained an admirable goal: The national debt disappeared, and, for the first and only time in American history, from 1835 to 1837, the government had a monetary surplus. But much of it consisted of questionable bank currencies—"bloated, diseased" currencies, in Jackson's vivid terminology.

Jackson decided to restrain the economy. In 1836, the Treasury Department issued the Specie Circular, an order that public land could be purchased only with hard money, federally coined gold and silver. In response, bankers started to reduce their loans, fearing a general contraction of the economy. Compounding the difficulty, the Bank of England also now insisted on hard-money payments for American loans, which had grown large since 1831 because of a trade imbalance. Failures in various crop markets, a downturn in cotton prices on the international market, and the silver glut, all unrelated to Jackson's fiscal policies, fed the growing economic crisis.

The familiar events of the panic of 1819 unfolded again, with terrifying rapidity. In April 1837, a wave of bank and business failures ensued, and the credit market tumbled like a house of cards. The Specie Circular was only one precipitating cause, but the Whig Party held it and Jackson responsible for the depression. For more than five years after the panic of 1837, the United States suffered from economic hard times.

Van Buren's One-Term Presidency

The election of 1836, which preceded the panic by six months, demonstrated the transformation of the Democrats from coalition to party. Jackson's personality had stamped the elections of 1824, 1828, and 1832. By 1836, the party apparatus was sufficiently developed to support itself. Local and state committees existed throughout the country. Democratic candidates ran in every state election, succeeding even in old Federalist states like Maine and New Hampshire. More than four hundred newspapers declared themselves Democratic. In 1836, the Democrats repeated an innovation begun in 1832: holding a national convention. They nominated Vice President Martin Van Buren of New York for president.

Sophisticated party organization was Martin Van Buren's specialty. Nicknamed the "Little Magician" for his consummate political skills, the New Yorker had built his career by pioneering many of the loyalty-enhancing techniques the Democrats used in the 1830s. After serving as senator and then governor, he became Jackson's secretary of state in 1828. Four years later he replaced Calhoun as Jackson's running mate. His eight years in the volatile Jackson administration required the full measure of his political deftness as he sought repeatedly to save Jackson from both his enemies and his own obstinacy.

Van Buren was a backroom politician, not a popular public figure, and the Whigs hoped that he might be defeatable. In many states, Whigs had captured high office in 1834, shedding the awkward National Republican label and developing statewide organizations to rival those of the Democrats. However, no figure commanded nationwide support, and so three regional candidates opposed Van Buren in 1836. Senator Daniel Webster of Massachusetts could deliver New England, home to reformers, merchants, and manufacturers; Senator Hugh Lawson White of Tennessee attracted proslavery (and thus anti–Van Buren) voters in the South; and the aging General William Henry Harrison of Indiana, memorable for his Indian war heroics in 1811, pulled in the western, anti-Indian vote. Not one of the three candidates could have won the presidency, but together they came close to denying Van Buren a majority vote. Their combined strength drew many Whigs into office at the state level. In the end, Van Buren had 170 electoral votes, while the other three received a total of 113.

Van Buren took office in March 1837, and a month later the panic hit. The new president called a special session of Congress to consider creating an independent treasury system to fulfill some of the functions of the defunct Bank of the United States. Such a system, funded by government deposits, would deal only in hard money, forcing commercial banks to restrict their issuance of paper currency, and it would not make loans, thus avoiding the danger of speculative meddling in the economy. In short, an independent treasury system could exert a powerful moderating influence on inflation and the credit market without itself being directly involved in the market. But Van Buren encountered strong resistance in Congress, even from Democrats. The treasury system finally won approval in 1840; by then, however, Van Buren's chances of a second term in office were virtually nil because of the tumultuous economy.

In 1840, the Whigs settled on William Henry Harrison, sixty-seven, to oppose Van Buren. The campaign drew on voter involvement as no presidential campaign ever had. The Whigs borrowed tricks from the Democrats: Harrison was touted as a common man born in a log cabin (in reality he was born on a Virginia plantation), and raucous campaign parades featured toy log cabins held aloft. His Indian-fighting days, now thirty years behind him, were played up to give him a Jacksonian aura. Whigs staged festive rallies all over the country, drumming up mass appeal with candlelight parades and song shows, and women participated in rallies as never before. Some 78 percent of eligible voters cast ballots—the highest percentage ever in American history. Harrison took 53 percent of the popular vote and won a resounding 234 electoral college votes to Van Buren's 60. A Democratic editor lamented, "We have taught them how to conquer us!"

REVIEW   How did Jackson's vision of democracy shape the policies of the Democratic Party?

Conclusion:
The Age of Jackson
or the Era of Reform?

Harrison's election closed a decade that had brought the common man and democracy to the forefront of American politics. Economic transformations loom large in explaining the fast-paced changes of the 1830s. Transportation advances put goods and people in circulation, augmenting urban growth and helping to create a national culture, and water-powered manufacturing began to change the face of wage labor. Trade and banking mushroomed, and western lands once occupied by Indians were auctioned off in a landslide of sales. Two economic downturns, the panics of 1819 and 1837, offered sobering lessons about speculative fever.

Andrew Jackson symbolized this age of opportunity for many. His fame as an aggressive general, Indian fighter, champion of the common man, and defender of slavery attracted growing numbers of voters to the emergent Democratic Party, which championed personal liberty, free competition, and egalitarian opportunity for all white men.

Jackson's constituency was challenged by a small but vocal segment of the population troubled by serious moral problems that Jacksonians preferred to ignore. Reformers drew sustenance from the message of the Second Great Awakening: that all men and women are free to choose salvation and that personal and societal sins can be overcome. Reformers targeted personal vices (illicit sex, intemperance) and social problems (prostitution, poverty, and slavery), and joined forces with evangelicals and wealthy lawyers and merchants North or South who appreciated a national bank and protective tariffs. The Whig Party was the party of activist moralism and state-sponsored entrepreneurship.

National politics in the 1830s were more divisive than at any other time since the 1790s. The new party system of Democrats and Whigs reached far deeper into the electorate than had the Federalists and Republicans. Stagecoaches and steamboats carried newspapers with their political coverage from the city to the backwoods, politicizing voters and creating party loyalty. Politics acquired immediacy and excitement, causing four out of five white men to cast ballots in 1840.

High rates of voter participation would continue into the 1840s and 1850s. Unprecedented urban growth, westward expansion, and early industrialism marked those decades, sustaining the Jacksonian-Whig split in the electorate. But critiques of slavery, concerns for free labor, and an emerging protest against women's second-class citizenship complicated the political scene of the 1840s, leading to third-party political movements. One of these third parties, called the Republican Party, would achieve dominance in 1860 with the election of an Illinois lawyer, Abraham Lincoln, to the presidency.

Suggestions for Further Reading

Patricia Cline Cohen, *The Murder of Helen Jewett: The Life and Death of a Prostitute in Nineteenth-Century New York* (1998). A true crime story of the underside of 1830s urban life, revealing in detail the sexual subculture protested by the Female Moral Reformers.

Daniel Feller, *The Jacksonian Promise: America, 1815–1840* (1995). An excellent one-volume narrative describing the energy and optimism of Jacksonian America's politics and society.

Paul E. Johnson and Sean Wilentz, *The Kingdom of Matthias: A Story of Sex and Salvation in Nineteenth-Century America* (1994). The bizarre but instructive tale of a self-proclaimed prophet operating at the margins of the Second Great Awakening.

Richard S. Newman, *The Transformation of American Abolitionism: Fighting Slavery in the Early Republic* (2002). An absorbing history of antislavery action in the United States from the 1780s to 1840, with close attention to race and gender.

Merrill D. Peterson, *The Great Triumvirate: Webster, Clay, and Calhoun* (1987). A vivid portrait of three powerful senators who also helped to define Jackson's decade.

Charles G. Sellers, *The Market Revolution: Jacksonian America, 1815–1846* (1991). A senior scholar's comprehensive synthesis of the economic, cultural, and political themes of the period.

▶ **For more books about topics in this chapter,** see the Online Study Guide at bedfordstmartins.com/roarkcompact.

▶ **For additional firsthand accounts of this period,** see Chapter 11 in Michael Johnson, ed., *Reading the American Past,* Third Edition.

▶ **For Web sites and documents related to topics and places in this chapter,** see "HistoryLinks," "DocLinks," and "PlaceLinks" at bedfordstmartins.com/roarkcompact.

REVIEWING THE CHAPTER

Follow these steps to review and strengthen your understanding of the chapter.

STEP 1: *Study the **Key Terms** and **Timeline** to identify the significance of each item listed.*

STEP 2: *Answer the **Review Questions**, drawing on key terms and dates to support your answers.*

STEP 3: *Drawing on the Key Terms, Timeline, and Review Questions, answer the broader **Making Connections** questions.*

KEY TERMS

Who

Andrew Jackson (p. 259)
Robert Fulton (p. 261)
John Quincy Adams (p. 266)
Charles Grandison Finney (p. 270)
David Walker (p. 272)
Maria Stewart (p. 272)
William Lloyd Garrison (p. 272)
Angelina and Sarah Grimké (p. 272)
Black Hawk (p. 276)
John C. Calhoun (p. 278)
Henry Clay (p. 279)
Martin Van Buren (p. 280)
William Henry Harrison (p. 280)

What

Erie Canal (p. 261)
Baltimore and Ohio Railroad (p. 262)
Lowell mills (p. 262)
second Bank of the United States (p. 264)
panic of 1819 (p. 264)
Hickory Clubs (p. 265)
Bucktails (p. 266)
Whigs (p. 266)
Democrats (p. 266)
Maysville Road veto (p. 267)
Second Great Awakening (p. 268)
separate spheres (p. 268)
American Temperance Society (p. 270)
American Temperance Union (p. 271)
Female Moral Reform Society (p. 271)

American Colonization Society (p. 272)
National Negro Convention (p. 272)
Liberator (p. 272)
New England Anti-Slavery Society (p. 272)
Indian Removal Act of 1830 (p. 276)
Black Hawk War (p. 276)
second Seminole War (p. 276)
Worcester v. Georgia (p. 277)
Trail of Tears (p. 277)
Tariff of Abominations (p. 278)
nullification (p. 278)
Force Bill (p. 278)
Specie Circular (p. 279)
panic of 1837 (p. 280)

TIMELINE

◄ **1807** • Robert Fulton's boat *Clermont* sets off steamboat craze.

1816 • Second Bank of the United States chartered.

1817 • American Colonization Society founded.

1818 • National Road links Baltimore to western Virginia.

1819 • Economic panic.

1821 • Mill town of Lowell, Massachusetts, founded.

1825 • Erie Canal in New York completed.

1826 • American Temperance Society founded.
• Schuylkill Canal in Pennsylvania completed.

1828 • Congress passes Tariff of Abominations.
• Democrat Andrew Jackson elected president.

REVIEW QUESTIONS

1. Why did the United States experience a market revolution after 1815? (pp. 260–65)

2. Why did Jackson defeat John Quincy Adams so dramatically in the 1828 election? (pp. 265–68)

3. How did evangelical Protestantism contribute to the social reform movements of the 1830s? (pp. 268–73)

4. How did Jackson's vision of democracy shape the policies of the Democratic Party? (pp. 273–80)

MAKING CONNECTIONS

1. Andrew Jackson's presidency coincided with important changes in American politics. Discuss how Jackson benefited from, and contributed to, the vibrant political culture of the 1830s. Cite specific national developments in your answer.

2. Describe the market revolution that began in the 1810s. How did it affect Americans' work and domestic lives? In your answer, be sure to consider how gender contributed to these developments.

3. While a volatile economy buffeted the nation, some Americans in the 1830s looked to reform the nation. Discuss the objectives and strategies of two reform movements. What was the relationship of these reform movements to larger political and economic trends of the 1830s?

4. Describe Andrew Jackson's response to the "Indian problem" during his presidency. How did his policies revise or continue earlier federal policies toward Native Americans? How did Native Americans respond to Jackson's actions?

> ► FOR PRACTICE QUIZZES, A CUSTOMIZED STUDY PLAN, AND OTHER STUDY TOOLS, see the Online Study Guide at bedfordstmartins.com/roarkcompact.

1829 • David Walker's *Appeal ... to the Coloured Citizens of the World* published.
• Baltimore and Ohio Railroad begun.

   1830 • Indian Removal Act.

      1831 • William Lloyd Garrison starts the *Liberator*.
• Charles G. Finney preaches in Rochester, New York.

         1832 • Massacre of Sauk and Fox Indians under Chief Black Hawk.
• *Worcester v. Georgia*.
• Jackson vetoes Bank of the United States charter.
• New England Anti-Slavery Society founded.

           1833 • Nullification declared in South Carolina.
• New York and Philadelphia antislavery societies founded.
• New York Female Moral Reform Society founded.
• Female mill workers strike in Lowell, Massachusetts.

               1836 • Jackson issues Specie Circular.
• Democrat Martin Van Buren elected president.

                  1837 • Economic panic.

                    1838 • Trail of Tears: Cherokees forced to relocate west.

                       1840 • Whig William Henry Harrison elected president.

GOLD NUGGETS
Gold! Nuggets like these scooped from a California river drove easterners crazy with excitement. A quarter of a million people joined the great rush for western riches in the five years after gold's discovery in 1848. Men from the East and around the world sought to escape routine jobs and mundane lives by "making their pile" in California. The carnival that was the gold rush fulfilled the hopes of only a few, but the rest participated in one of the great adventures of the nineteenth century and rarely regretted their experiences.
The Oakland Museum.

The New West and Free North

1840–1860

EARLY IN NOVEMBER 1842, Abraham Lincoln and his new wife, Mary, moved into their first home in Springfield, Illinois, a rented room measuring eight by fourteen feet on the second floor of the Globe Tavern, the nicest place Abraham had ever lived. Mary Todd Lincoln had grown up in Lexington, Kentucky, attended by slaves in the elegant home of her father, a prosperous merchant, banker, and politician. The small room above the Globe Tavern was the worst place she had ever lived. Fewer than twenty years later, in March 1861, the Lincolns moved into what would prove to be their last home, the presidential mansion in Washington, D.C. Abraham Lincoln climbed from the Globe Tavern to the White House by relentless work, unslaked ambition, and immense talent, traits he had honed since boyhood.

Born in a Kentucky log cabin in 1809, Lincoln grew up on small, struggling farms as his family migrated westward. His father, Thomas, had left Virginia, where he had been born, and settled in Kentucky. Thomas Lincoln never learned to read or, as his son recalled, "never did more in the way of writing than to bunglingly sign his own name." Lincoln's mother, Nancy, could neither read nor write. In December 1816, Thomas Lincoln moved his young family from Kentucky to the Indiana wilderness. They lived for two frozen months in a crude lean-to while Thomas, a skilled carpenter, built a cabin. On the Indiana farmstead, Abraham learned the arts of agriculture practiced by families throughout the nation. Although only eight years old, he "had an axe put into his hands at once" and used it "almost constantly" for the next fifteen years. When he could be spared from work, the boy attended school, less than a year in all. "There was absolutely nothing to excite ambition for education," Lincoln recollected. In contrast, Mary Todd, his future wife, received ten years of schooling in Lexington's best academies for young women.

By 1830, Thomas Lincoln decided to move farther west and start over again. The Lincolns hitched up the family oxen and headed to central Illinois, where they built another log cabin. The next spring Thomas Lincoln moved yet again, but this time Abraham stayed behind and set out on his own, a "friendless, uneducated, penniless boy," as he described himself.

By dogged striving, Lincoln gained an education and the respect of his Illinois neighbors, although a steady income eluded him for years. He and Mary received help from her father, including eighty acres of land and an allowance of about $1,100 for six years that helped them move out of their room above the Globe Tavern. Lincoln eventually built a thriving law practice in Springfield

Abraham Lincoln's Hat
Abraham Lincoln wore this stovepipe hat, made of beaver pelt, during his years as president of the United States. Stovepipe hats were worn by established, respectable, middle-class men in the 1850s. Workingmen and farmers would have felt out of place wearing such a hat, except perhaps on special occasions like weddings or funerals. Growing up in Kentucky, Indiana, and Illinois, Lincoln may have seen stovepipe hats on the leading men of his community, but he probably never owned one until he became an aspiring Illinois lawyer and politician. Wearing such a hat was a mark that one had achieved a certain success in life, in Lincoln's case the enormous social distance he had traveled from his backwoods origins to the White House. But even as president he continued a backwoods practice he had begun as a young postmaster in New Salem, Illinois, using his hat as a place to store letters and papers. Lincoln's law partner William Herndon termed Lincoln's hat "an extraordinary receptacle [that] served as his desk and memorandum book."

Smithsonian Institution, Washington, D.C.

and served in the Illinois legislature and then in Congress. His political activity and hard-driving ambition ultimately propelled him into the White House, the first president born west of the Appalachian Mountains.

Like Lincoln, millions of Americans believed they could make something of themselves, whatever their origins, so long as they were willing to work. Individuals who refused to work—who were lazy, undisciplined, or foolish—had only themselves to blame if they failed. Work was a prerequisite for success, not a guarantee. The promise of rewards from hard work spurred efforts that shaped the contours of America, pushing the boundaries of the nation south to the Rio Grande, north to the Great Lakes, and ever westward to the Pacific Ocean. During his presidency, Lincoln talked about moving west to California at the end of his term. The economic, political, and geographic expansion that Lincoln exemplified raised anew the question of whether slavery should also move west, the question that Lincoln and other Americans confronted again and again following the Mexican-American War, yet another outgrowth of the nation's ceaseless westward movement.

The Westward Movement

The 1840s ushered in a new era of rapid westward movement. Until then, the overwhelming majority of Americans lived east of the Mississippi River. Native Americans inhabited the plains, deserts, and rugged coasts to the west. The British claimed Oregon Country, and the Mexicans held the Southwest. But by 1850, the boundaries of the United States stretched to the Pacific, and by 1860, the great migration had carried four million Americans west of the Mississippi River.

The nation's revolution in transportation and communication, its swelling population, and its booming economy propelled the westward surge. But the emigrants themselves conquered the continent. **Frontier** settlers craving land took the soil and then, with the exception of the Mormons, lobbied their government to acquire the territories they settled in. The human cost of westward expansion was high. The young Mexican nation lost half of its territory. Two centuries of Indian wars east of the Mississippi ended during the 1830s, but the old, fierce struggle between native inhabitants and invaders continued for another half century in the West.

Manifest Destiny

Most Americans believed that the superiority of their institutions and white culture bestowed on them a God-given right to spread their civilization across the continent. They imagined the West as a howling wilderness, empty and undeveloped. If they recognized Indians and Mexicans at all, they dismissed them as primitive drags on progress who would have to be redeemed, shoved aside, or exterminated. The sense of mission and superiority had been bolstered by the United States's amazing success. The West needed the civilizing power of the hammer and plow, the ballot box and pulpit, that had transformed the East, most Americans believed.

In 1845, New York journalist John L. O'Sullivan coined the term **manifest destiny** as the latest justification for white settlers to take the land they coveted. O'Sullivan called on Americans to resist any foreign power—British, French, or Mexican—that attempted to thwart "the fulfillment of our manifest destiny to overspread the continent allotted by Providence for the free development of our yearly multiplying millions…[and] for the development of the great experiment of liberty and federative self-government entrusted to us." Almost overnight, the magic phrase *manifest destiny* swept the nation and provided an ideological shield for conquering the West.

As important as national pride and racial arrogance were to manifest destiny, economic gain made up its core. Land hunger drew hundreds of thousands of average Americans westward. Some politicians, moreover, had become convinced that national prosperity depended on capturing the rich trade of the Far East. To trade with Asia, the United States needed the Pacific coast ports that stretched from San Diego to Puget Sound. No one was more eager to extend American trade in the Pacific than Missouri's Senator Thomas Hart Benton. "The sun of civilization must shine across the sea: socially and commercially," he declared. The United States and Asia must "talk together, and trade together. Commerce is a great civilizer." In the 1840s, American economic expansion came wrapped in the rhetoric of uplift and civilization.

Oregon and the Overland Trail

Oregon Country—a vast region bounded on the west by the Pacific, on the east by the Rockies, on the south by the forty-second parallel, and on the north by Russian Alaska—caused the pulse of American expansionists to race (Map 12.1). But the British also coveted the area. They argued their claim lay with Sir Francis Drake's discovery of the Oregon coast in 1579. Americans countered with historic claims of their own. Unable to agree, the United States and Great Britain decided in 1818 on "joint occupation" that would leave Oregon "free and open" to settlement by both countries. A handful of American fur traders and "mountain men" roamed the region in the 1820s, but in the 1830s and 1840s expansionists made Oregon Country an early target of manifest destiny.

By the late 1830s, settlers began to trickle along the Oregon Trail (see Map 12.1). The first wagon trains headed west in 1841, and by 1843 about 1,000 emigrants a year set out from Independence, Missouri. By 1869, when the first transcontinental railroad was completed, approximately 350,000 migrants had traveled west to the Pacific in wagon trains.

Emigrants encountered Plains Indians, a quarter of a million Native Americans who populated the area between the Rocky Mountains and the Mississippi River. Some were farmers who lived peaceful, sedentary lives, but a majority—the Sioux, Cheyenne, Shoshone, and Arapaho of the central Plains and the Kiowa, Wichita, and Comanche in the southern Plains—were horse-mounted, nomadic, nonagricultural peoples whose warriors symbolized the "savage Indian" in the minds of whites.

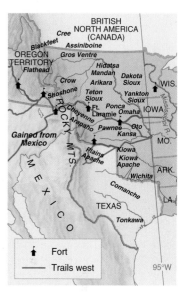

Plains Indians and Trails West in the 1840s and 1850s

Horses, which had been brought to North America by Spaniards in the sixteenth century, permitted the Plains tribes to become highly mobile hunters of buffalo. They came to depend on buffalo for most of their food, clothing, shelter, and fuel. Competition for buffalo led to war between the tribes. Young men were introduced to warfare early, learning to ride ponies at breakneck speed while firing off arrows and, later, rifles with astounding accuracy. "A Comanche on his feet is out of his element," observed western artist George Catlin, "but the moment he lays his hands upon his horse, his *face* even becomes handsome, and he gracefully flies away like a different being."

Plains Indians struck fear in the hearts of whites on the wagon trains. But Native Americans had far more to fear from whites. Indians killed fewer than 400 emigrants on the trail between 1840 and 1860, while whites brought alcohol and deadly epidemics of smallpox, measles, cholera, and scarlet fever. Moreover, whites killed the buffalo, often slaughtering them

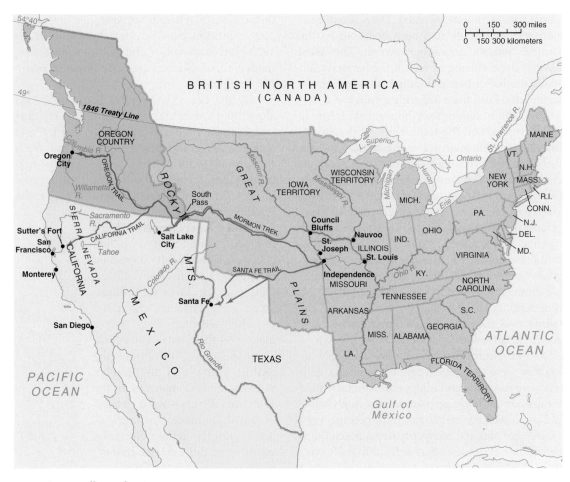

MAP 12.1 Trails to the West
In the 1830s, wagon trains began snaking their way to the Southwest and the Pacific coast. Deep ruts, some of which can still be seen today, soon marked the most popular routes.

for sport. Buffalo still numbered some twelve million in 1860, but the herds were shrinking rapidly, intensifying conflict among the Plains Indians.

Emigrants insisted that the federal government provide them more protection. The government responded by constructing a chain of forts along the Oregon Trail. More important, it adopted a new Indian policy: "concentration." First, the government rescinded the "permanent" buffer it had granted the Indians west of the ninety-fifth meridian. Then, in 1851, it called the Plains tribes to a conference at Fort Laramie, Wyoming. Some ten thousand Indians showed up, hopeful that something could be done to protect them from the ravages of the wagon trains. Instead, U.S. government negotiators

persuaded the chiefs to sign agreements that cleared a wide corridor for wagon trains by restricting Native Americans to specific areas that whites promised they would never violate. This policy of concentration became the seedbed for the subsequent policy of reservations. But whites would not keep out of Indian territory, and Indians would not easily give up their traditional ways of life. Competition meant warfare for decades to come.

Still, Indians threatened emigrants less than life on the trail did. The men, women, and children who headed west each spring could count on at least six months of grueling travel. With nearly two thousand miles to go and traveling no more than fifteen miles a day, the pioneers endured parching heat, drought, treacherous rivers, disease, physical and emotional exhaustion, and, if the snows closed the mountain passes before they got through, freezing and starvation. Women sometimes faced the dangers of trailside childbirth. It was said that a person could walk from Missouri to the Pacific stepping only on the graves of those who had died heading west. Such tribulations led one miserable woman, trying to keep her children dry in a rainstorm and to calm them as they listened to Indian shouts, to wonder "what had possessed my husband, anyway, that he should have thought of bringing us away out through this God forsaken country."

Men usually found Oregon "one of the greatest countries in the world." From "the Cascade mountains to the Pacific, the whole country can be cultivated," exclaimed one settler. When women reached Oregon, they found a wilderness. Things were in a "primitive state." One young wife set up housekeeping with her new husband with only one stew kettle and three knives. Necessity blurred the traditional division between men's and women's work. "I am maid of all traids," one busy woman remarked in 1853. Work seemed unending. "I am a very old woman," declared twenty-nine-year-old Sarah Everett. "My face is thin sunken and wrinkled, my hands bony withered and hard." Another settler observed, "A woman that can not endure almost as much as a horse has no business here." Despite the ordeal of the trail and the difficulties of starting from scratch, emigrants kept coming.

***Kee-O-Kuk, the Watchful Fox, Chief of the Tribe*, George Catlin, 1835**
In the 1830s, Pennsylvania-born artist George Catlin traveled the West painting Native American portraits, rituals, and landscapes. Although not the first artist to paint Indians, he was the first to portray them in their own environments and one of the few to present them as human beings, not savages. Convinced that western Indian cultures would soon disappear, Catlin sought to document Indian life through hundreds of paintings and prints. Keokuk, chief of the Sac and Fox, struggled with the warrior Black Hawk about the proper strategy for dealing with whites. Black Hawk fought American expansion; Keokuk believed war was fruitless and signed over land in Illinois, Missouri, and Wisconsin.
Smithsonian American Art Institution, Washington, D.C. Gift of Mrs. Joseph Harrison Jr.

The Mormon Exodus

Not every wagon train heading west was bound for the Pacific Slope. One remarkable group of religious emigrants halted near the Great Salt Lake in what was then Mexican territory. The Mormons deliberately chose the remote site as a refuge. After years of persecution in the East, they fled west to find religious freedom and communal security.

In 1830, Joseph Smith Jr., who was only twenty-four, published *The Book of Mormon* and founded the Church of Jesus Christ of Latter-Day Saints (the Mormons). A decade earlier, the upstate New York farm boy had begun to experience revelations that were followed, he said, by a visit from an angel who led him to golden tablets buried near his home. With the aid of magic stones, Smith translated the mysterious language on the tablets to produce *The Book of Mormon*. It told the story of an ancient Christian civilization in the New World and predicted the appearance of an American prophet who would reestablish Jesus Christ's undefiled kingdom in America. Converts, attracted to the promise of a pure faith in the midst of **antebellum** America's social turmoil and rampant materialism, flocked to the new church.

Neighbors branded Mormons heretics and drove Smith and his followers from New York to Ohio, then to Missouri, and finally in 1839 to Nauvoo, Illinois, where they built a prosperous community. But dissenters within the church accused Smith of advocating plural marriage (polygamy). Non-Mormons caught wind of the controversy and eventually arrested Smith and his brother. On June 27, 1844, a mob stormed the jail and shot both men dead.

Pioneer Family on the Trail West

In 1860, W. G. Chamberlain photographed these unidentified travelers momentarily at rest by the upper Arkansas River in Colorado. We do not know their fates, but we can hope that they fared better than the Sager family: Henry, Naomi, and their six children, who set out from St. Joseph, Missouri, in 1844. "Father," one of Henry and Naomi's daughters remembered, "was one of those restless men who are not content to remain in one place long at a time. [He] had been talking of going to Texas. But mother, hearing much said about the healthfulness of Oregon, preferred to go there." Still far from Oregon, Henry Sager died of fever; twenty-six days later, Naomi died, leaving seven children, the last delivered on the trail. The Sager children, under the care of other families in the wagon train, pressed on. After traveling 2,000 miles in seven months, the migrants arrived in Oregon, where Marcus and Narcissa Whitman, whose own daughter had drowned, adopted all seven of the Sager children.

Denver Public Library, Western History Division # F3226.

For more help analyzing this image, see the visual activity for this chapter in the Online Study Guide at **bedfordstmartins.com/roarkcompact**.

The embattled church turned to an extraordinary new leader, Brigham Young, who immediately began to plan a great exodus. In 1846, traveling in 3,700 wagons, 12,000 Mormons made their way to eastern Iowa; the following year they arrived at their new home beside the Great Salt Lake. Young described the region as a barren waste, "the paradise of the lizard, the cricket and the rattlesnake." Within ten years, however, the Mormons developed an irrigation system that made the desert bloom. They accomplished the feat through cooperative labor, not the individualistic and competitive enterprise common among most emigrants. Under Young's stern leadership, the Mormons built a thriving community.

In 1850, the Mormon kingdom was annexed to the United States as Utah Territory. The nation's attention focused on Utah in 1852 when Brigham Young announced that many Mormons practiced polygamy. Although only one Mormon man in five had more than one wife (Young had twenty-three), Young's statement caused a popular outcry that forced the U.S. government to establish its authority in Utah. In 1857, 2,500 U.S. troops invaded Salt Lake City in what was known as the Mormon War. The bloodless occupation illustrates that most Americans viewed the Mormons as a threat to American morality, law, and institutions. The invasion did not dislodge the Mormon Church from its central place in Utah, however, and for years to come most Americans perceived the Mormon settlement as strange and suitably isolated.

The Mexican Borderlands

In the Mexican Southwest, westward-moving Anglo-American pioneers confronted northern-moving Spanish-speaking frontiersmen. On this frontier as elsewhere, national cultures, interests, and aspirations collided. Since 1821, when Mexico won its independence from Spain, the Mexican flag had flown over the vast expanse that stretched from the Gulf of Mexico to the Pacific and from Oregon Country to Guatemala (Map 12.2). Mexico's borders remained ill defined, and its northern provinces were sparsely populated. Moreover, severe problems plagued the young nation: civil wars, economic crises, quarrels with the Roman Catholic Church, and devastating raids by the Comanche, Apache, and Kiowa. Mexico found it increasingly difficult to defend its borderlands, especially when faced with a northern neighbor convinced of its superiority and bent on territorial acquisition.

The American assault began quietly. In the 1820s, Anglo-American trappers, traders, and settlers drifted into Mexico's far northern provinces. Santa Fe, a remote outpost in the province of New Mexico, became a magnet for American enterprise. Each spring, American traders gathered at Independence, Missouri, for the long trek southwest along the Santa Fe Trail

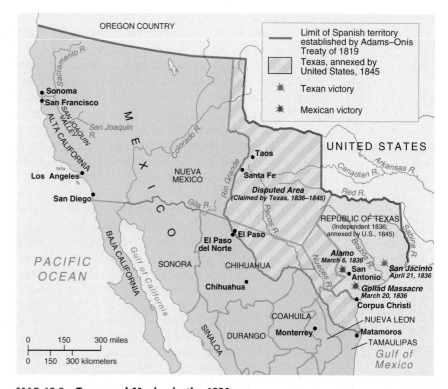

MAP 12.2 Texas and Mexico in the 1830s
As Americans spilled into lightly populated and loosely governed northern Mexico, Texas and then other Mexican provinces became contested territory.

(see Map 12.1). They crammed their wagons with inexpensive American manufactured goods and returned home with Mexican silver, furs, and mules.

The Mexican province of Texas attracted a flood of Americans who had settlement, not long-distance trade, on their minds (see Map 12.2). Wanting to populate and develop its northern territory, the Mexican government granted the American Stephen F. Austin a huge tract of land along the Brazos River. In the 1820s Austin became the first Anglo-American *empresario* (colonization agent) in Texas. Land was cheap—only ten cents an acre—and thousands of Americans poured across the border. Many brought cotton and slaves with them. By 1835, the settlers had established a thriving plantation economy in Texas. Americans numbered thirty-five thousand, while the *Tejano* (Spanish-speaking) population was less than eight thousand. Few Anglo-American settlers were Roman Catholic, spoke Spanish, or cared about assimilating into Mexican culture. In 1829, the Mexican government sought to halt further immigration by outlawing slavery, but the settlers sidestepped the decree by calling their slaves servants. The Americans increasingly complained about the puny voice they had in local government. General Antonio López de Santa Anna all but extinguished that voice when he seized political power and concentrated authority in Mexico City.

Texas War for Independence, 1836

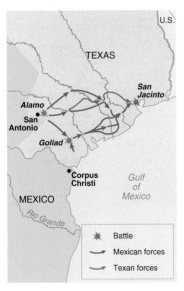

Faced with what they considered tyranny, the Texan settlers rebelled and declared the independent Republic of Texas. Santa Anna ordered the Mexican army northward and in February 1836 arrived at the outskirts of San Antonio. The rebels, who included the Tennessee frontiersman David Crockett and the Louisiana adventurer James Bowie, as well as a number of Tejanos, took refuge in a former Franciscan mission known as the Alamo. When Santa Anna's siege failed, he sent wave after wave of his 4,000-man army crashing against the walls until the attackers finally broke through and killed all 187 defenders. A few weeks later in the small town of Goliad, Mexican forces surrounded and captured a garrison of Texans. Following orders from Santa Anna, Mexican firing squads executed more than 300 of the men as "pirates." In April 1836 at San Jacinto, General Sam Houston's army adopted the massacre at Goliad as a battle cry and produced a crushing defeat of Santa Anna's troops. Texans had succeeded in establishing their Lone Star Republic, and the following year the United States recognized the independence of Texas from Mexico.

In California, the Mexican government sought to increase the number of Mexican immigrants. In 1824, it granted *ranchos*—huge estates devoted to cattle raising—to new settlers. *Rancheros* ruled over near-feudal empires worked by Indians whose condition sometimes approached that of slaves. Not satisfied, *rancheros* coveted the vast lands controlled by the Franciscan missions. In 1834, they persuaded the Mexican government to confiscate the missions and make their lands available to new settlement, a development that accelerated the decline of California Indians. Devastated by disease, the Indians, who numbered approximately 300,000

when the Spanish arrived in 1769, declined to half that number by 1846.

Despite the efforts of the Mexican government, California in 1840 counted a population of only 7,000 Mexican settlers. Non-Mexican settlers numbered only 380, but among them were Americans who championed manifest destiny. They sought to woo American emigrants to California. Wagon after wagon left the Oregon Trail to head southwest on the California Trail in the 1840s (see Map 12.1). As the trickle of Americans became a river, Mexican officials grew alarmed, for as a New York newspaper put it in 1845, "Let the tide of emigration flow toward California and the American population will soon be sufficiently numerous to play the Texas game." Only a few Americans in California looked forward to war for independence, but many dreamed of living again under the American flag.

The U.S. government made no secret of its desire to acquire California. In 1835, President Andrew Jackson tried unsuccessfully to purchase it. In 1846, American settlers in the Sacramento Valley took matters into their own hands. Prodded by John C. Frémont, a former army captain and explorer who had arrived with a party of sixty buckskin-clad frontiersmen spoiling for a fight, the Californians raised an independence movement known as the Bear Flag Revolt. By then, James K. Polk, a champion of expansion, sat in the White House.

> **REVIEW**   Why did westward migration expand dramatically in the mid-nineteenth century?

Expansion and the Mexican-American War

Although emigrants acted as the advance guard of American empire, there was nothing automatic about the U.S. annexation of territory in the West. Acquiring territory required political action. In the 1840s the politics of expansion became entangled with sectionalism and the slavery question. Texas, Oregon, and the Mexican borderlands thrust the United States into dangerous diplomatic crises with Great Britain and Mexico.

Aggravation between Mexico and the United States escalated to open antagonism in 1845 when the United States annexed Texas. Absorbing territory still claimed by Mexico ruptured diplomatic relations between the two countries and set the stage for war. But it was President James K. Polk's insistence on having Mexico's other northern provinces that made war certain. The war was not as easy as Polk anticipated, but it ended in American victory and the acquisition of a new American West.

The Politics of Expansion

Westward expansion ended up on the desk of John Tyler when he became president in April 1841. William Henry Harrison had been elected president in 1840 but died one month after taking office. The issue that stirred Tyler's blood, and that of much of the nation, was Texas. Texans had sought admission to the Union almost since winning their independence from Mexico in 1836. Tyler, an ardent expansionist, understood that Texas was a dangerous issue. Any suggestion of adding another slave state to the Union would enrage Northerners. Annexing Texas also risked precipitating war because Mexico had never relinquished its claim to its lost province.

Nevertheless, Tyler decided to risk annexing Texas. In April 1844, Secretary of State John C. Calhoun laid an annexation treaty before the Senate. But when Calhoun linked annexation to the defense of slavery, he doomed the treaty. Howls of protest erupted across the North. In Massachusetts, future senator Charles Sumner deplored the "insidious" plan to annex Texas and carve from it "great slaveholding states." The Senate soundly rejected the treaty, and it appeared that Tyler had succeeded only in inflaming sectional conflict.

The issue of Texas had not died down by the 1844 elections. In an effort to appeal to northern voters, Whig nominee for president Henry Clay came out against the immediate annexation of Texas. "Annexation and war with Mexico are identical," he declared. The Democrats chose Tennessean James K. Polk, who was as strong for the annexation of Texas as Clay was against it. To make Texas annexation palatable to Northerners, the Democrats shrewdly yoked Texas to Oregon, thus tapping the desire for expansion in the free states of the North as well as in the slave states of the South. The Democratic

Polk and Dallas Banner, 1844

In 1844, Democratic presidential nominee James K. Polk and vice presidential nominee George M. Dallas campaigned under this cotton banner. The extra star spilling over into the red and white stripes symbolizes Polk's vigorous support for annexing the huge slave republic of Texas, which had declared independence from Mexico eight years earlier. Henry Clay, Polk's Whig opponent, ran under a banner that was similar but conspicuously lacked the additional star.

Collection of Janice L. and David J. Frent.

platform called for the "reannexation of Texas" and the "reoccupation of Oregon." The suggestion that the United States was merely reasserting existing rights was poor history but good politics.

When Clay finally recognized the groundswell for expansion, he waffled, hinting that under certain circumstances he might accept the annexation of Texas. His retreat won little support in the South and succeeded only in alienating antislavery opinion in the North. James G. Birney, the candidate of the fledgling Liberty Party, picked up the votes of thousands of disillusioned Clay supporters. In the November election, Polk received 170 electoral votes and Clay 105. New York's 35 electoral votes proved critical to Clay's defeat. A shift of just one-third of Birney's 15,000 votes to Clay would have given Clay the state and the presidency.

On March 4, 1845, in his inaugural address, Polk confirmed his faith in America's manifest destiny. "This heaven-favored land," he declared, enjoyed the "most admirable and wisest system of well-regulated self-government...ever devised by human minds." And he asked, "Who shall assign limits to the achievements of free minds and free hands under the protection of this glorious Union?"

The nation did not have to wait for Polk's inauguration to see results from his victory. One month after the election, President Tyler announced that the triumph of the Democratic Party provided a mandate for the annexation of Texas "promptly and immediately." In February 1845, after a fierce debate between antislavery and proslavery forces, Congress approved a joint resolution offering the Republic of Texas admission to the United States. Texas entered as the fifteenth slave state.

Tyler delivered Texas, but Polk had promised Oregon, too. Westerners particularly demanded that the new president make good on the Democrats' pledge "Fifty-four Forty or Fight"— that is, all of Oregon, right up to Alaska (54°40′ was the southern latitude of Russian Alaska). But Polk was close to war with Mexico and could not afford a war with Britain over U.S. claims in Canada. After the initial bluster, therefore, Polk muted the all-of-Oregon refrain and renewed an old offer to divide Oregon along the forty-ninth parallel. When Britain accepted the compromise, some cried betrayal, but most Americans celebrated the agreement that gave the nation an enormous territory peacefully. Besides, when the Senate finally approved the treaty in June 1846, the United States and Mexico were already at war.

The Mexican-American War, 1846–1848

From the day he entered the White House, Polk craved Mexico's remaining northern provinces: California and New Mexico, land that today makes up California, Nevada, and Utah, most of New Mexico and Arizona, and parts of Wyoming and Colorado. Polk hoped to buy the territory, but when the Mexicans refused to sell, he concluded that military force would be needed to realize the United States's manifest destiny.

Polk had already ordered General Zachary Taylor to march his 4,000-man army from its position on the Nueces River, the southern boundary of Texas according to the Mexicans, 150 miles south, to the banks of the Rio Grande, the boundary claimed by Texans (Map 12.3). Viewing the American advance as aggression, the Mexican general in Matamoros ordered Taylor back to the

Nueces. Taylor refused, and on April 25 Mexican cavalry attacked a party of American soldiers, killing or wounding sixteen and capturing the rest. Even before news of the battle arrived in Washington, Polk had already obtained his cabinet's approval of a war message.

On May 11, 1846, the president told Congress, "Mexico has passed the boundary of the United States, has invaded our territory, and shed American blood upon American soil." Thus "war exists, and, notwithstanding all our efforts to avoid it, exists by the act of Mexico herself." Congress passed a declaration of war and began raising an army. Despite years of saber rattling toward Mexico and Britain, the U.S. army was pitifully small, only 8,600 soldiers. Faced with the nation's first foreign war, against a Mexican army that numbered more than 30,000, Polk called for volunteers. Eventually, more than 112,000 white Americans (blacks were banned) rushed to the colors, eager to fight in Mexico.

Despite the flood of volunteers, the war divided the nation. Northern Whigs in particular condemned the war as the bullying of a weak neighbor. The Massachusetts legislature claimed that the war was being fought for the "triple object of extending slavery, of strengthening the slave power, and of obtaining control of the free states." On January 12, 1848, a gangly freshman Whig representative from Illinois rose from his back-row seat in the House of Representatives to deliver his first important speech in Congress. Before Abraham Lincoln sat down, he had questioned Polk's intelligence, honesty, and sanity. The president simply ignored the upstart representative, but antislavery, antiwar Whigs kept up the attack throughout the conflict. In their effort to undercut national support, they labeled it "Mr. Polk's War."

Since most Americans backed the war, it was not really Polk's war, but the president acted as if it were and directed the war personally. He planned a short war in which U.S. armies would occupy Mexico's northern provinces and defeat the Mexican army in a decisive battle or two, after which Mexico would sue for peace and the United States would keep the territory its armies occupied.

At first, Polk's strategy seemed to work. In May 1846, Zachary Taylor's troops drove south from the Rio Grande and routed the Mexican army, first at Palo Alto, then at Resaca de la Palma (see Map 12.3). "Old Rough and Ready,"

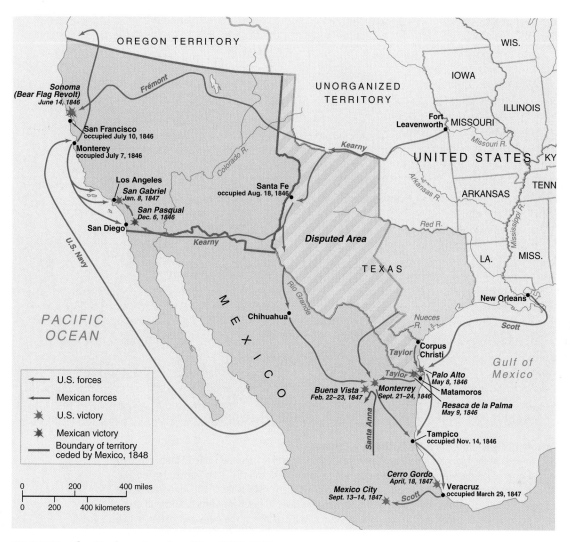

MAP 12.3   The Mexican-American War, 1846–1848
American and Mexican soldiers skirmished across much of northern Mexico, but the major battles took place between the Rio Grande and Mexico City.

as Taylor was affectionately known among his adoring troops, became an instant war hero. Polk rewarded Taylor for his victories by making him commander of the Mexican campaign.

A second prong of the campaign to occupy Mexico's northern provinces centered on Colonel Stephen Watts Kearny, who led a 1,700-man army from Missouri into New Mexico. Without firing a shot, U.S. forces took Santa Fe in August 1846. Polk then ordered Kearny to California. Pushing on with only 300 troops, Kearny three months later marched into San Diego and into a major Mexican rebellion against American rule. In January 1847, after several

clashes and severe losses, the U.S. forces occupied Los Angeles. California and New Mexico were in American hands.

By then, Taylor had driven deep into the interior of Mexico. In September 1846, after a five-day siege and house-to-house fighting, he took the fortified city of Monterrey. With reinforcements and fresh supplies, Taylor pushed his 5,000 troops southwest, where the Mexican hero of the Alamo, General Antonio López de Santa Anna, was concentrating an army of 21,000. On February 23, 1847, Santa Anna's troops attacked Taylor at Buena Vista. Superior American artillery and accurate musket fire won the day, but

Battala del Sacramento, Julio Michaud y Thomas
Most images of the Mexican-American War were created by artists from the United States, but Mexicans also recorded the war. In this hand-colored lithograph, Mexican artist Julio Michaud y Thomas offers his interpretation of the battle that took place in February 1847 when 1,100 American troops engaged 3,000 Mexicans on the banks of the Sacramento River in northern Mexico. Michaud accurately portrays the first moments of the bold Mexican cavalry charge at the American center, but he neglects to finish the story. American artillery forced the Mexican lancers to retreat, with "great confusion in their ranks." When the fighting ended, 700 Mexicans had been killed, wounded, or captured. American casualties amounted to one man killed and six wounded. The battle made a national hero of the American commander, Colonel Alexander Doniphan, who watched the battle with one leg hooked around his saddle horn, whittling a stick in full view of the enemy.
Yale Collection of Western Americana, Beinecke Rare Book and Manuscript Library.

the Americans suffered heavy casualties. The Mexicans suffered even greater losses (some 3,400 dead, wounded, and missing compared with 650 Americans). During the night Santa Anna withdrew his battered army from the battlefield, much to the "profound disgust of the troops," one Mexican officer remembered. "They are filled with grief that they were going to lose the benefit of all the sacrifices that they had made; that the conquered field would be abandoned, and that the victory would be given to the enemy." Retreat, he complained, fed the belief "that it was impossible to conquer the Americans."

The series of uninterrupted victories in northern Mexico certainly fed the American troops' sense of superiority. "No American force has ever thought of being defeated by any amount of Mexican troops," one soldier declared. The Americans worried about other hazards, however. "I can assure you that fighting is the least dangerous & arduous part of a soldier's life," one young man declared. Letters home told of torturous marches across arid wastes alive with tarantulas, scorpions, and rattlesnakes. Others recounted dysentery, malaria, smallpox, cholera, and yellow fever. Of the 13,000 American soldiers who died (some 50,000

Mexicans died), fewer than 2,000 fell to Mexican bullets and shells. Disease killed most of the others. Medicine was so primitive and conditions so harsh that as a Tennessee man observed, "nearly all who take sick die."

Victory in Mexico

Although Americans won battle after battle, President Polk's strategy misfired. Despite heavy losses on the battlefields, Mexico refused to trade land for peace. One American soldier captured the Mexican mood: "They cannot submit to be deprived of California after the loss of Texas, and nothing but the conquest of their Capital will force them to such a humiliation." Polk had arrived at the same conclusion. The president tapped another general to carry the war to Mexico City. While Taylor occupied the north, General Winfield Scott would land his army on the Gulf coast of Mexico and march 250 miles inland to the capital. Polk's plan entailed enormous risk because Scott would have to cut himself off from supplies and lead his men deep into enemy country against a much larger army.

After months of careful planning, an amphibious landing on March 9, 1847, near Veracruz put some 10,000 American troops ashore without the loss of a single life. After eighty-eight hours of furious shelling, Veracruz surrendered. In early April 1847, the U.S. army moved westward.

After the defeat at Buena Vista, Santa Anna had returned to Mexico City. He rallied his ragged troops and marched them east to set a trap for Scott in the mountain pass at Cerro Gordo. Knifing through Mexican lines, the Americans almost captured Santa Anna, who fled the field on foot. So complete was the victory that Scott gloated to Taylor, "Mexico no longer has an army." But Santa Anna, ever resilient, again rallied the Mexican army. Some 30,000 troops took up defensive positions on the outskirts of Mexico City and began melting down church bells to cast new cannon.

In August, Scott began his assault on the Mexican capital. The fighting proved the most brutal of the war. Santa Anna backed his army into the city, fighting each step of the way. At the battle of Churubusco, the Mexicans took 4,000 casualties in a single day and the Americans more than 1,000. At the castle of Chapultepec, American troops scaled the walls and fought the Mexican defenders hand to hand. After Chapultepec, Mexico City officials persuaded Santa Anna to evacuate the city to save it from

destruction, and on September 14, 1847, General Winfield Scott rode in triumphantly. The ancient capital of the Aztecs had fallen once again to an invading army.

On February 2, 1848, American and Mexican officials signed the Treaty of Guadalupe Hidalgo in Mexico City. Mexico agreed to give up all claims to Texas north of the Rio Grande and to cede the provinces of New Mexico and California—more than 500,000 square miles—to the United States (see Map 12.3). The United States agreed to pay Mexico $15 million and to assume $3.25 million in claims that American citizens had against Mexico. In March 1848 the Senate ratified the treaty. The last American soldiers left Mexico a few months later.

Golden California

The American triumph had enormous consequences. Less than three-quarters of a century after its founding, the United States had achieved its self-proclaimed manifest destiny to stretch from the Atlantic to the Pacific (Map 12.4). It would enter the industrial age with vast new natural resources and a two-ocean economy, while Mexico faced a sharply diminished economic future. Moreover, with the northern half of Mexico in American hands, California gold would pour into American and not Mexican pockets.

On a cold January morning in 1848, just weeks before the formal transfer of territory, James Marshall discovered gold in the American River in the foothills of the Sierra Nevada. Marshall's discovery set off the California gold rush, one of the wildest mining stampedes in the world's history. Between 1849 and 1852, more than 250,000 "forty-niners," as the would-be miners were known, descended on the Golden State. In less than two years, Marshall's discovery transformed California from foreign territory to statehood.

News of gold quickly spread around the world. Soon a stream of races and nationalities bent on getting rich arrived in California, where the forty-niners remade the quiet world of Mexican ranches into a raucous, roaring mining and town economy. (See "Historical Question," page 300.) Forty-niners rarely had much money or mining experience, but as one witness observed, "No capital is required to obtain this gold, as the laboring man wants nothing but his pick, shovel, and tin pan, with which to dig and wash the gravel; and many frequently pick gold

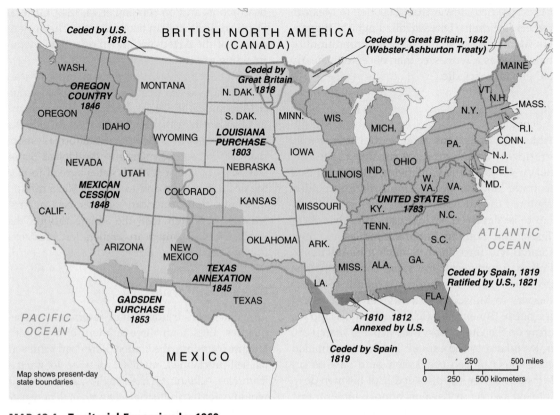

MAP 12.4   Territorial Expansion by 1860
Less than a century after its founding, the United States spread from the Atlantic seaboard
to the Pacific Ocean. War, purchase, and diplomacy had gained a continent.

out of the crevices of rock with their butcher knives in pieces from one to six ounces." Only a few struck it rich, and life in the gold fields was nasty, brutish, and often short. Men faced abysmal living conditions, sometimes living in holes and brush lean-tos. They also faced cholera and scurvy, exorbitant prices for food (eggs cost a dollar apiece), deadly encounters with claim jumpers, and endless backbreaking labor. Still, an individual with gold in his pocket could find temporary relief in the saloons, card games, dog fights, gambling dens, and brothels that flourished in the mining camps.

By 1853, San Francisco had grown into a raw, booming city of 50,000 that depended as much on gold as did the mining camps inland. It suffered from overcrowding, fire, crime, and violence, like all the towns that dotted the San Joaquin and Sacramento valleys, but enterprising individuals had learned that there was money to be made tending to the needs of the miners. Hotels, saloons, restaurants, laundries,

and shops and stores of all kinds exchanged services and goods for miners' gold.

San Francisco was no tamer than the mining camps. In 1851, the "Committee of Vigilance" determined to bring order to the city. Members pledged that "no thief, burglar, incendiary or assassin shall escape punishment, either by the quibbles of the law, the insecurity of prisons, the carelessness or corruption of the police, or a laxity of those who pretended to administer justice." Lynchings proved that the Committee meant business. In time, merchants, **artisans**, and professionals made the city their home and brought their families from back east. Gradually, gunfights declined and theaters sprouted, but many years would pass before anyone pacified San Francisco.

Bigotry and efforts to establish civic order brought the Chinese special scrutiny. By 1851, 25,000 Chinese lived in California, and their religion, language, dress, queues (long pigtails), eating habits, and opium convinced many Anglos that they were not fit citizens of the

Golden State. As early as 1852, opponents demanded a halt to Chinese immigration. Chinese leaders in San Francisco fought back. Admitting deep cultural differences, they insisted that "in the important matters we are good men. We honor our parents; we take care of our children; we are industrious and peaceable; we trade much; we are trusted for small and large sums; we pay our debts; and are honest, and of course must tell the truth." Their protestations, however, offered little protection, and racial violence braided with forty-niner optimism and energy.

Westward expansion did not stop at the California shore. A vast network of trade soon connected California and the Pacific. American seafarers and merchants traded furs, hides and tallow, and lumber and engaged in whaling and the China trade. Still, as California's first congressional representative observed, this new West was separated "by thousands of miles of plains, deserts, and almost impossible mountains" from the rest of the Union. Dreamers imagined a railroad that would someday connect the Golden State with the booming agriculture and thriving industry of the East.

> **REVIEW** Why was the annexation of Texas such a controversial policy?

Economic and Industrial Evolution

During the 1840s and 1850s, Americans lived amid profound economic transformation that had been under way since the start of the nineteenth century. Since 1800, the total output of the U.S. economy had multiplied twelvefold. Four fundamental changes in American society fueled this phenomenal economic growth.

First, millions of Americans—Abraham Lincoln among them—moved from farms to urban areas, although farmers still made up 80 percent of the nation's population in 1860. Second, more Americans worked in factories, which contributed to economic growth because, in general, factory workers produced twice as much as agricultural workers. Third, the shift from water to steam as a source of energy raised productivity and sped transportation on rails and ships. Fourth, the underlying change pro-

pelling America's economic development was the rise in agricultural productivity, which nearly doubled during Lincoln's lifetime. While cities, factories, and steam engines multiplied throughout the nation—especially in the North and West—the roots of America's economic growth lay in agriculture.

Historians often refer to this transformation as an industrial revolution. However, the profound changes occurring in these years did not cause a revolutionary discontinuity in the economy or society. The United States remained overwhelmingly agricultural. Old methods of production continued alongside the new. The process that the American economy underwent before 1860 might best be termed "industrial evolution."

Agriculture and Land Policy

Forests impeded agriculture. The labor required for farmers to clear land for planting took time and energy that might instead have gone to growing crops, thereby limiting agricultural productivity. But as farmers pushed westward, they encountered the Midwest's comparatively treeless prairie, where they could spend less time with an ax and more time with a plow or hoe. Farmers like the Lincolns migrated to the Midwest by the tens of thousands between 1830 and 1860. The population of Indiana, Illinois, Michigan, Wisconsin, and Iowa exploded tenfold between 1830 and 1860, four times faster than the growth of the nation as a whole.

Labor-saving improvements in farm implements also hiked agricultural productivity. The cast-iron plow in use since the 1820s proved too weak for the thick turf and dense soil of the midwestern prairie. In 1837, John Deere patented a strong, smooth steel plow that sliced through prairie soil so cleanly that farmers called it the "singing plow." Deere's company became the leading plow manufacturer in the Midwest, turning out more than ten thousand plows a year by the late 1850s. Better plows permitted farmers to break more ground and plant more crops.

Improvements in wheat harvesting also multiplied farmers' productivity. In 1850, most farmers harvested wheat by hand, cutting two or three acres a day with backbreaking labor. Cyrus McCormick and others experimented with designs for mechanical reapers. By the 1850s, a McCormick

Who Rushed for California Gold?

When news of James Marshall's discovery reached the East in the fall of 1848, gold proved irresistible. Newspapers went crazy with stories about prospectors who extracted half a pan of gold from every pan of gravel they scooped from western streams. Soon, cities reverberated with men singing:

> Oh Susannah, don't you cry for me;
> I'm gone to California with my
> wash-bowl on my knee.

Scores of ships sailed from East Coast ports, headed either around South America to San Francisco or across the Gulf of Mexico to Panama, where the passengers made their way by foot and canoe to the Pacific coast and waited for a ship to carry them north. Even larger numbers of gold seekers took riverboats to the Missouri River and then set out in wagons, on horseback, or by foot for the West.

Young men everywhere contracted gold fever. As stories of California gold circled the globe, Chinese and Germans, Mexicans and Irish, Australians and French, Chileans and Italians, and people of dozens of other nationalities set out to strike it rich. Louisa Knapp Clappe, wife of a minister and one of the few women in gold country, remarked that when she walked through Indian Bar, the little mining town where she lived, she heard English, French, Spanish, German, Italian, Kanaka (Hawaiian), Asian Indian, and American Indian languages. Hangtown, Hell's Delight, Gouge Eye, and a hundred other crude mining camps became temporary home to a diverse throng of nationalities and peoples.

One of the largest groups of new arrivals was the Chinese. Between 1848 and 1854, Chinese men numbering 45,000 (but almost no Chinese women) arrived in California. Most considered themselves "sojourners," temporary residents who planned to return home as soon as their savings allowed. The majority came under a Chinese-controlled contract labor system in which each immigrant worked out the cost of his transportation. In the early years, most became wage laborers in mining. By the 1860s, they dominated railroad construction in the West. Ninety percent of the Central Pacific Railroad's 10,000 workers were Chinese. The Chinese also made up nearly half of San Francisco's labor force, working in the shoe, tobacco, woolen, laundry, and sewing trades. By 1870, the Chinese population had grown to 63,200, including 4,500 women. They constituted nearly 10 percent of the state's people and 25 percent of its wage-earning force.

The presence of peoples from around the world shattered the Anglo-American dream of a racially and ethnically homogeneous West, but ethnic diversity did nothing to increase the tolerance of Anglo-American prospectors. In their eyes, no "foreigner" had a right to dig for gold. In 1850, the California legislature passed the Foreign Miners' Tax Law, which levied high taxes on non-Americans to drive them from the gold fields, except as hired laborers working on claims owned by Americans. Stubborn foreign miners were sometimes hauled before "Judge Lynch." Among the earliest victims of lynching in the gold fields were a Frenchman and a Chilean.

Anglo-Americans considered the Chinese devious and unassimilable. They also feared that hard-working, self-denying Chinese labor would undercut white labor and drive it from the country. As a consequence, the Chinese were segregated residentially and occupationally and made ineligible for citizenship. Along with blacks and Indians, Chinese were denied public education and the right to testify in court. In addition to exclusion, they suffered from violence. Mobs drove them from Eureka, Truckee, and other mining towns.

American prospectors swamped the *Californios*, Spanish and Mexican settlers who had lived in California for generations. Soon after the American takeover, raging prejudice and discriminatory laws pushed Hispanic *rancheros*, professionals,

Gold Mountain
This hardworking young man is wearing the typical dress of Chinese laborers, a blue cotton shirt and baggy pants. We cannot tell if a queue is hanging down his back. He bears the heavy tools of his trade of placer (surface) mining but still manages a smile. Although he probably did not strike it rich in Gum Sam (Gold Mountain), he did find a new world and a new way of life.
Nevada Historical Society.

merchants, and artisans into the ranks of unskilled labor. Americans took their land even though the U.S. government had pledged to protect Mexican and Spanish land titles after the cession of 1848. Anglo forty-niners branded Spanish-speaking miners, even native-born Californios, "foreigners" and drove them from the diggings. Mariano Vallejo, a leading Californio, said of the forty-niners: "The good ones were few and the wicked many."

For Native Americans, the gold rush was a catastrophe. Numbering about 150,000 in 1848, the Indian population of California fell to 25,000 in 1856. Californios had exploited the Native peoples, but the forty-niners wanted to eradicate them. Starvation, disease, and a declining birthrate took a heavy toll. Indians

also fell victim to wholesale murder. "That a war of extermination will continue to be waged between the two races until the Indian race becomes extinct must be expected," declared California governor Peter W. Burnett in 1851. The nineteenth-century historian Hubert Howe Bancroft described white behavior toward Indians during the gold rush as "one of the last human hunts of civilization, and the basest and most brutal of them all." To survive, Indians moved to the most remote areas of the state and tried to stay out of the way.

The forty-niners created dazzling wealth—in 1852, 81 million ounces of gold, nearly half of the world's production. Only a few prospectors—of whatever race and nationality—struck it rich, however.

The era of the prospector panning in streams quickly gave way to corporate-owned deep-shaft mining. The larger the scale of mining operations became, the smaller were the opportunities for individual miners. Most forty-niners eventually took up farming or opened small businesses or worked for wages for the corporations that pushed them out. But because of gold, an avalanche of people had roared into California. Anglo-Americans were most numerous, and Anglo dominance developed early. But the gold rush also brought a rainbow of nationalities. Anglo-American ascendancy *and* ethnic and racial diversity in the West both count among the most significant legacies of the gold rush. But because Anglo-Americans made the rules, not everyone shared equally.

Harvesting Grain with Cradles
This late-nineteenth-century painting shows the grain harvest during the mid-nineteenth century at Bishop Hill, Illinois, a Swedish community where the artist, Olof Krans, and his parents settled in 1850. The men swing cradles, slowly cutting a swath through the grain; the women gather the cut grain into sheaves to be hauled away later for threshing. Bishop Hill, a well-organized community, could call upon the labor of a large number of men and women at harvest time. Most farmers had only a few family members and a hired hand or two to help with the harvest. Notice that although the grain field appears level enough to be ideal for a mechanical reaper, all the work is done by hand; no machine is in sight.
Bishop Hill State Historic Site, Illinois Historic Preservation Agency.

reaper that cost between $100 and $150 allowed a farmer to harvest twelve acres a day. Although most farmers continued to cut their grain by hand, improved reapers and plows, mostly powered by horses or oxen, allowed farmers to cultivate more land, doubling the corn and wheat harvests between 1840 and 1860.

Federal land policy made possible the agricultural productivity that fueled the nation's economy. Up to 1860, the United States continued to be land-rich and labor-poor. During the nineteenth century, the nation became a great deal richer in land, acquiring more than a billion acres with the Louisiana Purchase (see chapter 10) and the annexation of Florida, Oregon, and vast territories following the Mexican-American War. The federal government made the land available for purchase to attract settlers and to generate revenues. Although a farmer could buy federal land for just $1.25 an acre, millions of Americans could not afford to pay $50 for a forty-acre farm. They squatted on unclaimed federal land and carved out a farm that they neither rented nor owned.

Government land policy also enriched wily speculators who found ways to claim large tracts of the most desirable plots and sell them to settlers at a generous markup. Nonetheless, by making land available to millions of ordinary people, the federal government achieved the goal of attracting settlers to the new territories in the West, which in due course joined the Union as new states. Above all, federal land policy created the basic precondition for the increase in agricultural productivity that underlay the nation's impressive economic growth.

Manufacturing and Mechanization

Changes in manufacturing arose from the nation's land-rich, labor-poor economy. England and other European countries had land-poor, labor-rich economies; there, meager opportunities in agriculture kept factory laborers plentiful and wages low. In the United States, western expansion and government land policies buoyed agriculture, keeping millions of people on the farm and thereby limiting the supply of workers for manufacturing and elevating wages. Because of this relative shortage of workers, manufacturers searched constantly for ways to save labor.

Mechanization allowed manufacturers to produce more with less labor. The practice of manufacturing and then assembling interchangeable parts spread from gun making to other industries and became known as the "American system." Mechanization became so integral to American manufacturing that some machinists specialized in what was called the machine tool industry, which made machines that made parts for other machines.

Manufacturing and agriculture meshed into a dynamic national economy. New England led the nation in manufacturing, shipping products such as clocks, guns, and axes west and south, while commodities such as wheat, pork, whiskey, tobacco, and cotton  moved north and east. Manufacturers specialized in producing for the gigantic domestic market rather than for export. British goods dominated the international market and, on the whole, they were cheaper and better than American-made products. U.S. manufacturers supported tariffs to minimize British competition, but their best protection from British competitors was to strive harder to please their American customers.

Throughout American manufacturing, hand labor continued to be essential despite advances in mechanization. Even in heavily mechanized industries, factories remained fairly small; few had more than twenty or thirty employees. The industrial evolution under way before 1860 would quicken later in the nineteenth century; railroads were a harbinger of that future.

Railroads: Breaking the Bonds of Nature

Railroads incorporated the most advanced developments of the age. They seemed to break the bonds of nature. When canals and rivers froze in winter or became impassable during summer droughts, trains steamed ahead. When becalmed sailing ships went nowhere, locomotives kept on chugging, averaging over twenty miles an hour during the 1850s. Above all, railroads offered cities not blessed with canals or navigable rivers a way to compete for the trade of the countryside.

By 1850, trains steamed along nine thousand miles of track, almost two-thirds of it in New England and the Middle Atlantic states. By 1860, several railroads had crossed the Mississippi River to link frontier farmers to the nation's 30,000 miles of track, approximately as much as in all the rest of the world combined (Map 12.5). This massive expansion of railroads helped the United States catapult into position as the world's second leading industrial power, behind Great Britain.

In addition to speeding transportation, railroads propelled the growth of the iron and coal industries. Iron production grew five times faster than the population during the decades up to 1860, in part to meet the demand for rails, wheels, axles, locomotives, and heavy, gravity-defying iron bridges. Railroads also stimulated the fledgling telegraph industry. In 1844, Samuel F. B. Morse persuasively demonstrated the potential of his telegraph by transmitting a series of dots and dashes that instantly conveyed  an electronic message along forty miles of wire strung between Washington and Baltimore. By 1861, more than fifty thousand miles of wire stretched across the continent to the Pacific, often alongside railroad tracks.

Almost all railroads were built and owned by private corporations rather than by governments. But privately owned railroads received massive government aid, especially federal **land grants**. Up to 1850, the federal government had

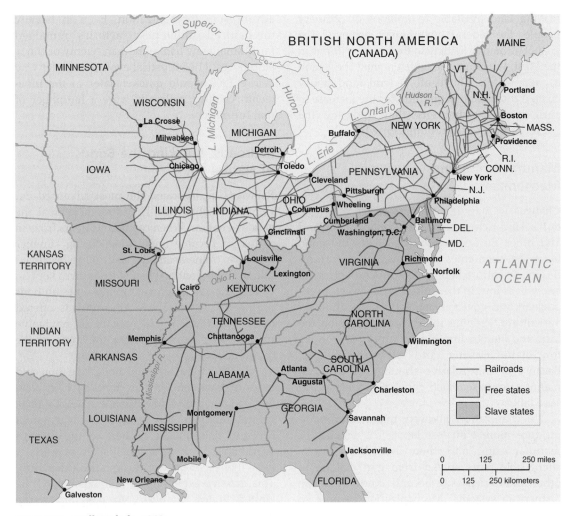

MAP 12.5 Railroads in 1860
Railroads were a crucial component of the revolutions in transportation and communications that transformed nineteenth-century America. The railroad system reflected the differences in the economies of the North and South.

READING THE MAP: In which sections of the country were most of the railroad tracks laid by the middle of the nineteenth century? What cities served as the busiest railroad hubs?
CONNECTIONS: How did the expansion of railroad networks affect the American economy? Why was the U.S. government willing to grant more than twenty million acres of public land to the private corporations that ran the railroads?

FOR MORE HELP ANALYZING THIS MAP, see the map activity for this chapter in the Online Study Guide at
bedfordstmartins.com/roarkcompact.

granted a total of seven million acres of federal land to various turnpike, highway, and canal projects. In 1850, Congress approved a precedent-setting grant to railroads of 6 square miles of federal land for each mile of track laid. By 1860, Congress had granted railroads more than twenty million acres of federal lands.

The railroad boom of the 1850s signaled the growing industrial might of the American econ-omy. But railroads, like other industries, suc-ceeded because they served farms as well as cities. And older forms of transportation re-mained significant. By 1857, for example, trains carried only about one-third of the mail; most of the rest still went by stagecoach or horseback. In 1860, most Americans were still far more familiar with four-legged horses than with iron horses.

The economy of the 1840s and 1850s linked an expanding, westward-moving population by muscles, animals, and farms as well as machines, steam, railroads, and cities. Abraham Lincoln split rails as a young man and defended railroad corporations as a successful attorney. His upward mobility illustrated the direction of economic change and the opportunities that change offered to enterprising individuals.

> **REVIEW** Why did the United States become a leading industrial power in the nineteenth century?

Free Labor: Promise and Reality

The nation's impressive economic performance did not reward all Americans equally. Native-born white men tended to do better than immigrants. With few exceptions, women were excluded from the opportunities open to men. Tens of thousands of women worked as seamstresses, laundresses, domestic servants, factory hands, and teachers but had little opportunity to aspire to higher-paying jobs. In the North and West, slavery was slowly eliminated in the half century after the American Revolution, but most free African Americans there found themselves relegated to dead-end jobs as laborers and servants. Discrimination against immigrants, women, and free blacks did not trouble most white men. With certain notable exceptions, they considered it proper and just.

The Free-Labor Ideal: Freedom plus Labor

During the 1840s and 1850s, leaders throughout the North and West emphasized a set of ideas that seemed to explain why the changes under way in their society benefited some more than others. They referred again and again to the advantages of what they termed **free labor**. (The word *free* referred to laborers who were not slaves; it did not mean laborers who worked for nothing.) By the 1850s, free-labor ideas described a social and economic ideal that accounted for both the successes and the shortcomings of the economy and society taking shape in the North and West.

Free-labor spokesmen celebrated hard work, self-reliance, and independence. They proclaimed that the door to success was open not just to those who inherited wealth or status but also to self-made men like Abraham Lincoln. The free-labor system, Lincoln argued, permitted farmers and artisans to enjoy the products of their own labor, and it also benefited wage workers. "The prudent, penniless beginner in the world," Lincoln asserted, "labors for wages awhile, saves a surplus with which to buy tools or land, for himself; then labors on his own account another while, and at length hires another new beginner to help him." Wage labor was the first rung on the ladder toward self-employment and, eventually, to hiring others.

The free-labor ideal affirmed an egalitarian vision of human potential. Lincoln and other spokesmen stressed the importance of universal education to permit "heads and hands [to] cooperate as friends." Throughout the North and West, communities supported public schools to make the rudiments of learning available to young children. By 1860, many cities and towns boasted that up to 80 percent of children ages seven to thirteen attended school at least for a few weeks each year. In rural areas, where the labor of children was more difficult to spare, schools typically enrolled no more than half the school-age children. Textbooks and teachers—most of whom were young women—drummed into students the lessons of the free-labor system: self-reliance, discipline, and, above all, hard work. "Remember that all the ignorance, degradation, and misery in the world is the result of indolence and vice," one textbook intoned. In school and out, free-labor ideology emphasized labor as much as freedom.

Economic Inequality

The free-labor ideal made sense to many Americans, especially in the North and West, because it seemed to describe their own experiences. Lincoln frequently referred to his humble beginnings as a hired laborer and implicitly invited his listeners to consider how far he had come. In 1860, his wealth of $17,000 easily placed him in the top 5 percent of the population. The opportunities presented by the expanding economy made a few men much, much richer. In 1860, the nation had about forty millionaires.

Most Americans, however, measured success in far more modest terms. The average wealth of adult white men in the North in 1860 barely topped $2,000. Nearly half of American men had no wealth at all; about 60 percent owned no land. Because property possessed by married women was normally considered to belong to their husbands, women had less wealth than men. Free African Americans had still less; 90 percent of them were propertyless.

Free-labor spokesmen considered these economic inequalities a natural outgrowth of freedom, the inevitable result of some individuals being more able, more willing to work, and luckier. These inequalities suggest, however, the gap between the promise and the performance of the free-labor ideal. Economic growth permitted many men to move from being landless squatters to landowning farmers and from being hired laborers to independent, self-employed producers. But many more Americans remained behind, landless and working for wages. Even those who realized their aspirations had a precarious hold on their independence. Bad debts, crop failure, sickness, or death could quickly eliminate a family's gains.

Seeking out new opportunities in pursuit of free-labor ideals created restless social and geographic mobility. Up to two-thirds of the residents of a rural area moved every decade, and the population turnover in cities was even greater. Such constant comings and goings weakened community ties to neighbors and friends and threw individuals even more on their own resources for help in times of trouble.

Immigrants and the Free-Labor Ladder

The risks and uncertainties of free labor did not deter millions of immigrants from entering the United States during the 1840s and 1850s. Almost 4.5 million immigrants arrived between 1840 and 1860, six times more than had come during the previous two decades (Figure 12.1). The half-million immigrants who came in 1854 accounted for nearly 2 percent of the entire U.S. population, a higher proportion than in any other single year of the nation's history. By 1860, foreign-born residents made up about one-eighth of the U.S. population, a fraction that held steady well into the twentieth century.

Nearly three out of four of the immigrants who arrived between 1840 and 1860 came from

FIGURE 12.1   Antebellum Immigration, 1820–1860
After increasing gradually for several decades, immigration shot up in the mid-1840s. Between 1848 and 1860, nearly 3.5 million immigrants entered the United States.

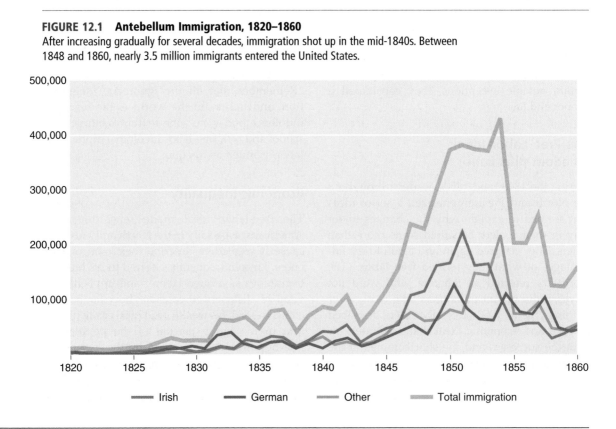

Germany or Ireland. The vast majority of the 1.4 million Germans who entered the United States during these years were skilled tradesmen and their families. They left Germany to escape deteriorating economic conditions, and they had little difficulty finding work in the expanding American economy. German butchers, bakers, beer makers, carpenters, shopkeepers, machinists, and others tended to congregate in cities, particularly in the Midwest. Roughly a quarter of German immigrants were farmers, most of whom scattered throughout the Midwest, although some settled in Texas. On the whole, German Americans settled into that middle stratum of sturdy independent producers celebrated by free-labor spokesmen; relatively few Germans occupied the bottom rung of the free-labor ladder as wage laborers or domestic servants.

Irish immigrants, in contrast, entered at the bottom of the free-labor ladder and had difficulty climbing up. Nearly 1.7 million Irish immigrants arrived between 1840 and 1860, nearly all of them desperately poor and often weakened by hunger and disease. Potato blight struck Ireland in 1845 and returned repeatedly in subsequent years, spreading a catastrophic famine throughout the island. Many of the lucky ones, half-starved, crowded into the holds of ships and set out for America, where they congregated in northeastern cities. As one immigrant group declared, "All we want is to get out of Ireland; we must be better anywhere than here."

Roughly three out of four Irish immigrants worked as laborers or domestic servants. Irish men dug canals, loaded ships, laid railroad track, and took what other work they could find. Irish women hired out to cook, wash and iron, mind children, and clean house. Almost all Irish immigrants were Catholic, a fact that set them apart from the overwhelmingly **Protestant** native-born residents. Many natives regarded the Irish as hard-drinking, obstreperous, half-civilized folk. Such views lay behind the discrimination reflected in job announcements that commonly stated, "No Irish need apply." Despite such prejudices, native residents hired Irish immigrants because they accepted low pay and worked hard.

In America's labor-poor economy, Irish laborers could earn far more than in Ireland. In America, one immigrant explained in 1853, there

was "plenty of work and plenty of wages plenty to eat and no land lords thats enough what more does a man want." But some immigrants wanted more, especially respect and decent working conditions. One immigrant complained that he was "a slave for the Americans as the generality of the Irish…are."

Such testimony illustrates that the free-labor system, whether for immigrants or native-born laborers, often did not live up to the optimistic vision outlined by Abraham Lincoln and others. Many wage laborers could not realistically aspire to become independent, self-sufficient property holders, despite the claims of free-labor proponents.

> **REVIEW** How did the free-labor ideal account for economic inequality?

Reforming Self and Society

The emphasis on self-discipline and individual effort at the core of the free-labor ideal pervaded America in the 1840s and 1850s. Many Americans believed that insufficient self-control caused the major social problems of the era. **Evangelical** Protestants struggled to control individuals' propensity to sin, and **temperance** advocates exhorted drinkers to control their urge for alcohol. In the midst of the worldly disruptions of geographic expansion and economic change, evangelicals brought more Americans than ever before into churches. Historians estimate that church members accounted for about one-third of the American population by midcentury. Most Americans remained outside churches, as did Abraham Lincoln. But the influence of evangelical religion reached far beyond those who belonged to churches. The evangelical temperament—a conviction of righteousness coupled with energy, self-discipline, and faith that the world could be improved—animated most reformers.

A few activists pointed out that certain fundamental injustices lay beyond the reach of individual self-control. Transcendentalists and utopians believed that perfection could be attained only by rejecting the competitive values of the larger society. Women's rights activists and abolitionists sought to reverse the subordination of women and to eliminate the enslavement of blacks by changing laws and social institutions as well as attitudes and customs. They confronted the daunting challenge of repudiating widespread assumptions about male supremacy and white supremacy and somehow subverting the entrenched institutions that reinforced those assumptions: the family and slavery.

The Pursuit of Perfection: Transcendentalists and Utopians

A group of New England writers that came to be known as transcendentalists believed that individuals should conform neither to the dictates of the materialistic world nor to the dogma of formal religion. Instead, people should look within themselves for truth and guidance. The leading transcendentalist, Ralph Waldo Emerson—an essayist, poet, and lecturer—proclaimed that the power of the solitary individual was nearly limitless. Henry David Thoreau, Margaret Fuller, and other transcendentalists agreed with Emerson that "if the single man plant himself indomitably on his instincts, and there abide, the huge world will come round to him." In many ways, transcendentalism represented less an alternative to the values of mainstream society than an exaggerated form of the rampant individualism of the age.

Unlike transcendentalists who sought to turn inward, a few reformers tried to change the world by organizing utopian communities as alternatives to prevailing social arrangements. Although these communities never attracted more than a few thousand people, the activities of their members demonstrated both dissatisfaction with the larger society and their efforts to realize their visions of perfection. Some communities functioned as retreats for those who did not want to sever ties with the larger society. Brook Farm, organized in 1841 in West Roxbury, Massachusetts, briefly provided a haven for a few literary and artistic New Englanders trying to balance bookish pursuits with manual labor.

Other communities set out to become models of perfection that they hoped would point the way toward a better life for everyone. During the 1840s, more than two dozen communities organized around the ideas of Charles Fourier, a French critic of contemporary society. Members of Fourierist phalanxes, as these communities were called, believed that individualism and competition were evils that denied the basic truth that "men…are brothers and not competitors." Fourierist phalanxes aspired to replace competition with harmonious cooperation based on communal ownership of property. But Fourierist communities failed to realize their lofty goals. Few survived more than two or three years.

The Oneida community went beyond the Fourierist notion of communalism. John Humphrey Noyes, the charismatic leader of Oneida, believed that American society's commitment to private property made people greedy and selfish. Noyes claimed that the root of private property lay in marriage, in men's conviction that their wives were their exclusive property. Drawing from a substantial inheritance, Noyes organized the Oneida community in New York in 1848 to abolish marital property rights through the practice of what he called "complex marriage." Sexual intercourse was not restricted to married couples but was permitted between any man and consenting woman in the community. Noyes also required all members to relinquish their economic property to the community, which developed a lucrative business manufacturing animal traps. Oneida's sexual and economic communalism attracted several hundred members, but most of their neighbors considered Oneidans adulterers, blasphemers, and worse. Yet the practices that set Oneida apart from its mainstream neighbors strengthened the community, and it survived long after the Civil War.

Women's Rights Activists

Women participated in the many reform activities that grew out of evangelical churches. Women church members outnumbered men two to one and worked to put their religious ideas into practice by joining peace, temperance, antislavery, and other societies. Involvement in reform organizations gave a few women activists practical experience in such political arts as speaking in public, running a meeting, drafting resolutions, and circulating petitions. Along with such experience came confidence. The abolitionist Lydia Maria Child pointed out in 1841 that "those who urged women to become missionaries and form tract societies…have changed the household utensil to a living energetic being and they have no spell to turn it into a broom again."

In 1848, about one hundred reformers led by Elizabeth Cady Stanton and Lucretia Mott gathered at Seneca Falls, New York, for the first national women's rights convention in the United States. The Seneca Falls Declaration of Sentiments proclaimed that "the history of mankind is a history of repeated injuries and usurpations on the part of man toward woman, having in direct object the establishment of an absolute tyranny over her." In the style of the Declaration of Independence (see appendix I, page A-1), the Seneca Falls Declaration demanded that women "have immediate admission to all the rights and privileges which belong to them as citizens of the United States," particularly the "inalienable right to the elective franchise."

Nearly two dozen other women's rights conventions assembled before 1860, repeatedly calling for **suffrage**. But they had difficulty receiving a respectful hearing, much less obtaining legislative action. No state came close to permitting women to vote. Politicians and editorialists sneered that a woman's place was in the home, rearing her children and civilizing her man. Nonetheless, the Seneca Falls Declaration served as a pathbreaking manifesto of dissent against male supremacy and of support for woman suffrage, which would become the focus of the women's rights movement during the next seventy years.

Abolitionists and the American Ideal

During the 1840s and 1850s, abolitionists continued to struggle to draw the nation's attention to the plight of slaves and the need for **emancipation**. Former slaves such as Frederick Douglass, Henry Bibb, and Sojourner Truth lectured to reform audiences throughout the North about the cruelties of slavery. Abolitionists published newspapers, held conventions, and petitioned Congress. But they never attracted a mass following among white Americans. Many white Northerners became convinced that slavery was wrong, but they still believed that blacks were inferior. Many other white Northerners shared the common view of white Southerners that slavery was necessary and even desirable. The geographic expansion of the nation during the 1840s offered abolitionists

Mary Cragin, Oneida Woman
A founding member of the Oneida community, Mary Cragin had a passionate sexual relationship with John Humphrey Noyes even before the community was organized. Within the bounds of complex marriage as practiced by the Oneidans, Cragin's magnetic sexuality made her a favorite partner of many men. In her journal, she confessed that "every evil passion was very strong in me from my childhood, sexual desire, love of dress and admiration, deceit, anger, pride." Oneida, however, transformed evil passion to holy piety. Cragin wrote, "In view of [God's] goodness to me and of his desire that I should let him fill me with himself, I yield and offer myself, to be penetrated by his spirit, and desire that love and gratitude may inspire my heart so that I shall sympathize with his pleasure in the thing, before my personal pleasure begins, knowing that it will increase my capability for happiness." Oneida's sexual practices were considered outrageous and sinful by almost all other Americans. Even Oneidans did not agree with all of Noyes's ideas about sex. "There is no reason why [sex] should not be done in public as much as music and dancing," he declared. It would display the art of sex, he explained, and watching "would give pleasure to a great many of the older people who now have nothing to do with the matter." Nonetheless, public sex never caught on among Oneidans.
Oneida Community Mansion House.

an opportunity to link their unpopular ideal to a goal that many white Northerners found much more attractive—limiting the geographic expansion of slavery, an issue that moved to the center of national politics during the 1850s (see chapter 14).

Abolitionist Meeting

This rare daguerreotype was made by Ezra Greenleaf Weld in August 1850 at an abolitionist meeting in Cazenovia, New York. Frederick Douglass, who had escaped from slavery in Maryland twelve years earlier, is seated on the platform next to the woman at the table. One of the nation's most brilliant and eloquent abolitionists, Douglass also supported equal rights for women. The man immediately behind Douglass gesturing with his outstretched arm is Gerrit Smith, a wealthy New Yorker and militant abolitionist whose funds supported many reform activities. Notice the two black women in similar clothing on either side of Smith and the white woman next to Douglass. Most white Americans considered such voluntary racial proximity scandalous and promiscuous. What messages did abolitionists attempt to convey by attending such protest meetings?

Collection of the J. Paul Getty Museum, Malibu, CA.

Black leaders rose to prominence in the abolitionist movement during the 1840s and 1850s. African Americans had actively opposed slavery for decades, but a new generation of leaders came to the forefront in these years. Frederick Douglass, Henry Highland Garnet, William Wells Brown, Martin R. Delany, and others became impatient with white abolitionists' appeals to the conscience of the white majority. Garnet proclaimed in 1843 that slaves should rise in insurrection against their masters, an idea that alienated almost all white people. To express their own uncompromising ideas, black abolitionists founded their own newspapers and held their own antislavery conventions, although they still cooperated with sympathetic whites.

The commitment of black abolitionists to battling slavery grew out of their own experiences with white supremacy. The 250,000 free African Americans in the North and West constituted less than 2 percent of the total population. They confronted the humiliations of racial discrimination in nearly every arena of daily life. Only Maine, Massachusetts, New Hampshire, and Vermont permitted black men to vote; New York imposed a special property-holding requirement on black—but not white—voters, effectively excluding most black men from the **franchise**. The pervasive racial discrimination both handicapped and energized black abolitionists. Some cooperated with the American Colonization Society's efforts to send freed slaves and other black Americans to Liberia in west Africa. Other black American leaders organized campaigns against segregation, particularly in transportation and education. Their most notable success came in 1855 when Massachusetts integrated public schools. Elsewhere white supremacy continued unabated.

Outside the public spotlight, free African Americans in the North and West contributed to the antislavery cause by quietly aiding fugitive slaves. Harriet Tubman escaped from slavery in Maryland in 1849 and repeatedly risked her freedom and her life to return to the South to escort slaves to freedom. When the opportunity arose, free blacks in the North provided fugitive slaves with food, a safe place to rest, and a helping hand. This "underground railroad" ran mainly through black neighborhoods, black churches, and black homes, an outgrowth of the antislavery sentiment and opposition to white supremacy that unified nearly all African Americans in the North.

> **REVIEW** Why were women especially prominent in many nineteenth-century reform efforts?

Conclusion: Free Labor, Free Men

In the 1840s, diplomacy and war handed the United States 1.2 million square miles and more than 1,000 miles of Pacific coastline. California almost immediately rewarded its new owners with mountains of gold. To most Americans, new territory and vast riches were appropriate accompaniments to the nation's stunning economic transformation. In the first half of the nineteenth century, a cluster of interrelated developments—steam power, railroads, and the growing mechanization of agriculture and manufacturing—meant greater productivity, a burst of output from farms and factories, and prosperity for many.

To Northerners, industrial evolution confirmed the choice they had made to eliminate slavery and to promote free labor as the key to independence, equality, and prosperity. Like Abraham Lincoln, millions could point to personal experience as evidence of the practical truth of the free-labor ideal. But millions of others had different stories to tell. They knew that in the free-labor system poverty and wealth continued to rub shoulders. By 1860, instead of social independence, more than half of the nation's free-labor workforce toiled for someone else. Free-labor enthusiasts denied that the problems were inherent in the system. They argued that most social ills—including poverty and dependency—sprang from individual deficiencies. Consequently, reformers focused on the lack of self-control and discipline, on sin and alcohol. They denied that free labor meant exploitation. Slaves, not free workers, suffered, they argued.

By midcentury, the nation was half slave and half free, and each region was animated by economic interests, cultural values, and political aims that were contrary to those of the other. Not even the victory over Mexico could bridge the deepening differences between North and South.

Suggestions for Further Reading

David Dary, *The Oregon Trail: An American Saga* (2004). A narrative based on the diaries and journals of the travelers who used the Oregon Trail.

Steven Mintz, *Moralists and Modernizers: America's Pre–Civil War Reformers* (1995). An informative survey of the many Americans eager to reform their world.

Malcolm Rohrbough, *Days of Gold: The California Gold Rush and the American Nation* (1997). A rollicking history of the forty-niners and the broad consequences of western gold.

Scott A. Sandage, *Born Losers: A History of Failure in America* (2005). The fascinating story of those who lost in America's free-labor economy.

Richard Bruce Winders, *Mr. Polk's Army: The American Military Experience in the Mexican War* (1997). An account of the war from the U.S. soldier's perspective.

Kenneth J. Winkle, *The Young Eagle: The Rise of Abraham Lincoln* (2001). The surprising story of Lincoln's rise from log cabin to lawyer and politician.

▶ FOR MORE BOOKS ABOUT TOPICS IN THIS CHAPTER, see the Online Bibliography at bedfordstmartins.com/roarkcompact.

▶ FOR ADDITIONAL FIRSTHAND ACCOUNTS OF THIS PERIOD, see Chapter 12 in Michael Johnson, ed., *Reading the American Past*, Third Edition.

▶ FOR WEB SITES AND DOCUMENTS RELATED TO TOPICS AND PLACES IN THIS CHAPTER, see "HistoryLinks," "DocLinks," and "PlaceLinks" at bedfordstmartins.com/roarkcompact.

REVIEWING THE CHAPTER

Follow these steps to review and strengthen your understanding of the chapter.

STEP 1: *Study the* **Key Terms** *and* **Timeline** *to identify the significance of each item listed.*

STEP 2: *Answer the* **Review Questions***, drawing on key terms and dates to support your answers.*

STEP 3: *Drawing on the Key Terms, Timeline, and Review Questions, answer the broader* **Making Connections** *questions.*

KEY TERMS

Who

Abraham Lincoln (p. 285)
John L. O'Sullivan (p. 287)
Joseph Smith Jr. (p. 289)
Brigham Young (p. 290)
Stephen F. Austin (p. 291)
Antonio López de Santa Anna (p. 292)
Sam Houston (p. 292)
John C. Frémont (p. 292)
James K. Polk (p. 293)
John Tyler (p. 293)
John C. Calhoun (p. 293)
Henry Clay (p. 293)
Zachary Taylor (p. 294)
Stephen Watts Kearny (p. 295)
Winfield Scott (p. 297)
John Deere (p. 299)
Cyrus McCormick (p. 299)
Samuel F. B. Morse (p. 303)
Ralph Waldo Emerson (p. 308)
Elizabeth Cady Stanton (p. 309)

Lucretia Mott (p. 309)
Frederick Douglass (p. 309)
Henry Highland Garnet (p. 310)
Harriet Tubman (p. 310)

What

manifest destiny (p. 287)
Oregon Trail (p. 287)
policy of concentration (p. 288)
Fort Laramie conference (p. 288)
The Book of Mormon (p. 289)
Church of Jesus Christ of Latter-Day Saints (p. 289)
Utah Territory (p. 291)
Mormon War (p. 291)
Santa Fe Trail (p. 291)
Republic of Texas (p. 292)
the Alamo (p. 292)
Goliad (p. 292)
San Jacinto (p. 292)
ranchos (p. 292)

California Trail (p. 292)
Bear Flag Revolt (p. 292)
Mexican-American War (p. 294)
Treaty of Guadalupe Hidalgo (p. 297)
California gold rush (p. 297)
industrial evolution (p. 299)
singing plow (p. 299)
mechanical reaper (p. 299)
American system (p. 303)
free-labor ideal (p. 305)
transcendentalism (p. 308)
utopian communities (p. 308)
Brook Farm (p. 308)
Fourierist phalanxes (p. 308)
Oneida community (p. 308)
Seneca Falls Declaration of Sentiments (p. 309)
American Colonization Society (p. 310)
underground railroad (p. 311)

TIMELINE

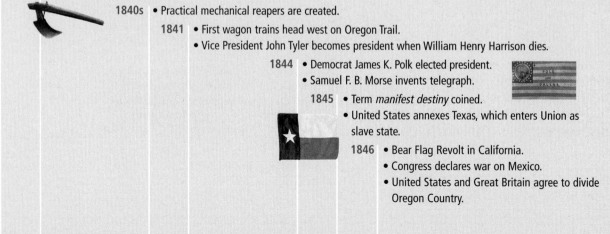

1836 • Texas declares independence from Mexico.

1837 • John Deere patents his steel plow.

1840s • Practical mechanical reapers are created.

1841 • First wagon trains head west on Oregon Trail.
• Vice President John Tyler becomes president when William Henry Harrison dies.

1844 • Democrat James K. Polk elected president.
• Samuel F. B. Morse invents telegraph.

1845 • Term *manifest destiny* coined.
• United States annexes Texas, which enters Union as slave state.

1846 • Bear Flag Revolt in California.
• Congress declares war on Mexico.
• United States and Great Britain agree to divide Oregon Country.

REVIEW QUESTIONS

1. Why did westward migration expand dramatically in the mid-nineteenth century? (pp. 286–92)

2. Why was the annexation of Texas such a controversial policy? (pp. 292–99)

3. Why did the United States become a leading industrial power in the nineteenth century? (pp. 299–305)

4. How did the free-labor ideal account for economic inequality? (pp. 305–07)

5. Why were women especially prominent in many nineteenth-century reform efforts? (pp. 307–11)

MAKING CONNECTIONS

1. How did the ideology of manifest destiny contribute to the mid-nineteenth-century drive for expansion? Discuss its implications for individual migrants and the nation. In your answer, consider how manifest destiny built on, or revised, earlier understandings of the nation's history and racial politics.

2. The Mexican-American War reshaped U.S. borders and more. Discuss the consequences of the war for national political and economic developments in subsequent decades. What resources did the new territory give the United States? How did debate over annexation revive older political disputes?

3. Varied political, economic, and technological factors promoted migration west in the mid-nineteenth century. Considering these factors, discuss migration to two different regions (e.g., Texas, Oregon, Utah, or California). What drew migrants to the region? How did the U.S. government contribute to their efforts?

4. Some nineteenth-century reform movements drew on the free-labor ideal, while others challenged it. Discuss the free-labor ideal in relation to two reform movements (abolitionism, utopian communalism, etc.). How did they draw on the ideal to pursue specific reforms? How did these minority movements try to influence national developments?

▶ For practice quizzes, a customized study plan, and other study tools, see the Online Study Guide at bedfordstmartins.com/roarkcompact.

1847 • Mormons settle in Utah.

1848 • Treaty of Guadalupe Hidalgo.
• Oneida community organized in New York.
• First U.S. women's rights convention takes place at Seneca Falls, New York.

1849 • California gold rush begins.

1850 • Mormon community annexed to United States as Utah Territory.

1851 • Conference in Laramie, Wyoming, marks the beginning of government policy of forcing Indians onto reservations.
• Massachusetts integrates public schools.

CLAY JUG

This ceramic water cooler, made in about 1840, is attributed to Thomas Chandler, a famous potter of Edgefield District, South Carolina. The relatively fine clothes of the African American man and woman portrayed on the vessel suggest that they are house servants. On the wall of the home of Alexander Stephens in Crawfordsville, Georgia, an intriguing letter from Stephens states that two of his favorite slaves are getting married and orders the plantation manager to butcher a hog for their wedding. This cooler, with its portrait of a couple, a hog, and a jug, may have been commissioned by Stephens to commemorate the union. Potters made vessels to be used—to hold water and food. Analysis of the form, decoration, and glazes of southern pottery suggests a blend of European, African, and Native American ceramic traditions. Some pottery went beyond the utilitarian and became art. The most renowned slave potter was an Edgefield man named Dave, who skillfully fashioned huge vessels, inscribed poems on their surfaces, and proudly and boldly signed them "Dave the potter."

Collection of the High Museum of Art, Atlanta. Purchase in honor of Audrey Shilt, President of the Members Guild of the High Museum of Art, 1996–1997, with funds from the Decorative Arts Endowment & Acquisition Trust 1996.132.

The Slave South
1820–1860

NAT TURNER WAS BORN A SLAVE in Southampton County, Virginia, in October 1800. People in his neighborhood claimed that he had always been different. His parents noticed special marks on his body, which they said were signs that he was "intended for some great purpose." His master said that he learned to read without being taught. As an adolescent, he adopted an austere lifestyle of Christian devotion and fasting. In his twenties, he received visits from the "Spirit," the same spirit, he believed, that had spoken to the ancient prophets. In time, Nat Turner began to interpret these things to mean that God had appointed him an instrument of divine vengeance for the sin of slaveholding.

In the early morning of August 22, 1831, he set out with six trusted friends—Hark, Henry, Sam, Nelson, Will, and Jack—to punish slave owners and free their suffering slaves. Turner struck the first blow, an ax to the head of his master, Joseph Travis. The rebels killed all of the white men, women, and children they encountered in each household they attacked. By noon, they had visited eleven farms and slaughtered fifty-seven whites and, along the way, added fifty or sixty men to their army. Word spread quickly, however, and soon the militia and hundreds of local whites gathered. By the next day, whites had captured or killed all of the rebels, except Nat Turner, who successfully hid out for about ten weeks before being captured in nearby woods. Within a week, he was tried, convicted, and executed. By then, forty-five slaves had stood trial, twenty had been convicted and hanged, and another ten had been transported from Virginia. Frenzied whites had killed another hundred or more blacks—insurgents and innocent bystanders—in their counterattack against the rebellion.

Virginia's governor John Floyd asked how Turner's band of "assassins and murderers" could have assaulted the "unsuspecting and defenseless" citizens of "one of the fairest counties in the Commonwealth." White Virginians prided themselves on having the "mildest" slavery in the South, but sixty black rebels on a rampage challenged the comforting theory of the contented slave. Nonetheless, whites found explanations that allowed them to feel safer. They placed the blame on outside agitators. In 1829, David Walker, a freeborn black man living in Boston, had published his *Appeal . . . to the Coloured Citizens of the World*, an invitation to slaves to rise up in bloody rebellion, and copies had fallen into the hands of Virginia slaves. Moreover, on January 1, 1831, in Boston, William Lloyd Garrison, the Massachusetts abolitionist, had published the first issue of the *Liberator*, his fiery newspaper. White Virginians also dismissed the rebellion's leader, Nat Turner, as insane. "He is a complete fanatic, or plays his part admirably," wrote Thomas R. Gray, the lawyer who was assigned to defend Turner.

Nat Turner

There are no known contemporary images of Nat Turner. This imagined portrait comes from William Still's *The Underground Railroad* (1872). Meeting secretly at night deep in a forest and thus well out of earshot of whites, an intense Turner passionately tries to convince four other slaves to join him in rebellion. What do their faces reveal? What considerations do you suppose entered their calculations about whether to join Turner? Significantly perhaps, they are holding work tools, not arms.

Library of Congress.

In the months following the insurrection, white Virginians debated the future of slavery in their state. While some expressed substantial doubts, the Virginia legislature reaffirmed the state's determination to preserve black bondage. Delegates passed a raft of laws strengthening the institution of slavery and further restricting free blacks. A thirty-year-old professor at the College of William and Mary, Thomas R. Dew, published a vigorous defense of slavery that became the bible of Southerners' proslavery arguments. More than ever, the nation was divided along the "Mason-Dixon line," the surveyors' mark that in colonial times had established the boundary between Maryland and Pennsylvania but half a century later divided the free North and slave South.

Black slavery increasingly molded the South into a distinctive region. In the decades after 1820, Southerners, like Northerners, raced westward, but unlike Northerners who spread small farms and free labor, Southerners spread slavery, cotton, and plantations. Geographic expansion meant that slavery became more vigorous and profitable than ever, embraced more people, and increased the South's political power. **Antebellum** Southerners included diverse peoples who at times found themselves at odds with one another—not only slaves and free people but also women and men; Indians, Africans, and Europeans; and aristocrats and common folk. Nevertheless, beneath this diversity of people, there was also forming a distinctively southern society and culture. The South became a slave society, and most white Southerners were proud of it.

The Growing Distinctiveness of the South

From the earliest settlements, inhabitants of southern colonies had shared a great deal with northern colonists. Most whites in both sections were British and **Protestant**, spoke a common language, and shared an exuberant pride in their victorious revolution against British rule. The creation of the new nation under the Constitution in 1789 forged strong political ties that bound all Americans. The beginnings of a national economy fostered economic interdependence and communication across regional boundaries. White Americans everywhere celebrated the achievements of the prosperous young nation, and they looked forward to its seemingly boundless future.

Despite these national similarities, Southerners and Northerners grew increasingly different. The French political observer Alexis de Tocqueville believed he knew why. "I could easily prove," he asserted in 1831, "that almost all the differences which may be noticed between the character of the Americans in the Southern and Northern states have originated in slavery." Slavery made the South different, and it was the differences between the North and South, not the similarities, that came to shape antebellum American history.

Cotton Kingdom, Slave Empire

In the first half of the nineteenth century, legions of Americans migrated west. In the South, the stampede began after the Creek War of 1813–1814, which divested the Creek Nation of

24 million acres and initiated the government campaign to remove Indian people living east of the Mississippi River to the West (see chapters 10 and 11). Eager slaveholders seeking virgin acreage for new plantations, struggling farmers looking for patches of land for small farms, herders and drovers pushing their hogs and cattle toward fresh pastures—anyone who was restless and ambitious felt the pull of Indian land. Southerners pushed westward relentlessly, until by midcentury the South encompassed nearly a million square miles, much of it planted in cotton.

The South's climate and geography were ideally suited for the cultivation of cotton. Advancing Southerners encountered a variety of terrain, soil, and weather, but cotton's requirements are minimal: two hundred frost-free days from planting to picking and plentiful rain, conditions found in much of the South. By the 1830s, cotton fields stretched from southern Virginia to central Texas. Heavy southern and westward migration led to statehood for Arkansas in 1836 and for Texas and Florida in 1845. Production soared from 300,000 bales in 1830 to nearly 5 million in 1860, when the South produced three-fourths of the world's supply. The South—especially that tier of states from South Carolina west to Texas known as the Lower South—had become the cotton kingdom (Map 13.1).

The cotton kingdom was also a slave empire. The South's cotton boom rested on the backs of slaves, who grew 75 percent of the crop on plantations, toiling in gangs in broad fields under the direct supervision of whites. As cotton agriculture expanded westward, whites shipped more than 300,000 slaves out of the old seaboard states. Victims of this brutal but thriving domestic slave trade marched hundreds of miles to new plantations in the Lower South. Cotton, slaves, and plantations moved west together.

The slave population grew enormously. Southern slaves numbered fewer than 700,000 in 1790, about 2 million in 1830, and over 4 million by 1860, an increase of almost 600 percent in seven decades. By 1860, the South contained more

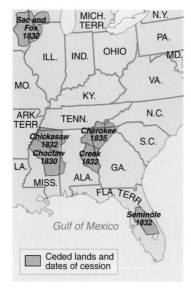

Frontier Land Opened by Indian Removal, 1830s

slaves than all the other slave societies in the New World combined. The extraordinary growth was not the result of the importation of slaves, which the federal government outlawed in 1808. Instead, the slave population grew through natural reproduction. By the nineteenth century, most slaves were native-born Southerners.

The South in Black and White

By 1860, one in every three Southerners was black (more than 4 million blacks and 8 million whites). In the Lower South states of Mississippi and South Carolina, blacks were the majority (Figure 13.1). The contrast with the North was striking: In 1860, only one Northerner in 76 was black (about 250,000 blacks to 19 million whites).

The presence of large numbers of African Americans had profound consequences for the South. Southern culture—language, food, music, religion, and even accents—was in part shaped by blacks. But the most direct consequence of the South's biracialism was southern whites' commitment to white supremacy. Northern whites believed in racial superiority, too, but they lived in a society in which blacks made up barely 1 percent of the population. Their dedication to white supremacy lacked the intensity and urgency increasingly felt by white Southerners who lived among millions of blacks. White Southerners despised blacks because they considered them members of an inferior race, further degraded by their status as slaves. They also feared blacks because they realized that slaves had every reason to hate them and to seek to end their oppression, as Nat Turner had, by any means necessary.

Attacks on slavery after 1820—from blacks and a handful of white antislavery advocates within the South and from abolitionists outside—jolted southern slaveholders into a distressing awareness that they lived in a dangerous and fragile world. In response, southern leaders initiated fresh efforts to strengthen slavery. State legislatures constructed slave codes (laws) that required the total submission of

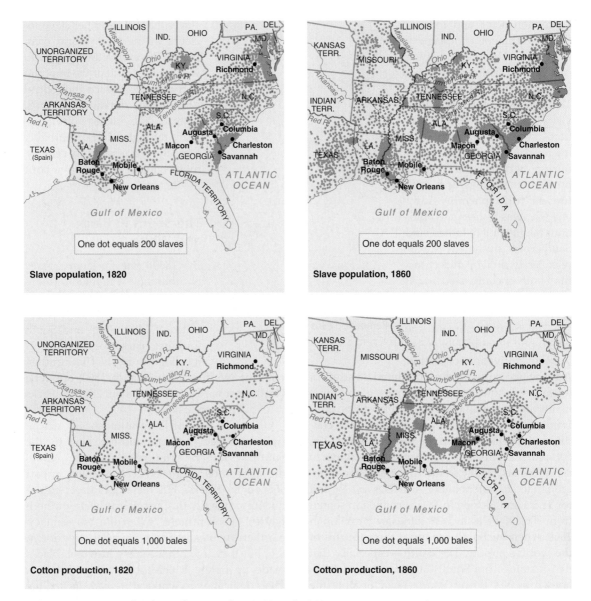

MAP 13.1   Cotton Kingdom, Slave Empire: 1820 and 1860
As the production of cotton soared, the slave population increased dramatically. Slaves continued to toil in tobacco and rice fields along the Atlantic seaboard, but increasingly they worked on cotton plantations in Alabama, Mississippi, and Louisiana.

slaves to their masters and to white society in general. As the Louisiana code stated, a slave "owes his master…a respect without bounds, and an absolute obedience." The laws underlined the authority of all whites, not just masters. Any white could "correct" slaves who did not stay "in their place."

Intellectuals joined legislators in the campaign to strengthen slavery. The South's academics, writers, and clergy constructed a proslavery argument that sought to unify the region's whites around slavery and provide ammunition for the emerging war of words with northern abolitionists. With the intellectuals' guidance, white Southerners gradually moved away from defending slavery as a "necessary evil"—the halfhearted argument popular in Jefferson's day—and toward a full-throated, aggressive defense of slavery as a "positive good." John C. Calhoun declared that in the states where slavery had been abolished "the condition of the African, instead of being improved, has become

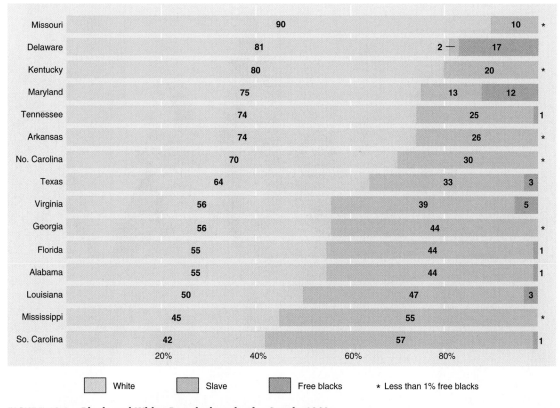

| | White | | Slave | | Free blacks | * Less than 1% free blacks |

FIGURE 13.1   Black and White Populations in the South, 1860
Blacks represented a much larger fraction of the population in the South than in the North, but considerable variation existed from state to state. Only one Missourian in ten, for example, was black, while Mississippi and South Carolina had black majorities. States in the Upper South were "whiter" than states in the Lower South, despite the Upper South's greater number of free blacks.

worse," while in the slave states the Africans "have improved greatly in every respect."

Slavery's champions employed every imaginable defense. In the South slaves were legal property, and wasn't the security of property the bedrock of American **liberty**? History also endorsed slavery, they claimed. Weren't the great civilizations—such as those of the Hebrews, Greeks, and Romans—slave societies? They argued that the Bible, properly interpreted, also sanctioned slavery. Old Testament patriarchs owned slaves, they observed, and in the New Testament Paul returned the runaway slave Onesimus to his master. Some proslavery spokesmen went on the offensive and attacked the economy and society of the North. George Fitzhugh of Virginia argued that behind the North's grand slogan of **free labor** lay a heartless philosophy: "Every man for himself, and the devil take the hindmost." Gouging capitalists exploited wage workers unmercifully, Fitzhugh

declared, and he contrasted the North's vicious free-labor system with the humane relations that he claimed prevailed between masters and slaves because slaves were valuable capital that masters sought to protect.

But at the heart of the defense of slavery lay the claim of black inferiority. Black enslavement was both necessary and proper, antebellum defenders argued, because Africans were lesser beings. Rather than exploitative, slavery was a mass civilizing effort that lifted lowly blacks from barbarism and savagery, taught them disciplined work, and converted them to soul-saving Christianity. According to Virginian Thomas R. Dew, most slaves were grateful. He declared that "the slaves of a good master are his warmest, most constant, and most devoted friends."

Black slavery encouraged whites to unify around race. The grubbiest, most tobacco-stained white man could proudly proclaim his superiority

THE FRUITS OF AMALGAMATION.

The Fruits of Amalgamation

White Southerners and Northerners alike generally agreed that giving blacks equal rights would lead to miscegenation (also known as "amalgamation"). In this lithograph from 1839, Edward W. Clay of Philadelphia attacked abolitionists by imagining the outcome of their misguided campaign. He drew a beautiful white woman with her two black children, one suckling at her breast while her dark-skinned, ridiculously overdressed husband, resting his feet in his wife's lap, reads an abolitionist newspaper. The couple is attended by a white servant. Another interracial couple—perhaps the man is abolitionist William Lloyd Garrison himself—has come calling. Hanging on the wall is a picture entitled *Othello & Desdemona*, based on the popular play *Othello*, a tragic tale about a couple who crossed the color line. A black dog and a white dog play indiscriminately on the floor. Abolitionists denied the charge of amalgamation and pointed to the lasciviousness of southern slaveholders as the true source of miscegenation in antebellum America.

Courtesy, American Antiquarian Society.

to all blacks and his equality with the most refined southern patrician. Because of racial slavery, Georgia attorney Thomas R. R. Cobb observed, every white Southerner "feels that he belongs to an elevated class. It matters not that he is no slaveholder; he is not of the inferior race; he is a freeborn citizen." Consequently, the "poorest meets the richest as an equal; sits at his table with him; salutes him as a neighbor; meets him in every public assembly, and stands on the same social platform." In the South, Cobb boasted, "there is no war of classes."

In reality, slavery did not create perfect harmony among whites. But by providing every antebellum white Southerner membership in the ruling race, slavery helped whites bridge differences in wealth, education, and culture. Slavery meant white dominance, white superiority, and white equality.

The Plantation Economy

As important as slavery was in unifying white Southerners, only about a quarter of the white population lived in slaveholding families. Most slaveholders owned fewer than five slaves. Only about 12 percent of slave owners owned twenty or more, the number of slaves that historians consider necessary to distinguish a **planter** from a farmer. Although hugely outnumbered, planters nevertheless dominated the southern economy. In 1860, 52 percent of the South's slaves lived and worked on plantations. Plantation slaves produced more than 75 percent of the South's export crops, the backbone of the region's economy. Although slavery was dying elsewhere in the New World, slave plantations increasingly dominated southern agriculture.

The South's major cash crops—tobacco, sugar, rice, and cotton—grew on plantations (Map 13.2). Tobacco, the original plantation crop in North America, had shifted westward in the nineteenth century from the Chesapeake to Tennessee and Kentucky. Large-scale sugar production began in 1795, when Étienne de Boré built a modern sugar mill in what is today New Orleans, and sugar plantations were confined almost entirely to Louisiana. Commercial rice production began in the seventeenth century, and like sugar, rice was confined to a small geographic area, a narrow strip of coast stretching from the Carolinas into Georgia.

If tobacco, sugar, and rice were the princes of plantation agriculture, cotton was king. Cotton became commercially significant after the advent of Eli Whitney's cotton gin in 1793, which removed sticky cotton seeds and thus dramatically increased the production of raw cotton. Cotton was relatively easy to grow and took little capital to get started—just enough for land, seed,

MAP 13.2   The Agricultural Economy of the South, 1860
Cotton dominated the South's agricultural economy, but the region grew a variety of crops and was largely self-sufficient in foodstuffs.

READING THE MAP: In what type of geographical areas were rice and sugar grown in 1860? After cotton, what crop commanded the greatest agricultural area in the South? In which region of the South was this crop predominantly found?
CONNECTIONS: What role did the South play in the U.S. economy in 1860? How did the economy of the South differ from that of the North?

FOR MORE HELP ANALYZING THIS MAP, see the map activity for this chapter in the Online Study Guide at bedfordstmartins.com/roarkcompact.

and simple tools. Thus, small farmers as well as planters grew the white fluffy stuff. But planters, whose fields were worked by slaves, produced three-quarters of the South's cotton. And cotton made planters rich.

Plantation slavery also enriched the nation. By 1840, cotton accounted for more than 60 percent of American exports. Much of the profit from sales of cotton overseas returned to planters, but some went to northern middlemen who bought, sold, insured, warehoused, and shipped cotton to the mills in Great Britain and elsewhere. As one New York merchant observed, "Cotton has enriched all through whose hands it has passed."

As middlemen invested their profits in the booming northern economy, industrial development received a burst of much-needed capital. Furthermore, southern plantations benefited northern industry by providing an important market for textiles, agricultural tools, and other manufactured goods.

The economies of the North and South steadily diverged. While the North developed a mixed economy—agriculture, commerce, and manufacturing—the South remained overwhelmingly agricultural. Since planters were earning healthy profits, they saw little reason to diversify. Year after year, they funneled the profits they earned from land and slaves back into more land and slaves. With its capital flowing into agriculture, the South did not develop many factories. By 1860, only 10 percent of the nation's industrial workers lived in the South. Some cotton mills sprang up, but the region that produced 100 percent of the nation's cotton manufactured less than 7 percent of its cotton textiles.

Without significant economic diversification, the South developed fewer cities than the North. In 1860, it was the least urban region in the country. While nearly 37 percent of New England's population lived in cities, less than 12 percent of Southerners were urban dwellers. Southern cities were mostly port cities on the periphery of the region and busy principally with exporting the agricultural products of plantations in the interior. Urban merchants provided agriculture with indispensable services, such as hauling, insuring, and selling cotton, rice, and sugar, but they were the tail on the plantation dog. Southern cities could claim something no northern city desired—140,000 slaves in 1860. In some cities, slaves made up half of the population, and they worked in nearly every conceivable occupation, helping the southern economy thrive.

Because the South had so few cities and industrial jobs, it attracted relatively small numbers of European immigrants. Seeking economic opportunity, not competition with slaves (whose labor would keep wages low), immigrants steered well north of the South's slave-dominated, agricultural economy. In 1860, 13 percent of all Americans were born abroad. But in nine of the fifteen slave states, only 2 percent or fewer were foreign-born.

Not every Southerner celebrated the region's plantation economy. Critics lambasted the excessive commitment to cotton and slaves and bemoaned what one called the "deplorable scarcity" of factories. Diversification, reformers promised, would make the South even more prosperous. State governments encouraged economic development by helping to create banking systems and by constructing railroads, but they also failed to create some of the essential services modern economies require. By the mid-nineteenth century, for example, no southern legislature had created a statewide public school system. Dominant slaveholders failed to see any benefit in educating small farmers, especially with their tax money. Despite the flurry of railroad building, the South's mileage in 1860 was less than half that of the North. Moreover, while railroads crisscrossed the North carrying manufactured goods as well as agricultural products, most railroads in the South ran from port cities back into farming areas and were built to export cotton (see Map 12.5, page 304).

Northerners claimed that slavery was a backward and doomed labor system, but few Southerners perceived economic weakness in their region. In fact, the planters' pockets were never fuller than in the 1850s. Compared with Northerners, Southerners invested less of their capital in industry, transportation, and public education. Planters' decisions to reinvest in agriculture ensured the momentum of the plantation economy and the political and social relationships rooted in it.

> **REVIEW**   Why did the nineteenth-century southern economy remain primarily agricultural while the northern economy grew increasingly diversified?

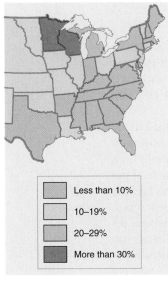

Immigrants as a Percentage of State Populations, 1860

- Less than 10%
- 10–19%
- 20–29%
- More than 30%

Masters, Mistresses, and the Big House

Nowhere was the contrast between northern and southern life more vivid than on the plantations of the South. Located on a patchwork of cleared fields and dense forests, a plantation typically included a "big house" and a slave quarter. Scattered about were numerous outbuildings, each with a special function. Near the big house were the kitchen, storehouse, smokehouse (for curing and preserving meat), and hen coop. More distant were the barns, toolsheds, **artisans'** workshops, and overseer's house. Large plantations sometimes had additional buildings such as an infirmary and a chapel for slaves. Depending on the crop, there was a tobacco shed, a rice mill, a sugar refinery, or a cotton gin house. Lavish or plain, plantations everywhere had an underlying similarity.

The plantation was the home of masters, mistresses, and slaves. Slavery shaped the lives of all the plantation's inhabitants, from work to leisure activities, but it affected each differently. A hierarchy of rigid roles and duties governed relationships. Presiding was the master, who ruled his wife, children, and slaves, none of whom had many legal rights and all of whom were designated by the state as dependents under his dominion and protection.

Plantation Masters

While smaller planters supervised the labor of their slaves themselves, larger planters hired overseers who went to the fields with the slaves, leaving planters free to concentrate on marketing, finance, and general plantation affairs. Planters also found time to escape to town to discuss cotton prices, to the courthouse and legislature to debate politics, and to the woods to hunt and fish.

Increasingly in the nineteenth century, planters characterized their mastery in terms of what they called "Christian guardianship" and what historians have called **paternalism**. The concept of paternalism denied that the form of slavery practiced in the South was brutal and exploitative. Instead, it defined southern slavery as a set of reciprocal obligations between masters and slaves. In exchange for the slaves' labor and obedience, masters provided basic care and necessary guidance. As owners of blacks, masters argued, they had the heavy responsibility of caring for a childlike, dependent people. In 1814, Thomas Jefferson captured the essence of the advancing ideal: "We should endeavor, with those whom fortune has thrown on our hands, to feed & clothe them well, protect them from ill usage, require such reasonable labor only as is performed voluntarily by freemen, and be led by no repugnancies to abdicate them, and our duties to them." A South Carolina rice planter insisted, "I manage them as my children."

Paternalism was part propaganda and part self-delusion. But it was also economically

Southern Man with Children and Their Mammy
Obviously prosperous and looking like a man accustomed to giving orders and being obeyed, this patriarch poses around 1848 with his young daughters and their nurse. The black woman is clearly a servant, a status indicated by her race and her attire. Why does she appear in the daguerreotype? The absent mother may be dead. Her death might account for the inclusion of the African American woman in the family circle. In any case, her presence signals her importance in the household. Fathers left the raising of children to mothers and nurses.
Collection of the J. Paul Getty Museum, Malibu, CA.

shrewd. Masters increasingly recognized slaves as valuable assets to be maintained, and they realized that the expansion of the slave labor force could come only from natural reproduction. The rising price of slaves led one planter to declare in 1849 that "it behooves those who own them to make them last as long as possible." Another planter instructed his overseer to pay attention to "whatever tends to promote their health and render them prolific."

One consequence of this paternalism and economic self-interest was a small improvement in slaves' welfare. Diet improved, although nineteenth-century slaves still mainly ate fatty pork and cornmeal. Housing improved, although the cabins still had cracks large enough, slaves said, for cats to slip through. Clothing improved, although slaves seldom received much more than two crude outfits a year and perhaps a pair of cheap shoes. In the fields, workdays remained sunup to sundown,

but planters often provided a rest period in the heat of the day. And most owners ceased the colonial practices of punishing slaves by branding and mutilation.

Paternalism should not be mistaken for "Ol' Massa's" kindness and goodwill. It encouraged better treatment because it made economic sense to provide at least minimal care for valuable slaves. Nor did paternalism require that planters put aside their whips. They could flail away and still claim that they were only fulfilling their responsibilities as guardians of their naturally lazy and at times insubordinate dependents. State laws gave masters nearly "uncontrolled authority over the body" of the slave, according to one North Carolina judge. Paternalism offered slaves some informal protection against the most brutal punishments, but whipping remained the planters' essential form of coercion. (See "Historical Question," page 326.)

With its notion that slavery imposed on masters a burden and a duty, paternalism provided slaveholders with a means of rationalizing their rule. But it also provided some slaves with leverage over the conditions of their lives. Slaves learned to manipulate a slaveholder's need to see himself as a good and decent master. To avoid a reputation as a cruel tyrant, planters sometimes negotiated with slaves, rather than just resorting to the whip. Masters sometimes granted slaves small garden plots in which they could work for themselves after their day in the fields or a few days off and a dance when they had gathered the last of the cotton.

The Virginia statesman Edmund Randolph argued that slavery created in white southern men a "quick and acute sense of personal liberty" and a "disdain for every abridgement of personal independence." Indeed, prickly individualism and aggressive independence became crucial features of the southern concept of honor. Social standing, political advancement, and even self-esteem rested on an honorable reputation. Defending honor became a male passion. Andrew Jackson's mother reportedly told her son, "Never tell a lie, nor take what is not your own, nor sue anybody for slander or assault and battery. Always settle them cases yourself." Southern boys were expected to master the "manly" arts, and among planters such advice sometimes led to duels. Dueling arrived from Europe in the eighteenth century. It died out in the North, but in the South, even after legislatures banned it, gentlemen continued to defend their honor with pistols at ten paces.

Slavery buttressed the power of white men, and planters brooked no opposition from any of their dependents, black or white. The master's absolute dominion sometimes led to **miscegenation**, the sexual mixing of the races. Laws prohibited interracial sex, and some masters practiced self-restraint. Others merely urged discretion. How many trips masters and their sons made to slave cabins is impossible to tell, but as long as slavery gave white men extraordinary power, slave women were forced to submit to the sexual appetites of the men who owned them.

Individualistic impulses were strong among planters, but duty to family was paramount. In time, as the children of one elite family married the children of another, ties of blood and kinship as well as economic interest and ideology linked planters to one another. Conscious of what they shared as slaveholders, planters worked together to defend their common interests. The values of the big house—slavery, honor, male domination—washed over the boundaries of plantations and flooded all of southern life.

Plantation Mistresses

Like their northern counterparts, southern ladies were expected to possess feminine virtues of piety, purity, chastity, and obedience within the context of marriage, motherhood, and domesticity. Southerners also expected ladies to mirror all that was best in plantation society. Countless toasts praised the southern lady as the perfect complement to her husband, the commanding patriarch. She was physically weak, "formed only for the less laborious occupations," and thus dependent on male protection. To gain this protection, she was naturally modest and delicate, possessed beauty and grace, and cultivated refinement and charm.

For women, this image of the southern lady was no blessing. Chivalry—the South's romantic ideal of male-female relationships—glorified the lady while it subordinated her. Chivalry's underlying assumptions about the weakness of women and the protective authority of men resembled the paternalistic defense of slavery. Indeed, the most articulate spokesmen for slavery also vigorously defended the subordination of women. George Fitzhugh insisted that "a woman, like children, has but one right and that is the right to protection. The right to protection involves the obligation to obey. A husband, a lord and master, nature designed for every woman.... If she be

***Bird Store, 626 Royal Street*, New Orleans**
Most elite white women in the antebellum South lived isolated existences on rural plantations. But some
lived in cities, while others visited them from time to time, and going shopping was a prominent feature
of such visits. Teenager Gertrude Clanton, who lived in Augusta, Georgia, wore store-bought clothes that
she described endlessly in letters to her friends. Here a wealthy mother and daughter shop for a pet in a
New Orleans bird store. The attentive proprietor and attractive shop provide everything they need—
birds, cages, bird food, even an inviting couch and blanket in case they want to rest before moving on.
Elite white women themselves were, in a way, like birds kept in golden cages. Could it be that they were
attracted to the thought of owning birds of their own, something they could care for, train, and control?
Historic New Orleans Collection.

obedient she stands little danger of maltreat-
ment." Just as the slaveholder's mastery was
written into law, so too were the paramount
rights of husbands. Once married, women found
divorce almost impossible.

Daughters of planters confronted chivalry's
demands at an early age. Their educations aimed
at fitting them to become southern ladies. At
their private boarding schools they read literature, learned languages, and studied the appropriate drawing-room arts. Elite women began
courting at a young age and married early. Kate
Carney exaggerated only slightly when she
despaired in her diary: "Today, I am seventeen,
getting quite old, and am not married." Yet mar-

riage meant turning their fates over to their husbands, and making enormous efforts to live up
to their region's lofty ideal.

Proslavery ideologues claimed that slavery
freed white women from drudgery. Surrounded
"by her domestics," declared Thomas R. Dew,
"she ceases to be a mere beast of burden" and
"becomes the cheering and animating center of
the family circle." In reality, however, having
servants required the plantation mistress to
work long hours. Like her husband, she had
managerial responsibilities. She managed the
big house, directly supervising as many as a
dozen slaves. But unlike her husband, the
mistress had no overseer. All house servants

How Often Were Slaves Whipped?

As important as this question is to historians, and obviously was to slaves, we have very little reliable evidence on the frequency of whipping. We know from white sources that whipping was the prescribed method of physical punishment on most antebellum plantations. Masters' instructions to overseers authorized whippings and often set limits on the number of strokes an overseer could administer. Some planters allowed fifteen lashes, some fifty, and some one hundred. But slave owners' instructions, as revealing as they are, tell us more about the severity of beatings than about their frequency.

Remembrances of former slaves confirm that whipping was widespread and frequent. In the 1930s, a government program gathered testimony from more than 2,300 elderly African Americans about their experiences as slaves. Their accounts offered grisly evidence of the cruelty of slavery. "You say how did our Master treat his slaves?" asked one woman. "Scandalous, they treated them just like dogs." She was herself whipped "till the blood dripped to the ground." A few slaves remembered kind masters and never personally felt the sting of the lash. Bert Strong was one such slave, but he also recalled hearing slaves on other farms "hollering when they get beat." He said, "They beat them till it a pity." Beatings occurred often, but how often?

A remarkably systematic record of whippings over a sustained period of time comes from the diary of Bennet H. Barrow, the master of Highland plantation in West Feliciana Parish, Louisiana. For a twenty-three-month period in 1840–1841, Barrow meticulously recorded every whipping he administered or ordered. On most large plantations, overseers handled the business of day-to-day management, but in 1838 Barrow concluded that overseers were "good for nothing" and "a perfect nuisance." He dismissed his white overseer and, assisted only by a black driver, began managing his own plantation.

What does the Barrow evidence show? In 1840, according to the federal census, Barrow owned 129 slaves. In the twenty-three-month period, Barrow recorded 160 whippings. That means that, on the average, a slave was whipped every four and a half days. Sixty of the 77 slaves who worked in the fields were whipped at least once. Most of the 17 field slaves who escaped being beaten were children and pregnant women. Eighty percent of male cotton pickers and 70 percent of female cotton pickers were whipped at least once in this period. Dave Barley received eight floggings, more than any other Barrow slave, and Patience received six whippings, more than any other female slave.

In most instances, Barrow recorded not only the fact of a whipping but also its cause. All sorts of "misconduct," "rascallity," and "disorderly acts" made Barrow reach for his whip. The provocations included family quarrels in the slave quarters, impudence, running away, and failure to keep curfew. But nearly 80 percent of the acts he recorded were related to poor work. Barrow gave beatings for "not picking as well as he can," for picking "very trashy cotton," and for failing to pick the prescribed weight of cotton. One slave claimed to have lost his eyesight and for months refused to work until Barrow "gave him 25 cuts yesterday morning & ordered him to work Blind or not."

Whippings should not be mistaken for spankings. Some planters used whips that raised welts, caused blisters, and bruised. Others resorted to rawhide and cowhide whips that broke the skin, caused scarring, and sometimes permanently maimed. Occasionally, slaves were beaten to death. Whipping was not Barrow's only means of inflicting pain. His diary mentions confining slaves to a plantation jail, putting them in chains, shooting them, breaking a "sword cane" over one slave's head, having slaves mauled by dogs, placing them in stocks, "staking down" slaves for hours, "hand sawing" them, holding their heads under water, and a variety of punishments

answered directly to her. She assigned them tasks each morning, directed their work throughout the day, and punished them when she found fault. In addition to supervising a complex household, women also bore the dangers of childbearing and responsibilities of child rearing. Southern ladies did not often lead lives of leisure.

Whereas masters used their status as slaveholders as a springboard into public affairs, the intending to ridicule and to shame, including making men wear women's clothing and do "women's work," such as the laundry. Still, Barrow's preferred instrument of punishment was the whip.

On the Barrow plantation, as on many others, whipping was public. Victims were often tied to a stake in the quarter, and the other slaves were made to watch. In a real sense, the entire slave population on the plantation experienced a whipping every four and a half days. Even though some never felt the lash personally, all were familiar with its terror and agony.

Was whipping effective? Did it produce a hardworking, efficient, and conscientious labor force? Not according to Barrow's own record. No evidence indicates that whipping changed the slaves' behavior. What Barrow considered bad work continued. Unabated whipping is itself evidence of the failure of punishment to achieve the master's will. Slaves knew the rules, yet they continued to act "badly." And they continued to suffer. It was a gruesome drama— the master seeking from his slaves hard labor and slaves denying their master what he most wanted, day after day.

Did Barrow whip with the same frequency as other planters? We simply do not know. As much as we would like to answer the question precisely, because of the lack of quantifiable evidence we will never know exactly how often whippings occurred. Still, the Barrow evidence allows us to speculate profitably on the frequency of whipping by large

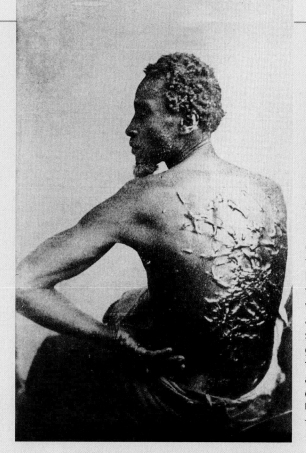

Gordon
This photograph of Gordon, a runaway slave from Baton Rouge, Louisiana, was taken on April 2, 1863, and sent home from the Civil War by Frederick W. Mercer, an assistant surgeon with the Forty-seventh Massachusetts Regiment. Mercer examined four hundred other runaways and found many "to be as badly lacerated." Masters claimed that they whipped only when they had to and only as hard as they had to, but slave testimony and photographic evidence refute their defense of slavery as a benign institution.
Courtesy of the Massachusetts Historical Society.

planters. We do know that Barrow did not consider himself a cruel man. He bitterly denounced his neighbor as "the most cruel Master i ever knew of" for castrating three of his slaves. Moreover, Barrow had dispensed with the overseers in part because of their "brutal feelings" toward slaves. Like most whites, he believed that the lash was essential to get work done. He used it no more than he believed absolutely necessary.

Most masters, including Barrow, tried to encourage work with promises of small gifts and brief holidays, but punishment was their most important motivator. We will

never know if the typical slave was beaten once a year as on the Barrow plantation, but the admittedly scanty evidence suggests that on large plantations the whip fell on someone's back every few days.

And former slaves remembered. More than a half century after emancipation, their sharpest recollections usually involved punishment. They remembered the pain, the injustice, and their bitter resentment. They evaluated their former masters according to how frequently they reached for the whip. According to one former slave, "some was good and some was bad, and about the most of them was bad."

mistress's life was circumscribed by the plantation. Masters left the plantation when they pleased, but plantation mistresses needed chaperones to travel. Women spent most days at home, where they often became lonely. In 1853,

Mary Kendall wrote how much she enjoyed her sister's letter: "For about three weeks I did not have the pleasure of seeing one white female face, there being no white family except our own upon the plantation."

The Price of Blood
This 1868 painting by T. S. Noble depicts a transaction between a slave trader and a rich planter. The trader nervously pretends to study the contract, while the planter waits impatiently for the completion of the sale. The planter's mulatto son, who is being sold, looks away. The children of white men and slave women were property and could be sold by the father/master. The tragedy of miscegenation, however, extended beyond the son shown here. Who is absent from the painting? Whose marriage has been betrayed? Who else's son is being sold away?
Morris Museum of Art, Augusta, GA.

FOR MORE HELP ANALYZING THIS IMAGE, see the visual activity for this chapter in the Online Study Guide at
bedfordstmartins.com/roarkcompact.

As members of slaveholding families, mistresses lived privileged lives. But they also had significant grounds for discontent. No feature of plantation life generated more rage and anguish among mistresses than miscegenation. Mary Boykin Chesnut of Camden, South Carolina, confided in her diary, "ours is a monstrous system, a wrong and iniquity. Like the patriarchs of old, our men live all in one house with their wives and their concubines; and the mulattos one sees in every family partly resemble the white children. Any lady is ready to tell you who is the father of all the mulatto children in everybody's household but her own. Those, she seems to think drop from the clouds."

But most planters' wives, including Mary Boykin Chesnut, accepted slavery. After all, the mistress's world rested on slave labor, just as the master's did. By acknowledging the realities of male power, mistresses enjoyed the rewards of their class and race. But these rewards came at a price. Still, the heaviest burdens of slavery fell not on those who lived in the big house but on those who toiled to support them.

REVIEW   Why did the ideology of paternalism gain currency among planters in the nineteenth century?

Slaves and the Quarter

On most plantations, only a few hundred yards separated the big house and the slave quarter. The distance was short enough to assure whites easy access to the labor of blacks, yet great enough to provide slaves with some privacy. Out of eyesight and earshot of the big house, slaves drew together and built lives of their own. They created families, worshipped God, and developed an African American community.

Despite the rise of plantations, a substantial minority of slaves lived and worked elsewhere. Most labored on small farms, where they wielded a hoe alongside another slave or two and perhaps their master. But by 1860, almost half a million slaves (one in eight) did not work in agriculture at all. Some were employed in towns and cities as domestics, day laborers, bakers, barbers, tailors, and more. Others, far from urban centers, toiled as fishermen, lumbermen, and railroad workers. Slaves could also be found in most of the South's factories. Nevertheless, a majority of slaves (52 percent) counted plantations as their homes and workplaces.

Work

Whites enslaved blacks for their labor, and all slaves who were capable of productive labor worked. Young children were introduced to the world of work as early as age five or six. Ex-slave Carrie Hudson recalled that children who were "knee high to a duck" were sent to the fields to carry water to thirsty workers or to protect ripening crops from hungry birds. Others helped in the slave nursery, caring for children even younger than themselves, or in the big house, where they swept floors or shooed flies in the dining room. When slave boys and girls reached the age of eleven or twelve, masters sent most of them to the fields, where they learned farm work by laboring alongside their parents. After a lifetime of labor, old women left the fields to care for the small children and spin yarn and old men moved on to mind livestock and clean stables.

The overwhelming majority of plantation slaves in 1860 worked as field hands. Planters sometimes assigned men and women to separate gangs, the women working at lighter tasks and the men doing the heavy work of clearing and breaking the land. But women also did heavy work. "I had to work hard," Nancy Boudry remembered, and "plow and go and split wood just like a man."

Haywood Dixon, Slave Carpenter
In this 1854 daguerreotype, Dixon (1826–c. 1889), a slave carpenter who worked in Greene County, North Carolina, poses with a symbol of his craft, the carpenter's square. When work was slow on the home plantation, masters could hire out their skilled artisans to neighbors who needed a carpenter, blacksmith, or mason.
Collection of William L. Murphy.

The backbreaking labor and the monotonous routines caused one ex-slave to observe, the "history of one day is the history of every day."

A few slaves (about one in ten) became house servants. And nearly all of those who did (nine of ten) were women. They cooked, cleaned house, babysat, washed clothes, and did the dozens of other tasks the master and mistress required. House servants enjoyed somewhat less physically demanding work than field hands, but they were constantly on call, with no time that was entirely their own. Since no servant could please constantly, most bore the brunt of white frustration and rage. Ex-slave Jacob Branch of Texas remembered, "My poor mama! Every washday old Missy give her a beating."

Even rarer than house servants were skilled artisans. In the cotton South, no more than one slave in twenty (almost all men) worked in a skilled trade. Most were blacksmiths and carpenters, but slaves also worked as masons, mechanics, millers, and shoemakers. Skilled slave fathers took pride in teaching their crafts to their sons. "My pappy was one of the black smiths and worked in the shop," John Mathews remembered. "I had to help my pappy in the shop when I was a child and I learnt how to beat out the iron and make wagon tires, and make plows."

Rarest of all slave occupations was that of slave driver. Probably no more than one male slave in a hundred worked in this capacity. These men were well named, for their primary task was driving other slaves to work harder in the fields. In some drivers' hands, the whip never rested. Ex-slave Jane Johnson of South Carolina called her driver the "meanest man, white or black, I ever see." But other drivers showed all the restraint they could. "Ole Gabe didn't like that whippin' business," West Turner of Virginia remembered. "When Marsa was there, he would lay it on 'cause he had to. But when old Marsa wasn't lookin', he never would beat them slaves."

Normally, slaves worked from what they called "can to can't," from "can see" in the morning to "can't see" at night. Even with a break at noon for a meal and rest, it made for a long day. For slaves, Lewis Young recalled, "work, work, work, 'twas all they do."

Family, Religion, and Community

From dawn to dusk, slaves worked for the master, but at night, when the labor was done, and all day Sundays and usually Saturday afternoons, slaves were left largely to themselves. Bone tired perhaps, they nonetheless used the time and space to develop and enjoy what mattered most: family, religion, and community.

In the quarter, slaves became husbands and wives, mothers and fathers, sons and daughters, preachers and singers, storytellers and conjurers. Over the generations, they created a community and a culture of their own that buoyed them up during long hours in the fields and brought them joy and hope in the few hours they had to themselves.

One of the most important consequences of the slaves' limited autonomy was the preservation and persistence of the family. Although severely battered, the black family survived slavery. No laws recognized slave marriage, and therefore no master or slave was legally obligated to honor the bond. Nevertheless, plantation records show that slave marriages were often long-lasting. Young men and women in the quarter fell in love, married, and set up housekeeping in cabins of their own. The primary cause of the ending of slave marriages was death, just as it was in white families. But the second most frequent cause of the end of slave marriages was the sale of the husband or wife, something no white family ever had to fear. Precise figures are unavailable, but in the years 1820 to 1860 sales destroyed

Slave Quarter, South Carolina

On large plantations, several score of African Americans lived in cabins that were often arranged along what slaves called "the street." The dwellings in this image by Civil War photographer George N. Barnard of a South Carolina plantation were better built than the typical rickety, one-room, dirt-floored slave cabin. Almost certainly posed, this photograph shows the inhabitants of the slave quarter—little children playing in the dirt, girls and women sitting on the steps talking and working at something, older boys and men driving carts and wagons. During the daylight hours of the workweek, when most men and women labored in the fields, the quarter was mostly empty. At night and on Sundays, it was a busy place.

Collection of the New-York Historical Society.

at least 300,000 slave marriages. Years after Moses Grandy was parted from his slave wife, he said, "I have never seen or heard of her from that day to this." And he added, "I loved her as I love my life."

Like families, religion also provided slaves with a refuge and a reason for living. Before the American Revolution, Baptists and Methodists began trying to convert slaves from their African beliefs. **Evangelicals** offered an emotional "religion of the heart" to which blacks (and many whites as well) responded enthusiastically. By the mid-nineteenth century, perhaps as many as one-quarter of all slaves claimed church membership, and many of the rest would not have objected to being called Christians.

Planters promoted Christianity in the quarter because they believed that the slaves' salvation was part of their obligation and that religion made slaves more obedient. South Carolina slaveholder Charles Colcock Jones, the leading missionary to the slaves, published his *Catechism for Colored Persons* in 1834. In it, he instructed blacks "to count their Masters 'worthy of all honour,' as those whom God has placed over them in this world." But slaves laughed up their sleeves at such messages. "That old white preacher just was telling us slaves to be good to our masters," one ex-slave chuckled. "We ain't cared a bit about that stuff he was telling us 'cause we wanted to sing, pray, and serve God in our own way."

Meeting in their cabins or secretly in the woods, slaves created an African American Christianity that served their needs, not the masters'. Laws prohibited teaching slaves to read, but a few could read enough to struggle with the Bible. They interpreted the Christian message themselves. Rather than obedience, their faith emphasized justice. Slaves believed that God kept score and that the accounts of this world would be settled in the next. "The idea of a revolution in the conditions of the whites and blacks is the corner-stone" of the slaves' religion, recalled one ex-slave. But the slaves' faith also spoke to their experiences in this world. In the Old Testament they discovered Moses, who delivered his people from slavery, and in the New Testament they found Jesus, who offered salvation to all. Jesus' message of equality provided a potent antidote to the planters' claim that blacks were an inferior people whom God condemned to slavery.

Christianity did not entirely drive out traditional African beliefs. Even slaves who were Christians sometimes continued to believe that conjurers, witches, and spirits possessed the power to injure and protect. Moreover, slaves' Christian music, preaching, and rituals reflected the influence of Africa, as did many of their secular activities, such as wood carving, quilt making, and storytelling. But by the mid-nineteenth century, black Christianity had assumed a central place in slaves' quest for freedom. In the words of one spiritual: "O my Lord delivered Daniel/O why not deliver me too?"

Gourd Fiddle
Found in St. Mary's County, Maryland, this slave-made gourd fiddle is an example of the many musical instruments that African Americans crafted and played throughout the South. Henry Wright, an ex-slave from Georgia, remembered: "I made a fiddle out of a large sized gourd—a long wooden handle was used as a neck, and the hair from a horse's tail was used for the bow. The strings were made of catgut." A hybrid of African and European elements, this fiddle offers material evidence of the cultural transformation of African slaves. Although Africans lost much in their forced journey to the Americas, Africa remained in their cultural memory. Black men and women drew on the traditions of their homeland and the South to create something new—an African American culture. Music, a crucial component of that sustaining culture, provided slaves with a creative outlet and relief from the rigors of slavery.
Smithsonian Institution / Aldo Tutino / Folio, Inc.

Resistance and Rebellion

Slaves did not suffer slavery passively. They were, as whites said, "troublesome property." Slaves understood that accommodation to what they could not change was the price of survival, but in a hundred ways they protested their bondage. Theoretically, the master was all-powerful and the slave powerless. But sustained by their families, religion, and community, slaves engaged in day-to-day resistance against their enslavers.

The spectrum of slave resistance ranged from mild to extreme. Telling a pointed story by the fireside in a slave cabin was probably the mildest form of protest. But when the weak got the better of the strong, as they did in tales of Br'er Rabbit and Br'er Fox (*Br'er* is a contraction of *Brother*), listeners could enjoy the thrill of a vicarious victory over their masters. Protest in the fields was riskier and included putting rocks in their cotton bags before having them weighed, feigning illness, and pretending to be so thickheaded that they could not understand the simplest instruction. Slaves broke so many hoes that owners outfitted hoes with oversized handles. Slaves so mistreated the work animals that masters switched from horses to mules, which could absorb more abuse. While slaves worked hard in the master's fields, they also sabotaged his interests.

Running away was a common form of protest. Some runaways sought the ultimate prize: freedom in the North or in Canada. Over the decades, thousands of slaves, almost all from the Upper South, made it. But escape from the Lower South was almost impossible, except in Texas, where several hundred slaves found freedom in Mexico. The overwhelming majority of runaways could hope only to escape for a few days. They usually stayed close to their plantation, keeping to the deep woods or swamps and slipping back into the quarter at night to get food. "Lying out," as it was known, usually ended when the runaway, worn out and ragged, gave up or was finally chased down by slave-hunting dogs.

While resistance was common, outright rebellion—a violent assault on slavery by large numbers of slaves—was very rare. The scarcity of revolts is not evidence of the slaves' contentedness, however. Rather, conditions gave rebels almost no chance of success. By 1860, whites in the South outnumbered blacks two to one and were heavily armed. Moreover, communication between plantations was difficult, and the South provided little protective wilderness into which rebels could retreat and defend themselves. Rebellion, as Nat Turner's experience showed, was virtual suicide.

Despite the rarity of slave revolts, whites believed that they were surrounded by conspiracies to rebel. In 1822, whites in Charleston accused Denmark Vesey, a free black carpenter, of conspiring with plantation slaves to slaughter Charleston's white inhabitants. The authorities rounded up scores of suspects, who, prodded by torture and the threat of death, implicated others in the plot "to riot in blood, outrage, and rapine." Although the city fathers never found any weapons and Vesey and most of the accused steadfastly denied the charges of conspiracy, officials hanged thirty-five black men, including Vesey, and banished another thirty-seven blacks from the state.

Masters boasted that their slaves were "instinctively contented," but steady resistance and occasional rebellion proved otherwise. Slaves did not have the power to end their bondage, but by asserting themselves, they affirmed their humanity and worth. By resisting their masters' will, slaves became actors in the plantation drama, helping to establish limits beyond which planters and overseers hesitated to go.

Still, slavery blunted and thwarted African Americans' hopes and aspirations. Slavery broke some and crippled others. But slavery's destructive power had to contend with the resiliency of the human spirit. Slaves fought back physically, culturally, and spiritually. They not only survived bondage, but they created in the quarter a vibrant African American culture and community that sustained them through more than two centuries of slavery and after.

REVIEW   Why did slave resistance rarely take the form of rebellion?

Black and Free: On the Middle Ground

Not every black Southerner was a slave. In 1860, some 260,000 (approximately 6 percent) of the region's 4.1 million African Americans were free (see Figure 13.1). What is surprising is not that their numbers were small but that they existed at all. "Free black" seemed increasingly a contradiction to most white Southerners. According to the emerging racial thinking, blacks were supposed to be slaves. Blacks who were free stood out, and whites made them more and more targets of oppression. Free blacks stood precariously between slavery and full freedom, on what a young free black artisan in Charleston in 1848 characterized as "a middle ground." But they made the most of their freedom, and a few found success despite the restrictions placed on them by white Southerners.

Precarious Freedom

The population of free blacks swelled after the Revolution, when the natural rights philosophy of the Declaration of Independence and the egalitarian message of evangelical Protestantism joined to challenge slavery. A brief flurry of **emancipation** visited the Upper South, where the ideological assault on slavery coincided with a deep depression in the tobacco economy. By 1810, free blacks in the South numbered more than 100,000, a fact that worried white Southerners, who, because of the cotton boom, wanted more slaves, not more free blacks.

In the 1820s and 1830s, state legislatures acted to stem the growth of the free black population and to shrink the liberty of those blacks who had already gained their freedom. Laws denied masters the right to free their slaves. Other laws humiliated and restricted free blacks by subjecting them to special taxes, requiring them to register annually with the state or to choose a white guardian, prohibiting them from interstate travel, denying them the right to have schools and to participate in politics, and requiring them to carry "freedom papers" to prove they were not slaves. Increasingly, whites subjected free blacks to the same laws as slaves. They could not testify under oath in a court of law or serve on juries. They were liable to whipping and the treadmill, like slaves. Free blacks were forbidden to strike whites, even to defend themselves. "Free negroes belong to a degraded caste of society," a South Carolina judge summed up in 1848. "They are in no respect on a perfect equality with the white man.... They ought, by law, to be compelled to demean themselves as inferiors."

The elaborate system of regulations confined most free African Americans to a constricted life of poverty and dependence. Typically, free blacks were rural, uneducated, unskilled agricultural

Freedom Paper
This legal document attests to the free status of the Rev. John F. Cook of Washington, D.C., his daughter Mary, and his son George. Cook was a free black man who kept his "freedom paper" in this watertight tin, which he probably carried with him at all times. Free blacks had to be prepared to prove their free status any time a white man challenged them, for southern law presumed that a black person was a slave unless he or she could prove otherwise. Without such proof, blacks risked enslavement.
Moorland-Spingarn Research Center, Howard University, Washington, D.C.

laborers and domestic servants. Opportunities of all kinds—for work, education, community—were slim. Planters looked on free blacks as degraded parasites, likely to set a bad example for slaves. They believed that free blacks subverted the racial subordination that was the essence of slavery.

Achievement despite Restrictions

Despite increasingly harsh laws and stepped-up persecution, free African Americans made the most of the advantages their status offered. Unlike slaves, free blacks could legally marry. They could protect their families from arbitrary disruption and pass on their heritage of freedom to their children. Freedom also meant that they could choose occupations and own property. For most, these economic rights proved only theoretical, for a majority of the South's free blacks remained propertyless.

Still, some free blacks escaped the poverty and degradation whites thrust on them. Particularly in urban areas—especially the cities of Charleston, Mobile, and New Orleans—a small elite of free blacks emerged. Urban whites enforced many of the restrictive laws only sporadically, allowing free blacks room to maneuver. The elite consisted overwhelmingly of light-skinned African Americans who worked at skilled trades, and their customers were prominent whites who appreciated their able, respectful service. The free black elite operated schools for their children and traveled in and out of their states, despite laws forbidding both activities. They worshipped with whites (in separate seating) in the finest churches and lived scattered about in white neighborhoods, not in ghettos. And like elite whites, some owned slaves. Blacks could own blacks because they had the right to own property, which in the South included human property. Of the 3,200 black slaveholders (barely 1 percent of the free black population), most owned only a few slaves, who were sometimes family members whom they could not legally free. But others owned slaves in large numbers and exploited them for labor.

One such free black slave owner was William Ellison of South Carolina. Ellison was born a slave in 1790, but in 1816 he bought his freedom and moved to a thriving plantation district about one hundred miles north of Charleston. He set up business as a cotton gin maker, a trade he had learned as a slave, and by 1835 he was prosperous enough to purchase the home of a former governor of the state. By the time of his death in 1861, he had become a cotton planter, with sixty-three slaves and an 800-acre plantation.

Most free blacks neither became slaveholders like Ellison nor sought to raise a slave rebellion, as whites accused Denmark Vesey of doing. Rather, most free blacks simply tried to preserve their freedom, which was under increasing attack. Free blacks clung to their precarious freedom by seeking to impress whites with their reliability, economic contribution, and good behavior.

> **REVIEW** Why did many state legislatures pass laws restricting free blacks' freedoms in the 1820s and 1830s?

The Plain Folk

Like most free blacks, most whites in the South did not own slaves, not even one. In 1860, more than 6 million of the South's 8 million whites lived in slaveless households. Most "plain folk" were small farmers. Perhaps three out of four were **yeomen**, small farmers who owned their own land. As in the North, farm ownership provided a family with an economic foundation, social respectability, and political standing. Unlike their northern counterparts, however, southern yeomen lived in a region whose economy and society were increasingly dominated by unfree labor.

In an important sense, the South had more than one white yeomanry. The huge southern landscape provided space enough for two yeoman societies, separated roughly along geographical lines. Yeomen throughout the South had much in common, but the life of a small farm family in the plantation belt—the flatlands that spread from South Carolina to east Texas—differed from the life of one in the upcountry—the area of hills and mountains.

Plantation Belt Yeomen

Plantation belt yeomen lived within the orbit of the planter class. Small farms actually outnumbered plantations in that great arc of fertile cotton land that spread from South Carolina to Texas, but they were dwarfed in importance. Small farmers grew mainly food crops, particularly corn, but they also devoted a portion of their land to cotton. With only family labor to draw upon, they produced only a few 400-pound bales each year, whereas large planters measured their crop in

The Cotton Belt

hundreds of bales. The small farmers' cotton tied them to planters. Unable to afford cotton gins or baling presses of their own, they relied on helpful neighborhood slave owners to gin and bale their small crops. With no link to merchants in the port cities, plantation belt yeomen turned to better-connected planters to ship and sell their cotton.

A dense network of relationships laced small farmers and planters together in patterns of reciprocity and mutual obligation. Planters hired out surplus slaves to ambitious yeomen who wanted to expand cotton production. They sometimes chose overseers from among the sons of local farm families. Plantation mistresses sometimes nursed ailing neighbors. Family ties could span class lines, making rich and poor kin as well as neighbors. On Sundays, plantation dwellers and plain folk came together in church to worship and afterward lingered to gossip and to transact small business.

Plantation belt yeomen may have envied, and at times even resented, wealthy slaveholders, but in general small farmers learned to accommodate. Planters made accommodation easier by going out of their way to provide necessary services, behave as good neighbors, and avoid direct exploitation of slaveless whites in their community. As a consequence, rather than raging at the oppression of the planter regime, the typical plantation belt yeoman sought entry into it. He dreamed of adding acreage to his farm, buying a few slaves of his own, and retiring from exhausting fieldwork.

Upcountry Yeomen

By contrast, the hills and mountains of the South resisted the penetration of slavery and plantations. In the western parts of Virginia, North Carolina, and South Carolina, northern Georgia and Alabama, and eastern Tennessee and Kentucky, the higher elevation, colder climate, rugged terrain, and poor transportation made it difficult for commercial agriculture to make headway. As a result, yeomen dominated these isolated areas, and planters and slaves were scarce.

At the core of this distinctive upcountry society was the independent farm family working its own patch of land;

Upcountry of the South

IOWA
MICH.
ILL. IND. OHIO PA.
N.J.
MD. DEL.
MO. KY. VA.
TENN. N.C.
ARK. S.C.
MISS. ALA. GA.
LA.
ATLANTIC OCEAN
FLA.
UPCOUNTRY
COASTAL PLAIN
Gulf of Mexico

raising hogs, cattle, and sheep; and seeking self-sufficiency and independence. Toward that end, all members of the family worked, their tasks depending on their sex and age. Husbands labored in the fields, and with their sons they cleared, plowed, planted, and cultivated primarily food crops. Although pressed into field labor at harvest time, wives and daughters of upcountry yeomen, like those of plantation belt yeomen, worked in and about the cabin most of the year. One upcountry farmer remembered that his mother "worked in the house cooking, spinning, weaving [and doing] patchwork." Women also tended the vegetable garden, kept a cow and some chickens, preserved foods, cleaned their homes, fed their families, and cared for their children. Male and female tasks were equally crucial to the farm's success, but as in other white southern households, the domestic sphere was subordinated to the will of the male patriarch.

The typical upcountry yeoman also grew a little cotton or tobacco, but production for home consumption was more important than production for the market. Not much currency changed hands in the upcountry. Barter was common. A yeoman might trade his cotton or tobacco to a country storeowner for a little salt, lead shot, needles, and nails. Or he might swap extra sweet potatoes with the blacksmith for a plow or with the tanner for leather. Networks of exchange and mutual assistance tied individual homesteads to the larger community. Farm families also joined together in logrolling, house- and barn-raising, and cornhusking.

Yeomen did not have the upcountry entirely to themselves. Even the hills had some plantations and slaves. But most upcountry counties were less than a quarter black, whereas counties in the plantation belt were more than half black. As a result, slaveholders had much less direct social and economic power, and yeomen had more. But yeoman domination did not mean that the upcountry opposed slavery. Yeomen there, like yeomen in the plantation belt, shared the planters' commitment to white supremacy and actively defended black subordination. In rural counties, nonslaveholding white men rode in slave patrols, which nightly scoured country roads for slaves who should have been in the quarter.

The Culture of the Plain Folk

Not all nonslaveholding farmers were yeomen who owned their own land. Perhaps one in four was landless and very poor. Some lived as tenants, renting land and struggling to make a go of it. Others strained to make a living by herding pigs and cattle or working as unskilled day laborers. Poor white men gained a reputation for unruly behavior and spontaneous violence. One visitor claimed that a "bowie-knife was a universal, and a pistol a not at all unusual companion." But most landless whites were ambitious people scratching to climb into the yeomanry. Many succeeded, but in the 1850s social mobility slowed. Profits from cotton allowed rich planters to expand their operations, often driving the price of land beyond the reach of poor families. Still, landless whites shared common cultural traits with yeoman farmers.

Situated on scattered farms and in tiny villages, rural plain folk lived isolated, local lives. Bad roads and a lack of newspapers meant that everyday life revolved around family, a handful of neighbors, the local church, and perhaps a country store. Work occupied most hours, but

plain folk still found time for pleasure. "Dancing they are all fond of," a visitor to North Carolina discovered, "especially when they can get a fiddle, or bagpipe." They also loved their tobacco. One visitor complained that the "use of tobacco is almost universal." Men smoked and chewed (and spat), while women dipped snuff. But the truly universal pastimes among men and boys were fishing and hunting. A traveler in Mississippi recalled that his host sent "two of his sons, little fellows that looked almost too small to shoulder a gun," for food. "One went off towards the river and the other struck into the forest, and in a few hours we were feasting on delicious venison, trout and turtle."

Plain folk did not usually associate "book learning" with the basic needs of life. A northern woman visiting the South in the 1850s observed, "Education is not extended to the masses here as at the North." Private academies charged fees that yeomen could not afford, and public schools were scarce. Although most people managed to pick up a basic knowledge of the "three R's," approximately one southern white man in five was illiterate in 1860, and the rate for white women was even higher. "People here prefer talking to reading," a Virginian remarked. Telling stories, reciting ballads, and singing hymns were important activities in yeoman culture.

Plain folk everywhere spent more hours in revival tents than in classrooms. Not all rural whites were religious, but many were, and the most characteristic feature of their evangelical Christian faith was the revival. The greatest of the early-nineteenth-century revivals occurred in 1801 at Cane Ridge, Kentucky, where some 20,000 people gathered to listen to a host of evangelical preachers who spoke day and night for a week. Ministers sought to save souls by bringing individuals to a personal conviction of sin. Revivalism crossed denominational lines, but Baptists and Methodists adopted it most readily and by midcentury had become the South's largest religious groups. By emphasizing free choice and individual worth, the plain folk's religion was hopeful and affirming. Hymns and spirituals provided guides to right and wrong—praising humility and steadfastness, condemning drunkenness and profanity.

***A Baptising on the South Branch of the Potomac near Franklin, Virginia* (detail), 1844**
In 1844, noted painter William Thompson Russell Smith undertook a geological expedition to Virginia, and there he encountered a rural baptism. Primarily a landscape painter, Smith portrayed the human figures as minor characters. If one of the participants had sketched the baptism, he or she might have emphasized the human drama, the emotional pitch of what was for evangelical Christians throughout the South a profound religious moment.
The Charleston Renaissance Gallery, Robert M. Hicklin Jr., Inc., Charleston, South Carolina.

Above all, hymns spoke of eventual release from worldly sorrows and the assurance of eternal salvation.

> **REVIEW**   Why did yeomen dominate the upcountry?

The Politics of Slavery

By the mid-nineteenth century, all southern white men—planters and plain folk alike—had gained the vote. But even after the South's politics became **democratic** for the white male population, political power remained unevenly distributed. The nonslaveholding white majority wielded less political power than their numbers indicated. The slaveholding white minority wielded more. Self-conscious, cohesive, and with a well-developed sense of class interest, slaveholders busied themselves with party politics, campaigns, and officeholding and made demands of state governments. As a result, they received significant benefits. Nonslaveholding whites were concerned mainly with preserving their liberties and keeping their taxes low. Collectively, they asked government for little of an economic nature, and they received little.

Slaveholders sometimes worried about nonslaveholders' loyalty to slavery, but since the eighteenth century, the majority of whites had accepted the planters' argument that the existing social order served all Southerners' interests. Slavery rewarded every white man—no matter how poor—with membership in the South's white ruling class. It also provided the means by which nonslaveholders might someday advance into the ranks of the planters. White men in the South fought furiously about many things, but they agreed that they should take land from Indians, promote agriculture, uphold white supremacy and masculine privilege, and defend slavery from its enemies.

The Democratization of the Political Arena

The political reforms that swept the nation in the first half of the nineteenth century reached deeply into the South. Southern politics became democratic politics—for white men. Southerners eliminated the wealth and property requirements that had once restricted political participation. By the early 1850s, every state had extended **suffrage** to all adult white males. Most southern states also removed the property requirements for holding state offices. To be sure, undemocratic features lingered. Plantation districts still wielded disproportionate power in several state legislatures. Nevertheless, southern politics took place within an increasingly democratic political structure.

White male suffrage ushered in an era of vigorous electoral competition. Eager voters rushed to the polls to exercise their new rights. High turnouts—often approaching 80 percent—became a hallmark of southern electoral politics. As politics became aggressively democratic, it also grew fiercely partisan. From the 1830s to the 1850s, Whigs and Democrats battled for the electorate's favor. In the South, both parties presented themselves as the plain white folk's best friend. All candidates declared their fervent commitment to **republican** equality and pledged to defend the people's liberty. Each party sought to portray the other as a collection of rich, snobbish, selfish men who had antidemocratic designs up their silk sleeves. Each, in turn, claimed for itself the mantle of humble "servant of the people."

Planter Power

Whether Whig or Democrat, southern officeholders were likely to be slave owners. The power slaveholders exerted over slaves did not translate directly into political authority over whites, however. In the nineteenth century, political power could be won only at the ballot box, and almost everywhere nonslaveholders were in the majority. Yet year after year, proud and noisily egalitarian common men elected wealthy slaveholders (Table 13.1).

By 1860, the percentage of slave owners in state legislatures ranged from 41 percent in Missouri to nearly 86 percent in North Carolina. Legislators not only tended to own slaves—they often owned large numbers. The percentage of planters (individuals with twenty or more slaves) in southern legislatures in 1860 ranged from 5.3 percent in Missouri to 55.4 percent in South Carolina. In North Carolina, where only 3 percent of the state's white families belonged to the planter class, more than 36 percent of the legislature were planters. The democratization of politics in the nineteenth century meant that

TABLE 13.1	PERCENT OF SLAVEHOLDERS AND PLANTERS IN SOUTHERN LEGISLATURES, 1860	
Legislature	Slaveholders	Planters*
Virginia	67.3%	24.2%
Maryland	53.4	19.3
North Carolina	85.8	36.6
Kentucky	60.6	8.4
Tennessee	66.0	14.0
Missouri	41.2	5.3
Arkansas	42.0	13.0
South Carolina	81.7	55.4
Georgia	71.6	29.0
Florida	55.4	20.0
Alabama	76.3	40.8
Mississippi	73.4	49.5
Louisiana	63.8	23.5
Texas	54.1	18.1

*Planters: Owned 20 or more slaves.

Source: Adapted from Ralph A. Wooster, *The People in Power: Courthouse and Statehouse in the Lower South, 1850–1860* (1969), 41; Wooster, *Politicians, Planters, and Plain Folks: Courthouse and Statehouse in the Upper South* (1975), 40. Courtesy of the University of Tennessee Press.

more ordinary citizens participated in elections, but yeomen and artisans remained rare sights in the halls of southern legislatures.

Upper-class dominance of southern politics reflected the elite's success in persuading the white majority that what was good for slaveholders was also good for them. In reality, the South had, on the whole, done well by the plain folk. Most had farms of their own. They participated as equals in a democratic political system. They enjoyed an elevated social status, above all blacks and in theory equal to all other whites. They commanded patriarchal authority over their households. And as long as slavery existed, they could dream of joining the planter class. Slaveless white men found much to celebrate in the slave South.

Most slaveholders took pains to win the plain folk's trust and to nurture their respect. One South Carolinian told his wealthy neighbor that he had a bright political future because he never thought himself "too good to sit down & talk to a poor man." South Carolinian Mary Boykin Chesnut complained about the fawning attention her slaveholding husband showed to poor men, including one who had "mud sticking up through his toes." Smart candidates found ways to convince wary plain folk of their democratic convictions and egalitarian sentiments,

whether they were genuine or not. When young John A. Quitman ran for a seat in the Mississippi legislature, he amazed a boisterous crowd of small farmers at one campaign stop by not only entering but winning contests in jumping, boxing, wrestling, and sprinting. For his finale he outshot the area's champion marksman. Then, demonstrating his deft political touch, he gave his prize, a fat ox, to the defeated rifleman. The electorate showed its approval by sending Quitman to the state capital.

Georgia politics illustrate how well planters protected their interests in state legislatures. In 1850, about half of the state's revenues came from taxes on slaves, the characteristic form of planter wealth. However, the tax rate on slaves was trifling, only about one-fifth the rate on land. Moreover, planters benefited far more than other groups from public spending. Financing railroads—which carried cotton to market—was the largest state expenditure. The legislature also established low tax rates on land, the characteristic form of yeoman wealth, which meant that the typical yeoman's annual tax bill was small. Still, relative to their wealth, large slaveholders paid less than did other whites. Relative to their numbers, they got more in return. A sympathetic slaveholding legislature protected planters' interests and gave the impression of protecting the small farmers' interests as well.

The South's elite defended slavery in other ways. In the 1830s, whites decided that slavery was too important to debate. "So interwoven is [slavery] with our interest, our manners, our climate and our very being," one man declared in 1833, "that no change can ever possibly be effected without a civil commotion from which the heart of a patriot must turn with horror." To end free speech on the slavery question, powerful whites dismissed slavery's critics from college faculties, drove them from pulpits, and hounded them from political life. Sometimes antislavery Southerners fell victim to vigilantes and mob violence. One could defend slavery; one could even delicately suggest mild reforms. But no Southerner could any longer safely call slavery evil or advocate its destruction.

In the South, therefore, the rise of the common man occurred alongside the continuing, even growing, power of the planter class. Rather than pitting slaveholders against nonslaveholders, elections remained an effective means of binding the region's whites together. Elections affirmed the sovereignty of white men, whether planter or plain folk, and the subordination of African Americans. Those twin themes played well among white women as well. Although unable to vote, white women supported equality for whites and slavery for blacks. In the antebellum South, the politics of slavery helped knit together all of white society.

> **REVIEW**   How did planters benefit from their control of state legislatures?

Conclusion: A Slave Society

By the early nineteenth century, northern states had either abolished slavery or put it on the road to extinction while southern states were aggressively building the largest slave society in the New World. Regional differences increased over time, not merely because the South became more and more dominated by slavery, but also because developments in the North rapidly propelled it in a very different direction.

One-third of the South's population was enslaved by 1860. Bondage saddled blacks with enormous physical and spiritual burdens: hard labor, harsh treatment, broken families, and most important, the denial of freedom itself. Although degraded and exploited, they were not defeated. Out of African memories and New World realities, blacks created a life-affirming African American culture that sustained and strengthened them. Their families, religion, and community provided antidotes to white racist ideas and even to white power. Defined as property, they refused to be reduced to things. Perceived as inferior beings, they rejected the notion that they were natural slaves. Slaves engaged in a war of wills with masters who sought their labor while the slaves sought to live dignified, autonomous lives.

By the mid-nineteenth century, slavery was crucial to the South's distinctiveness and to the loyalty and regional identification of its whites. The South was not merely a society with slaves; it had become a slave society: Slavery shaped the region's economy, culture, social structure, and politics. Whites south of the Mason-Dixon line believed that racial slavery was necessary and just.

By making all blacks a pariah class, all whites gained a measure of equality and harmony.

Racism did not erase stress along class lines. Nor did the other features of southern life that helped confine class tensions: the wide availability of land, rapid economic mobility, the democratic nature of political life, and patriarchal power among white men. Anxious slaveholders continued to worry that yeomen would defect from the proslavery consensus. But during the 1850s, a far more ominous division emerged—between "slave states" and "free states."

Suggestions for Further Reading

Ira Berlin, *Generations of Captivity: A History of African-American Slaves* (2003). A modern synthesis of the slave experience that emphasizes geographical diversity and change over time.

Drew G. Faust, *James Henry Hammond and the Old South: A Design for Mastery* (1982). A lively biography of one of the South's most compelling planter/politicians.

Peter Kolchin, *American Slavery, 1619-1877* (1993). A masterful survey of the historiography of slavery and reflection upon slavery's meaning for southern history.

Stephanie McCurry, *Masters of Small Worlds: Yeoman Households, Gender Relations, and the Political Culture of the Antebellum South* (1995). An insightful analysis of yeoman households that argues the centrality of patriarchy to southern politics.

Willie Lee Rose, ed., *A Documentary History of Slavery in North America* (1976). A collection of contemporary documents that vividly illustrates slaves' responses to bondage.

Adam Rothman, *Slave Country: American Expansion and the Deep South* (2005). A dramatic account of how and why slavery spread west from the original coastal southern states.

> ▶ **FOR MORE BOOKS ABOUT TOPICS IN THIS CHAPTER,** see the Online Bibliography at bedfordstmartins.com/roarkcompact.
>
> ▶ **FOR ADDITIONAL FIRSTHAND ACCOUNTS OF THIS PERIOD,** see Chapter 13 in Michael Johnson, ed., *Reading the American Past*, Third Edition.
>
> ▶ **FOR WEB SITES AND DOCUMENTS RELATED TO TOPICS AND PLACES IN THIS CHAPTER,** see "HistoryLinks," "DocLinks," and "PlaceLinks" at bedfordstmartins.com/roarkcompact.

REVIEWING THE CHAPTER

Follow these steps to review and strengthen your understanding of the chapter.

STEP 1: *Study the **Key Terms** and **Timeline** to identify the significance of each item listed.*

STEP 2: *Answer the **Review Questions**, drawing on key terms and dates to support your answers.*

STEP 3: *Drawing on the Key Terms, Timeline, and Review Questions, answer the broader **Making Connections** questions.*

KEY TERMS

Who

Nat Turner (p. 315)
David Walker (p. 315)
William Lloyd Garrison (p. 315)
Eli Whitney (p. 321)
Mary Boykin Chesnut (p. 328)
Charles Colcock Jones (p. 331)
Denmark Vesey (p. 332)
William Ellison (p. 334)

What

Nat Turner's insurrection (p. 315)
Mason-Dixon line (p. 316)
Creek War of 1813–1814 (p. 316)
cotton kingdom (p. 317)
slave codes (p. 317)
planter (p. 321)
plantation (p. 321)
overseer (p. 323)
paternalism (p. 323)

miscegenation (p. 324)
chivalry (p. 324)
slave driver (p. 330)
slave resistance (p. 332)
Vesey conspiracy (p. 332)
"free black" (p. 333)
emancipation (p. 333)
yeomen (p. 334)
plantation belt (p. 334)
upcountry (p. 335)

TIMELINE

◀ 1808 • External slave trade outlawed.

　　1810s–1850s • Suffrage extended throughout South to white males.

　　　　1813–1814 • Creek War opens Indian land to settlement.

　　　　　　1820s–1830s • Southern legislatures enact slave codes
　　　　　　　　　　to strengthen slavery.
　　　　　　　　• Southern legislatures enact laws to restrict
　　　　　　　　　growth of free black population.
　　　　　　　　• Southern intellectuals begin to fashion
　　　　　　　　　systematic defense of slavery.

　　　　　1820–1860 • Cotton production soars.

　　　　　　1822 • Denmark Vesey executed.

　　　　　　　　　1829 • *Appeal . . . to the Coloured
　　　　　　　　　　　　Citizens of the World* published.

　　　　　　　　　1830 • Southern slaves number
　　　　　　　　　　　　approximately 2 million.

REVIEW QUESTIONS

1. Why did the nineteenth-century southern economy remain primarily agricultural while the northern economy grew increasingly diversified? (pp. 316–22)

2. Why did the ideology of paternalism gain currency among planters in the nineteenth century? (pp. 322–28)

3. Why did slave resistance rarely take the form of rebellion? (pp. 329–32)

4. Why did many state legislatures pass laws restricting free blacks' freedoms in the 1820s and 1830s? (pp. 332–34)

5. Why did yeomen dominate the upcountry? (pp. 334–37)

6. How did planters benefit from their control of state legislatures? (pp. 337–39)

MAKING CONNECTIONS

1. By the mid-nineteenth century the South had become a "cotton kingdom." How did cotton's profitability shape the region's antebellum development? In your answer, discuss the region's distinctive demographic and economic features.

2. How did white southern legislators and intellectuals attempt to strengthen the institution of slavery in the 1820s? What prompted them to undertake this work? In your answer, be sure to explore regional and national influences.

3. Although bondage restricted slaves' autonomy and left slaves vulnerable to extreme abuse, they resisted slavery. Discuss the variety of ways in which slaves attempted to lessen the harshness of slavery. What were the short- and long-term effects of their efforts?

4. Despite vigorous political competition in the South, by 1860, legislative power was largely concentrated in the hands of a regional minority—slaveholders. Why were slaveholders politically dominant? In your answer, be sure to consider how the region's biracialism contributed to its politics.

▶ For practice quizzes, a customized study plan, and other study tools, see the Online Study Guide at bedfordstmartins.com/roarkcompact.

1831 • Nat Turner's slave rebellion.
      • First issue of *Liberator* published.

1834 • *Catechism for Colored Persons* published.

1836 • Arkansas admitted to the Union as a slave state.

1840 • Cotton accounts for more than 60 percent of the nation's exports.

1845 • Texas and Florida admitted to the Union as slave states.

1860
• Southern slaves number nearly 4 million, one-third of the South's population.

JOHN BROWN'S PIKES

Scorning what he called "milk-and-water" abolitionists who only talked about slavery, John Brown favored "action!" In 1859 when he brought his abolitionist war to Virginia, he carried with him 950 pikes, handsome but deadly spears made by a Connecticut blacksmith, which he expected to put into the hands of rebelling slaves. Bloody pikes, he thought, would end slavery in America. After Brown's failure at Harpers Ferry, townspeople sold many of the weapons as souvenirs.

Chicago Historical Society.

14

The House Divided

1846–1861

O THER THAN TWENTY CHILDREN, John Brown did not have much to show for his life in 1859. Grizzled, gnarled, and fifty-nine years old, he had for decades lived like a nomad, hauling his large family back and forth across six states as he tried desperately to better himself. He turned his hand to farming, raising sheep, running a tannery, and selling wool, but failure dogged him. The world had given John Brown some hard licks, but it had not budged his conviction that slavery was wrong and ought to be destroyed. He had learned to hate slavery at his father's knee, and in the wake of the fighting that erupted over the issue in Kansas in the 1850s, his beliefs turned violent. On May 24, 1856, he led an eight-man antislavery posse in the midnight slaughter of five allegedly proslavery men at Pottawatomie, Kansas. He told Mahala Doyle, whose husband and two oldest sons he killed, that if a man stood between him and what he thought right, he would take that man's life as calmly as he would eat breakfast.

After the killings, Brown slipped out of Kansas and reemerged in the East. More than ever, he was a man on fire for abolition. He spent thirty months begging money from New Englanders to support his vague plan for military operations against slavery. He captivated the genteel easterners, particularly the Boston elite. They were awed by his iron-willed determination and courage, but most could not accept violence. "These men are all talk," Brown declared. "What is needed is action—action!" But the hypnotic-eyed Brown convinced a handful that God had touched him for a great purpose, and they donated enough for him to gather a small band of antislavery warriors.

On the night of October 16, 1859, John Brown took his war against slavery into the South. With only twenty-one men, including five African Americans, he invaded Harpers Ferry, Virginia. His band quickly seized the town's armory and rifle works, but the invaders were immediately surrounded, first by local militia and then by Colonel Robert E. Lee, who commanded the U.S. troops in the area. When Brown refused to surrender, federal soldiers charged with bayonets. Seventeen men, two of whom were slaves, lost their lives. Although a few of Brown's raiders escaped, federal forces killed ten (including two of his sons) and captured seven, among them Brown.

"When I strike, the bees will begin to swarm," Brown told Frederick Douglass a few months before the raid. As slaves rushed to Harpers Ferry, Brown planned to arm them with the pikes he carried with him and with weapons stolen from the armory. They would then fight a war of liberation. Brown, however, neglected to inform the slaves that he had arrived in Harpers Ferry, and the few who knew of his arrival wanted nothing to do with his enterprise. "It was not a slave insurrection," Abraham Lincoln observed. "It was an attempt by white men to get up a revolt among slaves, in

John Brown

In this 1859 photograph, John Brown appears respectable, even statesmanlike, but contemporaries debated his mental state and moral character, and the debate still rages. Critics argue that he was a bloody terrorist, a religious fanatic who believed that he was touched by God for a great purpose, one for which he was willing to die. Admirers see a resolute and selfless hero, a rare white man who believed that black people were the equals of whites, a reformer who recognized that moral suasion would not end slavery in America. National Portrait Gallery, Smithsonian Institution / Art Resource, NY.

which the slaves refused to participate. In fact, it was so absurd that the slaves, with all their ignorance, saw plainly enough it could not succeed."

Although Brown's raid ended in utter defeat, white Southerners viewed it as proof of their growing suspicion that Northerners actively sought to incite slaves in bloody rebellion. For more than a decade, Northerners and Southerners had accused one another of hostile intentions, and by 1859, emotions were raw. Sectional tension was as old as the Constitution, but hostility had escalated with the outbreak of war with Mexico in May 1846 (see chapter 12). Only three months after the war began, national expansion and the slavery issue intersected when Representative David Wilmot introduced a bill to prohibit slavery from any territory that might be acquired as a result of the war. After that, the problem of slavery in the territories became the principal wedge that divided the nation.

"Mexico is to us the forbidden fruit," South Carolina senator John C. Calhoun declared at the war's outset. "The penalty of eating it [is] to subject our institutions to political death." For a decade and a half, the slavery issue intertwined with the fate of former Mexican land, poisoning national political debate. Slavery proved powerful enough to transform party politics into sectional politics. Rather than Whigs and Democrats confronting one another across party lines, Northerners and Southerners eyed one another hostilely across the Mason-Dixon line. Sectional politics encouraged the South's separatist impulses. A fitful tendency before the Mexican-American War, southern separatism gained strength with each confrontation. As the nation lurched from crisis to crisis, southern disaffection and alienation mounted, and support for compromise and conciliation eroded. The era began with a crisis of Union and ended with the Union in even graver peril. As Abraham Lincoln predicted in 1858, "A house divided against itself cannot stand."

The Bitter Fruits of War

Between 1846 and 1848, the nation grew by 1.2 million square miles, an incredible two-thirds. By 1850, the gold rush had transformed the sleepy **frontier** of California into a booming, thriving economy (see chapter 12). The 1850s witnessed new "rushes," for gold in Colorado and silver in Nevada's Comstock Lode. People from around the world flocked to the West where they produced a vibrant agriculture as well as tons of gold and silver. But it quickly became clear that Northerners and Southerners had very different visions of the West, particularly the place of slavery in its future.

History provided contradictory precedents for handling slavery in the territories. In 1787, the Northwest Ordinance banned slavery north of the Ohio River. In 1803, slavery was allowed to remain in the newly acquired Louisiana Territory. The Missouri Compromise of 1820 prohibited slavery in part of that territory but allowed it in the rest. In 1846, when the war with Mexico suggested new territory for the United States, politicians offered various plans. But when the war ended in 1848, Congress had made no headway in solving the issue of slavery in the western territories. In 1850, Congress patched together a settlement, one that Americans hoped would be permanent.

The Wilmot Proviso and the Expansion of Slavery

Most Americans agreed that the Constitution had left the issue of slavery to the individual states to decide. Northern states had done away with slavery, while southern states had retained it. But what about slavery in the nation's territories? The Constitution states that "Congress shall have power to…make all needful rules and regulations respecting the territory…belonging to the United States." The debate about slavery, then, turned toward Congress.

In August 1846 the young Democratic representative from Pennsylvania, David Wilmot, proposed that Congress bar slavery from all lands acquired in the war with Mexico. The Mexicans had already abolished slavery in their country, and Wilmot declared, "God forbid that we should be the means of planting this institution upon it."

Regardless of party affiliation, Northerners lined up behind Wilmot's proviso. Many supported **free soil**, by which they meant territory from which slavery would be prohibited, on the basis of egalitarian principle. They wanted to preserve the West for **free labor**, for hard-working, self-reliant free men, not for slaveholders and slaves. But support also came from those who were simply anti-South. New slave territories would eventually mean new slave states, and they opposed magnifying the political power of Southerners. Wilmot himself said he saw his proposal as a means of blunting "the *power* of slaveholders" in the national government.

Additional support for free soil came from Northerners who were hostile to blacks and wanted to reserve new lands for whites. Wilmot understood what one Indiana man put bluntly: "The American people are emphatically a *Negro-hating* people." Wilmot himself blatantly encouraged racist support when he declared, "I would preserve for free white labor a fair country, a rich inheritance, where the sons of toil, of my own race and own color, can live without the disgrace which association with negro slavery brings upon free labor." It is no wonder that some called the Wilmot Proviso the White Man's Proviso.

The thought that slavery might be excluded outraged almost all white Southerners. They regarded the West as a ladder for economic and social opportunity. They also believed that the exclusion of slavery was a slap in the face to southern veterans of the Mexican-American War. "When the war-worn soldier returns home," one Alabaman asked, "is he to be told that he cannot carry his property to the country won by his blood?"

Mexican Cession, 1848

In addition, southern leaders understood the need for political parity with the North to protect the South's interests, especially slavery. James Henry Hammond of South Carolina predicted that ten new states would be carved from the acquired Mexican land. If free soil won, the North would "ride over us rough shod" in Congress, he claimed. "Our only safety is in *equality* of POWER."

The two sides squared off in the nation's capital. Because Northerners had a majority in the House, they easily passed the Wilmot Proviso. In the Senate, however, where slave states outnumbered free states fifteen to fourteen, Southerners defeated it. Senator John C. Calhoun of South Carolina denied that Congress had constitutional authority to

John C. Calhoun
Hollow-cheeked and dark-eyed in this 1850 daguerreotype by Mathew Brady, Calhoun had only months to live. Still, his passion and indomitable will come through. British writer Harriet Martineau once described the champion of southern rights as "the cast-iron man who looks as if he had never been born and could never be extinguished."
National Portrait Gallery, Smithsonian Institution/Art Resource, NY.

exclude slavery from the nation's territories. He argued that Congress could not justly deprive any state of equal rights in the territories and therefore could not bar citizens of one state from migrating with their property (including slaves) to the territories. Whereas Wilmot demanded that Congress slam shut the door to slavery, Calhoun called on Congress to hold the door wide open.

Senator Lewis Cass of Michigan offered a compromise through the doctrine of **popular sovereignty**, by which the people who settled the territories would decide for themselves slavery's fate. This solution, Cass argued, sat squarely in the American tradition of **democracy** and local self-government. It had the added attraction of removing the incendiary issue of the expansion of slavery from the nation's capital.

Popular sovereignty's most attractive feature was its ambiguity about the precise moment when settlers could determine slavery's fate. Northern advocates believed that the decision on slavery could be made as soon as the first territorial legislature assembled. With free-soil majorities likely because of the North's greater population, they would shut the door to slavery almost before the first slave arrived. Southern supporters declared that popular sovereignty guaranteed that slavery would be unrestricted throughout the entire territorial period. Only at the very end, when settlers in the territory drew up a constitution and applied for statehood, could they decide the issue of slavery. By then, slavery would have sunk deep roots. As long as the matter of timing remained vague, popular sovereignty gave hope to both sides.

When Congress ended its session in 1848, no plan had won a majority in both houses. Northerners who demanded no new slave territory anywhere, ever, and Southerners who demanded entry for their slave property into all territories, or else, staked out their extreme positions. Unresolved in Congress, the territorial question naturally became an issue in the presidential election of 1848.

The Election of 1848

When President Polk—worn out and ailing—chose not to seek reelection, the Democratic convention nominated Lewis Cass of Michigan, the man most closely associated with popular sovereignty. But in an effort to keep peace between their proslavery and antislavery factions, the Democrats adopted a platform that avoided a firm position on slavery in the territories. The

Whigs followed a different strategy and nominated a Mexican-American War hero, General Zachary Taylor. The Whigs bet that the combination of a military hero and total silence on the slavery issue would carry the day, and thus they declined to adopt a party platform. Taylor, who owned more than 100 slaves on plantations in Mississippi and Louisiana, was hailed by Georgia politician Robert Toombs as a "Southern man, a slaveholder, a cotton planter."

Antislavery Whigs balked and looked for an alternative. The time seemed ripe for a major political realignment. Senator Charles Sumner called for "one grand Northern party of Freedom," and in the summer of 1848 antislavery Whigs and antislavery Democrats founded the Free-Soil Party. Nearly 15,000 noisy Free-Soilers gathered in Buffalo, New York, where they nominated a Democrat, Martin Van Buren, for president and a Whig, Charles Francis Adams, for vice president. The platform boldly proclaimed, "Free soil, free speech, free labor, and free men."

The November election dashed the hopes of the Free-Soilers. Although they succeeded in making slavery the campaign's central issue, they did not carry a single state. The major parties went through contortions to present their candidates favorably in both North and South, and their evasions succeeded. Taylor won the all-important electoral vote, 163 to 127, carrying eight of the fifteen slave states and seven of the fifteen free states (Map 14.1). (Wisconsin had entered the Union earlier in 1848 as the fifteenth free state.) Northern voters proved they were not yet ready for Sumner's "one grand Northern party of Freedom," but the struggle over slavery in the territories had shaken the major parties badly.

Debate and Compromise

Southern slaveholder Zachary Taylor entered the White House in March 1849 and almost immediately shocked the nation by championing a free-soil solution to the Mexican cession. Believing that he could avoid further sectional strife if California and New Mexico skipped the territorial stage, he sent agents west to persuade the settlers to apply for admission to the Union as states. Predominately antislavery, the settlers began writing free-state constitutions. "For the first time," Mississippian Jefferson Davis

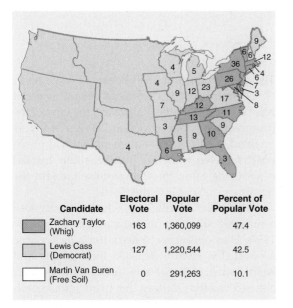

Candidate	Electoral Vote	Popular Vote	Percent of Popular Vote
Zachary Taylor (Whig)	163	1,360,099	47.4
Lewis Cass (Democrat)	127	1,220,544	42.5
Martin Van Buren (Free Soil)	0	291,263	10.1

MAP 14.1 The Election of 1848
When Congress convened in December 1849, anxious citizens packed the galleries, eager for the "Great Debate." They witnessed what proved to be one of the longest, most contentious, and most significant sessions in the history of Congress.

lamented, "we are about permanently to destroy the balance of power between the sections."

Congress convened in December 1849, beginning one of the most contentious and most significant sessions in its history. President Taylor urged Congress to admit California as a free state immediately and to admit New Mexico, which lagged behind a few months, as soon as it applied. Southerners exploded. In their eyes, Taylor had betrayed his region. Southerners who would "consent to be thus degraded and enslaved," a North Carolinian declared, "ought to be whipped through their fields by their own negroes."

In stepped Senator Henry Clay of Kentucky, the architect of Union-saving compromises in the Missouri and **nullification** crises. Clay offered a series of resolutions meant to answer and balance "all questions in controversy between the free and slave states, growing out of the subject of slavery." Admit California as a free state, he proposed, but organize the rest of the Southwest without restrictions on slavery. Require Texas to abandon its claim to parts of New Mexico, but compensate it by assuming its preannexation debt. Abolish the domestic slave trade in Washington, D.C., but confirm slavery itself in the nation's capital. Reassert Congress's lack of authority to interfere with the interstate

slave trade. And enact a more effective fugitive slave law.

Both antislavery advocates and "fire-eaters" (as radical Southerners who urged secession from the Union were called) savaged Clay's plan. Senator Salmon Chase of Ohio ridiculed it as "sentiment for the North, substance for the South." Senator Henry S. Foote of Mississippi denounced it as more offensive to the South than the speeches of abolitionists William Lloyd Garrison, Wendell Phillips, and Frederick Douglass combined. The most ominous response came from Calhoun, who argued that the fragile political unity of North and South depended on continued equal representation in the Senate, which Clay's plan for a free California destroyed. "As things now stand," he said in February 1850, the South "cannot with safety remain in the Union."

Senator Daniel Webster of Massachusetts then addressed the Senate. Like Clay, Webster sought to build a constituency for compromise. He appealed for an end to reckless proposals and, to the dismay of many Northerners, mentioned by name the Wilmot Proviso. A legal ban on slavery in the territories was unnecessary, he said, because the harsh climate effectively prohibited the expansion of cotton and slaves into the new American Southwest.

Free-soil forces recoiled from what they saw as Webster's desertion. In Boston, the clergyman and abolitionist Theodore Parker could only conclude that "the Southern men" must have offered Webster the presidency. In Washington, Senator William H. Seward of New York responded that Webster's and Clay's compromise with slavery was "radically wrong and essentially vicious." He flatly rejected Calhoun's argument that Congress lacked constitutional authority to exclude slavery from the territories. In any case, Seward said, in the most sensational moment in his address, there was a "higher law than the Constitution"—the law of God—to ensure freedom in all the public domain. Claiming that God was a Free-Soiler did nothing to cool the superheated political atmosphere.

In May, a Senate committee produced a bill that joined Clay's resolutions into a single comprehensive package, known as the Omnibus Bill because it was a vehicle on which "every sort of passenger" could ride. Clay bet that a majority of Congress wanted compromise and that each member would vote for the package to gain an overall settlement of sectional issues. But the omnibus strategy backfired. Free-Soilers and proslavery Southerners voted down the comprehensive plan.

Fortunately for those who favored a settlement, Senator Stephen A. Douglas, a rising Democratic star from Illinois, stepped in. He broke the bill into its various parts and skillfully ushered each through Congress. The agreement Douglas won in September 1850 was very much the one Clay had proposed in January. California entered the Union as a free state. New Mexico and Utah became territories where slavery would be decided by popular sovereignty. Texas accepted its boundary with New Mexico and received $10 million from the federal government. Congress ended the slave trade in the District of Columbia but enacted a more stringent fugitive slave law. In September, Millard Fillmore, who had become president when Zachary Taylor died suddenly in July, signed into law each bill, collectively known as the Compromise of 1850 (Map 14.2).

Actually, the Compromise of 1850 was not a true compromise at all. Douglas's parliamentary skill, not a spirit of conciliation, was responsible for the legislative success. Still, the nation breathed a sigh of relief, for the Compromise preserved the Union and peace for the moment.

> **REVIEW** Why did response to the Wilmot Proviso split along sectional rather than party lines?

The Sectional Balance Undone

The Compromise of 1850 began to come apart almost immediately. The thread that unraveled it was not slavery in the Southwest, the crux of the disagreement, but runaway slaves in New England, a part of the settlement that had previously received relatively little attention. Instead of restoring calm, the Compromise brought the horrors of slavery into the North.

Millions of Northerners who had never seen a runaway slave confronted slavery in the early 1850s. Harriet Beecher Stowe's *Uncle Tom's Cabin,* a novel that vividly depicted the brutality and heartlessness of the South's "peculiar institution," aroused passions so deep that many found goodwill toward white Southerners nearly impossible. But no groundswell of antislavery sentiment compelled Congress to reopen the slavery controversy: Politicians did it themselves. Four years after Congress delicately stitched the sectional compromise together, it ripped the threads out. Once again it posed the question of slavery in the territories, the deadliest of all sectional issues.

The Fugitive Slave Act

The Fugitive Slave Act proved the most explosive of the Compromise measures. The issue of runaways was as old as the Constitution, which contained a provision for the return of any "person held to service or labor in one state" who escaped to another. In 1793, a federal law gave muscle to the provision by authorizing slave owners to enter other states to recapture their slave property. Proclaiming the 1793 law a license to kidnap free blacks, northern states in the 1830s began passing "personal liberty laws" that provided fugitives with some protection.

Some northern communities also formed vigilance committees to help runaways and to obstruct white Southerners who came north to reclaim them. Each year, a few hundred slaves escaped into free states and found friendly northern "conductors" who put them aboard the "underground railroad," which was not a railroad at all but a series of secret "stations" (hideouts) on the way to Canada. Harriet Tubman, an escaped slave from Maryland, returned to the South more

MAP 14.2 The Compromise of 1850

The patched-together sectional agreement was both clumsy and unstable. Few Americans—in either North or South—supported all five parts of the Compromise.

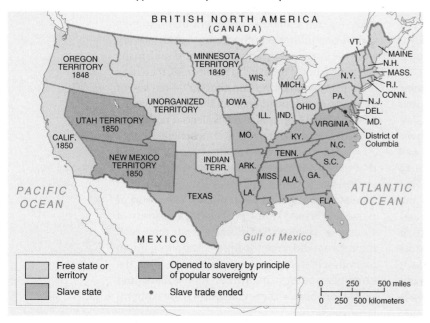

than a dozen times and guided more than 300 slaves to freedom in this way.

Furious about northern interference, Southerners in 1850 insisted on the stricter fugitive slave law that was passed as part of the Compromise. To seize an alleged slave, a slaveholder simply had to appear before a commissioner and swear that the runaway was his. The commissioner earned $10 for every black returned to slavery but only $5 for those set free. Most galling to Northerners, the law stipulated that all citizens were expected to assist officials in apprehending runaways.

In Boston in February 1851, an angry crowd overpowered federal marshals and snatched a runaway named Shadrach from a courtroom, put him on the underground railroad, and whisked him off to Canada. Three years later, when another Boston crowd rushed the courthouse in a failed attempt to rescue Anthony Burns, who had recently fled slavery in Richmond, a guard was shot dead. To white Southerners, it seemed that fanatics of the "higher law" creed had whipped Northerners into a frenzy of massive resistance. Such spectacular rescues were rare. The overwhelming majority of fugitives claimed before federal commissioners were reenslaved peacefully. But brutal enforcement of the unpopular law had a radicalizing effect in the North, particularly in New England. And to Southerners it seemed that Northerners had betrayed the Compromise. "The continued existence of the United States as one nation," warned the *Southern Literary Messenger,* "depends upon the full and faithful execution of the Fugitive Slave Bill."

Uncle Tom's Cabin

The spectacle of shackled African Americans being herded south seared the conscience of every Northerner who witnessed such a scene. But even more Northerners were turned against slavery by a fictional account, a novel. Harriet Beecher Stowe, a Northerner who had never seen a plantation, made the South's slaves into flesh-and-blood human beings almost more real than life.

A member of a famous clan of preachers, teachers, and reformers, Stowe despised the slave catchers and wrote to expose the sin of slavery. Published as a book in 1852, *Uncle Tom's Cabin, or Life among the Lowly* became a blockbuster hit and sold 300,000 copies in its first year and more than 2 million copies within ten years.

Stowe's characters leaped from the page. Here was the gentle slave Uncle Tom, a Christian saint who forgave those who beat him to death; the courageous slave Eliza, who fled with her child across the frozen Ohio River; and the fiendish overseer Simon Legree, whose Louisiana plantation was a nightmare of torture and death. Mother of seven children, Stowe aimed her most powerful blows at slavery's destructive impact on the family. Her character Eliza succeeds in keeping her son from being sold away, but other mothers are not so fortunate. When told that her infant has been sold, Lucy drowns herself. Driven half mad by the sale of a son and daughter, Cassy decides "never again [to] let a child live to grow up!" She gives her third child an opiate and watches as "he slept to death."

In the North, common people and literary giants alike shed tears and sang praises to *Uncle Tom's Cabin.* But what Northerners accepted as truth, Southerners denounced as slander. Virginian George F. Holmes proclaimed Stowe a member of the "Woman's Rights" and "Higher Law" schools and dismissed the novel as a work of "intense fanaticism." Although it is impossible to measure precisely the impact of a novel on public opinion, *Uncle Tom's Cabin* clearly helped to crystallize northern sentiment against slavery and to confirm white Southerners' suspicion that they no longer had any sympathy in the free states.

Uncle Tom's Cabin
The cover drawing on this early illustrated edition of Harriet Beecher Stowe's novel shows a runaway slave mother racing across ice floes to escape dogs and slave catchers. During the 1850s, at least ten individuals, including Harriet Beecher Stowe herself, dramatized the novel. Stowe's moral indictment of slavery translated well to the stage. Scenes of Eliza crossing the ice with bloodhounds in pursuit, the cruelty of Simon Legree, and Little Eva borne to heaven on puffy clouds gripped the imagination of audiences in America and Britain and fueled the growing antislavery crusade.
Picture Research Consultants & Archives.

Other writers—ex-slaves who knew life in slave cabins firsthand—also produced stinging indictments of slavery. Solomon Northup's compelling *Twelve Years a Slave* (1853) sold 27,000 copies in two years, and the powerful *Narrative of the Life of Frederick Douglass, as Told by Himself* (1845) eventually sold more than 30,000 copies. But no work touched the North's conscience like the novel by a free white woman. A decade after its publication, when Stowe visited Abraham Lincoln at the White House, he reportedly said, "So you are the little woman who wrote the book that made this great war."

The Kansas-Nebraska Act

As national elections approached in 1852, Democrats and Whigs sought to close the sectional rifts that had opened within their parties. For their presidential nominee, the Democrats turned to Franklin Pierce of New Hampshire. Pierce's most valuable asset was his well-known sympathy with southern views on public issues. His leanings caused northern critics to include him among the "doughfaces," northern men malleable enough to champion southern causes. The Whigs were less successful in bridging differences. Adopting the formula that had proved successful in 1848, they chose another Mexican-American War hero, General Winfield Scott of Virginia. But the Whigs were hopelessly divided between their northern and southern factions and suffered a humiliating defeat. The Democrat Pierce carried twenty-seven states to Scott's four, 254 electoral votes to 42. In the afterglow of the Compromise of 1850, the Free-Soil Party lost almost half of the voters who had turned to it in the tumultuous atmosphere of 1848.

Eager to leave the sectional controversy behind, the new president turned swiftly to foreign expansion. **Manifest destiny** remained robust. (See "Beyond America's Borders," page 352.) Pierce's major objective was Cuba, which was owned by Spain and in which slavery flourished, but his clumsy diplomatic efforts galvanized antislavery Northerners, who blocked Cuba's acquisition to keep more slave territory from entering the Union. Pierce's fortunes improved in Mexico. In 1853, he sent diplomat James Gadsden to negotiate a $15 mil-

lion purchase of some 30,000 square miles of territory south of the Gila River in present-day Arizona and New Mexico. The Gadsden Purchase stemmed from the dream of a transcontinental railroad to California and Pierce's desire for a southern route through Mexican territory. The booming population of the Pacific coast made it obvious that the vast, loose-jointed republic needed a railroad to bind it together. Talk of a railroad ignited rivalries in cities from New Orleans to Chicago as they maneuvered to become the eastern terminus. The desire for a transcontinental railroad evolved into a sectional contest, which by the 1850s inevitably involved slavery.

No one played the railroad game more enthusiastically than Illinois's Democratic senator Stephen A. Douglas. He badly wanted the transcontinental railroad for Chicago and his home state, and his chairmanship of the Senate Committee on Territories provided him with an opportunity. Any railroad that ran west from Chicago would pass through a region that Congress in 1830 had designated a "permanent" Indian reserve. Douglas proposed giving this vast area between the Missouri River and the Rocky Mountains an Indian name, Nebraska, and then throwing the Indians out. Once the region achieved territorial status, whites could survey and sell the land, establish civil government, and build a railroad.

Nebraska lay within the Louisiana Purchase and, according to the Missouri Compromise of 1820, was closed to slavery (see chapter 10). Since Douglas could not count on New England to back western economic development, he needed southern votes to pass his Nebraska legislation. But Southerners had no incentive to create another free territory or to help a northern city win the transcontinental railroad. Southerners, however, agreed to help organize Nebraska for a price: nothing less than repeal of the Missouri Compromise. Southerners insisted that Congress organize Nebraska according to popular sovereignty. That meant giving slavery a chance in the Nebraska Territory and reopening the dangerous issue of slavery expansion, which Douglas himself had so ably helped to resolve only four years earlier.

In January 1854, Douglas introduced his bill to organize the Nebraska Territory, leaving to the settlers themselves the decision

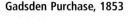

Gadsden Purchase, 1853

about slavery. At southern insistence, and even though he knew it would "raise a hell of a storm," Douglas added an explicit repeal of the Missouri Compromise. Indeed, the Nebraska bill raised a storm of controversy. Free-Soilers branded Douglas's plan "a gross violation of a sacred pledge" and an "atrocious plot" to transform free land into a "dreary region of despotism, inhabited by masters and slaves."

Undaunted, Douglas skillfully shepherded the explosive bill through Congress in May 1854. Nine-tenths of all southern members (Whigs and Democrats) and half of the northern Democrats cast votes in favor. In its final form, the Kansas-Nebraska Act divided the huge territory in two: Nebraska west of the free state of Iowa and Kansas west of the slave state of Missouri (Map 14.3). With this act, the government pushed the Plains Indians farther west, making way for farmers and railroads.

> **REVIEW** Why did the Fugitive Slave Act provoke such strong opposition in the North?

Realignment of the Party System

The Kansas-Nebraska Act marked a fateful escalation of the sectional conflict. Douglas's controversial measure had several consequences, none more crucial than the realignment of the nation's political parties. Since the rise of the Whigs in the early 1830s, Whigs and Democrats had organized and channeled political conflict in the nation. This party system dampened sectionalism and strengthened the Union. To achieve national political power, Whigs and Democrats had to retain strength in both North and South. Strong northern and southern wings required that each party compromise and find positions acceptable to both wings.

The Kansas-Nebraska controversy shattered this stabilizing political system. In place of two national parties with bisectional strength, the mid-1850s witnessed the development of one party heavily dominated by one section and another party entirely limited to the other section. Rather

than "national" parties, the country had what one critic disdainfully called "geographic" parties. Parties now sharpened ideological and policy differences between the sections and no longer muffled moral issues, like slavery. But the new party system also thwarted political compromise and instead promoted political polarization that further jeopardized the Union.

The Old Parties: Whigs and Democrats

Distress signals could be heard from the Whig camp as early as the Mexican-American War, when members clashed over the future of slavery in annexed Mexican lands. By 1852, the Whig Party could please its proslavery southern wing or its antislavery northern wing but not both. The Whigs' miserable showing in the election of 1852 made clear that they were no longer a strong national party. By 1856, after more than two decades of contesting the Democrats, they were hardly a party at all (Map 14.4).

The collapse of the Whig Party left the Democrats as the country's only national party. Although the Democrats were not immune to the

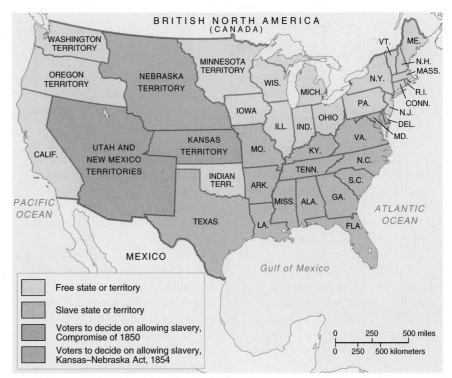

MAP 14.3   The Kansas-Nebraska Act, 1854
Americans hardly thought twice about dispossessing the Indians of lands guaranteed them by treaty, but many worried about the outcome of repealing the Missouri Compromise and opening up lands to slavery.

Filibusters: The Underside of Manifest Destiny

Each year the citizens of Caborca, Mexico, a small town in the northern state of Sonora, celebrate the defeat there in 1857 of an American army. The invaders did not wear the uniform of the U.S. army but marched as a private army, the "Arizona Colonization Company." Their commander, Henry A. Crabb, a Mississippian who followed the gold rush to California, saw fresh opportunity in the civil disorder that reigned south of the border. Fierce fighting between Mexicans and Apache and Yaqui Indians made life precarious in Sonora and divided the Mexicans. When the governor of Sonora faced an insurrection, he invited Crabb, who was married to a Sonoran woman, to help him repress his enemies in exchange for mineral rights and land.

Crabb marched his band of sixty-eight heavily armed ex-miners south from Los Angeles into Mexico. But by the time the Americans arrived, the governor had put down the insurgency, and he turned on the invaders. Every American except one died either in battle or at the hands of Mexican firing squads. Crabb's head was preserved in alcohol and placed on display as a symbol of victory.

Henry Crabb was one of thousands of American adventurers, known as "filibusters" (from Spanish *filibustero,* meaning "freebooter" or "pirate"), who in the mid-nineteenth century joined private armies that invaded foreign countries in North America, Central America, South America, and the Caribbean. Although these expeditions were illegal and violated the U.S. Neutrality Act of 1818, private American armies attacked Canada, Mexico, Ecuador, Honduras, Cuba, and Nicaragua and planned invasions of places as far away as the Hawaiian kingdom. The federal government occasionally winked at the actions of filibusters, but more often it cracked down, fearful that private invasions would jeopardize legitimate diplomatic efforts to promote trade and acquire territory.

Filibusters joined invading armies for a variety of reasons ranging from personal gain to validating manhood. Many saw themselves as carrying on the work of manifest destiny, extending America's reach beyond Texas, California, and Oregon, the prizes of the 1830s and 1840s. In addition, during the 1840s and 1850s when Northerners insisted on containing slavery's spread to the North and West, Southerners joined filibustering expeditions to expand slavery south beyond U.S. borders. Although filibusters came from all regions of the country, their greatest numbers and support came from the proslavery forces of the South. The leading proslavery ideologue, George Fitzhugh, sought to blunt criticism of filibustering by defending it through historical comparison: "They who condemn the modern filibuster, to be consistent, must also condemn the discoverers and settlers of America, of the East Indies of Holland, and of the Indian and Pacific Oceans." Such arguments, deeply rooted in manifest destiny, failed to convince many, including the ambassador from Costa Rica, who called filibustering America's "social cancer." Northerners claimed (with some justification) that filibustering was a southern campaign to extend "the empire of the lash."

One of the most vigorous filibusters to appeal to southern interests was not an American: Narciso Lopez was a Venezuelan-born Cuban who dedicated himself to the liberation of Cuba from Spanish rule. In his first attempt in 1849, he recruited an army of several hundred would-be liberators but got no farther than New York harbor, where U.S. marshals intercepted his fleet. Thereafter, he resolved to "rest his hopes on the men of the bold West and chivalric South." Lopez claimed that Spain was planning to free Cuba's slaves, and he told Southerners that "self-preservation" demanded that they seize the island. When Governor John Quitman of Mississippi joined his scheme, Lopez shifted his headquarters to New Orleans. Early in 1850, Lopez and an army of more than 500 landed on the northwest coast of Cuba, but Spanish troops quickly drove them off. Two months later, with 450 troops, he tried again. This

Filibustering in Nicaragua

In this image of a pitched battle in Nicaragua in 1856, Costa Ricans on foot fight American filibusters on horseback. Costa Rican soldiers and their Central American allies defeated William Walker's *filibusteros* in 1857, but before then the Pierce administration had extended diplomatic recognition to Walker's regime, and white Southerners had cheered Walker's attempt to "introduce civilization" in Nicaragua and to develop its rich resources "with slave labor."

London Illustrated Times, May 24, 1856.

time, the Spanish crushed the invasion, killing 200 filibusters, shipping 160 prisoners to Spain, executing 50 invaders by firing squad, and publicly garroting Lopez. John Quitman gathered another army of several thousand, but federal authorities seized one of his ships and ended the threat to Cuba.

The most successful of all filibusters was William Walker of Tennessee, a restless dreamer who longed for an empire of his own south of the border. Walker cut his filibustering teeth with expeditions to Baja California and Sonora, but when they failed, he turned to

Central America. He believed that Southerners paid too much attention to Kansas and that instead they should expand slavery in tropical America. In May 1855, Walker and an army of fifty-six men sailed from San Francisco to the west coast of Nicaragua. Two thousand reinforcements and a civil war in Nicaragua gave Walker his victory. He had himself proclaimed president, legalized slavery, and called on Southerners to come raise cotton, sugar, and coffee in "a magnificent country." Hundreds of Southerners took up **land grants**, but Walker's regime survived only until 1857, when a

coalition of Central American countries allied with the Nicaraguans and sent Walker packing. Walker doggedly launched four other attacks on Nicaragua; then in 1860, Honduran forces captured and shot him.

Filibustering had lost steam by 1861, but the battle-hardened adventurers found new employment in the armies of the Civil War, particularly in the service of the Confederate military. The Confederacy paid a diplomatic price for its association with filibustering, however. The Guatemalan minister Antonio Jose de Irisarri declared that there was "no foreign Nation which can have less cause for sympathy with the enemies of the American Union, than the Republics of Central America, because from the Southern States were set on foot those filibustering expeditions." No Central American nation recognized Confederate independence.

A century and more later, the peoples of Central America and the Caribbean, like the inhabitants of Sonora, harbor bitter memories of filibusters' private wars of **imperialism** and honor those who fought off American advances. When U.S. marines occupied Nicaragua in the 1920s, insurgents found inspiration in their country's defeat of William Walker's army of freebooters eighty years earlier. In 1951, on the centennial of Lopez's invasion, Cubans erected a monument at the very spot where his ill-fated army came ashore. Costa Ricans celebrate Juan Santamaria as their national martyr for his courage in battling William Walker. Memories of the invasions by nineteenth-century filibusters set the stage for anti-American sentiment in Latin America that lingers to this day.

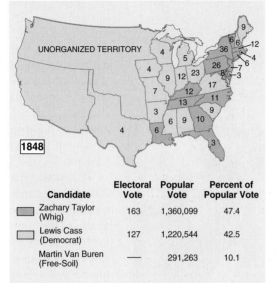

Candidate	Electoral Vote	Popular Vote	Percent of Popular Vote
Zachary Taylor (Whig)	163	1,360,099	47.4
Lewis Cass (Democrat)	127	1,220,544	42.5
Martin Van Buren (Free-Soil)	—	291,263	10.1

Candidate	Electoral Vote	Popular Vote	Percent of Popular Vote
Franklin Pierce (Democrat)	254	1,601,274	50.9
Winfield Scott (Whig)	42	1,386,580	44.1
John P. Hale (Free-Soil)	5	155,825	5.0

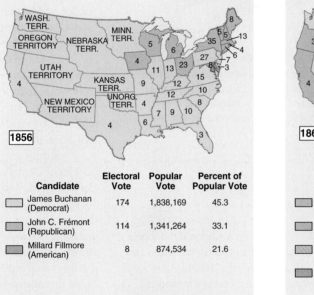

Candidate	Electoral Vote	Popular Vote	Percent of Popular Vote
James Buchanan (Democrat)	174	1,838,169	45.3
John C. Frémont (Republican)	114	1,341,264	33.1
Millard Fillmore (American)	8	874,534	21.6

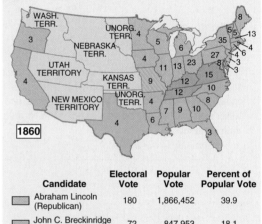

Candidate	Electoral Vote	Popular Vote	Percent of Popular Vote
Abraham Lincoln (Republican)	180	1,866,452	39.9
John C. Breckinridge (Southern Democrat)	72	847,953	18.1
Stephen A. Douglas (Northern Democrat)	12	1,375,157	29.4
John Bell (Constitutional Union)	39	590,631	12.6

MAP 14.4 Political Realignment, 1848–1860

In 1848, slavery and sectionalism began hammering the country's party system. The Whig Party was an early casualty. By 1860, national parties—those that contended for votes in both North and South—had been replaced by regional parties.

READING THE MAP: Which states did the Democrats pick up in the 1852 election over the previous election? Which of the states won in 1852 were lost to the Democrats in 1856? Compare the general geographical location of the states won by the Republicans in 1860 and in 1856.

CONNECTIONS: In the 1860 election, which party benefited the most from the addition of western and midwestern states added to the Union since 1848? Why would these states choose to back the Republicans over the Democrats?

FOR MORE HELP ANALYZING THIS MAP, see the map activity for this chapter in the Online Study Guide at bedfordstmartins.com/roarkcompact.

disruptive pressures of the territorial question, they discovered in popular sovereignty a doctrine that many Democrats could support. Even so, popular sovereignty very nearly undid the party. When Stephen Douglas applied the doctrine to the part of the Louisiana Purchase where slavery had been barred, he divided northern Democrats and destroyed the dominance of the Democratic Party in the free states. After 1854, the Democrats became a southern-dominated party. Nevertheless, the Democrats, unlike the Whigs, remained a national political organization. Gains in the South more than balanced Democratic losses in the North. During the 1850s, Democrats elected two presidents and won majorities in Congress in almost every election.

The breakup of the Whigs and the disaffection of significant numbers of northern Democrats set many Americans politically adrift. As they searched for new political harbors, Americans found that the death of the old party system created a multitude of fresh political alternatives. The question was which party would attract the drifters.

The New Parties: Know-Nothings and Republicans

Dozens of new political organizations vied for voters' attention. Out of the confusion two emerged as true contenders. One grew out of the slavery controversy, a spontaneous coalition of indignant antislavery Northerners. The other arose from an entirely different split in American society, between Roman Catholic immigrants and native **Protestants**.

The tidal wave of immigrants that broke over America from 1845 to 1855 produced a nasty backlash among Protestant Americans, who believed that the American Republic was about to drown in a sea of Roman Catholics from Ireland and Germany (see Figure 12.1, page 306). Most immigrants became Democrats because they perceived that party as more tolerant of newcomers than were the Whigs. But in the 1850s they met sharp political opposition when **nativists** (individuals who were anti-immigrant) began to organize, first into secret fraternal societies and then into a political party. Recruits swore never to vote for either foreign-born or Roman Catholic candidates and not to reveal any information about the organization. When questioned, they said: "I know nothing." Officially, they were named the American Party, but most Americans called them Know-Nothings.

The Know-Nothings exploded onto the political stage in 1854 and 1855 with a series of dazzling successes. They captured state legislatures in the Northeast, West, and South and claimed dozens of seats in Congress. Members of both traditional parties described the phenomenal success of the Know-Nothings as a "tornado," a "hurricane," and "a freak of political insanity." By 1855, an observer might reasonably have concluded that the Know-Nothings had emerged as the successor to the Whigs.

Know-Nothings were not the only new party making noise, however. One of the new antislavery organizations provoked by the Kansas-Nebraska Act called itself **Republican**. Republicans attempted to unite all the dissidents and political orphans—Whigs, Free-Soilers, anti-Nebraska Democrats, even Know-Nothings—who opposed the extension of slavery into any territory of the United States.

The Republican creed tapped into the basic beliefs and values of the northern public. Slavery, the Republicans argued, degraded the dignity of white labor by associating work with blacks and servility. They warned that the insatiable slaveholders of the South, whom antislavery Northerners called the "Slave Power," were

Know-Nothing Banner
Convinced that the incendiary issue of slavery had blinded Americans to the greater dangers of uncontrolled immigration and foreign influence, the Know-Nothing Party in 1856 ran Millard Fillmore for president. There is more than a little irony in this banner's appeal to "Native Americans" to stem the invasion from abroad. Know-Nothings meant native-born Americans, but bona fide Native Americans, American Indians, also faced an invasion and to them it made little difference whether the aggressors were fresh off the boat or born in the U.S.A.
Milwaukee County Historical Society.

conspiring through their control of the Democratic Party to expand slavery, subvert **liberty**, and undermine the Constitution. Only if slavery were restricted to the South, Republicans believed, could the system of free labor flourish elsewhere. The ideal of free labor respected the dignity of work and provided anyone willing to toil an opportunity for a decent living and for advancement (see chapter 12). These powerful images of liberty and opportunity attracted a wide range of Northerners to the Republican cause.

The Election of 1856

The election of 1856 revealed that the Republicans had become the Democrats' main challenger and slavery in the territories, not nativism, the election's principal issue. When the Know-Nothings insisted on a platform that endorsed the Kansas-Nebraska Act, most Northerners walked out and the party came apart. The few Know-Nothings who remained nominated ex-president Millard Fillmore.

The Republicans adopted a platform that focused almost exclusively on "making every territory free." When they labeled slavery a "relic of barbarism," Republicans signaled that they had written off the South. For president, they nominated the dashing soldier and California adventurer John C. Frémont, "Pathfinder of the West." Frémont lacked political credentials, but political know-how resided in his wife, Jessie, who, as a daughter of Senator Thomas Hart Benton of Missouri, knew the political map as well as her husband knew western trails. Although careful to maintain a proper public image, the vivacious young mother and antislavery zealot helped draw ordinary women into politics.

The Democrats chose another "doughface," James Buchanan of Pennsylvania. The Democrats took refuge in the ambiguity of popular sovereignty and portrayed Republicans as extremists ("Black Republican Abolitionists") whose support for the Wilmot Proviso risked pushing the South out of the Union.

The Democratic strategy carried the day for Buchanan, but Frémont did astonishingly well. Buchanan won 174 electoral votes against Frémont's 114 and Fillmore's 8. Campaigning under the banner "Free soil, Free men, Fremont," the Republican carried all but five of the states north of the Mason-Dixon line. The election made clear that the Whigs had disintegrated, the Know-Nothings would not ride nativism to national power, and the Republicans were a power to be reckoned with (see Map 14.4). Sectionalism had fashioned a new party system, one that spelled danger for the Republic (Figure 14.1). Indeed, war had already broken out between proslavery and antislavery forces in distant Kansas Territory.

> **REVIEW**   Why did the Whig Party disintegrate in the 1850s?

Freedom under Siege

Events in Kansas Territory in the mid-1850s provided the young Republican organization with an enormous boost and help explain its strong showing in the election of 1856. Republicans organized around the premise that the slaveholding South

John and Jessie Frémont Poster
The election of 1856 marked the first time a candidate's wife appeared on campaign items. Smart and ambitious, Jessie Benton Frémont made the breakthrough. In this poster—made from paper letters and figures cut from an English hunting print—Jessie and her husband, John C. Frémont, Republican Party presidential nominee, ride spirited horses. The scene emphasizes their youth (John was 43 and Jessie 31), their vigor, and their outdoor exuberance. Jessie helped plan Frémont's campaign, coauthored his election biography, and drew northern women into political activity as never before. "What a shame that women can't vote!" declared abolitionist Lydia Maria Child. "We'd carry 'our Jessie' into the White House on our shoulders, wouldn't we." Critics of Jessie's violation of women's traditional sphere ridiculed both Frémonts. A man who met the couple in San Francisco pronounced her "the better man of the two." Jessie Frémont was, as Abraham Lincoln observed ambivalently, "quite a female politician."
Museum of American Political Life.

provided a profound threat to "free soil, free labor, and free men," and now Kansas reeled with violence that Republicans argued was southern in origin. Kansas, Republicans claimed, opened a window to southern values and intentions. Republicans also pointed to the brutal beating by a Southerner of a respected northern senator on the floor of Congress. Even the Supreme Court, in the Republicans' view, reflected the South's drive toward tyranny and minority rule. Then, in 1858, the issues dividing North and South received an extraordinary airing in a senatorial contest in Illinois, when the nation's foremost Democrat debated a resourceful Republican.

"Bleeding Kansas"

Three days after the House of Representatives approved the Kansas-Nebraska Act in 1854, Senator William H. Seward of New York boldly challenged the South. "Come on then, Gentlemen of the Slave States," he cried, "since there is no escaping your challenge, I accept it in behalf of the cause of freedom. We will engage in competition for the virgin soil of Kansas, and God give the victory to the side which is stronger in numbers as it is in right." Because of Stephen Douglas, popular sovereignty would determine whether Kansas became slave or free. Free-state and slave-state settlers each sought majorities at the ballot box, claimed God's blessing, and kept their rifles ready.

In both North and South, emigrant aid societies sprang up to promote settlement from free states or slave states. Missourians, already bordered on the east by the free state of Illinois and on the north by the free state of Iowa, especially thought it important to secure Kansas for slavery. Thousands of rough frontiersmen, egged on by Missouri senator David Rice Atchison, invaded Kansas. "There are eleven hundred coming over from Platte County to vote," Atchison reported, "and if that ain't enough we can send five thousand—enough to kill every God-damned abolitionist in the Territory." Not surprisingly, proslavery candidates swept the elections in November 1854. When Kansas's first territorial legislature met, it enacted a raft of proslavery laws. Ever-pliant President Pierce endorsed the work of the fraudulently elected legislature. Free-soil Kansans did not. They elected their own legislature, which promptly banned both slaves and free blacks from the territory. Organized into two rival governments and armed to the teeth, Kansans verged on civil war.

Fighting broke out on the morning of May 21, 1856, when several hundred proslavery men

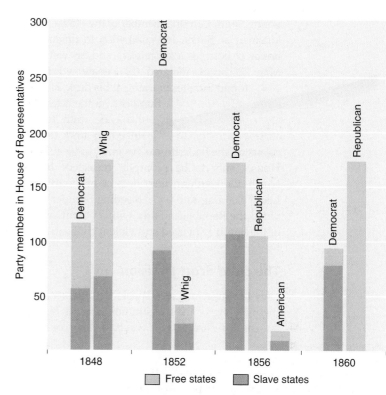

FIGURE 14.1 Changing Political Landscape, 1848–1860
The polarization of American politics between free states and slave states occurred in little more than a decade.

raided the town of Lawrence, the center of free-state settlement. Only one man died, but the "Sack of Lawrence," as free-soil forces called it, inflamed northern opinion. Elsewhere in Kansas, news of events in Lawrence provoked John Brown, a free-soil settler, to "fight fire with fire." He led the posse that massacred five allegedly proslavery settlers along the Pottawatomie Creek. After that, **guerrilla war** engulfed the territory.

Just as "Bleeding Kansas" gave the fledgling Republican Party fresh ammunition for its battle against the Slave Power, so, too, did an event that occurred in the national capital. In May 1856, Senator Charles Sumner of Massachusetts delivered a speech entitled "The Crime against Kansas" that included a scalding personal attack on the South Carolina senator Andrew P. Butler, whom Sumner described as a "Don Quixote" who had taken as his mistress "the harlot, slavery." Preston Brooks, a

"Bleeding Kansas," 1850s

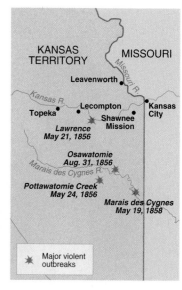

young South Carolina member of the House and a kinsman of Butler, felt compelled to defend the honor of both his aged relative and his state. On May 22, Brooks entered the Senate, where he found Sumner working at his desk. He beat Sumner over the head with his cane until he lay bleeding and unconscious on the floor. Brooks resigned his seat in the House, only to be promptly reelected. In the North, the southern hero became an archvillain. Like "Bleeding Kansas," "Bleeding Sumner" provided the Republican Party with a potent symbol of the South's "twisted and violent civilization."

The *Dred Scott* Decision

Only the Supreme Court speaks definitively about the meaning of the Constitution, and in 1857, in the case of *Dred Scott v. Sandford*, the Court an-nounced its judgment of the issue of slavery in the territories. The Court's decision demonstrated that it enjoyed no special immunity from the sectional and partisan passions that convulsed the land.

In 1833, John Emerson, an army doctor, bought the slave Dred Scott in St. Louis, Missouri, and took him as his personal servant to Fort Armstrong, Illinois. Two years later, Scott accompanied Emerson when he transferred to Fort Snelling in Wisconsin Territory. Emerson eventually returned Scott to St. Louis, where in 1846, Scott, with the help of white friends, sued to prove that he and his family were legally entitled to their freedom. Scott based his claim on his travels and residences in a free state and a free territory.

In 1857, the U.S. Supreme Court ruled in the case. Chief Justice Roger B. Taney hated Republicans and detested racial equality, and the Court's majority decision, which he wrote, reflected those prejudices. First, the Court ruled that Dred Scott could not legally claim violation of his constitutional rights because he was not a citizen of the United States. When the Constitution was written, Taney said, blacks "were regarded as beings of an inferior order…so far inferior, that they had no rights which the white man was bound to respect." Second, the laws of Dred Scott's home state, Missouri, determined his status, and thus his travels in free areas did not make him free. Third, Congress's power to

The Dred Scott Family

The *Dred Scott* case in 1857 not only produced a fierce political storm but also fueled enormous curiosity about the family suing for freedom. The correspondent for the popular *Frank Leslie's Illustrated Newspaper* met Dred Scott in St. Louis and reported: "We found him on examination to be a pure-blooded African, perhaps fifty years of age, with a shrewd, intelligent, good-natured face, of rather light frame, being not more than five feet six inches high." Northerners wanted to see all of the Scotts: Harriet, who was a slave when Dred Scott married her in Wisconsin Territory in about 1836; daughter Eliza, who was born in 1838 on board a ship traveling in free territory north of Missouri; and daughter Lizzie, born after the Scotts returned to St. Louis.
Library of Congress.

make "all needful rules and regulations" for the territories did not include the right to prohibit slavery. The Court explicitly declared the Missouri Compromise unconstitutional, even though it had already been voided by the Kansas-Nebraska Act.

The Taney Court's extreme proslavery decision outraged Republicans. By denying the federal government the right to exclude slavery in the territories, it cut the ground out from under the Republican Party. Moreover, as the *New York Tribune* lamented, the decision cleared the way for "all our Territories...to be ripened into Slave States." Particularly frightening to African Americans in the North was the Court's declaration that blacks were not citizens and had no rights.

The Republican rebuttal to the *Dred Scott* ruling relied heavily on the dissenting opinion of Justice Benjamin R. Curtis. Scott *was* a citizen of the United States, Curtis argued. At the time of the writing of the Constitution, free black men could vote in five states and participated in the ratification process. Scott *was* free. Because slavery was prohibited in Wisconsin, the "involuntary servitude of a slave, coming into the Territory with his master, should cease to exist." The Missouri Compromise *was* constitutional. The Founders had meant exactly what they said: Congress had the power to make "*all* needful rules and regulations" for the territories, including barring slavery.

Rejecting Curtis's arguments, a seven-to-two majority of the justices validated an extreme statement of the South's territorial rights. John C. Calhoun's claim that Congress had no authority to exclude slavery became the law of the land. White Southerners cheered, but the *Dred Scott* decision actually strengthened the young Republican Party. It provided dramatic evidence of the Republicans' claim that a hostile Slave Power conspired against northern liberties. Only the capture of the Supreme Court by the "slavocracy," Republicans argued, could explain the tortured and historically inaccurate decision.

Prairie Republican: Abraham Lincoln

By re-igniting the sectional flames, the *Dred Scott* case provided Republican politicians with fresh challenges and fresh opportunities. Abraham Lincoln had long since put behind him his hardscrabble log-cabin beginnings in Kentucky and Indiana. He lived in a fine two-story house in Springfield, Illinois, and earned good money as a lawyer. The law provided Lincoln's living, but politics was his life. "His ambition was a little engine that knew no rest," observed his law partner William Herndon. Lincoln had served as a Whig in the Illinois state legislature and in the House of Representatives, but he had not held public office since 1849.

The disintegration of the Whig Party meant that Lincoln had no political home. His credo—opposition to "the *extension* of slavery"—made the Republicans his only choice, and in 1856 Lincoln joined the party. Convinced that slavery was a "monstrous injustice," a "great moral wrong," and an "unqualified evil to the negro, the white man, and the State," Lincoln condemned Douglas's Kansas-Nebraska Act of 1854 for giving slavery a new life. He accepted that the Constitution permitted slavery in those states where it existed, but he believed that Congress could contain its spread. Penned in, Lincoln believed, plantation slavery would wither, and in time Southerners would end slavery themselves. By providing fresh land in the territories, Douglas had put slavery "on the high road to extension and perpetuity."

Lincoln held what were, for his times, moderate racial views. Like a majority of Republicans, Lincoln defended black humanity without challenging white supremacy. While he denounced slavery as immoral, he also viewed black equality as impractical and unachievable. "Negroes have natural rights...as other men have," he said, "although they cannot enjoy them here." Insurmountable white prejudice made it impossible to extend full citizenship and equality to blacks in America, he believed. In Lincoln's mind, social stability and black progress required that slavery end and that blacks leave the country.

Lincoln envisioned the western territories as "places for poor people to go to, and better their conditions." But slavery's expansion threatened free men's basic right to succeed. The Kansas-Nebraska Act and the *Dred Scott* decision persuaded him that slaveholders were engaging in a dangerous conspiracy to nationalize slavery. The next step, Lincoln warned, would be "another Supreme Court decision, declaring that the Constitution of the United States does not permit a State to exclude slavery from its limits." Unless the citizens of Illinois woke up, he warned, the Supreme Court would make "Illinois a slave State."

In Lincoln's view, the nation could not "endure, permanently half slave and half free." Either opponents of slavery would arrest its spread and place it on the "course of ultimate extinction," or its advocates would see that it became legal in "*all* the States, *old* as well as *new*— *North* as well as *South*." Lincoln's convictions that slavery was wrong, that Congress must stop its spread, and that it must be put on the road to extinction formed the core of the Republican ideology. Lincoln so impressed his fellow Republicans in Illinois that in 1858 they chose him to challenge the nation's premier Democrat, who was seeking reelection to the U.S. Senate.

The Lincoln-Douglas Debates

When Stephen Douglas learned that the Republican Abraham Lincoln would be his opponent for the Senate, he confided in a fellow Democrat: "He is the strong man of the party—full of wit, facts, dates—and the best stump speaker, with his droll ways and dry jokes, in the West. He is as honest as he is shrewd, and if I beat him my victory will be hardly won."

Not only did Douglas have to contend with a formidable foe, but he also carried the weight of a burden not of his own making. The previous year, the nation's economy experienced a sharp downturn. Prices plummeted, thousands of businesses failed, and unemployment rose. As a Democrat, Douglas had to go before the voters as a member of the party whose policies stood accused of causing the "panic of 1857."

Douglas's response to another crisis in 1857, however, helped shore up his standing in Illinois. Proslavery forces in Kansas met in the town of Lecompton, drafted a proslavery constitution, and applied for statehood. Everyone knew that Free-Soilers outnumbered proslavery settlers, but President Buchanan instructed Congress to admit Kansas as the sixteenth slave state. Republicans denounced the "Lecompton swindle." Senator Douglas broke with the Democratic administration and came out against the Lecompton constitution; Congress killed the Lecompton bill. (When Kansans reconsidered the Lecompton constitution in an honest election, they rejected it six to one. Kansas entered the Union in 1861 as a free state.) By denouncing the fraudulent proslavery constitution, Douglas declared his independence from the South and, he hoped, made himself acceptable at home.

A relative unknown and a decided underdog in the Illinois election, Lincoln challenged Douglas to debate him face-to-face. The two met in seven communities for what would become a legendary series of debates. Thousands stood straining to see and hear as they debated the central issues of the age—slavery and freedom. They showed the citizens of Illinois (and much of the nation because of widespread press coverage) the difference between an anti-Lecompton Democrat and a true Republican.

Lincoln badgered Douglas with the question of whether he favored the spread of slavery. He tried to force Douglas into the damaging admission that the Supreme Court had repudiated Douglas's own territorial solution, popular sovereignty. In the debate at Freeport, Illinois, Douglas admitted that settlers could not now pass legislation barring slavery, but he argued that they could ban slavery just as effectively by not passing protective laws, such as those found in slave states. Southerners condemned Douglas's "Freeport Doctrine" and charged him with trying to steal the victory they had gained with the *Dred Scott* decision. Lincoln chastised his opponent for his "don't care" attitude about slavery, for "blowing out the moral lights around us."

Douglas worked the racial issue. He called Lincoln an abolitionist and an egalitarian enamored with "our colored brethren." Put on the defensive, Lincoln came close to staking out positions on race that were as conservative as Douglas's. Lincoln reaffirmed his faith in white rule: "I will say, then, that I am not, nor ever have been, in favor of bringing about in any way the social and political equality of the white and black race." But unlike Douglas, who told racist jokes, Lincoln was no negrophobe. He tried to steer the debate back to what he considered the true issue: the morality and future of slavery. "Slavery is wrong," Lincoln repeated, because "a man has the right to the fruits of his own labor."

As Douglas predicted, the election was hard-fought and closely contested. Until the adoption of the Seventeenth Amendment in 1911, citizens voted for state legislators, who in turn selected U.S. senators. Since Democrats won a slight majority in the Illinois legislature, the members returned Douglas to the Senate. But the debates thrust Lincoln, the prairie Republican, into the national spotlight.

> **REVIEW**   Why did the *Dred Scott* decision strengthen northern suspicions of a "Slave Power" conspiracy?

The Union Collapses

Lincoln's thesis that the "slavocracy" conspired to make slavery a national institution now seems exaggerated. But from the northern perspective, the

Kansas-Nebraska Act, the Brooks-Sumner affair, the *Dred Scott* decision, and the Lecompton constitution amounted to irrefutable evidence of the South's aggressiveness. White Southerners, of course, saw things differently. They were the ones who were under siege, they declared. Signs were everywhere, they believed, that the North planned to use its numerical advantage to attack slavery, and not just in the territories. Republicans had made it clear that they were unwilling to accept the *Dred Scott* ruling as the last word on the issue of slavery expansion. And John Brown's attempt to incite a slave insurrection in Virginia in 1859 proved that Northerners were unwilling to be bound by Christian decency and reverence for life.

Threats of secession increasingly laced the sectional debate. Talk of leaving the Union had been heard for years, but until the final crisis, Southerners had used secession as a ploy to gain concessions within the Union, not to destroy it. Then the 1850s delivered powerful blows to Southerners' confidence that they could remain Americans and protect slavery. When the Republican Party won the White House in 1860, many Southerners concluded that they would have to leave.

The Aftermath of John Brown's Raid

For his attack on Harpers Ferry, John Brown stood trial for treason, murder, and incitement of slave insurrection. "To hang a fanatic is to make a martyr of him and fledge another brood of the same sort," cautioned one newspaper, but on December 2, 1859, Virginia executed Brown. In life, Brown was a ne'er-do-well, but he died with courage and dignity. He told his wife that he was "determined to make the utmost possible out of a defeat." He told the court: "If it is deemed necessary that I should forfeit my life for the furtherance of the ends of justice, and mingle my blood further with the blood of…millions in this slave country whose rights are disregarded by wicked, cruel, and unjust enactments, I say, let it be done."

After Brown's heroic death, northern denunciation of Brown as a dangerous fanatic gave way to grudging respect. Some even celebrated his "splendid martyrdom." Abolitionist Lydia Maria Child likened Brown to Christ and declared that he made "the scaffold…as glorious as the Cross of Calvary." Some abolitionists explicitly endorsed Brown's resort to violence. Abolitionist William Lloyd Garrison, who usually professed pacifism, announced, "I am pre-pared to say 'success to every slave insurrection at the South and in every country.'"

Most Northerners did not advocate bloody rebellion, however. Like Lincoln, they concluded that Brown's noble antislavery ideals could not "excuse violence, bloodshed, and treason." Still, when many in the North marked John Brown's execution with tolling bells, hymns, and prayer vigils, white Southerners contemplated what they had in common with people who "regard John Brown as a martyr and a Christian hero, rather than a murderer and robber." Georgia senator Robert Toombs announced solemnly that Southerners must "never permit this Federal government to pass into the traitorous hands of the black Republican party." At that moment, the presidential election was only months away.

Republican Victory in 1860

Events between Brown's hanging and the presidential election only heightened sectional hostility and estrangement. A southern business convention meeting in Nashville shocked the nation (including many Southerners) by calling for the reopening of the African slave trade. Chief Justice Taney provoked new indignation when the Supreme Court ruled northern personal liberty laws unconstitutional and reaffirmed the Fugitive Slave Act. Then, the normally routine business of electing a Speaker of the House threatened to turn bloody as Democrats and Republicans battled over control of the office. After two months of acrimonious debate left the House deadlocked, one congressman observed that the "only persons who do not have a revolver and a knife are those who have two revolvers." A last-minute compromise may have averted a shootout.

When Democrats converged on Charleston for their convention in April 1860, fire-eating Southerners denounced Stephen Douglas and demanded a platform that included federal protection of slavery in the territories. But northern Democrats knew that northern voters would not stomach a federal slave code. When the delegates approved a platform with popular sovereignty, representatives from the entire Lower South and Arkansas stomped out of the convention. The remaining Democrats adjourned to meet a few weeks later in Baltimore, where they nominated Douglas for president.

When southern Democrats met, they nominated Vice President John C. Breckinridge of Kentucky for president and approved a platform

***John Brown Going to His Hanging,* Horace Pippin, 1942**
The grandparents of Horace Pippin, a Pennsylvania artist, were slaves. His grandmother witnessed the hanging of John Brown, and here Pippin recalls the scene she so often described to him. He uses a muted palette to establish the bleak setting and to tell the grim story, but he manages to convey a striking intensity nevertheless. Historically accurate, the painting depicts Brown tied and sitting erect on his coffin, passing resolutely before the silent, staring white men. The black woman in the lower right corner is presumably Pippin's grandmother.

Romare Bearden, a leading twentieth-century African American artist, recalled the central place of John Brown in black memory: "Lincoln and John Brown were as much a part of the actuality of the Afro-American experience, as were the domino games and the hoe cakes for Sunday morning breakfast. I vividly recall the yearly commemorations for John Brown and see my grandfather reading Brown's last speech to the court, which was a regular part of the ceremony at Pittsburgh's Shiloh Baptist Church."
Pennsylvania Academy of Fine Arts, Philadelphia. John Lambert Fund.

FOR MORE HELP ANALYZING THIS IMAGE, see the visual activity for this chapter in the Online Study Guide at bedfordstmartins.com/roarkcompact.

with a federal slave code. Southern moderates, however, refused to support Breckinridge. They formed a new party to provide voters a Unionist choice. Instead of adopting a platform and confronting the slavery question, the Constitutional Union Party merely approved a vague resolution pledging "to recognize no political principle other than *the Constitution…the Union…and the Enforcement of the Laws.*" For president they picked former senator John Bell of Tennessee.

The Republicans smelled victory. But they estimated that they needed to carry nearly all the free states to win. To make their party more appealing, they expanded their platform beyond antislavery. They hoped that free homesteads, a protective tariff, a transcontinental railroad, and a guarantee of immigrant political rights would provide an economic and social agenda broad enough to unify the North. While reasserting their commitment to stop the spread of slavery, they also denounced John Brown's raid as "among the gravest of crimes" and confirmed the security of slavery in the South.

Republicans cast about for a moderate candidate to go with their evenhanded platform. The foremost Republican, William H. Seward, had made enemies with his radical "higher law" doctrine and "irrepressible conflict" speech. Lincoln, however, since bursting onto the national scene in 1858 had demonstrated his clear purpose, good judgment, and solid Republican credentials. That, and his residence in Illinois, a crucial state, made him attractive to the party. On the third ballot, the delegates chose Lincoln. Defeated by Douglas in a state contest less than two years earlier, Lincoln now stood ready to take him on for the presidency.

The election of 1860 was like none other in American politics. It took place in the midst of the nation's severest crisis. Four major candidates crowded the presidential field. Rather than a four-cornered contest, however, the election broke into two contests, each with two candidates. In the North, Lincoln faced Douglas; in the South, Breckinridge confronted Bell. Southerners did not even permit Lincoln's name to appear on the ballot in ten of the fifteen slave states, so outrageous did they consider the Republican Party.

On November 6, 1860, Lincoln swept all of the eighteen free states except New Jersey, which split its electoral votes between him and Douglas. While Lincoln received only 39 percent of the popular vote, he won easily in the electoral balloting, gaining 180 votes, 28 more than he needed for victory. Lincoln did not win because his opposition was splintered. Even if the votes of his three opponents had been combined, Lincoln would still have won. He won because his votes were concentrated in the free states, which contained a majority of electoral votes. Ominously, however, Breckinridge, running on a southern-rights platform, won the entire Lower South plus Delaware, Maryland, and North Carolina (Map 14.5).

Secession Winter

The telegraphs had barely stopped tapping out the news of Lincoln's victory when anxious Southerners began debating what to do. Although Breckinridge had carried the South, a vote for "southern rights" was not necessarily a vote for secession. Besides, slightly more than half of the Southerners who had voted cast ballots for Douglas and Bell, two stout defenders of the Union.

Abraham Lincoln
Lincoln actively sought the Republican presidential nomination in 1860. When in New York City to give a political address, he had his photograph taken by Mathew Brady. "While I was there I was taken to one of the places where they get up such things," Lincoln explained, sounding more innocent than he was, "and I suppose they got my shadow, and can multiply copies indefinitely." Multiply they did. Later, Lincoln credited his victory to his New York speech and to this dignified photograph by Brady.
The Lincoln Museum, Fort Wayne, Indiana. Photo: #0-17.

Southern Unionists tried to calm the fears that Lincoln's election triggered. Let the dust settle, they pleaded. Former congressman Alexander Stephens of Georgia asked what Lincoln had done to justify something as extreme as secession. Had he not promised to respect slavery where it existed? In Stephens's judgment, the fire-eater cure would be worse than the Republican disease. Secession might lead to war, which would loosen the hinges of southern society, possibly even open the door to slave insurrection. "Revolutions are much easier started

Candidate	Electoral Vote	Popular Vote	Percent of Popular Vote
Abraham Lincoln (Republican)	180	1,866,452	39.9
J.C. Breckenridge (Southern Democrat)	72	847,953	18.1
Stephen A. Douglas (Northern Democrat)	12	1,375,157	29.4
John Bell (Constitutional Union)	39	590,631	12.6

MAP 14.5   The Election of 1860

than controlled," he warned. "I consider slavery much more secure in the Union than out of it."

Secessionists emphasized the dangers of delay. "Mr. Lincoln and his party assert that this doctrine of equality applies to the negro," former Georgia governor Howell Cobb declared, "and necessarily there can exist no such thing as property in our equals." Lincoln's election without a single electoral vote from the South meant that Southerners were no longer able to defend themselves within the Union, Cobb argued. Why wait, he said, for Lincoln to send abolitionist emissaries to the South. As for war, there would be none. The Union was a voluntary compact, and Lincoln would not coerce patriotism. If Northerners did resist with force, secessionists argued, one southern woodsman could whip five of Lincoln's greasy mechanics.

For all their differences, southern whites were generally united in their determination to defend slavery. They disagreed about whether the mere presence of a Republican in the White House made it necessary to exercise what they considered a legitimate right to secede.

South Carolina seceded from the Union on December 20, 1860. By February 1861, the six other

Secession of the Lower South, December 1860–February 1861

Lower South states marched in South Carolina's footsteps. In some states, the vote was close. In general, slaveholders spearheaded secession, while nonslaveholders in the Piedmont and mountain counties, where slaves were relatively few, displayed the greatest attachment to the Union. On February 4, representatives from South Carolina, Georgia, Florida, Alabama, Mississippi, Louisiana, and Texas met in Montgomery, Alabama, where three days later they celebrated the birth of the Confederate States of America. Jefferson Davis became president, and Alexander Stephens, who had spoken so eloquently about the dangers of revolution, became vice president.

Lincoln's election had split the Union. Now secession split the South. Seven slave states seceded during the winter, but the eight slave states of the Upper South rejected secession, at least for the moment. The fact was that the Upper South had a smaller stake in slavery. Just over half as many white families in the Upper South held slaves (21 percent) as did those in the Lower South (37 percent). Slaves represented twice as large a percentage of the population in the Lower South (48 percent) as in the Upper South (23 percent). Consequently, whites in the Upper South had fewer fears that Republican ascendancy meant economic catastrophe, social chaos, and racial war. Lincoln would need to do more than just be elected to provoke them into secession.

The nation had to wait until March 4, 1861, when Lincoln took office, to see what he would do. (Presidents-elect waited four months to take office until 1933, when the Twentieth Amendment to the Constitution shifted the inauguration forward to January 20.) After his election, Lincoln chose to stay in Springfield and to say nothing. "Lame-duck" president James Buchanan sat in Washington and did nothing. Buchanan demonstrated, William H. Seward said mockingly, that "it is the President's duty to enforce the laws, unless somebody opposes him." In Congress, efforts at cobbling together a peace-saving compromise came to nothing.

Lincoln began his inaugural address with reassurances to the South. He had "no lawful right" to interfere with slavery where it existed, he declared again, adding for emphasis that he had "no inclination to do so." Conciliatory about slavery, Lincoln proved inflexible about the Union. The Union, he declared, is "perpetual." Secession was "anarchy" and "legally void." The Constitution required him to execute the law "in all the States." He would hold federal property, collect federal duties, and deliver the mails.

The decision for civil war or peace rested in the South's hands, Lincoln declared. "You can have no conflict, without being yourselves the aggressors. *You* have no oath registered in Heaven to destroy the government, while *I* shall have the most solemn one to 'preserve, protect, and defend' it." What Confederates in Charleston held in their hands at that very moment were the cords for firing the cannons aimed at the federal garrison at Fort Sumter.

> **REVIEW** Why did some southern states secede immediately after Lincoln's election?

Conclusion: Slavery, Free Labor, and the Failure of Political Compromise

As their economies, societies, and cultures diverged in the nineteenth century, Northerners and Southerners expressed different concepts of the American promise and the role of slavery within it. Their differences crystallized into political form in 1846 when David Wilmot proposed banning slavery in any territory won in the Mexican-American War. "As if by magic," a Boston newspaper observed, "it brought to a head the great question that is about to divide the American people." Discovery of gold and other precious metals in the West added urgency to the controversy over slavery in the territories. Although Congress addressed the issue with the Compromise of 1850, the Fugitive Slave Act quickly brought conflict between free and slave states. Matters worsened with the 1852 publication of *Uncle Tom's Cabin*, which further hardened northern sentiments against slavery and confirmed southern suspicions of northern ill will. The bloody violence that erupted in Kansas in 1856 and the incendiary *Dred Scott* decision in 1857 further eroded hope for a solution to this momentous question.

During the extended crisis of the Union that stretched from 1846 to 1861, the slavery question braided with national politics. The traditional Whig and Democratic parties struggled to hold together, as new parties, most notably the Republican Party, emerged. Politicians fixed their attention on the expansion of slavery, but from the beginning the nation recognized that the controversy had less to do with slavery in the territories than with the future of slavery in America.

For more than seventy years, statesmen had found compromises that accepted slavery and preserved the Union. But as each section grew increasingly committed to its labor system and the promise it provided, Americans discovered that accommodation had limits. In 1859, John Brown's militant antislavery pushed white Southerners to the edge. In 1860, Lincoln's election convinced whites in the Lower South that slavery and the society they had built on it were at risk in the Union, and they seceded. In his inaugural, Lincoln pleaded, "We are not enemies but friends. We must not be enemies." By then, however, the seven southern states had ceased to sing what he called "the chorus of the Union." It remained to be seen whether disunion would mean war.

Suggestions for Further Reading

Charles B. Dew, *Apostles of Disunion: Southern Secession Commissioners and the Causes of the Civil War* (2001). An analysis that places slavery at the center of the decision to secede.

Don E. Fehrenbacher, *The Slaveholding Republic: An Account of the United States Government's Relations to Slavery* (2001). An insightful discussion of the federal government's changing relationship with slavery from the Constitution to the Civil War.

Eric Foner, *Free Labor, Free Soil, Free Men: The Ideology of the Republican Party before the Civil War* (1970). A probing analysis of the rise of the Republican Party.

Michael Holt, *Fate of Their Country: Politicians, Slavery Extension, and the Coming of the Civil War* (2004). A clear discussion of the political origins of the Civil War.

Bruce C. Levine, *Half Slave and Half Free: The Roots of the Civil War* (1992). A vivid narrative that describes the growing divergence between North and South.

David S. Reynolds, *John Brown, Abolitionist: The Man Who Killed Slavery, Sparked the Civil War, and Seeded Civil Rights* (2005). A provocative biography of one of the era's most controversial figures.

> ▶ **FOR MORE BOOKS ABOUT TOPICS IN THIS CHAPTER,** see the Online Bibliography at bedfordstmartins.com/roarkcompact.
>
> ▶ **FOR ADDITIONAL FIRSTHAND ACCOUNTS OF THIS PERIOD,** see Chapter 14 in Michael Johnson, ed., *Reading the American Past*, Third Edition.
>
> ▶ **FOR WEB SITES AND DOCUMENTS RELATED TO TOPICS AND PLACES IN THIS CHAPTER,** see "HistoryLinks," "DocLinks," and "PlaceLinks" at bedfordstmartins.com/roarkcompact.

REVIEWING THE CHAPTER

Follow these steps to review and strengthen your understanding of the chapter.
STEP 1: *Study the* **Key Terms** *and* **Timeline** *to identify the significance of each item listed.*
STEP 2: *Answer the* **Review Questions**, *drawing on key terms and dates to support your answers.*
STEP 3: *Drawing on the Key Terms, Timeline, and Review Questions, answer the broader* **Making Connections** *questions.*

KEY TERMS

Who

John Brown (p. 343)
David Wilmot (p. 345)
John C. Calhoun (p. 345)
Lewis Cass (p. 346)
Martin Van Buren (p. 346)
Zachary Taylor (p. 346)
Henry Clay (p. 347)
Daniel Webster (p. 347)
William H. Seward (p. 347)
Stephen A. Douglas (p. 348)
Millard Fillmore (p. 348)
Harriet Beecher Stowe (p. 349)
Franklin Pierce (p. 350)
Winfield Scott (p. 350)
James Gadsden (p. 350)
John C. Frémont (p. 356)
Jessie Frémont (p. 356)

James Buchanan (p. 356)
Charles Sumner (p. 357)
Roger B. Taney (p. 358)
Abraham Lincoln (p. 359)
John C. Breckinridge (p. 361)
Jefferson Davis (p. 364)

What

John Brown's raid on Harpers Ferry
  (p. 343)
Wilmot Proviso (p. 345)
popular sovereignty (p. 346)
Democratic Party (pp. 346, 351)
Whig Party (pp. 346, 351)
Free-Soil Party (p. 346)
Omnibus Bill (p. 347)
Compromise of 1850 (p. 348)
Fugitive Slave Act (p. 348)

underground railroad (p. 348)
Uncle Tom's Cabin (p. 349)
Gadsden Purchase (p. 350)
Kansas-Nebraska Act (p. 351)
Know-Nothing Party (p. 355)
Republican Party (p. 355)
free labor (p. 356)
"Bleeding Kansas" (p. 357)
"Sack of Lawrence" (p. 357)
"Bleeding Sumner" (p. 358)
Dred Scott decision (p. 358)
panic of 1857 (p. 360)
Lecompton constitution (p. 360)
Lincoln-Douglas debates (p. 360)
Constitutional Union Party (p. 362)
Confederate States of America (p. 364)

TIMELINE

◀ 1820 • Missouri Compromise.

1846 • Wilmot Proviso introduced in Congress.

1847 • Wilmot Proviso defeated in Senate.
     • Compromise of "popular sovereignty" offered.

1848 • Free-Soil Party founded.
     • Whig General Zachary Taylor elected president.

1849 • California gold rush.

1850 • Taylor dies; Vice President Millard Fillmore becomes president.
     • Compromise of 1850 becomes law.

1852 • *Uncle Tom's Cabin* published.
     • Democrat Franklin Pierce elected president.

1853 • Gadsden Purchase.

1854 • American Party (Know-Nothings) emerges.
     • Kansas-Nebraska Act.
     • Republican Party emerges.

REVIEW QUESTIONS

1. Why did response to the Wilmot Proviso split along sectional rather than party lines? (pp. 344–48)

2. Why did the Fugitive Slave Act provoke such strong opposition in the North? (pp. 348–51)

3. Why did the Whig Party disintegrate in the 1850s? (pp. 351–56)

4. Why did the *Dred Scott* decision strengthen northern suspicions of a "Slave Power" conspiracy? (pp. 356–60)

5. Why did some southern states secede immediately after Lincoln's election? (pp. 360–65)

MAKING CONNECTIONS

1. The process of compromise that had successfully contained tensions between slave and free states since the nation's founding collapsed with secession. Why did compromise fail at this moment? In your answer, address specific political conflicts and attempts to solve them between 1846 and 1861.

2. In the 1850s many Americans supported popular sovereignty as the best solution to the explosive question of slavery in the western territories. Why was this solution so popular, and why did it ultimately prove inadequate? In your answer, be sure to address popular sovereignty's varied critics as well as champions.

3. In the 1840s and 1850s, the United States witnessed the realignment of its long-standing two-party system. Why did the old system fall apart, what emerged to take its place, and how did this process contribute to the coming of the Civil War?

4. Abraham Lincoln believed he had staked out a moderate position on the question of slavery, avoiding the extremes of immediate abolitionism and calls for unlimited protection of slavery. Why, then, did some southern states determine that his election necessitated the radical act of secession?

▶ **FOR PRACTICE QUIZZES, A CUSTOMIZED STUDY PLAN, AND OTHER STUDY TOOLS,** see the Online Study Guide at bedfordstmartins.com/roarkcompact.

1856 • "Bleeding Kansas."
  • Preston Brooks canes Charles Sumner.
  • Pottawatomie massacre.
  • Democrat James Buchanan elected president.
  1857 • *Dred Scott* decision.
    • Congress rejects Lecompton constitution.
    • Panic of 1857.
    1858 • Abraham Lincoln and Stephen A. Douglas debate slavery; Douglas wins Senate seat.
      1859 • John Brown raids Harpers Ferry, Virginia.
      1860 • Republican Abraham Lincoln elected president.
        • South Carolina secedes from Union.
        1861 • Six other deep South states secede.
          • The Confederate States of America is formed.
          • Lincoln takes office.

FORT SUMTER STARS AND STRIPES

This U.S. flag flew over Fort Sumter throughout the
Confederate bombardment that started the Civil War on
April 12, 1861. Shrapnel from thirty-three hours of cannon
fire shredded the flag, but when the Union major Robert
Anderson surrendered on April 13, he and his men marched
out of the fort under this tattered banner. The governor of
South Carolina cheered what he called the humbling of the
flag of the United States. Northerners bridled at this insult,
and within days flags sprouted across the Union. The Civil
War stitched the flag and American nationalism together
and made the Stars and Stripes the powerful symbol it is
today. When Anderson returned to Fort Sumter in April 1865,
he triumphantly raised this very flag.

Confederate Museum, United Daughters of the Confederacy.

The Crucible of War
1861–1865

O N THE RAINY NIGHT OF SEPTEMBER 21, 1862, in Wilmington, North Carolina, twenty-four-year-old William Gould and seven other black men crowded into a small boat on Cape Fear River and quietly pushed away from the dock. Knowing that the authorities would sound the alarm for eight runaway slaves at daybreak, they rowed hard throughout the night. By dawn, the runaways had traveled twenty-eight miles to where the river flowed into the Atlantic Ocean. They plunged into the swells and made for the Union navy patrolling offshore to disrupt the flow of goods in and out of Wilmington, a major Confederate port. At 10:30 that morning, the U.S.S. *Cambridge* took the men aboard.

Astonishingly, on the same day that Gould reached the federal ship, President Abraham Lincoln announced to his cabinet in Washington, D.C., that he intended to issue a proclamation of **emancipation** freeing slaves in the Confederate states. Because the proclamation would not take effect until January 1863, Gould was not legally free in the eyes of the U.S. government. But the U.S. navy, suffering from a shortage of sailors, cared little about the formal status of runaway slaves. Within days, all eight runaways became sailors "for three years," Gould said, "first taking the Oath of Allegiance to the Government of Uncle Samuel."

Unlike most slaves, William Gould could read and write, and he began making almost daily entries in a remarkable diary, apparently the only diary kept during the war by a sailor who had been a slave. In some ways, Gould's naval experience looked like that of white sailors. He found duty on a ship in the blockading squadron both boring and exhilarating. He often recorded "All hands painting, cleaning" and "Cruised as usual." But long days of tedious work were sometimes interrupted by a "period of daring exploit" as enemy ships engaged in combat. When Gould's ship closed in on one Confederate vessel, he declared that "we told them good morning in the shape of a shot." In a five-day period in 1862, his ship and two other blockaders captured four blockade runners and ran another aground. In October 1863, Gould transferred to the U.S.S. *Niagara* and sailed for European waters to search for Confederate cruisers abroad.

But Gould's Civil War experience was shaped by his race. Most whites fought to preserve their government and society, while most black men in the Union military saw service as an opportunity to fight slavery. From the beginning, Gould linked union and freedom, which he called "the holiest of all causes." Nevertheless, Gould witnessed a number of racial incidents on federal ships. When a black regiment came aboard, "they were treated verry rough by the crew," he declared. White sailors "refused to let them eat off the mess pans and calld them all kinds of names[;]…in all they was treated

Newly Recruited Contrabands, 1862
The U.S. navy recruited men with little regard for status or color. Blacks initially served only as coal heavers, cooks, and stewards, but within a year, some black sailors joined their ships' gun crews. As this photograph of newly recruited ex-slaves reveals, naval service was not limited to young men.
Courtesy of the New Hampshire Historical Society.

shamefully." Recording another incident, Gould stated, "This Morning four or fiv[e] white fellows beat Jerry Jones (co[lored]). He was stabd in his left shoulder. Verry bad."

Still, Gould was proud of his service in the navy and monitored the progress of racial equality during the war. On shore leave in 1863, he cheered the "20th Regmt of U.S. (collard [colored]) Volunteers, the first collard Regement raised in New York pronounce[d] by all to be A splendid Regement." In March 1865, he celebrated the "passage of an amendment of the Con[sti]tution prohibiting slavery througho[ut] the United States." And a month later, he thrilled to the "Glad Tidings that the Stars and Stripe[s] had been planted over the Capital of the D—nd Confederacy by the invincible Grant." He added, we must not forget the "Mayrters to the cau[se] of Right and Equality."

Slaves like the eight runaways from Wilmington took the first steps toward making the war for union also a war for freedom. Early in the fighting, black abolitionist Frederick Douglass challenged the friends of freedom to "*be up and doing;—now is your time.*" For the first eighteen months of the war, Union soldiers

fought solely to uphold the Constitution and preserve the nation. But with the Emancipation Proclamation the northern war effort took on a dual purpose: to save the Union and to free the slaves.

Even if the Civil War had not touched slavery, the conflict still would have transformed America. As the world's first modern war, it mobilized the entire populations of North and South, harnessed the productive capacities of both economies, and produced battles that fielded 200,000 soldiers and created casualties in the tens of thousands. The carnage lasted four years and cost the nation an estimated 633,000 lives. The war helped mold the modern American nation-state and encouraged industrialization. The federal government emerged with new power and responsibility over national life. The war tore families apart and pushed women into new roles. But because the war for Union also became a war against slavery, the northern victory had truly revolutionary meaning. Defeat and emancipation destroyed the slave society of the Old South and gave birth to a different southern society.

Recalling the Civil War years, Frederick Douglass said, "It is something to couple one's name with great occasions." It *was* something—for William Gould and millions of other Americans. Whether they fought for the Confederacy or for the Union, whether they labored behind the lines to supply Yankee or rebel soldiers, whether they prayed for the safe return of Northerners or Southerners, all Americans experienced the crucible of war. But the war affected no group more than the four million African Americans who saw its beginning as slaves and emerged as free people.

"And the War Came"

Abraham Lincoln faced the worst crisis in the history of the nation: the threat of disunion. He revealed his strategy on March 4, 1861, in his inaugural address, firm yet conciliatory. First, he determined to avoid any act that would push the skittish Upper South (North Carolina, Virginia, Maryland, Delaware, Kentucky, Tennessee, Missouri, and Arkansas) out of the Union. Second, he reassured the Lower South (South Carolina, Georgia, Florida, Alabama, Mississippi, Louisiana, and Texas) that the Republicans would not abolish slavery. Lincoln believed that Unionists there would assert themselves and overturn the secession decision. Always, Lincoln denied the right of secession and upheld Union.

His counterpart, Jefferson Davis, fully intended to establish the Confederate States of America as an independent republic. To achieve permanence, Davis had to sustain the secession fever that had carried the Lower South out of the Union. Even if the Lower South held firm, however, the Confederacy would remain weak without additional states. Davis watched for opportunities to add new stars to the Confederate flag.

Neither man sought war. Both wanted to achieve their objectives peacefully. But as Lincoln later observed, "Both parties deprecated war, but one of them would *make* war rather than let the nation survive, and the other would *accept* war rather than let it perish. And the war came."

Attack on Fort Sumter

Major Robert Anderson and some eighty U.S. soldiers occupied Fort Sumter at the entrance to Charleston harbor. The fort with its American flag became a hated symbol of the nation that Southerners had abandoned, and they wanted federal troops out. Sumter was also a symbol to Northerners, a beacon affirming federal sovereignty in the seceded states.

Lincoln decided to hold Fort Sumter, but to do so, he had to provision it, for Anderson was running dangerously short of food. In the first week of April 1861, Lincoln authorized a peaceful expedition to bring supplies, but not military reinforcements, to the fort. The president understood that he risked war, but his plan honored his inaugural promises to defend federal property and to avoid using military force unless first attacked. Masterfully, Lincoln had shifted the fateful decision of war or peace to Jefferson Davis.

On April 9, Jefferson Davis and his cabinet met to consider the situation in Charleston harbor. The territorial integrity of the Confederacy demanded the end of the federal presence, Davis argued. But his secretary of state, Robert Toombs of Georgia, pleaded against military action. "Mr. President," he declared, "at this time it is suicide, murder, and will lose us every friend at the North. You will wantonly strike a hornet's nest which extends from mountain to ocean, and legions now

Fort Sumter after the Bombardment
Located on an artificial island inside the entrance to Charleston harbor, Fort Sumter had walls eight to twelve feet thick. The fort was so undermanned that when Confederate shells began raining down on April 12, U.S. troops could answer back with only a few of the fort's forty-eight guns. Confederate artillery lobbed more than 4,000 rounds. Cannonballs pulverized the walls, while hot shot ignited the wooden buildings inside.
Minnesota Historical Society.

quiet will swarm out and sting us to death." Davis rejected Toombs's prophecy and sent word to Confederate troops in Charleston to take the fort before the relief expedition arrived. Thirty-three hours of bombardment on April 12 and 13 reduced the fort to rubble. Miraculously, not a single Union soldier died. On April 14, with the fort ablaze, Major Anderson offered his surrender and lowered the U.S. flag. The Confederates had Fort Sumter, but they also had war.

On April 15, when Lincoln called for 75,000 militiamen to serve for ninety days to put down the rebellion, several times that number rushed to defend the flag. Democrats responded as fervently as Republicans. Stephen A. Douglas, the recently defeated Democratic candidate for president, pledged his support. "There are only two sides to the question," he said. "Every man must be for the United States or against it. There can be no neutrals in this war, *only patriots—or traitors.*" But the people of the Upper South found themselves torn.

The Upper South Chooses Sides

The Upper South faced a horrendous choice: either to fight against the Lower South or to fight against the Union. Many who only months earlier had rejected secession now embraced the Confederacy. To vote against southern independence was one thing, to fight fellow Southerners another. As one man concluded, "this is no time now to discuss the causes, but it is the duty of all who regard Southern institutions of value to side with the South, make common cause with the Confederate States and sink or swim with them."

One by one the states of the Upper South jumped off the fence. Within weeks, Virginia, Arkansas, Tennessee, and North Carolina had joined the Confederacy (Map 15.1). But in the border states of Delaware, Maryland, Kentucky, and Missouri, Unionism triumphed. Only in Delaware, where slaves accounted for less than 2 percent of the population, was the victory easy. In Maryland, Unionism needed a helping hand. Lincoln suspended the writ of habeas corpus, essentially setting aside constitutional guarantees that protect citizens from illegal and arbitrary arrest and detention, and he ordered U.S. troops into Baltimore. Maryland's legislature rejected secession.

The struggle turned violent in the West. In Missouri, Unionists won a narrow victory, but southern-sympathizing **guerrilla** bands roamed the state for the duration of the war, terrorizing civilians and soldiers alike. In Kentucky, Unionists also narrowly defeated secession, but a prosouthern minority claimed otherwise. The Confederacy, not especially careful about counting votes, eagerly made Missouri and Kentucky the twelfth and thirteenth stars on the Confederate flag.

Throughout the border states, but especially in Kentucky, the Civil War was truly a "brother's war." Seven of Henry Clay's grandsons fought: four for the Confederacy and three for the Union. Lincoln understood that the border states—particularly Kentucky—contained indispensable resources, population, and wealth and also controlled major rivers and railroads. "I think to lose Kentucky is nearly the same as to lose the whole game," Lincoln said. "Kentucky gone, we can not hold Missouri, nor, as I think, Maryland. These all against us,...we would as well consent to separation at once."

In the end, only eleven of the fifteen slave states joined the Confederate States of America. Moreover, the four seceding Upper South states contained significant numbers of people who felt little affection for the Confederacy.

MAP 15.1 Secession, 1860–1861
After Lincoln's election, the fifteen slave states debated what to do. Seven states quickly left the Union, four left after the firing on Fort Sumter, and four remained loyal to the Union.

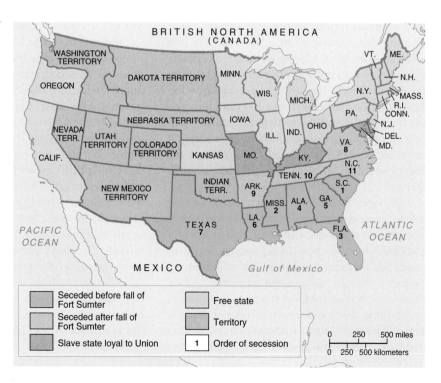

Dissatisfaction was so rife in the western counties of Virginia that in 1863 citizens there voted to create the separate state of West Virginia, loyal to the Union. Still, the acquisition of four new states greatly strengthened the Confederacy's drive for national independence.

> **REVIEW** Why did both the Union and the Confederacy consider control of the border states crucial?

The Combatants

Only slaveholders had a direct economic stake in preserving slavery (estimated at some $3 billion in 1860), but most whites in the Confederacy defended the institution, the way of life built on it, and the Confederacy itself. The degraded and subjugated status of blacks elevated the status of the poorest whites. Moreover, Yankee "aggression" was no longer a mere threat; it was real and at the South's door.

For Northerners, rebel "treason" threatened to destroy the best government on earth. The South's failure to accept the **democratic** election of a president and its firing on the nation's flag challenged the rule of law, the authority of the Constitution, and the ability of the people to govern themselves. As an Indiana soldier told his wife, a "good government is the best thing on earth. Property is nothing without it, because it is not protected; a family is nothing without it, because they cannot be educated."

While both sides claimed the lion's share of virtue, census figures show that the North's resources far surpassed the South's. Yankees took heart at their superior power, but the rebels believed they had advantages that nullified every northern strength. Both sides mobilized swiftly in 1861, and each devised what it believed would be a winning military and diplomatic strategy.

How They Expected to Win

The balance sheet of northern and southern resources reveals enormous advantages for the Union (Figure 15.1). The twenty-three states remaining in the

Union had a population of 22.3 million; the eleven Confederate states had a population of only 9.1 million, of whom 3.67 million (40 percent) were slaves. The North's economic advantages were even more overwhelming. So mismatched were Union and Confederacy that the question becomes why the South made war at all. Was not the South's cause lost before Confederates fired the first rounds at Fort Sumter? The answer quite simply is "no." Southerners expected to win—for some good reasons—and they came very close to doing so.

Southerners knew they bucked the military odds, but hadn't the **liberty**-loving colonists in 1776 also done so? "Britain could not conquer three million," a Louisianan proclaimed, and "the world cannot conquer the South." How could anyone doubt the outcome of a contest between lean, hard, country-born rebel warriors defending family, property, and liberty, and soft, flabby, citified Yankee mechanics waging an unconstitutional war?

The South's confidence also rested on its belief that northern prosperity depended on the

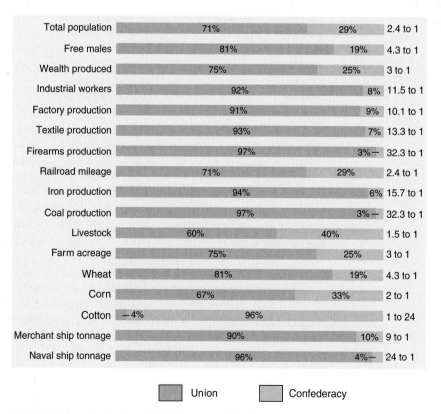

Total population	71%	29%	2.4 to 1
Free males	81%	19%	4.3 to 1
Wealth produced	75%	25%	3 to 1
Industrial workers	92%	8%	11.5 to 1
Factory production	91%	9%	10.1 to 1
Textile production	93%	7%	13.3 to 1
Firearms production	97%	3%–	32.3 to 1
Railroad mileage	71%	29%	2.4 to 1
Iron production	94%	6%	15.7 to 1
Coal production	97%	3%–	32.3 to 1
Livestock	60%	40%	1.5 to 1
Farm acreage	75%	25%	3 to 1
Wheat	81%	19%	4.3 to 1
Corn	67%	33%	2 to 1
Cotton	–4%	96%	1 to 24
Merchant ship tonnage	90%	10%	9 to 1
Naval ship tonnage	96%	4%–	24 to 1

◼ Union ◼ Confederacy

FIGURE 15.1 Resources of the Union and Confederacy
The Union's enormous statistical advantages failed to convince Confederates that their cause was doomed.

South's cotton. It followed then that without cotton, New England textile mills would stand idle. And without southern **planters** purchasing northern manufactured goods, northern factories would drown in their own unsold goods. A Virginian spoke for most Confederates when he declared that in the South's ability to "withhold the benefits of our trade, we hold a power over the North more powerful than a powerful army in the field."

Cotton would also make Europe a powerful ally of the Confederacy, Southerners reasoned. After all, they said, England's economy (and to a lesser degree France's) also depended on cotton. Of the 900 million pounds of cotton England imported annually, more than 700 million came from the South. If the supply were interrupted, sheer economic need would make England (and perhaps France) a Confederate ally. And because the British navy ruled the seas, the North would find Britain a formidable foe.

Southerners' confidence may seem naive today, but even tough-minded European military observers picked the South to win. Offsetting the Union's power was the Confederacy's expanse. The North, Europeans predicted, could not conquer the vast territory (750,000 square miles). To defeat the South, the Union would need to raise and equip a massive invading army and protect supply lines that would stretch farther than any in modern history.

Indeed, the South enjoyed major advantages, and the Confederacy devised a military strategy to exploit them. It recognized that a Union victory required the North to defeat and subjugate the South, but a Confederate victory required only that the South blunt invasions, avoid battles that risked annihilating its army, and outlast the North's will to fight. When an opportunity presented itself, the South would strike the invaders. Like the American colonists, the South could win independence by not losing the war.

If the North did nothing, the South would by default establish itself as a sovereign nation. The Lincoln administration therefore adopted an offensive strategy that applied pressure at many points. Lincoln declared a naval blockade of the Confederacy to deny the South the advantages offered by its most valuable commodity — cotton. Without the sale of cotton abroad, the South would have far fewer dollars to pay for war goods. Lincoln also ordered the Union army into Virginia, at the same time planning a march through the Mississippi valley that would cut the Confederacy in two. This ambitious strategy took advantage of the Union's superior resources.

Neither side could foresee the magnitude and duration of the war. Americans thought of war in terms of their most recent experience, the Mexican-American War of the 1840s. In Mexico, fighting had taken place between relatively small armies, had cost relatively few lives, and had inflicted only light damage on the countryside. On the eve of the Civil War, they could not know that four ghastly years of bloodletting lay ahead.

Lincoln and Davis Mobilize

Mobilization required effective political leadership, and at first glance the South appeared to have the advantage. Jefferson Davis brought to the Confederate presidency a distinguished political career, including experience in the U.S. Senate. He was also a West Point graduate, a combat veteran and authentic hero of the Mexican-American War, and a former secretary of war. In contrast, Abraham Lincoln brought to the White House one term in the House of Representatives, and his sole brush with anything military was as a captain in the militia in the Black Hawk War, a brief struggle in Illinois in 1832 in which whites expelled the last Indians from the state. The lanky, disheveled Illinois lawyer-politician looked anything but military or presidential in his bearing.

Davis, however, proved to be less than he appeared. Although he worked hard, Davis had no gift for military strategy yet intervened often in military affairs. He was an even less able political leader. Quarrelsome and proud, he had an acid tongue that made enemies the Confederacy could ill afford. He insisted on dealing with every scrap of paper that came across his desk, and he grew increasingly unbending and dogmatic.

With Lincoln, in contrast, the North got far more than met the eye. He proved himself a master politician and a superb leader. When forming his cabinet, Lincoln appointed the ablest men, no matter that they were often his chief rivals and critics. He appointed Salmon P. Chase secretary of the treasury, knowing that Chase had presidential ambitions. As secretary of state, he chose his chief opponent for the Republican nomination in 1860, William H. Seward. Despite his civilian background, Lincoln displayed an innate understanding of military strategy. No one was more crucial in mapping the Union war plan.

Minié Ball

The Union army was one of the best equipped armies in history. None of its weaponry proved more vital than a French innovation: Captain Claude Minié's new bullet. In 1848, Minié created an inch-long slug that was rammed down a rifled barrel and would spin at great speed as it left the muzzle. The spin gave the bullet greater distance and accuracy than bullets fired from smoothbore weapons. When the war began, most soldiers carried smoothbore muskets; but by 1863, infantry on both sides fought with rifles. Bullets caused more than 90 percent of battle wounds, and minié balls proved extremely destructive to human bodies on impact.

Picture Research Consultants & Archives.

Further, Lincoln galvanized Union citizens in defense of the nation he called "the last best hope of earth."

Lincoln and Davis began gathering their armies. Confederates had to build almost everything from scratch, and Northerners had to channel their superior numbers and industrial resources to purposes of war. In 1860, the federal army numbered only 16,000 men, most of them scattered over the West subjugating Indians. One-third of the officers followed the example of the Virginian Robert E. Lee, resigning their commissions and heading south. The U.S. navy was in better shape. Forty-two ships were in service, and a large merchant marine would in time provide more ships and sailors for the Union cause. Possessing a much weaker navy, the South pinned its hopes on its armies.

The Confederacy made prodigious efforts to build new factories to produce tents, blankets, shoes, and its gray uniforms, but many rebel soldiers slept in the open air without proper clothes and sometimes without shoes. Even when factories managed to produce what the soldiers needed, southern railroads often could not deliver the goods. And each year more railroads were captured, destroyed, or left in disrepair. Food production proved less of a problem, but food sometimes rotted before it reached the soldiers. The one bright spot was the Confederacy's Ordnance Bureau, headed by Josiah Gorgas, a near miracle worker when it came to manufacturing gunpower, cannon, and rifles. In April 1864, Gorgas proudly observed: "Where three years ago we were not making a gun, a pistol nor a sabre, no shot nor shell…—a pound of powder—we now make all these in quantities to meet the demands of our large armies."

Recruiting and supplying huge armies required enormous new revenues. At first, the Union and the Confederacy sold war bonds, which essentially were loans from patriotic citizens. In addition, both sides turned to taxes. The North raised one-fifth of its wartime revenue from taxes; the South raised only one-twentieth. Eventually, both began printing paper money. Inflation soared, but the Confederacy suffered more because it financed a greater part of its wartime costs through the printing press. Prices in the Union rose by about 80 percent during the war, while inflation in the Confederacy topped 9,000 percent.

Within months, both sides found men to fight and ways to supply and support them. But the underlying strength of the northern economy gave the Union the decided advantage. With their military and industrial muscles beginning to ripple, Northerners became itchy for action. They wanted an invasion that once and for all would smash the rebellion. Horace Greeley's *New York Tribune* began to chant: "Forward to Richmond! Forward to Richmond!"

REVIEW   Why did the South believe it could win the war despite numerical disadvantages?

Battling It Out, 1861–1862

During the first year and a half of the war, armies fought major campaigns in both East and West. Because the rival capitals—Richmond and Washington, D.C.—were only ninety miles apart and each was threatened more than once with capture, the eastern campaign was especially dramatic. But the battles in the West proved more decisive. As Yankee and rebel armies pounded each other on land, the navies of each side fought on the seas and in the rivers of the South. In Europe, Confederate and U.S. diplomats competed for advantage in the corridors of power. All the while, casualty lists reached appalling lengths.

Stalemate in the Eastern Theater

Irvin McDowell, commanding general of the Union army assembling outside Washington, had no thought of taking his raw recruits into battle during the summer of 1861. Lincoln, however, ordered him to prepare his 35,000 troops for an attack on the 20,000 Confederates defending Manassas, a railroad junction in Virginia about thirty miles southwest of Washington. On July 21, the Union army forded Bull Run, a branch of the Potomac River, and engaged the southern forces effectively (Map 15.2). But fast-moving southern reinforcements blunted the Union attack and then counterattacked. What began as an orderly Union retreat turned into a panicky stampede. Demoralized federal troops ran over shocked civilians as the soldiers raced back to Washington.

By Civil War standards, casualties (wounded and dead) at Bull Run (or Manassas, as

---

MAP 15.2   The Civil War, 1861–1862

While eyes focused on the eastern theater, especially the 90-mile stretch of land between the U.S. capital at Washington and the Confederate capital at Richmond, Union troops were winning strategic victories in the West.

READING THE MAP: In which states did the Confederacy and the Union each win the most battles in this period? Which side used or followed water routes most for troop movements and attacks?

CONNECTIONS: Which major cities in the South and West fell to Union troops in 1862? Which strategic area did those Confederate losses place in Union hands? How did this outcome affect the later movement of troops and supplies?

FOR MORE HELP ANALYZING THIS MAP, see the visual activity for this chapter in the Online Study Guide at bedfordstmartins.com/roarkcompact.

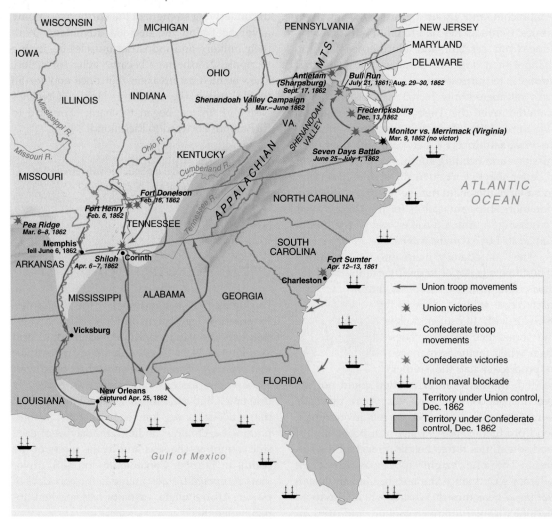

Southerners called the battle) were light. The significance of the battle lay in the lessons Northerners and Southerners drew from it. For Southerners, it confirmed the superiority of rebel fighting men and the inevitability of Confederate nationhood. Manassas was *"one of the decisive battles of the world,"* a Georgian proclaimed. It *"has secured our independence."* While victory elevated southern pride, defeat sobered Northerners. It was a major setback, admitted the *New York Tribune*, but "Let us go to work, then, with a will." Bull Run taught Lincoln that victory would be neither quick nor easy. Within four days of the disaster, the president authorized the enlistment of one million men for three years.

Lincoln also found a new general, replacing McDowell with young George B. McClellan. Born in Philadelphia of well-to-do parents, graduating from West Point second in his class, the thirty-four-year-old McClellan believed that he was a great soldier and that Lincoln was a dunce, the "original Gorilla." A superb administrator and organizer, McClellan came to Washington as commander of the newly named Army of the Potomac. McClellan energetically whipped his dispirited army into shape but was reluctant to send his soldiers into battle. For all his energy, McClellan lacked decisiveness. Lincoln wanted a general who would advance, take risks, and fight, but McClellan went into winter quarters. "If General McClellan does not want to use the army I would like to *borrow* it," Lincoln declared in frustration.

Finally, in May 1862, McClellan launched his long-awaited offensive. He transported his highly polished army, now 130,000 strong, to the mouth of the James River and began moving up the Yorktown peninsula toward Richmond. When he was within six miles of the Confederate capital, General Joseph Johnston hit him like a hammer. In the assault, Johnston was wounded and was replaced by Robert E. Lee, who would become the

The Battle of Savage's Station, Robert Knox Sneden, 1862

In 1862, thirty-year-old Robert Sneden joined the Fortieth New York Volunteers and soon found himself in Virginia, part of George McClellan's peninsula campaign. A gifted artist in watercolor as well as an eloquent writer, Sneden captures here an early Confederate assault in what became known as the Seven Days Battle. "The immense open space in front of Savage's [house] was densely thronged with wagon trains, artillery, caissons, ammunition trains, and moving troops," Sneden observed. The "storm of lead was continuous and deadly on the approaching lines of the Rebels. They bravely rushed up, however, to within twenty feet of our artillery, when bushels of grape and canister from the cannon laid them low in rows." Over the next three years, Sneden produced hundreds of vivid drawings and eventually thousands of pages of remembrance, providing one of the most complete accounts of a Union soldier's Civil War experience.

© 1996, Lora Robbins Collection of Virginia Art, Virginia Historical Society.

South's most celebrated general. Lee named his command the Army of Northern Virginia.

The contrast between Lee and McClellan could hardly have been greater. McClellan brimmed with conceit and braggadocio; Lee was courteous and reserved. On the battlefield, McClellan grew timid and irresolute, and Lee became audaciously, even recklessly, aggressive. And Lee had at his side in the peninsula campaign military men of real talent: Thomas J. Jackson, nicknamed "Stonewall" for holding the line at Manassas, and James E. B. (Jeb) Stuart, a dashing twenty-nine-year-old cavalry commander who rode circles around Yankee troops.

Lee's assault initiated the Seven Days Battle (June 25–July 1)

Peninsula Campaign, 1862

and began McClellan's march back down the peninsula. By the time McClellan reached the safety of the Union navy, 30,000 men from both sides had died or been wounded. Although Southerners suffered twice the casualties of Northerners, Lee had saved Richmond and achieved a strategic success. Lincoln wired McClellan to abandon the peninsula campaign and replaced him with General John Pope.

In August, north of Richmond, at the second battle of Bull Run, Lee's smaller army battered Pope's forces and sent them scurrying back to Washington. Lincoln had not changed his mind about McClellan's capacity as a warrior, but he restored him to command. "If he can't fight himself, he excels in making others ready to fight," Lincoln admitted.

Sensing that he had the enemy on the ropes, Lee sought to land the knockout punch. He pushed his army across the Potomac and invaded Maryland. A victory on northern soil would dislodge Maryland from the Union, Lee reasoned, and might even cause Lincoln to sue for peace. On September 17, 1862, McClellan's forces engaged Lee's army at Antietam Creek (see Map 15.2). The Union army did severe damage. With "solid shot…cracking skulls like eggshells," according to one observer, the armies went after each other. By nightfall, 6,000 men lay dead or dying on the battlefield, and 17,000 more had been wounded. The battle of Antietam would be the bloodiest day of the war. Instead of being the war-winning fight Lee had anticipated when he came north, Antietam sent the battered Army of Northern Virginia limping back home. McClellan claimed to have saved the North, but Lincoln again removed him from command of the Army of the Potomac and appointed General Ambrose Burnside.

Although bloodied, Lee found an opportunity in December to punish the enemy at Fredericksburg, Virginia, where Burnside's 122,000 Union troops faced 78,500 Confederates dug in behind a stone wall on the heights above the Rappahannock River. Half a mile of open ground separated the armies. "A chicken could not live on that field when we open on it," a Confederate artillery officer predicted. Yet Burnside ordered a frontal assault. When the shooting ceased, the Federals counted nearly 13,000 casualties, the Confederates fewer than 5,000. The battle of Fredericksburg was one of the Union's worst defeats. As 1862 ended, the North seemed no nearer to ending the rebellion than it had been when the war began. Rather than checkmate, military struggle in the East had reached stalemate.

Union Victories in the Western Theater

While most eyes focused on events in the East, the decisive early encounters of the war were taking place between the Appalachian Mountains and the Ozarks (see Map 15.2). Confederates wanted Missouri and Kentucky, states they claimed but did not control. Federals wanted to split Arkansas, Louisiana, and Texas from the Confederacy by taking control of the Mississippi River and to occupy Tennessee, one of the Confederacy's main producers of food, mules, and iron—all vital resources.

Before Union forces could march on Tennessee, they needed to secure Missouri to the west. Union troops commanded by General Samuel R. Curtis swept across Missouri to the border of Arkansas, where in March 1862, they encountered General Earl Van Dorn's 16,000-man Confederate army, which included three regiments of Indians from the Five Civilized Nations in Indian Territory. Curtis's victory at the battle of Pea Ridge left Missouri free of Confederate troops, but Missouri was not free of Confederate guerrillas. Guerrilla bands led by the notorious William Clarke Quantrill and "Bloody Bill" Anderson burned, tortured, scalped, and murdered Union civilians and soldiers until the final year of the war.

Even farther west, Confederate armies sought to fulfill Jefferson Davis's vision of a slaveholding empire stretching all the way to the Pacific. Both sides recognized the immense value of the gold and silver mines of California, Nevada, and Colorado. A quick strike by Texas troops took Santa Fe, New Mexico, in the winter of 1861–62. Then in March 1862, a band of Colorado miners ambushed and crushed southern forces at Glorieta Pass, outside Santa Fe. Confederate military

Battle of Glorieta Pass, 1862

Native American Recruits

Both the Union and the Confederacy sought soldiers from tribes in Indian Territory. Here a Union recruiter swears in Indian recruits, but it was the Confederacy that signed treaties with the so-called Five Civilized Tribes—the Choctaw, Chickasaw, Creek, Seminole, and Cherokee—in 1861. Confederates promised to assume the financial obligations of the old treaties with the United States, guarantee slavery, respect the independence of the tribes, and permit the tribes to send delegates to Richmond. John Ross, chief of the Cherokee Nation, prayed that he had chosen the right side. "We are in the situation of a man standing upon a low naked spot of ground," he said, "with the water rising all around him.... The tide carries by him, in its mad course, a drifting log.... By refusing it he is a doomed man. By seizing hold of it he has a chance for his life." Several thousand Indians fought in blue and in gray uniforms. In some battles in Arkansas, Indians fought Indians.

Wisconsin Historical Society.

failures in the far West meant that there would be no Confederate empire beyond Texas.

The principal western battles took place in Tennessee, where General Ulysses S. Grant emerged as the key northern commander. Grant had graduated from West Point and served bravely in Mexico. When the Civil War began, he was a thirty-nine-year-old dry-goods clerk in Galena, Illinois. Gentle at home, he became pugnacious on the battlefield. "The art of war is simple," he said. "Find out where your enemy is, get at him as soon as you can and strike him as hard as you can, and keep moving on." Grant's philosophy of war as attrition would take a huge toll in human life, but it played to the North's strength: superiority in manpower. In his private's uniform and slouch hat, Grant did not look much like a general. But Lincoln, who did not look much like a president, learned his worth. Later, to critics who wanted the president to sack Grant because of his drinking, Lincoln would say: *"I can't spare this man. He fights."*

In February 1862, Grant captured Fort Henry on the Tennessee River and Fort Donelson on the Cumberland (see Map 15.2). Defeat forced the Confederates to withdraw from all of Kentucky and most of Tennessee, but Grant followed. On April 6, General Albert Sidney Johnston's army surprised him at Shiloh Church in Tennessee. Grant's troops were badly mauled the first day, but Grant remained cool and brought up reinforcements throughout the night. The next morning, the Union army counterattacked, driving the Confederates before it. The battle of Shiloh was terribly costly to both sides; there were 20,000 casualties, among them General Johnston. Grant later said that after Shiloh he "gave up all idea of saving the Union except by complete conquest."

Although no one knew it at the time, Shiloh ruined the Confederacy's bid to control the theater of operations in the West. In short order, the Yankees captured the strategic town of Corinth, Mississippi, the river city of Memphis, and the South's largest city, New Orleans. By the end of 1862, the far West and most—but not all—of the Mississippi valley lay in Union hands. At the same time, the outcome of the struggle in another theater of war was also becoming clearer.

Major Battles of the Civil War, 1861–1862

April 12–13, 1861	Attack on Fort Sumter
July 21, 1861	First battle of Bull Run (Manassas)
February 6, 1862	Battle of Fort Henry
February 16, 1862	Battle of Fort Donelson
March 9, 1862	Battle of the *Merrimack* (the *Virginia*) and the *Monitor*
March 26, 1862	Battle of Glorieta Pass
March 28, 1862	Battle of Pea Ridge
May–July 1862	McClellan's peninsula campaign
April 6–7, 1862	Battle of Shiloh
June 6, 1862	Fall of Memphis
June 25–July 1, 1862	Seven Days Battle
August 29–30, 1862	Second battle of Bull Run (Manassas)
September 17, 1862	Battle of Antietam
December 13, 1862	Battle of Fredericksburg

War and Diplomacy in the Atlantic Theater

At the beginning of the war, the U.S. navy's blockade fleet consisted of about three dozen ships to patrol more than 3,500 miles of southern coastline, and rebel merchant ships were able to slip in and out of southern ports nearly at will. Taking on cargoes in the Caribbean, sleek, fast Confederate blockade runners brought in vital supplies—guns and medicine. But with the U.S. navy commissioning a new blockader almost weekly, the naval fleet eventually numbered 150 ships on duty, and the Union navy dramatically improved its score.

Unable to build a conventional navy equal to the expanding U.S. fleet, Confederates experimented with a radical new maritime design: the ironclad warship. At Norfolk, Virginia, they layered the wooden hull of the frigate *Merrimack* with two-inch-thick armor plate. Rechristened *Virginia*, the ship steamed out in March 1862 and sank two large federal ships, killing at least 240 Union sailors (see Map 15.2). When the *Virginia* returned to finish off the federal blockaders, it was challenged by the *Monitor*, a federal ironclad of even more radical design, topped with a revolving turret holding two eleven-inch guns. On March 9, the two ships hurled shells at each other for two hours, but neither could penetrate the other's armor and the battle ended in a draw.

The Confederacy never found a way to break the Union blockade despite exploring many naval innovations including a new underwater vessel—the submarine. Each month the Union fleet tightened its noose. The growing effectiveness of the federal blockade, a southern naval officer observed, "shut the Confederacy out from the world, deprived it of supplies, weakened its military and naval strength." By 1865, the blockaders were intercepting about half of the southern ships attempting to break through.

What Confederates could not achieve on saltwater, they sought to achieve through foreign policy. In theory, King Cotton meant that cotton-starved European nations would have to break the Union blockade and recognize the Confederacy. Some European nations granted the Confederacy "belligerent" status, which enabled it to buy goods and build ships in European ports, but none challenged the blockade or recognized the Confederate States of America as a nation, a bold act that probably would have drawn them into war with the United States.

King Cotton diplomacy failed for several reasons. A bumper cotton crop in 1860 meant that the warehouses of British textile manufacturers bulged with surplus cotton throughout 1861. When a cotton shortage did occur, European manufacturers found new sources in Egypt and India. In addition, the development of a brisk trade between the Union and Britain—British war materiel for American grain and flour—helped offset the decline in textiles and encouraged Britain to remain neutral. Union military successes in the West also made Britain and France think twice about linking their fates to the Confederacy. Finally, in September 1862, five days after the Union victory at Antietam, Lincoln announced a new policy that made an alliance with the Confederacy an alliance with slavery, an alliance the French and British were not willing to make.

> **REVIEW** Why did King Cotton diplomacy fail?

Union *and* Freedom

For a year and a half, Lincoln insisted that the war was strictly to save the Union. But despite Lincoln's repeated pronouncements, the war for union became a war for African American freedom. Each month the conflict dragged on, it became clearer that the Confederate war machine depended heavily on slavery. Rebel armies used slaves to build fortifications, haul materiel, tend horses, and perform camp chores. On the home front, slaves labored in ironworks and shipyards, and they grew the food that fed both soldiers and civilians. Slavery undergirded the Confederacy as certainly as it had the Old South. Union military commanders and politicians alike gradually realized that to defeat the Confederacy, the North would have to destroy slavery. "I am a slow walker," Lincoln said, "but I never walk back."

From Slaves to Contraband

Lincoln detested human bondage, but as president he felt compelled to act prudently in the interests of the Union. He doubted his right under the Constitution to tamper with the "domestic institutions" of any state, even states in rebellion. An astute politician, Lincoln worked within the tight limits of public opinion. The issue of black freedom was particularly explosive in the loyal border states, where slaveholders threatened to jump into the arms of the Confederacy at even the hint of emancipation. Black freedom also raised alarms in the free states. The Democratic Party gave notice that emancipation would make the war strictly a Republican affair.

Moreover, many white Northerners were not about to risk their lives to satisfy abolitionist "fanaticism." "We Won't Fight to Free the Nigger," one popular banner read. They feared that emancipation would propel "two or three million semi-savages" northward, where they would crowd into white neighborhoods, compete for white jobs, and mix with white "sons and daughters." Thus, a surge of anti-emancipation, antiblack sentiment threatened to dislodge the loyal slave states from the Union, alienate the Democratic Party, deplete the armies, and perhaps even spark race warfare.

Yet proponents of emancipation pressed Lincoln as relentlessly as the anti-emancipation forces. Abolitionists argued that by seceding Southerners had forfeited their right to the protection of the Constitution, and that Lincoln could—as the price of their treason—legally confiscate their property in slaves. When Lincoln refused, abolitionists scalded him. Frederick Douglass labeled him "the miserable tool of traitors and rebels."

The Republican-dominated Congress declined to leave slavery policy entirely in Lincoln's hands. In August 1861, Congress approved the Confiscation Act, which allowed the seizure of any slave employed directly by the Confederate military. It also fulfilled the **free-soil** dream of prohibiting slavery in the territories and abolished slavery in Washington, D.C. Democrats and border-state representatives voted against even these mild measures, but Congress's attitude stiffened as it cast about for a just and practical slavery policy.

Slaves, not politicians, became the most insistent force for emancipation. By escaping their masters by the tens of thousands and running away to Union lines, they forced slavery on the North's wartime agenda. Runaways precipitated a series of momentous decisions. Were the runaways now free, or were they still slaves who, according to the fugitive slave law, had to be returned to their masters? At first, Yankee military officers sent the fugitives back. But Union armies needed laborers, and some officers accepted the runaways and put them to work. At Fort Monroe, Virginia, General Benjamin F. Butler refused to turn them over to their owners, calling them "contraband of war," meaning "confiscated property." Congress made Butler's practice national policy in March 1862 when it forbade returning fugitive slaves to their masters. Slaves were still not legally free, but there was a tilt toward emancipation.

Lincoln's policy of noninterference with slavery gradually crumbled. To calm Northerners' racial fears, Lincoln offered **colonization**, the deportation of African Americans from the United States to Haiti, Panama, or elsewhere. Congress voted a small amount of money to underwrite colonization, but after one miserable experiment on a small island in the Caribbean, practical limitations and black opposition sank further efforts.

While Lincoln was developing his own initiatives, he snuffed out actions that he believed would jeopardize northern unity. He was particularly alert to Union commanders who tried to dictate slavery policy from the field. In August 1861, when John C. Frémont freed the slaves belonging to Missouri rebels, Lincoln forced the general to revoke his edict and then removed him from command. The following May, when General David Hunter freed slaves in Georgia, South Carolina, and Florida, Lincoln countermanded his order. Events moved so rapidly, however, that Lincoln found it impossible to control federal policy on slavery.

From Contraband to Free People

On August 22, 1862, Lincoln replied to an angry abolitionist who demanded that he attack slavery. "My paramount objective in this struggle *is* to save the Union," Lincoln said deliberately, "and is *not* either to save or destroy slavery. If I could save the Union without freeing *any* slave I would do it, and if I could save it by freeing *all* the slaves I would do it; and if I could save it by freeing some and leaving others alone I would also do that." Instead of simply restating his old position that union was the North's sole objective, Lincoln now added that he would emancipate every slave if doing so would preserve the Union.

By the summer of 1862, events were tumbling rapidly toward emancipation. On July 17, Congress adopted a second Confiscation Act. The first had confiscated slaves employed by the Confederate military; the second declared all slaves of rebel masters "forever free of their servitude." In theory, this breathtaking measure freed most Confederate slaves, for slaveholders formed the backbone of the rebellion. Congress had traveled far since the war began.

Lincoln had, too. On July 21, the president informed his cabinet that he was ready "to take some definitive steps in respect to military action and slavery." The next day, he read a draft of a preliminary emancipation proclamation that promised to free *all* slaves in the seceding states on January 1, 1863. Lincoln described emancipation as an "act of justice," but it was the lengthening casualty lists that finally brought him around. Emancipation, he declared, was "a military necessity, absolutely essential to the preservation of the Union." On September 22, Lincoln issued his preliminary Emancipation Proclamation promising freedom to slaves in areas still in rebellion on January 1, 1863.

The limitations of the proclamation—it exempted the loyal border states and Union-occupied areas of the Confederacy—caused some to ridicule the act. The *London Times* observed cynically, "Where he has no power Mr. Lincoln will set the negroes free, where he retains power he will consider them as slaves." But Lincoln had no power to free slaves in loyal states, and invading Union armies would liberate slaves in the Confederacy as they advanced.

By presenting emancipation as a "military necessity," Lincoln hoped he had disarmed his **conservative** critics. Emancipation would deprive the Confederacy of valuable slave laborers, shorten the war, and thus save lives. Democrats, however, fumed that the "shrieking and howling abolitionist faction" had captured the White House and made it "a nigger war." Democrats made political hay out of Lincoln's action in the November 1862 elections, gaining thirty-four congressional seats. House Democrats quickly proposed a resolution branding emancipation "a high crime against the Constitution." The Republicans, who maintained narrow majorities in both houses of Congress, beat it back.

As promised, on New Year's Day 1863, Lincoln issued the final Emancipation Proclamation. In addition to freeing the slaves in the rebel states, the edict also committed the federal government to the fullest use of African Americans to defeat the Confederate enemy.

War of Black Liberation

Even before Lincoln proclaimed freedom a Union war aim, African Americans in the North had volunteered to fight. But the War Department, doubtful of their abilities and fearful of white reaction to serving side by side with them, refused to make black men soldiers. Instead, the army employed black men as manual laborers; black women sometimes found employment as laundresses and cooks. The navy, however, accepted blacks from the outset, including runaway slaves like William Gould.

As the Union experienced manpower shortages, Northerners gradually and reluctantly turned to African Americans to fill the Union army's blue uniforms. After the Emancipation Proclamation, whites—like it or not—were fighting and dying for black freedom, and few insisted that blacks remain out of harm's way behind the lines. Indeed, whites insisted that blacks share the danger, especially after March 1863, when Congress resorted to the **draft** to fill the Union army.

The military was far from color-blind. The Union army established segregated black regiments, paid black soldiers $10 per month rather than the $13 it paid to whites, refused blacks the opportunity to become commissioned officers, punished blacks as if they were slaves, and assigned blacks to labor battalions rather than to combat units. Still, when the war ended, 179,000 African American men—more than half ex-slaves—had served in the Union military, approximately 10 percent of the army total. An astounding 71 percent of black men ages eighteen to forty-five in the free states wore Union blue, a participation rate that was substantially higher than that of white men.

In time, whites allowed blacks to put down their shovels and to shoulder rifles. At the battles of Port Hudson and Milliken's Bend on the Mississippi River and at Fort Wagner in Charleston harbor, black courage under fire finally dispelled notions that African Americans could not fight. More than 38,000 black soldiers died in the Civil War, a mortality rate that was higher than that of white troops. Blacks played a crucial role in the triumph of the Union and the destruction of slavery in the South.

> REVIEW Why did the Union change policy in 1863 to allow black men to serve in the army?

The South at War

By seceding, Southerners brought on themselves a firestorm of unimaginable fury. Monstrous losses on the battlefields nearly bled the Confederacy to death. White Southerners on the home front also suffered, even at the hands of their own government. Efforts by the Davis administration in Richmond to centralize power to fight the war effectively convinced some men and women that the Confederacy had betrayed them. Wartime economic changes hurt everyone, some more than others. By 1863, planters and **yeomen** who had stood together began to drift apart. Most disturbing of all, slaves became open participants in the destruction of slavery and the Confederacy.

Revolution from Above

As one Confederate general observed, Southerners were engaged in a total war "in which the whole population and the whole production... are to be put on a war footing, where every institution is to be made auxiliary to war." Jefferson Davis faced the task of building an army and navy from scratch, supplying them from factories that were scarce and anemic, and paying for it all from a treasury that did not exist. Finding eager soldiers proved easiest. Very quickly, the Confederacy developed formidable striking power.

The Confederacy's economy and finances proved tougher problems. Because of the Union blockade, the government had no choice but to

Guard Detail of the 107th U.S. Colored Infantry, Arlington, Virginia, 1865

A white man's war when it began, the Civil War eventually gained color, as this photograph of the soldiers of the 107th U.S. Colored Infantry attests. The Lincoln administration was slow to accept black soldiers, in part because of lingering doubts about their ability to fight. Colonel Thomas W. Higginson, a white Massachusetts clergyman and abolitionist, commanded the First South Carolina Infantry, which was made up of former slaves. After his regiment's first skirmish with Confederate troops, Higginson celebrated his men's courage: "No officer in this regiment now doubts that the key to the successful prosecution of this war lies in the unlimited employment of black troops....Instead of leaving their homes and families to fight they are fighting for their homes and families." After the spring of 1863, the federal government did all it could to maximize the number of black soldiers. Eventually, ex-slaves and free blacks filled 145 Union regiments. Throughout the war, however, policy required that blacks serve under white commissioned officers.

© Bettmann / Corbis.

build an industrial sector itself. Government-owned clothing and shoe factories, mines, arsenals, and powder works sprang up. The government also harnessed private companies to the war effort. Paying for the war became the most difficult task. A flood of paper money caused debilitating inflation. By 1863, Charlestonians paid ten times more for food than they had paid at the start of the war. By Christmas 1864, a Confederate soldier's monthly pay no longer bought a pair of socks. Despite bold measures, the Davis administration failed to transform the agricultural economy into a modern industrial one. The Confederacy never produced all that the South needed. Each month, the gap between the North's and the South's production widened.

Richmond's war-making effort brought unprecedented government intrusion into the private lives of Confederate citizens. In April 1862, the Confederate Congress passed the first **conscription** (draft) law in American history. All

Confederate Soldiers and Their Slaves
Soldiers of the Seventh Tennessee Cavalry pose with their slaves. Many slaveholders took "body servants" with them to war. These slaves cooked, washed, and cleaned for the white soldiers. In 1861, James H. Langhorne reported to his sister: "Peter...is charmed with being with me & 'being a soldier.' I gave him my old uniform overcoat & he says he is going to have his picture taken...to send to the servants." Do you think Peter was "puttin' on ol' massa" or just glad to be free of plantation labor?
Daguerreotype courtesy of Tom Farish. Photographed by Michael Latil.

FOR MORE HELP ANALYZING THIS IMAGE, see the visual activity for this chapter in the Online Study Guide at bedfordstmartins.com/roarkcompact.

able-bodied white males between the ages of eighteen and thirty-five (later seventeen and fifty) were liable to serve in the rebel army. The government adopted a policy of impressment, which allowed officials to confiscate food, horses, wagons, and whatever else they wanted from private citizens and to pay for them at below-market rates. After March 1863, the Confederacy legally impressed slaves, employing them as military laborers.

War necessitated much of the government's unprecedented behavior, but citizens found it arbitrary and inequitable. Richmond's centralizing efforts ran head-on into the South's traditional values of **states' rights** and unfettered individualism. The states lashed out at what Georgia governor Joseph E. Brown denounced as the "dangerous usurpation by Congress of the reserved right of the States." Richmond and the states struggled for control of money, supplies, and soldiers, with damaging consequences for the war effort. Individual citizens also remembered that Davis had promised to defend southern "liberty" against Republican "despotism."

Hardship Below

Hardships on the home front fell most heavily on the poor. Flour that cost three or four cents a pound in 1861 cost thirty-five cents in 1863. The draft stripped yeoman farms of men, leaving the women and children to grow what they ate. Government agents took 10 percent of farm

wives' harvests as a "tax-in-kind" on agriculture. Like inflation, shortages afflicted the entire population, but the rich lost luxuries while the poor lost necessities. In the spring of 1863, bread riots broke out in a dozen cities and villages across the South. In Richmond, a mob of nearly a thousand hungry women broke into shops and took what they needed.

"Men cannot be expected to fight for the Government that permits their wives & children to starve," a southern leader observed in November 1862. While a few wealthy individuals shared their bounty and the Confederate and state governments made efforts at social welfare, every attempt fell short. In late 1864, one desperate farm wife told her husband: "I have always been proud of you, and since your connection with the Confederate army, I have been prouder of you than ever before. I would not have you do anything wrong for the world, but before God, Edward, unless you come home, we must die." When the war ended, one-third of the soldiers had already gone home. A Mississippi deserter explained, "We are poor men and are willing to defend our country but our families [come] first."

Yeomen perceived a profound inequality of sacrifice. They called it "a rich man's war and a poor man's fight." The draft law permitted a man who had money to hire a substitute to take his place. Moreover, the "twenty-Negro law" exempted one white man on every plantation with twenty or more slaves. The government intended this law to provide protection for white women and to see that slaves tended the crops, but yeomen perceived it as rich men evading military service. A Mississippian complained that stay-at-home planters sent

Maria Isabella ("Belle") Boyd, Spy
Most white southern women, in addition to keeping their families fed and safe, served the Confederate cause by sewing uniforms, knitting socks, rolling bandages, and nursing the sick and wounded. But Belle Boyd became a spy. Only seventeen when the war broke out, she became in the words of a northern journalist "insanely devoted to the rebel cause." Her first act for the Confederacy came on July 3, 1861, when she shot a drunken federal soldier who barged into her Virginia home and insulted her mother. Her relations with occupying northern troops improved, and soon this compelling young woman was eavesdropping on officers' conversations and slipping messages to Confederate armies. Boyd's information handed Stonewall Jackson an easy victory at Front Royal, Virginia, in May 1862. "I thank you," the general wrote Boyd, "…for the immense service that you have rendered your country today." Imprisoned several times for spying, Boyd took up a theatrical career when the war ended.
Courtesy Warren Rifles Confederate Museum, Front Royal, VA.

their slaves into the fields to grow cotton while in plain view "poor soldiers' wives are plowing with *their own* hands to make a subsistence for themselves and children—while their husbands are suffering, bleeding and dying for their country." In fact, most slaveholders went

off to war, but the extreme suffering of common folk and the relative immunity of planters fueled class animosity.

The Richmond government hoped that the crucible of war would mold a region into a nation. Officials and others worked to promote a southern **nationalism** that would "excite in our citizens an ardent and enduring attachment to our Government and its institutions." Clergymen assured their congregations that God had blessed slavery and the new nation. Patriotic songwriters, poets, authors, and artists extolled southern culture. But these efforts failed to win over thousands of die-hard Unionists. And friction between yeomen and planters increased rather than decreased. The war also threatened to rip the southern social fabric along its racial seam.

The Disintegration of Slavery

The legal destruction of slavery was the product of presidential proclamation, congressional legislation, and eventually constitutional amendment, but the practical destruction of slavery was the product of war, what Lincoln called war's "friction and abrasion." War exposed the illusion of slave contentment. Slaves took advantage of the upheaval to reach for freedom. Some half a million of the South's four million slaves ran away to northern military lines. More than 100,000 men fled bondage, took up arms as federal soldiers and sailors, and attacked slavery directly. Other men and women stayed in the slave quarter, where they staked their claim to more freedom.

War disrupted slavery in a dozen ways. Almost immediately, it called the master away, leaving white women to assume responsibility for the plantations. But mistresses could not maintain traditional standards of slave discipline in wartime, and the balance of power shifted. Slaves got to the fields late, worked indifferently, and quit early. Some slaveholders responded violently; most saw no alternative but to strike bargains—offering gifts or part of the crop—to keep slaves at home and at work. Slaveholders had believed that they "knew" their slaves but learned they did not. When the war began, a North Carolina woman praised her slaves as "diligent and respectful." When it ended, she said, "As to the idea of a *faithful servant, it is all a fiction.*"

As military action sliced through the South's farms and plantations, some slaveholders fled, leaving their slaves behind. Many more took their slaves with them, but flight meant additional chaos and offered slaves new opportunities to resist bondage. But whites' greatest fear—retaliatory violence—rarely occurred. Slaves who stayed home steadily undermined white mastery and expanded control over their own lives.

> **REVIEW**   How did wartime hardship in the South contribute to class animosity?

The North at War

While the North was largely untouched by the fighting, Northerners could not avoid being touched by war. Almost every family had a son, a husband, a brother in uniform. Moreover, total war blurred the distinction between home front and battlefield. As in the South, men marched off to fight, but preserving the country was also women's work. For civilians as well as soldiers, for women as well as men, war was transforming.

The need to build and fuel the Union war machine boosted the economy. The Union sent nearly 2 million men into the military and still increased production in almost every area. But because the rewards and burdens of patriotism were distributed unevenly, the North experienced sharp, even violent, divisions. Workers confronted employers, whites confronted blacks, and Democrats confronted Republicans. Still, Northerners on the home front remained fervently attached to the Union.

The Government and the Economy

When the war began, the United States had no national banking system, no national currency, and no federal income or excise taxes. But the secession of eleven slave states cut the Democrats' strength in Congress in half and destroyed their capacity to resist Republican economic programs. The Legal Tender Act of February 1862 created a national currency, paper money that Northerners called "greenbacks." With passage of the National Banking Act in February 1863, Congress created a system of national banks that by the 1870s had largely replaced the **antebellum** system of decentralized state banks. Congress also enacted a series of sweeping tax laws. By revolutionizing the country's banking, monetary, and tax structures, the Republicans generated enormous economic power.

The Republicans' wartime legislation also aimed at integrating the West more thoroughly into the Union. In May 1862, Congress approved the Homestead Act, which offered 160 acres of public land to settlers who would live and labor on it. The Homestead Act bolstered western loyalty and in time resulted in more than a million new farms. The Pacific Railroad Act in July 1862 provided massive federal assistance for building a transcontinental railroad that ran from Omaha to San Francisco when completed in 1869. Congress further bound East and West by subsidizing the Pony Express mail service and a transcontinental telegraph.

Two additional initiatives had long-term consequences for agriculture and industry. Congress created a Department of Agriculture and passed the Land-Grant College Act (also known as the Morrill Act after its sponsor, Representative Justin Morrill of Vermont), which set aside public lands to support universities that emphasized "agriculture and mechanical arts." The Lincoln administration immeasurably strengthened the North's effort to win the war, but its ideas also permanently changed the nation.

Women and Work on the Home Front

More than a million farm men were called to the military, so farm women added men's chores to their own. "I met more women driving teams on the road and saw more at work in the fields than men," a visitor to Iowa reported in the fall of 1862. Rising production figures testified to their success in plowing, planting, and harvesting. Rapid mechanization assisted farm women in their new roles. Cyrus McCormick sold 165,000 of his reapers during the war years. The combination of high prices for farm products and increased production ensured that war and prosperity joined hands in the rural North.

A few industries, such as textiles (which depended on southern cotton), declined during the war, but many more grew. Huge profits prompted one Pennsylvania ironmaster to remark, "I am in no hurry for peace." With orders pouring in and a million nonfarm workers at war, unemployment declined and wages often rose. The boom proved friendlier to owners than to workers, however. Inflation and taxes cut so deeply into workers' paychecks that their standard of living actually fell.

In cities, women stepped into jobs vacated by men, particularly in manufacturing, and also into essentially new occupations such as government secretaries and clerks. Women made up about one-quarter of the manufacturing workforce when the war began and one-third when it ended. But in 1864 New York seamstresses working fourteen-hour days earned only $1.54 a week. Urban workers resorted increasingly to strikes to wrench decent salaries from their employers, but their protests rarely succeeded. Nevertheless, tough times failed to undermine the patriotism of most workers.

Most middle-class white women stayed home and contributed to the war effort in traditional ways. They sewed, wrapped bandages, and sold homemade goods at local fairs to raise money to aid the soldiers. Other women expressed their patriotism in an untraditional way—as wartime nurses. Thousands of women on both sides defied prejudices about female delicacy and volunteered to nurse the wounded. Many northern female volunteers worked through the U.S. Sanitary Commission, a civilian organization that bought and distributed clothing, food, and medicine and recruited doctors and nurses.

Some volunteers went on to become paid military nurses. For example, Dorothea Dix, well known for her efforts to reform insane asylums, was named superintendent of female nurses in April 1861. Eventually, some 3,000 women served under her. Most nurses worked in hospitals behind the battle lines, but some, like Clara Barton, who later founded the American Red Cross, worked in battlefield units. At Antietam, as Barton was giving a wounded man a drink, a bullet ripped through her sleeve, striking and killing the soldier. Women who served in the war went on to lead the postwar movement to establish training schools for female nurses.

Union Ordnance, Yorktown, Virginia
As the North successfully harnessed its enormous industrial capacity to the needs of war, cannon, mortars, and shells poured out of its factories. A fraction of that abundance is seen here in 1862 at Yorktown, ready for transportation to Union troops in the field. Two years later, Abraham Lincoln observed that the Union was "gaining strength, and may if need be maintain the contest indefinitely.... Material resources are now more complete and abundant than ever.... The national resources are unexhausted, and, as we believe, inexhaustible." Library of Congress.

Politics and Dissent

At first, the bustle of economic and military mobilization seemed to silence politics, but bipartisan unity did not last. Within a year, Democrats were labeling the Republican administration a "reign of terror," and Republicans were calling Democrats the party of "Dixie, Davis, and the Devil." Democrats denounced Republican policies— emancipating the slaves, subsidizing private business, and expanding federal power—as unconstitutional. In September 1862, in an effort to stifle opposition to the war, Lincoln placed under military arrest any person who discouraged enlistments, resisted the draft, or engaged in "disloyal" practices. Before the war ended, his administration imprisoned nearly 14,000 individuals, most in the border states. The campaign fell short of a reign of terror, for the majority of the prisoners were not northern Democratic opponents but Confederates, blockade runners, and citizens of foreign countries, and most of those arrested gained quick release. Still, the administration's heavy-handed tactics did suppress free speech.

When the Republican-dominated Congress enacted the draft law in March 1863, Democrats had another grievance. The law required that all men between the ages of twenty and forty-five enroll and make themselves available for a lottery that would decide who went to war. What poor men found particularly galling were provisions that allowed a draftee to hire a substitute or simply to pay a $300 fee and get out of his military obligation. As in the South, common folk could be heard chanting, "A rich man's war and a poor man's fight."

Linking the draft and emancipation, Democrats argued that Republicans employed an unconstitutional means (the draft) to achieve an unconstitutional end (emancipation). In the summer of 1863, antidraft, antiblack mobs went on rampages in northern cities. In New York City, Democratic Irish workingmen—crowded into filthy tenements, gouged by inflation, enraged by the draft, and dead set against fighting to free blacks—erupted in four days of rioting that killed at least 105 people, most of them black, and left the Colored Orphan Asylum a smoking ruin.

Racist mobs failed to achieve their purpose: the subordination of African Americans. Free black leaders had lobbied aggressively for emancipation, and after Lincoln's proclamation they fanned out over the North agitating for equality. They won few victories, however. Significant progress toward black equality would have to wait until the war ended.

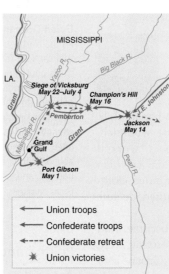

Vicksburg Campaign, 1863

REVIEW   Why was the U.S. Congress able to pass such a bold legislative agenda during the war?

Grinding Out Victory, 1863–1865

In the early months of 1863, the Union's prospects looked bleak, and the Confederate cause stood at high tide. Then in July 1863, the tide began to turn. The military man most responsible for this shift was Ulysses S. Grant. Lifted from obscurity by his successes in the West, Grant became the "great man of the day," one man observed in July 1864, "perhaps of the age." Elevated to supreme command, Grant knit together a powerful war machine that integrated a sophisticated command structure, modern technology, and complex logistics and supply systems. But the arithmetic of this plain man remained unchanged: Killing more of the enemy than he kills of you equaled "the complete overthrow of the rebellion."

The North ground out the victory, battle by bloody battle. The balance tipped in the Union's favor in 1863, but Southerners were not deterred. The fighting escalated in the last two years of the war. As national elections approached in the fall of 1864, Lincoln expected a war-weary North to reject him. Instead, northern voters declared their willingness to continue the war in the defense of the ideals of union and freedom.

Vicksburg and Gettysburg

Vicksburg, Mississippi, situated on the eastern bank of the Mississippi River, stood between Union forces and complete control of the river. Union forces under Grant attacked the city in May 1863, but when the Confederates beat back the assault, Grant decided to lay siege and starve out the enemy. Civilian residents of Vicksburg moved into caves to escape the incessant Union bombardment, and as the attack dragged on, they had to eat mules and rats to survive. After six weeks, on July 4, 1863, nearly 30,000 rebels marched out of Vicksburg, stacked their arms, and surrendered unconditionally. A Yankee captain wrote home to his wife: "The backbone of the Rebellion is this day broken. The Confederacy is divided.... Vicksburg is ours. The Mississippi

River is opened, and Gen. Grant is to be our next President."

On the same Fourth of July, word arrived that Union forces had crushed General Lee at Gettysburg, Pennsylvania (Map 15.3). Emboldened by his victory at Chancellorsville in May and hoping to relieve Virginia of the burden of the fighting, Lee and his 75,000-man army invaded Pennsylvania. On June 28, Union forces under General George G. Meade intercepted the Confederates at the small town of Gettysburg, where Union soldiers occupied the high ground. Three days of furious fighting involving 165,000 troops could not dislodge the Federals from the hills. Lee ached for a decisive victory, and on July 3 he ordered a major assault against the Union center on Cemetery Ridge. Open, rolling fields provided the dug-in Yankees with three-quarters of a mile of clear vision, and they raked the mile-wide line of Confederate soldiers under General George E. Pickett with cannon and rifle fire. Gettysburg cost Lee more than one-third of his army— 28,000 casualties. "It's all my fault," he lamented. In a drenching rain on the night of July 4, 1863, he marched his battered army back to Virginia.

The twin disasters at Vicksburg and Gettysburg proved to be the turning point of the war. The Confederacy could not replace the nearly 60,000 soldiers who were captured, wounded, or killed. Lee never launched another major offensive north of the Mason-Dixon line. It is hindsight, however, that permits us to see the pair of battles as decisive. At the time, the Confederacy still controlled the heartland of the South, and Lee still had a vicious sting. War-weariness threatened to erode the North's will to win before Union armies could destroy the Confederacy's ability to go on.

Grant Takes Command

Toward the end of September 1863, Union general William Rosecrans placed his army in a dangerous situation in Chattanooga, Tennessee, where he had retreated after defeat at the battle of

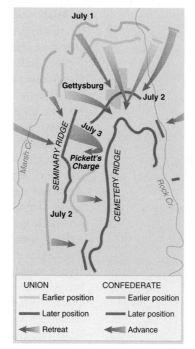

Battle of Gettysburg, July 1–3, 1863

Chickamauga earlier in the month (see Map 15.3). Rebels surrounded the disorganized bluecoats and threatened to starve them into submission. Grant, now commander of Union forces between the Mississippi River and the Appalachians, arrived in Chattanooga in October. Within weeks, he opened an effective supply line, broke the siege, and routed the Confederate army. The victory at Chattanooga on November 25 opened the door to Georgia. It also confirmed Lincoln's estimation of Grant. In March 1864, the president asked Grant to come east to become the general in chief of all Union armies.

In Washington, Grant implemented his grand strategy for a war of attrition. He ordered a series of simultaneous assaults from Virginia to Louisiana. Two actions proved more significant than the others. In one, General William Tecumseh Sherman, whom Grant appointed his successor to command the western armies, plunged southeast toward Atlanta. In the other, Grant, who took control of the Army of the Potomac, went head-to-head with Lee for almost four straight weeks in Virginia.

Grant and Lee met in the first week of May 1864 in northern Virginia in a dense tangle of scrub oaks and small pines. Often unable to see more than ten paces, the armies pounded away at each other until approximately 18,000 Yankees and 11,000 rebels had fallen. The savagery of the Battle of the Wilderness did not compare with that at Spotsylvania Court House a few days later. Frenzied men fought hand to hand for eighteen hours in the rain. One veteran remembered men "piled upon each other in some places four layers deep, exhibiting every ghastly phase of mutilation." Spotsylvania cost Grant another 18,000 casualties and Lee 10,000, but the Yankee bulldog would not let go. Grant kept moving and tangled with Lee again at Cold Harbor, where he suffered 13,000 additional casualties to Lee's 5,000. (See "Historical Question," page 392.)

Twice as many Union soldiers as rebel soldiers died in four weeks of fighting in Virginia in May and June, but because Lee had only half as

Grant at Cold Harbor
Seated next to his chief of staff, John A. Rawlins, at his Cold Harbor, Virginia, headquarters, Ulysses S. Grant plots his next move against Robert E. Lee. On June 3, 1864, Grant ordered frontal assaults against entrenched Confederate forces, resulting in enormous Union losses. "I am disgusted with the generalship displayed," young Brigadier General Emory Upton exclaimed. "Our men have, in many cases, been foolishly and wantonly slaughtered." Years later, Grant said that he regretted the assault at Cold Harbor, but in 1864 he kept pushing toward Richmond.
Chicago Historical Society.

many troops as Grant, his losses were equivalent to Grant's. Grant knew that the South could not replace the losses. Moreover, the campaign carried Grant to the outskirts of Petersburg, just south of Richmond, where he abandoned the costly tactic of the frontal assault and began a siege that immobilized both armies and dragged on for nine months.

Simultaneously, Sherman invaded Georgia. Grant instructed Sherman to "get into the interior of the enemy's country as far as you can, inflicting all the damage you can against their War resources." In early May, Sherman moved 100,000 men south against the 65,000 rebels. Skillful maneuvering, constant skirmishing, and one pitched battle, at Kennesaw Mountain, brought Sherman to Atlanta, which fell on September 2.

Intending to "make Georgia howl," Sherman marched out of Atlanta on November 15 with 62,000 battle-hardened veterans, heading for Savannah, 285 miles away on the Atlantic coast. One veteran remembered, "[We] destroyed all we could not eat, stole their niggers, burned their cotton & gins, spilled their sorghum, burned & twisted their R. Roads and raised Hell generally." Sherman's "March to the Sea" aimed at destroying the will of the southern people. A few weeks earlier, General Philip H. Sheridan had carried out his own scorched-earth campaign in the Shenandoah Valley, complying with Grant's order to turn the valley into "a barren waste...so that crows flying over it for the balance of this season will have to carry their provender [food] with them." When Sherman's troops entered an undefended Savannah in mid-December, the general telegraphed Lincoln that he had "a Christmas gift" for him. A month earlier, Union voters had bestowed on the president an even greater gift.

The Election of 1864

In the summer 1864, with Sherman temporarily checked outside Atlanta and Grant bogged down in the siege of Petersburg, the Democratic Party smelled victory in the fall elections. Rankled by inflation, the draft, the attack on civil liberties, and the commitment to blacks, Northerners appeared ready for a change. Lincoln himself concluded, "It seems exceedingly probable that this administration will not be re-elected."

Democrats were badly divided, however. "Peace" Democrats insisted on an armistice, while "war" Democrats supported the conflict but opposed Republican means of fighting it. The party tried to paper over the chasm by nominating a war

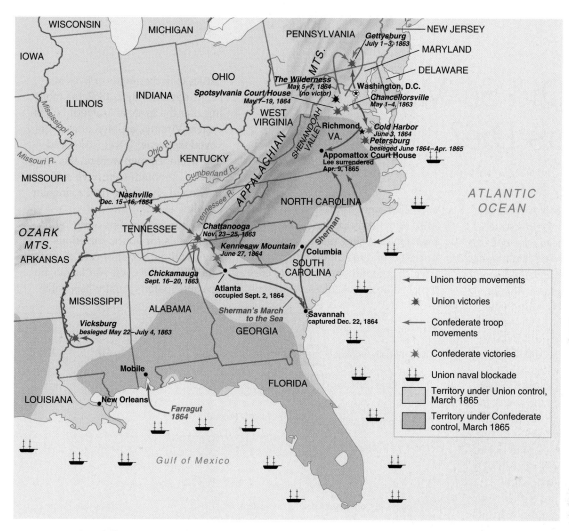

MAP 15.3   The Civil War, 1863–1865
Ulysses S. Grant's victory at Vicksburg divided the Confederacy at the Mississippi River. William Tecumseh Sherman's march from Chattanooga to Savannah divided it again. In northern Virginia, Robert E. Lee fought fiercely, but Grant's larger, better-supplied armies prevailed.

candidate, General George McClellan, but adopting a peace platform that demanded that "immediate efforts be made for a cessation of hostilities." Republicans denounced the peace plank as a sellout that "virtually proposed to surrender the country to the rebels in arms against us."

The capture of Atlanta on September 2 turned the political tide in favor of the Republicans. Lincoln received 55 percent of the popular vote, but his electoral margin was a whopping 212 to McClellan's 21. Republicans also gained large margins over the Democrats in the congressional elections. Lincoln's party won a resounding victory, one that gave him a mandate to continue the war until slavery and the Confederacy were dead.

The Confederacy Collapses

As 1865 dawned, military disaster littered the Confederate landscape. With the destruction of John B. Hood's army at Nashville in December 1864, the interior of the Confederacy lay in Yankee hands (see Map 15.3). Sherman's troops, resting momentarily in Savannah, eyed South Carolina hungrily. Farther north, Grant had Lee's army pinned down in Petersburg, a few miles from Richmond.

More and more Confederates turned their backs on the rebellion. News from the battlefields made it difficult not to conclude that the Yankees had beaten them. Soldiers' wives begged their husbands to return home to keep their families

Why Did So Many Soldiers Die?

From 1861 to 1865, Americans killed Americans on a scale never before seen. Not until the First World War, a half century later, would the world match (and surpass) the killing fields at Shiloh, Antietam, and Gettysburg (Figure 15.2). Why were the Civil War totals so horrendous? Why did 260,000 rebel soldiers and 373,000 Union soldiers die?

By the mid-nineteenth century, the balance between the ability to kill and the ability to save lives had tipped disastrously toward death. The sheer size of the armies—some battles involved more than 200,000 soldiers—ensured that battlefields would turn red with blood. Moreover, armies fought with antiquated Napoleonic strategy. In the generals' eyes, the ideal soldier was trained to advance with his comrades in a compact, close-order formation. Theory also emphasized frontal assaults. In classrooms at West Point and on the high plains of Mexico in the 1840s, men learned that infantry advancing shoulder to shoulder, supported by artillery, carried the day.

By the 1860s, modern technology had made such strategy appallingly deadly. Weapons with rifled barrels (that is, with spiral grooves cut into the bore) were replacing smoothbore muskets and cannon. Rifles propelled spinning bullets four times as far as muskets—about 320 yards. The rifle's greater range and accuracy,

and rifled cannons firing canisters filled with flesh-ripping, bone-breaking steel shot, made sitting ducks of charging infantry units and gave an enormous advantage to entrenched defensive forces. As a result,

battles took thousands of lives in a single day. On July 2, 1862, the morning after the battle at Malvern Hill in eastern Virginia, a Union officer surveyed the scene: "Over 5,000 dead and wounded men were on the ground…enough were alive and moving to give to the field a singular crawling effect."

Wounded soldiers often lay on battlefields for hours, sometimes days, without water or care of any kind. When the Civil War began, no one anticipated casualty lists with

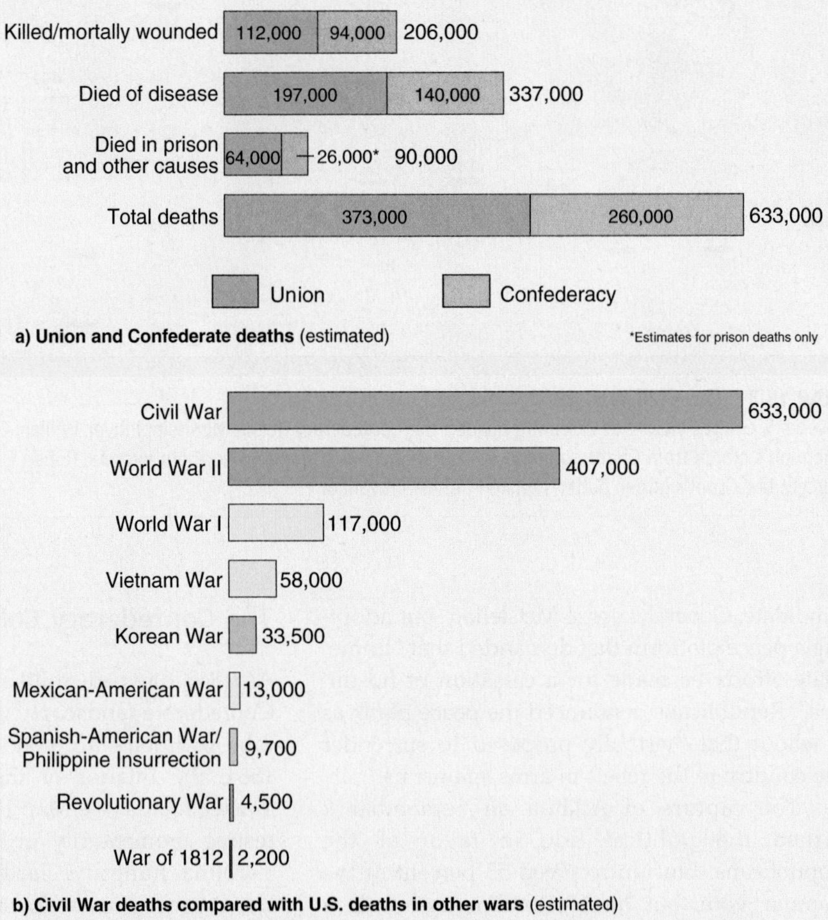

a) **Union and Confederate deaths** (estimated)   *Estimates for prison deaths only

Killed/mortally wounded	112,000 / 94,000 / 206,000
Died of disease	197,000 / 140,000 / 337,000
Died in prison and other causes	64,000 — 26,000* / 90,000
Total deaths	373,000 / 260,000 / 633,000

Union   Confederacy

b) **Civil War deaths compared with U.S. deaths in other wars** (estimated)

Civil War	633,000
World War II	407,000
World War I	117,000
Vietnam War	58,000
Korean War	33,500
Mexican-American War	13,000
Spanish-American War/Philippine Insurrection	9,700
Revolutionary War	4,500
War of 1812	2,200

FIGURE 15.2   Civil War Deaths
The loss of life in the Civil War was almost equal to the losses in all other American wars.

thousands of names. Union and Confederate medical departments could not cope with skirmishes, much less large-scale battles. They had no ambulance corps to remove the wounded from the scene. They had no field hospitals. Early in the war, someone in the U.S. Quartermaster Department, which was responsible for constructing Union hospitals, responded to demands that it do something to improve the care of the wounded by saying: "Men need guns, not beds." Only the shock of massive casualties compelled reform. A lack of resources meant that the South lagged behind the North, but gradually both North and South organized effective ambulance corps, built hospitals, and hired trained surgeons and nurses.

Soldiers did not always count speedy transportation to a field hospital as a blessing. As one Union soldier said, "I had rather risk a battle than the Hospitals." Real danger lurked behind the lines. While the technology of killing advanced to very high standards, medicine remained primitive. Physicians gained a reputation as butchers, and soldiers dreaded the operating table more than they did entrenched riflemen. Serious wounds to a leg or an arm usually meant amputation, the best way doctors knew to save lives. After major battles, surgeons worked among piles of severed limbs.

A wounded man's real enemy was not doctors' callousness but medical ignorance. Physicians had almost no knowledge of the cause and transmission of disease or the benefits of antiseptics. Not aware of basic germ theory, they spread infection almost every time they operated.

Doctors wore the same bloody smocks for days and washed their hands and their scalpels and saws in buckets of dirty water. When they had difficulty threading their needles, they wet the thread with their own saliva. Soldiers often did not survive amputations, not because of the operation but because of the infection that inevitably followed. Of the Union soldiers whose legs were amputated above the knee, more than half died. A Union doctor discovered in 1864 that bromine (previously used in combination with other elements as a sedative) arrested gangrene, but the best that most amputees could hope for was maggots, which ate dead flesh on the stump and thus inhibited the spread of infection. During the Civil War, nearly one of every five wounded rebel soldiers died, and one of every six Yankees. A century later, in Vietnam, the proportion of deaths was one wounded American soldier in four hundred.

Soldiers who avoided battlefield wounds and hospital infections still faced sickness. Deadly diseases swept through crowded army camps, where latrines were often dangerously close to drinking-water supplies. The principal killers were dysentery and typhoid, but pneumonia and malaria also cut down thousands. Doctors did what they could, but often their treatments only added to the misery. They prescribed doses of turpentine for patients with typhoid, they fought respiratory problems with mustard plasters, and they attacked intestinal disorders by blistering the skin with sulfuric acid.

Thousands of female nurses, including Dorothea Dix, Clara Barton, and Juliet Ann Opie Hopkins, im-

Doctor's Surgical Kit
With simple instruments like these, not unlike the tools of the butcher's trade, northern and southern surgeons performed approximately 60,000 amputations. Approximately 45,000 of the amputees survived.
Chicago Historical Society.

proved the wounded men's odds and alleviated their suffering. Civilian relief agencies, such as the U.S. Sanitary Commission and the Women's Relief Society of the Confederacy, promoted hygiene in army camps and made some headway. Nevertheless, as Figure 15.2 shows, disease killed nearly twice as many soldiers as did combat. Many who died of disease were prisoners of war. Approximately 30,000 Northerners died in Confederate prisons, and approximately 26,000 Southerners died in Union prisons. No northern prison, however, could equal the horror of Andersonville in southern Georgia. In August 1864, about 33,000 emaciated men lived in unspeakable conditions in a 26-acre barren stockade with no shelter except what the prisoners were able to construct. More than 13,000 perished.

In the end, 633,000 northern and southern soldiers died, a staggering toll.

from starving, and the stream of deserters became a flood. In most cases, white Southerners lost the will to continue not so much because they lost faith in independence but because they had been battered into submission. They had demonstrated remarkable endurance for their cause. Half of the 900,000 Confederate soldiers had been killed or wounded, and ragged, hungry women and children had sacrificed throughout the bloodiest war then known to history.

The end came with a rush. On February 1, 1865, Sherman's troops stormed out of Savannah into South Carolina, the "cradle of the Confederacy." In Virginia, Lee abandoned Petersburg, and Richmond fell. Grant pursued Lee until he surrendered on April 9, 1865, at Appomattox Court House, Virginia. Grant offered generous peace terms. He allowed Lee's men to return home and to keep their horses to help "put in a crop to carry themselves and their families through the next winter." With Lee gone, the remaining Confederate armies lost hope and gave up within two weeks. After four years, the war was over.

No one was more relieved than Lincoln, but his celebration was restrained. He told his cabinet that his postwar burdens would weigh almost as heavily as those of wartime. Seeking

Ruins of Richmond

A Union soldier and a small boy wearing a Union cap contemplate the silence and devastation of the Confederacy's capital. On their way out of the city on the evening of April 2, 1865, Confederate demolition squads set fire to tobacco warehouses and ammunition dumps. Huge explosions tore holes in the city, and windswept fires destroyed much of what was left standing. As one Confederate observed, "The old war-scarred city seemed to prefer annihilation to conquest."

Library of Congress.

Major Battles of the Civil War, 1863–1865

May 1–4, 1863	Battle of Chancellorsville
July 1–3, 1863	Battle of Gettysburg
July 4, 1863	Fall of Vicksburg
September 16–20, 1863	Battle of Chickamauga
November 23–25, 1863	Battle of Chattanooga
May 5–7, 1864	Battle of the Wilderness
May 7–19, 1864	Battle of Spotsylvania Court House
June 3, 1864	Battle of Cold Harbor
June 27, 1864	Battle of Kennesaw Mountain
September 2, 1864	Fall of Atlanta
November–December 1864	Sheridan sacks Shenandoah Valley Sherman's "March to the Sea"
December 15–16, 1864	Battle of Nashville
December 22, 1864	Fall of Savannah
April 2–3, 1865	Fall of Petersburg and Richmond
April 9, 1865	Lee surrenders at Appomattox Court House

distraction, Lincoln attended Ford's Theatre on the evening of Good Friday, April 14, 1865. John Wilkes Booth, an actor with southern sympathies, slipped into the president's box and shot Lincoln in the head. He died at 7:22 the following morning. Vice President Andrew Johnson became president. The man who had led the nation through the war would not lead it during the postwar search for a just peace.

> **REVIEW** Why were the siege of Vicksburg and the battle of Gettysburg crucial to the outcome of the war?

Conclusion: The Second American Revolution

A transformed nation emerged from the crucible of war. Antebellum America was decentralized politically and loosely integrated economically. To accommodate Union victory, Congress enacted legislation that reshaped the nation's political and economic character. It created national currency and banking systems and turned to free land, a transcontinental railroad, and miles of telegraph lines to bind the West to the rest of the nation. Congress also established the sovereignty of the federal government and permanently increased its power. To most citizens before the war, Washington meant the post office and little more; during the war years, the federal government drafted, taxed, and judged Americans in unprecedented ways. The massive changes brought about by war—the creation of a national government, a national economy, and a national spirit—led one historian to call the American Civil War the "Second American Revolution."

The Civil War also had a profound effect on individual lives. When the war began in 1861, millions of men dropped their hoes, hammers, and pencils, put on blue or gray uniforms, and fought and suffered for what they passionately believed was right. The war disrupted families, leaving women at home with additional responsibilities while offering new opportunities to others for wartime work in factories, offices, and hospitals. It offered blacks new and more effective ways to resist slavery and agitate for equality.

The war devastated the South. Three-fourths of southern white men of military age served in the Confederate army, and at least half of them were captured, wounded, or killed or died of disease. The war destroyed two-fifths of the South's livestock, wrecked half of the farm machinery, and blackened dozens of cities and towns. The immediate impact of the war on the North was more paradoxical. The struggle cost the North a heavy price: 373,000 lives. But rather than devastating the land, war set the countryside and cities humming with business activity. The radical shift in power from South to North signaled a new direction in American development: the long decline of agriculture and the rise of industrial capitalism.

Most revolutionary of all, the war ended slavery. Ironically, the South's war to preserve slavery destroyed it. Ex-slaves like William Gould dedicated their wartime service to its eradication. Because slavery was both a labor and a racial system, the institution was entangled in almost every aspect of southern life. Slavery's uprooting inevitably meant fundamental change. But the full meaning of abolition remained unclear in 1865. Determining the new economic, political, and social status of four million ex-slaves would be the principal task of reconstruction.

Suggestions for Further Reading

Ira Berlin et al., eds., *Freedom: A Documentary History of Emancipation, 1861–1867*, 4 vols. (1982–1993). A monumental collection of contemporary documents that recount the black experience in the war.

Richard J. Carwardine, *Lincoln* (2003). A fresh biography of Lincoln as war leader.

Catherine Clinton and Nina Silber, eds., *Divided Houses: Gender and the Civil War* (1992). Essays that demonstrate that the Civil War was more than a "brother's war."

Gary W. Gallagher, *The Confederate War* (1997). A lively account of white Southerners' steadfast commitment to the Confederate cause.

William B. Gould IV, ed., *Diary of a Contraband: The Civil War Passage of a Black Sailor* (2002). A remarkable account of an ex-slave's service in the Union navy.

Margaret M. Storey, *Loyalty and Loss: Alabama's Unionists in the Civil War and Reconstruction* (2004). A new understanding of divided loyalties on the Confederate home front.

▶ **FOR MORE BOOKS ABOUT TOPICS IN THIS CHAPTER,** see the Online Bibliography at bedfordstmartins.com/roarkcompact.

▶ **FOR ADDITIONAL FIRSTHAND ACCOUNTS OF THIS PERIOD,** see Chapter 15 in Michael Johnson, ed., *Reading the American Past,* Third Edition.

▶ **FOR WEB SITES AND DOCUMENTS RELATED TO TOPICS AND PLACES IN THIS CHAPTER,** see "HistoryLinks," "DocLinks," and "PlaceLinks" at bedfordstmartins.com/roarkcompact.

REVIEWING THE CHAPTER

Follow these steps to review and strengthen your understanding of the chapter.

STEP 1: *Study the* **Key Terms** *and* **Timeline** *to identify the significance of each item listed.*

STEP 2: *Answer the* **Review Questions**, *drawing on key terms and dates to support your answers.*

STEP 3: *Drawing on the Key Terms, Timeline, and Review Questions, answer the broader* **Making Connections** *questions.*

KEY TERMS

Who

Frederick Douglass (p. 370)
Abraham Lincoln (pp. 370, 374)
Jefferson Davis (pp. 371, 374)
Salmon P. Chase (p. 374)
William H. Seward (p. 374)
George B. McClellan (p. 377)
Joseph Johnston (p. 377)
Robert E. Lee (p. 377)
Ambrose Burnside (p. 378)
Samuel R. Curtis (p. 378)
William Clarke Quantrill (p. 378)
"Bloody Bill" Anderson (p. 378)
Ulysses S. Grant (p. 379)
Benjamin F. Butler (p. 381)
Dorothea Dix (p. 387)
Clara Barton (p. 387)
George G. Meade (p. 389)
George E. Pickett (p. 389)
William Tecumseh Sherman (p. 389)
Philip H. Sheridan (p. 390)

What

Fort Sumter (p. 371)
battle of Bull Run/Manassas (p. 376)
Virginia peninsula campaign (p. 377)
Seven Days Battle (p. 377)
battle of Antietam (p. 378)
battle of Fredericksburg (p. 378)
battle of Pea Ridge (p. 378)
Fort Henry (p. 379)
Fort Donelson (p. 379)
battle of Shiloh (p. 379)
Union blockade (p. 380)
Merrimack/Virginia (p. 380)
Monitor (p. 380)
King Cotton diplomacy (p. 380)
Confiscation Act (p. 381)
contraband of war (p. 381)
second Confiscation Act (p. 382)
Emancipation Proclamation (p. 382)
bread riots (p. 384)
National Banking Act (p. 386)

Homestead Act (p. 386)
Pacific Railroad Act (p. 386)
Land-Grant College Act (Morrill Act) (p. 386)
U.S. Sanitary Commission (p. 387)
American Red Cross (p. 387)
Union draft law (p. 388)
New York City draft riots (p. 388)
siege of Vicksburg (p. 388)
battle of Gettysburg (p. 389)
battle of Chattanooga (p. 389)
Battle of the Wilderness (p. 389)
Sherman's "March to the Sea" (p. 390)
"peace" Democrats (p. 390)

TIMELINE

1861 • **April.** Attack on Fort Sumter.
• **April–May.** Four Upper South states join Confederacy.
• **July.** Union forces routed in first battle of Bull Run.
• **August.** First Confiscation Act.

1862 • Grant captures Fort Henry and Fort Donelson.
• **March.** Confederates defeated at battle of Glorieta Pass.
• Union victory at battle of Pea Ridge.
• **April.** Battle of Shiloh in Tennessee ends Confederate bid to control Mississippi valley.
• Confederate Congress authorizes draft.
• **May.** Homestead Act.
• **May–July.** Union forces defeated during Virginia peninsula campaign.
• **July.** Second Confiscation Act.
• Militia Act.
• **September.** Battle of Antietam stops Lee's advance into Maryland.

REVIEW QUESTIONS

1. Why did both the Union and the Confederacy consider control of the border states crucial? (pp. 370–73)

2. Why did the South believe it could win the war despite numerical disadvantages? (pp. 373–75)

3. Why did King Cotton diplomacy fail? (pp. 375–80)

4. Why did the Union change policy in 1863 to allow black men to serve in the army? (pp. 380–83)

5. How did wartime hardship in the South contribute to class animosity? (pp. 383–86)

6. Why was the U.S. Congress able to pass such a bold legislative agenda during the war? (pp. 386–88)

7. Why were the siege of Vicksburg and the battle of Gettysburg crucial to the outcome of the war? (pp. 388–95)

MAKING CONNECTIONS

1. Despite loathing slavery, Lincoln embraced emancipation as a war objective late and with great caution. Why? In your answer, trace the progression of Lincoln's position, considering how legal, political, military, and moral concerns influenced his policies.

2. The Emancipation Proclamation did not accomplish the destruction of slavery on its own. How did a war over union bring about the end of slavery? In your answer, consider the direct actions of slaves and Union policymakers as well as indirect factors within the Confederacy.

3. In addition to restoring union and destroying slavery, what other significant changes did the war produce on the home front and in the nation's capital? In your answer, discuss economic, governmental, and social developments, being attentive to regional variations.

4. Brilliant military strategy alone did not determine the outcome of the war; victory also depended on generating revenue, material mobilization, diplomacy, and politics. In light of these considerations, explain why the Confederacy believed it would succeed, and why it ultimately failed.

> ▶ For practice quizzes, a customized study plan, and other study tools, see the Online Study Guide at bedfordstmartins.com/roarkcompact.

1863 • **January.** Emancipation Proclamation becomes law.
• **February.** National Banking Act.
• **March.** Congress authorizes draft.
• **July.** Fall of Vicksburg to Union forces.
• Lee defeated at battle of Gettysburg.
• New York City antidraft riots.

1864 • **March.** Grant appointed Union general in chief.
• **May–June.** The Wilderness campaign.
• **September.** Fall of Atlanta to Sherman.
• **November.** Lincoln reelected.
• **December.** Fall of Savannah to Sherman.

1865 • **April 2–3.** Fall of Petersburg and Richmond.
• **April 9.** Lee surrenders to Grant.
• **April 15.** Lincoln dies from bullet wound.
• Vice President Andrew Johnson becomes president.

CARPETBAG

A carpetbag was a nineteenth-century suitcase made from carpet, often brightly colored. Applied first to wildcat bankers on the western frontier, "carpetbagger" was a derogatory name for rootless and penniless adventurers who could carry everything they owned in a single carpetbag. Critics of Republican administrations in the South hurled the name "carpetbaggers" at white Northerners who moved South during reconstruction and became active in politics. According to white Southerners, carpetbaggers exploited gullible ex-slaves to gain power and wealth. In fact, many Northerners who came to the South joined with blacks and some southern whites to form Republican state and local governments that were among the most progressive anywhere in the nineteenth century.

Private Collection/Picture Research Consultants & Archives.

16

Reconstruction

1863–1877

"**Y**ORK DISAPPEARED on yesterday morning," David Golightly Harris noted in his journal on June 6, 1865. "I suppose that he has gone to the yankey. I wish they would give him a good whipping & hasten him back." York, a black field hand, had once belonged to Harris, a white slaveholder in Spartanburg District, South Carolina. When York disappeared, the war had been over for two months, and York was a free man. In Harris's mind, however, simply declaring York free did not make him so. In July, Harris noted that another field hand, Old Will, had left "to try to enjoy the freedom the Yankey's have promised the negroes." Two weeks later, black freedom still seemed in doubt. "There is much talk about freeing the negroes. Some are said already to have freed them," Harris declared. But Harris had not freed anyone. He did not inform his former slaves of their freedom until federal military authorities forced him to. "Freed the Negroes," he declared on August 16, four months after Appomattox and more than two and a half years after the Emancipation Proclamation.

Like many ex-slaveholders, Harris had trouble coming to grips with **emancipation**. "Family well, Horses well, Cattle well, Hogs well & everything else are well so far as I know, if it was not for the free negroes," Harris declared on September 17. "On their account everything is turned upside down. So much so that we do not know what to do with our land, nor who to hire if we want it worked.... We are in the midst of troublesome times & do not know what will turn up." Harris had owned ten slaves, and now he faced what seemed to him an insoluble problem. He needed blacks to cultivate his farm, but like most whites he did not believe that African Americans would work much when free. Some kind of compulsion would be needed, but slavery was gone, leaving the South upside down. White men in Harris's neighborhood sought to set it straight again. "In this district several negroes have been badly whipped & several have been hung by some unknown persons," he noted in November. "This has a tendency to keep them in their proper bounds & make them more humble." But the violence did not keep ex-slaves from acting like free people. On Christmas Day 1865, Harris recorded, "The negroes leave today to hunt themselves a new home while we will be left to wait upon ourselves."

Across the South, ex-masters predicted that emancipation would mean economic collapse and social anarchy. Carl Schurz, a Union general who undertook a fact-finding mission to the former Confederate states in the summer of 1865, encountered this dire prediction often enough to conclude that the Civil War was a "revolution but half accomplished." Northern victory had freed the slaves, but it had not changed former slaveholders' minds about the need for slavery. Left to themselves, Schurz believed, whites would "introduce some new system of forced labor, not perhaps exactly slavery in its old form but something similar to it." To defend their freedom, blacks would need federal protection, land of their own, and voting rights, Schurz concluded. Until whites "cut loose from the past, it will be a dangerous experiment to put Southern society upon its own legs." Schurz discovered that the end of the war did not mean the beginning of peace. Instead, the nation entered one of its most chaotic and violent eras—Reconstruction, an era that would define the status of the defeated South within the Union and the meaning of freedom for ex-slaves.

The status of the South and the contours of black freedom were determined in the nation's capital, where the federal government played an active role, but also in the state legislatures and county seats of the South. Moreover, on farms and plantations from Virginia to Texas, ex-slaves like York and Old Will, who were determined to become free people, battled with whites like David Golightly Harris, who clung to the Old South. In the midst of the racial flux and chaos, a small band of crusading women sought to achieve gender equality. The years of reconstruction witnessed an enormous struggle to determine the consequences of Confederate defeat and emancipation. Although white Southerners prevailed, their **New South** was a very different South from the one to which whites like David Golightly Harris wished to return.

Wartime Reconstruction

Reconstruction did not wait for the end of war. As the odds of a northern victory increased, thinking about reunification quickened. Immediately, a question arose: Who had authority to devise a plan for reconstructing the Union? Lincoln believed firmly that reconstruction was a matter of executive responsibility. Congress just as firmly asserted its jurisdiction. Fueling the argument about who had authority to set the terms of reconstruction were significant differences about the terms themselves. Lincoln's primary aim was the restoration of national unity, which he sought through a program of speedy, forgiving political reconciliation. Congress feared that the president's program amounted to restoring the old southern ruling class to power. It wanted greater assurances of white loyalty and greater guarantees of black rights.

Black Woman in Cotton Fields, Thomasville, Georgia

Few images of everyday black women during the Reconstruction era survive. This photograph was taken in 1895, but it nevertheless goes to the heart of the labor struggle after the Civil War. Before emancipation black women worked in the fields, and after emancipation white landlords wanted them to continue working there. Freedom allowed some women to escape field labor, but not this Georgian, who probably worked to survive. The photograph reveals a strong person with a clear sense of who she is. Though worn to protect her head and body from the fierce heat, her intricately wrapped headdress dramatically expresses her individuality. Her bare feet also reveal something about her life.

Courtesy, Georgia Department of Archives and History, Atlanta, Georgia.

In their eagerness to formulate a plan for political reunification, neither Lincoln nor Congress gave much attention to the South's land and labor problems. But as the war rapidly eroded slavery and traditional plantation agriculture, Yankee military commanders in the

Union-occupied areas of the Confederacy had no choice but to oversee the emergence of a new labor system.

"To Bind Up the Nation's Wounds"

On March 4, 1865, President Abraham Lincoln delivered his second inaugural address. He surveyed the history of the long, deadly war and then looked ahead to peace. "With malice toward none; with charity for all; with firmness in the right, as God gives us to see the right," Lincoln said, "let us strive on to finish the work we are in; to bind up the nation's wounds…to do all which may achieve and cherish a just, and a lasting peace." Lincoln had contemplated re-union for nearly two years. While deep compassion for the enemy guided his thinking about peace, his plan for reconstruction aimed primarily at shortening the war and ending slavery.

In his Proclamation of Amnesty and Reconstruction, issued in December 1863, Lincoln offered a full pardon to rebels willing to renounce secession and to accept emancipation. (Pardons were valuable because they restored all property, except slaves, and full political rights.) When merely 10 percent of a state's voting population had taken an oath of allegiance, the state could organize a new government. Lincoln's plan did not require ex-rebels to extend social or political rights to ex-slaves, nor did it anticipate a program of long-term federal assistance to freedmen. Clearly, the president looked forward to the speedy restoration of the broken Union.

Lincoln's easy terms enraged abolitionists like Bostonian Wendell Phillips, who charged that the president "makes the negro's freedom a mere sham." He "is willing that the negro should be free but seeks nothing else for him," Phillips declared. Phillips and other northern radicals called instead for a thorough overhaul of southern society. Their ideas proved to be too drastic for most Republicans during the war years, but Congress agreed that Lincoln's plan was inadequate. In July 1864, Congress put forward a plan of its own.

Congressman Henry Winter Davis of Maryland and Senator Benjamin Wade of Ohio jointly sponsored a bill that demanded that at least half of the voters in a conquered rebel state take the oath of allegiance before reconstruction could begin. Moreover, the Wade-Davis bill banned ex-Confederates from participating in the drafting of new state constitutions. Finally, the bill guaranteed the equality of freedmen before the law. When Lincoln exercised his right not to sign the bill and let it die instead, Wade and Davis published a manifesto charging the president with usurpation of power. They warned Lincoln to confine himself to "his executive duties—to obey and execute, not make the laws—to suppress by arms armed rebellion, and leave political organization to Congress."

Undeterred, Lincoln continued to nurture the formation of loyal state governments under his own plan. Four states—Louisiana, Arkansas, Tennessee, and Virginia—fulfilled the president's requirements, but Congress refused to seat representatives from the "Lincoln states." In his last public address in April 1865, Lincoln defended his plan but for the first time expressed publicly his endorsement of **suffrage** for southern blacks, at least "the very intelligent, and… those who serve our cause as soldiers." The announcement demonstrated that Lincoln's thinking about reconstruction was still evolving. Four days later, he was dead.

Land and Labor

Of all the problems raised by the North's victory in the war, none proved more critical than the South's transition from slavery to **free labor**. As federal armies invaded and occupied the Confederacy, hundreds of thousands of slaves became free workers. Union armies controlled vast territories in the South where legal title to land had become unclear. The wartime Confiscation Acts punished "traitors" by taking away their property. The question of what to do with federally occupied land and how to organize labor on it engaged former slaves, former slaveholders, Union military commanders, and federal government officials long before the war ended.

Up and down the Mississippi valley, occupying federal troops announced a new labor code. The code required slaveholders to sign contracts with ex-slaves and to pay wages. It obligated employers to provide food, housing, and medical care. It outlawed whipping, but it reserved to the army the right to discipline blacks who refused to work. The code required black laborers to enter into contracts, work diligently, and remain subordinate and obedient. Military leaders clearly had no intention of promoting a social or economic revolution. Instead, they sought to restore plantation agriculture with wage labor. The effort resulted in a hybrid system that one contemporary called "compulsory free labor," something that satisfied no one.

Planters complained because the new system fell short of slavery. Blacks could not be "transformed by proclamation," a Louisiana sugar planter warned. Yet under the new system, blacks "are expected to perform their new obligations without coercion, & without the fear of punishment which is essential to stimulate the idle and correct the vicious." Without the right to whip, he concluded, the new labor system did not have a chance.

African Americans found the new regime too reminiscent of slavery to be called free labor, and they lamented its failure to provide them land of their own. "What's the use of being free if you don't own land enough to be buried in?" one man asked. Freedmen believed they had a moral right to land because they and their ancestors had worked it without compensation for more than two centuries. Moreover, several wartime developments led them to believe that the federal government planned to undergird black freedom with landownership.

In January 1865, General William Tecumseh Sherman set aside part of the coast south of Charleston for black settlement. By June 1865, some 40,000 freedmen sat on 400,000 acres of "Sherman land." In addition, in March 1865, Congress passed a bill establishing the Bureau of Refugees, Freedmen, and Abandoned Lands. The Freedmen's Bureau, as it was called, distributed food and clothing to destitute Southerners and eased the transition of blacks from slaves to free persons. Congress also authorized the agency to divide abandoned and confiscated land into 40-acre plots, to rent them to freedmen, and eventually to sell them "with such title as the United States can convey." By June 1865, the bureau had situated nearly 10,000 black families on a half million acres abandoned by fleeing planters. Hundreds of thousands of other ex-slaves eagerly anticipated farms of their own.

Despite the flurry of activity, wartime reconstruction failed to produce agreement about whether the president or Congress had the authority to devise and direct policy or what proper policy should be. As Lincoln anticipated, the nation faced postwar dilemmas almost as trying as those of the war.

The African American Quest for Autonomy

Ex-slaves never had any doubt about what they wanted from freedom. They had only to contemplate what they had been denied as slaves. (See "Documenting the American Promise," page 404.) Slaves had to remain on their plantations; freedom allowed blacks to go wherever they pleased. Thus, in the first heady weeks after emancipation, freedmen often abandoned their plantations just to see what was on the other side of the hill. Slaves had to be at work in the fields by dawn; freedom permitted blacks to taste the formerly forbidden pleasure of sleeping through a sunrise. Freedmen also tested the etiquette of racial subordination. "Lizzie's maid passed me today when I was coming from church *without speaking to me,*" huffed one plantation mistress.

To whites, emancipation looked like pure anarchy. Blacks, they said, had reverted to their natural condition: lazy, irresponsible, and wild. Actually, these former slaves were experimenting with freedom, but they could not long afford to roam the countryside, neglect work, and casually provoke whites. Soon, most were back at work in the kitchens and fields.

But other items on ex-slaves' agenda of freedom endured. They dreamed of land of their own. "The way we can best take care of ourselves is to have land," an ex-slave declared in 1865, "and turn it and till it by our own labor." Another explained that he wanted land, "not a Master or owner[,] Neither a driver with his Whip." In addition, freedmen wanted to learn to read and write. "I wishes the Childern all in School," a black Union army veteran asserted. "It is beter for them then to be their Sureing a mistes [mistress]."

Another persistent black aspiration was secure and complete families. Thousands of black men and women took to the roads in 1865 to look for kin who had been sold away or to free those who were being held illegally as slaves. A black soldier from Missouri wrote his daughters that he was coming for them. "I will have you if it cost me my life," he declared. "Your Miss Kitty said that I tried to steal you," he told them. "But I'll let her know that god never intended for a man to steal his own flesh and blood." And he swore that "if she meets me with ten thousand soldiers, she [will] meet her enemy."

Another hunger was for independent worship. Blacks greeted freedom with a mass exodus from white churches. Some joined the newly established southern branches of all-black northern churches, such as the African Methodist Episcopal Church. Others formed black versions of

the major southern denominations, Baptists and Methodists. Freedmen interpreted the events of the Civil War and reconstruction as Christian people. One black woman thanked Lincoln for the Emancipation Proclamation, declaring, "When you are dead and in Heaven, in a thousand years that action of yours will make the Angels sing your praises I know it."

> **REVIEW** Why did Congress object to Lincoln's wartime plan for reconstruction?

Presidential Reconstruction

Abraham Lincoln died on April 15, 1865, just hours after John Wilkes Booth shot him at a Washington, D.C., theater. Chief Justice Salmon P. Chase immediately administered the oath of office to Vice President Andrew Johnson of Tennessee. Congress had adjourned in March, which meant that legislators were away from Washington when Lincoln was killed. They would not reconvene until December. Throughout the summer and fall, therefore, the "accidental president" made critical decisions about the future of the South without congressional input. Like Lincoln, Johnson believed that responsibility for restoring the Union lay with the president. With dizzying speed, he drew up and executed a plan of reconstruction.

Congress returned to the capital in December to find that, as far as the president and former Confederates were concerned, reconstruction was already decided. Most Republicans, however, thought Johnson's modest demands of ex-rebels made a mockery of the sacrifice of Union soldiers. It appeared to them that Johnson had acted as midwife to the rebirth of the Old South and the stillbirth of black liberty. To let his program stand, Republican legislators said, would mean that the North's dead had indeed died in vain. They proceeded to dismantle it and substitute a program of their own, one that southern whites found ways to resist.

Johnson's Program of Reconciliation

Born in 1808 in Raleigh, North Carolina, Andrew Johnson was the son of illiterate parents. Self-educated and ambitious, Johnson moved to Tennessee, where he worked as a tailor, accumu-

lated a fortune in land, acquired five slaves, and built a career in politics championing the South's common white people and assailing its "illegitimate, swaggering, bastard, scrub aristocracy." The only senator from a Confederate state to remain loyal to the Union, Johnson held the planter class responsible for secession. Less than two weeks before he became president, he made it clear what he would do to planters if he ever had the chance: "I would arrest them—I would try them—I would convict them and I would hang them."

Despite such statements, Johnson was no friend of the Republicans. A southern Democrat all his life, Johnson occupied the White House only because the Republican Party in 1864 had needed a vice presidential candidate who would appeal to loyal, Union-supporting Democrats. Johnson favored traditional Democratic causes, vigorously defending **states' rights** (but not secession) and opposing Republican efforts to expand the power of the federal government. A steadfast defender of slavery, Johnson had owned slaves until 1862, when Tennessee rebels, angry at his Unionism, confiscated them. He only grudgingly accepted emancipation. When he did, it was more because he hated planters than sympathized with slaves. "Damn the negroes," he said. "I am fighting those traitorous aristocrats, their masters." At a time when the nation confronted the future of black Americans, the new president harbored unshakable racist convictions. Africans, Johnson said, were "inferior to the white man in point of intellect—better calculated in physical structure to undergo drudgery and hardship."

Like Lincoln, Johnson stressed reconciliation between the Union and the defeated Confederacy and rapid restoration of civil government in the South. Like Lincoln, he promised to pardon most, but not all, ex-rebels. Johnson recognized the state governments created by Lincoln but set out his own requirements for restoring the other rebel states to the Union. All that the citizens of a state had to do was to renounce the right of secession, deny that the debts of the Confederacy were legal and binding, and ratify the Thirteenth Amendment abolishing slavery, which became part of the Constitution in December 1865. Johnson's plan ignored Lincoln's acceptance near the end of his life of some form of limited black voting.

Johnson's eagerness to restore relations with southern states and his lack of sympathy for blacks also led him to return to pardoned

The Meaning of Freedom

On New Year's Day 1863, President Abraham Lincoln issued the Emancipation Proclamation. It states that "all persons held as slaves" within the states still in rebellion "are, and henceforward shall be, free." Although the Proclamation in and of itself did not free any slaves, it transformed the character of the war. Despite often intolerable conditions, black people focused on the possibilities of freedom.

DOCUMENT 1
Letter from John Q. A. Dennis to Edwin M. Stanton, July 26, 1864

John Q. A. Dennis, formerly a slave in Maryland, wrote to ask Secretary of War Edwin M. Stanton for help in reuniting his family.

Boston
Dear Sir I am Glad that I have the Honour to Write you afew line I have been in troble for about four yars my Dear wife was taken from me Nov 19th 1859 and left me with three Children and I being a Slave At the time Could Not do Anny thing for the poor little Children for my master it was took me Carry me some forty mile from them So I Could Not do for them and the man that they live with half feed them and half Cloth them & beat them like dogs & when I was admitted to go to see them it use to brake my heart & Now I say again I am Glad to have the honour to write to you to see if you Can Do Anny thing for me or for my poor little Children I was keap in Slavy untell last Novr 1863. then the Good

lord sent the Cornel borne [federal Colonel William Birney?] Down their in Marland in worsester Co So as I have been recently freed I have but letle to live on but I am Striveing Dear Sir but what I went too know of you Sir is it possible for me to go & take my Children from those men that keep them in Savery if it is possible will you pleas give me a permit from your hand then I think they would let them go....

Hon sir will you please excuse my Miserable writeing & answer me as soon as you can I want get the little Children out of Slavery, I being Criple would like to know of you also if I Cant be permited to rase a Shool Down there & on what turm I Could be admited to Do so No more At present Dear Hon Sir

SOURCE: Ira Berlin, Joseph P. Reidy, and Leslie S. Rowland, eds., *Freedom: A Documentary History of Emancipation, 1861–1867,* ser. 1, vol. 1, *The Destruction of Slavery,* 386. Copyright © 1985. Reprinted with the permission of Cambridge University Press.

DOCUMENT 2
Report from Reverend A. B. Randall, February 28, 1865

Freedom prompted ex-slaves to seek legal marriages, which under slavery had been impossible. Writing from Little Rock, Arkansas, to the adjutant general of the Union army, A. B. Randall, the white chaplain of a black regiment, affirmed the importance of marriage to freed slaves and emphasized their conviction that emancipation was only the first step toward full freedom.

Weddings, just now, are very popular, and abundant among the Colored People. They have just learned, of the Special Order No. 15. of Gen Thomas [Adjutant General Lorenzo Thomas] by which, they may not only be lawfully married, but have their Marriage Certificates, Recorded; in a book furnished by the Government. This is most desirable.... Those who were captured...at Ivy's Ford, on the 17th of January, by Col Brooks, had their Marriage Certificates, taken from them; and destroyed; and then were roundly cursed, for having such papers in their posession. I have married, during the month, at this Post; Twenty five couples; mostly, those, who have families; & have been living together for years. I try to dissuade single men, who are soldiers, from marrying, till their time of enlistment is out: as that course seems to me, to be most judicious.

The Colord People here, generally consider, this war not only; their exodus, from bondage; but the road, to Responsibility; Competency; and an honorable Citizenship—God grant that their hopes and expectations may be fully realized.

SOURCE: Ira Berlin, Joseph P. Reidy, and Leslie S. Rowland, eds., *Freedom: A Documentary History of Emancipation, 1861–1867,* ser. 2, vol. 1, *The Black Military Experience,* 712. Copyright © 1982. Reprinted with the permission of Cambridge University Press.

DOCUMENT 3
Petition "to the Union Convention of Tennessee Assembled in the Capitol at Nashville," January 9, 1865

Early efforts at political reconstruction prompted petitions from former slaves

demanding civil and political rights. In January 1865, black Tennesseans petitioned a convention of white Unionists debating the reorganization of state government.

We the undersigned petitioners, American citizens of African descent, natives and residents of Tennessee, and devoted friends of the great National cause, do most respectfully ask a patient hearing of your honorable body in regard to matters deeply affecting the future condition of our unfortunate and long suffering race.

First of all, however, we would say that words are too weak to tell how profoundly grateful we are to the Federal Government for the good work of freedom which it is gradually carrying forward; and for the Emancipation Proclamation which has set free all the slaves in some of the rebellious States, as well as many of the slaves in Tennessee....

We claim freedom, as our natural right, and ask that in harmony and co-operation with the nation at large, you should cut up by the roots the system of slavery, which is not only a wrong to us, but the source of all the evil which at present afflicts the State. For slavery, corrupt itself, corrupted nearly all, also, around it, so that it has influenced nearly all the slave States to rebel against the Federal Government, in order to set up a government of pirates under which slavery might be perpetrated.

In the contest between the nation and slavery, our unfortunate people have sided, by instinct, with the former. We have little fortune to devote to the national cause, for a hard fate has hitherto forced us to live in poverty, but we do devote to its success, our hopes, our toils, our whole heart, our sacred honor, and our lives. We will work, pray, live, and, if need be, die for the Union, as cheerfully as ever a white patriot died for his country. The color of our skin does not lessen in the least degree, our love either for God or for the land of our birth....

We know the burdens of citizenship, and are ready to bear them. We know the duties of the good citizen, and are ready to perform them cheerfully, and would ask to be put in a position in which we can discharge them more effectually....

This is a democracy—a government of the people. It should aim to make every man, without regard to the color of his skin, the amount of his wealth, or the character of his religious faith, feel personally interested in its welfare. Every man who lives under the Government should feel that it is his property, his treasure, the bulwark and defence of himself and his family, his pearl of great price, which he must preserve, protect, and defend faithfully at all times, on all occasions, in every possible manner.

This is not a Democratic Government if a numerous, law-abiding, industrious, and useful class of citizens, born and bred on the soil, are to be treated as aliens and enemies, as an inferior degraded class, who must have no voice in the Government which they support, protect and defend, with all their heart, soul, mind, and body, both in peace and war....

The possibility that the negro suffrage proposition may shock popular prejudice at first sight, is not a conclusive argument against its wisdom and policy. No proposition ever met with more furious or general opposition than the one to enlist colored soldiers in the United States army. The opponents of the measure exclaimed on all hands that the negro was a coward; that he would not fight; that one white man, with a whip in his hand could put to flight a regiment of them; that the experiment would end in the utter rout and ruin of the Federal army. Yet the colored man has fought so well, on almost every occasion, that the rebel government is prevented, only by its fears and distrust of being able to force him to fight for slavery as well as he fights against it, from putting half a million of negroes into its ranks.

The Government has asked the colored man to fight for its preservation and gladly has he done it. It can afford to trust him with a vote as safely as it trusted him with a bayonet.

SOURCE: Ira Berlin, Joseph P. Reidy, and Leslie S. Rowland, eds., *Freedom: A Documentary History of Emancipation, 1861–1867,* ser. 2, vol. 1, *The Black Military Experience,* 811–16. Copyright © 1982. Reprinted with the permission of Cambridge University Press.

QUESTIONS FOR ANALYSIS AND DEBATE

1. How does John Q. A. Dennis interpret his responsibility as a father?

2. Why do you think ex-slaves wanted their marriages legalized?

3. Why, according to petitioners to the Union Convention of Tennessee, did blacks deserve voting rights?

ex-Confederates all confiscated and abandoned land, even if it was in the hands of freedmen. Reformers were shocked. They had expected the president's hatred of planters to mean the permanent confiscation of the South's plantations and the distribution of the land to loyal freedmen. Instead, his instructions canceled the promising beginnings made by General Sherman and the Freedmen's Bureau to settle blacks on land of their own. As one freedman observed, "Things was hurt by Mr. Lincoln getting killed."

White Southern Resistance and Black Codes

In the summer of 1865, delegates across the South gathered to draw up the new state constitutions required by Johnson's plan of reconstruction. Rather than take their medicine, delegates choked on even the president's mild requirements. Refusing to renounce secession, the South Carolina and Georgia conventions

The Black Codes
Titled "Selling a Freeman to Pay His Fine at Monticello, Florida," this 1867 drawing from a northern magazine equates the black codes with the reinstitution of slavery. The laws stopped short of reenslavement but sharply restricted blacks' freedom. In Florida, as in other southern states, certain acts, such as breaking a labor contract, were made criminal offenses, the penalty for which could be involuntary plantation labor for a year.
Library of Congress.

merely "repudiated" their secession ordinances, preserving in principle their right to secede. South Carolina and Mississippi refused to disown their Confederate war debts. Mississippi rejected the Thirteenth Amendment outright, and Alabama rejected it in part. Despite these defiant acts, Johnson did nothing. By failing to draw a hard line, he rekindled southern resistance. White Southerners began to think that by standing up for themselves they—not victorious Northerners—would shape reconstruction. In the fall of 1865, newly elected southern legislators set out to reverse what they considered the "retreat into barbarism" that followed emancipation.

State governments across the South adopted a series of laws known as black codes, which made a travesty of black freedom. The codes sought to keep ex-slaves subordinate to whites by subjecting them to every sort of discrimination. Several states made it illegal for blacks to own a gun. Mississippi made insulting gestures and language by blacks a criminal offense. The codes barred blacks from jury duty. Not a single southern state granted any black—no matter how educated, wealthy, or refined—the right to vote.

At the core of the black codes, however, lay the matter of labor. Faced with the death of slavery, legislators sought to hustle freedmen back to the plantations. South Carolina attempted to limit blacks to either farmwork or domestic service by requiring them to pay annual taxes of $10 to $100 to work in any other occupation. Mississippi declared that blacks who did not possess written evidence of employment could be declared vagrants and be subject to involuntary plantation labor. Most states allowed judges to bind black children—orphans and others whose parents they deemed unable to support them—to white employers. Under these so-called apprenticeship laws, courts bound thousands of black children to work for planter "guardians."

Johnson refused to intervene. A staunch defender of states' rights, he believed that the citizens of every state should be free to write their own constitutions and laws. Moreover, since Johnson was as eager as other white Southerners to restore white supremacy and black subordination, the black codes did not offend him.

But Johnson also followed the path that he believed would offer him the greatest political return. A **conservative** Tennessee Democrat at the head of a northern Republican Party, he began to look southward for political allies.

Despite tough talk about punishing traitors, he personally pardoned 14,000 wealthy or high-ranking ex-Confederates. By pardoning powerful whites, by acquiescing in the black codes, and by accepting governments even when they failed to satisfy his minimal demands, he won useful southern friends.

In the elections of 1865, white Southerners dramatically expressed their mood. To represent them in Congress, they chose former Confederates, not loyal Unionists. Of the eighty senators and representatives they sent to Washington, fifteen had served in the Confederate army, ten of them as generals. Another sixteen had served in civil and judicial posts in the Confederacy. Nine others had served in the Confederate Congress. One— Alexander Stephens—had been vice president of the Confederacy. In December, this remarkable group arrived on the steps of the nation's Capitol building to be seated in Congress. As one Georgian remarked, "It looked as though Richmond had moved to Washington."

Expansion of Federal Authority and Black Rights

Southerners had blundered monumentally. They had assumed that what Andrew Johnson was willing to accept Republicans would accept as well. But southern intransigence compelled even moderates to conclude that ex-rebels were a "generation of vipers," still untrustworthy and dangerous.

The black codes became a symbol of southern intentions to "restore all of slavery but its name." Northerners were hardly saints when it came to racial justice, but black freedom had become a hallowed war aim. "We tell the white men of Mississippi," the *Chicago Tribune* roared, "that the men of the North will convert the State of Mississippi into a frog pond before they will allow such laws to disgrace one foot of the soil in which the bones of our soldiers sleep and over which the flag of freedom waves."

The moderate majority of the Republican Party wanted only assurance that slavery and treason were dead. They did not champion black equality or the confiscation of plantations or black voting, as did the radicals, a minority within the party. But southern obstinacy had succeeded in forging unity (at least temporarily) among Republican factions. In December 1865, exercising Congress's right to determine the qualifications of its members, Republicans refused to seat the southern representatives. Rather than accept Johnson's claim that the "work of restoration" was done, Congress challenged his executive power. Congressional Republicans enjoyed a three-to-one majority over the Democrats, and if they could agree on a program of reconstruction, they could easily pass legislation and even override presidential vetoes.

Senator Lyman Trumbull of Illinois declared that the president's policy meant that the ex-slave would "be tyrannized over, abused, and virtually reenslaved without some legislation by the nation for his protection." Early in 1866, the moderates produced two bills that strengthened the federal shield. The first, the Freedmen's Bureau bill, prolonged the life of the agency established by the previous Congress. Since the end of the war, it had distributed food, supervised labor contracts, and sponsored schools for freedmen. Arguing that the Constitution never contemplated a "system for the support of indigent persons," President Andrew Johnson vetoed the bill. Congress failed by a narrow margin to override the president's veto.

The moderates designed their second measure, the Civil Rights Act, to nullify the black codes by affirming African Americans' rights to "full and equal benefit of all laws and proceedings for the security of person and property as is enjoyed by white citizens." The act boldly required the end of legal discrimination in state laws and represented an extraordinary expansion of black rights and federal authority. The president argued that the civil rights bill amounted to "unconstitutional invasion of states' rights" and vetoed it. In essence, he denied that the federal government possessed authority to protect the civil rights of blacks.

In April 1866, an incensed Republican Party again pushed the civil rights bill through Congress and overrode the presidential veto. In July, it passed another Freedmen's Bureau bill and overrode Johnson's veto. For the first time in American history, Congress had overridden presidential vetoes of major legislation. As a worried South Carolinian observed, Johnson had succeeded in uniting the Republicans and probably touched off "a fight this fall such as has never been seen."

REVIEW How did the North respond to the passage of black codes in the southern states?

Congressional Reconstruction

By the summer of 1866, President Andrew Johnson and Congress had dropped their gloves and stood toe to toe in a bare-knuckled contest unprecedented in American history. Johnson made it clear that he would not budge on either constitutional issues or policy. Moderate Republicans responded by amending the Constitution. But the obstinacy of Johnson and white Southerners pushed Republican moderates ever closer to the radicals and to acceptance of additional federal intervention in the South. In time, Congress debated whether to give the ballot to black men. Outside of Congress, blacks championed color-blind voting rights, while women sought to make voting sex-blind as well.

The Fourteenth Amendment and Escalating Violence

In June 1866, Congress passed the Fourteenth Amendment to the Constitution, and two years later it gained the necessary ratification of three-fourths of the states. The most important provisions of this complex amendment made all native-born or naturalized persons American citizens and prohibited states from abridging the "privileges and immunities" of citizens, depriving them of "life, liberty, or property without due process of law," and denying them "equal protection of the laws." By making blacks national citizens, the amendment provided a national guarantee of equality before the law. In essence, it protected blacks against violation by southern state governments.

The Fourteenth Amendment also dealt with voting rights. It gave Congress the right to reduce the congressional representation of states that withheld suffrage from some of its adult male population. In other words, white Southerners could either allow black men to vote or see their representation in Washington slashed.

Republicans stood to benefit from the Fourteenth Amendment. If southern whites granted voting rights to freedmen, Republicans, entirely a northern party, would gain valuable black votes, establish a wing in the South, and secure their national power. But if whites refused, representation of southern Democrats would plunge, and Republicans would still gain political power.

The Fourteenth Amendment's suffrage provisions completely ignored the small band of politicized and energized women who had emerged from the war demanding "the ballot for the two disenfranchised classes, negroes and women." Founding the American Equal Rights Association in 1866, Susan B. Anthony and Elizabeth Cady Stanton lobbied for "a government by the people, and the whole people; for the people and the whole people." They felt betrayed when their old antislavery allies, who now occupied positions of national power, proved to be fickle and refused to work for their goals. "It was the Negro's hour," Frederick Douglass later explained. Charles Sumner suggested that woman suffrage could be "the great question of the future."

The Fourteenth Amendment dashed women's expectations. It provided for punishment of any state that excluded voters on the basis of race but not on the basis of sex. The amendment also introduced the word *male* into the Constitution when it referred to a citizen's right to vote. Stanton predicted that "if that word 'male' be inserted, it will take us a century at least to get it out."

Tennessee approved the Fourteenth Amendment in July, and Congress promptly welcomed the state's representatives and senators back. Had Johnson counseled other southern states to ratify this relatively mild amendment and warned them that they faced the fury of an outraged Republican Party if they refused, they might have listened. Instead, Johnson advised Southerners to reject the Fourteenth Amendment and to rely on him to trounce the Republicans in the fall congressional elections.

Johnson had decided to make the Fourteenth Amendment the overriding issue of the 1866 congressional elections and to gather its white opponents into a new conservative party, the National Union Party. The president's strategy suffered a setback when whites in several southern cities went on rampages against blacks—an escalation of the violence that had never really ceased. When a mob in New Orleans assaulted delegates to a black suffrage convention, 34 blacks died. In Memphis, white mobs crashed through the black sections of town, killing at least 46 people. The slaughter shocked Northerners and renewed skepticism about Johnson's claim that southern whites could be trusted. "Who doubts that the Freedmen's Bureau ought to be abolished forthwith," a New Yorker observed sarcasti-

Susan B. Anthony
Like many outspoken suffragists, Anthony, depicted here in 1852, began her public career working on behalf of temperance and abolition. But she grew tired of laboring under the direction of male clergymen—"white orthodox little saints," she called them—who controlled the reform movements and routinely dismissed the opinions of women. Anthony's continued passion for other causes—improving working conditions for labor, for example—led some conservatives to oppose women's political rights because they equated the suffragist cause with radicalism in general. Women could not easily overcome such views, and the long struggle for the vote eventually drew millions of women into public life.
Susan B. Anthony House, Inc.

cally, "and the blacks remitted to the paternal care of their old masters, who 'understand the nigger, you know, a great deal better than the Yankees can.'"

The 1866 election resulted in an overwhelming Republican victory in which the party retained its three-to-one congressional majority. Johnson had bet that Northerners would not support federal protection of black rights and that a racist backlash would blast the Republican Party. But the war was still fresh in northern minds, and as one Republican explained, southern whites "with all their intelligence were traitors, the blacks with all their ignorance were loyal."

Radical Reconstruction and Military Rule

The elections of 1866 should have taught southern whites the folly of relying on Andrew Johnson to guide them through reconstruction. But when Johnson continued to urge Southerners to reject the Fourteenth Amendment, every southern state except Tennessee voted it down. "The last one of the sinful ten," thundered Representative James A. Garfield of Ohio, "has flung back into our teeth the magnanimous offer of a generous nation." After the South rejected the moderates' program, the radicals seized the initiative.

Each act of defiance by southern whites had boosted the standing of the radicals within the Republican Party. Except for freedmen themselves, no one did more to make freedom the "mighty moral question of the age." Radicals like Massachusetts senator Charles Sumner and Pennsylvania representative Thaddeus Stevens did not speak with a single voice, but they united in demanding civil and political equality. They insisted on extending to ex-slaves the same opportunities that northern working people enjoyed under the free-labor system. Southern states were "like clay in the hands of the potter," Stevens declared in January 1867, and he called on Congress to begin reconstruction all over again.

In March 1867, Congress overturned the Johnson state governments and initiated military rule of the South. The Military Reconstruction Act (and three subsequent acts) divided the ten unreconstructed Confederate states into five military districts. Congress placed a Union general in charge of each district and instructed him to "suppress insurrection, disorder, and violence" and to begin political reform. After the military had completed voter registration, which would include black men, voters in each state would elect delegates to conventions that would draw up new state constitutions. Each constitution would guarantee black suffrage. When the voters of each state had approved the

Reconstruction Military Districts, 1867

constitution and the state legislature had ratified the Fourteenth Amendment, the state could submit its work to Congress. If Congress approved, the state's senators and representatives could be seated, and political reunification would be accomplished.

Radicals proclaimed the provision for black suffrage "a prodigious triumph," for it extended far beyond the limited suffrage provisions of the Fourteenth Amendment. Republicans united in the conviction that only the voting power of ex-slaves could bring about a permanent revolution in the South. Indeed, suffrage provided blacks with a powerful instrument of change and self-protection. When combined with the disfranchisement of thousands of ex-rebels, it promised to cripple any neo-Confederate resurgence and guarantee Republican state governments in the South.

Despite its bold suffrage provision, the Military Reconstruction Act of 1867 disappointed those who advocated the confiscation and redistribution of southern plantations to ex-slaves. Thaddeus Stevens, who believed that at bottom reconstruction was an economic problem, agreed with the freedman who said, "Give us our own land and we take care of ourselves, but without land, the old masters can hire us or starve us, as they please." But most Republicans believed they had already provided blacks with what they needed: equal legal rights and the ballot. If blacks were to get forty acres, they would have to gain the land themselves.

Declaring that he would rather sever his right arm than sign such a formula for "anarchy and chaos," Andrew Johnson vetoed the Military Reconstruction Act. Congress overrode his veto the very same day, dramatizing the shift in power from the executive to the legislative branch of government. With the passage of the Reconstruction Acts of 1867, congressional reconstruction was virtually completed. Congress left whites owning most of the South's land but, in a departure that justified the term "radical reconstruction," had given black men the ballot. In 1867, the nation began an unprecedented experiment in interracial democracy—at least in the South, for Congress's plan did not touch the North. But before the spotlight swung away from Washington to the South, the president and Congress had one more scene to play.

Impeaching a President

Despite his defeats, Andrew Johnson had no intention of yielding control of reconstruction. In a dozen ways he sabotaged Congress's will and encouraged white belligerence and resistance. He issued a flood of pardons to undermine efforts at political and economic change. He waged war against the Freedmen's Bureau by removing officers who sympathized too fully with ex-slaves. And he replaced Union generals eager to enforce Congress's Reconstruction Acts with conservative men eager to defeat them. Johnson claimed that he was merely defending the "violated Constitution." At bottom, however, the president subverted congressional reconstruction to protect southern whites from what he considered the horrors of "Negro domination."

Radicals argued that Johnson's abuse of constitutional powers and his failure to fulfill constitutional obligations were impeachable offenses, but moderates interpreted the constitutional provision to mean violation of criminal statutes. According to the Constitution, the House of Representatives can impeach and the Senate can try any federal official for "treason, bribery, or other high crimes and misdemeanors." As long as Johnson refrained from breaking a law, **impeachment** remained a faint hope.

Then in August 1867, Johnson suspended Secretary of War Edwin M. Stanton from office. As required by the Tenure of Office Act, which required the approval of the Senate for the removal of any government official who had been appointed with Senate approval, the president requested the Senate to consent to the dismissal. When the Senate balked, Johnson removed Stanton anyway. "Is the President crazy, or only drunk?" asked a dumbfounded Republican moderate. "I'm afraid his doings will make us all favor impeachment."

News of Johnson's open defiance of the law convinced every Republican in the House to vote for a resolution impeaching the president. Supreme Court Chief Justice Salmon Chase presided over the Senate trial, which lasted from March until May 1868. Chase refused to allow Johnson's opponents to raise broad issues of misuse of power and forced them to argue their case exclusively on the narrow legal grounds of Johnson's removal of Stanton. Johnson's lawyers argued that the president had not committed a criminal offense, that the Tenure of Office Act was unconstitutional, and that in any case it did not apply to Stanton, who had been appointed by Lincoln. When the critical vote came, 35 senators voted guilty and 19 not guilty. The impeachment forces fell one vote short of the two-thirds needed to convict.

Although Johnson survived, he did not come through the ordeal unscathed. After his trial he called a truce, and for the remaining ten months of his term congressional reconstruction proceeded unhindered by presidential interference. Without interference from Johnson, Congress revisited the suffrage issue.

The Fifteenth Amendment and Women's Demands

In February 1869, Republicans passed the Fifteenth Amendment to the Constitution, which prohibited states from depriving any citizen of the right to vote because of "race, color, or previous condition of servitude." The Reconstruction Acts of 1867 already required black suffrage in the South; the Fifteenth Amendment extended black voting nationwide. Partisan advantage played an important role in the amendment's passage. Gains by northern Democrats in the 1868 elections worried Republicans, and black voters now represented the balance of power in several northern states. By giving ballots to northern blacks, Republicans could lessen their political vulnerability. As one Republican congressman observed, "Party expediency and exact justice coincide for once."

Some Republicans, however, found the final wording of the Fifteenth Amendment "lame and halting." Rather than absolutely guaranteeing the right to vote, the amendment merely prohibited exclusion on grounds of race. The distinction would prove to be significant. In time, inventive white Southerners would devise tests of literacy and property and other apparently nonracial measures that would effectively disfranchise blacks yet not violate the Fifteenth Amendment. But an amendment that fully guaranteed the right to vote courted defeat outside the South. Rising antiforeign sentiment—against the Chinese in California and against European immigrants in the Northeast—caused states to resist giving up total control of suffrage requirements. In March 1870, after three-fourths of the states had ratified it, the Fifteenth Amendment became part of the Constitution. Republicans generally breathed a sigh of relief, confident that black suffrage was "the last great point that remained to be settled of the issues of the war."

Woman suffrage advocates, however, were sorely disappointed with the Fifteenth Amendment's failure to extend voting rights to women.

Major Reconstruction Legislation, 1865–1875

1865	
Thirteenth Amendment (ratified 1865)	Abolishes slavery.
1865 and 1866	
Freedmen's Bureau Acts	Establish the Freedmen's Bureau to distribute food and clothing to destitute Southerners and help freedmen with labor contracts and schooling.
Civil Rights Act of 1866	Affirms the rights of blacks to enjoy "full and equal benefit of all laws and proceedings for the security of person and property as is enjoyed by white citizens" and effectively requires the end of legal discrimination in state laws.
Fourteenth Amendment (ratified 1868)	Makes native-born blacks citizens and guarantees all citizens "equal protection of the laws." Threatens to reduce representatives of a state that denies suffrage to any of its male inhabitants.
1867	
Military Reconstruction Acts	Impose military rule in the South, establish rules for readmission of ex-Confederate states to the Union, and require those states to guarantee the vote to black men.
1869	
Fifteenth Amendment (ratified 1870)	Prohibits racial discrimination in voting rights in all states in the nation.
1875	
Civil Rights Act of 1875	Outlaws racial discrimination in transportation, public accommodations, and juries.

Although women fought hard to include the word *sex* (as they had fought hard to keep the word *male* out of the Fourteenth Amendment), the amendment denied states the right to forbid suffrage only on the basis of race. Elizabeth Cady Stanton and Susan B. Anthony condemned the Republicans' "negro first" strategy and concluded that woman "must not put her trust in man." The Fifteenth Amendment severed the early **feminist** movement from its abolitionist roots. Over the next several decades, women would establish an independent suffrage crusade that drew millions of women into political life.

Republicans took enough satisfaction in the Fifteenth Amendment to promptly scratch the "Negro question" from the agenda of national politics. Even that steadfast crusader for equality, Wendell Phillips, concluded that the black man now held "sufficient shield in his own hands.... Whatever he suffers will be largely now, and in future, his own fault." Northerners had no idea of the violent struggles that lay ahead.

REVIEW   Why did Johnson urge southern states to reject the Fourteenth Amendment?

The Struggle in the South

Northerners believed they had discharged their responsibilities with the Reconstruction Acts and the amendments to the Constitution, but Southerners knew that the battle had just begun. Black suffrage established the foundation for the rise of the Republican Party in the South. Gathering together outsiders and outcasts, southern Republicans won elections, wrote new state constitutions, and formed new state governments. Challenging the established class for political control was dangerous business. Equally dangerous were the confrontations that took place on farms and plantations in the countryside, where blacks sought to give practical, everyday meaning to their newly won legal and political equality. Ex-masters like David Golightly Harris and other whites had their own ideas about the social and economic arrangements that should replace slavery. Freedom remained contested territory, and Southerners fought pitched battles with one another to determine the contours of their new world.

Freedmen, Yankees, and Yeomen

African Americans made up the majority of southern Republicans. After gaining voting rights in 1867, nearly every eligible black man registered to vote. Almost all registered as Republicans, grateful to the party that had freed them and granted them the **franchise**. Black women, like white women, remained disfranchised but mobilized along with black men. In the 1868 presidential election, they bravely wore buttons supporting the Republican candidate, former Union general Ulysses S. Grant. Southern

blacks did not have identical political priorities, but they united in their desire for education and equal treatment before the laws.

Northern whites who made the South their home after the war were a second element of the South's Republican Party. Conservative white Southerners called them "carpetbaggers," men so poor that they could stuff all their earthly belongings in a single carpet-sided suitcase and swoop southward like buzzards to "fatten on our misfortunes." But most Northerners who moved south were restless, relatively well-educated young men who looked upon the South as they did the West—as a promising place to make a living. They expected that the South without slavery would prosper, and they wanted to be part of it. Northerners in the southern Republican Party consistently supported programs that encouraged vigorous economic development along the lines of the northern free-labor model.

Southern whites made up the third element of the South's Republican Party. Approximately one out of four white Southerners voted Republican. The other three condemned the one who did as a traitor to his region and his race and called him a "scalawag," a term for runty horses and low-down, good-for-nothing rascals. **Yeoman** farmers accounted for the majority of southern white Republicans. Some were Unionists who emerged from the war with bitter memories of Confederate persecution. Others were small farmers who wanted to end state governments' favoritism toward plantation owners. Yeomen usually supported initiatives for public schools and for expanding economic opportunity in the South.

The South's Republican Party, then, was made up of freedmen, Yankees, and yeomen—an improbable coalition. The mix of races, regions, and classes inevitably meant friction as each group maneuvered to define the party. But Reconstruction represents an extraordinary moment in American politics: Blacks and whites joined together in the Republican Party to pursue political change. Formally, of course, only men participated in politics—casting ballots and holding offices—but women also played parts in the political struggle by joining in parades and rallies, attending stump speeches, and even campaigning.

Reconstruction politics was not for cowards. Activity on behalf of Republicans in particular took courage. Most whites in the South condemned reconstruction politics as illegitimate and felt justified in doing whatever they could to stamp out

Republicanism. Violence against blacks—the "white terror"—took brutal institutional form in 1866 with the formation in Tennessee of the Ku Klux Klan, a social club of Confederate veterans that quickly developed into a paramilitary organization supporting Democrats. The Klan went on a rampage of whipping, hanging, shooting, burning, and throat-cutting to restore white supremacy. Rapid demobilization of the Union army after the war left only 20,000 troops to patrol the entire South, a vast territory. Without effective military protection, southern Republicans had to take care of themselves.

Republican Rule

In the fall of 1867, southern states held elections for delegates to state constitutional conventions, as required by the Reconstruction Acts. About 40 percent of the white electorate stayed home because they had been disfranchised or because they had decided to boycott politics. Republicans won three-fourths of the seats. About 15 percent of the Republican delegates to the conventions were Northerners who had moved south, 25 percent were African Americans, and 60 percent were white Southerners. As a British visitor observed, the delegate elections reflected "the mighty revolution that had taken place in America." But Democrats described the state conventions as zoos of "baboons, monkeys, mules…and other jackasses." In fact, the conventions brought together serious, purposeful men who hammered out the legal framework for a new order.

The reconstruction constitutions introduced two broad categories of changes in the South: those that reduced aristocratic privilege and increased **democratic** equality and those that expanded the state's responsibility for the general welfare. In the first category, the constitutions adopted universal male suffrage, abolished property qualifications for holding office, and made more offices elective and fewer appointed. In the second category, they enacted prison reform; made the state responsible for caring for orphans, the insane, and the deaf and mute; and exempted debtors' homes from seizure.

These forward-looking state constitutions provided blueprints for a new South but stopped short of the specific reforms advocated by some. Despite the wishes of virtually every former slave, no southern constitution confiscated and redistributed land. And despite the prediction of Unionists that unless all former Confederates were banned from politics they would storm back and wreck reconstruction, no state constitution disfranchised ex-rebels wholesale.

Democrats, however, were blind to the limits of the Republican program. They thought they faced wild revolution. According to Democrats, Republican victories initiated "black and tan" (ex-slave and mulatto) governments across the South.

Congressman John R. Lynch

Although whites almost always maintained control of reconstruction politics, over 600 blacks served in legislatures in the South. Ex-slaves made up the majority of the black legislators. The Union army freed John R. Lynch of Mississippi, and he gained an education at a Natchez freedmen's school. Lynch (1847–1939) was only twenty-four when he became speaker of Mississippi's house of representatives. In 1872, he joined six other African Americans in Congress in Washington, D.C., where in support of civil rights legislation he described his personal experience of being forced to ride in railroad smoking cars with gamblers and drunks. After reconstruction ended, Lynch practiced law and wrote a history of the reconstruction legislatures, which, he argued, were the "best governments those States ever had." Natchez photographer Henry C. Norman took this powerful photograph, probably in the early 1870s.

Collection of Thomas H. Gandy and Joan W. Gandy.

But the claims of "Negro domination" had almost no validity. While four out of five Republican voters were black men, more than four out of five Republican officeholders were white. Southerners sent fourteen black congressmen and two black senators to Washington, but only 6 percent of Southerners in Congress during Reconstruction were black (Figure 16.1). With the exception of South Carolina, where blacks briefly held a majority in one house of the legislature, no state experienced "Negro rule," despite black majorities in the populations of some states.

In almost every state, voters ratified the new constitutions and swept Republicans into power. When the former Confederate states ratified the Fourteenth Amendment, Congress readmitted them. Southern Republicans then turned to a staggering array of problems. Wartime destruction—burned cities, shattered bridges, broken levees—still littered the landscape. The South's share of the nation's wealth had fallen from 30 to only 12 percent. Manufacturing limped along at a fraction of prewar levels, agricultural production remained anemic, and the region's railroads lay devastated. Without the efforts of the

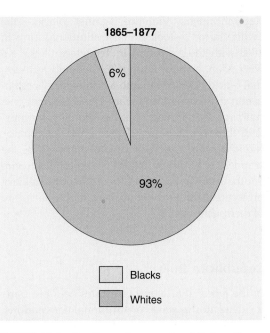

FIGURE 16.1 Southern Congressional Delegations, 1865–1877
The statistics contradict the myth of black domination of congressional representation during Reconstruction.

Freedmen's Bureau, black and white Southerners would have starved. Making matters worse, racial harassment and reactionary violence dogged Southerners who sought reform. In this desperate context, Republicans struggled to breathe life into their new state governments.

Republican activity focused on three areas—education, civil rights, and economic development. Every state inaugurated a system of public education. Before the Civil War, whites had deliberately kept slaves illiterate, and planter-dominated governments rarely spent tax money to educate

One-Cent Primer
"The people are hungry and thirsty after knowledge," a former slave observed after the Civil War. Future African American leader Booker T. Washington remembered "a whole race trying to go to school. Few were too young, and none too old, to make the attempt to learn." Inexpensive elementary textbooks (this eight-page primer cost a penny) offered ex-slaves the basic elements of literacy. For people long forbidden to learn to read and write, literacy symbolized freedom and allowed the deeply religious to experience the joy of Bible reading. It also permitted African Americans to understand labor agreements, sign contracts, and participate knowledgeably in politics.
Gladstone Collection.

the children of yeomen. By 1875, half of Mississippi's and South Carolina's eligible children (the majority of whom were black) were attending school. Despite underfunding and dilapidated facilities, literacy rates rose sharply. Although public schools were racially segregated, education remained for many blacks a tangible, deeply satisfying benefit of freedom and Republican rule.

State legislatures also attacked racial discrimination and defended civil rights. Republicans especially resisted efforts to segregate blacks from whites in public transportation. Mississippi levied fines of up to $1,000 and three years in jail for railroads, steamboats, hotels, and theaters that denied "full and equal rights" to all citizens. But passing color-blind laws was one thing; enforcing them another. Despite the law, segregation—later called **Jim Crow**—developed at white insistence and became a feature of southern life long before the end of the Reconstruction era.

Republican governments also launched ambitious programs of economic development. They envisioned a South of diversified agriculture, roaring factories, and booming towns. Republican legislatures chartered scores of banks and industrial companies, appropriated funds to fix ruined levees and to drain swamps, and went on a railroad-building binge. These efforts fell far short of solving the South's economic troubles, however. Republican spending to stimulate economic growth also meant rising taxes and enormous debt that drained funds from schools and other programs.

The southern Republicans' record, then, was mixed. To their credit, the biracial party took up an ambitious agenda to change the South under trying circumstances. Money was scarce, the Democrats continued their harassment, and factionalism threatened the Republican Party from within. However, corruption infected Republican governments in the South. Public morality reached new lows everywhere in the nation after the Civil War, and the chaos and disruption of the postwar South proved fertile soil for bribery, fraud, and influence peddling. Despite problems and shortcomings, however, the Republican Party made headway in its efforts to purge the South of aristocratic privilege and racist oppression. Republican governments had less success in overthrowing the long-established white oppression of black farm laborers in the rural South.

White Landlords, Black Sharecroppers

In the countryside, clashes occurred daily between ex-slaves who wished to escape slave labor and ex-masters who wanted to reinstitute old ways. Except for having to put down the whip and pay subsistence wages, planters had not been required to offer many concessions to emancipation. They continued to believe that African Americans were inherently lazy and would not work without coercion. Whites moved quickly to restore the antebellum world of work gangs, white overseers, field labor for black women and children, clustered cabins, minimal personal freedom, and even whipping whenever they could get away with it.

Ex-slaves resisted every effort to roll back the clock. They argued that if any class could be described as "lazy," it was the planters, who, as one ex-slave noted, "lived in idleness all their lives on stolen labor." Land of their own would anchor their economic independence, they believed, and end planters' interference in their personal lives. They could then, for example, make their own decisions about whether women and children would labor in the fields. Indeed, within months after the war, perhaps one-third of black women abandoned field labor to work on chores in their own cabins just as poor white women did. With freedom to decide how to use family time, hundreds of thousands of black children enrolled in school. But landownership proved to be beyond the reach of most blacks once the federal government abandoned plans to redistribute Confederate property. Without land, ex-slaves had little choice but to work on plantations.

Although they were forced to return to the planters' fields, freedmen resisted efforts to restore slavelike conditions. In his South Carolina neighborbood, David Golightly Harris discovered that few freedmen were "willing to hire by the day, month or year." Instead of working for wages, "the negroes all seem disposed to rent land," which would increase their independence from whites. By rejecting wage labor, by striking, and by abandoning the most reactionary employers, blacks sought to force concessions. Out of this tug-of-war between white landlords and black laborers emerged a new system of southern agriculture.

Sharecropping was a compromise that offered both ex-masters and ex-slaves something but satisfied neither. Under the new system, planters divided their cotton plantations into

Black Family, 1870s

"If a man got to go crost de riber, and he can't git a boat, he take a log," a South Carolina freedman declared after President Andrew Johnson allowed planters to repossess their land. "If I can't own de land, I'll hire or lease land, but I won't contract." Determined to "set up for himself," almost every freedman in the cotton South preferred the economic independence and personal freedom of share-cropping to the dependency of wage labor. The members of this black family posed in front of their dilapidated home are clearly proud and undefeated, but optimism was hard to sustain in the postwar rural South. "We thought we was goin' to be richer than the white folks," recalled a former slave in Texas, "cause we was stronger and knowed how to work, and the whites didn't and they didn't have us to work for them anymore. But it didn't turn out that way."

Roll, Jordan, Roll by Doris Ullmann 1933.

small farms of twenty-five to thirty acres that freedmen rented, paying with a share of each year's crop, usually half. Sharecropping gave blacks more freedom than the system of wages and labor gangs and released them from the day-to-day supervision of whites. Black families abandoned the old slave quarters and scattered over plantations, building separate cabins for themselves on the patches of land they rented (Map 16.1). Black families now decided who would work, for how long, and how hard. Still, most blacks remained dependent on white landlords, who had the power to expel them at the end of each growing season. For planters, sharecropping offered a way to resume agricultural production, but it did not allow them to restore the old slave plantation.

Sharecropping introduced a new figure—the country merchant—into the agricultural equation. Landlords supplied sharecroppers with land, mules, seeds, and tools, but blacks also needed credit to obtain essential food and clothing before they harvested their crops. Thousands of small crossroads stores sprang up to offer credit. Under an arrangement called a crop lien, a merchant would advance goods to a sharecropper in exchange for a lien, or legal claim, on the farmer's future crop. Some merchants charged exorbitant rates of interest, as much as 60 percent, on the goods they sold. At the end of the growing season, after the landlord had taken half of the farmer's crop for rent, the merchant took most of the rest. Sometimes, the farmer's debt to the merchant exceeded the income he received from his remaining half of the crop, and the farmer would have no choice but to borrow more from the merchant and begin the cycle all over again.

An experiment at first, sharecropping spread quickly and soon dominated the cotton South. Lien merchants forced tenants to plant cotton, which was easy to sell, instead of food crops. The result was excessive production of cotton and falling cotton prices, developments that cost thousands of small white farmers their land and pushed them into the great army of sharecroppers. The new sharecropping system of agriculture took shape just as the political power of Republicans in the South began to buckle under Democratic pressure.

> **REVIEW** Why was the Republican Party in the South a coalition party?

Reconstruction Collapses

By 1870, after a decade of war and reconstruction, Northerners wanted to turn to their own affairs and put "the southern problem" behind them. Increasingly, practical, business-minded men came to the forefront of the Republican Party, replacing the band of reformers and idealists who had been prominent in the 1860s. While northern commitment to defend black freedom eroded, southern commitment to white supremacy intensified. Without northern protection, southern Republicans were no match for the Democrats' economic coercion, political corruption, and bloody violence. One by one, Republican state governments fell in the South.

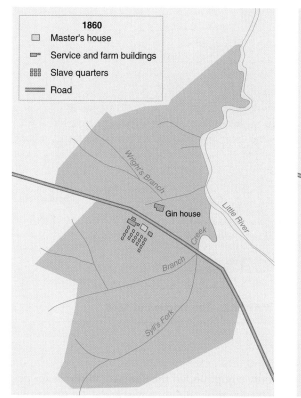

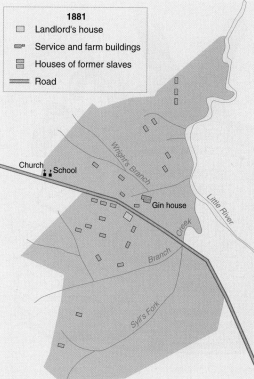

MAP 16.1   A Southern Plantation in 1860 and 1881

These maps of the Barrow plantation in Georgia illustrate some of the ways in which ex-slaves expressed their freedom. Freed men and women deserted the clustered living quarters behind the master's house, scattered over the plantation, built family cabins, and farmed rented land. The former Barrow slaves also worked together to build a school and a church.

READING THE MAP: Compare the number and size of the slave quarters in 1860 with the homes of the former slaves in 1881. How do they differ? Which buildings were prominently located along the road in 1860, and which could be found along the road in 1881?

CONNECTIONS: How might the former master feel about the new configuration of buildings on the plantation in 1881? In what ways did the new system of sharecropping replicate the old system of plantation agriculture? In what ways was it different?

FOR MORE HELP ANALYZING THIS MAP, see the map activity for this chapter in the Online Study Guide at bedfordstmartins.com/roarkcompact.

The election of 1876 both confirmed and completed the collapse of reconstruction.

Grant's Troubled Presidency

In 1868, the Republican Party's presidential nomination went to Ulysses S. Grant, the North's favorite general. Hero of the Civil War and a supporter of congressional reconstruction, Grant was the obvious choice. His Democratic opponent, Horatio Seymour of New York, ran on a platform that blasted congressional reconstruction as "a flagrant usurpation of power...unconstitu-

tional, revolutionary, and void." The Republicans answered by "waving the **bloody shirt**"—that is, they reminded voters that the Democrats were "the party of rebellion." During the campaign, the Ku Klux Klan erupted in a reign of terror, murdering hundreds of southern Republicans. Violence in the South cost Grant votes, but he gained a narrow 309,000-vote margin in the popular vote and a substantial victory (214 votes to 80) in the electoral college (Map 16.2).

Grant hoped to forge a policy that secured both sectional reconciliation and justice for blacks. But he took office at a time when a majority of

"I BEG TO REPEAT THAT THESE FRAUDS ON THE GOVERNMENT SHALL BE PROBED TO THE VERY BOTTOM."

Grant and Scandal

In this anti-Grant cartoon, Thomas Nast, the nation's most celebrated political cartoonist, shows the president falling headfirst into the barrel of fraud and corruption that tainted his administration. During Grant's eight years in the White House, many members of his administration failed him. Sometimes duped, sometimes merely loyal, Grant stubbornly defended wrongdoers, even to the point of perjuring himself to keep an aide out of jail.
Library of Congress.

FOR MORE HELP ANALYZING THIS IMAGE, see the visual activity for this chapter in the Online Study Guide at bedfordstmartins.com/roarkcompact.

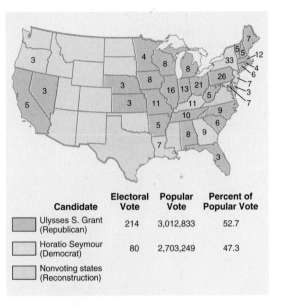

Candidate	Electoral Vote	Popular Vote	Percent of Popular Vote
Ulysses S. Grant (Republican)	214	3,012,833	52.7
Horatio Seymour (Democrat)	80	2,703,249	47.3
Nonvoting states (Reconstruction)			

MAP 16.2   The Election of 1868

white Northerners had grown weary of the "Southern Question" and were increasingly willing to let southern whites manage their own affairs. Moreover, Grant was not as good a president as he was a general. The talents he had demonstrated on the battlefield—decisiveness, clarity, and resolution—were less obvious in the White House. Able advisers might have helped, but he surrounded himself with fumbling kinfolk and old cronies from his army days. He also made a string of dubious appointments that led to a series of damaging scandals. Charges of corruption tainted his vice president, Schuyler Colfax, and brought down two of his cabinet officers. Grant's dogged loyalty to liars and cheats

only compounded the damage. While never personally implicated in any scandal, Grant was aggravatingly naive and his administration filled with rot.

In 1872 anti-Grant Republicans bolted and launched the Liberal Party. To clean up the graft and corruption, Liberals proposed ending the **spoils system**, by which victorious parties rewarded loyal workers with public office, and replacing it with a nonpartisan **civil service** commission that would oversee competitive examinations for appointment to office. Moreover, they demanded that the federal government remove its troops from the South and restore "home rule" (southern white control). Democrats liked the Liberals' southern policy and endorsed the Liberal presidential candidate, Horace Greeley, the longtime editor of the *New York Tribune*. However, the nation still felt enormous affection for the man who had saved the Union and reelected Grant with 56 percent of the popular vote.

Grant's ambitions for his administration extended beyond reconstruction, but not even foreign affairs could escape the problems of the South. The annexation of Santo Domingo in the Caribbean was Grant's greatest passion. He argued that the acquisition of this tropical land would permit the United States to expand its trade and also provide a new home for the South's blacks, who were so desperately harassed by the Klan. Aggressive foreign policy had not originated with the Grant administration.

Lincoln and Johnson's secretary of state, William H. Seward, had thwarted French efforts to set up a puppet empire under Maximilian in Mexico, and his purchase of Alaska ("Seward's Ice Box") from Russia in 1867 for only $7 million fired Grant's **imperialist** ambition. But in the end, Grant could not convince Congress to approve the treaty annexing Santo Domingo. The South preoccupied Congress and undermined Grant's initiatives.

Grant's Proposed Annexation of Santo Domingo

Northern Resolve Withers

While Grant genuinely wanted to see blacks' civil and political rights protected, he understood that most Northerners had grown weary of reconstruction. Average citizens wanted to shift their attention to other issues, especially after the nation slipped into a devastating economic depression in 1873. More than eighteen thousand businesses collapsed, leaving more than a million workers without jobs. Northern businessmen who wanted to invest in the South believed that recurrent federal intrusion was itself a major cause of instability in the region. Republican leaders began to question the wisdom of their party's alliance with the South's lower classes—its small farmers and sharecroppers. Grant's secretary of the interior, Jacob D. Cox of Ohio, proposed allying with the "thinking and influential native southerners…the intelligent, well-to-do, and controlling class."

Congress, too, wanted to leave reconstruction behind, but southern Republicans made that difficult. When the South's Republicans begged for federal protection from Klan violence, Congress enacted three laws in 1870 and 1871 that were intended to break the back of white terrorism. The severest of the three, the Ku Klux Klan Act (1871), made interference with voting rights a felony and authorized the use of the army to enforce it. Intrepid federal marshals arrested thousands of Klansmen, and the government came close to destroying the Klan but did not end terrorism against blacks. Congress also passed the Civil Rights Act of 1875, which boldly outlawed racial discrimination in transportation, public accommodations, and juries. But federal authorities never enforced the law aggressively, and segregated facilities remained the rule throughout the South.

By the early 1870s, the Republican Party had lost its principal spokesmen for African American rights to death or defeat at the polls. Others in Congress concluded that the quest for black equality was mistaken or hopelessly naive. In May 1872, Congress restored the right of officeholding to all but three hundred ex-rebels. In the opinion of many, traditional white leaders offered the best hope for honesty, order, and prosperity in the South.

Underlying the North's abandonment of reconstruction was unyielding racial prejudice. During the war, Northerners had learned to accept black freedom, but deep-seated prejudice prevented many from following freedom with equality. Even the actions they took on behalf of blacks often served partisan political advantage. Northerners generally supported Indiana senator Thomas A. Hendricks's harsh declaration that "this is a white man's Government, made by the white man for the white man."

The U.S. Supreme Court also did its part to undermine reconstruction. The Court issued a series of decisions that significantly weakened the federal government's ability to protect black Southerners under the Fourteenth and Fifteenth Amendments. In the *Slaughterhouse* cases (1873), the Court distinguished between national and state citizenship and ruled that the Fourteenth Amendment protected only those rights that stemmed from the federal government, such as voting in federal elections and interstate travel. Since the Court decided that most rights derived from the states, it sharply curtailed the federal government's authority to protect black citizens. Even more devastating, the *United States v. Cruikshank* ruling (1876) said that the reconstruction amendments gave Congress power to legislate against discrimination only by states, not by individuals. The "suppression of ordinary crime," such as assault, remained a state responsibility. The Supreme Court did not declare reconstruction unconstitutional but undermined its legal foundation.

The mood of the North found political expression in the election of 1874, when for the first time in eighteen years the Democrats gained control of the House of Representatives. As one Republican observed, the people had grown tired of the "negro question, with all its complications, and the reconstruction of Southern States, with all its interminable embroilments." Reconstruction had come apart. The people were tired of it. Grant grew increasingly unwilling to enforce it. Congress gradually abandoned it. The Supreme Court busily denied the constitutionality of significant parts of it. Rather than defend reconstruction from its southern enemies, Northerners steadily backed away from the challenge. After the early 1870s, southern blacks faced the forces of reaction largely on their own.

White Supremacy Triumphs

Republican state and local governments in the South attracted more bitterness and hatred than any other political regimes in American history. In the eyes of the majority of whites, Republican rule meant intolerable insults: Black militiamen patrolled town streets, black laborers negotiated contracts with former masters, black maids stood up to former mistresses, black voters cast ballots, and black legislators enacted laws. The northern retreat from reconstruction permitted southern Democrats to harness this white rage to politics. Taking the name "Redeemers," they promised to replace "bayonet rule" (some federal troops continued to be stationed in the South) with "home rule." They branded Republican governments a carnival of extravagance, waste, and fraud and promised that honest, thrifty Democrats would supplant the irresponsible tax-and-spend Republicans. Above all, Redeemers swore to save southern civilization from a descent into African "barbarism" and "negro rule." As one man put it, "We must render this either a white man's government, or convert the land into a Negro man's cemetery."

Southern Democrats adopted a two-pronged racial strategy to overthrow Republican governments. First, they sought to polarize the parties around color. They went about gathering all the South's white voters into the Democratic Party, leaving the Republicans to depend on blacks. The "straight-out" appeal to whites promised great advantage because whites made up a majority of the population in every southern state except Mississippi, South Carolina, and Louisiana.

To dislodge whites from the Republican Party, Democrats fanned the flames of racial prejudice. A South Carolina Democrat crowed that his party appealed to the "proud Caucasian race, whose sovereignty on earth God has proclaimed." Ostracism also proved effective. Local newspapers published the names of whites who kept company with blacks. So complete was the ostracism that one of its victims said, "No white man can live in the South in the future and act with any other than the Democratic party unless he is willing and prepared to live a life of social isolation."

Democrats also exploited the severe economic plight of small white farmers by blaming it on Republican financial policy. Government spending soared during reconstruction, and small farmers saw their tax burden skyrocket. "This is tax time," David Golightly Harris observed. "We are nearly all on our head about them. They are so high & so little money to pay with." Farmers without enough cash to pay their taxes began "selling every egg and chicken they can get." In 1871, Mississippi reported that one-seventh of the state's land—3.3 million acres—had been forfeited for nonpayment of taxes. The small farmers' economic distress had a racial dimension. Because few

"White Man's Country"
White supremacy emerged as a central tenet of the Democratic Party before the Civil War, and Democrats kept up a vicious racist attack on Republicans as long as reconstruction lasted. On this silk ribbon from the 1868 presidential election between Republican Ulysses S. Grant and his Democratic opponent, New York governor Horatio Seymour, the Democrats openly declare their racial goal. During the campaign, Democratic vice presidential nominee Francis P. Blair Jr. promised that a Seymour victory would restore "white people" to power by declaring the reconstruction governments in the South "null and void." The Democrats' promotion of white supremacy reached new levels of shrillness in the 1870s, when northern support for reconstruction began to waver.
Collection of Janice L. and David J. Frent.

freedmen succeeded in acquiring land, they rarely paid taxes. In Georgia in 1874, blacks made up 45 percent of the population but paid only 2 percent of the taxes. From the perspective of a small white farmer, Republican rule meant that he was paying more taxes and paying them to aid blacks. Democrats asked whether it was not time for hard-pressed yeomen to join the white man's party.

If racial pride, social isolation, and Republican financial policies proved insufficient to drive yeomen from the Republican Party, Democrats turned to terrorism. "Night riders" targeted white Republicans as well as blacks for murder and assassination. "A dead Radical is very harmless," South Carolina Democratic leader Martin Gary told his followers. By the 1870s, only a handful of white Republicans remained.

The second prong of Democratic strategy aimed at the complete intimidation of black voters. Violence escalated to unprecedented levels. In 1873 a clash between black militiamen and gun-toting whites killed two white men and an estimated seventy black men in Louisiana. Whites slaughtered half of the black men after they surrendered. Although the federal government indicted more than one hundred white men, local juries failed to convict anyone.

Even before adopting the all-out white supremacist tactics of the 1870s, Democrats had already taken control of the governments of Virginia, Tennessee, and North Carolina. The new campaign brought fresh gains. The Redeemers retook Georgia in 1871, Texas in 1873, and Arkansas and Alabama in 1874. Mississippi became a scene of open, unrelenting, and often savage intimidation of black voters and their few remaining white allies. As the state election approached in 1876, Governor Adelbert Ames appealed to Washington for federal troops to control the violence, only to hear from the attorney general that the "whole public are tired of these annual autumnal outbreaks in the South." Abandoned, Mississippi Republicans succumbed to the Democratic onslaught in the fall elections.

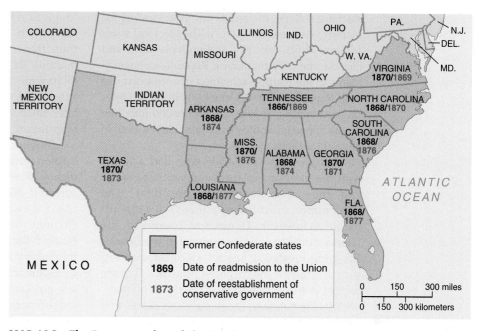

MAP 16.3 The Reconstruction of the South

Myth has it that Republican rule of the former Confederacy was not only harsh but long. In most states, however, conservative southern whites stormed back into power in a few months or a very few years. By the election of 1876, Republican governments could be found in only three states. And they soon fell.

By 1876, only three Republican state governments—in Florida, Louisiana, and South Carolina—survived (Map 16.3).

An Election and a Compromise

The centennial year of 1876 witnessed one of the most tumultuous elections in American history. Its chaos and confusion provided a fitting conclusion to the experiment known as reconstruction. The election took place in November, but not until March 2 of the following year did the nation know who would be inaugurated president on March 4.

The Democrats nominated New York's governor, Samuel J. Tilden, who immediately targeted the corruption of the Grant administration and the despotism of Republican reconstruction. The Republicans put forward Rutherford B. Hayes, governor of Ohio. Privately, Hayes considered "bayonet rule" a mistake but concluded that waving the "bloody shirt"—reminding voters that the Democrats were the "party of rebellion"—remained the Republicans' best political strategy.

On election day, Tilden tallied 4,300,000 votes to Hayes's 4,036,000. But in the all-important electoral college, Tilden fell one vote short of the majority required for victory. The electoral votes of three states—South Carolina, Louisiana, and Florida, the only remaining Republican governments in the South—remained in doubt because both Republicans and Democrats in those states claimed victory. To win, Tilden needed only one of the nineteen contested votes. Hayes had to have all of them.

Congress had to decide who had actually won the elections in the three southern states and thus who would be president. The Constitution provided no guidance for this situation. Moreover, Democrats controlled the House, and Republicans controlled the Senate. Congress created a special electoral commission to arbitrate the disputed returns. All of the commissioners voted their party affiliation, giving every state to the Republican Hayes and putting him over the top in electoral votes (Map 16.4).

Some outraged Democrats vowed to resist Hayes's victory. Rumors flew of an impending coup and renewed civil war. But the impasse was broken when negotiations behind the scenes between Hayes's lieutenants and some moderate southern Democrats resulted in an informal understanding, known as the Compromise of 1877. In exchange for a Democratic promise not to block Hayes's inauguration and to deal fairly with the freedmen, Hayes vowed to refrain from using the army to uphold the remaining Republican regimes in the South and to provide the South with substantial federal subsidies for internal improvements. Two days later, the nation celebrated Hayes's peaceful inauguration.

Stubborn Tilden supporters bemoaned the "stolen election" and damned "His Fraudulency," Rutherford B. Hayes. Old-guard radicals such as William Lloyd Garrison denounced Hayes's bargain as a "policy of compromise, of credulity, of weakness, of subserviency, of surrender." But the nation as a whole celebrated, for the country had weathered a grave crisis. The last three Republican state governments in the South fell quickly once Hayes abandoned them and withdrew the U.S. army. Reconstruction came to an end.

> **REVIEW** How did the Supreme Court undermine the Fourteenth and Fifteenth Amendments?

Conclusion: "A Revolution But Half Accomplished"

In 1865, when General Carl Schurz visited the South, he discovered "a revolution but half accomplished." White Southerners resisted the passage from slavery to free labor, from white racial despotism to equal justice, and from white political **monopoly** to biracial democracy. Ex-masters like David Golightly Harris had trouble seeing former slaves like York and Old Will as free people. The old elite wanted to get "things back as near to slavery as possible," Schurz reported, while ex-slaves and some whites were eager to exploit the revolutionary implications of defeat and emancipation.

The northern-dominated Republican Congress pushed the revolution along. Although it refused to provide for blacks' economic welfare, through constitutional amendments Congress required ex-Confederates to accept legal equality and share political power with black men. Congress was not willing to extend such power to women. Conservative southern whites fought

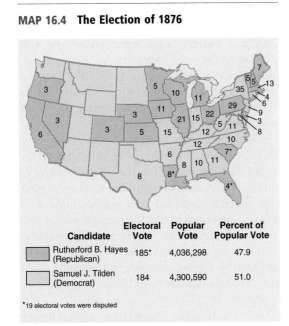

MAP 16.4 The Election of 1876

Candidate	Electoral Vote	Popular Vote	Percent of Popular Vote
Rutherford B. Hayes (Republican)	185*	4,036,298	47.9
Samuel J. Tilden (Democrat)	184	4,300,590	51.0

*19 electoral votes were disputed

ferociously to recover their power and privilege. When Democrats regained control of politics, whites used both state power and private violence to wipe out many of the gains of reconstruction, leading one observer to conclude that the North had won the war but the South had won the peace.

The Redeemer counterrevolution, however, did not mean a return to slavery. Northern victory in the Civil War ensured abolition, and ex-slaves gained the freedom to not be whipped or sold, to send their children to school, to worship in their own churches, and to work independently on their own rented farms. Even sharecropping, with all its hardships, provided more autonomy and economic welfare than bondage had. It was limited freedom, to be sure, but it was not slavery.

The Civil War and emancipation set in motion the most profound upheaval in the nation's history, and nothing whites did entirely erased its revolutionary impact. War destroyed the largest slave society in the New World. War also gave birth to a modern nation-state. For the first time sovereignty rested uncontested in the federal government, and Washington increased its role in national affairs. When the South returned to the Union, it did so as a junior partner. The victorious North now possessed the power to establish the nation's direction, and it set the nation's compass toward the expansion of industrial capitalism.

Despite massive changes, the Civil War remained only a "half accomplished" revolution. By not fulfilling the promises the nation seemed to hold out to black Americans at war's end, Reconstruction represents a tragedy of enormous proportions. The failure to protect blacks and guarantee their rights had enduring consequences. Almost a century after Reconstruction, the nation would embark on what one observer called a "second reconstruction." The solid achievements of the Thirteenth, Fourteenth, and Fifteenth Amendments to the Constitution would provide a legal foundation for the renewed commitment. It is worth remembering, though, that it was only the failure of the first reconstruction that made the modern civil rights movement necessary.

Suggestions for Further Reading

Jane Turner Censer, *The Reconstruction of White Southern Womanhood, 1865–1895* (2003). A lively investigation of the consequences of the Civil War for white southern women.

Eric Foner, *Reconstruction: America's Unfinished Revolution, 1863–1877* (1988). A masterful, comprehensive survey that makes African Americans the central actors in the Reconstruction era.

Stephen Kantrowitz, *Ben Tillman and the Reconstruction of White Supremacy* (2000). An eloquent biography of a leading white supremacist in South Carolina.

Philip N. Racine, ed., *Piedmont Farmer: The Journals of David Golightly Harris, 1855–1870* (1990). A skillfully edited journal that captures one slaveholder's confrontation with emancipation.

Brooks D. Simpson, *The Reconstruction Presidents* (1998). A thoughtful interpretation that emphasizes the differences between the policies and styles of presidents Lincoln, Johnson, Grant, and Hayes.

Michael Wayne, *The Reshaping of Plantation Society: The Natchez District, 1860–1880* (1983). A careful analysis of ex-slaves' and ex-masters' struggles to shape postwar economic and social relationships.

▶ **For more books about topics in this chapter,** see the Online Bibliography at bedfordstmartins.com/roarkcompact.

▶ **For additional firsthand accounts of this period,** see Chapter 16 in Michael Johnson, ed., *Reading the American Past,* Third Edition.

▶ **For Web sites and documents related to topics and places in this chapter,** see "HistoryLinks," "DocLinks," and "PlaceLinks" at bedfordstmartins.com/roarkcompact.

REVIEWING THE CHAPTER

Follow these steps to review and strengthen your understanding of the chapter.

STEP 1: *Study the **Key Terms** and **Timeline** to identify the significance of each item listed.*

STEP 2: *Answer the **Review Questions**, drawing on key terms and dates to support your answers.*

STEP 3: *Drawing on the Key Terms, Timeline, and Review Questions, answer the broader **Making Connections** questions.*

KEY TERMS

Who

Carl Schurz (p. 399)
Abraham Lincoln (p. 401)
Wendell Phillips (p. 401)
Henry Winter Davis (p. 401)
Benjamin Wade (p. 401)
William Tecumseh Sherman (p. 402)
John Wilkes Booth (p. 403)
Salmon P. Chase (p. 403)
Andrew Johnson (p. 403)
Susan B. Anthony (p. 408)
Elizabeth Cady Stanton (p. 408)
Charles Sumner (p. 409)
Thaddeus Stevens (p. 409)
Edwin M. Stanton (p. 410)
Ulysses S. Grant (p. 417)
Horatio Seymour (p. 417)
Schuyler Colfax (p. 418)
Horace Greeley (p. 418)
William H. Seward (p. 419)
Jacob D. Cox (p. 419)

Redeemers (p. 420)
night riders (p. 421)
Samuel J. Tilden (p. 421)
Rutherford B. Hayes (p. 421)

What

Proclamation of Amnesty and
  Reconstruction (p. 401)
Wade-Davis bill (p. 401)
Confiscation Acts (p. 401)
compulsory free labor (p. 401)
Freedmen's Bureau (p. 402)
black codes (p. 406)
apprenticeship laws (p. 406)
Civil Rights Act of 1866 (p. 407)
Fourteenth Amendment (p. 408)
American Equal Rights Association
  (p. 408)
National Union Party (p. 408)
Memphis riots (p. 408)
Military Reconstruction Act (p. 409)

black suffrage (p. 409)
Reconstruction Acts of 1867 (p. 410)
impeachment (p. 410)
Tenure of Office Act (p. 410)
Fifteenth Amendment (p. 411)
woman suffrage (p. 411)
carpetbagger (p. 412)
scalawag (p. 412)
Ku Klux Klan (p. 413)
sharecropping (p. 415)
country merchant (p. 416)
crop lien (p. 416)
bloody shirt (p. 417)
Liberal Party (p. 418)
civil service commission (p. 418)
Ku Klux Klan Act (p. 419)
Civil Rights Act of 1875 (p. 419)
Slaughterhouse cases (p. 419)
United States v. Cruikshank (p. 419)
Compromise of 1877 (p. 422)

TIMELINE

1863 • Proclamation of Amnesty and Reconstruction.

    1864 • Wade-Davis bill.

        1865 • Freedmen's Bureau established.
               • Lincoln shot, dies on April 15, succeeded by Andrew Johnson.
               • Black codes enacted.
               • Thirteenth Amendment becomes part of Constitution.

            1866 • Congress approves Fourteenth Amendment.
                   • Civil Rights Act.
                   • Equal Rights Association founded.
                   • Ku Klux Klan founded.

                1867 • Military Reconstruction Act.
                       • Tenure of Office Act.

                    1868 • Impeachment trial of President Johnson.
                         • Republican Ulysses S. Grant elected president.

                        1869 • Congress approves Fifteenth Amendment.

REVIEW QUESTIONS

1. Why did Congress object to Lincoln's wartime plan for reconstruction? (pp. 400–03)

2. How did the North respond to the passage of black codes in the southern states? (pp. 403–07)

3. Why did Johnson urge southern states to reject the Fourteenth Amendment? (pp. 408–12)

4. Why was the Republican Party in the South a coalition party? (pp. 412–16)

5. How did the Supreme Court undermine the Fourteenth and Fifteenth Amendments? (pp. 416–22)

MAKING CONNECTIONS

1. Reconstruction succeeded in advancing black civil rights but failed to secure them over the long-term. Why and how did the federal government retreat from defending African Americans' civil rights in the 1870s? In your answer, cite specific actions by Congress and the Supreme Court.

2. Why was distributing plantation land to former slaves such a controversial policy? In your answer, discuss why landownership was important to freedpeople and why Congress rejected redistribution as a general policy.

3. At the end of the Civil War, it remained to be seen exactly how emancipation would transform the South. How did emancipation change political and labor organization in the region? In your answer, discuss how ex-slaves exercised their new freedoms and how white southerners attempted to limit them.

4. The Republican Party shaped Reconstruction through its control of Congress and state legislatures in the South. How did the identification of the Republican Party with Reconstruction policy affect the party's political fortunes in the 1870s? In your answer, be sure to address developments on the federal and state levels.

> ► **FOR PRACTICE QUIZZES, A CUSTOMIZED STUDY PLAN, AND OTHER STUDY TOOLS**, see the Online Study Guide at bedfordstmartins.com/roarkcompact.

1871 • Ku Klux Klan Act.

    1872 • Liberal Party formed; calls for end of government corruption.
            • President Grant reelected.

        1873 • Economic depression sets in for remainder of decade.
                • *Slaughterhouse* cases.

            1874 • Democrats win majority in House of Representatives.

                1875 • Civil Rights Act.

                    1876 • *United States v. Cruikshank.*

                        1877 • Republican Rutherford B. Hayes elected president; Reconstruction era ends.

Documents

For additional documents see the DocLinks feature at **bedfordstmartins.com/roarkcompact**.

THE DECLARATION OF INDEPENDENCE

In Congress, July 4, 1776,

THE UNANIMOUS DECLARATION OF THE
THIRTEEN UNITED STATES OF AMERICA

When in the course of human events, it becomes necessary for one people to dissolve the political bands which have connected them with another, and to assume, among the powers of the earth, the separate and equal station to which the laws of nature and of nature's God entitle them, a decent respect to the opinions of mankind requires that they should declare the causes which impel them to the separation.

We hold these truths to be self-evident, that all men are created equal; that they are endowed by their Creator with certain unalienable rights; that among these, are life, liberty, and the pursuit of happiness. That, to secure these rights, governments are instituted among men, deriving their just powers from the consent of the governed; that, whenever any form of government becomes destructive of these ends, it is the right of the people to alter or to abolish it, and to institute a new government, laying its foundation on such principles, and organizing its powers in such form, as to them shall seem most likely to effect their safety and happiness. Prudence, indeed, will dictate that governments long established, should not be changed for light and transient causes; and, accordingly, all experience hath shown, that mankind are more disposed to suffer, while evils are sufferable, than to right themselves by abolishing the forms to which they are accustomed. But, when a long train of abuses and usurpations, pursuing invariably the same object, evinces a design to reduce them under absolute despotism, it is their right, it is their duty, to throw off such government and to provide new guards for their future security. Such has been the patient sufferance of these colonies, and such is now the necessity which constrains them to alter their former systems of government. The history of the present King of Great Britain is a history of repeated injuries and usurpations, all having, in direct object, the establishment of an absolute tyranny over these States. To prove this, let facts be submitted to a candid world:

He has refused his assent to laws the most wholesome and necessary for the public good.

He has forbidden his governors to pass laws of immediate and pressing importance, unless suspended in their operation till his assent should be obtained; and, when so suspended, he has utterly neglected to attend to them.

He has refused to pass other laws for the accommodation of large districts of people, unless those people would relinquish the right of representation in the legislature; a right inestimable to them, and formidable to tyrants only.

He has called together legislative bodies at places unusual, uncomfortable, and distant from the depository of their public records, for the sole purpose of fatiguing them into compliance with his measures.

He has dissolved representative houses repeatedly for opposing, with manly firmness, his invasions on the rights of the people.

He has refused, for a long time after such dissolutions, to cause others to be elected; whereby the legislative powers, incapable of annihilation, have returned to the people at large for their exercise; the state remaining in the mean-time exposed to all the danger of invasion from without, and convulsions within.

He has endeavoured to prevent the population of these States; for that purpose, obstructing the laws for naturalization of foreigners, refusing to pass others to encourage their migration hither, and raising the conditions of new appropriations of lands.

He has obstructed the administration of justice, by refusing his assent to laws for establishing judiciary powers.

He has made judges dependent on his will alone, for the tenure of their offices, and the amount and payment of their salaries.

He has erected a multitude of new offices, and sent hither swarms of officers to harass our people, and eat out their substance.

He has kept among us, in times of peace, standing armies, without the consent of our legislature.

He has affected to render the military independent of, and superior to, the civil power.

He has combined, with others, to subject us to a jurisdiction foreign to our Constitution, and unacknowledged by our laws; giving his assent to their acts of pretended legislation:

For quartering large bodies of armed troops among us:

For protecting them by a mock trial, from punishment, for any murders which they should commit on the inhabitants of these States:

For cutting off our trade with all parts of the world:

For imposing taxes on us without our consent:

For depriving us, in many cases, of the benefit of trial by jury:

For transporting us beyond seas to be tried for pretended offences:

For abolishing the free system of English laws in a neighbouring province, establishing therein an arbitrary government, and enlarging its boundaries, so as to render it at once an example and fit instrument for introducing the same absolute rule into these colonies:

For taking away our charters, abolishing our most valuable laws, and altering, fundamentally, the powers of our governments:

For suspending our own legislatures, and declaring themselves invested with power to legislate for us in all cases whatsoever.

He has abdicated government here, by declaring us out of his protection, and waging war against us.

He has plundered our seas, ravaged our coasts, burnt our towns, and destroyed the lives of our people.

He is, at this time, transporting large armies of foreign mercenaries to complete the works of death, desolation, and tyranny, already begun, with circumstances of cruelty and perfidy scarcely paralleled in the most barbarous ages, and totally unworthy the head of a civilized nation.

He has constrained our fellow citizens, taken captive on the high seas, to bear arms against their country, to become the executioners of their friends, and brethren, or to fall themselves by their hands.

He has excited domestic insurrections amongst us, and has endeavoured to bring on the inhabitants of our frontiers, the merciless Indian savages, whose known rule of warfare is an undistinguished destruction of all ages, sexes, and conditions.

In every stage of these oppressions, we have petitioned for redress; in the most humble terms; our repeated petitions have been answered only by repeated injury. A prince, whose character is thus marked by every act which may define a tyrant, is unfit to be the ruler of a free people.

Nor have we been wanting in attention to our British brethren. We have warned them, from time to time, of attempts made by their legislature to extend an unwarrantable jurisdiction over us. We have reminded them of the circumstances of our emigration and settlement here. We have appealed to their native justice and magnanimity, and we have conjured them, by the ties of our common kindred, to disavow these usurpations, which would inevitably interrupt our connections and correspondence. They, too, have been deaf to the voice of justice and consanguinity. We must, therefore, acquiesce in the necessity which denounces our separation, and hold them as we hold the rest of mankind, enemies in war, in peace, friends.

We, therefore, the representatives of the United States of America, in general Congress assembled, appealing to the Supreme Judge of the world for the rectitude of our intentions, do, in the name, and by authority of the good people of these colonies, solemnly publish and declare, that these united colonies are, and of right ought to be, free and independent states: that they are absolved from all allegiance to the British Crown, and that all political connection between them and the state of Great Britain is, and ought to be, totally dissolved; and that, as free and independent states, they have full power to levy war, conclude peace, contract alliances, establish commerce, and to do all other acts and things which independent states may of right do. And, for the support of this declaration, with a firm reliance on the protection of Divine Providence, we mutually pledge to each other our lives, our fortunes, and our sacred honor.

The foregoing Declaration was, by order of Congress, engrossed, and signed by the following members:

JOHN HANCOCK

New Hampshire
Josiah Bartlett
William Whipple
Matthew Thornton

Massachusetts Bay
Samuel Adams
John Adams
Robert Treat Paine
Elbridge Gerry

Rhode Island
Stephen Hopkins
William Ellery

Connecticut
Roger Sherman
Samuel Huntington
William Williams
Oliver Wolcott

New York
William Floyd
Phillip Livingston
Francis Lewis
Lewis Morris

New Jersey
Richard Stockton
John Witherspoon
Francis Hopkinson
John Hart
Abraham Clark

Pennsylvania
Robert Morris
Benjamin Rush
Benjamin Franklin
John Morton
George Clymer
James Smith
George Taylor
James Wilson
George Ross

Delaware	North Carolina	Virginia	Georgia
Caesar Rodney	William Hooper	George Wythe	Button Gwinnett
George Read	Joseph Hewes	Richard Henry Lee	Lyman Hall
Thomas M'Kean	John Penn	Thomas Jefferson	George Walton
		Benjamin Harrison	
Maryland	**South Carolina**	Thomas Nelson, Jr.	
Samuel Chase	Edward Rutledge	Francis Lightfoot Lee	
William Paca	Thomas Heyward, Jr.	Carter Braxton	
Thomas Stone	Thomas Lynch, Jr.		
Charles Carroll,	Arthur Middleton		
of Carrollton			

Resolved, That copies of the Declaration be sent to the several assemblies, conventions, and committees, or councils of safety, and to the several commanding officers of the continental troops; that it be proclaimed in each of the United States, at the head of the army.

THE CONSTITUTION OF THE UNITED STATES*

Agreed to by Philadelphia Convention, September 17, 1787. Implemented March 4, 1789.

Preamble

We the people of the United States, in order to form a more perfect union, establish justice, insure domestic tranquility, provide for the common defense, promote the general welfare, and secure the blessings of liberty to ourselves and our posterity, do ordain and establish this Constitution for the United States of America.

Article I

Section 1 All legislative powers herein granted shall be vested in a Congress of the United States, which shall consist of a Senate and a House of Representatives.

Section 2 The House of Representatives shall be composed of members chosen every second year by the people of the several States, and the electors in each State shall have the qualifications requisite for electors of the most numerous branch of the State Legislature.

No person shall be a Representative who shall not have attained to the age of twenty-five years, and been seven years a citizen of the United States, and who shall not, when elected, be an inhabitant of that State in which he shall be chosen.

Representatives and direct taxes shall be apportioned among the several States which may be included within this Union, according to their respective numbers, *which shall be determined by adding to the whole number of free persons, including those bound to service for a term of years and excluding Indians not taxed, three-fifths of all other persons.* The actual enumeration shall be made within three years after the first meeting of the Congress of the United States, and within every subsequent term of ten years, in such manner as they shall by law direct. The number of Representatives shall not exceed one for every thirty thousand, but each State shall have at least one Representative; *and until such enumeration shall be made, the State of New Hampshire shall be entitled to choose three, Massachusetts eight, Rhode Island and Providence Plantations one, Connecticut five, New York six, New Jersey four, Pennsylvania eight, Delaware one, Maryland six, Virginia ten, North Carolina five, South Carolina five, and Georgia three.*

When vacancies happen in the representation from any State, the Executive authority thereof shall issue writs of election to fill such vacancies.

The House of Representatives shall choose their Speaker and other officers; and shall have the sole power of impeachment.

Section 3 The Senate of the United States shall be composed of two Senators from each State, *chosen by the legislature thereof,* for six years; and each Senator shall have one vote.

Immediately after they shall be assembled in consequence of the first election, they shall be divided as equally as may be into three classes. The seats of the Senators of the first class shall be vacated at the expiration of the second year, of the second class at the expiration of the fourth year, and of the third class at the expiration of the sixth year, so that one-third may be chosen every second year; and if vacancies happen by resignation or otherwise, during the recess of the legislature of any State, the Executive thereof may make temporary appointments until the next meeting of the legislature, which shall then fill such vacancies.

---

* Passages no longer in effect are in italic type.

No person shall be a Senator who shall not have attained to the age of thirty years, and been nine years a citizen of the United States, and who shall not, when elected, be an inhabitant of that State for which he shall be chosen.

The Vice-President of the United States shall be President of the Senate, but shall have no vote, unless they be equally divided.

The Senate shall choose their other officers, and also a President *pro tempore,* in the absence of the Vice-President, or when he shall exercise the office of President of the United States.

The Senate shall have the sole power to try all impeachments. When sitting for that purpose, they shall be on oath or affirmation. When the President of the United States is tried, the Chief Justice shall preside: and no person shall be convicted without the concurrence of two-thirds of the members present.

Judgment in cases of impeachment shall not extend further than to removal from the office, and disqualification to hold and enjoy any office of honor, trust or profit under the United States: but the party convicted shall nevertheless be liable and subject to indictment, trial, judgment and punishment, according to law.

Section 4 The times, places and manner of holding elections for Senators and Representatives shall be prescribed in each State by the legislature thereof; but the Congress may at any time by law make or alter such regulations, except as to the places of choosing Senators.

The Congress shall assemble at least once in every year, and such meeting *shall be on the first Monday in December, unless they shall by law appoint a different day.*

Section 5 Each house shall be the judge of the elections, returns and qualifications of its own members, and a majority of each shall constitute a quorum to do business; but a smaller number may adjourn from day to day, and may be authorized to compel the attendance of absent members, in such manner, and under such penalties, as each house may provide.

Each house may determine the rules of its proceedings, punish its members for disorderly behavior, and with the concurrence of two-thirds, expel a member.

Each house shall keep a journal of its proceedings, and from time to time publish the same, excepting such parts as may in their judgment require secrecy; and the yeas and nays of the members of either house on any question shall, at the desire of one-fifth of those present, be entered on the journal.

Neither house, during the session of Congress, shall, without the consent of the other, adjourn for more than three days, nor to any other place than that in which the two houses shall be sitting.

Section 6 The Senators and Representatives shall receive a compensation for their services, to be ascertained by law and paid out of the treasury of the United States. They shall in all cases except treason, felony and breach of the peace, be privileged from arrest during their attendance at the session of their respective houses, and in going to and returning from the same; and for any speech or debate in either house, they shall not be questioned in any other place.

No Senator or Representative shall, during the time for which he was elected, be appointed to any civil office under the authority of the United States, which shall have been created, or the emoluments whereof shall have been increased, during such time; and no person holding any office under the United States shall be a member of either house during his continuance in office.

Section 7 All bills for raising revenue shall originate in the House of Representatives; but the Senate may propose or concur with amendments as on other bills.

Every bill which shall have passed the House of Representatives and the Senate, shall, before it become a law, be presented to the President of the United States; if he approve he shall sign it, but if not he shall return it with objections to that house in which it shall have originated, who shall enter the objections at large on their journal, and proceed to reconsider it. If after such reconsideration two-thirds of that house shall agree to pass the bill, it shall be sent, together with the objections, to the other house, by which it shall likewise be reconsidered, and, if approved by two-thirds of that house, it shall become a law. But in all such cases the votes of both houses shall be determined by yeas and nays, and the names of the persons voting for and against the bill shall be entered on the journal of each house respectively. If any bill shall not be returned by the President within ten days (Sundays excepted) after it shall have been presented to him, the same shall be a law, in like manner as if he had signed it, unless the Congress by their adjournment prevent its return, in which case it shall not be a law.

Every order, resolution, or vote to which the concurrence of the Senate and House of Representatives may be necessary (except on a question of adjournment) shall be presented to the President of the United States; and before the same shall take effect, shall be approved by him, or being disapproved by him, shall be repassed by two-thirds of the Senate and House of Representatives, according to the rules and limitations prescribed in the case of a bill.

Section 8 The Congress shall have power

To lay and collect taxes, duties, imposts, and excises, to pay the debts and provide for the common defense and general welfare of the United States;

but all duties, imposts and excises shall be uniform throughout the United States;

To borrow money on the credit of the United States;

To regulate commerce with foreign nations, and among the several States, and with the Indian tribes;

To establish an uniform rule of naturalization, and uniform laws on the subject of bankruptcies throughout the United States;

To coin money, regulate the value thereof, and of foreign coin, and fix the standard of weights and measures;

To provide for the punishment of counterfeiting the securities and current coin of the United States;

To establish post offices and post roads;

To promote the progress of science and useful arts by securing for limited times to authors and inventors the exclusive right to their respective writings and discoveries;

To constitute tribunals inferior to the Supreme Court;

To define and punish piracies and felonies committed on the high seas and offences against the law of nations;

To declare war, grant letters of marque and reprisal, and make rules concerning captures on land and water;

To raise and support armies, but no appropriation of money to that use shall be for a longer term than two years;

To provide and maintain a navy;

To make rules for the government and regulation of the land and naval forces;

To provide for calling forth the militia to execute the laws of the Union, suppress insurrections and repel invasions;

To provide for organizing, arming, and disciplining the militia, and for governing such part of them as may be employed in the service of the United States, reserving to the States respectively the appointment of the officers, and the authority of training the militia according to the discipline prescribed by Congress;

To exercise exclusive legislation in all cases whatsoever, over such district (not exceeding ten miles square) as may, by cession of particular States, and the acceptance of Congress, become the seat of the government of the United States, and to exercise like authority over all places purchased by the consent of the legislature of the State, in which the same shall be, for erection of forts, magazines, arsenals, dock-yards, and other needful buildings; — and

To make all laws which shall be necessary and proper for carrying into execution the foregoing powers, and all other powers vested by this Constitution in the government of the United States, or in any department or officer thereof.

Section 9 *The migration or importation of such persons as any of the States now existing shall think proper to admit shall not be prohibited by the Congress prior to the year one thousand eight hundred and eight; but a tax or duty may be imposed on such importation, not exceeding ten dollars for each person.*

The privilege of the writ of habeas corpus shall not be suspended, unless when in cases of rebellion or invasion the public safety may require it.

No bill of attainder or ex post facto law shall be passed.

No capitation, or other direct, tax shall be laid, unless in proportion to the census or enumeration herein before directed to be taken.

No tax or duty shall be laid on articles exported from any State.

No preference shall be given by any regulation of commerce or revenue to the ports of one State over those of another; nor shall vessels bound to, or from, one State be obliged to enter, clear, or pay duties in another.

No money shall be drawn from the treasury, but in consequence of appropriations made by law; and a regular statement and account of the receipts and expenditures of all public money shall be published from time to time.

No title of nobility shall be granted by the United States: and no person holding any office of profit or trust under them, shall, without the consent of the Congress, accept of any present, emolument, office, or title, of any kind whatever, from any king, prince, or foreign state.

Section 10 No State shall enter into any treaty, alliance, or confederation; grant letters of marque and reprisal; coin money; emit bills of credit; make anything but gold and silver coin a tender in payment of debts; pass any bill of attainder, ex post facto law, or law impairing the obligation of contracts, or grant any title of nobility.

No State shall, without the consent of Congress, lay any imposts or duties on imports or exports, except what may be absolutely necessary for executing its inspection laws: and the net produce of all duties and imposts, laid by any State on imports or exports, shall be for the use of the treasury of the United States; and all such laws shall be subject to the revision and control of the Congress.

No State shall, without the consent of Congress, lay any duty of tonnage, keep troops, or ships of war in time of peace, enter into any agreement or compact with another State, or with a foreign power, or engage in war, unless actually invaded, or in such imminent danger as will not admit of delay.

Article II

Section 1 The executive power shall be vested in a President of the United States of America. He shall hold his office during the term of four years, and, together with the Vice-President, chosen for the same term, be elected as follows:

Each State shall appoint, in such manner as the legislature thereof may direct, a number of electors, equal to the whole number of Senators and Representatives to which the State may be entitled in the Congress; but no Senator or Representative, or person holding an office of trust or profit under the United States, shall be appointed an elector.

The electors shall meet in their respective States, and vote by ballot for two persons, of whom one at least shall not be an inhabitant of the same State with themselves. And they shall make a list of all the persons voted for, and of the number of votes for each; which list they shall sign and certify, and transmit sealed to the seat of government of the United States, directed to the President of the Senate. The President of the Senate shall, in the presence of the Senate and House of Representatives, open all the certificates, and the votes shall then be counted. The person having the greatest number of votes shall be the President, if such number be a majority of the whole number of electors appointed; and if there be more than one who have such majority, and have an equal number of votes, then the House of Representatives shall immediately choose by ballot one of them for President; and if no person have a majority, then from the five highest on the list said house shall in like manner choose the President. But in choosing the President the votes shall be taken by States, the representation from each State having one vote; a quorum for this purpose shall consist of a member or members from two-thirds of the States, and a majority of all the States shall be necessary to a choice. In every case, after the choice of the President, the person having the greatest number of votes of the electors shall be the Vice-President. But if there should remain two or more who have equal votes, the Senate shall choose from them by ballot the Vice-President.

The Congress may determine the time of choosing the electors, and the day on which they shall give their votes; which day shall be the same throughout the United States.

No person except a natural-born citizen, *or a citizen of the United States at the time of the adoption of this Constitution,* shall be eligible to the office of President; neither shall any person be eligible to that office who shall not have attained to the age of thirty-five years, and been fourteen years a resident within the United States.

In cases of the removal of the President from office or of his death, resignation, or inability to discharge the powers and duties of the said office, the same shall devolve on the Vice-President, and the Congress may by law provide for the case of removal, death, resignation, or inability, both of the President and Vice-President, declaring what officer shall then act as President, and such officer shall act accordingly, until the disability be removed, or a President shall be elected.

The President shall, at stated times, receive for his services a compensation, which shall neither be increased nor diminished during the period for which he shall have been elected, and he shall not receive within that period any other emolument from the United States, or any of them.

Before he enter on the execution of his office, he shall take the following oath or affirmation: — "I do solemnly swear (or affirm) that I will faithfully execute the office of the President of the United States, and will to the best of my ability preserve, protect and defend the Constitution of the United States."

Section 2 The President shall be commander in chief of the army and navy of the United States, and of the militia of the several States, when called into the actual service of the United States; he may require the opinion, in writing, of the principal officer in each of the executive departments, upon any subject relating to the duties of their respective offices, and he shall have power to grant reprieves and pardons for offences against the United States, except in cases of impeachment.

He shall have power, by and with the advice and consent of the Senate, to make treaties, provided two-thirds of the Senators present concur; and he shall nominate, and by and with the advice and consent of the Senate, shall appoint ambassadors, other public ministers and consuls, judges of the Supreme Court, and all other officers of the United States, whose appointments are not herein otherwise provided for, and which shall be established by law: but Congress may by law vest the appointment of such inferior officers, as they think proper, in the President alone, in the courts of law, or in the heads of departments.

The President shall have power to fill up all vacancies that may happen during the recess of the Senate, by granting commissions which shall expire at the end of their next session.

Section 3 He shall from time to time give to the Congress information of the state of the Union, and recommend to their consideration such measures as he shall judge necessary and expedient; he may, on extraordinary occasions, convene both houses, or either of them, and in case of disagreement between them, with respect to the time of adjournment, he may adjourn them to such time as he shall think proper; he shall receive ambassadors and other public ministers; he shall take care that the laws be faithfully executed, and shall commission all the officers of the United States.

Section 4 The President, Vice-President and all civil officers of the United States shall be removed from office on impeachment for, and on conviction of, treason, bribery, or other high crimes and misdemeanors.

Article III

Section 1 The judicial power of the United States shall be vested in one Supreme Court, and in such

THE CONSTITUTION OF THE UNITED STATES

inferior courts as the Congress may from time to time ordain and establish. The judges, both of the Supreme and inferior courts, shall hold their offices during good behavior, and shall, at stated times, receive for their services a compensation which shall not be diminished during their continuance in office.

Section 2 The judicial power shall extend to all cases, in law and equity, arising under this Constitution, the laws of the United States, and treaties made, or which shall be made, under their authority; — to all cases affecting ambassadors, other public ministers and consuls; — to all cases of admiralty and maritime jurisdiction; — to controversies to which the United States shall be a party; — to controversies between two or more States; — *between a State and citizens of another State;* — between citizens of different States; — between citizens of the same State claiming lands under grants of different States, and between a State, or the citizens thereof, and foreign states, citizens or subjects.

In all cases affecting ambassadors, other public ministers and consuls, and those in which a State shall be party, the Supreme Court shall have original jurisdiction. In all the other cases before mentioned, the Supreme Court shall have appellate jurisdiction, both as to law and fact, with such exceptions, and under such regulations, as the Congress shall make.

The trial of all crimes, except in cases of impeachment, shall be by jury; and such trial shall be held in the State where said crimes shall have been committed; but when not committed within any State, the trial shall be at such place or places as the Congress may by Law have directed.

Section 3 Treason against the United States shall consist only in levying war against them, or in adhering to their enemies, giving them aid and comfort. No person shall be convicted of treason unless on the testimony of two witnesses to the same overt act, or on confession in open court.

The Congress shall have power to declare the punishment of treason, but no attainder of treason shall work corruption of blood, or forfeiture except during the life of the person attainted.

Article IV

Section 1 Full faith and credit shall be given in each State to the public acts, records, and judicial proceedings of every other State. And the Congress may by general laws prescribe the manner in which such acts, records, and proceedings shall be proved, and the effect thereof.

Section 2 The citizens of each State shall be entitled to all privileges and immunities of citizens in the several States.

A person charged in any State with treason, felony, or other crime, who shall flee from justice, and be found in another State, shall on demand of the executive authority of the State from which he fled, be delivered up, to be removed to the State having jurisdiction of the crime.

No Person held to service or labor in one State, under the laws thereof, escaping into another, shall, in consequence of any law or regulation therein, be discharged from such service or labor, but shall be delivered up on claim of the party to whom such service or labor may be due.

Section 3 New States may be admitted by the Congress into this Union; but no new State shall be formed or erected within the jurisdiction of any other State; nor any State be formed by the junction of two or more States, or parts of States, without the consent of the legislatures of the States concerned as well as of the Congress.

The Congress shall have power to dispose of and make all needful rules and regulations respecting the territory or other property belonging to the United States; and nothing in this Constitution shall be so construed as to prejudice any claims of the United States, or of any particular State.

Section 4 The United States shall guarantee to every State in this Union a republican form of government, and shall protect each of them against invasion; and on application of the legislature, or of the executive (when the legislature cannot be convened), against domestic violence.

Article V

The Congress, whenever two-thirds of both houses shall deem it necessary, shall propose amendments to this Constitution, or, on the application of the legislatures of two-thirds of the several States, shall call a convention for proposing amendments, which, in either case, shall be valid to all intents and purposes, as part of this Constitution, when ratified by the legislatures of three-fourths of the several States, or by conventions in three-fourths thereof, as the one or the other mode of ratification may be proposed by the Congress; provided *that no amendments which may be made prior to the year one thousand eight hundred and eight shall in any manner affect the first and fourth clauses in the ninth section of the first article;* and that no State, without its consent, shall be deprived of its equal suffrage in the Senate.

Article VI

All debts contracted and engagements entered into, before the adoption of this Constitution, shall be as valid against the United States under this Constitution, as under the Confederation.

This Constitution, and the laws of the United States which shall be made in pursuance thereof; and all treaties made, or which shall be made, under the authority of the United States, shall be the supreme law of the land; and the judges in every State shall be bound thereby, anything in the Constitution or laws of any State to the contrary notwithstanding.

The Senators and Representatives before mentioned, and the members of the several State legislatures, and all executive and judicial officers, both of the United States and of the several States, shall be bound by oath or affirmation to support this Constitution; but no religious test shall ever be required as a qualification to any office or public trust under the United States.

GEORGE WASHINGTON
PRESIDENT AND DEPUTY FROM VIRGINIA

Article VII

The ratification of the conventions of nine States shall be sufficient for the establishment of this Constitution between the States so ratifying the same.

Done in convention by the unanimous consent of the States present, the seventeenth day of September in the year of our Lord one thousand seven hundred and eighty-seven and of the Independence of the United States of America the twelfth. In witness whereof we have hereunto subscribed our names.

New Hampshire	**New Jersey**	**Delaware**	**North Carolina**
John Langdon	William Livingston	George Read	William Blount
Nicholas Gilman	David Brearley	Gunning Bedford, Jr.	Richard Dobbs Spaight
	William Paterson	John Dickinson	Hugh Williamson
Massachusetts	Jonathan Dayton	Richard Bassett	
Nathaniel Gorham		Jacob Broom	**South Carolina**
Rufus King			John Rutledge
	Pennsylvania	**Maryland**	Charles Cotesworth
Connecticut	Benjamin Franklin	James McHenry	Pinckney
William Samuel	Thomas Mifflin	Daniel of St.	Charles Pinckney
Johnson	Robert Morris	Thomas Jenifer	Pierce Butler
Roger Sherman	George Clymer	Daniel Carroll	
	Thomas FitzSimons		
	Jared Ingersoll	**Virginia**	**Georgia**
New York	James Wilson	John Blair	William Few
Alexander Hamilton	Gouverneur Morris	James Madison, Jr.	Abraham Baldwin

AMENDMENTS TO THE CONSTITUTION WITH ANNOTATIONS
(including the six unratified amendments)

IN THEIR EFFORT TO GAIN Antifederalists' support for the Constitution, Federalists frequently pointed to the inclusion of Article 5, which provides an orderly method of amending the Constitution. In contrast, the Articles of Confederation, which were universally recognized as seriously flawed, offered no means of amendment. For their part, Antifederalists argued that the amendment process was so "intricate" that one might as easily roll "sixes an hundred times in succession" as change the Constitution.

The system for amendment laid out in the Constitution requires that two-thirds of both houses of Congress agree to a proposed amendment, which must then be ratified by three-quarters of the legislatures of the states. Alternatively, an amendment may be proposed by a convention called by the legislatures of two-thirds of the states. Since 1789, members of Congress have proposed thousands of amendments. Besides the seventeen amendments added since 1789, only the six "unratified" ones included here were approved by two-thirds of both houses and sent to the states for ratification.

Among the many amendments that never made it out of Congress have been proposals to declare dueling, divorce, and interracial marriage unconstitutional as well as proposals to establish a national university, to acknowledge the sovereignty of Jesus Christ, and to prohibit any person from possessing wealth in excess of $10 million.*

_____

* Richard B. Bernstein, *Amending America* (New York: Times Books, 1993), 177–81.

Among the issues facing Americans today that might lead to constitutional amendment are efforts to balance the federal budget, to limit the number of terms elected officials may serve, to limit access to or prohibit abortion, to establish English as the official language of the United States, and to prohibit flag burning. None of these proposed amendments has yet garnered enough support in Congress to be sent to the states for ratification.

Although the first ten amendments to the Constitution are commonly known as the Bill of Rights, only Amendments 1–8 actually provide guarantees of individual rights. Amendments 9 and 10 deal with the structure of power within the constitutional system. The Bill of Rights was promised to appease Antifederalists who refused to ratify the Constitution without guarantees of individual liberties and limitations to federal power. After studying more than two hundred amendments recommended by the ratifying conventions of the states, Federalist James Madison presented a list of seventeen to Congress, which used Madison's list as the foundation for the twelve amendments that were sent to the states for ratification. Ten of the twelve were adopted in 1791. The first on the list of twelve, known as the Reapportionment Amendment, was never adopted (see page A-11). The second proposed amendment was adopted in 1992 as Amendment 27 (see page A-20).

Amendment I

Congress shall make no law respecting an establishment of religion, or prohibiting the free exercise thereof; or abridging the freedom of speech, or of the press; or the right of the people peaceably to assemble, and to petition the government for a redress of grievances.

♦♦♦

The First Amendment is a potent symbol for many Americans. Most are well aware of their rights to free speech, freedom of the press, and freedom of religion and their rights to assemble and to petition, even if they cannot cite the exact words of this amendment.

The First Amendment guarantee of freedom of religion has two clauses: the "free exercise clause," which allows individuals to practice or not practice any religion, and the "establishment clause," which prevents the federal government from discriminating against or favoring any particular religion. This clause was designed to create what Thomas Jefferson referred to as "a wall of separation between church and state." In the 1960s, the Supreme Court ruled that the First Amendment prohibits prayer (see Engel v. Vitale, *online) and Bible reading in public schools.*

Although the rights to free speech and freedom of the press are established in the First Amendment, it was not until the twentieth century that the Supreme Court began to explore the full meaning of these guarantees. In 1919, the Court ruled in Schenck v. United States *(online) that the government could suppress free expression only where it could cite a "clear and present danger." In a decision that continues to raise controversies, the Court ruled in 1990, in* Texas v. Johnson, *that flag burning is a form of symbolic speech protected by the First Amendment.*

Amendment II

A well-regulated militia being necessary to the security of a free State, the right of the people to keep and bear arms shall not be infringed.

♦♦♦

Fear of a standing army under the control of a hostile government made the Second Amendment an important part of the Bill of Rights. Advocates of gun ownership claim that the amendment prevents the government from regulating firearms. Proponents of gun control argue that the amendment is designed only to protect the right of the states to maintain militia units.

In 1939, the Supreme Court ruled in United States v. Miller *that the Second Amendment did not protect the right of an individual to own a sawed-off shotgun, which it argued was not ordinary militia equipment. Since then, the Supreme Court has refused to hear Second Amendment cases, while lower courts have upheld firearms regulations. Several justices currently on the bench seem to favor a narrow interpretation of the Second Amendment, which would allow gun control legislation. The controversy over the impact of the Second Amendment on gun owners and gun control legislation will certainly continue.*

Amendment III

No soldier shall, in time of peace, be quartered in any house without the consent of the owner, nor in time of war, but in a manner to be prescribed by law.

♦♦♦

The Third Amendment was extremely important to the framers of the Constitution, but today it is nearly forgotten. American colonists were especially outraged that they were forced to quarter British troops in the years before and during the American Revolution. The philosophy of the Third Amendment has been viewed by some justices and scholars as the foundation of the modern constitutional right to privacy. One example of this can be found in Justice William O. Douglas's opinion in Griswold v. Connecticut *(online).*

Amendment IV

The right of the people to be secure in their persons, houses, papers, and effects, against unreasonable searches and seizures, shall not be violated, and no warrants shall issue but upon probable cause, supported by oath or affirmation, and particularly describing the place to be searched, and the persons or things to be seized.

◆ ◆ ◆

In the years before the Revolution, the houses, barns, stores, and warehouses of American colonists were ransacked by British authorities under "writs of assistance" or general warrants. The British, thus empowered, searched for seditious material or smuggled goods that could then be used as evidence against colonists who were charged with a crime only after the items were found.

The first part of the Fourth Amendment protects citizens from "unreasonable" searches and seizures. The Supreme Court has interpreted this protection as well as the words search *and* seizure *in different ways at different times. At one time, the Court did not recognize electronic eavesdropping as a form of search and seizure, though it does today. At times, an "unreasonable" search has been almost any search carried out without a warrant, but in the two decades before 1969, the Court sometimes sanctioned warrantless searches that it considered reasonable based on "the total atmosphere of the case."*

The second part of the Fourth Amendment defines the procedure for issuing a search warrant and states the requirement of "probable cause," which is generally viewed as evidence indicating that a suspect has committed an offense.

The Fourth Amendment has been controversial because the Court has sometimes excluded evidence that has been seized in violation of constitutional standards. The justification is that excluding such evidence deters violations of the amendment, but doing so may allow a guilty person to escape punishment.

Amendment V

No person shall be held to answer for a capital, or otherwise infamous crime, unless on a presentment or indictment of a grand jury, except in cases arising in the land or naval forces, or in the militia, when in actual service in time of war or public danger; nor shall any person be subject for the same offence to be twice put in jeopardy of life or limb; nor shall be compelled in any criminal case to be a witness against himself, nor be deprived of life, liberty, or property, without due process of law; nor shall private property be taken for public use without just compensation.

◆ ◆ ◆

The Fifth Amendment protects people against government authority in the prosecution of criminal offenses. It prohibits the state, first, from charging a person with a serious crime without a grand jury hearing to decide whether there is sufficient evidence to support the charge and, second, from charging a person with the same crime twice. The best-known aspect of

the Fifth Amendment is that it prevents a person from being "compelled ... to be a witness against himself." The last clause, the "takings clause," limits the power of the government to seize property.

Although invoking the Fifth Amendment is popularly viewed as a confession of guilt, a person may be innocent yet still fear prosecution. For example, during the Red-baiting era of the late 1940s and 1950s, many people who had participated in legal activities that were associated with the Communist Party claimed the Fifth Amendment privilege rather than testify before the House Un-American Activities Committee because the mood of the times cast those activities in a negative light. Since "taking the Fifth" was viewed as an admission of guilt, those people often lost their jobs or became unemployable. (See chapter 26.) Nonetheless, the right to protect oneself against self-incrimination plays an important role in guarding against the collective power of the state.

Amendment VI

In all criminal prosecutions, the accused shall enjoy the right to a speedy and public trial, by an impartial jury of the State and district wherein the crime shall have been committed, which district shall have been previously ascertained by law, and to be informed of the nature and cause of the accusation; to be confronted with the witnesses against him; to have compulsory process for obtaining witnesses in his favor, and to have the assistance of counsel for his defence.

◆ ◆ ◆

The original Constitution put few limits on the government's power to investigate, prosecute, and punish crime. This process was of great concern to the early Americans, however, and of the twenty-eight rights specified in the first eight amendments, fifteen have to do with it. Seven rights are specified in the Sixth Amendment. These include the right to a speedy trial, a public trial, a jury trial, a notice of accusation, confrontation by opposing witnesses, testimony by favorable witnesses, and the assistance of counsel.

Although this amendment originally guaranteed these rights only in cases involving the federal government, the adoption of the Fourteenth Amendment began a process of applying the protections of the Bill of Rights to the states through court cases such as Gideon v. Wainwright *(online).*

Amendment VII

In suits at common law, where the value in controversy shall exceed twenty dollars, the right of trial by jury shall be preserved, and no fact tried by a jury shall be otherwise reexamined in any court of the United States, than according to the rules of the common law.

◆ ◆ ◆

This amendment guarantees people the same right to a trial by jury as was guaranteed by English common law in 1791. Under common law, in civil trials (those involving money damages) the role of the judge was to settle questions of law and that of the jury was to settle questions of fact. The amendment does not specify the size of the jury or its role in a trial, however. The Supreme Court has generally held that those issues be determined by English common law of 1791, which stated that a jury consists of twelve people, that a trial must be conducted before a judge who instructs the jury on the law and advises it on facts, and that a verdict must be unanimous.

Amendment VIII

Excessive bail shall not be required, nor excessive fines imposed, nor cruel and unusual punishments inflicted.

♦ ♦ ♦

The language used to guarantee the three rights in this amendment was inspired by the English Bill of Rights of 1689. The Supreme Court has not had a lot to say about "excessive fines." In recent years it has agreed that despite the provision against "excessive bail," persons who are believed to be dangerous to others can be held without bail even before they have been convicted.

Although opponents of the death penalty have not succeeded in using the Eighth Amendment to achieve the end of capital punishment, the clause regarding "cruel and unusual punishments" has been used to prohibit capital punishment in certain cases (see Furman v. Georgia, *online) and to require improved conditions in prisons.*

Amendment IX

The enumeration in the Constitution, of certain rights, shall not be construed to deny or disparage others retained by the people.

♦ ♦ ♦

Some Federalists feared that inclusion of the Bill of Rights in the Constitution would allow later generations of interpreters to claim that the people had surrendered any rights not specifically enumerated there. To guard against this, Madison added language that became the Ninth Amendment. Interest in this heretofore largely ignored amendment revived in 1965 when it was used in a concurring opinion in Griswold v. Connecticut *(online). While Justice William O. Douglas called on the Third Amendment to support the right to privacy in deciding that case, Justice Arthur Goldberg, in the concurring opinion, argued that the right to privacy regarding contraception was an unenumerated right that was protected by the Ninth Amendment.*

In 1980, the Court ruled that the right of the press to attend a public trial was protected by the Ninth

Amendment. While some scholars argue that modern judges cannot identify the unenumerated rights that the framers were trying to protect, others argue that the Ninth Amendment should be read as providing a constitutional "presumption of liberty" that allows people to act in any way that does not violate the rights of others.

Amendment X

The powers not delegated to the United States by the Constitution, nor prohibited by it to the States, are reserved to the States respectively, or to the people.

♦ ♦ ♦

The Antifederalists were especially eager to see a "reserved powers clause" explicitly guaranteeing the states control over their internal affairs. Not surprisingly, the Tenth Amendment has been a frequent battleground in the struggle over states' rights and federal supremacy. Prior to the Civil War, the Democratic Republican Party and Jacksonian Democrats invoked the Tenth Amendment to prohibit the federal government from making decisions about whether people in individual states could own slaves. The Tenth Amendment was virtually suspended during Reconstruction following the Civil War. In 1883, however, the Supreme Court declared the Civil Rights Act of 1875 unconstitutional on the grounds that it violated the Tenth Amendment. Business interests also called on the amendment to block efforts at federal regulation.

The Court was inconsistent over the next several decades as it attempted to resolve the tension between the restrictions of the Tenth Amendment and the powers the Constitution granted to Congress to regulate interstate commerce and levy taxes. The Court upheld the Pure Food and Drug Act (1906), the Meat Inspection Acts (1906 and 1907), and the White Slave Traffic Act (1910), all of which affected the states, but struck down an act prohibiting interstate shipment of goods produced through child labor. Between 1934 and 1935, a number of New Deal programs created by Franklin D. Roosevelt were declared unconstitutional on the grounds that they violated the Tenth Amendment. (See chapter 24.) As Roosevelt appointees changed the composition of the Court, the Tenth Amendment was declared to have no substantive meaning. Generally, the amendment is held to protect the rights of states to regulate internal matters such as local government, education, commerce, labor, and business, as well as matters involving families such as marriage, divorce, and inheritance within the state.

Unratified Amendment

Reapportionment Amendment (proposed by Congress September 25, 1789, along with the Bill of Rights)

After the first enumeration required by the first article of the Constitution, there shall be one Representative for every thirty thousand, until the number shall amount to one hundred, after which the proportion shall be so regulated by Congress, that there shall be not less than one hundred Representatives, nor less than one Representative for every forty thousand persons, until the number of Representatives shall amount to two hundred; after which the proportion shall be so regulated by Congress, that there shall not be less than two hundred Representatives, nor more than one Representative for every fifty thousand persons.

◆ ◆ ◆

If the Reapportionment Amendment had passed and remained in effect, the House of Representatives today would have more than 5,000 members rather than 435.

Amendment XI
[Adopted 1798]

The judicial power of the United States shall not be construed to extend to any suit in law or equity, commenced or prosecuted against one of the United States by citizens of another State, or by citizens or subjects of any foreign state.

◆ ◆ ◆

In 1793, the Supreme Court ruled in favor of Alexander Chisholm, executor of the estate of a deceased South Carolina merchant. Chisholm was suing the state of Georgia because the merchant had never been paid for provisions he had supplied during the Revolution. Many regarded this Court decision as an error that violated the intent of the Constitution.

Antifederalists had long feared a federal court system with the power to overrule a state court. When the Constitution was being drafted, Federalists had assured worried Antifederalists that section 2 of Article 3, which allows federal courts to hear cases "between a State and citizens of another State," did not mean that the federal courts were authorized to hear suits against a state by citizens of another state or a foreign country. Antifederalists and many other Americans feared a powerful federal court system because they worried that it would become like the British courts of this period, which were accountable only to the monarch. Furthermore, Chisholm v. Georgia *prompted a series of suits against state governments by creditors and suppliers who had made loans during the war.*

In addition, state legislators and Congress feared that the shaky economies of the new states, as well as the country as a whole, would be destroyed, especially if loyalists who had fled to other countries sought reimbursement for land and property that had been seized. The day after the Supreme Court announced its decision, a resolution proposing the Eleventh Amendment, which overturned the decision in Chisholm v. Georgia, *was introduced in the U.S. Senate.*

Amendment XII
[Adopted 1804]

The electors shall meet in their respective States, and vote by ballot for President and Vice-President, one of whom, at least, shall not be an inhabitant of the same State with themselves; they shall name in their ballots the person voted for as President, and in distinct ballots the person voted for as Vice-President, and they shall make distinct lists of all persons voted for as President, and of all persons voted for as Vice-President, and of the number of votes for each, which lists they shall sign and certify, and transmit sealed to the seat of government of the United States, directed to the President of the Senate; — the President of the Senate shall, in the presence of the Senate and House of Representatives, open all the certificates and the votes shall then be counted; — the person having the greatest number of votes for President shall be the President, if such number be a majority of the whole number of electors appointed; and if no person have such majority, then from the persons having the highest numbers not exceeding three on the list of those voted for as President, the House of Representatives shall choose immediately, by ballot, the President. But in choosing the President, the votes shall be taken by States, the representation from each State having one vote; a quorum for this purpose shall consist of a member or members from two-thirds of the States, and a majority of all the States shall be necessary to a choice. And if the House of Representatives shall not choose a President whenever the right of choice shall devolve upon them, before *the fourth day of March* next following, then the Vice-President shall act as President, as in the case of the death or other constitutional disability of the President.

The person having the greatest number of votes as Vice-President shall be the Vice-President, if such number be a majority of the whole number of electors appointed; and if no person have a majority, then from the two highest numbers on the list the Senate shall choose the Vice-President; a quorum for the purpose shall consist of two-thirds of the whole number of Senators, and a majority of the whole number shall be necessary to a choice. But no person constitutionally ineligible to the office of President shall be eligible to that of Vice-President of the United States.

◆ ◆ ◆

The framers of the Constitution disliked political parties and assumed that none would ever form. Under the original system, electors chosen by the states would each vote for two candidates. The candidate who won the most votes would become president, while the person who won the second-highest number of votes would become vice president. Rivalries between Federalists and Antifederalists led to the formation of political parties, however, even before George Washington had left office. Though Washington was elected unanimously in 1789 and 1792, the elections of 1796 and 1800 were procedural disasters because of party maneuvering (see chapters 9 and 10). In 1796, Federalist John Adams was chosen as president, and his great rival, the Antifederalist Thomas Jefferson (whose party was called the Republican Party), became his vice president. In 1800, all the electors cast their two votes as one of two party blocs. Jefferson and his fellow Republican nominee, Aaron Burr, were tied with 73 votes each. The contest went to the House of Representatives, which finally elected Jefferson after 36 ballots. The Twelfth Amendment prevents these problems by requiring electors to vote separately for the president and vice president.

Unratified Amendment

Titles of Nobility Amendment (proposed by Congress May 1, 1810)

If any citizen of the United States shall accept, claim, receive or retain any title of nobility or honor or shall, without the consent of Congress, accept and retain any present, pension, office or emolument of any kind whatever, from any emperor, king, prince or foreign power, such person shall cease to be a citizen of the United States, and shall be incapable of holding any office of trust or profit under them or either of them.

♦ ♦ ♦

This amendment would have extended Article 1, section 9, clause 8 of the Constitution, which prevents the awarding of titles by the United States and the acceptance of such awards from foreign powers without congressional consent. Historians speculate that general nervousness about the power of the emperor Napoleon, who was at that time extending France's empire throughout Europe, may have prompted the proposal. Though it fell one vote short of ratification, Congress and the American people thought the proposal had been ratified and it was included in many nineteenth-century editions of the Constitution.

The Civil War and Reconstruction Amendments (Thirteenth, Fourteenth, and Fifteenth Amendments)

In the four months between the election of Abraham Lincoln and his inauguration, more than 200 proposed constitutional amendments were presented to Congress as part of a desperate attempt to hold the rapidly dissolving Union together. Most of these were efforts to appease the southern states by protecting the right to own slaves or by disfranchising African Americans through constitutional amendment. None were able to win the votes required from Congress to send them to the states. The relatively innocuous Corwin Amendment seemed to be the only hope for preserving the Union by amending the Constitution.

The northern victors in the Civil War tried to restructure the Constitution just as the war had restructured the nation. Yet they were often divided in their goals. Some wanted to end slavery; others hoped for social and economic equality regardless of race; others hoped that extending the power of the ballot box to former slaves would help create a new political order. The debates over the Thirteenth, Fourteenth, and Fifteenth Amendments were bitter. Few of those who fought for these changes were satisfied with the amendments themselves; fewer still were satisfied with their interpretation. Although the amendments put an end to the legal status of slavery, it took nearly a hundred years after the amendments' passage before most of the descendants of former slaves could begin to experience the economic, social, and political equality the amendments had been intended to provide.

Unratified Amendment

Corwin Amendment (proposed by Congress March 2, 1861)

No amendment shall be made to the Constitution which will authorize or give to Congress the power to abolish or interfere, within any State, with the domestic institutions thereof, including that of persons held to labor or service by the laws of said State.

♦ ♦ ♦

Following the election of Abraham Lincoln, Congress scrambled to try to prevent the secession of the slaveholding states. House member Thomas Corwin of Ohio proposed the "unamendable" amendment in the hope that by protecting slavery where it existed, Congress would keep the southern states in the Union. Lincoln indicated his support for the proposed amendment in his first inaugural address. Only Ohio and Maryland ratified the Corwin Amendment before it was forgotten.

Amendment XIII

[Adopted 1865]

Section 1   Neither slavery nor involuntary servitude, except as a punishment for crime whereof the party shall have been duly convicted, shall exist within the United States, or any place subject to their jurisdiction.

Section 2   Congress shall have power to enforce this article by appropriate legislation.

♦ ♦ ♦

Although President Lincoln had abolished slavery in the Confederacy with the Emancipation Proclamation of 1863, abolitionists wanted to rid the entire country of slavery. The Thirteenth Amendment did this in a clear and straightforward manner. In February 1865, when the proposal was approved by the House, the gallery of the House was newly opened to black Americans who had a chance at last to see their government at work. Passage of the proposal was greeted by wild cheers from the gallery as well as tears on the House floor, where congressional representatives openly embraced one another.

The problem of ratification remained, however. The Union position was that the Confederate states were part of the country of thirty-six states. Therefore, twenty-seven states were needed to ratify the amendment. When Kentucky and Delaware rejected it, backers realized that without approval from at least four former Confederate states, the amendment would fail. Lincoln's successor, President Andrew Johnson, made ratification of the Thirteenth Amendment a condition for southern states to rejoin the Union. Under those terms, all the former Confederate states except Mississippi accepted the Thirteenth Amendment, and by the end of 1865 the amendment had become part of the Constitution and slavery had been prohibited in the United States.

Amendment XIV

[Adopted 1868]

Section 1   All persons born or naturalized in the United States, and subject to the jurisdiction thereof, are citizens of the United States and of the State wherein they reside. No State shall make or enforce any law which shall abridge the privileges or immunities of citizens of the United States; nor shall any State deprive any person of life, liberty, or property, without due process of law; nor deny to any person within its jurisdiction the equal protection of the laws.

Section 2   Representatives shall be appointed among the several States according to their respective numbers, counting the whole number of persons in each State, excluding Indians not taxed. But when the right to vote at any election for the choice of Electors for President and Vice-President of the United States, Representatives in Congress, the executive and judicial officers of a State, or the members of the legislature thereof, is denied to any of the male inhabitants of such State, being twenty-one years of age and citizens of the United States, or in any way abridged, except for participation in rebellion, or other crime, the basis of representation therein shall be reduced in the proportion which the number of such male citizens shall bear to the whole number of male citizens twenty-one years of age in such State.

Section 3   No person shall be a Senator or Representative in Congress, or Elector of President and Vice-President, or hold any office, civil or military, under the United States, or under any State, who, having previously taken an oath, as a member of Congress, or as an officer of the United States, or as a member of any State legislature, or as an executive or judicial officer of any State, to support the Constitution of the United States, shall have en-

gaged in insurrection or rebellion against the same, or given aid or comfort to the enemies thereof. Congress may, by a vote of two-thirds of each house, remove such disability.

Section 4   The validity of the public debt of the United States, authorized by law, including debts incurred for payment of pensions and bounties for services in suppressing insurrection or rebellion, shall not be questioned. But neither the United States nor any State shall assume or pay any debt or obligation incurred in aid of insurrection or rebellion against the United States, or any claim for the loss or emancipation of any slave; but all such debts, obligations, and claims shall be held illegal and void.

Section 5   The Congress shall have power to enforce, by appropriate legislation, the provisions of this article.

◆◆◆

Without Lincoln's leadership in the reconstruction of the nation following the Civil War, it soon became clear that the Thirteenth Amendment needed additional constitutional support. Less than a year after Lincoln's assassination, Andrew Johnson was ready to bring the former Confederate states back into the Union with few changes in their governments or politics. Anxious Republicans drafted the Fourteenth Amendment to prevent that from happening. The most important provisions of this complex amendment made all native-born or naturalized persons American citizens and prohibited states from abridging the "privileges or immunities" of citizens; depriving them of "life, liberty, or property, without due process of law"; and denying them "equal protection of the laws." In essence, it made all ex-slaves citizens and protected the rights of all citizens against violation by their own state governments.

As occurred in the case of the Thirteenth Amendment, former Confederate states were forced to ratify the amendment as a condition of representation in the House and the Senate. The intentions of the Fourteenth Amendment, and how those intentions should be enforced, have been the most debated point of constitutional history. The terms due process *and* equal protection *have been especially troublesome. Was the amendment designed to outlaw racial segregation? Or was the goal simply to prevent the leaders of the rebellious South from gaining political power?*

The framers of the Fourteenth Amendment hoped Article 2 would produce black voters who would increase the power of the Republican Party. The federal government, however, never used its power to punish states for denying blacks their right to vote. Although the Fourteenth Amendment had an immediate impact in giving black Americans citizenship, it did nothing to protect blacks from the vengeance of whites once Reconstruction ended. In the late nineteenth and early twentieth centuries, section 1 of the Fourteenth Amendment was often used to protect business inter-

ests and strike down laws protecting workers on the grounds that the rights of "persons," that is, corporations, were protected by "due process." More recently, the Fourteenth Amendment has been used to justify school desegregation and affirmative action programs, as well as to dismantle such programs.

Amendment XV

[Adopted 1870]

Section 1   The right of citizens of the United States to vote shall not be denied or abridged by the United States or by any State on account of race, color, or previous condition of servitude.

Section 2   The Congress shall have power to enforce this article by appropriate legislation.

♦ ♦ ♦

The Fifteenth Amendment was the last major piece of Reconstruction legislation. While earlier Reconstruction acts had already required black suffrage in the South, the Fifteenth Amendment extended black voting rights to the entire nation. Some Republicans felt morally obligated to do away with the double standard between North and South since many northern states had stubbornly refused to enfranchise blacks. Others believed that the freedman's ballot required the extra protection of a constitutional amendment to shield it from white counterattack. But partisan advantage also played an important role in the amendment's passage, since Republicans hoped that by giving the ballot to northern blacks, they could lessen their political vulnerability.

    Many women's rights advocates had fought for the amendment. They had felt betrayed by the inclusion of the word male *in section 2 of the Fourteenth Amendment and were further angered when the proposed Fifteenth Amendment failed to prohibit denial of the right to vote on the grounds of sex as well as "race, color, or previous condition of servitude." In this amendment, for the first time, the federal government claimed the power to regulate the franchise, or vote. It was also the first time the Constitution placed limits on the power of the states to regulate access to the franchise. Although ratified in 1870, the amendment was not enforced until the twentieth century.*

The Progressive Amendments (Sixteenth–Nineteenth Amendments)

No amendments were added to the Constitution between the Civil War and the Progressive Era. America was changing, however, in fundamental ways. The rapid industrialization of the United States after the Civil War led to many social and economic problems. Hundreds of amendments were proposed, but none received enough support in Congress to be sent to the states. Some scholars believe that regional differences and rivalries were so strong during this period that it was almost impossible to gain a consensus on a constitutional amendment. During the Progressive Era, however, the Constitution was amended four times in seven years.

Amendment XVI

[Adopted 1913]

The Congress shall have power to lay and collect taxes on incomes, from whatever source derived, without apportionment among the several States, and without regard to any census or enumeration.

♦ ♦ ♦

Until passage of the Sixteenth Amendment, most of the money used to run the federal government came from customs duties and taxes on specific items, such as liquor. During the Civil War, the federal government taxed incomes as an emergency measure. Pressure to enact an income tax came from those who were concerned about the growing gap between rich and poor in the United States. The Populist Party began campaigning for a graduated income tax in 1892, and support continued to grow. By 1909, thirty-three proposed income tax amendments had been presented in Congress, but lobbying by corporate and other special interests had defeated them all. In June 1909, the growing pressure for an income tax, which had been endorsed by Presidents Roosevelt and Taft, finally pushed an amendment through the Senate. The required thirty-six states had ratified the amendment by February 1913.

Amendment XVII

[Adopted 1913]

Section 1   The Senate of the United States shall be composed of two Senators from each State, elected by the people thereof, for six years; and each Senator shall have one vote. The electors in each State shall have the qualifications requisite for electors of [voters for] the most numerous branch of the State legislatures.

Section 2   When vacancies happen in the representation of any State in the Senate, the executive authority of such State shall issue writs of election to fill such vacancies: Provided, that the Legislature of any State may empower the executive thereof to make temporary appointments until the people fill the vacancies by election as the Legislature may direct.

Section 3   This amendment shall not be so construed as to affect the election or term of any Senator chosen before it becomes valid as part of the Constitution.

♦ ♦ ♦

The framers of the Constitution saw the members of the House as the representatives of the people and the members of the Senate as the representatives of the states. Originally senators were to be chosen by the state legislators. According to reform advocates, however, the growth of private industry and transportation conglomerates during the Gilded Age had created a network of corruption in which wealth and power were exchanged for influence and votes in the Senate. Senator Nelson Aldrich, who represented Rhode Island in the late nineteenth and early twentieth centuries, for example, was known as "the senator from Standard Oil" because of his open support of special business interests.

Efforts to amend the Constitution to allow direct election of senators had begun in 1826, but since any proposal had to be approved by the Senate, reform seemed impossible. Progressives tried to gain influence in the Senate by instituting party caucuses and primary elections, which gave citizens the chance to express their choice of a senator who could then be officially elected by the state legislature. By 1910, fourteen of the country's thirty senators received popular votes through a state primary before the state legislature made its selection. Despairing of getting a proposal through the Senate, supporters of a direct-election amendment had begun in 1893 to seek a convention of representatives from two-thirds of the states to propose an amendment that could then be ratified. By 1905, thirty-one of forty-five states had endorsed such an amendment. Finally, in 1911, despite extraordinary opposition, a proposed amendment passed the Senate; by 1913, it had been ratified.

Amendment XVIII

[Adopted 1919; repealed 1933 by Amendment XXI]

Section 1   After one year from the ratification of this article the manufacture, sale, or transportation of intoxicating liquors within, the importation thereof into, or the exportation thereof from the United States and all territory subject to the jurisdiction thereof, for beverage purposes, is hereby prohibited.

Section 2   The Congress and the several States shall have concurrent power to enforce this article by appropriate legislation.

Section 3   This article shall be inoperative unless it shall have been ratified as an amendment to the Constitution by the legislatures of the several States, as provided by the Constitution, within seven years from the date of the submission thereof to the States by the Congress.

◆ ◆ ◆

The Prohibition Party, formed in 1869, began calling for a constitutional amendment to outlaw alcoholic beverages in 1872. A prohibition amendment was first proposed in the Senate in 1876 and was revived eighteen times before 1913. Between 1913 and 1919, another thirty-nine attempts were made to prohibit liquor in the United States through a constitutional amendment. Prohibition became a key element of the progressive agenda as reformers linked alcohol and drunkenness to numerous social problems, including the corruption of immigrant voters. While opponents of such an amendment

argued that it was undemocratic, supporters claimed that their efforts had widespread public support. The admission of twelve "dry" western states to the Union in the early twentieth century and the spirit of sacrifice during World War I laid the groundwork for passage and ratification of the Eighteenth Amendment in 1919. Opponents added a time limit to the amendment in the hope that they could thus block ratification, but this effort failed. (See also Amendment XXI.)

Amendment XIX

[Adopted 1920]

Section 1   The right of citizens of the United States to vote shall not be denied or abridged by the United States or by any State on account of sex.

Section 2   Congress shall have the power to enforce this article by appropriate legislation.

◆ ◆ ◆

Advocates of women's rights tried and failed to link woman suffrage to the Fourteenth and Fifteenth Amendments. Nonetheless, the effort for woman suffrage continued. Between 1878 and 1912, at least one and sometimes as many as four proposed amendments were introduced in Congress each year to grant women the right to vote. While over time women won very limited voting rights in some states, at both the state and federal levels opposition to an amendment for woman suffrage remained very strong. President Woodrow Wilson and other officials felt that the federal government should not interfere with the power of the states in this matter. Others worried that granting suffrage to women would encourage ethnic minorities to exercise their own right to vote. And many were concerned that giving women the vote would result in their abandoning traditional gender roles. In 1919, following a protracted and often bitter campaign of protest in which women went on hunger strikes and chained themselves to fences, an amendment was introduced with the backing of President Wilson. It narrowly passed the Senate (after efforts to limit the suffrage to white women failed) and was adopted in 1920 after Tennessee became the thirty-sixth state to ratify it.

Unratified Amendment

Child Labor Amendment (proposed by Congress June 2, 1924)

Section 1   The Congress shall have power to limit, regulate, and prohibit the labor of persons under eighteen years of age.

Section 2   The power of the several States is unimpaired by this article except that the operation of State laws shall be suspended to the extent necessary to give effect to legislation enacted by Congress.

◆ ◆ ◆

Throughout the late nineteenth and early twentieth centuries, alarm over the condition of child workers grew. Opponents of child labor argued that children worked in dangerous and unhealthy conditions, that they took jobs from adult workers, that they depressed wages in certain industries, and that states that allowed child labor had an economic advantage over those that did not. Defenders of child labor claimed that children provided needed income in many families, that working at a young age developed character, and that the effort to prohibit the practice constituted an invasion of family privacy.

In 1916, Congress passed a law that made it illegal to sell goods made by children through interstate commerce. The Supreme Court, however, ruled that the law violated the limits on the power of Congress to regulate interstate commerce. Congress then tried to penalize industries that used child labor by taxing such goods. This measure was also thrown out by the courts. In response, reformers set out to amend the Constitution. The proposed amendment was ratified by twenty-eight states, but by 1925, thirteen states had rejected it. Passage of the Fair Labor Standards Act in 1938, which was upheld by the Supreme Court in 1941, made the amendment irrelevant.

Amendment XX

[Adopted 1933]

Section 1   The terms of the President and Vice-President shall end at noon on the 20th day of January, and the terms of Senators and Representatives at noon on the 3rd day of January, of the years in which such terms would have ended if this article had not been ratified; and the terms of their successors shall then begin.

Section 2   The Congress shall assemble at least once in every year, and such meeting shall begin at noon on the 3rd day of January, unless they shall by law appoint a different day.

Section 3   If, at the time fixed for the beginning of the term of the President, the President-elect shall have died, the Vice-President-elect shall become President. If a President shall not have been chosen before the time fixed for the beginning of his term, or if the President-elect shall have failed to qualify, then the Vice-President-elect shall act as President until a President shall have qualified; and the Congress may by law provide for the case wherein neither a President-elect nor a Vice-President-elect shall have qualified, declaring who shall then act as President, or the manner in which one who is to act shall be selected, and such person shall act accordingly until a President or Vice-President shall have qualified.

Section 4   The Congress may by law provide for the case of the death of any of the persons from whom the House of Representatives may choose a President whenever the right of choice shall have devolved upon them, and for the case of the death of any of the persons from whom the Senate may choose a Vice-President whenever the right of choice shall have devolved upon them.

Section 5   Sections 1 and 2 shall take effect on the 15th day of October following the ratification of this article.

Section 6   This article shall be inoperative unless it shall have been ratified as an amendment to the Constitution by the Legislatures of three-fourths of the several States within seven years from the date of its submission.

♦ ♦ ♦

Until 1933, presidents took office on March 4. Since elections are held in early November and electoral votes are counted in mid-December, this meant that more than three months passed between the time a new president was elected and when he took office. Moving the inauguration to January shortened the transition period and allowed Congress to begin its term closer to the time of the president's inauguration. Although this seems like a minor change, an amendment was required because the Constitution specifies terms of office. This amendment also deals with questions of succession in the event that a president- or vice president-elect dies before assuming office. Section 3 also clarifies a method for resolving a deadlock in the electoral college.

Amendment XXI

[Adopted 1933]

Section 1   The eighteenth article of amendment to the Constitution of the United States is hereby repealed.

Section 2   The transportation or importation into any State, Territory, or Possession of the United States for delivery or use therein of intoxicating liquors, in violation of the laws thereof, is hereby prohibited.

Section 3   This article shall be inoperative unless it shall have been ratified as an amendment to the Constitution by conventions in the several States, as provided in the Constitution, within seven years from the date of the submission thereof to the States by the Congress.

♦ ♦ ♦

Widespread violation of the Volstead Act, the law enacted to enforce prohibition, made the United States a nation of lawbreakers. Prohibition caused more problems than it solved by encouraging crime, bribery, and corruption. Further, a coalition of liquor and beer manufacturers, personal liberty advocates, and constitutional scholars joined forces to challenge the amendment. By 1929, thirty proposed repeal amendments had been introduced in Congress, and the Democratic Party made repeal part of its platform in the 1932 presidential campaign. The

Twenty-first Amendment was proposed in February 1933 and ratified less than a year later. The failure of the effort to enforce prohibition through a constitutional amendment has often been cited by opponents to subsequent efforts to shape public virtue and private morality.

Amendment XXII

[Adopted 1951]

Section 1   No person shall be elected to the office of the President more than twice, and no person who has held the office of President, or acted as President, for more than two years of a term to which some other person was elected President shall be elected to the office of President more than once. But this article shall not apply to any person holding the office of President when this Article was proposed by the Congress, and shall not prevent any person who may be holding the office of President, or acting as President, during the term within which this Article becomes operative from holding the office of President or acting as President during the remainder of such term.

Section 2   This article shall be inoperative unless it shall have been ratified as an amendment to the Constitution by the legislatures of three-fourths of the several States within seven years from the date of its submission to the States by the Congress.

♦ ♦ ♦

George Washington's refusal to seek a third term of office set a precedent that stood until 1912, when former President Theodore Roosevelt sought, without success, another term as an independent candidate. Democrat Franklin Roosevelt was the only president to seek and win a fourth term, though he did so amid great controversy. Roosevelt died in April 1945, a few months after the beginning of his fourth term. In 1946, Republicans won control of the House and the Senate, and early in 1947 a proposal for an amendment to limit future presidents to two four-year terms was offered to the states for ratification. Democratic critics of the Twenty-second Amendment charged that it was a partisan posthumous jab at Roosevelt.

Since the Twenty-second Amendment was adopted, however, the only presidents who might have been able to seek a third term, had it not existed, were Republicans Dwight Eisenhower and Ronald Reagan, and Democrat Bill Clinton. Since 1826, Congress has entertained 160 proposed amendments to limit the president to one six-year term. Such amendments have been backed by fifteen presidents, including Gerald Ford and Jimmy Carter.

Amendment XXIII

[Adopted 1961]

Section 1   The District constituting the seat of Government of the United States shall appoint in such manner as the Congress may direct: A number of electors of President and Vice-President equal to the whole number of Senators and Representatives in Congress to which the District would be entitled if it were a State, but in no event more than the least populous State; they shall be in addition to those appointed by the States, but they shall be considered for the purposes of the election of President and Vice-President, to be electors appointed by a State; and they shall meet in the District and perform such duties as provided by the twelfth article of amendment.

Section 2   The Congress shall have the power to enforce this article by appropriate legislation.

♦ ♦ ♦

When Washington, D.C., was established as a federal district, no one expected that a significant number of people would make it their permanent and primary residence. A proposal to allow citizens of the district to vote in presidential elections was approved by Congress in June 1960 and was ratified on March 29, 1961.

Amendment XXIV

[Adopted 1964]

Section 1   The right of citizens of the United States to vote in any primary or other election for President or Vice-President, for electors for President or Vice-President, or for Senator or Representative in Congress, shall not be denied or abridged by the United States or any State by reason of failure to pay any poll tax or other tax.

Section 2   The Congress shall have the power to enforce this article by appropriate legislation.

♦ ♦ ♦

In the colonial and Revolutionary eras, financial independence was seen as necessary to political independence, and the poll tax was used as a requirement for voting. By the twentieth century, however, the poll tax was used mostly to bar poor people, especially southern blacks, from voting. While conservatives complained that the amendment interfered with states' rights, liberals thought that the amendment did not go far enough because it barred the poll tax only in national elections and not in state or local elections. The amendment was ratified in 1964, however, and two years later, the Supreme Court ruled that poll taxes in state and local elections also violated the equal protection clause of the Fourteenth Amendment.

Amendment XXV

[Adopted 1967]

Section 1   In case of the removal of the President from office or of his death or resignation, the Vice-President shall become President.

Section 2   Whenever there is a vacancy in the office of the Vice-President, the President shall nominate a Vice-President who shall take office upon confirmation by a majority vote of both Houses of Congress.

Section 3   Whenever the President transmits to the President pro tempore of the Senate and the Speaker of the House of Representatives his written declaration that he is unable to discharge the powers and duties of his office, and until he transmits to them a written declaration to the contrary, such powers and duties shall be discharged by the Vice-President as Acting President.

Section 4   Whenever the Vice-President and a majority of either the principal officers of the executive departments or of such other body as Congress may by law provide, transmit to the President pro tempore of the Senate and the Speaker of the House of Representatives their written declaration that the President is unable to discharge the powers and duties of his office, the Vice-President shall immediately assume the powers and duties of the office as Acting President.

Thereafter, when the President transmits to the President pro tempore of the Senate and the Speaker of the House of Representatives his written declaration that no inability exists, he shall resume the powers and duties of his office unless the Vice-President and a majority of either the principal officers of the executive department[s] or of such other body as Congress may by law provide, transmit within four days to the President pro tempore of the Senate and the Speaker of the House of Representatives their written declaration that the President is unable to discharge the powers and duties of his office. Thereupon Congress shall decide the issue, assembling within forty-eight hours for that purpose if not in session. If the Congress, within twenty-one days after receipt of the latter written declaration, or, if Congress is not in session, within twenty-one days after Congress is required to assemble, determines by two-thirds vote of both Houses that the President is unable to discharge the powers and duties of his office, the Vice-President shall continue to discharge the same as Acting President; otherwise, the President shall resume the powers and duties of his office.

◆ ◆ ◆

The framers of the Constitution established the office of vice president because someone was needed to preside over the Senate. The first president to die in office was William Henry Harrison, in 1841. Vice President John Tyler had himself sworn in as president, setting a precedent that was followed when seven later presidents died in office. The assassination of President James A. Garfield in 1881 posed a new problem, however. After he was shot, the president was incapacitated for two months before he died; he was unable to lead the country, while his vice president, Chester A. Arthur, was unable to assume leadership. Efforts to resolve questions of succession in the event of a presidential disability thus began with the death of Garfield.

In 1963, the assassination of President John F. Kennedy galvanized Congress to action. Vice President Lyndon Johnson was a chain smoker with a history of

heart trouble. According to the 1947 Presidential Succession Act, the two men who stood in line to succeed him were the seventy-two-year-old Speaker of the House and the eighty-six-year-old president of the Senate. There were serious concerns that any of these men might become incapacitated while serving as chief executive. The first time the Twenty-fifth Amendment was used, however, was not in the case of presidential death or illness, but during the Watergate crisis. When Vice President Spiro T. Agnew was forced to resign following allegations of bribery and tax violations, President Richard M. Nixon appointed House Minority Leader Gerald R. Ford vice president. Ford became president following Nixon's resignation eight months later and named Nelson A. Rockefeller as his vice president. Thus, for more than two years, the two highest offices in the country were held by people who had not been elected to them.

Amendment XXVI

[Adopted 1971]

Section 1   The right of citizens of the United States, who are eighteen years of age or older, to vote shall not be denied or abridged by the United States or by any State on account of age.

Section 2   The Congress shall have power to enforce this article by appropriate legislation.

◆ ◆ ◆

Efforts to lower the voting age from twenty-one to eighteen began during World War II. Recognizing that those who were old enough to fight a war should have some say in the government policies that involved them in the war, Presidents Eisenhower, Johnson, and Nixon endorsed the idea. In 1970, the combined pressure of the antiwar movement and the demographic pressure of the baby boom generation led to a Voting Rights Act lowering the voting age in federal, state, and local elections.

In Oregon v. Mitchell (1970), the state of Oregon challenged the right of Congress to determine the age at which people could vote in state or local elections. The Supreme Court agreed with Oregon. Since the Voting Rights Act was ruled unconstitutional, the Constitution had to be amended to allow passage of a law that would lower the voting age. The amendment was ratified in a little more than three months, making it the most rapidly ratified amendment in U.S. history.

Unratified Amendment

Equal Rights Amendment (proposed by Congress March 22, 1972; seven-year deadline for ratification extended June 30, 1982)

Section 1   Equality of rights under the law shall not be denied or abridged by the United States or by any State on account of sex.

Section 2   The Congress shall have the power to enforce, by appropriate legislation, the provisions of this article.

Section 3   This amendment shall take effect two years after the date of ratification.

♦ ♦ ♦

In 1923, soon after women had won the right to vote, Alice Paul, a leading activist in the woman suffrage movement, proposed an amendment requiring equal treatment of men and women. Opponents of the proposal argued that such an amendment would invalidate laws that protected women and would make women subject to the military draft. After the 1964 Civil Rights Act was adopted, protective workplace legislation was removed anyway.

The renewal of the women's movement, as a by-product of the civil rights and antiwar movements, led to a revival of the Equal Rights Amendment (ERA) in Congress. Disagreements over language held up congressional passage of the proposed amendment, but on March 22, 1972, the Senate approved the ERA by a vote of 84 to 8, and it was sent to the states. Six states ratified the amendment within two days, and by the middle of 1973 the amendment seemed well on its way to adoption, with thirty of the needed thirty-eight states having ratified it. In the mid-1970s, however, a powerful "Stop ERA" campaign developed. The campaign portrayed the ERA as a threat to "family values" and traditional relationships between men and women. Although thirty-five states ultimately ratified the ERA, five of those state legislatures voted to rescind ratification, and the amendment was never adopted.

Unratified Amendment

D.C. Statehood Amendment (proposed by Congress August 22, 1978)

Section 1   For purposes of representation in the Congress, election of the President and Vice-President, and article V of this Constitution, the District constituting the seat of government of the United States shall be treated as though it were a State.

Section 2   The exercise of the rights and powers conferred under this article shall be by the people of the District constituting the seat of government, and as shall be provided by Congress.

Section 3   The twenty-third article of amendment to the Constitution of the United States is hereby repealed.

Section 4   This article shall be inoperative, unless it shall have been ratified as an amendment to the Constitution by the legislatures of three-fourths of the several states within seven years from the date of its submission.

♦ ♦ ♦

The 1961 ratification of the Twenty-third Amendment, giving residents of the District of Columbia

the right to vote for a president and vice president, inspired an effort to give residents of the district full voting rights. In 1966, President Lyndon Johnson appointed a mayor and city council; in 1971, D.C. residents were allowed to name a nonvoting delegate to the House; and in 1981, residents were allowed to elect the mayor and city council. Congress retained the right to overrule laws that might affect commuters, the height of federal buildings, and selection of judges and prosecutors. The district's nonvoting delegate to Congress, Walter Fauntroy, lobbied fiercely for a congressional amendment granting statehood to the district. In 1978, a proposed amendment was approved and sent to the states. A number of states quickly ratified the amendment, but, like the ERA, the D.C. Statehood Amendment ran into trouble. Opponents argued that section 2 created a separate category of "nominal" statehood. They argued that the federal district should be eliminated and that the territory should be reabsorbed into the state of Maryland. Although these theoretical arguments were strong, some scholars believe that racist attitudes toward the predominantly black population of the city was also a factor leading to the defeat of the amendment.

Amendment XXVII
[Adopted 1992]

No law, varying the compensation for the services of the Senators and Representatives, shall take effect, until an election of Representatives shall have intervened.

♦ ♦ ♦

While the Twenty-sixth Amendment was the most rapidly ratified amendment in U.S. history, the Twenty-seventh Amendment had the longest journey to ratification. First proposed by James Madison in 1789 as part of the package that included the Bill of Rights, this amendment had been ratified by only six states by 1791. In 1873, however, it was ratified by Ohio to protest a massive retroactive salary increase by the federal government. Unlike later proposed amendments, this one came with no time limit on ratification. In the early 1980s, Gregory D. Watson, a University of Texas economics major, discovered the "lost" amendment and began a single-handed campaign to get state legislators to introduce it for ratification. In 1983, it was accepted by Maine. In 1984, it passed the Colorado legislature. Ratifications trickled in slowly until May 1992, when Michigan and New Jersey became the thirty-eighth and thirty-ninth states, respectively, to ratify. This amendment prevents members of Congress from raising their own salaries without giving voters a chance to vote them out of office before they can benefit from the raises.

Facts and Figures: Government, Economy, and Demographics

PRESIDENTIAL ELECTIONS

Year	Candidates	Parties	Popular Vote	Percentage of Popular Vote	Electoral Vote	Percentage of Voter Participation
1789	**GEORGE WASHINGTON (Va.)***				69	
	John Adams				34	
	Others				35	
1792	**GEORGE WASHINGTON (Va.)**				132	
	John Adams				77	
	George Clinton				50	
	Others				5	
1796	**JOHN ADAMS (Mass.)**	Federalist			71	
	Thomas Jefferson	Democratic-Republican			68	
	Thomas Pinckney	Federalist			59	
	Aaron Burr	Dem.-Rep.			30	
	Others				48	
1800	**THOMAS JEFFERSON (Va.)**	Dem.-Rep.			73	
	Aaron Burr	Dem.-Rep.			73	
	John Adams	Federalist			65	
	C. C. Pinckney	Federalist			64	
	John Jay	Federalist			1	
1804	**THOMAS JEFFERSON (Va.)**	Dem.-Rep.			162	
	C. C. Pinckney	Federalist			14	
1808	**JAMES MADISON (Va.)**	Dem.-Rep.			122	
	C. C. Pinckney	Federalist			47	
	George Clinton	Dem.-Rep.			6	
1812	**JAMES MADISON (Va.)**	Dem.-Rep.			128	
	De Witt Clinton	Federalist			89	
1816	**JAMES MONROE (Va.)**	Dem.-Rep.			183	
	Rufus King	Federalist			34	
1820	**JAMES MONROE (Va.)**	Dem.-Rep.			231	
	John Quincy Adams	Dem.-Rep.			1	
1824	**JOHN Q. ADAMS (Mass.)**	Dem.-Rep.	108,740	30.5	84	26.9
	Andrew Jackson	Dem.-Rep.	153,544	43.1	99	
	William H. Crawford	Dem.-Rep.	46,618	13.1	41	
	Henry Clay	Dem.-Rep.	47,136	13.2	37	
1828	**ANDREW JACKSON (Tenn.)**	Democratic	647,286	56.0	178	57.6
	John Quincy Adams	National Republican	508,064	44.0	83	

*State of residence when elected president.

Year	Candidates	Parties	Popular Vote	Percentage of Popular Vote	Electoral Vote	Percentage of Voter Participation
1832	**ANDREW JACKSON (Tenn.)**	Democratic	687,502	55.0	219	55.4
	Henry Clay	National Republican	530,189	42.4	49	
	John Floyd	Independent			11	
	William Wirt	Anti-Mason	33,108	2.6	7	
1836	**MARTIN VAN BUREN (N.Y.)**	Democratic	765,483	50.9	170	57.8
	W. H. Harrison	Whig			73	
	Hugh L. White	Whig	739,795	49.1	26	
	Daniel Webster	Whig			14	
	W. P. Mangum	Whig			11	
1840	**WILLIAM H. HARRISON (Ohio)**	Whig	1,274,624	53.1	234	80.2
	Martin Van Buren	Democratic	1,127,781	46.9	60	
	J. G. Birney	Liberty	7,069		—	
1844	**JAMES K. POLK (Tenn.)**	Democratic	1,338,464	49.6	170	78.9
	Henry Clay	Whig	1,300,097	48.1	105	
	J. G. Birney	Liberty	62,300	2.3	—	
1848	**ZACHARY TAYLOR (La.)**	Whig	1,360,967	47.4	163	72.7
	Lewis Cass	Democratic	1,222,342	42.5	127	
	Martin Van Buren	Free-Soil	291,263	10.1	—	
1852	**FRANKLIN PIERCE (N.H.)**	Democratic	1,601,117	50.9	254	69.6
	Winfield Scott	Whig	1,385,453	44.1	42	
	John P. Hale	Free-Soil	155,825	5.0	—	
1856	**JAMES BUCHANAN (Pa.)**	Democratic	1,832,995	45.3	174	78.9
	John C. Frémont	Republican	1,339,932	33.1	114	
	Millard Fillmore	American	871,731	21.6	8	
1860	**ABRAHAM LINCOLN (Ill.)**	Republican	1,865,593	39.8	180	81.2
	Stephen A. Douglas	Democratic	1,382,713	29.5	12	
	John C. Breckinridge	Democratic	848,356	18.1	72	
	John Bell	Union	592,906	12.6	39	
1864	**ABRAHAM LINCOLN (Ill.)**	Republican	2,206,938	55.0	212	73.8
	George B. McClellan	Democratic	1,803,787	45.0	21	
1868	**ULYSSES S. GRANT (Ill.)**	Republican	3,012,833	52.7	214	78.1
	Horatio Seymour	Democratic	2,703,249	47.3	80	
1872	**ULYSSES S. GRANT (Ill.)**	Republican	3,597,132	55.6	286	71.3
	Horace Greeley	Democratic; Liberal Republican	2,834,125	43.9	66	
1876	**RUTHERFORD B. HAYES (Ohio)**	Republican	4,036,572	48.0	185	81.8
	Samuel J. Tilden	Democratic	4,284,020	51.0	184	
1880	**JAMES A. GARFIELD (Ohio)**	Republican	4,454,416	48.5	214	79.4
	Winfield S. Hancock	Democratic	4,444,952	48.1	155	
1884	**GROVER CLEVELAND (N.Y.)**	Democratic	4,879,507	48.5	219	77.5
	James G. Blaine	Republican	4,850,293	48.2	182	
1888	**BENJAMIN HARRISON (Ind.)**	Republican	5,439,853	47.9	233	79.3
	Grover Cleveland	Democratic	5,540,309	48.6	168	
1892	**GROVER CLEVELAND (N.Y.)**	Democratic	5,555,426	46.1	277	74.7
	Benjamin Harrison	Republican	5,182,690	43.0	145	
	James B. Weaver	People's	1,029,846	8.5	22	
1896	**WILLIAM McKINLEY (Ohio)**	Republican	7,104,779	51.1	271	79.3
	William J. Bryan	Democratic-People's	6,502,925	47.7	176	
1900	**WILLIAM McKINLEY (Ohio)**	Republican	7,207,923	51.7	292	73.2
	William J. Bryan	Dem.-Populist	6,358,133	45.5	155	

PRESIDENTIAL ELECTIONS

Year	Candidates	Parties	Popular Vote	Percentage of Popular Vote	Electoral Vote	Percentage of Voter Participation
1904	**THEODORE ROOSEVELT (N.Y.)**	Republican	7,623,486	57.9	336	65.2
	Alton B. Parker	Democratic	5,077,911	37.6	140	
	Eugene V. Debs	Socialist	402,283	3.0	—	
1908	**WILLIAM H. TAFT (Ohio)**	Republican	7,678,908	51.6	321	65.4
	William J. Bryan	Democratic	6,409,104	43.1	162	
	Eugene V. Debs	Socialist	420,793	2.8	—	
1912	**WOODROW WILSON (N.J.)**	Democratic	6,293,454	41.9	435	58.8
	Theodore Roosevelt	Progressive	4,119,538	27.4	88	
	William H. Taft	Republican	3,484,980	23.2	8	
	Eugene V. Debs	Socialist	900,672	6.1	—	
1916	**WOODROW WILSON (N.J.)**	Democratic	9,129,606	49.4	277	61.6
	Charles E. Hughes	Republican	8,538,221	46.2	254	
	A. L. Benson	Socialist	585,113	3.2	—	
1920	**WARREN G. HARDING (Ohio)**	Republican	16,143,407	60.5	404	49.2
	James M. Cox	Democratic	9,130,328	34.2	127	
	Eugene V. Debs	Socialist	919,799	3.4	—	
1924	**CALVIN COOLIDGE (Mass.)**	Republican	15,725,016	54.0	382	48.9
	John W. Davis	Democratic	8,386,503	28.8	136	
	Robert M. La Follette	Progressive	4,822,856	16.6	13	
1928	**HERBERT HOOVER (Calif.)**	Republican	21,391,381	58.2	444	56.9
	Alfred E. Smith	Democratic	15,016,443	40.9	87	
	Norman Thomas	Socialist	267,835	0.7	—	
1932	**FRANKLIN D. ROOSEVELT (N.Y.)**	Democratic	22,809,638	57.4	472	56.9
	Herbert Hoover	Republican	15,758,901	39.7	59	
	Norman Thomas	Socialist	881,951	2.2	—	
1936	**FRANKLIN D. ROOSEVELT (N.Y.)**	Democratic	27,751,597	60.8	523	61.0
	Alfred M. Landon	Republican	16,679,583	36.5	8	
	William Lemke	Union	882,479	1.9	—	
1940	**FRANKLIN D. ROOSEVELT (N.Y.)**	Democratic	27,244,160	54.8	449	62.5
	Wendell Willkie	Republican	22,305,198	44.8	82	
1944	**FRANKLIN D. ROOSEVELT (N.Y.)**	Democratic	25,602,504	53.5	432	55.9
	Thomas E. Dewey	Republican	22,006,285	46.0	99	
1948	**HARRY S. TRUMAN (Mo.)**	Democratic	24,105,695	49.5	303	53.0
	Thomas E. Dewey	Republican	21,969,170	45.1	189	
	J. Strom Thurmond	States'-Rights Democratic	1,169,021	2.4	38	
	Henry A. Wallace	Progressive	1,156,103	2.4	—	
1952	**DWIGHT D. EISENHOWER (N.Y.)**	Republican	33,936,252	55.1	442	63.3
	Adlai Stevenson	Democratic	27,314,992	44.4	89	
1956	**DWIGHT D. EISENHOWER (N.Y.)**	Republican	35,575,420	57.6	457	60.6
	Adlai Stevenson	Democratic	26,033,066	42.1	73	
	Other	—	—	—	1	
1960	**JOHN F. KENNEDY (Mass.)**	Democratic	34,227,096	49.9	303	62.8
	Richard M. Nixon	Republican	34,108,546	49.6	219	
	Other	—	—	—	15	
1964	**LYNDON B. JOHNSON (Texas)**	Democratic	43,126,506	61.1	486	61.7
	Barry M. Goldwater	Republican	27,176,799	38.5	52	
1968	**RICHARD M. NIXON (N.Y.)**	Republican	31,770,237	43.4	301	60.9
	Hubert H. Humphrey	Democratic	31,270,533	42.7	191	
	George Wallace	American Indep.	9,906,141	13.5	46	
1972	**RICHARD M. NIXON (N.Y.)**	Republican	47,169,911	60.7	520	55.2
	George S. McGovern	Democratic	29,170,383	37.5	17	
	Other	—	—	—	1	

Year	Candidates	Parties	Popular Vote	Percentage of Popular Vote	Electoral Vote	Percentage of Voter Participation
1976	JIMMY CARTER (Ga.)	Democratic	40,828,587	50.0	297	53.5
	Gerald R. Ford	Republican	39,147,613	47.9	241	
	Other	—	1,575,459	2.1	—	
1980	RONALD REAGAN (Calif.)	Republican	43,901,812	50.7	489	54.0
	Jimmy Carter	Democratic	35,483,820	41.0	49	
	John B. Anderson	Independent	5,719,722	6.6	—	
	Ed Clark	Libertarian	921,188	1.1	—	
1984	RONALD REAGAN (Calif.)	Republican	54,455,075	59.0	525	53.1
	Walter Mondale	Democratic	37,577,185	41.0	13	
1988	GEORGE H. W. BUSH (Texas)	Republican	47,946,422	54.0	426	50.2
	Michael S. Dukakis	Democratic	41,016,429	46.0	112	
1992	WILLIAM J. CLINTON (Ark.)	Democratic	44,908,254	42.3	370	55.9
	George H. W. Bush	Republican	39,102,282	37.4	168	
	H. Ross Perot	Independent	19,721,433	18.9	—	
1996	WILLIAM J. CLINTON (Ark.)	Democratic	47,401,185	49.2	379	49.0
	Robert Dole	Republican	39,197,469	40.7	159	
	H. Ross Perot	Independent	8,085,294	8.4	—	
2000	GEORGE W. BUSH (Texas)	Republican	50,456,062	47.8	271	51.2
	Al Gore	Democratic	50,996,862	48.4	267	
	Ralph Nader	Green Party	2,858,843	2.7	—	
	Patrick J. Buchanan	—	438,760	.4	—	
2004	GEORGE W. BUSH (Texas)	Republican	61,872,711	50.6	286	60.3
	John F. Kerry	Democratic	58,894,584	48.1	251	
	Other	—	1,582,185	1.3	—	

PRESIDENTS, VICE PRESIDENTS, AND SECRETARIES OF STATE

The Washington Administration (1789–1797)

Vice President	John Adams	1789–1797
Secretary of State	Thomas Jefferson	1789–1793
	Edmund Randolph	1794–1795
	Timothy Pickering	1795–1797

The John Adams Administration (1797–1801)

Vice President	Thomas Jefferson	1797–1801
Secretary of State	Timothy Pickering	1797–1800
	John Marshall	1800–1801

The Jefferson Administration (1801–1809)

Vice President	Aaron Burr	1801–1805
	George Clinton	1805–1809
Secretary of State	James Madison	1801–1809

The Madison Administration (1809–1817)

Vice President	George Clinton	1809–1813
	Elbridge Gerry	1813–1817
Secretary of State	Robert Smith	1809–1811
	James Monroe	1811–1817

The Monroe Administration (1817–1825)

Vice President	Daniel Tompkins	1817–1825
Secretary of State	John Quincy Adams	1817–1825

The John Quincy Adams Administration (1825–1829)

Vice President	John C. Calhoun	1825–1829
Secretary of State	Henry Clay	1825–1829

The Jackson Administration (1829–1837)

Vice President	John C. Calhoun	1829–1833
	Martin Van Buren	1833–1837
Secretary of State	Martin Van Buren	1829–1831
	Edward Livingston	1831–1833
	Louis McLane	1833–1834
	John Forsyth	1834–1837

The Van Buren Administration (1837–1841)

Vice President	Richard M. Johnson	1837–1841
Secretary of State	John Forsyth	1837–1841

PRESIDENTS, VICE PRESIDENTS, AND SECRETARIES OF STATE

The William Harrison Administration (1841)

Vice President	John Tyler	1841
Secretary of State	Daniel Webster	1841

The Tyler Administration (1841–1845)

Vice President	None	
Secretary of State	Daniel Webster	1841–1843
	Hugh S. Legaré	1843
	Abel P. Upshur	1843–1844
	John C. Calhoun	1844–1845

The Polk Administration (1845–1849)

Vice President	George M. Dallas	1845–1849
Secretary of State	James Buchanan	1845–1849

The Taylor Administration (1849–1850)

Vice President	Millard Fillmore	1849–1850
Secretary of State	John M. Clayton	1849–1850

The Fillmore Administration (1850–1853)

Vice President	None	
Secretary of State	Daniel Webster	1850–1852
	Edward Everett	1852–1853

The Pierce Administration (1853–1857)

Vice President	William R. King	1853–1857
Secretary of State	William L. Marcy	1853–1857

The Buchanan Administration (1857–1861)

Vice President	John C. Breckinridge	1857–1861
Secretary of State	Lewis Cass	1857–1860
	Jeremiah S. Black	1860–1861

The Lincoln Administration (1861–1865)

Vice President	Hannibal Hamlin	1861–1865
	Andrew Johnson	1865
Secretary of State	William H. Seward	1861–1865

The Andrew Johnson Administration (1865–1869)

Vice President	None	
Secretary of State	William H. Seward	1865–1869

The Grant Administration (1869–1877)

Vice President	Schuyler Colfax	1869–1873
	Henry Wilson	1873–1877
Secretary of State	Elihu B. Washburne	1869
	Hamilton Fish	1869–1877

The Hayes Administration (1877–1881)

Vice President	William A. Wheeler	1877–1881
Secretary of State	William M. Evarts	1877–1881

The Garfield Administration (1881)

Vice President	Chester A. Arthur	1881
Secretary of State	James G. Blaine	1881

The Arthur Administration (1881–1885)

Vice President	None	
Secretary of State	F. T. Frelinghuysen	1881–1885

The Cleveland Administration (1885–1889)

Vice President	Thomas A. Hendricks	1885–1889
Secretary of State	Thomas F. Bayard	1885–1889

The Benjamin Harrison Administration (1889–1893)

Vice President	Levi P. Morton	1889–1893
Secretary of State	James G. Blaine	1889–1892
	John W. Foster	1892–1893

The Cleveland Administration (1893–1897)

Vice President	Adlai E. Stevenson	1893–1897
Secretary of State	Walter Q. Gresham	1893–1895
	Richard Olney	1895–1897

The McKinley Administration (1897–1901)

Vice President	Garret A. Hobart	1897–1901
	Theodore Roosevelt	1901
Secretary of State	John Sherman	1897–1898
	William R. Day	1898
	John Hay	1898–1901

The Theodore Roosevelt Administration (1901–1909)

Vice President	Charles Fairbanks	1905–1909
Secretary of State	John Hay	1901–1905
	Elihu Root	1905–1909
	Robert Bacon	1909

The Taft Administration (1909–1913)

Vice President	James S. Sherman	1909–1913
Secretary of State	Philander C. Knox	1909–1913

The Wilson Administration (1913–1921)

Vice President	Thomas R. Marshall	1913–1921
Secretary of State	William J. Bryan	1913–1915
	Robert Lansing	1915–1920
	Bainbridge Colby	1920–1921

The Harding Administration (1921–1923)

Vice President	Calvin Coolidge	1921–1923
Secretary of State	Charles E. Hughes	1921–1923

The Coolidge Administration (1923–1929)

Vice President	Charles G. Dawes	1925–1929
Secretary of State	Charles E. Hughes	1923–1925
	Frank B. Kellogg	1925–1929

The Hoover Administration (1929–1933)

Vice President	Charles Curtis	1929–1933
Secretary of State	Henry L. Stimson	1929–1933

The Franklin D. Roosevelt Administration (1933–1945)

Vice President	John Nance Garner	1933–1941
	Henry A. Wallace	1941–1945
	Harry S. Truman	1945
Secretary of State	Cordell Hull	1933–1944
	Edward R. Stettinius Jr.	1944–1945

The Truman Administration (1945–1953)

Vice President	Alben W. Barkley	1949–1953
Secretary of State	Edward R. Stettinius Jr.	1945
	James F. Byrnes	1945–1947
	George C. Marshall	1947–1949
	Dean G. Acheson	1949–1953

The Eisenhower Administration (1953–1961)

Vice President	Richard M. Nixon	1953–1961
Secretary of State	John Foster Dulles	1953–1959
	Christian A. Herter	1959–1961

The Kennedy Administration (1961–1963)

Vice President	Lyndon B. Johnson	1961–1963
Secretary of State	Dean Rusk	1961–1963

The Lyndon Johnson Administration (1963–1969)

Vice President	Hubert H. Humphrey	1965–1969
Secretary of State	Dean Rusk	1963–1969

The Nixon Administration (1969–1974)

Vice President	Spiro T. Agnew	1969–1973
	Gerald R. Ford	1973–1974
Secretary of State	William P. Rogers	1969–1973
	Henry A. Kissinger	1973–1974

The Ford Administration (1974–1977)

Vice President	Nelson A. Rockefeller	1974–1977
Secretary of State	Henry A. Kissinger	1974–1977

The Carter Administration (1977–1981)

Vice President	Walter F. Mondale	1977–1981
Secretary of State	Cyrus R. Vance	1977–1980
	Edmund Muskie	1980–1981

The Reagan Administration (1981–1989)

Vice President	George H. W. Bush	1981–1989
Secretary of State	Alexander M. Haig	1981–1982
	George P. Shultz	1982–1989

The George H. W. Bush Administration (1989–1993)

Vice President	J. Danforth Quayle	1989–1993
Secretary of State	James A. Baker III	1989–1992
	Lawrence S. Eagleburger	1992–1993

The Clinton Administration (1993–2001)

Vice President	Albert Gore	1993–2001
Secretary of State	Warren M. Christopher	1993–1997
	Madeleine K. Albright	1997–2001

The George W. Bush Administration (2001–)

Vice President	Richard Cheney	2001–
Secretary of State	Colin Powell	2001–2005
	Condoleezza Rice	2005–

SUPREME COURT JUSTICES

Name	Service	Appointed by	Name	Service	Appointed by
John Jay*	1789–1795	Washington	Lucius Q. C. Lamar	1888–1893	Cleveland
James Wilson	1789–1798	Washington	**Melville W. Fuller**	1888–1910	Cleveland
John Blair	1789–1796	Washington	David J. Brewer	1889–1910	B. Harrison
John Rutledge	1790–1791	Washington	Henry B. Brown	1890–1906	B. Harrison
William Cushing	1790–1810	Washington	George Shiras	1892–1903	B. Harrison
James Iredell	1790–1799	Washington	Howell E. Jackson	1893–1895	B. Harrison
Thomas Johnson	1791–1793	Washington	Edward D. White	1894–1910	Cleveland
William Paterson	1793–1806	Washington	Rufus W. Peckham	1896–1909	Cleveland
John Rutledge†	1795	Washington	Joseph McKenna	1898–1925	McKinley
Samuel Chase	1796–1811	Washington	Oliver W. Holmes	1902–1932	T. Roosevelt
Oliver Ellsworth	1796–1799	Washington	William R. Day	1903–1922	T. Roosevelt
Bushrod Washington	1798–1829	J. Adams	William H. Moody	1906–1910	T. Roosevelt
Alfred Moore	1799–1804	J. Adams	Horace H. Lurton	1910–1914	Taft
John Marshall	1801–1835	J. Adams	Charles E. Hughes	1910–1916	Taft
William Johnson	1804–1834	Jefferson	Willis Van Devanter	1910–1937	Taft
Henry B. Livingston	1806–1823	Jefferson	**Edward D. White**	1910–1921	Taft
Thomas Todd	1807–1826	Jefferson	Joseph R. Lamar	1911–1916	Taft
Gabriel Duval	1811–1836	Madison	Mahlon Pitney	1912–1922	Taft
Joseph Story	1811–1845	Madison	James C. McReynolds	1914–1941	Wilson
Smith Thompson	1823–1843	Monroe	Louis D. Brandeis	1916–1939	Wilson
Robert Trimble	1826–1828	J. Q. Adams	John H. Clarke	1916–1922	Wilson
John McLean	1829–1861	Jackson	**William H. Taft**	1921–1930	Harding
Henry Baldwin	1830–1844	Jackson	George Sutherland	1922–1938	Harding
James M. Wayne	1835–1867	Jackson	Pierce Butler	1923–1939	Harding
Roger B. Taney	1836–1864	Jackson	Edward T. Sanford	1923–1930	Harding
Philip P. Barbour	1836–1841	Jackson	Harlan F. Stone	1925–1941	Coolidge
John Catron	1837–1865	Van Buren	**Charles E. Hughes**	1930–1941	Hoover
John McKinley	1837–1852	Van Buren	Owen J. Roberts	1930–1945	Hoover
Peter V. Daniel	1841–1860	Van Buren	Benjamin N. Cardozo	1932–1938	Hoover
Samuel Nelson	1845–1872	Tyler	Hugo L. Black	1937–1971	F. Roosevelt
Levi Woodbury	1845–1851	Polk	Stanley F. Reed	1938–1957	F. Roosevelt
Robert C. Grier	1846–1870	Polk	Felix Frankfurter	1939–1962	F. Roosevelt
Benjamin R. Curtis	1851–1857	Fillmore	William O. Douglas	1939–1975	F. Roosevelt
John A. Campbell	1853–1861	Pierce	Frank Murphy	1940–1949	F. Roosevelt
Nathan Clifford	1858–1881	Buchanan	**Harlan F. Stone**	1941–1946	F. Roosevelt
Noah H. Swayne	1862–1881	Lincoln	James F. Byrnes	1941–1942	F. Roosevelt
Samuel F. Miller	1862–1890	Lincoln	Robert H. Jackson	1941–1954	F. Roosevelt
David Davis	1862–1877	Lincoln	Wiley B. Rutledge	1943–1949	F. Roosevelt
Stephen J. Field	1863–1897	Lincoln	Harold H. Burton	1945–1958	Truman
Salmon P. Chase	1864–1873	Lincoln	**Frederick M. Vinson**	1946–1953	Truman
William Strong	1870–1880	Grant	Tom C. Clark	1949–1967	Truman
Joseph P. Bradley	1870–1892	Grant	Sherman Minton	1949–1956	Truman
Ward Hunt	1873–1882	Grant	**Earl Warren**	1953–1969	Eisenhower
Morrison R. Waite	1874–1888	Grant	John Marshall Harlan	1955–1971	Eisenhower
John M. Harlan	1877–1911	Hayes	William J. Brennan Jr.	1956–1990	Eisenhower
William B. Woods	1880–1887	Hayes	Charles E. Whittaker	1957–1962	Eisenhower
Stanley Matthews	1881–1889	Garfield	Potter Stewart	1958–1981	Eisenhower
Horace Gray	1882–1902	Arthur	Byron R. White	1962–1993	Kennedy
Samuel Blatchford	1882–1893	Arthur	Arthur J. Goldberg	1962–1965	Kennedy
			Abe Fortas	1965–1969	L. Johnson
			Thurgood Marshall	1967–1991	L. Johnson
			Warren E. Burger	1969–1986	Nixon

***Chief Justices appear in bold type.**
†Acting Chief Justice; Senate refused to confirm appointment.

Name	Service	Appointed by		Name	Service	Appointed by
Harry A. Blackmun	1970–1994	Nixon		David H. Souter	1990–	G. H. W. Bush
Lewis F. Powell Jr.	1972–1988	Nixon		Clarence Thomas	1991–	G. H. W. Bush
William H. Rehnquist	1972–1986	Nixon				
John Paul Stevens	1975–	Ford		Ruth Bader Ginsburg	1993–	Clinton
Sandra Day O'Connor	1981–2006	Reagan				
William H. Rehnquist	1986–2005	Reagan		Stephen Breyer	1994–	Clinton
				John G. Roberts Jr.	2005–	G. W. Bush
Antonin Scalia	1986–	Reagan		Samuel Anthony Alito Jr.	2006–	G. W. Bush
Anthony M. Kennedy	1988–	Reagan				

FEDERAL SPENDING AND THE ECONOMY, 1790–2002

Year	Gross National Product (in billions)	Foreign Trade (in millions) Exports	Imports	Federal Budget (in billions)	Federal Surplus/Deficit (in billions)	Federal Debt (in billions)
1790	NA	20	23	0.004	0.00015	0.076
1800	NA	71	91	0.011	0.0006	0.083
1810	NA	67	85	0.008	0.0012	0.053
1820	NA	70	74	0.018	−0.0004	0.091
1830	NA	74	71	0.015	0.100	0.049
1840	NA	132	107	0.024	−0.005	0.004
1850	NA	152	178	0.040	0.004	0.064
1860	NA	400	362	0.063	−0.01	0.065
1870	7.4	451	462	0.310	0.10	2.4
1880	11.2	853	761	0.268	0.07	2.1
1890	13.1	910	823	0.318	0.09	1.2
1900	18.7	1,499	930	0.521	0.05	1.2
1910	35.3	1,919	1,646	0.694	−0.02	1.1
1920	91.5	8,664	5,784	6.357	0.3	24.3
1930	90.4	4,013	3,500	3.320	0.7	16.3
1940	99.7	4,030	7,433	9.6	−2.7	43.0
1950	284.8	10,816	9,125	43.1	−2.2	257.4
1960	503.7	19,600	15,046	92.2	0.3	286.3
1970	977.1	42,700	40,189	195.6	−2.8	371.0
1980	2,631.7	220,600	244,871	590.9	−73.8	907.7
1990	5,832.2	393,600	495,300	1,253.2	−221.2	3,266.1
2000	9,848.0	1,070,054	1,445,438	1,788.8	236.4	5,701.9
2002	10,436.7	974,107	1,392,145	2,011.0	−157.8	6,255.4

SOURCE: *Historical Statistics of the U.S., Colonial Times to 1970* (1975), *Statistical Abstract of the U.S., 1996* (1996), *Statistical Abstract of the U.S., 1999* (1999), and *Statistical Abstract of the U.S., 2003* (2003).

POPULATION GROWTH, 1630–2000

Year	Population	Percent Increase	Year	Population	Percent Increase
1630	4,600	—	1820	9,638,453	33.1
1640	26,600	473.3	1830	12,866,020	33.5
1650	50,400	89.1	1840	17,069,453	32.7
1660	75,100	49.0	1850	23,191,876	35.9
1670	111,900	49.1	1860	31,443,321	35.6
1680	151,500	35.4	1870	39,818,449	26.6
1690	210,400	38.9	1880	50,155,783	26.0
1700	250,900	19.3	1890	62,947,714	25.5
1710	331,700	32.2	1900	75,994,575	20.7
1720	466,200	40.5	1910	91,972,266	21.0
1730	629,400	35.0	1920	105,710,620	14.9
1740	905,600	43.9	1930	122,775,046	16.1
1750	1,170,800	30.0	1940	131,669,275	7.2
1760	1,593,600	36.1	1950	150,697,361	14.5
1770	2,148,100	34.8	1960	179,323,175	19.0
1780	2,780,400	29.4	1970	203,302,031	13.4
1790	3,929,214	41.3	1980	226,542,199	11.4
1800	5,308,483	35.1	1990	248,718,302	9.8
1810	7,239,881	36.4	2000	281,422,509	13.1

SOURCE: *Historical Statistics of the U.S.* (1960), *Historical Statistics of the U.S., Colonial Times to 1970* (1975), *Statistical Abstract of the U.S., 1996* (1996), and *Statistical Abstract of the U.S., 2003* (2003).

Birthrate, 1820–2000

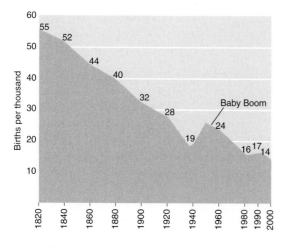

SOURCE: Data from *Historical Statistics of the U.S., Colonial Times to 1970* (1975) and *Statistical Abstract of the U.S., 2003* (2003).

Life Expectancy, 1900–2000

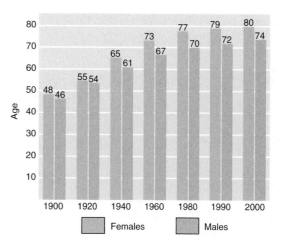

SOURCE: Data from *Historical Statistics of the U.S., Colonial Times to 1970* (1975) and *Statistical Abstract of the U.S., 2003* (2003).

Major Trends in Immigration, 1820–2000

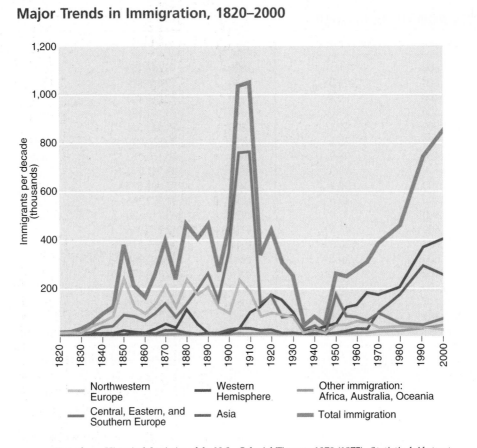

SOURCE: Data from *Historical Statistics of the U.S., Colonial Times to 1970* (1975), *Statistical Abstract of the U.S., 1999* (1999), and *Statistical Abstract of the U.S., 2003* (2003).

Research Resources in U.S. History

For help refining your research skills, finding what you need on the Web, and using it effectively, see "Online Research and Reference Aids" at bedfordstmartins.com/roarkcompact.

WHILE DOING RESEARCH IN HISTORY, you will use the library to track down primary and secondary sources and to answer questions that arise as you learn more about your topic. This appendix suggests helpful indexes, references, periodicals, and sources of primary documents. It also offers an overview of electronic resources available through the Internet. The materials listed here are not carried at all libraries, but they will give you an idea of the range of sources available. Remember, too, that librarians are an extremely helpful resource. They can direct you to useful materials throughout your research process.

Bibliographies and Indexes

American Historical Association Guide to Historical Literature. 3rd ed. New York: Oxford University Press, 1995. Offers 27,000 citations to important historical literature, arranged in forty-eight sections covering theory, international history, and regional history. An indispensable guide recently updated to include current trends in historical research.

American History and Life. Santa Barbara: ABC-Clio, 1964–. Covers publications of all sorts on U.S. and Canadian history and culture in a chronological/regional format, with abstracts and alphabetical indexes. Available in computerized format. The most complete ongoing bibliography for American history.

Freidel, Frank Burt. *Harvard Guide to American History.* Cambridge: Harvard University Press, Belknap Press, 1974. Provides citations to books and articles on American history published before 1970. The first volume is arranged topically, the second chronologically. Though it does not cover current scholarship, it is a classic and remains useful for tracing older publications.

Prucha, Francis Paul. *Handbook for Research in American History: A Guide to Bibliographies and Other Reference Works.* 2nd rev. ed. Lincoln: University of Nebraska Press, 1994. Introduces a variety of research tools, including electronic ones. A good source to consult when planning an in-depth research project.

General Overviews

Dictionary of American Biography. New York: Scribner's, 1928–1937, with supplements. Gives substantial biographies of prominent Americans in history.

Dictionary of American History. New York: Scribner's, 1976. An encyclopedia of terms, places, and concepts in U.S. history; other more specialized sets include the *Encyclopedia of North American Colonies* and the *Encyclopedia of the Confederacy.*

Encyclopedia of American Social History. New York: Scribner's, 1993. Surveys topics such as religion, class, gender, race, popular culture, regionalism, and everyday life from pre-Columbian to modern times.

Encyclopedia of the United States in the Twentieth Century. New York: Scribner's, 1996. An overview of American cultural, social, and intellectual history in articles arranged topically with useful bibliographies for further research.

Specialized Information

Black Women in America: An Historical Encyclopedia. Brooklyn: Carlson, 1993. A scholarly compilation of biographical and topical articles that constitute a definitive history of African American women.

Carruth, Gordon. *The Encyclopedia of American Facts and Dates.* 10th ed. New York: HarperCollins, 1997. Covers American history chronologically from 1986 to the present, offering information on treaties, battles, explorations, popular culture, philosophy, literature, and so on, mixing significant events with telling trivia. Tables allow for reviewing a year from a variety of angles. A thorough index helps pinpoint specific facts in time.

Cook, Chris. *Dictionary of Historical Terms.* 2nd ed. New York: Peter Bendrick, 1990. Covers a wide variety of terms—events, places, institutions, and topics—in history for all periods and places in a remarkably small package. A good place for quick identification of terms in the field.

Dictionary of Afro-American Slavery. New York: Greenwood, 1985. Surveys important people, events, and topics, with useful bibliographies; similar works include *Dictionary of the Vietnam War, Historical Dictionary of the New Deal,* and *Historical Dictionary of the Progressive Era.*

Knappman-Frost, Elizabeth. *The ABC-Clio Companion to Women's Progress in America.* Santa Barbara: ABC-Clio, 1994. Covers American women who were notable for their time as well as topics and organizations that have been significant in women's quest for equality. Each article is brief; there are a chronology and a bibliography at the back of the book.

United States Bureau of the Census. *Historical Statistics of the United States, Colonial Times to 1970.* Washington, D.C.: Government Printing Office, 1975. Offers vital statistics, economic figures, and social data for the United States. An index at the back helps locate tables by subject. For statistics since 1970, consult the annual *Statistical Abstract of the United States.*

Primary Resources

There are many routes to finding contemporary material for historical research. You may search your library catalog using the name of a prominent historical figure as an author; you may also find anthologies covering particular themes or periods in history. Consider also the following special materials for your research.

THE PRESS

American Periodical Series, 1741–1900. Ann Arbor: University Microfilms, 1946–1979. Microfilm collection of periodicals from the colonial period to 1900. An index identifies periodicals that focused on particular topics.

Herstory Microfilm Collection. Berkeley: Women's History Research Center, 1973. A microfilm collection of alternative feminist periodicals published between 1960 and 1980. Offers an interesting documentary history of the women's movement.

New York Times. New York: New York Times, 1851–. Many libraries have this newspaper on microfilm going back to its beginning in 1851. An index is available to locate specific dates and pages of news stories; it also provides detailed chronologies of events as they were reported in the news.

Readers' Guide to Periodical Literature. New York: Wilson, 1900–. This index to popular magazines started in 1900; an earlier index, *Poole's Index to Periodical Literature,* covers 1802–1906, though it does not provide such thorough indexing.

DIARIES, PAMPHLETS, BOOKS

The American Culture Series. Ann Arbor: University Microfilms, 1941–1974. A microfilm set, with a useful index, featuring books and pamphlets published between 1493 and 1875.

American Women's Diaries. New Canaan: Readex, 1984–. A collection of reproductions of women's diaries. There are different series for different regions of the country.

The March of America Facsimile Series. Ann Arbor: University Microfilms, 1966. A collection of more than ninety facsimiles of travel accounts to the New World published in English or English translation from the fifteenth through the nineteenth century.

Women in America from Colonial Times to the Twentieth Century. New York: Arno, 1974. A collection of reprints of dozens of books written by women describing women's lives and experiences in their own words.

GOVERNMENT DOCUMENTS

Congressional Record. Washington, D.C.: Government Printing Office, 1874–. Covers daily debates and proceedings of Congress. Earlier series were called *Debates and Proceedings in the Congress of the United States* and *The Congressional Globe.*

Foreign Relations of the United States. Washington, D.C.: Department of State, 1861–. A collection of documents from 1861, including diplomatic papers, correspondence, and memoranda, that provides a documentary record of U.S. foreign policy.

Public Papers of the Presidents. Washington, D.C.: Office of the Federal Register, 1957–. Includes major documents issued by the executive branch from the Hoover administration to the present.

Serial Set. Washington, D.C.: Government Printing Office, 1789–1969. A huge collection of congressional documents, available in many libraries on microfiche, with a useful index.

LOCAL HISTORY COLLECTIONS

State and county historical societies often house a wealth of historical documents; consider their resources when planning your research — you may find yourself working with material that no one else has analyzed before.

Internet Resources

The Internet has been a useful place for scholars to communicate and publish information in recent years. Electronic discussion lists, electronic journals, and primary texts are among the resources available to historians. The following sources are good places to find historical information. You can also search the Web using any of a number of search engines. However, bear in mind that there is no board of editors screening Internet sites for accuracy or usefulness. Be critical of all of your sources, particularly those found on the Internet. Note that when

INTERNET RESOURCES

this book went to press, the sites listed below were active and maintained.

The American Civil War Homepage. <http://sunsite.utk.edu/civil-war/warweb.html> A comprehensive resource bank on the American Civil War. Maintained by George Hoemann of the University of Tennessee, the site contains letters, documents, photographs, information about battles, links to other sites, and regiment rosters.

American Memory: Historical Collections for the National Digital Library Program. <http://memory.loc.gov/ammem.html> A Web site that features digitized primary source materials from the Library of Congress, among them African American pamphlets, Civil War photographs, documents from the Constitutional Convention of 1774–1790, materials on woman suffrage, and oral histories.

Douglass Archives of American Public Address. <http://douglassarchives.org> An electronic archive of American speeches and documents by a variety of people from Jane Addams to Jonathan Edwards to Theodore Roosevelt.

Historical Text Archive. <http://historicaltextarchive.com/> One of the oldest and largest Internet archives of historical documents, articles, photographs, and more. Includes sections on Native American, African American, and U.S. history, in which can be found texts of the Declaration of Independence, the Constitution of Iroquois Nations, World War II surrender documents, and a great deal more.

Index of Native American Resources on the Internet. <http://www.hanksville.org/NAresources> A vast index of Native American resources organized by category. Within the history category, links are organized under subcategories: oral history, written history, geographical areas, timelines, and photographs and photographic archives. A central place to come in the search for information on Native American history.

Internet Resources for Students of Afro-American History and Culture. <http://www.libraries.rutgers.edu/rul/rr_gateway/research_guides/history/afrores.shtml> A good place to begin research on topics in African American history. The site is indexed and linked to a wide variety of sources, including primary documents, text collections, and archival sources on African American history. Individual documents such as slave narratives and petitions, and speeches by W. E. B. Du

Bois and Martin Luther King Jr. are categorized by century.

NativeWeb. <http://www.nativeweb.org> One of the best organized and most accessible sites available on Native American issues, *NativeWeb* combines an events calendar and message board with history, statistics, a list of news sources, archives, new and updated related sites each week, and documents.

Perry-Castañeda Library Map Collection. <http://www.lib.utexas.edu/maps/> The University of Texas at Austin library has put over seven hundred United States maps on the Web along with hundreds of other maps from around the world. The collection includes both historical and contemporary maps.

Smithsonian Institution. <http://www.si.edu> Organized by subject, such as military history or Hispanic/Latino American resources, this site offers selected links to sites hosted by Smithsonian museums and organizations. Content includes graphics of museum pieces and relevant textual information, book suggestions, maps, and links.

Supreme Court Collection. <http://www.law.cornell.edu/supct/> This database can be used to search for information on various Supreme Court cases. Although the site primarily covers cases that occurred after 1990, there is information on some earlier historic cases. The justices' opinions, as originally written, are also included.

United States Holocaust Memorial Museum. <http://www.ushmm.org> This site contains information about the Holocaust Museum in Washington, D.C., in particular and the Holocaust in general, and it lists links to related sites.

Women's History Resources. <http://www.mcps.k12.md.us/curriculum/socialstd/Women_Bookmarks.html> An extensive listing of women's history sources available on the Internet. The site indexes resources on subjects as diverse as woman suffrage, women in the workplace, and celebrated women writers. Some of the links are to equally vast indexes, providing an overwhelming wealth of information.

WWW-VL History Index. <http://www.ukans.edu/history/VL> A vast list of more than 1,700 links to sites of interest to historians, arranged by general topic and by continent and country. The United States history page includes links to online research tools as well as links arranged by topic and historical period.

A Note to Students: This list of terms is provided to help you with the vocabulary of historians and economists. Many of these terms refer to broad, enduring concepts that you may encounter not only in further studies of history but also when following current events. The terms appear in bold at their first use in each chapter. In the glossary, the page numbers of those chapter-by-chapter appearances are provided so you can look up the terms' uses in various periods and contexts. For definitions and discussions of words not included here, consult a dictionary and the book's index, which will point you to topics covered at greater length in the book.

antebellum A term that means "before a war" and commonly refers to the period prior to the Civil War. (pp. 289, 316, 386)

antinomian A person who does not obey societal or religious law. In colonial Massachusetts, Puritan authorities accused Anne Hutchinson of antinomianism because she believed that Christians could achieve salvation by faith alone; they further asserted, incorrectly, that Hutchinson also held the belief that it was not necessary to follow God's laws as set forth in the Bible. (p. 89)

archaeology A social science devoted to learning about people who lived in the past through the study of physical artifacts created by humans. Most but not all archaeological study focuses on the history of people who lived before the use of the written word. (p. 3)

Archaic America Various hunting and gathering cultures that descended from Paleo-Indians. The term also refers to the period of time when these cultures dominated ancient America, roughly from 8000 BP to between 2000 and 1000 BP. (p. 10)

artifacts Material remains studied and used by archaeologists and historians to support their interpretations of human history. Examples of artifacts include bones, pots, baskets, jewelry, furniture, tools, clothing, and buildings. (p. 3)

artisan A term commonly used prior to 1900 to describe a skilled craftsman, such as a cabinetmaker. (pp. 43, 94, 106, 164, 201, 298, 323)

Bill of Rights The commonly used term for the first ten amendments to the U.S. Constitution. The Bill of Rights (the last of which was ratified in 1791) guarantees individual liberties and defines limitations to federal power. Many states made the promise of the prompt addition of a bill of rights a precondition for their ratification of the Constitution. (pp. 206, 213)

bloody shirt A refrain used by Republicans in the late nineteenth century to remind the voting public that the Democratic Party, dominated by the South, was largely responsible for the Civil War and that the Republican Party had led the victory to preserve the Union. Republicans urged their constituents to "Vote the way you shot." (p. 417)

Calvinism The religious doctrine of which the primary tenet is that salvation is predestined by God. Founded by John Calvin of Geneva during the Protestant Reformation, Calvinism required its adherents to live according to a strict religious and moral code. The Puritans who settled in colonial New England were devout Calvinists. (p. 85) *See also* predestination.

checks and balances A system in which the executive, legislative, and judicial branches of the government curb each other's power. Checks and balances were written into the U.S. Constitution during the Constitutional Convention of 1787. (p. 207)

civil service The administrative service of a government. This term often applies to reforms following passage of the Pendleton Act in 1883, which set qualifications for U.S. government jobs and sought to remove such jobs from political influence. (p. 418) *See also* spoils system.

colonization The process by which a country or society gains control over another, primarily through settlement. (pp. 31, 55, 80, 272, 381)

Columbian exchange The transatlantic exchange of goods, peoples, and ideas that began when Columbus arrived in the Caribbean, ending the age-old separation of the hemispheres. (p. 34)

conscription Compulsory military service. Americans were first subject to conscription during the Civil War. The Draft Act of 1940 marked the first peacetime use of conscription. (p. 383) *See also* draft.

conservatism A political and moral outlook dating back to Alexander Hamilton's belief in a strong central government resting on a solid banking foundation. Currently associated with the Republican Party, conservatism today places a high premium on military preparedness, free-market economics, low taxes, and strong sexual morality. (pp. 382, 406)

covenant An agreement or pact; in American history, a religious agreement. The Pilgrims used this term in the Mayflower Compact to refer to the agreement among themselves to establish a law-abiding community in which all members would work together for the common good. Later, New England Puritans used this term to refer to the agreement they made with God and each other to live according to God's will as revealed through Scripture. (pp. 77, 106) *See also* Halfway Covenant.

democracy   A system of government in which the people have the power to rule, either directly or indirectly through their elected representatives. Believing direct democracy dangerous, the framers of the Constitution created a government that gave direct voice to the people only in the House of Representatives and placed a check on the voice of the people in the Senate by offering unlimited six-year terms to senators, elected by the state legislatures to protect them from the whims of democratic majorities. The framers further curbed the perceived dangers of democracy by giving each of the three branches of government (legislative, executive, and judicial) the ability to check the power of the other two. (pp. 164, 189, 212, 248, 265, 337, 346, 373, 413) *See also* checks and balances.

draft (draftee)   A system for selecting individuals for compulsory military service. A draftee is an individual selected through this process. (pp. 167, 382) *See also* conscription.

emancipation   The act of freeing from slavery or bondage. The emancipation of American slaves, a goal shared by slaves and abolitionists alike, occurred with the passage of the Thirteenth Amendment in 1865. (pp. 192, 250, 272, 309, 333, 369, 399)

English Reformation   *See* Reformation.

Enlightenment   An eighteenth-century philosophical movement that emphasized the use of reason to reevaluate previously accepted doctrines and traditions. (p. 119)

evangelicalism   The trend in Protestant Christianity stressing salvation through conversion, repentance of sin, adherence to Scripture, and the importance of preaching over ritual. During the Second Great Awakening, in the 1830s, evangelicals worshipped at camp meetings and religious revivals led by exuberant preachers. (pp. 260, 307, 331) *See also* Second Great Awakening.

feminism   The belief that men and women have an inherent right to equal social, political, and economic opportunities. The suffrage movement and second-wave feminism of the 1960s and 1970s were the most visible and successful manifestations of feminism, but feminist ideas were expressed in a variety of statements and movements as early as the late eighteenth century and continue to be expressed in the twenty-first. (pp. 218, 411)

franchise   The right to vote. The franchise was gradually widened in the United States to include groups such as women and African Americans, who had no vote when the Constitution was ratified. (pp. 310, 412) *See also* suffrage.

free labor   Work conducted free from constraint and in accordance with the laborer's personal inclinations and will. Prior to the Civil War, free labor became an ideal championed by Republicans (who were primarily Northerners) to articulate individuals' right to work how and where they wished, and to accumulate property in their own name. The ideal of free labor lay at the heart of the North's argument that slavery should not be extended into the western territories. (pp. 272, 305, 319, 345, 401)

free soil   The idea advanced in the 1840s that Congress should prohibit slavery within western territories. "Free soil, free speech, free labor, and free men" became the rallying cry of the short-lived Free-Soil Party. (pp. 345, 381)

frontier   A borderland area. In U.S. history, the borderland between the areas primarily inhabited by Europeans or their descendants and the areas solely inhabited by Native Americans. (pp. 31, 63, 90, 132, 166, 243, 259, 286, 344)

government bonds   Promissory notes issued by a government in order to borrow money from members of the public. Such bonds are redeemable at a set future date. Bondholders earn interest on their investment. (p. 173)

Great Awakening   The widespread movement of religious revitalization in the 1730s and 1740s that emphasized vital religious faith and personal choice. It was characterized by large, open-air meetings at which emotional sermons were given by itinerant preachers. (p. 119)

guerrilla warfare   Fighting carried out by an irregular military force usually organized into small, highly mobile groups. Guerrilla combat was common in the Vietnam War and during the American Revolution. Guerrilla warfare is often effective against opponents who have greater material resources. (pp. 160, 357, 372)

Halfway Covenant   A Puritan compromise that allowed the unconverted children of the "visible saints" to become "halfway" members of the church and to baptize their own children even though they were not full members of the church themselves because they had not experienced full conversion. Massachusetts ministers accepted this compromise in 1662, though the compromise remained controversial throughout the seventeenth century. (p. 91)

hard currency (hard money)   Money coined directly from, or backed in full by, precious metals (particularly gold). (pp. 173, 196, 217, 264)

impeachment   The process by which formal charges of wrongdoing are brought against a president, a governor, or a federal judge. (p. 410)

imperialism   The system by which great powers gain control of overseas territories. The United States became an imperialist power by gaining control of Puerto Rico, Guam, the Philippines, and Cuba as a result of the Spanish-American War. (pp. 353, 419)

indentured servitude   A system that committed poor immigrants to four to seven years of labor in exchange for passage to the colonies and food and shelter after they arrived. An indenture is a type of contract. (pp. 54, 105)

Jim Crow   The system of racial segregation that developed in the post–Civil War South and extended well into the twentieth century; it replaced slavery as the chief instrument of white supremacy. Jim Crow laws segregated African Americans in public facilities such as trains and streetcars and denied them basic civil rights, including the right to vote. It was also at this time that the doctrine of "separate but equal" became institutionalized. (p. 415)

land grant A gift of land from a government, usually intended to encourage settlement or development. The British government issued several land grants to encourage development in the American colonies. In the mid-nineteenth century the U.S. government issued land grants to encourage railroad development and through passage of the Land-Grant College Act (also known as the Morrill Act) in 1863 set aside public lands to support universities. (pp. 55, 92, 167, 303, 353, 430)

liberty The condition of being free or enjoying freedom from control. This term also refers to the possession of certain social, political, or economic rights such as the right to own and control property. Eighteenth-century American colonists evoked the principle to argue for strict limitations on government's ability to tax its subjects. (pp. 78, 132, 159, 189, 215, 238, 260, 319, 356, 373)

manifest destiny A term coined by journalist John O'Sullivan in 1845 to express the popular nineteenth-century belief that the United States was destined to expand westward to the Pacific Ocean and had an irrefutable right and God-given responsibility to do so. This idea provided an ideological rationale for westward expansion and masked the economic and political motivations of many of those who championed it. (pp. 287, 350)

mercantilism A set of policies that regulated colonial commerce and manufacturing for the enrichment of the mother country. Mercantilist policies ensured that the American colonies in the mid-seventeenth century produced agricultural goods and raw materials to be shipped to Britain, where they would increase wealth in the mother country through reexportation or manufacture into finished goods that would then be sold to the colonies and elsewhere. (p. 66)

Middle Passage The crossing of the Atlantic (as a slave destined for auction) in the hold of a slave ship in the eighteenth and nineteenth centuries. Conditions were unimaginably bad, and many slaves died during these voyages. (pp. 72, 112)

miscegenation The sexual mixing of races. In slave states, despite social stigma and legal restrictions on interracial sex, masters' almost unlimited power over their female slaves meant that liaisons inevitably occurred. Many states maintained laws against miscegenation into the 1950s. (p. 324)

monopoly Exclusive control and domination by a single business entity over an entire industry through ownership, command of supply, or other means. (pp. 29, 260, 422)

Monroe Doctrine President James Monroe's 1823 declaration that the Western Hemisphere was closed to any further colonization or interference by European powers. In exchange, Monroe pledged that the United States would not become involved in European struggles. Although Monroe could not back his policy with action, it was an important formulation of national goals. (p. 251)

nationalism A strong feeling of devotion and loyalty toward one nation over others. Nationalism encourages the promotion of the nation's common culture, language, and customs. (pp. 248, 385)

nativism Bias against immigrants and in favor of native-born inhabitants. American nativists especially favor persons who come from white, Anglo-Saxon, Protestant lines over those from other racial, ethnic, and religious heritages. Nativists may include former immigrants who view new immigrants as incapable of assimilation. Many nativists, such as members of the Know-Nothing Party in the nineteenth century and the Ku Klux Klan through the contemporary period, voice anti-immigrant, anti-Catholic, and anti-Semitic sentiments. (p. 355)

New South A vision of the South promoted after the Civil War by Henry Grady, editor of the *Atlanta Constitution,* who urged the South to abandon its dependence on agriculture and use its cheap labor and natural resources to compete with northern industry. Many southerners migrated from farms to cities in the late nineteenth century, and northerners and foreigners invested a significant amount of capital in railroads, cotton and textiles, mining, lumber, iron, steel, and tobacco in the region. (p. 400)

nullification The idea that states can disregard federal laws when those laws represent an overstepping of congressional powers. The controversial idea was first proposed by opponents of the Alien and Sedition Acts of 1798 and later by South Carolina politicians in 1828 as a response to the Tariff of Abominations. (pp. 229, 239, 278, 347)

paternalism The idea that slavery was a set of reciprocal obligations between masters and slaves, with slaves providing labor and obedience and masters providing basic care and direction. The concept of paternalism denied that the slave system was brutal and exploitative. While paternalism did provide some protection against the worst brutality, it did not guarantee decent living conditions, reasonable work, or freedom from physical punishment. (p. 323)

planters Owners of large farms (or more specifically plantations) that were worked by twenty or more slaves. By 1860, planters had accrued a great deal of local, statewide, and national political power in the South despite the fact that they represented a minority of the white electorate in those states. Planters' dominance of southern politics demonstrated both the power of tradition and stability among southern voters and the planters' success at convincing white voters that the slave system benefited all whites, even those without slaves. (pp. 59, 95, 112, 139, 161, 225, 244, 272, 321, 374, 402)

popular sovereignty The idea that government is subject to the will of the people; before the Civil War, the idea that the residents of a territory should determine, through their legislatures, whether to allow slavery. (p. 346)

predestination The idea that individual salvation or damnation is determined by God at, or just prior to, a person's birth. The concept of predestination invalidated the idea that salvation could be obtained through either faith or good works. (p. 85) *See also* Calvinism.

Protestant Reformation *See* Reformation.

Protestantism A powerful Christian reform movement that began in the sixteenth century with Martin Luther's critiques of the Roman Catholic Church. Over the centuries, Protestantism has taken many different forms, branching into numerous denominations with differing systems of worship. (pp. 47, 64, 79, 106, 150, 249, 268, 307, 316, 355)

Puritanism The ideas and religious principles held by dissenters from the Church of England, including the belief that the church needed to be purified by eliminating the elements of Catholicism from its practices. (pp. 64, 78, 105)

Reformation The reform movement that began in 1517 with Martin Luther's critiques of the Roman Catholic Church, which led to the formation of Protestant Christian groups. The English Reformation began with Henry VIII's break with the Roman Catholic Church, which established the Protestant Church of England. Henry VIII's decision was politically motivated; he had no particular quarrel with Catholic theology and remained an orthodox Catholic in most matters of religious practice. (pp. 46, 78)

republicanism The belief that the unworkable model of European-style monarchy should be replaced with a form of government in which supreme power resides in the hands of citizens with the right to vote and is exercised by a representative government answerable to this electorate. In Revolutionary-era America, republicanism became a social philosophy that embodied a sense of community and called individuals to act for the public good. (pp. 164, 186, 213, 237, 337, 355)

Second Great Awakening A popular religious revival that preached that salvation was available to anybody who chose to take it. The revival peaked in the 1830s, and its focus on social perfection inspired many of the reform movements of the Jacksonian era. (p. 268) *See also* evangelicalism.

separate spheres A concept of gender relations that developed in the Jacksonian era and continued well into the twentieth century, holding that women's proper place was in the private world of hearth and home (the private sphere) and men's was in the public world of commerce and politics (the public sphere). The doctrine of separate spheres eroded slowly over the nineteenth and twentieth centuries as women became more and more involved in public activities. (p. 268)

spoils system An arrangement in which party leaders reward party loyalists with government jobs. This slang term for *patronage* comes from the phrase "To the victor go the spoils." Widespread government corruption during the Gilded Age spurred reformers to curb the spoils system through the passage of the Pendleton Act in 1883, which created the Civil Service Commission to award government jobs on the basis of merit. (pp. 267, 418) *See also* civil service.

states' rights A strict interpretation of the Constitution that holds that federal power over states is limited and states hold ultimate sovereignty. First expressed in 1798 through the passage of the Virginia and Kentucky Resolutions, which were based on the assumption that states have the right to judge the constitutionality of federal laws, the states' rights philosophy became a cornerstone of the South's resistance to federal control of slavery. (pp. 202, 252, 277, 384, 403)

suffrage The right to vote. The term *suffrage* is most often associated with the efforts of American women to secure voting rights. (pp. 190, 268, 309, 337, 401) *See also* franchise.

temperance movement The reform movement to end drunkenness by urging people to abstain from the consumption of alcohol. Begun in the 1820s, this movement achieved its greatest political victory with the passage of a constitutional amendment in 1919 that prohibited the manufacture, sale, and transportation of alcohol. That amendment was repealed in 1933. (pp. 271, 307)

virtual representation The notion, propounded by British Parliament in the eighteenth century, that the House of Commons represented all British subjects — wherever they lived and regardless of whether they had directly voted for their representatives. Prime Minister George Grenville used this idea to argue that the Stamp Act and other parliamentary taxes on colonists did not constitute taxation without representation. American colonists rejected this argument, insisting that political representatives derived authority only from explicit citizens' consent indicated by elections, and that members of a distant government body were incapable of adequately representing their interests. (p. 142)

War Hawks Young Republicans elected to the U.S. Congress in the fall of 1810 who were eager for war with England in order to legitimize attacks on Indians, end impressment, and avenge foreign insults. (p. 244)

yeoman A farmer who owned a small plot of land sufficient to support a family and tilled by family members and perhaps a few servants. (pp. 65, 116, 279, 334, 383, 412)

Embedded Artifact Credits

A note about the index:

Names of individuals appear in boldface; biographical dates are included for major historical figures.

Letters in parentheses following page numbers refer to:
(i)   illustrations, including photographs and artifacts, as well as information in picture captions
(f)   figures, including charts and graphs
(m) maps
(b) boxed features (such as "Historical Question")
(t)   tables
(n) notes

at Harpers Ferry, 343
in Indian conflicts, 222–225, 223(m), 224(i), 277, 375
in Mexican-American War, 294–297, 295(m), 296(i)
militia in, 199, 200, 200(i), 200(m)
private, 199–200, 200(i), 200(m)
in Quasi-War with France, 228
rum ration, 270
stationed in the South (Reconstruction), 413, 418, 420, 422
volunteer, 294
women and, 223
Army of Northern Virginia, 377. *See also* Confederate Army
Army of the Potomac, 377. *See also* Union army
Arnold, Benedict (*1741–1801*), 168, 169(m), 178, 178(i)
Art. *See also* Artists
in American Revolution, 152(i), 165(i)
political, 148(i), 149(i), 151(i), 165(i), 234(i), 253(i), 320(i), 328(i)
religious, 68, 68(i), 79(i), 87(i), 92(i)
Articles of Confederation (*1781*), 184(i), 186–189
taxation under, 187, 196
weaknesses of, 186, 187–189, 193, 196, 200
western lands issue, 186, 187–188, 188(m), 197–199, 198(m), 207
Artisans, 108, 109, 164, 298
clockmakers, 210(i)
free black, 332, 333, 334
in Jamestown, 57
in Middle Colonies, 94, 104(i), 110, 164
in New England, 81, 84(i), 90(i), 106–107
printers and publishers, 103, 106, 110–111, 148(i), 164
shipbuilders, 106
slave, 102(i), 314(i), 323, 329–330, 329(i)
Spanish, 43
woodworkers, 84(i), 106, 130(i), 246(b), 247(b), 247(i), 258(i), 329(i), 332
Artist(s)
portray Indians, 243(i), 289(i)
slave, 314(i), 331, 331(i)
society portrait painters, 54(i), 90(i), 104(i), 114(i), 171(i), 186(i), 197(i), 212(i), 228(i), 242(i)
war, 126(i), 152(i), 165(i), 224(i), 296(i), 377(i)
Asante culture, 112
Ashley Creek, Utah, petroglyph, 17(i)
Asia, 8(b)–9(b)
luxury trade with, 28–31, 29(m), 287
Paleo-Indian migrants from, 5–7, 8(b), 9(b)
Asian American(s). *See individual nationalities*
Atahualpa, Incan emperor, 37
Athapascan tribes, 20
Atkinson, David Rice, 357
Atlanta, Ga., fall of (*1864*), 390, 391, 391(m), 394(t)

Attucks, Crispus (*c. 1723–1770*), 147, 148(i)
Augusta, Ga., 177, 325(i)
Austin, Stephen F. (*1793–1836*), 291
Ayllón, Lucas Vázquez de, 33(m), 37
Aztecs. *See* Mexica

Bacon, Nathaniel (*1647–1676*), 66–67
Bacon's Rebellion (*1676*), 66–68
Balboa, Vasco Núñez de (*1475–1519*), 33(m), 34
Baltimore, Lord (George Calvert) (*c. 1580–1632*), 64, 98
Baltimore, Md.
British attack, 245, 245(m)
transportation and, 260, 303, 304(m)
Baltimore and Ohio Railroad, 262
Bambara culture, 112
Bancroft, Hubert Howe, 301(b)
Bank of England, 220, 279
Bank of North America (*1781*), 196
Bank of the United States
chartered (*1791*), 220–221, 264
second (*1816*), 264, 264–265, 278–279, 280
Banks and banking system, 196, 208(b), 216–217, 220–221
collapse of, 260, 280
Jackson's policy on, 258(i), 278–280, 281
national banking system, 386
state, 264, 265, 279, 332, 386
Bantus, 113(m)
Baptist(s), 119, 249
revivalism in, 270, 336
"Baptizing on the South Branch of the Potomac near Franklin, Virginia" (Smith), 336(i)
Barbados, 71(m), 137(m)
slavery in, 69–70, 71, 72
sugar plantations in, 69–70
Barley, Dave, 326(b)
Barnard, George N., 330(i)
Barrow, Bennet H., 326(b)–327(b)
Barton, Clara, 387, 393(b)
Basket making, 11, 13, 20
Taino zemi basket, 26(i)
Baton Rouge, La., 318(m)
"Battala del Sacramento" (Michaud y Thomas), 296(i)
"Battle of Savage's Station, The" (Sneden), 377(i)
Bear Flag Revolt (*1846*), 292, 295(m)
Bearden, Romare, 362(i)
Beecher, Lyman, 270
Beissel, Johann Conrad, 108(i)
Bell, John, 354(m), 361, 363, 364(m)
Benin, 29(m), 31(i), 115(i)
Benton, Thomas Hart (*1889–1975*), 287, 356
Beringia, 5–7, 6, 8(b)–9(b), 18, 22
Berkeley, William (*1606–1677*), 65, 66, 67
Bernard, Francis, 143, 145, 147
Bestes, Peter, 194(b)
Bethlehem, Penn., founding (*1740*), 111(i)
Biafra, Bight of, 112–113, 113(m), 114
Bibb, Henry, 309

Bible, the
Puritans and, 76(i), 79, 79(i), 91
reading, 414(i)
slavery and, 331
Big Knives, Shawnee epithet for Americans, 235
Bill of Rights (first ten amendments to U.S. Constitution), 189–190, 190–191, 191–193, 213, 214–215, 230
vs. Alien and Sedition Acts, 228–230
Bills of rights, state, 189–193, 206
Birney, James G., 293
Birney, William, 404(b)
Birthrate
Native American, 301(b)
slave, 114, 275(b), 317, 323
Bison, giant, fossils of, 3–4, 3(i), 9(b), 10(i), 12. *See also* Buffalo
Black(s), 252(i), 359. *See also* African Americans; Free blacks (freedmen)
Creole, 114
education, 192, 269(i), 334
families, 333–334, 404(b), 416(i), 423
fight in Civil War, 369–370, 370(i), 382–383, 383(i)
on frontier, 3, 4(i), 252(i)
population, 319(f), 332
racial discrimination outlawed, 407, 411(t)
racism and, 272, 305, 309, 310, 317, 339, 403
in Reconstruction, 413–415, 413(i), 414(f)
sharecroppers, 415–416, 416(i), 417(m)
Black churches, 192, 331, 334, 362(i), 402–403
Black codes, adopted across South (*1865*), 406–407, 406(i), 407
Blackfeet tribe, 19(m), 20
Black Hawk, chief, 276, 289(i)
Black Hawk War (*1832*), 276, 276(m), 374
"Bleeding Kansas" (*1856*), 357–358, 357(m), 365
"Bleeding Sumner," 358
"Bloody shirt" tactic, 417, 421
Blue Jacket, Shawnee chief, 224
Board of Trade (Britain), 126
Book of Mormon, The (Smith), 289
Books. *See* Publishing; Writers
Boonesborough, Ky., 175, 176(m)
Booth, John Wilkes, 394, 403
Borders. *See also* Westward expansion
with Canada, 225, 244, 245, 287(m), 288(m), 292, 294, 298(m)
Louisiana Purchase and (*1803*), 239–241, 240(m)
with Mexico, 291, 291(m), 292, 295(m), 298(m), 350, 350(m)
in Proclamation of *1763*, 137(m), 138, 142
in Treaty of Paris (*1783*), 179
Boré, Étienne de, 321
Boston, Mass., 90(i), 96(m), 103, 105, 122(m)
abolitionists in, 272, 275(b), 343, 349, 401
battle of Bunker Hill (*1775*), 161, 164, 164(m)
Breed's Hill in, 164(m)

Concord, Mass., battle of (*1775*), 152(i),
153, 153(m), 160, 163(b), 169(m)
Conestoga Indians, 141(b)
Confederate States of America (CSA),
353(b), 364. *See also* South, the
belligerent status of, 380
casualties in, 370, 378, 379, 389–390,
392(b), 393(b), 394, 395
Civil War strategy of, 373–374, 373(f),
377, 378, 383–384, 384–385
congress of, 383–384
diplomacy in Europe, 374, 375, 380
dissatisfaction in, 373, 384–385
as independent republic, 371, 372, 377
Indians in, 378, 379(i)
inflation in, 375, 383, 384
naval blockade of, 374, 380, 391(m)
naval strength of, 373(f), 376(m), 380,
380(t)
Ordnance Bureau of, 375
resources of, 373–374, 373(f), 383–385,
395
slavery undergirds, 369, 380–381, 382,
384(i), 385–386
supplying, 371(i), 375, 375(i), 380, 383,
384, 389–390, 391, 394
war effort in, 383–384, 389–390, 391,
394, 395
Confiscation Acts
First (*1861*), 381
Second (*1862*), 381, 382
Congo, 29(m), 31, 32, 113(m), 114
Congregational Church, 119, 270. *See also*
Puritans
Congress, U.S. *See also* House of
Representatives, U.S.; Senate, U.S.
Bill of Rights in, 213, 214–215
blacks in, 413(i), 414, 414(f)
challenges executive power of
president, 401, 402, 403, 406–407,
408–410
Civil War and, 381, 382, 395
debate over Revolutionary War debt,
211–213, 217, 220, 230
declares war, 294
integrates West into Union, 386, 395
judicial review and, 239
North–South divide over slavery in
(*1820–1860*), 250–251, 251(m), 293,
294, 346–348, 348(m), 348–351,
355–357, 357(f), 360–365
powers of, 202, 203, 220–221, 229–230,
346, 347, 358–359, 395, 401, 402
on qualification of its members, 401,
407, 408, 409–410, 421(m)
Reconstruction under, 401, 402, 407,
408–410, 409(m), 411(t), 412,
422–423
states' rights to nullify, 229–230
Connecticut, 122(m), 123, 126, 130(m),
172(m), 304(m)
blacks in, 167
cession of western lands, 187, 188(m)
economy of, 106, 107
emancipation in, 192(m)
founding (*1636*), 89

government in, 189, 192, 192(m)
ratifies Constitution, 204, 205(m)
Connecticut River valley, 89, 216, 220(i)
Conquest, Spanish. *See also* New Spain
Columbian exchange in, 34, 35(i), 43,
45, 49
forced labor in, 34, 39, 44–45
gold and silver from, 36, 37, 39, 39(m),
40(b), 42, 43(f), 46(i), 47
of Inca (Peru), 33(m), 37
justifying, 40(b)–41(b)
of Mexica, 21, 35–37, 36(i), 36(m),
38–43
participants in, 36, 37, 38, 42–43, 44(i)
Conscientious objectors, 214
Conscription (draft)
in Confederacy, 383–384, 384
resistance to, 388
in Union, 388, 390
"Constantia" essays (Murray), 215(i)
Constitution, U.S. (*1788*), 184(i), 186,
212(i), 316
amendments to, 206, 213, 214–215, 227.
See also individual amendments
Antifederalists and, 204–206, 205(m),
214, 238
Bill of Rights in, 206, 213, 214–215
checks and balances in, 203, 207
Federalists and, 204, 205, 205(m), 206
judicial review and, 239
provisions of, 201–203, 206, 207
ratification of, 203–206, 205(m)
slave trade banned from *1808*, 274(b),
275(b)
three-fifths clause, 202–203, 213(i)
Constitution (ship), 258(i)
Constitutional Convention (*1787*),
200–203, 201(i), 202(i)
democracy vs. republicanism, 203, 214
New Jersey Plan, 201, 202
Virginia Plan, 201–202
Constitutional Union Party, 354(m), 362
Consumer culture, 213(i), 268
Consumer goods, colonial, 104(i),
106–108, 110–111, 116, 117, 118(f),
119, 145, 146
Consumption
of British imports, 106, 110, 146, 213(i),
221, 241, 244
of colonial products, 60(b)–61(b),
117–120, 188(f). *See also* Tobacco
industry and; Trade and trading
of consumer durables, 246(b)–247(b),
247(i), 265, 303
of domestic manufactures, 221,
246(b)–247(b)
Navigation Acts control access to
products, 66, 95, 116, 117, 139
nonconsumption (boycott) as protest,
145–147, 146(i), 148, 170, 173,
218(i)
patterns of, 268
taxes on, 131, 145–147, 148. *See also*
Parliament, revenue acts; Tariff(s)
of tea, 146, 147, 148–150, 149(i)
Continental Association (*1774*), 151

Continental Congress, First (*1774*),
150–151, 160
as response to Coercive Acts, 150,
150–151
Continental Congress, Second
(*1775–1781*), 152, 159, 160–161,
164, 166, 167, 181, 185–186, 186(i),
191(i), 201(i), 202(i), 207
agrees on Articles of Confederation,
184(i), 185–186, 186–188
authorizes Constitutional Convention,
200–201
currency of, 158(i), 161, 172–173, 193,
193(i), 197
declares war, 161
diplomacy and, 160, 164
foreign relations and, 187, 197(i)
home of, 189
legislation of, 187, 199
military authority of, 158(i), 160, 161,
162(b), 163(b), 172, 175
political authority of, 160, 161, 172,
199–200, 213
war debts, 193, 196, 199
weaknesses as confederation
government, 186, 187, 188–189,
193, 196, 200–201
Coode, John, 98
Cook, George, John F., and Mary, 333(i)
Cookstove, 246(b)–247(b), 247(i)
Corbin, Hannah, 190
Corinth, Miss., fall of (*1862*), 376(m), 379
Corn, 302
as currency, 96(i)
in early colonies, 56, 57, 80
Indian cultivation of, 7(f), 13, 19, 20,
27, 34
in North, 373(f)
in South, 321(m), 334, 373(f)
Cornstalk, Shawnee chief, 175
Cornwallis, Lord (Charles) (*1738–1805*),
177, 177(m), 178, 179
Coronado, Francisco Vásquez de
(*1510–1554*), 33(m), 37–38,
38(i), 45
Corporations, 264
"Corrupt bargain" (*1824*), 254, 266
Corruption
during American Revolution, 173,
174, 178
financial, 221, 228
political, 237, 254, 266, 357, 360, 415,
418, 418(i), 421
Cortés, Hernán (*1485–1547*), 35, 35–37,
36(i), 36(m), 38, 46, 47, 68
Cosway, Maria, 197(i)
Cotton. *See also* Textile industry
in Civil War strategy, 373–374, 373(f),
380, 386
export of, 216, 242, 278, 321–322, 374
free field laborers, 399, 400(i), 400,
415–416
gin invented (*1793*), 216, 321
plantations, 326(b)–327(b), 333, 334,
400(i), 415–416, 417(m)
prices, 265, 279–280

Instructor's Resources for *The American Promise: A Compact History*, Third Edition

See the preface for full descriptions of these supplements.

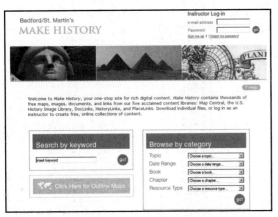

- **Make History** at **bedfordstmartins.com/makehistory**
  Provides access to Map Central, U.S. History Image Library, DocLinks, HistoryLinks, and PlaceLinks for one-stop searching by keyword, topic, date, or book chapter and easy downloading of the maps, images, documents, and Web links found.

- ***Instructor's Resource Manual,*** ISBN 0–312–44840–6
  Includes model answers for review questions, lecture strategies, a guide addressing common misconceptions and difficult topics, film suggestions, discussion starters, in-class activities, a survival guide for first-time teaching assistants, and more.

- **Transparencies,** ISBN 0–312–41737–3
  Includes over 160 full-color acetate transparencies of all full-sized maps and many images from both the full-length and compact editions of the text.

- **Book Companion site** at **bedfordstmartins.com/roarkcompact**
  Gathers all the electronic resources for the text, including the Online Study Guide and related Quiz Gradebook, at a single Web address. The resources on this Web site are also formatted for use with **course management systems** such as Blackboard, WebCT, Angel, and Desire2Learn.

- **Computerized Test Bank CD-ROM,** ISBN 0–312–44838–4

- **Instructor's Resource CD-ROM,** ISBN 0–312–44839–2
  Features PowerPoint presentations built around chapter outlines, maps, figures, and selected images from the textbook, plus the *Instructor's Resource Manual*, and more.

- ***Using the Bedford Series in History and Culture in the U.S. History Survey*** at **bedfordstmartins.com/usingseries**

- An assortment of **videos and multimedia** for qualified adopters

- ***The American Promise* for Distance Learning via Telecourse**